# The West and the World

# The West and the World

## A TOPICAL HISTORY OF CIVILIZATION

Kevin Reilly
SOMERSET COUNTY COLLEGE

**HARPER & ROW, PUBLISHERS, New York**
Cambridge, Hagerstown, Philadelphia, San Francisco,
London, Mexico City, São Paulo, Sydney

To My Mother and Father

Sponsoring Editor: John L. Michel
Project Editor: Claudia Kohner
Designer: Robert Sugar
Senior Production Manager: Kewal K. Sharma
Photo Researcher: Myra Schachne
Compositor: Maryland Linotype Composition Co., Inc.
Printer and Binder: Halliday Lithograph Corporation
Maps: Jean Paul Tremblay
Part openers: *Part I* Museum of Aquitaine, Bordeaux, Scala, EPA.
*Part II* Musei Vaticani.
*Part III* The Metropolitan Museum of Art, The Cloisters Collection, Purchase, 1937.
*Part IV* Alinari, EPA.
*Part V* Segal, George. *The Bus Driver* (1962). Figure of plaster over cheesecloth; bus parts including coin box, steering wheel, driver's seat, railing, dashboard, etc. Figure 53½ x 26⅞ x 45"; wood platform, 5⅛ x 51⅝ x 6'3⅝"; overall height, 6'3". Collection, The Museum of Modern Art, New York, Philip Johnson Fund.
Cover: Bruegel, Pieter the Elder, *Wedding Banquet*, Panel (c. 1567), Granger.

**The West and the World**



Library of Congress Cataloging in Publication Data
Reilly, Kevin, Date —
The West and the world.

Bibliography: p.
Includes index.
1. Civilization, Occidental. 2. Civilization—History. I. Title.
CB245.R44 1980 909'.09821 80–11828
ISBN 0–06–045345–1

# Contents

**MAPS**

# Topical Outline

## The Self and Others



## Community and Class



## Nations, Nature, and Markets

# Preface

This book, published in one-volume and two-volume editions, is designed to meet the needs of Western Civilization and World Civilization courses. Its topical organization is the result of different assumptions about historical understanding and the process of education. Most traditional texts on either Western or world history are based on the assumption that historical understanding is the possession of information (facts and ideas) and that education is the transfer of this information to the student.

The ancient Greeks spoke of "historia" as a process of inquiry. History was a verb. It was a way of thinking, an inquiry about human change. Today, when change cries out for understanding, history has become a subject matter. One learns history instead of learning to think historically. One memorizes it instead of understanding it. We have lost our ability to think about change.

This book begins with the assumptions of the twentieth-century intellectual revolution: knowledge is created, not given; each fact is created (from an infinite number of other possibilities) out of interest, perspective, values, and involvement; we never have all the facts about the most minor event; particular facts have neither intrinsic value nor priority of importance, but only meaning in terms of the questions we ask; education is learning to create and test facts and interpretations, to ask and answer useful questions, to create meaning, to evaluate accuracy, and to think critically and clearly.

If education is training in thinking, history education is training in thinking about the past, about the relation of the past to the present. That is the purpose of this book: to encourage students to think more critically, sharply, and clearly about the ways things change. The book adopts two strategies for achieving this goal. First, it asks historical questions about topics of current interest for the students and society. Each chapter, and topical group of chapters, explores a current issue—sexism, racism, cities, ecology, and others—in order to encourage students to think more historically about that issue. Second, the particular historical interpretation of each issue is obviously a partial view, not a final answer. The author's interpretations sometimes deliberately depart from the mainstream in order to prod the student to challenge them and devise alternatives. (The instructor's manual explains each chapter's assumptions and aims, as well as alternative ways of discussing and testing its content.) Thus, the deficiency of traditional texts—their implicit message that they are the final authority—is avoided. Instead, students are engaged to think for themselves about issues that concern them.

A topical approach not only cultivates interest and thinking skills but it also suggests a response to the issue of teaching Western versus world history. We are interested in the problems of the Western world (the European-American world) because they are our own problems. Thus, the topics chosen for this book are phrased in Western terms. We ask, for instance, about "Love and Sex" because the relationship of the two is a current Western problem. We do not ask about the problem of "Women and Islamic Law" or the issue of "Caste and Ritual Purity." On the other hand, most Western problems are not uniquely our own, certainly not even love and sex. If we categorically ignored the historical experiences of the rest of the world, we would be as foolish as someone who read only the green books in the library. The history of Western civilization may tell us more about Western problems than the history of other civilizations, but the whole world has much to tell us about who we are and how things change. A topical approach to the history of civilization can make that discovery possible, exciting, and meaningful.

## Acknowledgments

One remembers a cherished few teachers and friends who taught one how to think. From my own college days at Rutgers, I remember Eugene Meehan (now at the University of Missouri), Warren Susman, Traian Stoianovich, and my friend, Robert Rosen (now at UCLA). All of them also made graduate school a rare period of discovery. Without them, and without the kind guidance of Donald Weinstein (now at the University of Arizona), the intellectually exhilarating friendship of Abdelwahab Elmessiri, and the love and assistance of Phyllis Reilly, this book would not have been written.

My debts to most of my favorite scholars are compounded by using their work in the text. The assistance of friends and colleagues can be mentioned here. Emily Berleth suggested the book and shepherded my proposal to Harper & Row. Roger Cranse, Vermont Department of Education, and Brock Haussamen, Somerset County College, gave me editorial help and encouragement from the beginning. The following people, while at the institutions listed, read parts or all of the manuscript and made constructive comments: Robert G. Clouse, Indiana State University; Steven Gosch, University of Wisconsin at Eau Claire; Alan Kirshner, Ohlone College; Fred A. Lloyd, III, Danville Community College; John McFarland, Sierra College; Herbert McGuire, Gulf Coast Community College; Andrew Mikus, Glendale Community College; Francis J. Moriarty, Franklin Pierce College; Thomas N. Pappas, Anderson College; and Larry Story, Tarrant County Junior College. Steven Kaufman corrected my most glaring anthropological misconceptions. Dennis Reilly contributed an artist's eye; he and Dave Fowler helped with illustrations. My good friends Mark Bezanson, David Massie, and Gerald Stern listened to my ideas even when they were their own. My students kept me going. Somerset County College gave me a sabbatical year for a trip around the world. Everyone I worked with at Harper & Row was more insightful and helpful than I could have expected. Linda Edwards made typing a new art form. And Marjorie and Charles Colvin gave me the necessary time and space as their "writer in residence" to finish the difficult final stages.

Kevin Reilly

# PERMISSIONS ACKNOWLEDGMENTS

*(The numbers in italics preceding each credit are page numbers in this text.)*

## Text Credits

*6, 7, 8:* Mead quote is from *Sex and Temperament in Three Primitive Societies* by Margaret Mead. Reprinted by permission of William Morrow & Company, Inc.; *15:* Campbell quote is from *Masks of God:* Primitive Mythology by Joseph Campbell. Reprinted by permission of Viking Penguin, Inc.; *24, 25, 31, 70, 80, 81, 83, 85, 85–86, 251–252, 261, 262:* Mumford quotes are excerpts from *The City in History* by Lewis Mumford. Reprinted by permission of Harcourt Brace Jovanovich, Inc.; copyright © 1961 by Lewis Mumford; *35:* Poem quoted is from the Chinese *Classic for Girls,* translated by Isaac T. Headland in *Home Life in China,* published in 1914. Reprinted by permission of Gordon Press, New York. Excerpted from *Marriage, East and West* by David and Vera Mace. Copyright © 1959, 1960 by David and Vera Mace. Reprinted by permission of Doubleday & Company, Inc.; *40:* Poem quoted is from *The Archarnians* by Aristophanes, translated by Douglass Parker, edited by William Arrowsmith. Copyright © 1961 by William Arrowsmith. Reprinted by arrangement with The New American Library, Inc., New York, N.Y.; *79, 241–243:* Toynbee quotes are from *Cities of Destiny,* Arnold Toynbee, ed., 1967. Selections from "Changan" by Arnold F. Wright and "Alexandria Under the Ptolemies" by Claire Preaux. Reprinted by permission of Thames and Hudson Ltd.; *93, 96, 98, 102, 105, 186, 189, 192, 193, 194:* Hunt quotes are from *The Natural History of Love* by Morton Hunt. Reprinted by permission of the author; *106–108:* Ovid quotes are from Ovid's *The Art of Love,* translated by Rolfe Humphries, published by Indiana University Press. Reprinted by permission of Indiana University Press; *139–140:* Homer quotes are reprinted by permission from *The Iliad* by Homer, from The World's Great Classics series, Grolier Incorporated. Bk. XXII, trans. by Andrew Lang, Walter Leaf, and Ernest Myers (N.Y.: Grolier, 1969); *141–142:* McNeill quote is from *A World History* by William McNeill. Copyright © 1967 by Oxford University Press. Reprinted by permission; *160:* Asoka quote is from *Asoka: The Buddhist Emperor of India* translated by Vincent A. Smith (1920). Reprinted by permission of Oxford University Press; *166–167, 171:* Use of J. G. A. Pocock's scholarship in *Politics, Language and Time* by permission of Atheneum Publishers; *170:* Taoist poetry from *The Way and Its Power* by Arthur Waley. Published by George Allen & Unwin, Publishers, Ltd. Reprinted by permission; *225:* Arab poetry is quoted from *The Medieval World* by Friedrich Heer (New York: New American Library, 1961); *232, 232–234:* Huizinga quotes are from *The Waning of the Middle Ages* by J. Huizinga © 1967. Reprinted by permission of St. Martin's Press, Inc. and Edward Arnold Publishers Ltd.; *245:* Quote is from *Daily Life in China on the Eve of the Mongol Invasion 1250–1276* by Jacques Gernet. Translation © George Allen & Unwin, Publishers, Ltd., 1962. Reprinted with permission of Macmillan; *256–257:* Quote is from Helene Wieruszowski, "Art and the Commune in the Time of Dante," *Speculum,* Volume XIX, No. 1, January 1944. Reprinted by permission of the Medieval Academy of America; *270–271:* Two Toynbee quotes are from "The Religious Background of the Present Environmental Crisis" by Arnold Toynbee which originally appeared in the *International Journal of Environmental Studies,* 3 (1972), 141–146. Reprinted by permission of the author and the *Journal.* Quoted from *Ecology and Religion in History* edited by David and Eileen Spring. Used by permission of Harper & Row, Publishers, Inc. and Gordon & Breach Science Publishers; *271–272, 272:* White quotes are from "The Historical Roots of Our Ecologic Crisis" by Lynn White, Jr. which originally appeared in *Science,* 155 (10 March 1967), 1203–1207. Copyright 1967 by the American Association for the Advancement of Science. Reprinted by permission of *Science* and the author. This article was delivered at a meeting of the American Association for the Advancement of Science in Washington, D.C., 26 December 1966. Quoted from *Ecology and Religion in History* edited by David and Eileen Spring. Used by permission of Harper & Row, Publishers, Inc.; *271:* White quoted in Spring's *Ecology and Religion in History* is from the Introduction of David and Eileen Spring's *Ecology and Religion in History,* used by permission of Harper & Row, Publishers, Inc.; *275:* Poems quoted from *Masks of God:* Oriental Mythology by Joseph Campbell. Reprinted by permission of Viking Penguin, Inc.; *276,*

*277, 278:* Quoted in Yi-Fu Tuan, "Discrepancies Between Environmental Attitude and Behavior: Examples from Europe and China," *The Canadian Geographer,* 12, no. 3 (1968), quoted in Spring, *Ecology and Religion; 285–286, 386, 387–388, 395:* Mumford quotes are excerpts from *Technics and Civilization* by Lewis Mumford. Reprinted by permission of Harcourt Brace Jovanovich, Inc.; copyright © 1934 by Harcourt Brace Jovanovich Inc.; copyright © 1962 by Lewis Mumford; *298, 300, 301:* Machiavelli quotes are from Niccolo Machiavelli, *The Prince,* translated by Luigi Ricci (Modern Library, 1940). Reprinted by permission of Oxford University Press; *302, 303, 307:* Cassirer quotes are from Ernst Cassirer's *The Myth of the State,* 1946. Reprinted by permission of Yale University Press; *317–318:* Hobbes's quotes are taken from *The Political Theory of Possessive Individualism* by C. B. Macpherson (1962). Reprinted by permission of Oxford University Press; *341:* Table is from a section of "Table I" from B. H. Slicher Van Bath's *The Agrarian History of Western Europe.* Reprinted by permission of Edward Arnold Publishers Ltd.; *400:* Commager quote is from Henry Steele Commager, "America's Heritage of Bigness," *Saturday Review,* July 4, 1970. Reprinted by permission of the *Saturday Review; 401:* Murray quote is excerpted from an article by Bertram G. Murray, Jr., "What the Ecologists Can Teach Economists," which appeared in the *New York Times* Magazine, December 10, 1972. © 1972 by *The New York Times Company.* Reprinted by permission; *415–416, 416, 417–418:* Quotes reprinted from *The Defense of Gracchus Babeuf before the High Court of Vendome,* edited and translated by John Anthony Scott, copyright © 1967 by the University of Massachusetts Press; *419, 421, 422, 423, 424:* Quotes from *The Utopian Vision of Charles Fournier: Selected Texts on Work, Love and Passionate Attraction* edited by Jonathan Beecher and Richard Bienvenu, published by Beacon Press, Boston, Massachusetts; *438, 439, 440–441: Communist Manifesto* quotes from Karl Marx and Friedrich Engels, *The Communist Manifesto,* ed., Samuel H. Beer, 1955. Reprinted by permission of AMH Publishing Corporation; *454–456:* Quote from the James Hamilton article "Some Dynamics of Anti-Negro Prejudice" which appeared in *The Psychoanalytic Review,* Volume LIII (1966–1967). Reprinted by permission of *The Psychoanalytic Review; 475–476, 481, 482–483:* Quotes reprinted by permission of G. P. Putman's Sons from *By the Sweat of Thy Brow* by Melvin Kranzberg and Joseph Gies. Copyright © 1975 by Melvin Kranzberg and Joseph Gies; *508, 510, 511, 512, 514, 515, 515–516, 517, 519:* Commoner quotes from *The Closing Circle: Nature, Man and Technology* by Barry Commoner. Copyright © 1971 by Barry Commoner. Reprinted by permission of Alfred A. Knopf, Inc. Portions of this book originally appeared in *The New Yorker; 519:* Schrag quote from Peter Schrag, "Who Owns the Environment?" *Saturday Review,* July 4, 1970. Reprinted by permission of the *Saturday Review.*

## Map Credits

*55, 56:* Figures taken from *History of Mankind: Cultural and Scientific Developments, Vol. I: Prehistory and the Beginning of Civilization, Part I* by Jacquetta Hawkes and Sir Leonard Wooley. George Allen & Unwin, 1963. © UNESCO 1963. Reproduced by permission of UNESCO; *71, 82:* Redrawn by permission of Macmillan Publishing Co., Inc. from *The Western Heritage,* Vol. I by Donald Kagan, Frank M. Turner, and Steven E. Ozment. Copyright © 1979 Macmillan Publishing Co., Inc.; *76:* From *Cities of Destiny,* edited by Arnold Toynbee. © 1967 Thames and Hudson Limited; *242:* T'ang China map is from Hilda Hookham's *A Short History of China.* Copyright © 1969, 1970 The Longman Group Ltd. By permission of The Longman Group Limited. The Changan map is used by permission of The British Library; *348:* Redrawn by permission of Macmillan Publishing Co., Inc., from *British History Atlas* by Martin Gilbert, cartography by Arthur Banks. Copyright © 1968 by Martin Gilbert; *488:* Redrawn by permission of Macmillan Publishing Co., Inc., from *Recent History Atlas* by Martin Gilbert, cartography by John Flower. Copyright © 1966 by Martin Gilbert; *494–495:* Adapted from *A World History,* B. L. Linder, E. Selzer, and B. M. Berk © 1979, Science Research Associates, Inc. By permission of the publisher.

# I

# PART I

# THE ANCIENT WORLD

## To 1000 B.C.

# Chapter 1

# Masculine and Feminine

## Nature and History

> He is playing masculine. She is playing feminine.
>
> He is playing masculine *because* she is playing feminine. She is playing feminine *because* he is playing masculine.
>
> He is playing the kind of man that she thinks the kind of woman she is playing ought to admire. She is playing the kind of woman that he thinks the kind of man he is playing ought to desire.
>
> If he were not playing masculine, he might well be more feminine than she is—except when she is playing very feminine. If she were not playing feminine, she might well be more masculine than he is—except when he is playing very masculine.
>
> So he plays harder. And she plays . . . softer.[1]

We have all played masculine/feminine. We've been taught it from birth. Only recently has it occurred to us that it might be a game.

Many of us have been prompted by women's movements and homosexual groups in the last few years to question some of our traditional ideas about what is "natural" for men and women. We are used to thinking that there is something natural in men being strong, logical, athletic, tough, ambitious, and unemotional while women are naturally moody, intuitive, passive, and emotional.

## An Anthropologist Discovers Culture

These expectations run so deep that the American anthropologist Margaret Mead set out in the 1930s to find out not whether men and women have different temperaments, but what those differences are. She landed in New Guinea and lived with three primitive societies which she chose quite accidentally. She was astonished by what she found, and the lessons she learned are just as instructive today as they were 40 years ago.

The first society she visited called themselves the Arapesh. This isolated mountain tribe evidently had no idea that women were supposed to have different personalities from men—so they didn't. Both Arapesh men and women displayed what we would call feminine and maternal personality traits. For both, the main business of life was conceiving and "growing" children. The Arapesh verb meaning "to bear a child" is used for the father or the mother. The father is thought to labor as hard as the mother in bringing the child into the world. Though children are made of the father's semen and the mother's blood, the "life soul" of the infant can come from either parent. From the moment the child is born, the father shares all of the tasks in caring for the baby. He even lies down next to his wife, carefully placing his head on a wooden pillow to protect his elaborate headdress, and is said by the other natives to be "in bed having a baby."[2]

As the child grows, the father assists its mother in all of the trying details:

> Fathers show as little embarrassment as mothers in disposing of the very young child's excreta, and as much patience as their wives in persuading a young child to eat soup from one of the clumsy coconut spoons that are always too large for the child's mouth. The minute day-by-day care of little children, with its routine, its exasperations, its wails of misery that cannot be correctly interpreted, these are as congenial to the Arapesh men as they are to the Arapesh women. And in recognition of this care, as well as in recognition of the father's initial contribution, if one comments upon a middle-aged man as good-looking, the people answer: Good-looking? Ye-e-s! But you should have seen him before he bore all those children.[3]

From our perspective, Arapesh men are even more "feminine" than the women. As already suggested, it is the men who take hours fixing their hair. They are also the ones who decorate themselves, wear special ceremonial clothing, and dance. Only the men are thought capable of painting in color, so men are the more artistic of the Arapesh.

Arapesh women, however, do not feel compelled to have opposite personalities. Both men and women are trained to be "co-operative, unaggressive, responsive to the needs and demands of others. We found no idea that sex was a powerful driving force either for men or for women."[4]

The second tribe Margaret Mead visited was the Mundugumor. Located less than a hundred miles away, but in a low-lying river valley, the Mundugumor were like the Arapesh in only one way: they too expected men and women to have the same personalities. But their expectations were exactly the reverse of those of the Arapesh.

> We found among the Mundugumor that both men and women developed as ruthless, aggressive, positively sexed individuals, with the maternal cherishing aspects of personality at a minimum. Both men and women approximated to a personality type that we in our culture would find only in an undisciplined and very violent male. . . . The Mundugumor ideal is the violent aggressive man married to the violent aggressive woman.[5]

Mundugumor men and women were equally bored and exasperated by raising children. They treated them viciously or indifferently when young, and as sexual competitors or objects of gratification when older.

We might imagine Margaret Mead's refreshing surprise when she came to the third tribe, again chosen accidentally and located on a lake between the Arapesh and Mundugumor. Here at last was a tribe that insisted, as we do, that men and women had different, even opposite, personalities. Like us, this tribe, the Tchambuli, expected men to be men and women to be women without any annoying, fuzzy in-between shades of gray.

Imagine her astonishment, then, when she discovered that the Tchambuli men were models of American femininity and the women were all taught to be what we would call "masculine."

> In the third tribe, the Tchambuli, we found a genuine reversal of the sex-attitudes of our own culture, with the woman the dominant, impersonal, managing partner, the man the less responsible and the emotionally dependent person.[6]

Tchambuli women fish and gather food while the men arrange their curls and beautify their masks or practice their flute playing. The arts—dancing, carving, and painting—are unimportant to the women, but they are the most important activities possible for the men. Tchambuli men cultivate the mincing step and the charming, nervous sensitivity of the actress. Most of their lives are played out self-consciously as if they were performing roles on the stage which they would hope the women would enjoy. Tchambuli women work together in an atmosphere of comradeship and almost boisterous good fun. In contrast, relationships between the men are always strained and watchful, and their remarks are usually catty. The women create the wealth of Tchambuli society by making and selling mosquito nets. The men do the shopping, dressed up in their finest feathers and shell ornaments, haggling over every purchase, but continually mindful that they are using the women's property.

> Real property, which one actually owns, one receives from women, in return for languishing looks and soft words. . . . The women's attitude towards the men is one of kindly tolerance and appreciation. They enjoy the games that the men play, they particularly enjoy the theatricals that the men put on for their benefit.[7]

Women are the ones who are expected to initiate sexual activity. Men await women's advances, sometimes coyly and sometimes in shame and fear. If a widow does not immediately take another lover, people are surprised at her restraint.

> Has she not a vulva? they ask. This is the comment that is continually made in Tchambuli: Are women passive sexless creatures who can be expected to wait upon the dilly-dallying . . . [of men?][8]

The implicit Tchambuli answer is "not if they are normal."

The beliefs and behavior of these three tribes are probably not typical of most primitives, but there is enough variety to suggest that nothing at all is normal or "natural" for either men or women. One Philippine tribe is convinced that "no man can keep a secret." The Manus, another Pacific tribe, believe that "only men enjoy playing with babies." Another, the Toda, maintain that "almost all domestic work" is "too sacred for women."[9]

Examples of human diversity abound. Men and women are born with the potential to be hard or soft, aggressive or passive, even "masculine" or "feminine." They have to be taught to be like one sex or the other. And different societies teach different things.

The investigations of Margaret Mead and other anthropologists into the styles of life of the few remaining primitive tribes of the world reveal a potential for modification, if not elimination, of our own sexual stereotypes. The demands of women and homosexuals for less oppressively narrow conceptions of what it is to be a man or woman are not unrealistic. They are not asking us to destroy anything that is natural; they are only asking that we change something that has been shaped by human beings.

Once we know such change is possible, we are free to ask if it is desirable or likely. Therefore, we have to know how changes in sexual styles come about. To know how flexible or inflexible our social customs are, we have to ask how and when they originated. To know how they can be changed, we have to know what made things this way. What brought us to this juncture? If we chose one out of many life-styles, when did we make that choice? Why? What were the alternatives? Why weren't they chosen?

Most of these are the questions of the historian. History is not the study of the past for its own sake. It is the study of change, the study of how the past did, or did not, become the present.

In the rest of this chapter we will ask how the relationship of men and women has changed over time. The anthropologist can show us that there is nothing "natural" in the way we do things, but that does not explain why we do things our way. We must study the past to understand the general direction of human change.

## Archeologists Discover Change

When we ask how the roles and relationships of men and women have changed, we must examine the most basic changes in human history. We must attempt to outline the changes that occurred in male and female roles over the longest possible duration. This is much more difficult than asking about the relationship of city people and country people, for example. To answer that question we only have to look at the last five thousand years because there have only been cities that long. In contrast, there have been men and women as long as there have been human beings.

Since we are attempting to discover the broadest outlines of human change, we must ask the help of archeologists as well as historians. Historians normally study only written records of human change, and writing was only invented about five thousand years ago, in the first cities. Archeologists dig beneath these ancient cities for the silent records—the broken pieces of pottery and huts, the charred animal remains, the fragments of human bone, the painted shells, the stone axes and digging sticks—which reveal something about the earliest human societies before the invention of writing and city life. Archeologists have been able not only to dig up the remains of earlier human groups, but they have also been able to reconstruct the general development and most basic changes of the human past. Let us turn, then, to examine the methods and conclusions of these archeologists.

Since it is impossible for any society to bury its garbage over its head, archeologists can chart the stages of human development simply by digging. To dig deeper is always to go backward in time. In this way, archeologists have discovered roughly three stages of human history: hunting-gathering, farming, and city life. They find the remains of these three stages in reverse order when they dig. Directly below the oldest cities they find the tools of farmers, and below the remains of farmers they always find the tools of older hunting-gathering groups. They can even give approximate dates to the tools and bones they discover because they know that all organic (human, vegetable, and animal) matter loses half of its carbon radioactivity every five or six thousand years. This method of radiocarbon dating tells them that the earliest human cities were created about five thousand years ago, and the earliest farming villages go back about ten thousand years.

We can summarize all of human history, then, in very rough terms. First, all humans were hunters of wild animals or gatherers of wild plants and insects. In their dependence on wild foods, their lives were not very different from that of apes. Then, gradually after 8000 B.C., people began to learn to grow their own food and tame animals. Only about .001 percent of the world's population today has not yet entered this second or "farming stage" of history. Then, soon after 3000 B.C. (at least in the areas of the Middle East which had first developed farming), the "city stage" of history began. In these societies farming was so efficient (largely because of the invention of a heavy plow drawn by animals) that large numbers of people could live and work without themselves farming. We might even add a recent "fourth" stage, which we will call the "industrial stage," to this outline. In the last two hundred years, Europe and North America have undergone an industrial revolution which has been productive enough to allow 80 percent of the population to live without farming.

It is safe to say that no changes in human history have been as important as these. Obviously, not all hunters, or all farmers, are alike. But the differences between hunters and farmers are much greater than the differences between any two groups of either. Similarly, although there are still farmers in city societies (since people have to eat), the lives of these farmers are usually transformed by city markets, governments, tools, culture, and communications that make them very different people from the farmers before 3000 B.C. If anything in the roles and relationships of men and women is normal, we should expect to find it changed little as humanity evolved from hunting-gathering to farming to city living.

## Hunters and Gatherers: The Paleolithic Period

The earliest human societies were unlike the Arapesh, Mundugumor, and Tchambuli, who were all farmers. Before the first human beings learned the complicated process of planting seeds to make things grow around ten thousand years ago, all people had been hunters and gatherers. In these earliest of human societies the men probably did most of the hunting. Women probably moved around less than men since they periodically gave birth and nursed the children. While small bands of men followed the larger wild animals, women gathered grains, seeds, nuts, fruit, roots, eggs, grubs, small animals, and insects. Women's work was steady and regular. Except in periods of extreme hardship, it provided the group with an adequate amount of food and allowed the group to avoid starvation even when the men came home with nothing. Men's work was more spectacular, but its rewards were less regular. Importantly, a society which could not afford to save its food, or lacked knowledge about preserving it, required the daily regularity of women's work more than the occasional luxury of men's provisions.

Women, of course, not only sustained life by regularly gathering enough food to survive, they also produced life from their own bodies. The magic of childbirth must have haunted primitive men. The oldest human art testifies to the importance of female fertility in the minds of these hunters and gatherers. The oldest statues that archeologists have found are statues of women, or, more accurately, since they do not show individual features, they are statues of pregnant, fertile womankind. Typical of these is the Venus of Willendorf with full breasts, belly, buttocks, and thighs. This statue (made fifteen thousand years ago) and the many others like it seem to have been objects of worship. This is indicated by some of the features common to most of these female statues. They are painted with a red clay which seems to have been reserved for the sacred. Many of them have been found near what appear to be altar fires next to charred bones (possibly the remains of animal sacrifices). Finally, they all emphasize the life-giving and life-sustaining functions which are normally associated

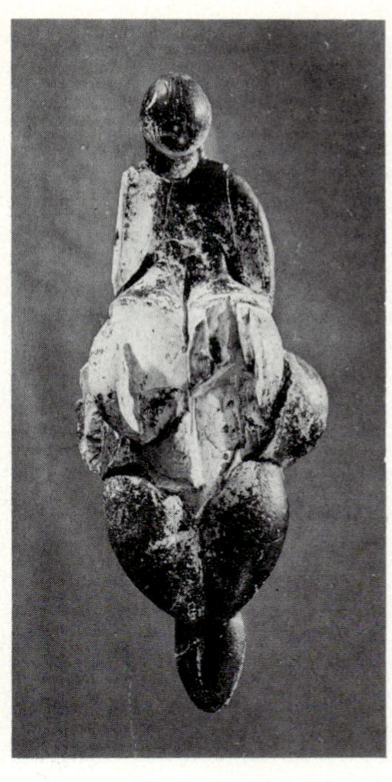

■ *Paleolithic Venuses like these are the oldest sculptural representations of the human form. They testify to the religious importance of female fertility in the Old Stone Age when the deities may have been goddesses. The Venus of Willendorf (bottom) is the one with the braided head. The rough, squatting figure (top, left) is one of many found in excavations at Jarmo (Iraq). The Venus of Lespugue (top, right) and the Venus of Laussel (Part I opening page) were found in France. (Naturhistorisches Museum, Wien; Oriental Institute, University of Chicago; Musée de L'homme, Scala, EPA)*

with the divine. Although there are very few statues of men from the end of this Paleolithic period, none of those which have been found display any of these supernatural characteristics.

It seems very likely, then, that in the oldest human societies the gods were not gods at all, but goddesses. The most magical and mysterious of human experiences was the giving of life, and that was woman's work. The fertility goddess enshrined woman's magical "labor" and her regular daily work: producing life and sustaining it.

## A Paleolithic Matriarchy?

Some people have concluded that if primitive gods were women, then women must have been like gods in primitive society. In defense of this position, it is certainly difficult to imagine a male-dominated society that worshiped women, and certainly there must have been some resemblance between the image that Paleolithic people had of women and the role that women actually played in Paleolithic society.

But we should be careful of assuming that the religion of Paleolithic people was only a mirror image of their society. Imagine archeologists thousands of years from now digging up the ruins of our own society and trying to interpret how we think and feel on the basis of our art. Imagine those archeologists coming upon the ruins of one of our newsstands and congratulating themselves on the value of such a find. How astonished they would probably be at discovering that much of our "art" seemed to be devoted to photographing the female nude, especially large breasts. It might not be a mistake for those future archeologists to conclude that twentieth-century Americans worshiped the female form. But they would surely be wrong if they concluded that these Americans must have lived in a society dominated by women. The existence of so many pornographic magazines and the attraction of so many movie "goddesses" in the film magazines, the scandal sheets, and even the daily newspapers would tell the archeologists very little about the actual power and position of women in our society.

Therefore, we should be careful about assuming that women were goddesses in Paleolithic society simply because the few bits of evidence that we have indicate that the gods were women. We should be all too conscious of the way in which a preoccupation with femininity (in the *Playboy* manner) can be just another aspect of the exploitation of women in general and of the actual weakness of women in the society. We should be well aware of the capacities of men to put women on a pedestal in order to keep them out of the real world.

The question we have to ask is to what extent Paleolithic institutions show the dominance of women. Modern anthropologists speak of such institutions as "matrilineal" and "matrilocal." A matrilineal group is one in which the line of descent (and inheritance) is figured through the women's line rather than the men's (as in our society). A matrilocal group is one in which the husband comes to live with his wife's family, rather than the wife living with the husband's family or in the husband's place of residence (as in our society). Some anthropologists have even argued that "matriarchy" (by which they mean matrilineality and matrilocality) was the original state of human affairs.

Now, we can't know what was original. There is little evidence about the ways of life of these hunter-gatherer societies thousands of years ago. To make things worse, words like "matriarchy" for societies where women are in control and "patriarchy" for societies dominated by men are somewhat fuzzy. No society is ruled entirely by either men or women. Certainly, both mothers and fathers have some influence in any society, both inside and outside of the family. No group of people can exclude half the population (the other sex) from all power, position, or influence. Even in societies where women are not allowed to have jobs outside of the home, their influence on the children, the family, and home life is bound to be considerable. Some writers have even called modern American society mom-oriented precisely because our most important values and ideas are developed as children while our fathers spend most of their time outside of the home in the "real" world of work.

But the fact that most of the important jobs in our society are performed by men, and the fact that women feel compelled at all to demand equality with men, indicate that we live in more of a patriarchy than a matriarchy. Most people would still rather have sons than daughters. Most people (even women) prefer men to "wear the pants" in the family and make the more important decisions in the world of politics, business, and society. A mark of women's oppression (only twenty years ago) was the conclusion of women's magazine editors that most women can "identify completely with the victims of blindness, deafness, physical maiming, cerebral palsy, paralysis, cancer, or approaching death" while they have difficulty identifying with ambitious women in meaningful careers.[10]

We live then in a predominantly patriarchal society. Our custom of patrilineality (women generally take the name of their fathers and husbands; men rarely take the name of their mothers or wives) and our custom of patrilocality (wives almost always live near the husband's job, if not with his family) are both signs of the dominance of the male in modern society. They are also both very old customs—but they are not eternal.

## Some Evidence

At least some hunting societies were matrilineal and matrilocal. This may have been necessitated by the demands of the hunt. Since groups of men may frequently have been chasing wild animals, the lives of women—gathering wild foods—may have been the only link to a permanent area and a continuing tradition.

In other cases, the male hunters, especially if they were successful at providing the society's main source of food, may have been able to impose their own control. In *The Second Sex*, the French feminist Simone de Beauvoir argues that the most important value of hunting society must have been the taking of life (men's work) rather than the giving of life (women's work). Many of these bands of hunters formed aggressively masculine clubs (not too unlike modern fraternities and fraternal lodges) which created religious beliefs and practices that excluded women and dominated the whole society. But it is interesting even here how defensive these men's secret societies appear. A scholar of primitive mythology, Joseph Campbell, has observed:

> It is, in fact, most remarkable how many of these primitive hunting races have the legend of a still more primitive age than their own, in which the women were the sole possessors of the magical art. Among the Ona of Tierra del Fuego, for example, the idea is fundamental to the origin legend of the lodge or *Hain* of the men's secret society.[11]

The origin legend of these Ona Indians on the desolate southern tip of South America can be summarized briefly as follows:

In the days long ago before the parakeet painted the forests with its colors, and mountains were still sleeping giants, in those distant days, only women knew the secrets of magic and witchcraft. They kept their own lodge in which they taught their daughters how to bring sickness and death; and men were frightened and powerless. Finally, the women's tyranny became so great that the men got together and massacred all of the women. They left only the young girls who had not yet begun their studies in witchcraft. And while they waited for the girls to grow up to replace their wives, they wondered how they might prevent them from reestablishing the tyranny of their mothers. So they created their own lodge (the *Hain*) to take the place of the women's lodge, and they banished all women from their secret activities, under penalty of death. Then, they invented a new group of demons which they said hated women, and they dressed up to look like these creatures to scare the women away.[12]

Among the hunting tribes of Australia who are today often patriarchal, there are also signs of a previous age dominated by women.

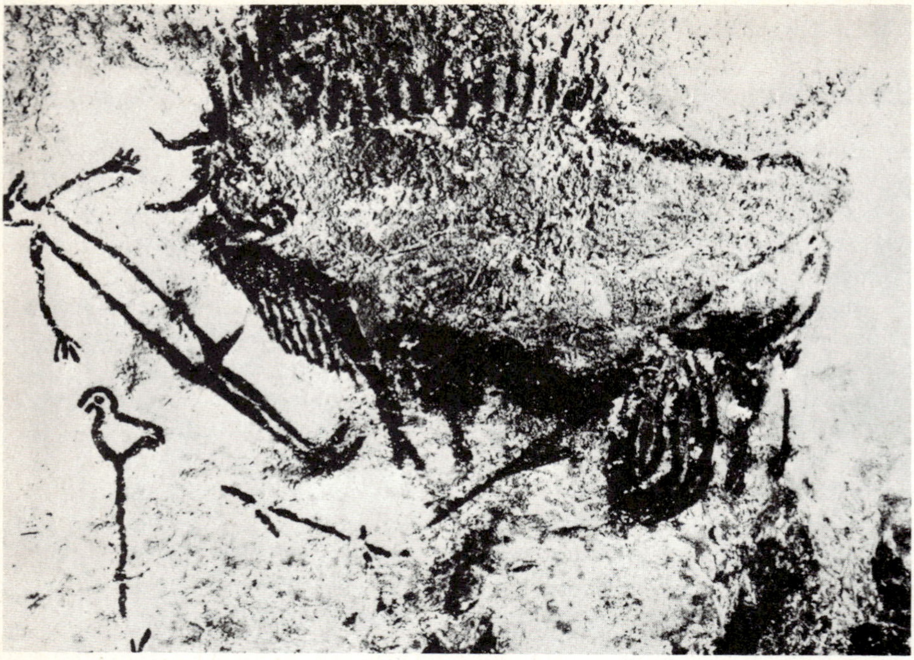

■ *The violence and beauty of the male, Paleolithic hunt is captured in these cave paintings from Lascaux, France. (Wide World; Granger)*

Some of the most sacred spots of these Australian aborigines are said by the natives to mark the place where women performed the magic in mythological times, and the cave drawings are almost exclusively of women. Even in some of the men's lodges, which are today the center of male power in the society, the most important divinities are frequently female, and the supreme being itself is thought of as an Earth Mother. On closer examination of these secret men's societies which initiate young boys into manhood, the men's sense of inferiority for which they are trying to overcompensate is evident.

> The basic theme of the initiatory cult . . . is that women, by virtue of their ability to make children, hold the secrets of life. Men's role is uncertain, undefined, and perhaps unnecessary. By a great effort man has hit upon a method of compensating himself for his basic inferiority. Equipped with various mysterious noise-making instruments, whose potency rests upon their actual forms being unknown to those who hear the sounds—that is, the women and children must never know they are really bamboo flutes, or hollow logs, or bits of elliptoid wood whirled on strings—they get the male children away from the women, brand them as incomplete, and themselves turn boys into men. Women, it is true, make human beings, but only men can make men. Sometimes more overtly, sometimes less, these imitations of birth go on, as the initiates are swallowed by the crocodile that represents the men's group and come out new-born at the other end; as they are housed in wombs, or fed on blood, fattened, hand-fed, and tended by male "mothers." Behind the cult lies the myth that in some way all of this was stolen from the women; sometimes women were killed to get it. Men owe their manhood to a theft and a theatrical mime, which would fall to the ground in a moment as mere dust and ashes if its true constituents were known.[13]

Hunting societies, also are usually oriented to the moon rather than the sun, and the lunar spirits are imagined to be particularly sensitive to female needs (as they are obviously attuned to women's biological rhythms). Paleolithic hunters relied on the moon for evening light and for measuring time, and saw it as the source of not only women's sexuality but also the mysterious powers of the witch.

It is unlikely, of course, that all human societies developed in the same way. Among the .001 percent of today's world population that still lives a Paleolithic life, more are patrilineal and patrilocal than are matrilineal and matrilocal. Whether these signs of patriarchy are outweighed by religious signs of matriarchy is only speculation. Whether these current Paleolithic societies were preceded by more matriarchal societies, as some of the legends suggest, is also speculation. Some anthropologists have speculated that the older Paleolithic world that produced the Venus figurines was replaced, with the retreat of the last ice age (around 15,000 to 12,000 years ago), with a world that produced more aggressively masculine cave paintings, and that these paintings suggest a renewed patriarchy. But these theories encourage further study rather than conclusions. The evidence is still too limited.

## Human Nature and Human History

The comic-strip image of the brawny caveman pulling a woman by the hair into his cave for an evening's entertainment is an image which answers a modern need to believe in human nature. In a society like ours, where everything is changing constantly, we are eager for images of an unchanging, universal, human nature. But the modern experience of change has also prompted the discovery by anthropologists that people act in terms of their particular "culture," and that there are a large number of different cultures in the world. Almost anything is "natural" for the humans of a culture somewhere in the past or present world. The study of archeology (also nourished by the changing modern world) has taught us to see fundamental changes (some have even said "stages") in human history. Taken together, the discovery of the importance of culture and of the fundamental changes in human experience has meant a discovery of cultural change in human history that is often so fundamental from one era to another that the idea of human nature seems inadequate. We have begun, in the last hundred years or so, to see that what we want to call "human nature" is only a particular cultural example of human history.

Fifty years ago, the archeologist V. Gordon Childe expressed the idea that there is no human nature other than those worked out in human history by titling his classic study of Paleolithic, Neolithic, and early urban life *Man Makes Himself*. Today, we might say with the aid of more recently cultivated sensitivities that history is the account of how men and women make and remake themselves and each other.

The process by which men and women make their "natures," as Childe pointed out, has much to do with the tools they shape to mold their worlds. Tools change the maker as well as the world, and the new world calls for different people, with different abilities and different possibilities. The Paleolithic technological system created not only a hunting-gathering social system, but also fostered the science, sensitivities, superstitions, and sexual roles which seemed to make that society work. Our knowledge of that Paleolithic human nature is one of the many modern tools we have for making ourselves.

## *For Further Reading*

There is an abundance of anthropological literature on men and women. Margaret Mead is a good place to start. We have relied on **Sex and Temperament in Three Primitive Societies,*** but the student might also want to consult her **Male and Female*** bearing in mind that some feminists (e.g., Betty Friedman in **The Feminine Mystique***) find this and Mead's other later work reflecting a more "sexist" bias.

The anthropological classics that first suggested the existence of an ancient matriarchy are dated but still worth reading. If one does not go all the way back to J. J. Bachofen's **Mutterrecht (Mother Right)*** of 1861, it might be interesting to look at the early suggestions of the American Lewis Henry Morgan in **Ancient Society*** (1877) if only because it was adopted by Marx and Engels in the latter's **The Origin of the Family, Private Property, and the State*** (1884) and thus influenced generations of Marxists and communists. Even more interesting is Robert Briffault's **The Mothers*** (1927) or the abridgement of the three volumes into a single volume by Gordon Rattray Taylor. For recent anthropological criticisms of this tradition, one might want to consult the writings of Robin Fox or Lionel Tiger, especially the latter's **Men in Groups.*** There is also a recent collection of articles by women called **Woman, Culture & Society,*** edited by Michelle Zimbalist Rosaldo and Louise Lamphere, which objects to the idea of an ancient matriarchy, but in general supports the argument of Engels and others that women's power in society has usually been related to her contributions to the important work of the society. (It seems to me that that is what "matriarchy" means in Neolithic society.)

One of the best archeological studies of the Paleolithic age is Jacquetta Hawkes's **Prehistory.*** Aside from her, archeologists have been less willing than anthropologists to generalize about Paleolithic sexuality, partly because the nature of their "hard evidence" is less conclusive. Specialists in other areas, however, have offered some interesting interpretations of archeological findings which relate to our study of men and women. The art historian, S. Gideon, for instance, in **The Eternal Present: The Beginnings of Art** has a lot of fascinating things to say about Paleolithic cave painting, fertility symbols, and Venus figurines. Similarly, Joseph Campbell's **The Masks of God: Primitive Mythology*** is full of insight regarding Paleolithic sexual symbolization.

Unfortunately most of the recent literature growing out of the women's movement is either not historical or concerned with modern history. One notable exception is the work of Evelyn Reed.* Most of the histories of women devote only an introductory chapter to the Paleolithic era. Some of the exceptions are more polemical than historical: Elaine Morgan's **The Descent of Women*** and Elizabeth Gould Davis's **The First Sex*** overtax the credibility of most men and Amaury de Riencourt's **Sex and Power in History*** would equally infuriate most women. Short, incisive discussions of

* Available in paperback.

the problem can be found in the introductory sections of Kate Millett's **Sexual Politics*** and Lewis Mumford's **The City in History.*** A promising addition at the time of this writing is Michel Foucault's multivolume **The History of Sexuality.**

## *Notes*

1. Betty Roszak and Theodore Roszak, *Masculine/Feminine* (New York: Harper & Row, 1969), p. vii.
2. Margaret Mead, *Sex and Temperament in Three Primitive Societies* (New York: Dell, 1935, 1950, 1963), p. 50.
3. *Ibid.*, p. 55.
4. *Ibid.*, p. 259.
5. *Ibid.*
6. *Ibid.*
7. *Ibid.*, p. 239.
8. *Ibid.*, p. 243.
9. *Ibid.*, p. 16.
10. Betty Friedan, *The Feminine Mystique* (New York: Dell, 1963, 1970), p. 46.
11. Joseph Campbell, *The Masks of God: Primitive Mythology* (New York: Viking Press, 1959, 1969), p. 315.
12. *Ibid.*, pp. 315–316 (adapted).
13. Mead, *Male and Female* (New York: Morrow, 1949), pp. 102–103.

# Chapter 2

# Matriarchy and Patriarchy

## Agricultural and Urban Power

Women's movements in the last few years have alerted us not only to the sexual stereotyping of masculine and feminine personalities for boys and girls. They have also called our attention to the unequal power of men and women in adult society. Economic power on the job, political power in public office, social power in the community have all been held by men in greater proportion than their numbers would warrant.

How long has it been a "man's world"? Were women ever the leaders of society? Have men always been in charge? Where does men's power come from? If we live in a patriarchy, when did it originate? What were its historical causes?

These are some of the questions raised in this chapter. We cannot answer all of them. We can, however, put these questions in an historical context and offer some theories.

One of our theories is that the patriarchy, as we know it, does not go back to the beginning of time. Although Paleolithic society might have often been patriarchical, it does not seem that Neolithic society was. That is not to say that Neolithic society was matriarchal, though we will examine some of the evidence for that assertion. Neolithic society at least seems to have reversed some of the patriarchal institutions of the Paleolithic period. In many ways Neolithic society seems to have provided women with considerable prestige and status. Our theory is that our modern patriarchy developed after the Neolithic Age—in the first city civilizations of the ancient world. We will offer some evidence for this theory, and then let the student decide.

## Farmers and Herders: The Neolithic Period

The most important breakthrough in human history (at least until the last couple of hundred years) was the invention of agriculture. This was women's invention, and it probably elevated the position of women in many of the societies in which it occurred.

Paleolithic hunters and gatherers were forced to rely on whatever nature provided. With the invention of agriculture, people took their first giant step to control nature. Women who had spent their days picking wild fruits, nuts, and grains learned that they could plant some of these "seeds" in the ground and grow more than happened to grow naturally. At about the same time that women learned they could "tame" and control the natural vegetable world, men learned ways of taming and controlling the animals that they previously had to chase.

These events—the domestication of plants and animals—occurred first about ten thousand years ago in parts of the Middle East, India, and China, and soon after in other parts of the world. By 1500 B.C. 99 percent of the people in the world were living this Neolithic or New Stone Age way of life.

In the early stages of the Neolithic period, the invention of agriculture was even more important than the domestication of animals. In fact, it was probably not until men were able to take over much of the agricultural work (with the aid of their animals) that women were relegated to a secondary position in society.

## Women's Work

Women were the inventors of agriculture. Since they had been the gatherers, they were more familiar with the world of plants. They knew which plants were edible, which were poisonous, which grew the easiest, or which provided the most food. They were also equipped with the oldest human tool, the digging stick, which could be used to plant seeds as well as to uproot the harvest. The work routine of agriculture was also very much like that of gathering. It was steady, regular, and tedious; it lacked excitement, but usually provided a predictable, basic food supply.

Agriculture created the first economy of abundance: the first economy where people could have more food than they had to eat immediately. But this could only come about through saving and planning. In the early stages, women probably had to keep some of the grains and other seeds that they gathered away from the men. Notably, the invention of planting required the first systematic saving and planning for the future. It was eventually so successful that human populations were able to multiply to hundreds of times the density of gathering populations.

The Neolithic revolution was more than the invention of planting, though. It was a whole set of interrelated inventions that made farming efficient and increased the uses of the harvest. Most of this was women's work. One expert summarizes the achievement this way:

> To accomplish the neolithic revolution mankind, or rather womankind, had not only to discover suitable plants and appropriate methods for their cultivation, but must also devise special implements for tilling the soil, reaping and storing the crop, and converting it into foods. . . .
>
> It is an essential element in the neolithic economy that sufficient food shall be gathered at each harvest and stored to last till the next crop is ripe, normally in a year's time. Granaries or storehouses were accordingly a prominent feature. . . . Wheat and barley need to be separated from the husk by threshing and winnowing, and then ground into flour. The grinding could be done by pounding in a mortar, but the standard procedure was to rub the grains on a saucer-shaped or saddle-shaped stone with a bun-shaped or sausage-shaped rubbing-stone. . . .
>
> The flour can be easily converted into porridge or into flat cakes, but to make it into bread requires a knowledge of some biochemistry—the use of the microorganism, yeast—and also a specially constructed oven. Moreover, the same biochemical process as was used to make bread rise opened to mankind a new world of enchantment.[1]

The source of enchantment that the author refers to is woman's invention of beer, wine, and liquor which they made by adding yeast to liquified grains or grapes. Alcoholic drinks must have been an especially convincing demonstration of the magical power of woman's agricultural efforts. The earliest priests and priestesses in ancient Mesopotamia and Egypt drank and offered these intoxicants to their gods and goddesses to increase their power over the crops.

The invention of fermented liquors meant the invention of permanent, often elaborate, containers.

> By 3000 B.C., indeed, intoxicants had become necessities to most societies in Europe and Hither Asia, and a whole service of jars, jugs, beakers, strainers, and drinking-tubes had come into fashion for their ceremonial consumption.
>
> All the foregoing inventions and discoveries were . . . the work of the women. To that sex, too, may by the same token be credited the chemistry of pot-making, the physics of spinning, the mechanics of the loom, and the botany of flax and cotton.[2]

## Sexuality of Tools?

Lewis Mumford, in *The City in History*, has suggested that the very sexuality of woman is evident in women's inventions throughout the Neolithic village:

> Woman's presence made itself felt in every part of the village: not least in its physical structures, with their protective enclosures, whose further symbolic meanings psychoanalysis has now tardily brought to light. Security, receptivity, enclosure, nurture—these functions belong to woman; and they take structural expression in every part of the village, in the house and the oven, the byre and the bin, the cistern, the storage pit, the granary, and from there pass on to the city, in the wall and the moat, and all inner spaces, from the atrium to the cloister. House and village, eventually the town itself, are woman writ large. If this seems a wild psychoanalytic conjecture, the ancient Egyptians stand ready to vouch for the identification. In Egyptian hieroglyphics, "house" or "town" may stand for symbols for "mother," as if to confirm the similarity of the individual and collective nurturing function. In line with this, the more primitive structures—houses, rooms, tombs—are usually round ones: like the original bowl described in Greek myth, which was modelled on Aphrodite's breast.[3]

We don't have to agree with Freud's notion that "anatomy is destiny" or even accept Mumford's inference that "security, receptivity, enclosure, nurture" are normally woman's function. Women, like men, can understand themselves primarily in terms of their sexual characteristics or in terms of something else (their occupation, special talents, personality, nationality, or whatever). It is very likely, however, that both women and men five, ten, or fifteen thousand years ago understood themselves and others primarily in terms of sex. Paleolithic artists have left us statues of women with highly exaggerated sexual organs and, later, cave paintings of stick figures with protruding penises or breasts which clearly indicate sex, but little else. We might prefer a world where people are not defined above all by their sex, but Neolithic woman did not have that choice. Consequently, Mumford's psychoanalytic interpretation of the Neolithic period might be much more perceptive than such an interpretation of our own age would be. Margaret Mead has reminded us that there is nothing "natural" in the personalities of men and women. Mumford reminds us that most people thought there was.

Archeologists have called the age of farming Neolithic (meaning "new stone") because they noticed that the remains of these first farming settlements usually contained not only the first human evidence of pottery and weaving, villages and permanent buildings, but also highly polished stone tools which were much finer than the chipped stone tools of Paleolithic (meaning "old stone") peoples. This was no accident. The polished stone was much more efficient at clearing away trees so that farming could be developed in fertile areas (that is, those areas which were fertile enough to produce trees).

Mumford suggests that even this invention of polished stone tools, the hallmark as it were of the Neolithic revolution, was either women's invention or the achievement of a culture which, under the dominance of women, had become "feminized." Since his thesis is as fascinating as it is unusual, we should let him tell it:

> With the village came a new technology: the masculine weapons and tools of the hunter and miner—the spear, the bow, the hammer, the ax, the knife—were supplemented by typically neolithic forms, of feminine origin: even the very smoothness of ground tools, in contrast to chipped forms, may be considered a feminine trait. . . .
>
> Paleolithic tools and weapons mainly were addressed to movements and muscular efforts: instruments of chipping, hacking, digging, burrowing, cleaving, dissecting, exerting force swiftly at a distance; in short, every manner of aggressive activity. The bones and muscles of the male dominate his technical contributions: even his limp penis is useless, sexually speaking, until it is as hard as a bone—as vulgar speech recognizes. But in woman the soft internal organs are the center of her life: her arms and legs serve less significantly for movement than for holding and enclosing, whether it be a lover or a child; and it is in the orifices and sacs, in mouth, vulva, vagina, breast, womb, that her sexually individualized activities take place.
>
> Under woman's dominance, the neolithic period is pre-eminently one of containers: it is an age of stone and pottery utensils, of vases, jars, vats, cisterns, bins, barns, granaries, house, not least great collective containers, like irrigation ditches and villages.[4]

## Twilight of the Gods?

There is abundant other evidence that the Neolithic Age was an age dominated by women's culture, and even women's sexuality. For example, the ancient Paleolithic mother and "Venus" goddesses which had become less important in the later Paleolithic era return with a vengeance at the discovery of agriculture. In the Neolithic Age women were unquestionably the source of life. They possessed not only the magical properties of the moon which enabled them to give birth to human beings, but they had also gained control of the earth and the sun in order to feed the life they gave. Neolithic women seemed to be the source of all fertility, all life. The major divinities of agricultural peoples were Earth Mothers, goddesses who caused the earth to flower and bear fruit. The ancient Mesopotamians worshiped the mother goddesses Tiamat, Ninhursag, and Ishtar; the ancient Indian Hindus, the goddess Kali; and the Egyptians, Isis.

■ *Isis, the Egyptian goddess, stretches out her winged arms to protect all creatures. Worship of this Neolithic Earth Mother survived well into the age of male-dominated civilizations, when birds had become words, as this tomb painting of 1292 B.C. attests.* (Granger)

Many Neolithic societies worshiped the Earth Mother and the young virgin daughter ("virgin" in those days simply meant "independent," rather than infertile or inexperienced). The ancient Greek version of this was Demeter, the Great Mother of the earth, and Persephone, the daughter, who rose from the dead each fruitful spring. According to Greek legend, the Earth Mother, Demeter or Melaina, was

> "mistress of the earth and sea": black like the black-earth. . . . Wearing black robes and a horse's head . . . [she retires to a cave] . . . to mourn the disappearance of her daughter Persephone. The fruits of the earth perish and famine threatens. But a miracle occurs. The god of the underworld restores Persephone to her earthly abode in exchange for her promise to rejoin him annually. Upon her return the earth dons a garment of green, fruits grow again, life is joy.[5]

Even today in agricultural societies, the fertility of the earth is associated with the fecundity of women.

> Women should plant [corn] because women know how to produce children. The sterile wife . . . is injurious to a garden. Many customs connect a new bride with corn: corn is thrown over her or she is crowned with it. In New Zealand, the same ritual precautions apply to a pregnant woman as apply to one who is cultivating a patch of sweet potatoes. Many peoples believe that seed grows best when planted by a pregnant woman.[6]

In other societies only bare-breasted women are supposed to harvest the crops, presumably because that will insure an abundant harvest. Of course, we still throw rice at brides because our ancestors used to think that it insured fertility.

## A Neolithic Matriarchy?

Was the Neolithic Age matriarchal? Did Neolithic women's economic and religious importance translate into political power in the clan, village, or tribe? We just do not know. The best answer is that there was probably some translation to the political realm in some Neolithic societies, but that in general the notion of a matriarchy exaggerates the power of women in the Neolithic age.

The combination of women doing the most important work, goddesses worshiped as the most important deities, and both matrilineal descent and matrilocal residence as the governing kinship institutions must have muted male dominance considerably in the Neolithic world. Such a combination existed among the Navaho Indians, for example.

While Navaho men did some of the farming, Navaho women were engaged in the more profitable pottery making and rug and blanket weaving. The most important Navaho deity was Changing Woman, the benevolent giver of corn and mother of the Twin Heroes. Navaho society was both matrilineal and matrilocal. Names and property were women's, passed down from mother to daughter. Men came as strangers to the clans of their wives. The power of men in such a society was severely curtailed. Imagine the confusion of the American government and military officials in the nineteenth century who insisted on making territorial treaties with the Navaho men only to discover that the men had no such authority.

Matrilineal descent and matrilocal residence certainly increased in the Neolithic world. But such societies might have been outnumbered by patrilineal and patrilocal ones. At least the distribution of descent patterns among tribal societies in today's world suggests that. Among the hunting-gathering tribes in the world today, about 10 percent are matrilineal, 20 percent are patrilineal, and most of the rest figure descent bilineally through mother and father. Among the farming tribes today, almost 25 percent are matrilineal, about 40 percent are patrilineal, and the rest bilineal. We have no way of knowing how representative these tribes in today's world are of ancient Paleolithic and Neolithic societies, but they do suggest that the Neolithic revolution involved less of a change in descent and inheritance patterns than in work and religious patterns.

Further, as critics of the idea of a Neolithic matriarchy have pointed out, the combination of matrilineal descent and matrilocal residence does not always translate into women's power. In over half of the matrilineal and matrilocal tribes today, men retain their authority by practicing a form of "village endogamy," by which they marry women from the other half of the village (rather than a foreign village). In that way men remain influential in village activities as a whole even though they leave their side of the village at marriage. In such societies property is still owned by women, but it is often administered by men. The separation of economic and political power was, in any case, more feasible in ancient societies that were used to a sexual division of labor and placed little value on ownership.

With these qualifications in mind, it is still "tempting to be convinced" with Jacquetta Hawkes, one of the leading scholars of the Neolithic Age, "that the earliest Neolithic societies throughout their range in time and space gave woman the highest status she has ever known."[7] The inventiveness of women's work, the prestige of women's deities, the awe of women's magic, must have given them status and respect considerably beyond what they had known in the Paleolithic Age. Even if the Neolithic Age was not a matriarchy, the importance of women was such that we can speak of the emergence of our own patriarchy in the twilight of the Neolithic or the dawn of urban civilization.

## Man's Place

We have said very little so far of the male contribution to the Neolithic Age. Men domesticated wild animals. However, this achievement was less important than women's achievement of domesticating plants. This was because agriculture was the more basic source of the food supply; it was regular and reliable, and it led (at least at first) to other more important inventions: stable communities or villages, permanent dwellings, polished tools, containers, liquors, weaving, potting, etc. The woman's agricultural revolution also brought about the most basic changes in society and culture: female-centered fertility religions, more matrilineal and matrilocal social systems, and a general concern with (what was then perceived as) the female function—birth, growth, nurturing, production, and reproduction.

While women developed the art of hoe farming after 8000 B.C. in the river valleys of the Middle East and North Africa, and soon after in parts of India and China, men were increasing their knowledge of wild animals. Gradually men learned to keep animals in controlled herds so that they would reproduce in the captivity of the range. In this way, sheep, goats, cows, horses, and oxen were most successfully domesticated. By 3000 B.C. these herds could supply enough food to sustain much denser populations than the earliest Neolithic villages. Even more significantly, however, men learned to use some of these animals (especially oxen) to plow large fields whereas, previously, women cultivated small plots by hand.

As men invented the heavy plough and tied their world of animals to women's world of farming (both in the earliest places around 3000 B.C.), human beings were able for the first time to support cities. And these cities became far more patriarchal than the early Neolithic villages had been matriarchal.

## The Heavy Plow and Cities: The Origins of Our Patriarchy

The first Neolithic villages included men and women in equal proportions. But, since the main business of these farming communities was women's work, men's role was often subordinate. On the other hand, in the pasture land around these first villages, herders led a very different style of life. They moved around more frequently than the villagers; they had few permanent possessions, and their lives were usually harder and more violent. Women, of course, also lived with the herdsmen, but in these nomadic bands it was the women who were subordinate. Two-thirds of today's pastural tribes are patrilineal. Less than 10 percent are matrilineal.

Cities were the children of the marriage of these two different Neolithic cultures: the female-influenced agricultural communities and the male-dominated bands of herders. The farm culture was more inventive and more complex than the pastural culture. Indeed, the herders lived lives that were not much more advanced than the Paleolithic culture of hunters. But, when the two cultures were forced to live peacefully together, and when that union was complete enough to bring the herders and their animals into the farming—the actual source of women's prestige—the men usually took over.

Villages could become cities only when agriculture was efficient enough to support large, dense populations of people, many of whom did not have to spend their lives in the fields. It is no accident, then, that archeologists have discovered the remains of the first ox-drawn heavy plows side by side with the remains of the first cities—in many of the same areas where the first Neolithic villages originated, but about five thousand years later.

The marriage of these two cultures took thousands of years to occur in these initial areas. In other parts of the world it occurred only recently. American Westerns remind us that the conflict between farmers and cattle ranchers was one of the main themes of our own history just a hundred years ago. The process may not have been too different in ancient Mesopotamia, Egypt, China, or India. In some cases, bands of herders probably took over scattered farming communities by force and stumbled upon a system of using animals to plow fields more efficiently. In other cases, the husbands may have aided their wives in farming: first, just clearing the land; later, pulling a heavier plow than their wives could manage; and, finally, adopting oxen or horses to do the hard work. In either case, individual men and the age-old male life-style were integrated into farming communities.

## Sky Fathers

As men increasingly did the important work, they asserted themselves in the society, controlled the developing cities, and reformed the culture in their own image. Goddesses were replaced by gods. Even the deities associated with agriculture became men: Osiris in Egypt and

Bacchus in Greece, for instance. Gods even replaced Mother Earth deities as the source of life and procreation. The Sky Father became as important as the Earth Mother. Rain was now often imagined to be the fertilizing sperm of the Sky Father. The Egyptians in one myth even denied the female role in conception completely. The Egyptian god Atum was thought to have created the universe out of his own body, by masturbation. As Mumford points out, "The proud male could scarcely have used plainer words to indicate that, in the new scheme of life, women no longer counted."[8]

## City Skylines

Mumford finds the city itself to be the characteristic work of male sexuality just as the Neolithic village reflects female sexuality.

> Male symbolisms and abstructions now become manifest: they show themselves in the insistent straight line, the rectangle, the firmly bounded geometric plan, the phallic tower and the obelisk, finally, in the beginnings of mathematics and astronomy. . . . It is perhaps significant that while the early cities seem largely circular in form, the ruler's citadel and the sacred precinct are more usually enclosed by a rectangle.
>
> In the city, new ways, rigorous, efficient, often harsh, even sadistic, took the place of ancient customs and comfortable easy-paced routine. Work itself was detached from other activities and canalized into the "working day" of unceasing toil under a taskmaster. . . . Struggle, domination, mastery, conquest were the new themes: not the protectiveness and prudence, the holding fast or the passive endurance of the village. With this all-too-plenteous enlargement of power, the isolated village—even a thousand isolated villages—could not cope: it existed as a container for more limited functions and more strictly maternal and organic concerns.[9]

Certainly straight lines and rectangular forms predominate in the city just as round forms are typical of the first villages. These may not always be symbols of male and female sexuality respectively, but the possibility is fascinating. We can observe a similar change in the symbolism of right and left. People have almost universally regarded the right side as masculine and the left as feminine, but it was not until the first cities that the left was thought to be inferior to the right. The inhabitants of the city of Rome have given us our modern meaning of left as "sinister" from the Latin *sinistra*. In contrast, the Neolithic priests and priestesses of the Egyptian Great Mother goddess Isis used to carry sculptured large left hands in their religious processions. Similarly, religious seals which the Neolithic Mesopotamians apparently worshiped show pictures of deities and left hands.

## City Fathers

The primacy of male symbols was a reflection of men's power. Significantly, cities gave us our first kings. Indeed, it was the men of these cities who created the institution of kingship. Neolithic villages had no permanent leaders. Though some men might be appointed or elected temporarily to positions of power in an emergency, these villages were usually very democratic.

The plow seems to have made possible not only cities dominated by kings, but also families dominated by fathers. The plow cultures of today's world that have still not developed cities are as patrilineal as pastoral cultures. Two-thirds are patrilineal. Less than 10 percent are matrilineal. The development of patrilineality and patrilocality in the city cultures which evolved after 3000 B.C. meant a marked decline in the position of women.

The reason for these changes was that men had successfully cut away the economic basis of women's status—not only by making farming men's work but also by depriving women of their role in other crafts. The men of the cities, for instance, invented a wheel which was a more efficient method for making pots, and (in almost every case) they became the potters. Further, as men gained access to more useful and efficient craft tools (like the potter's wheel), they could move around from one place to another and start their own families where they chose. They were not then bound to a woman's clan, and, thus, they were able to make the family (rather than the clan) the new basis of social organization.

As men increased their power over women, they began to make laws to ensure and legitimitize that power. One of the oldest complete codes of laws which has come down to us from these first cities is that of King Hammurabi of Babylon in Mesopotamia. Hammurabi's code, a combination of old customs and new ideas when it was written around 1750 B.C., shows us how the earliest cities treated women. According to these laws women were the property of their husbands or fathers. The husband could freely divorce his wife or, if he preferred, declare her his slave. As his slave, his wife would be forced by law to obey not only her husband but any of the free servants in the household. A husband could also turn over his wife to his creditors as security for his debts. He was not required by law to repay his debts as long as his wife was held as security—a period initially limited to three years, but later extended indefinitely. This system of going into debt, and then using the wife as security, actually became a very profitable system of slave trading. Even free women were faced with a legal death penalty if they should be unfaithful to their husbands, while their husbands could commit adultery without penalty.

■ *The top of the pillar of Hammurabi's Code reveals the symbols of the urban patriarchy: the Sky Father, male kingship, and written law. Even the phallic tower is symbolic of a male age, with Hammurabi at the head—above the law.* (Louvre, Paris)

## The Roman Patriarchy

While similar practices were frequently found in ancient Egypt and Greece, it was probably the Romans who developed the patriarchal state most fully. Roman law is important to us because it gave final form to the patriarchal family in which we still live, and because its laws (more than those of any other society) became the basis for our own.

The earliest Neolithic inhabitants of Italy lived in clans which were usually matriarchal, but as the city of Rome became a vast empire the father-dominated family became the basis of Roman life. To the Romans the *familia* meant the property, possessions, and people which the father ruled. It was not just a system of biological relationships as in the Neolithic clan. In this case, a person was a member of a particular clan because of blood relationship to other people, usually women. The Roman family, on the other hand, might include strangers that a man decided to adopt, the servants that he employed, and even the property that he owned. It is difficult to escape the conclusion that Roman fathers frequently thought of their wives and daughters as part of that property. Women were always under the power of either their fathers or their husbands. And this power was usually absolute. The emperor Constantine as late as the fourth century A.D. called it the "right of life and death." The father was the sole legal entity of the family. All family members took their identity from him.

Thus, Roman women gave up their Neolithic role as the symbol of the clan. They not only identified themselves as the possession of some man, but that was the only identity they had. They had no individual names. They were known simply by the feminine form of their family (or father's) name. A daughter of Julio Claudius, for instance, would be called only Claudia. So would all her sisters. They might be distinguished by such impersonal phrases as "the elder Claudia" or "the fourth Claudia," but they had no personal names like our own given names. This was not merely something that Roman men forgot to develop. They were not stupid. They gave each one of their sons separate individual names as well as the family name. Clearly, Roman women were only to think of themselves as one of virtually indistinguishable aspects of their father's *familia*.[10]

The first city societies (or "civilizations" in the technical, not moral sense) were almost universally dominated by men. In China and India, just as in the Near East, Greece, and Rome, women were deprived of the status they had enjoyed in Neolithic society, and were relegated to the status of property, servants, or helpers. The tombstones which some of the more devout Roman husbands erected for their wives show what men thought of them: "She loved her husband. . . . She bore two sons. . . . She kept the house and worked in wool."[11] This was how women were remembered.

## Eastern Patriarchies

The early civilizations of the East added a few demeaning institutions which were at least less common in the West, but the intention was everywhere the same.

The women of ancient Indian civilization were often expected to commit suicide (suttee) at their husband's death. Indian religion (Hinduism) not only condoned, but encouraged this practice, until quite recently.

The purdah system of ancient India also treated women as the property of their husbands. This system isolated women in the airless, crowded, poorly furnished rooms in the back of the house. Windows were shuttered so that no other man could see the Indian wife or daughters who were shut in. These women internalized the fears of men (that they would be tempted by the outside world) so completely that it became a matter of pride for a Hindu woman to be able to boast that not even the eye of the sun had ever seen her face.

Chinese women were also confined to their own quarters, but instead of locking the doors Chinese men found a more imaginative solution. They crippled the feet of girls by tightly binding them from an early age. A long piece of cloth was wrapped around the foot so that toes were held securely underneath; then, the whole foot was bound tightly enough to stop circulation and retard growth. The resulting mass of distorted flesh and broken bones was considered an object of beauty by Chinese men and women alike. The more successfully bound feet fitted into fashionable three-inch shoes which were admiringly described as dainty "golden lilies." The principle was much the same as the Western style of high-heeled shoes: it was supposed to emphasize women's sexual attractiveness. But the Chinese were sometimes very frank about the real reason for the custom. According to the famous Chinese *Classic for Girls:*

> Have you ever learned the reason
> For the binding of your feet?
> 'Tis from fear that 'twill be easy
> To go out upon the street.[12]

Foot binding was one of the few traditions that the Japanese did not borrow from the Chinese, but Japanese men often kept their wives in a kind of "house arrest" in the back rooms. The polite Japanese word for wife, *okusama,* actually means "the lady of the back parlor." The Japanese husband's servants occupied the rooms in the front of the house, effectively cutting off the wife's access to the street and the outside world.

These extreme patriarchal customs of the East—sutee, purdah, foot binding, and other forms of seclusion—were most developed in cities and among the upper classes. The patriarchal upper classes (that gave us our first cities and profited most from city life) attempted to impose their ideas of women on the poorer peasants of the countryside, but often without success. Peasant women were needed to assist their husbands in the fields even after the men had assumed the management of agriculture. Poor peasants could not afford to isolate their wives in back rooms or make them almost incapable of walking and lifting. In many cases, peasant women benefited from the greater activity that country life allowed. But some of the wives of very poor peasants might have envied the painful inactivity of their city sisters. A Jesuit missionary to China before the communist revolution saw a poor farmer guide a plow which was pulled by his wife and an ass. Similarly, an American visitor to Japan was told of country girls who, after marriage, were harnessed to the plow with an ox. There, less symbolically, is the meaning of the heavy plow and cities for women.

## *For Further Reading*

The literature on women's role in Neolithic and early urban society is much richer than that on "primitive" or Paleolithic society. Lewis Mumford's **The City in History*** is still a fascinating interpretive beginning. And Joseph Campbell's **The Masks of God: Primitive Mythology*** is still stimulating and useful, as are his volumes **The Masks of God: Oriental Mythology** and **The Masks of God: Occidental Mythology.*** Jacquetta Hawkes's **Prehistory** is also as thorough an introduction to Neolithic society as it is to the Paleolithic era. Her study of ancient Crete, **Dawn of the Gods*** is especially valuable for an understanding of the role of women in what was perhaps the most matriarchal of early civilizations. Robert Briffault's **The Mothers*** and Sir James Frazer's **The Golden Bough,** abridged by Theodor Gaster as **The New Golden Bough,*** are fascinating collections of anthropological data from the last century. That anthropological tradition became even more controversial and stimulating in the intuitive Jungian psychological interpretations of Erich Neumann in the 1950s, especially **The Great Mother: An Analysis of the Archetype*** and **Amor and Psyche: The Psychic Development of the Feminine.*** Neumann's theory of a uniquely feminine psychology can be found (despite Margaret Mead's **Sex and Temperament**) in

* Available in paperback.

a more sober form in Simone de Beauvoir's **The Second Sex,*** and Amaury de Riencourt's **Sex and Power in History.***

Archeological studies are generally more useful for this period than anthropological ones. We have already mentioned the work of Jacquetta Hawkes as a general introduction. But perhaps the best study of the archeological remains of gods and goddesses is Marija Gimbutas's recent **The Gods and Goddesses of Old Europe 7000 to 3500 BC: Myths, Legends and Cult Images,** a marvelous study of the greater Balkan area from Crete to what became southern Russia (on the east) and southern Italy (on the west). Other valuable studies are J. Boardman's **Pre-classical, From Crete to Archaic Greece,** Stuart Piggott's **Ancient Europe, From the Beginnings of Agriculture to Classical Antiquity,** L. R. Palmer's **Mycenaeans and Minoans,** and James Mellaart's, **Catal Hüyük, a Neolithic Town in Anatolia.**

There are also a number of good studies of ancient religion which relate directly to our topic. Mircea Eliade's many books are full of information and suggestions for a general understanding of ancient religion. His **Gods, Goddesses, and Myths of Creation*** is perhaps the easiest introduction. More challenging are **Birth and Rebirth, Images and Symbols,* The Myth of the Eternal Return,* Myths, Dreams and Mysteries,*** and **Patterns in Comparative Religion.*** Studies of the goddesses of the ancient Greek and Balkan world include J. N. Coldstream's **Demeter,** O. G. S. Crawford's **The Eye Goddess,** W. K. C. Guthrie's **The Religion and Myth of the Greeks,** Ester Harding's **Woman's Mysteries: Ancient and Modern,** Jane E. Harrison's classic **Themis: A Study of the Social Origins of Greek Religion,*** Rachel G. Levy's **Religious Conceptions of the Stone Age and Their Influence upon European Thought,** originally published as **The Gate of Horn,** Donald Mackenzie's **Myths of Crete and Pre-Hellenic Europe,** Grant Showerman's **The Great Mother of the Gods,** and Donald J. Sobol's **The Amazons of Greek Mythology.**

Finally, for an excellent discussion of the emergence of kingship and male gods in the first civilizations, see Henri Frankfort's **Kingship and the Gods.***

## Notes

1. V. G. Childe, *What Happened in History* (Baltimore: Penguin, 1942), p. 65.
2. *Ibid.*, p. 66.
3. Lewis Mumford, *The City in History* (New York: Harcourt Brace Jovanovich, 1961), pp. 12–13.
4. *Ibid.*, pp. 15–16.
5. Traian Stoianovich, *A Study in Balkan Civilization* (New York: Knopf, 1967), pp. 7–8.
6. Robert Briffault, *The Mothers,* abridged by C. R. Taylor (London: Allen & Unwin, 1927, 1959), p. 363.
7. Jacquetta Hawkes, *Prehistory* (New York: New American Library, 1963), pp. 356–357.
8. Mumford, *op. cit.*, p. 25. Much of the argument here is taken from Mumford.
9. *Ibid.*, p. 27.

10. See M. I. Finley, "The Silent Women of Rome," *Horizons* 7, no. 1 (Winter 1965): pp. 56–64. Reprinted in M. I. Finley, *Aspects of Antiquity* (New York: Viking, 1969) as ch. 10.
11. *Horizons*, p. 64.
12. Trans. Isaac T. Headland, *Home Life in China* (New York: Macmillan, 1914), p. 77. Quoted in David and Vera Mace, *Marriage: East & West* (New York: Doubleday, 1959, 1960), p. 70.

# Chapter 3

# Cities and Civilization

## Civility and Class

The words "city" and "civilization" do not ring well in the modern ear. Cities seem to be impossible places to live for all but the very wealthy. Urban ghettos have become prisons for the poor. The middle class works for a home in the suburbs. The young seek salvation in the country. Civilization is no longer an ideal. The word conjures up images of technological narrowness or upper-class snobbery.

This chapter confronts some of these ideas. It argues on behalf of both cities and civilization, accepting the common origins that the words imply. It argues that city life has been largely responsible for the achievements of civilization, and that those achievements have enhanced human life enormously. The chapter does not deny that cities are ridden by class differences. Nor does it deny that civilization has been largely the product of upper-class interests. It argues, in fact, that class differences were at the root of the urbanizing and civilizing process.

Our examination of the origins of ancient civilization suggests, however, that one of the achievements of ruling classes was to make themselves superfluous and create new possibilities for us all.

## Before There Were Cities

The "urban revolution" began only about five thousand years ago, and it has spread considerably only within the last few hundred years. For thousands of years before the development of cities, most of the world's people lived in small village settlements. Some people even continued a pre-Neolithic (before herding and farming) life of hunting and food gathering.

We have already accepted Lewis Mumford's suggestion that the first cities were the fruits of a "marriage" between the rough, male-dominated pastoral society and the settled, female-centered village society of the farmers. At times it must have been a marriage of convenience. Most frequently, however, it must have been a forceful abduction.

Only force can explain why some self-sufficient farming villages turned over enough of their crops to support new classes of specialists—chiefs, kings, priests, soldiers, administrators, and craftsmen—who grew no food themselves. It is difficult to imagine the conservative farming villagers, attuned as they were to the eternal, natural rhythms of planting and harvesting, suddenly deciding that their lives should become more complicated.

Even if village life were not the golden age that later city poets imagined, it was certainly more peaceful and egalitarian than city life was to become. One Sumerian poet wrote that in the village even the wolf and lion were not dangerous. That seems too unlikely to be taken literally, but it does appear that institutionalized warfare was absent from village life. Ancient dramatists often put their peace speeches in the mouths of the villagers:

> I fix my eyes upon my fields and lust for Peace.
> I loathe the stingy, greedy city. I long
> for my own ungrudging countryside, my generous
> village,
> my openhearted home sweet home. *It* never barked,
> "Buy Coal! Buy Oil! Buy Vinegar!" Gratis it gave me
> everything, unstintingly supplied my wants, and that
> blasted
> city byword "BUY"—
> Goodbye to that![1]

The village raised no armies and drafted no soldiers. Nor did the village make people buy things. Money, buying and selling, and the market were inventions of the city. The village supplied the wants of its members gratis (free of charge) because each of the villagers contributed to the communal storage. The average villagers did not try to avoid work because everyone gained equally from the advantages of work. Work was life—everyone's life. Villagers could not afford to allow any of their members to monopolize the communal resources. There were no leisure classes or families who lived on the work of others. Even a taste for idle luxury, special privilege, private property, or greater power seems to have been absent. Village crops were varied and ample. There was rarely enough of a surplus to allow the development of a special class of nonfarming administrators—but there often was enough of a surplus to tempt the nomadic herders. Perhaps the very success of village life proved to be its undoing.

It is unlikely that villagers would have freely chosen to create the class of specialists, rulers, tax collectors, and armies that made the first cities possible. It is also unlikely that the force for such a change would have been raised in the stable, nurturing village itself. The drives for acquisition and power and conquest were much more typical of the herders than of the villagers.

It is also unlikely that all villages would have eventually grown large enough to be cities. We make a mistake when we think of a city as only an overgrown or especially populated village. There were some very large villages in the ancient world that never became cities. In some places with particularly fertile soil, a village might support a couple of thousand inhabitants, most of whom were farmers.

Villages did not gradually evolve into cities. A few villages were forged into the first cities, probably by conquering herders from the surrounding grasslands. This explains the suddenness of the change and the character of the first cities. In many ways the city still bears the stamp of that forge.

## Village to City

The earliest cities were, of course, towns that retained much of village life. They were still small in size and population, had a limited variety of nonsubsistence occupations, and were still pretty classless and democratic. (At least the graves are all the same.) One of the oldest of these that archeologists have discovered is the biblical Jericho. If a wall marks the difference between a village and a city, then Jericho was a city almost ten thousand years ago—at the beginning of the

**The Spread of Civilization**

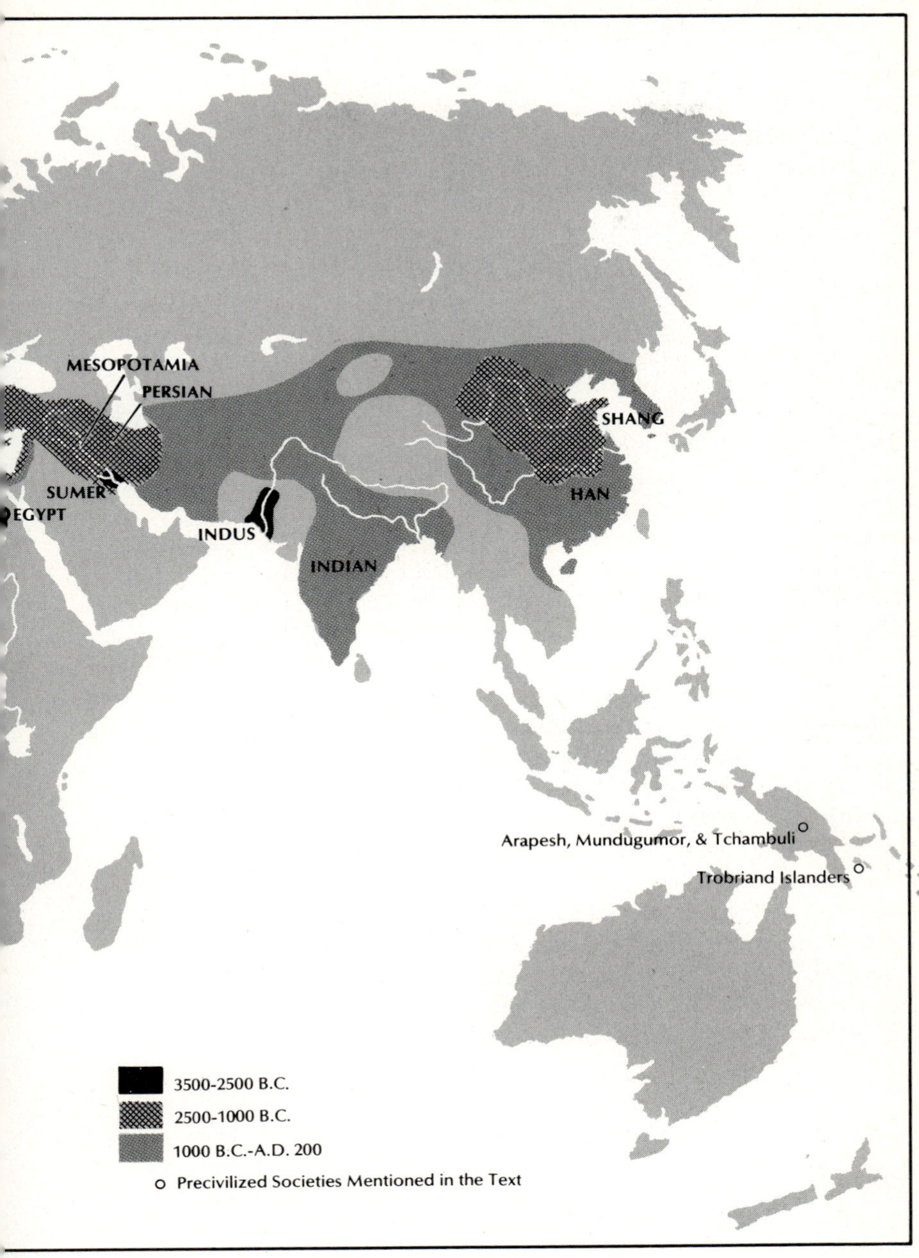
MESOPOTAMIA
PERSIAN
SHANG
SUMER
EGYPT
HAN
INDUS
INDIAN
Arapesh, Mundugumor, & Tchambuli
Trobriand Islanders
3500-2500 B.C.
2500-1000 B.C.
1000 B.C.-A.D. 200
Precivilized Societies Mentioned in the Text

Neolithic period. Possibly the first city wall ever constructed, Jericho's wall of 8000 B.C. was constructed of stones dragged from a riverbed half a mile away to protect the desert oasis of about ten acres and possibly a couple of thousand inhabitants. Five thousand years before the construction of the Sumerian temples and the Egyptian pyramids (and six and a half thousand years before Joshua's Israelite army destroyed a later wall at Jericho) the urban revolution may have begun. If we prefer Lewis Mumford's distinction between the round cottages of villages and the rectangular buildings of cities, then Jericho was a city after 7000 B.C. Suddenly after that date the houses of Jericho showed the shape of things to come.

Jericho is probably not unique. It has received more extensive archeological work because of the biblical story. Other mounds in ancient Palestine, Turkey, Syria, Iraq, and Iran have already, or no doubt will, yield the remains of fairly permanent, defended settlements from the period between 8000 and 3000 B.C.

It may be preferable, however, to limit the word "city" to some of the settlements that achieved maturity closer to 3000 B.C. The Sumerian settlements from this period show a much more developed Neolithic technology. (The Jericho of 8000 B.C. did not even know pottery.) And more significantly, the settlements of Sumer had by the period of 4000–3000 B.C. begun the process of an urban technological revolution that far surpassed the Neolithic. The perfection of Neolithic technology between 6000 and 4000 B.C. involved such inventions as the ox-drawn plow, the wheeled cart, the sailboat, metallurgy, irrigation, and the domestication of new plants, all of which made agriculture productive enough to support settlements of tens of thousands of inhabitants in a particular area.

"True" cities were possible when these advanced Neolithic settlements used their increased agricultural productivity to create specialized artists, metalworkers, architects, writers, accountants, bureaucrats, physicians, and scientists, and to institutionalize their skills and achievements. This is what happened along the Euphrates River at a number of places shortly before 3000 B.C.

## The Urban Revolution: Civilization and Class

The full-scale urban revolution occurred not in the rain-watered lands that first turned some villages into cities, but in the potentially more productive river valleys of Mesopotamia around 3500 B.C. Situated along the Tigris and Euphrates rivers, large villages like Eridu, Erech, Lagash, Kish, and later Ur and Babylon built irrigation systems that increased farm production enormously. Settlements like these were able to support five, even ten thousand people, and still allow something like 10 percent of the inhabitants to work full time at nonfarming occupations.

A change of this scale was a revolution, certainly the most important revolution in human living since the invention of agriculture five thousand years earlier. The urban revolution was prepared by a whole series of technological inventions in agricultural society. Between 6000 and 3000 B.C people learned not only how to harness the power of oxen and the wind with the plow, the wheeled cart, and the sailboat; they also discovered the physical properties of metals, learned how to smelt copper and bronze, and began to work out a calendar based on the movements of the sun. River valleys like those of the Tigris and Euphrates were muddy swamps that had to be drained and irrigated to take advantage of the rich soil deposits. The dry land had literally to be built by teams of organized workers.

Therefore, cities required an organizational revolution that was every bit as important as the technological one. This was accomplished under the direction of the new class of rulers and managers—probably from the grasslands—who often treated the emerging cities as a conquered province. The work of irrigation itself allowed the rulers ample opportunity to coerce the inhabitants of these new cities. Rain knows no social distinctions. Irrigated water must be controlled and channeled.

It is no wonder then that the first cities gave us our first kings and our first class societies. Almost everywhere that cities spread (or were again invented) after 3000 B.C.—along the Nile of Egypt, on the Indus River in Pakistan, in Turkey and China, and later in Middle America—the king is usually described as the founder of cities. Almost everywhere these kings were able to endow their control with religious sanction. In Egypt and America the king was god. In Mesopotamia a new class of priests carried out the needs of the king's religion of control.

In some cities the new priesthood would appoint the king. In others, they were merely his lieutenants. When they were most loyal, the religion of the priests served to deify the king. The teachings of the new class of Mesopotamian priests, for instance, were that their god had created the people solely to work for the king and make his life easier. But even when the priesthood attempted to wrest some of the king's power from him, they taught the people to accept the divided society which benefited king and priesthood as providers of a natural god-given order. The priesthood, after all, was responsible for measuring time, bounding space, and predicting seasonal events. The mastery of people was easy for those who controlled time and space.

■ *This reconstruction shows how the pyramids were built. Stone blocks were pulled over slippery, milky surfaces and rollers to be prodded into place at ever higher levels of the inclined plane that became the pyramid. The pharaoh's dream of a monumental tomb was realized by architects and court officials directing the enforced labor of peasants and craftspeople. (Museum of Science, Boston)*

The priesthood was only one of the new classes that insured the respectability of the warrior-chieftain turned king. Other palace intellectuals—scribes (or writers), doctors, magicians, and diviners—also struggled to maintain the king's prestige and manage his kingdom. This new class was rewarded, like the priests, with leisure, status, and magnificent buildings, all of which further exalted the majesty of the king and his city.

Beneath the king, the priesthood, and the new class of intellectuals-managers was another new class charged with maintaining the king's law and order. Soldiers and police were also inventions of the first cities. Like the surrounding city wall, the king's military guard served a double function: they provided defense from outside attack and an obstacle to internal rebellion.

That these were the most important classes of city society can be seen from the physical remains of the first cities. The archeologist's spade has uncovered the monumental buildings of these classes in virtually all of the first cities. The palace, the temple, and the citadel (or fort) are, indeed, the monuments that distinguish cities from villages. Further, the size of these buildings and the permanency of their construction (compared with the small, cheaply built homes of the farmers) attest to the fundamental class divisions of city society.

## Civilization: Security and Variety

The most obvious achievements of the first civilizations are the monuments—the pyramids, temples, palaces, statues, and treasures—that were created for the new ruling class of kings, nobles, priests, and their officials. But civilized life is much more than the capacity to create monuments.

Civilized life is secure life. At the most basic level this means security from the sudden destruction that village communities might suffer. Civilized life gives the feeling of permanence. It offers regularity, stability, order, even routine. Plans can be made. Expectations can be realized. People can be expected to act predictably, according to the rules.

The first cities were able to attain stability with walls that shielded the inhabitants from nomads and armies, with the first codes of law that defined human relationships, with police and officials that enforced the laws, and with institutions that functioned beyond the lives of their particular members. City life offered considerably more permanence and security than village life.

Civilization involves more than security, however. A city that provided only order would be more like a prison than a civilization. The first cities provided something that the best-ordered villages lacked. They provided far greater variety: more races and ethnic groups were speaking more languages, engaged in more occupations, and living a greater variety of life-styles. The abundance of choice, the opportunities for new sensations, new experiences, knowledge—these have always been the appeals of city life. The opportunities for growth and enrichment were far greater than the possibilities of plow and pasture life.

Security plus variety equals creativity. At least the possibility of a more creative, expressive life was available in the protected, semi-permanent city enclosures which drew, like magnets, foreign traders and diplomats, new ideas about gods and nature, strange foods and customs, and the magicians, ministers, and mercenaries of the king's court. Civilization is the enriched life which this dynamic urban setting permitted and the human creativity and opportunity which it encouraged. At the very least, cities made even the most common slave think and feel a greater range of things than the tightly knit, clanish agricultural village allowed. That was (and still is) the root of innovation and creativity—of civilization itself.

The variety of people and the complexity of city life required new and more general means of communication. The villager knew everyone personally. Cities brought together people who often did not even speak the same language. Not only law codes but written language itself became a way to bridge the many gaps of human variety. Cities invented writing so that strangers could communicate, and so that those communications could become permanent—remembered publically, officially recorded. Emerson was right when he said that the city lives by memory, but it was the official memory which enabled the city to carry on its business or religion beyond the lifetime of the village elders. Written symbols that everyone could recognize became the basis of laws, invention, education, taxes, accounting, contracts, and obligations. In short, writing and records made it possible for each generation to begin on the shoulders of the ancestors. Village life and knowledge often seemed to start from scratch. Thus, cities cultivated not only memory and the past, but hope and the future as well. City civilizations invented not only history and record keeping but also prophecy and social planning.

Writing was one city invention that made more general communication possible. Money was another. Money made it possible to deal with anyone just as an agreed-upon public language did. Unnecessary in the village climate of mutual obligations, money was essential in the city society of strangers. Such general media of communication as writing and money vastly increased the number of things that could be said and thought, bought and sold. As a consequence, city life was more impersonal than village life, but also more dynamic and more exciting.

## The "Eye" and "I"

Marshall McLuhan has written that "civilization gave the barbarian an eye for an ear." We might add that civilization also gave an "I" for an "us." City life made the "eye" and the "I" more important than they had been in the village. The invention of writing made knowledge more visual. The eye had to be trained to recognize the minute differences in letters and words. Eyes took in a greater abundance of detail: laws, prices, the strange cloak of the foreigner, the odd type of shoes made by the new craftsman from who-knows-where, the colors of the fruit and vegetable market, elaborate painting in the temple, as well as the written word. In the village one learned by listening. In the city seeing was believing. In the new city courts of law an "eyewitness account" was believed to be more reliable than "hearsay evidence." In some villages even today, the heard and the spoken are thought more reliable than the written and the seen. In the city, even spoken language took on the uniformity and absence of emotion that is unavoidable in the written word. Perhaps emotions themselves became less violent. "Civilized" is always used to mean emotional restraint, control of the more violent passions, and a greater understanding, even tolerance, of the different and foreign.

Perhaps empathy (the capacity to put yourself in someone else's shoes) increased in cities—so full of so many different others that had to be understood. When a Turkish villager was recently asked "What would you do if you were president of your country?" he stammered: "My God! How can you ask such a thing? How can I . . . I cannot . . . president of Turkey . . . master of the whole world?" He was completely unable to imagine himself as president. It was as removed from his experience as if he were master of the world. Similarly, a Lebanese villager who was asked what he would do if he were editor of a newspaper accused the interviewer of ridiculing him, and frantically waved the interviewer on to another question. Such a life was beyond his comprehension. It was too foreign to imagine. The very variety of city life must have increased the capacity of the lowest commoner to imagine, empathize, sympathize, and criticize.

The oral culture of the village reinforced the accepted by saying and singing it almost monotonously. The elders, the storytellers, and the minstrels must have had a prodigious memory. But their stories changed only gradually and slightly. The spoken word was sacred. To say it differently was to change the truth. The written culture of cities taught "point of *view*." An urban individual did not have to remember everything. That was done permanently on paper. Knowledge became a recognition of different interpretations and the capacity to look up things. The awareness of variety meant the possibility of criticism, analysis, and an ever-newer synthesis. It is no wonder that the technical and scientific knowledge of cities increased at a geometric rate compared to the knowledge of villages. The multiplication of knowledge was implicit in the city's demand to recognize difference and variety. Civilization has come to mean that ever-expanding body of knowledge and skill. Its finest achievements have been that knowledge, its writing, and its visual art. The city and civilization (like the child) are to be seen and not heard.

It may seem strange to say that the impersonal life of cities contributed greatly to the development of personality—the "I" as well as the "eye." Village life was in a sense much more personal. Everything was taken personally. Villagers deal with each other not as "the blacksmith," "the baker," "that guy who owes me a goat," or "that no good bum." They do not even "deal" with each other. They know each other by name and family. They love, hate, support, and murder each other because of who they are, because of personal feelings, because of personal and family responsibility. They have full, varied relationships with each member of the village. They do not merely buy salt from this person, talk about the weather with this other person, and discuss personal matters with only this other person. They share too much with each other to divide up their relationships in that way.

City life is a life of separated, partial relationships. In a city you do not know about the butcher's life, wife, kids, and problems. You do not care. You are in a hurry. You have too many other things to do. You might discuss the weather—but while he's cutting. You came to buy meat. Many urban relationships are like that. There are many business, trading, or "dealing" relationships because there are simply too many people to know them all as relatives.

The impersonality of city life is a shame in a way. (It makes it easier to get mugged by someone who does not even hate you.) But the luxurious variety of impersonal relationships (at least some of the time) provide the freedom for the individual personality to emerge. Maybe that is why people have often dreamed of leaving family and friends (usually for a city) in the hope of "finding themselves." Certainly, the camaraderie and community of village life had a darker side of surveillance and conformity. When everything was known about everyone, it was difficult for the individual to find his or her individuality. Family ties and village custom were often obstacles to asserting self-identity. The city offered its inhabitants a huge variety of possible relationships and personal identities. The urban inhabitant was freer than his village cousin to choose friends, lovers, associates, occupation, housing, and life-style. The city was full of choices that the village could not afford or condone. The village probably provided more security in being like everyone else and doing what was expected. But the city provided the variety of possibilities that could allow the individual to follow the "inner self" and cultivate inner gardens.

The class divisions of city society made it difficult for commoners to achieve an effective or creative individuality. But the wealthy and

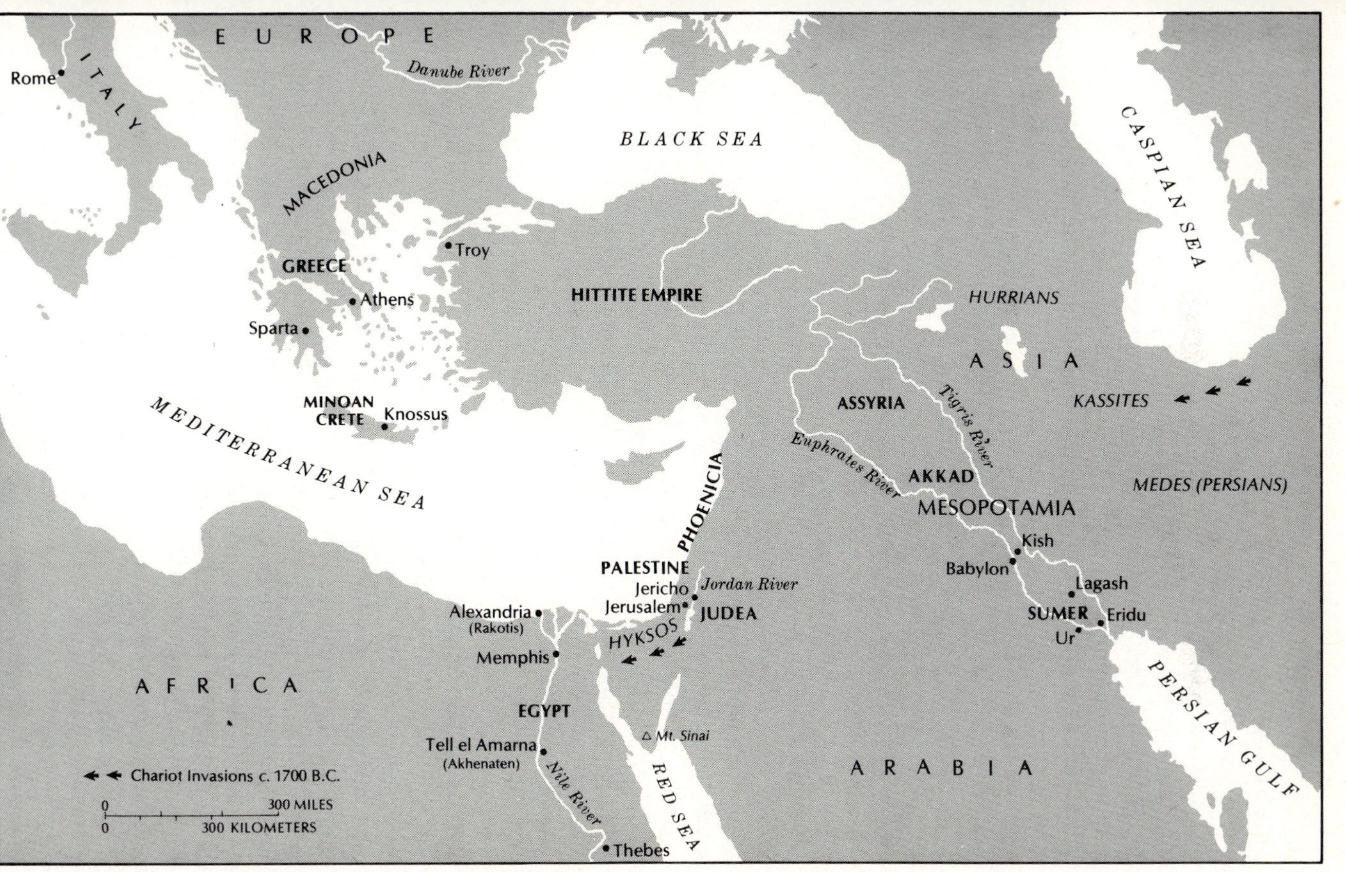


**The Ancient Middle East**
*Mesopotamian, Egyptian, and Greek Civilizations.*

powerful—especially the king—were able to develop models of individuality and personality that were revolutionary. No one before had ever achieved such a sense of the self, and the model of the king's power and freedom became a goal for the rest of the society. The luxury, leisure, and opportunity of the king was a revolutionary force. Unlike a village elder, the king could do whatever he wanted. Recognizing that, more and more city inhabitants asked, "Why can't we?" City revolutions have continually extended class privilege and opportunities ever since.

Once a society has achieved a level of abundance, once it can offer the technological means, the educational opportunities, the creative outlets necessary for everyone to lead meaningful, happy, healthy lives, then classes may be a hindrance. Class divisions were, however, a definite stimulus to productivity and creativity in the early city civilizations. The democratic villagers preferred stability to improvement. As a result, their horizons were severely limited. They died early, lived precipitously, and suffered without much hope. The rulers of the first cities discovered the possibilities of leisure, creation, and the good life. They invented heaven and utopia—first for themselves. Only very gradually has the invention of civilization, of human potential, sifted down to those beneath the ruling class. In many cases, luxury, leisure, freedom, and opportunity are still the monopolies of the elite. But once the powerful have exploited the poor enough to establish their own paradise on earth and their own immortality after death, the poor also have broader horizons and plans.

## Mesopotamian and Egyptian Civilizations: A Tale of Two Rivers

Experts disagree as to whether Mesopotamian or Egyptian civilization is older. Mesopotamian influence in Egypt was considerable enough to suggest slightly earlier origins, but both had evolved distinct civilizations by 3000 B.C. Indeed, the difference between the two civilizations attests to the existence of multiple routes to civilized life. In both cases, river valleys provided the necessary water and silt for an agricultural surplus large enough to support classes of specialists who did not have to farm. But the differing nature of the rivers had much to do with the different types of civilization that evolved.

The Egyptians were blessed with the easier and more reliable of the two rivers. The Nile overflowed its banks predictably every year on the parched ground in the autumn after August 15, well after the harvest had been gathered, depositing its rich sediment, and withdrawing by early October, leaving little salt or marsh, in time for the sowing of winter crops. Later sowings for summer crops required only simple canals that tapped the river upstream and the natural drainage of the Nile Valley. Further, transportation on the Nile was simplified by the fact that the prevailing winds blew from the north while the river flowed from the south, making navigation a matter of using sails upstream and dispensing with them coming downstream.

The Euphrates offered none of these advantages as it cut its way through Mesopotamia. The Euphrates flowed high above the flood plain (unlike the neighboring Tigris) so that its waters could be used, but it flooded suddenly and without warning in the late spring, after the summer crops had been sown and before the winter crops could be harvested. Thus, the flooding of the Euphrates offered no natural irrigation. Its waters were needed at other times, and its flooding was destructive. Canals were necessary to drain off water for irrigation when the river was low, and these canals had to be adequately blocked, and the banks reinforced, when the river flooded. Further, since the Euphrates was not as easily navigable as the Nile, the main canals had to serve as major transportation arteries as well.

In Mesopotamia the flood was the enemy. The Mesopotamian deities who ruled the waters, Nin-Girsu and Tiamat, were feared. The forces of nature were often evil. Life was a struggle. In Egypt, on the other hand, life was viewed as a cooperation with nature. Even the Egyptian god of the flood, Hapi, was a helpful deity who provided the people's daily bread. Egyptian priests and philosophers were much more at ease with their world than their Mesopotamian counterparts. And, partly because of their different experiences with their rivers, the Mesopotamians developed a civilization based on cities, while the Egyptians did not. From the first Sumerian city-states on the lower Euphrates to the later northern Mesopotamian capital of Babylon, civilization was the product and expression of city life. Egyptian civilization, in contrast, was the creation of the pharaoh's court rather than of cities. Beyond the court, which was moved from one location to another, Egypt remained a country of peasant villages.

A prime reason for Egypt's lack of urbanization was the ease of farming on the banks of the Nile. Canal irrigation was a relatively simple process which did not demand much organization. Small market towns were sufficient for the needs of the countryside. They housed artisans, shopkeepers, the priests of the local temple, and the agents of the pharaoh, but they never swelled with a large middle class and never developed large-scale industry or commerce.

In Sumer, and later in Mesopotamia, the enormous task of fighting the Euphrates required a complex social organization with immediate local needs. Only communal labor could build and maintain the network of subsidiary canals for irrigation and drainage. Constant supervision was necessary to keep the canals free of silt, to remove salt deposits, to maintain the river banks at flood-time, and to prevent any farmer from monopolizing the water in periods of drought. Life on the Euphrates required cooperative work and responsibility that never ceased. It encouraged absolute, administrative control over an area larger than the village, and it fostered participation and loyalty to an irrigated area smaller than the imperial state. The city-state was the political answer to the economic problems of Sumer and Mesopotamia.

The religious practices of the Euphrates Valley reflected and supported city organization. Each local area worshiped its local god while recognizing the existence of other local gods in a larger Sumerian, and eventually Mesopotamian, pantheon of gods. The priests of the local temple supervised canal work, the collection of taxes, and the storage of written records, as well as the proper maintenance of religious rituals. Thus, religious loyalty reinforced civic loyalty. Peasant and middle-class Sumerians thought of themselves as citizens of their particular city, worshipers of their particular city god, subjects of their particular god's earthly representative, but not as Sumerian nationals. By contrast, the Egyptian peasant was always an Egyptian, a subject of the pharaoh, but never a citizen.

The local, civic orientation of Mesopotamian cities can be seen in the physical structure of the capital city of Sumer, the city of Ur. Like other cities on the Euphrates, Ur was surrounded by a wall. It was dominated by the temple of Nannar, the moon-god who owned the city, and the palace complex beneath the temple. The residential areas were situated outside of the sacred Temenos, or temple compound, but within the walls, between the river and the main canal. The well-excavated remains of Ur of the seventeenth century B.C. show a residential street plan that looks like many Middle Eastern cities of today. A highly congested area of winding alleys and broad streets sheltered one- and two-story houses of merchants, shopkeepers, tradespeople, and occasional priests and scribes that suggest a large, relatively prosperous middle class. Most houses were built around a central courtyard that offered shade throughout the day, with mud-brick, often even plastered, outside walls that protected a number of interior rooms from the sun and the eyes of the tax inspector. The remains of seventeenth-century Ur show both the variety and density of modern city life. There are specialized districts throughout the city. Certain trades have their special quarters: a bakers' square, probably special areas for the dyers, tanners, potters, and metalworkers. But life is mixed together as well. Subsidiary gods have temples outside the Temenos. Small and large houses are jumbled next to each other. There seems to be a slum area near the Temenos, but there are small houses for workers, tenant farmers, and the poor throughout the city. And no

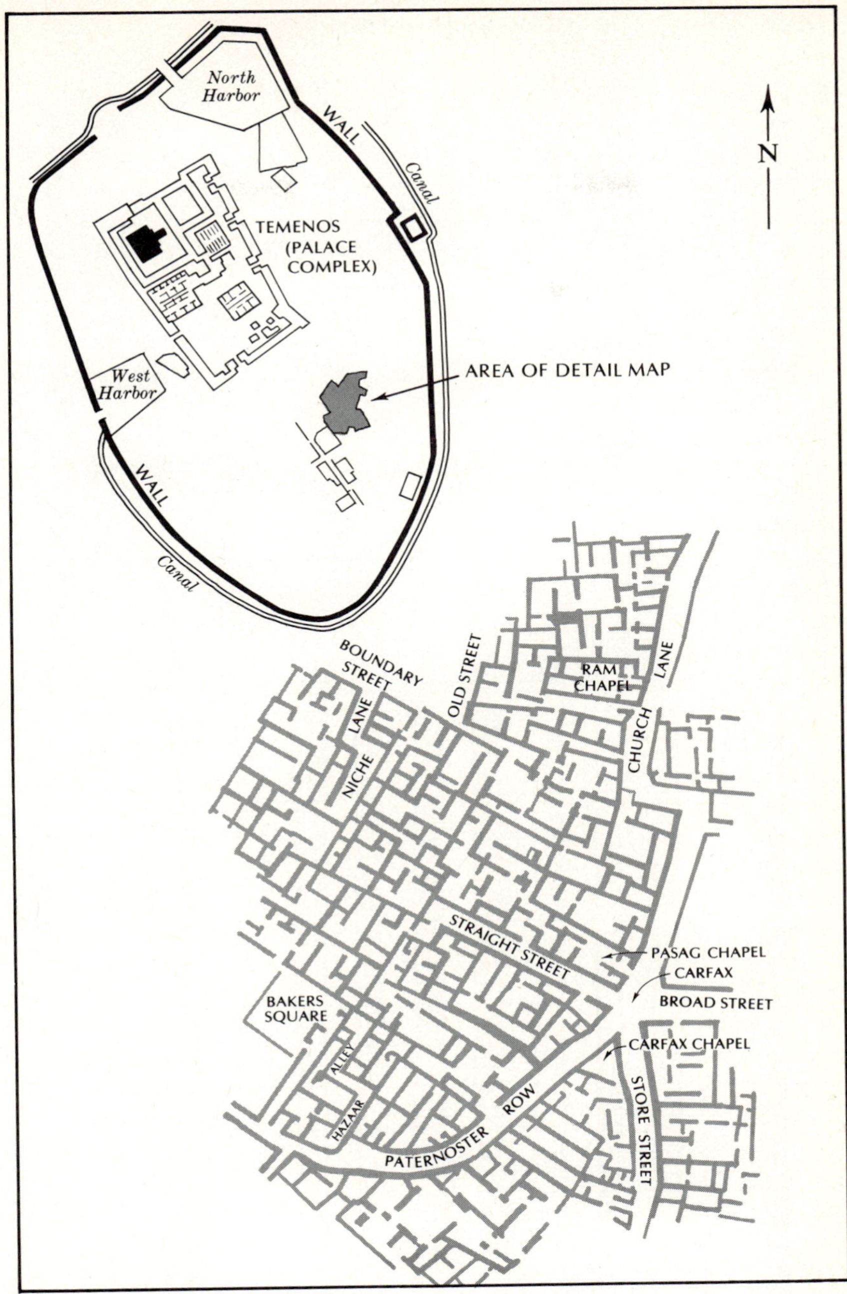


**Sumerian Ur: The Walled City and Opened Life**
*The walled city of Ur (shown in the top portion of the map) required civic participation of its citizens. This can be sensed in the winding streets and neighborhoods of the working quarters (shown in detail in the bottom portion of the map).*

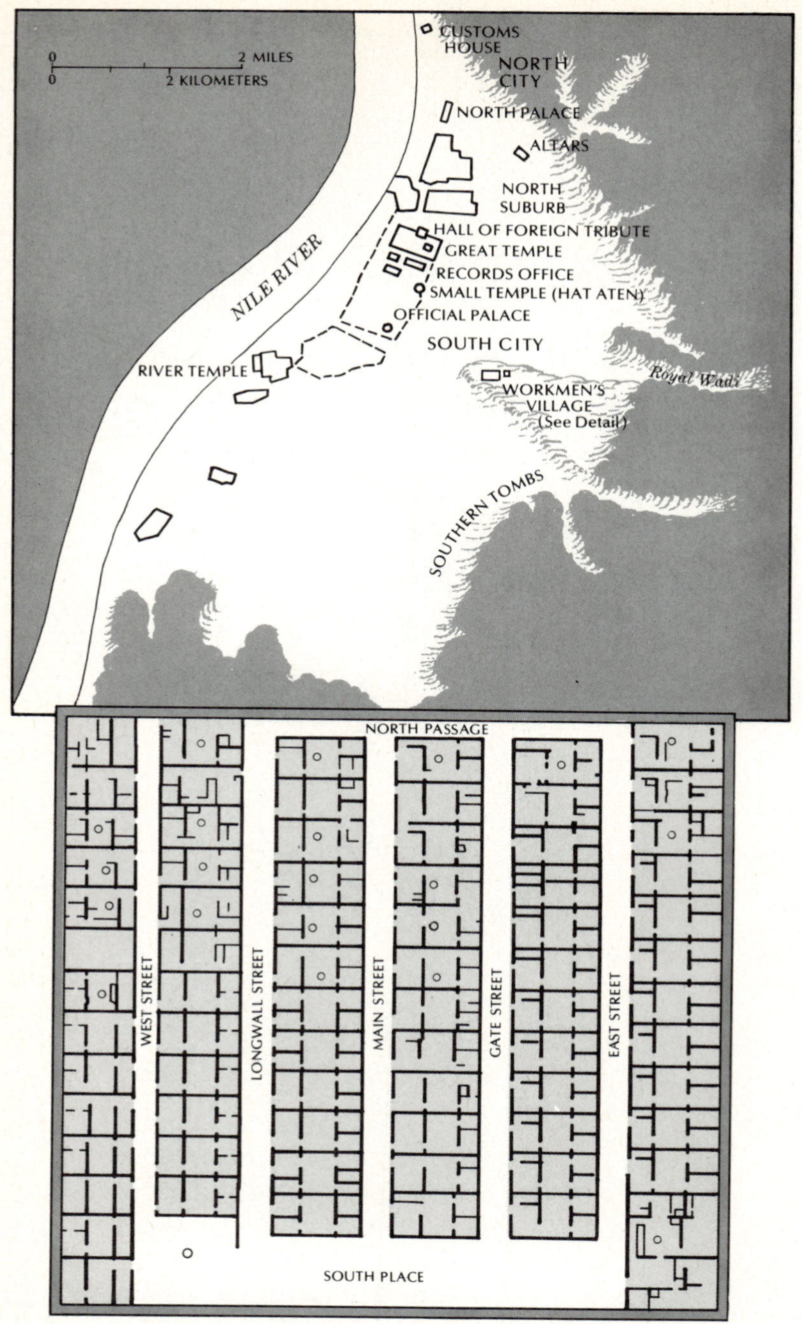


**Egyptian Akhetaton: Open Spaces and Imperial Order**

*The unwalled city of Akhetaton was the pharaoh's court city. The absence of civic life can be seen in the administrative simplicity and small size of the housing of the worker's quarters (shown in detail in the bottom portion of the map).*

shop or urban professional was more than a short walking distance away. The entire size of the walled city was an oval that extended three-quarters of a mile long and a half a mile wide.

A well-excavated Egyptian city from roughly the same period (the fourteenth century B.C.) offers some striking contrasts. Akhetaton, or Tell el Amarna, Pharaoh Akhenaton's capital on the Nile, was not enclosed by walls or canals. It merely straggled down the eastern bank of the Nile for five miles and faded into the desert. Without the need for extensive irrigation or protection, Tell el Amarna shows little of the crowded, vital density of Ur. Its layout lacks any sense of urgency. The North Palace of the pharaoh is a mile and a half north of the temple complex and offices, which are three and a half miles from the official pleasure garden. The palaces of the court nobility and the large residences of the court's officials front one of the two main roads which parallel the river, or they are situated at random. There is plenty of physical space (and social space) between these and the bunched villages of workers' houses. The remains suggest very little in the way of a middle class or a merchant or professional class beyond the pharaoh's specialists and retainers. Life for the wealthy was, judging from the housing, more luxurious than at Ur, but for the majority of the population city life was less rich. In many ways, the pharaoh's court at Tell el Amarna was not a city at all.

## Diversity, Diffusion, and Development of Civilization

Within a short time after the establishment of Mesopotamian and Egyptian civilizations, other civilizations developed in the Middle East, on the Indus River in India, and on the Yellow River in China. We know relatively little of the earliest Indian and Chinese civilizations. The Indian cities of Harappa and Mohenjo-daro flourished from about 2500 B.C to 1500 B.C. when they were burned, destroyed, and left in rubble by invading Aryan-speaking tribes from the north. The ruins suggest a highly organized, class-divided society run by priests: the streets follow a strict grid plan, most of the housing is quite small, and the remains of a temple quarter and large temple residences stood above the rest of the city.

A much more pleasant style of life must have developed in the courtly, sea-borne civilization of Minoan Crete. The paintings found in the palace of Minos (first built about 1900 B.C.) show an exhilarating spontaneity, elaborate dress, and fondness for nature and life that reminds us of the courtly Egyptian society that the Cretans knew through trade. In some ways, however, Minoan Crete reminds us more

■ *The "Snake Goddess" of Minoan Crete wears the traditional dress of Minoan Civilization, but the snake recalls an older Neolithic cult of fear and fertility, birth and rebirth.* (Alinari, EPA)

of a Neolithic society. The chief deity seems to have been a Great Mother goddess. Women, in their ornate, open-breasted gowns appear to play prominent roles, and there appears to be a gaiety, charm, and peacefulness (neither city walls nor military imagery) that is far removed from the struggles of other Middle Eastern civilizations.

The civilization of Sumer passed upriver as the delta soil became salted or merely as less civilized armies upstream conquered by controlling the water supply. Akkad dominated Sumer after 2250 B.C., and both were controlled by Hammurabi's Babylon further north by the eighteenth century B.C. Their northern Semitic languages replaced Sumerian, but they retained enough of Sumerian culture to be called Mesopotamian.

By 2000 B.C. Mesopotamian civilization was circled by various satellite civilizations—Kassites, Hittites, Canaanites, Hurrians, and Assyrians—whose pastoral-military organization made conquest and imitation easier than permanent rule, but who became civilized in the process. The periodic invasions of these protocivilized tribes (especially around 1700, 1500, and 1200 B.C.) probably resulted more in the diffusion of civilization to the new conquerors, and the development of civilized life in the rain-watered lands from which they came, than in the destruction of civilized ways of life. Even when the native inhabitants regained their lands, as the Egyptians did from the Hyksos in the sixteenth century B.C., the resulting native dynasties (like those of the New Kingdom or Empire in Egypt, 1600–1200 B.C.) often displayed the same militarism and lack of inventiveness shown by their former conquerors. By the advent of the first Iron Age invasions after 1200 B.C., the civilization of cities—bronze, ploughs, and writing—was no longer the monopoly of a few vulnerable river valleys. Its diffusion meant its ultimate survival, even after particular cities, peoples, or writing systems had long been forgotten.

If the first millenium of civilization building (about 3500 to 2500 B.C.) had produced in rapid succession most of the technological and organizational achievements of the Bronze Age, the second millenium insured the continuance of that accomplishment through diffusion. Bureaucratization, militarization, and war may have slowed the pace of technological development between 2500 and 1200 B.C., or it may have been that the potentialities and limits of the Bronze Age were reached rather early. Whatever the case, the Egyptian Middle Kingdom (2050–1750 B.C.) did little more than imitate the pyramid-building and institutions of kingship of the Old Kingdom (3000–2250 B.C.), and the Semitic empires of northern Mesopotamia (like Babylon) mainly enlarged and militarized the achievements of the earlier Sumerians.

Culturally, however, the period between 2500 B.C. and the development of Iron Age technology around 1200 B.C. was more innovative. One thinks, for instance, of developments in law, religion, and writing that opened the possibilities of cultural achievement even within the boundaries of Mesopotamian and Egyptian civilization. The law codes of Hammurabi (1750 B.C.) enshrined patriarchal power and class rule, but even in doing so provided a measure of certainty and justice lacking in more traditional tribal societies. Further, the efficiency of a bureaucratic empire required a responsible as well as powerful ruling class. Thus, Hammurabi's code stipulated heavier punishment of nobles convicted of certain crimes, as well as heavier punishment for crimes committed against nobles. The nobility were expected to conduct themselves better than subjects.

In Egypt, the concrete (or stone) expression of personal immortality during the main period of pyramid building (2700–2500 B.C.) filtered down to the rest of the society in cults of the god Osiris by 2000 B.C. Osiris, who himself had been restored to life by his loving wife Isis, after being dismembered by his wicked brother Seth, was pictured as a god of the underworld who weighed the souls of all deceased Egyptians against the feather symbol of justice. Immortality was opened to those beyond the family of the pharaoh, and a person's worth could no longer be measured by wealth and social position. Osiris worship became so common in the New Kingdom (1600–1200 B.C.) that the priests attempted to counteract its democratic implications by devising fees and duties that would ensure a light heart (or a heavy feather). That was one of the corruptions that Akhenaton (c. 1375–1358 B.C.) attempted to reform by his espousal of one god, Aton, who demanded moral goodness of his worshipers. Akhenaton's monotheism may have even been a source of the Judeo-Christian idea of a single almighty deity, since this was the period of the Hebrew presence in Egypt. If so, it departed with the Hebrew exodus. Akhenaton's young successor, Tutankhamen, allowed the priests to abandon the revolutionary doctrine and its capital at Tell el Amarna.

Like law and religion, the art of writing also achieved greater flexibility after 2000 B.C. The pictorial Egyptian hieroglyphic and Mesopotamian cuneiform writing were still the standards for international trade and the models of classic style. The Hittites and Minoans actually copied the pictorial style so that their inscriptions could look as impressive as those of the Egyptians. But increasingly after 1600 B.C., pictorial writing was replaced in everyday work by phonetic (sound) systems instead of pictures. Phonetic systems are much simpler because the human voice makes fewer sounds than the human imagination makes pictures. That means a smaller set of symbols. Pictorial writing can be cumbersome if everything is drawn, or it can be confusing if detail is omitted. What is the meaning, for example, of a stick-figure man leaning on a stick? Does it mean "leaning" or "walking" or "soldier" or "old age"? The transition from pictorial to

■ *Akhenaton, his wife Queen Nefertiti, and one of their daughters stand with offerings to the sun-god Aton at the Pharaoh's new city of Aton, Akhetaton (Tell el Amarna today).* (Metropolitan Museum of Art)

phonetic writing was very gradual. At first the pictorial images were used to do double duty as sounds as well as pictures. This led to an elaborate system of visual puns. An English equivalent would be writing the word "belief" with a picture of a bee and a picture of a leaf. Gradually, certain symbols became standard for certain sounds, first symbols for syllables, then symbols for consonants, and finally the alphabet of separate symbols for consonants and vowels.

The development of phonetic writing was not complete by 1000 B.C. It is not used in China today. By 1000 B.C. in the Middle East, symbols for syllables instead of pictures and puns were increasingly used. But even that much of a transition opened the mastery of writing to a broader population than the priests and scribes. As with the idea of legal justice and the idea of individual moral responsibility, the ruling class of the ancient world had devised more efficient tools for ruling subjects and empires. But like any tools, once devised they could not remain the property of a dynasty, a civilization, or a class.

## *For Further Reading*

There are a number of interesting books on the development of the first city societies or civilizations by archeologists and historians. V. Gordon Childe's **Man Makes Himself*** first outlined the importance of the Neolithic and urban revolutions and, although dated, it is still absorbing. Dora Jane Hamblin and the editors of Time-Life books update the older interpretation in a beautifully illustrated collection of essays on specific cities entitled **The First Cities.*** Another well-illustrated, readable introduction is Glyn Daniel's **The First Civilizations: The Archaeology of Their Origins.*** For a short, well-argued, comparative history with a cyclical perspective, the student might try Rushton Coulborn's **The Origin of Civilized Societies.*** A much fuller comparative treatment can be found in Jacquetta Hawkes's **The First Great Civilizations** and in Sir Leonard Woolley's **The Beginnings of Civilization,*** also published as Hawkes and Woolley, **Prehistory and the Beginnings of Civilization.** For vivid histories of archeological discovery which are also studies of ancient civilizations, Leonard Cottrell's volumes on Egypt **(The Lost Pharaohs),*** Crete **(The Bull of Minos),*** and his **Lost Cities*** make exciting reading. A catchy series of urban "firsts" is recorded in Samuel Noah Kramer's **History Begins at Sumer.*** A more sophisticated analysis of the philosophy and mythology of the ancient civilizations of the Middle East can be found in the volume by Henri Frankfort and others called **Before Philosophy*** and in S. H. Hooke's **Middle Eastern Mythology.***

For students who wish to explore the history of a particular ancient civilization, there are a wide range of possibilities. For ancient Mesopotamia, besides some of the titles already mentioned, there are J. Mellaart's **Earliest**

* Available in paperback.

**Civilizations in the Near East,*** W. W. Hallo and W. K. Simpson's **The Ancient Near East,*** Milton Covensky's **The Ancient Near Eastern Tradition,*** Cyrus H. Gordon's **The Ancient Near East,*** C. Leonard Woolley's **Ur of the Chaldees,** Samuel Noah Kramer's **The Sumerians: Their History, Culture, and Character,** A. Leo Oppenheim's **Ancient Mesopotamia: A Portrait of a Dead Civilization,*** Henri Frankfort's **The Birth of Civilization in the Near East,*** and H. W. F. Sagg's **The Greatness That Was Babylon.***

On ancient Egyptian civilization, besides sections of some of the books already mentioned, there are C. Aldred's **The Egyptians, Ancient Peoples and Places,** Elizabeth Riefstahl's **Thebes in the Time of Amunhotep III,*** Sir Alan Gardiner's **Egypt of the Pharaohs,*** Barbara Mertz's **Temples, Tombs and Hieroglyphs: The Story of Egyptology,*** Torgny Save-Soderbergh's **Pharaohs and Mortals,** and John A. Wilson's **The Burden of Egypt*** and **The Culture of Ancient Egypt.*** The classic works of James Henry Breasted, **The Development of Religion and Thought in Ancient Egypt*** and the enormous **A History of Egypt,*** are still superb after 50 years. A good collection of primary sources can be found in **The Literature of Ancient Egypt, An Anthology of Stories, Instructions, and Poetry,*** edited by W. K. Simpson. Pyramid buffs would enjoy Ahmed Fakhry's **The Pyramids.***

Other ancient Middle Eastern civilizations are treated in O. R. Gurney's **The Hittites,** D. B. Harden's **The Phoenicians,** R. W. Hutchinson's **Prehistoric Crete,** W. A. McDonald's **Progress Into the Past: The Rediscovery of Mycenaean Civilization,*** and A. T. Olmstead's **History of the Persian Empire.***

On India there are Stuart Piggott's **Prehistoric India,** Sir Mortimer Wheeler's **The Indus Civilization,*** W. T. DeBray's **Sources of Indian Tradition,** Romila Thapar's **A History of India,*** and O. I. Chavarria-Aguilar's **Traditional India.**

On China there are W. A. Fairservis, Jr.'s **Origins of Oriental Civilization,** C. P. Fitzgerald's **China: A Short Cultural History,*** W. Eichhorn's **Chinese Civilization: An Introduction,** James T. C. Liu and Wei-ming Tu's **Traditional China,** W. Watson's **China Before the Han Dynasty,** Chun-shu Chang, ed., **The Making of China,** and Hefflee G. Creel's **The Birth of China.***

## *Notes*

1. Aristophanes, *The Archarnians,* trans. Douglass Parker (New York: New American Library, 1961), pp. 16–17.

## CHRONOLOGICAL CONTEXT OF
# The Ancient World: to 1000 B.C.

| | |
|---|---|
| Before 8000 B.C. | Paleolithic (Old Stone) Age: hunting and gathering. |
| 8000 B.C. | Beginning of Neolithic (New Stone) Age: farming and herding. |
| 8000–1500 B.C. | Diffusion of Neolithic revolution through 99 percent of world population. Neolithic inventions: polished stone tools, planting, seed use, hoe, containers, pottery, yeast for bread, alcoholic drinks, plant knowledge, spinning and weaving, settled life, villages, Earth Mother goddesses, domestication of animals. |
| 6000–4000 B.C. | Perfection of Neolithic technology. Early metallurgy, wheeled carts, sailboats, irrigation, plows, small cities. |
| 3500–3000 B.C. | Urban revolution in Sumer. Beginnings of Mesopotamian and Egyptian civilizations. Development of irrigation, calendars, writing, kingship, priests, classes, urban occupations, mathematics, rudimentary astronomy, bureaucracies, royal culture, patriarchal institutions and religion. |
| 3000 B.C. | Unification of Egypt. Old Kingdom, 3000–2250 B.C. |
| 2700–2500 B.C. | Pyramid building in Egypt. Beginning of Minoan and Indus civilizations, Neolithic farming in China. |
| 2250 B.C. | Beginning of empire of Sargon of Akkad in Mesopotamia. |
| 2000 B.C. | Emergence of satellite civilizations on rain-watered land in Middle East. Egyptian Middle Kingdom 2050–1750 B.C. |
| 1750 B.C. | Hammurabi's Mesopotamian Empire and law code. |
| 1700–1500 B.C. | Nomadic tribes in chariots invade civilizations. Minoan and Indus civilizations destroyed. Egyptian New Kingdom (1600–1200 B.C.) after defeat of Hyksos. Shang dynasty begins in China (1500 B.C.) |
| 1600–1300 B.C. | Early development of alphabetic writing. Osiris worship in Egypt spreads idea of personal immortality. |
| 1375–1358 B.C. | Akhenaton's monotheistic reforms. Capital at Tell el Amarna. |
| 1200–1000 B.C. | Iron Age invasions. Dorians in Greece. Chou dynasty in China. |

# II

# PART II

# THE CLASSICAL WORLD

## 1000 B.C.–A.D. 500

# Chapter 4

# City-State and Capital City

## Athens to Rome

We are used to thinking of cities in terms of numbers. We define a city as an area with so many people. We identify the problems of cities with overcrowding, congestion, and vertical living. Cities seem to have too much of everything: too many people, too much traffic, too much pollution. The sheer weight of numbers seems to make city life too fast and frantic.

Sometimes we have to be reminded that it is not population size, but population density that defines a city and contributes to its problems. Density is more of a problem than simple size or numbers of people. But decreasing population density does not by itself make a city more habitable, any more than decreasing the number of people. Modern cities like New York and Tokyo, for instance, have about one-fifth the density of population as the ancient, compact, walled cities.

Cities may have become larger in population and smaller in

density, but if their problems have increased we may have to look elsewhere for the reasons. This chapter will look at the history of ancient cities to explore a different kind of distinction—that of *function* rather than numbers. The ancient world distinguished between city-states and imperial capital cities, and this may be a useful distinction for us even today.

The city-state was different from the capital city in the functions it performed. It served the needs of the inhabitants in town and country, and it often functioned quite autonomously and even democratically (at least for its citizens). The function of the capital city, on the other hand, was usually to magnify the power of the ruler, rather than to serve the interests of the inhabitants. The two types of cities were often different in size and density, but their differences in function said a lot more for the possibilities of life that they offered.

Athens was the most famous city-state of the ancient world. Alexandria and Rome were the best examples of the capital, foreign and domestic. The choice is one we confront everyday. Are we choosing Rome and Alexandria?

## Athens: The City-State and the Good Life

Aristotle said that "men come together in the city to live; they remain there in order to live the good life." He was writing about the city in general, but he must have been thinking of his native Athens. By "the good life" Aristotle most certainly did not mean physical comforts and material possessions. One Greek visitor remarked:

> The road to Athens is a pleasant one, running between cultivated fields the whole way. The city is dry and ill supplied with water. The streets are nothing but miserable old lanes, the houses mean, with a few better ones among them. On his first arrival a stranger would hardly believe this is the Athens of which he has heard so much.[1]

The sanitary facilities that ancient Sumerian Ur or Indian Harappa had enjoyed two thousand years before were virtually unknown in Athens. The houses of the city were made of unbaked brick with tile roofs or even of mud and straw. There was no paving to prevent the narrow streets from turning into mud in the spring and dust in the summer. The charcoal fires never seemed to take the chill out of the winter, and the small closely built one-story houses worked like ovens in the summer.

Athens lacked the amenities of big city life. Like earlier city-states it was really something of a small town. It was only a 15 minute walk from the center to the outskirts. It was a city of peasant farmers, many of whom still walked to the surrounding fields to tend their plots. In terms of technology, comforts, physical layout, and the lives of the inhabitants, Athens was not very far removed from the peasant village. That, in fact, may have been its great strength.

The democratic ways of the village continued in most of the early city-states, but in Athens they were taken especially seriously. Power was exercised by a far larger proportion of the population than in any other city. At its largest there were probably about forty thousand male citizens, another hundred and fifty thousand free women, children, and foreigners, and another hundred thousand slaves. The exclusion of women from citizenship and the creation of a slave class were less democratic than village life, of course. But all cities excluded

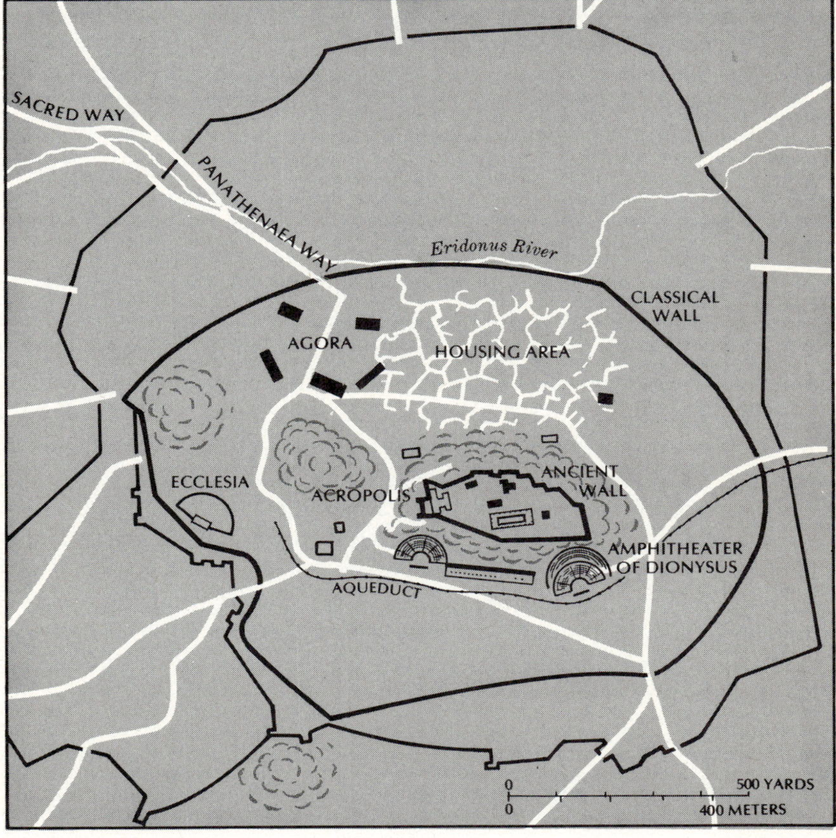


**Athens, c. Fifth Century B.C.**
*Classical Athens was a city of public meeting places of civic significance and of narrow, winding streets.*

women and captured slaves. The uniquely democratic character of Athens lay in the rough equality of its male citizens and the degree of their participation in political life.

If we concentrate on that unusually large one-seventh of the population that consisted of the citizens, the Athenian political system seems extremely democratic—perhaps even more than our own. These citizens were chosen by lot (like a lottery) to serve on virtually all of the governing bodies of the city. This avoided some of the pitfalls of elections: it minimized the importance of the "big names" of the traditional aristocracy, slowed the growth of political machines, and gave many more citizens the opportunity and experience of public service than an election system; it allowed greater flexibility in changing government policy without confronting entrenched deadwood bureaucrats or damaging the egos of the authors of the old policy; and it forced citizens to keep in touch with public affairs since they might suddenly find themselves on the town council. More than a representative democracy, the Athenian system of lot selection made public service the education and creation of the citizens.

When special knowledge or skill was necessary (managing finances or building docks) special boards of "professionals" were appointed. But the Athenians understood (perhaps better than we do) that governing does not require expertise as much as an active, informed citizenry.

The big choices (the laws, decisions of war and peace, the determination of how much money to collect and what to spend it on) were made by the Ecclesia or mass assembly. Unlike our Congress, this legislative body consisted of all of the citizens. Anyone could speak. Everyone had a vote. The town council prepared most of the issues for this assembly, but the assembled citizens were the final judges of what was to be done.

It is appropriate that the Greek word for city-state, polis, is the root of our word for politics. Athens showed the potential of the democratic city, but more fundamentally it taught the possibility of the participatory city and the creative city. That is what Pericles, the great Athenian statesman who was *elected* general from 443 to 430 B.C., meant when he said that Athens was "an education to Greece." We would add: "and to the world."

## Athens: Acropolis, Agora, and Amphitheater

The Ecclesia was only one center of Athenian social life. There were also the acropolis, the agora, and the amphitheater to enrich public life. The acropolis, the home of the gods, presides over Athens today on a high bluff in the center of the city just as it did in the time

■ *The ruins of the Athenian Acropolis as it still presides over Athens. (Hirmer Fotoarchiv)*

of Pericles when the present temples were built. The contrast must have been even more striking then: the new majestic, colored buildings and the rubble of houses beneath. Before it became the museum of marble art (and the most beautiful in the world), it was the Athenian's source of life, identity, and meaning. In the most important city festival, the Panathenaea, the Athenians marched in a winding processional up the slopes to the acropolis where they gathered to present their gifts to the goddess Athena. This festival, like many others, was a kind of celebration that occurred often in the ancient city-state. Special times for collective rejoicing, gaiety, and festivity served to rededicate the people to their city and to each other—just as the Ecclesia sharpened their sense of political participation.

The female goddess, the sacred mountain, caves, springs, and shrines connected the acropolis with the magic and rituals of a Neolithic past. Similarly, the agora, the market and meeting place, affirmed the continuity of the "village square" or, more appropriately, the central, circular open space where all the villagers gathered and some spread out their wares. The market was secondary to the meeting place. Homer's *Iliad* first describes the agora as a "place of assembly" where "town folk gathered around" as the elders "seated on polished stones in the midst of the hallowed circle" rendered their judgement of an accused villager. In the city the meeting place became more of a marketplace, but the exchange of ideas and gossip must have kept pace with the exchange of goods. The agora was the most vital element of the city. The large square swarmed with activity: between the fountain and the ceramic stalls the sausage seller and the silversmith compete for space; on the steps between the fish market and the temple Socrates has buttonholed Alcibiades to talk about "the different types of virtue"—and to escape from his wife; the argument of a group of men about freedom in Sparta grows louder with the approach of two young boys who are playing flutes; a peasant and his donkey jostle Plato who pauses to watch the intricate work of a carpenter in his open shop.

The Athenian amphitheater, a huge semicircle of steps carved out of a sloping hill, is another outlet for sociability that connects the public concerns of the city with the ritual of ancient religion. In the century before Sophocles died in 406 B.C., twelve hundred plays were written and produced, one hundred by Sophocles himself. Like many of those of Euripides, Aeschylus, and Aristophanes (to name a few), they are enthralling even today. Under the open sky the Greek tragedies and comedies put human foibles, political policy, and the eternal dramas of human life on stage for all to see. The performance was both an opportunity for social intercourse and a stimulus to self-examination. The amphitheater, like the acropolis and the agora, involved an enormous expense of public energy. Many Athenians played a part at some time or another. There was little distinction between performer and audience. Often the playwright expressed public sentiment in parts designed for a "chorus." Contests were held. Prizes were awarded. Some plays were booed off the stage. But despite the public expense and enthusiasm, the drama was still close enough to its primitive sacred origins to be prized at its most controversial. During the Peloponnesian War, while Athens was being conquered by Sparta, Aristophanes was able to perform *The Archarnians,* a play in which the hero makes his "private peace" with the enemy. Athenians found public space and time in order to deepen private consciousness and free expression.

Popular participation on such a high level naturally required a certain amount of leisure time. The city, Aristotle said, "should be such as may enable the inhabitants to live at once temperately and liberally in the enjoyment of leisure." Much of the citizen's leisure was no doubt provided by the slaves who worked in the mines and ships, or who served in the city police or the homes of the wealthy. But the average peasant or craftsman owned no slaves, the moderately wealthy owned only a dozen, even the very rich owned no more than 50. Leisure was due not only to slavery. It was also the result of the acceptance of a temperate technological standard of living which enabled the citizens to live "the good life" of public participation, reflective conversation, and artistic expression more "liberally." Leisure was after all a village value. Farmers have always probably had more free time than city people. The Athenians insisted on using that leisure to expand the possibilities of human life. They did so at the expense of slaves, but before we criticize them in terms of modern morality we might notice that we usually use our much more productive machines to increase work and hurry time. And we use our cities for private exploitation. At least for the Athenian citizens, the enrichment of human life was the goal. And the polis made it possible.

## The Greek Imperial City: Alexandrian Capitals of Culture

In his discussion of ideal cities, Aristotle was more appreciative of variety, plurality, and particular local needs than his teacher, Plato. Plato's ideal city would have been a geometric absolute: exactly 5,040 citizens and 5,040 lots; three classes of people, educated and living separately; twelve sections to the city, each with a separate god and temple; each of the houses lined up like a wall, "the form of the city being like a single dwelling." In short, everything was to be regular and uniform. Plato admired the discipline and military organization of Sparta. Aristotle was less taken by ideal forms, and more concerned (possibly because of his extensive study of biological organisms) with process, purpose, function, growth, and potential—in short, the kinds of living produced by certain cities rather than the "ideal" shell.

The future was designed by Aristotle's most famous student, Alexander the Great. However, Alexander's design was closer to Plato's. By the time the 33-year-old Alexander died in 323 B.C., he had founded 70 cities, most of which he named Alexandria. Many have not survived. The Alexandria that served as the capital of Alexander's North African empire has. Now it shows us what the other cities of this Hellenistic Age must have looked like, and then it performed a more valuable service than the rest: it preserved much of the learning of the earlier Hellenic culture of the Greek city-states. Its design was the

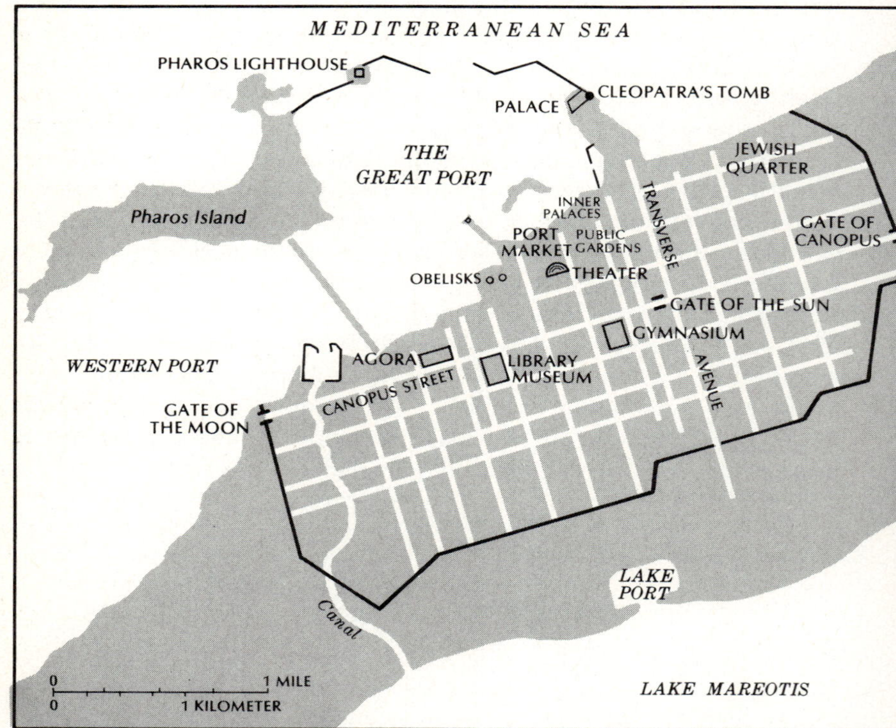


**Alexandria Under the Ptolemies**
*Alexandria was an emperor's city, laid out for easy access and control. The monuments were for the enjoyment of the court and the admiration of the inhabitants.*

model of future city planning even for the next rulers of the Mediterranean, the Romans. And at the same time, it recaptured the design and style of the ancient imperial cities of the Middle East—of Babylonia, Assyria, Crete, and Egypt.

It was an ideal site. Maybe Alexander remembered Homer's mention in the *Odyssey* of "an island in the surging sea in front of Egypt, and men call it Pharos. . . . Therein is a harbour with good anchorage, whence men launch the shapely ships into the sea." The island (whose name was probably a corruption of the Egyptian word for pharaoh) protected a narrow strip of land between the Mediterranean and a large Egyptian lake. Alexander decided to build his city on that strip. A canal joined the Mediterranean to the lake. Another canal gave access to the Nile. Broad streets were laid out in a rectangular grid pattern, the long ones running east and west along the strip and the shorter ones running north and south from the sea to the lake. Most of the streets were 18 to 19 feet wide, but the main east-west street, Canopus Street, was probably a hundred feet wide. Thus, everything was designed for easy, direct movement. Alexandria was to be a model of efficiency and clarity. It was the dream of a city founder who could not take time to learn the lay of the land. It was the ideal of a world ruler who desired to show the extent and evenness of his control. It was the model of the foreign general who feared the potential threat of tight native quarters protected by narrow winding streets. And it was the envy of the foreign merchants and visitors who could do their business, see the sights, and never get lost.

## Alexandria: Sights, Seeing, and Spectacles

And what sights there were! One visitor, the Greek novelist Achilles Tatius, reminds us that the spectacular city could be a feast for the eyes:

> After a voyage lasting for three days, we arrived at Alexandria. I entered it by the Sun Gate, as it is called, and was instantly struck by the splendid beauty of the city, which filled my eyes with delight. From the Sun Gate to the Moon Gate—these are the guardian divinities of the entrances—led a straight double row of columns, about the middle of which lies the open part of the town, and in it so many streets that walking in them you would fancy yourself abroad while still at home. Going a few hundred yards further, I came to the quarter called after Alexander, where I saw a second town; the splendour of this was cut into squares, for there was a row of columns intersected by another as long at right angles. I tried to cast my eyes down every street, but my gaze was still unsatisfied, and I could not grasp all the beauty of the

■ *A reconstruction of ancient Alexandria as it is believed to have appeared when viewed from the harbor. (From* Cities of Destiny, *edited by Arnold Toynbee. © 1967 Thames and Hudson Limited)*

> spot at once; some parts I saw, some I was on the point of seeing, some I earnestly desired to see, some I could not pass by; that which I actually saw kept my gaze fixed, while that which I expected to see would drag it on to the next. I explored therefore every street, and at last, my vision unsatisfied, exclaimed in weariness, "Ah, my eyes, we are beaten." Two things struck me as especially strange and extraordinary—it was impossible to decide which was the greatest, the size of the place or its beauty, the city itself, or its inhabitants; for the former was larger than a continent, the latter outnumbered a whole nation. Looking at the city, I doubted whether any race of men would ever fill it; looking at the inhabitants, I wondered whether any city could ever be found large enough to hold them all. The balance seemed exactly even.[2]

Exaggeration probably came easy to visitors of Alexandria. Within a hundred years of its founding by Alexander in 331 B.C., it was the largest city in the world. By the second century B.C., it was the first city in human history to number between a hundred and a hundred and fifty thousand people. It's inhabitants came from India and the Iberian Peninsula. They included Arabians, Babylonians, Assyrians, Medes, Persians, Carthaginians, Italians, and Gauls. But besides the cosmopolitan population of three continents, there were distinct native quarters—the Greek royal quarter on the harbor, the native Egyptian quarter on the west, and the Jewish quarter on the east—that were separate cities in themselves. A visit to Alexandria was a visit to three foreign countries and to "the city of the world."

Architecturally, it was unique. Even the ordinary dwellings were built, like the finer residences, of stone, with foundations of masonry, vaulted arches, and cisterns connected to the Nile. The absence of wood (even for floors and timbers) made Alexandria more fireproof than both other ancient cities and many modern ones. But it was probably the monumental buildings that attracted the eye of the visitor.

Alexander and each of the successive rulers (called the Ptolemies) built their own palaces as a way of continually enhancing the city's magnificence. The palaces alone occupied one-quarter to one-third of the entire city. There was also a giant stadium, an amphitheater, beautiful public gardens, two obelisks (called "Cleopatra's Needles"—after the last of the Ptolemies—now in London and New York), a light house that the ancients considered one of the seven wonders of the world, and many elaborate gates and temples. The Greek geographer Strabo had seen much of the Mediterranean world when he visited Alexandria in 24 B.C., but he was still impressed:

> The city is full of public and sacred buildings, but the most beautiful of them is the Gymnasium, which has porticoes more than a stadium [200 yards] in length. And in the middle [of the city] there are both the court of justice and the groves. Here, too, is the Paneum, a man-made eminence; it has the shape of a fir-cone, resembles a rocky hill, and is ascended by a spiral road; and from the summit one can see the whole of the city lying below it on all sides.[3]

Alexandria's greatest contributions to civilization took place in another monument—the palace museum, which was actually a kind of research university with the largest library of antiquity (over seven hundred thousand volumes). It was there that 72 scholars from Jerusalem, invited by Ptolemy, translated the Old Testament into the Greek edition that was spread by Christianity. The library catalogued and collected the most accurate editions of classical literature, preserving much of what remains today:

> It was there that Eratosthenes, assembling the information brought back by the explorers sent into Africa and Arabia, prepared his map of the world. This served as a basis for Ptolemy's map. It was there also that Euclid codified geometry and that Aristarchus of Samos ventured on the conjecture that the Earth moves around the Sun. . . . Herophilus and Erasistratus gained accurate knowledge of the anatomy of the brain, of the heart, and of the eye, and this opened up possibilities of more efficient surgery.[4]

## Alexandria: Spectacles and Spectators

Under the Ptolemies, even (after Cleopatra) under the Romans, Alexandria was the cultural capital of the Mediterranean world. It preserved the ancient heritage and, especially in science, increased human knowledge far beyond the capacity of the city-state. In many ways Alexandria achieved a level of intellectual sophistication which was unmatched for another thousand years.

Alexandria points to what the Hellenistic city, or the capital city, could do toward the embellishment of life as monument, art, intellect, and power. But it shares with other cities built by Alexander (or other founders, for that matter) and other monumental cities of the Hellenistic Age (or any age, for that matter) in causing a deadening effect on the human spirit.

All rectangular cities lost something in human interaction and spontaneity in order to achieve artificial regularity and order. No capital city could allow self-government to the extent that it might threaten the rule of the palace or the vested interests of wider dominion. All monumental cities substituted (to some degree) monuments for men, museums for muses, and palaces for poets. When the city itself became a work of art, the people became the spectators. Lewis Mumford observes:

> Consider the kind of urban "arena" necessary for the coronation of Ptolemy Philadelphus, a not untypical monarch of the period at its best. To mount that spectacle there were 57,000 infantrymen, 23,000 cavalry, innumerable chariots, of which 400 bore vessels of silver, 800 were filled with perfumes; a gigantic chariot of Silenus, drawn by 300 men, was followed by chariots drawn by antelopes, buffaloes, ostriches, and zebras. What later circus could compare with this prototype? Such a parade could not have found its way through the streets of fifth-century Athens even in broken order.[5]

But the Athenians would not have held such a brash display of power. That is Mumford's point. "Democracies are often too stingy in spending money for public purposes, for its citizens feel that the money is theirs. Monarchies and tyrannies can be generous because they dip their hands freely into other people's pockets."[6]

Further, it was not only the coronation but all of life that was a spectacle in the spectacular city. And we have been living in such places since the decline of the city-state. To quote Mumford again:

> The city thus ceased to be a stage for a significant drama in which everyone had a role, with lines to speak: it became, rather, a pompous show place for power; and its streets properly presented only two-dimensional facades that served as a mask for a pervasive system of regimentation and exploitation. What paraded as town planning in the Hellenistic Age was not unrelated to the kind of smooth lies and insidious perversions that go under the name of public relations and advertising in the American economy today.[7]

## The Roman Imperial City: Caesarian Capital of Power

If Alexandria shows the capital city or the city of the Hellenistic Age at its best, Rome shows it at its worst. Rome, even more than the other regimented Hellenistic cities, was a "show place for power." And unlike Alexandria, Rome cannot apologize that it was born that way. The earliest Rome was an Etruscan village and then a city-state. Even in the early days of the Roman Republic, before the imperial expansion of the second century B.C., Rome retained many of the features of the city-state. The empire itself changed all of that. Let us look at the Rome of the Caesars, the capital city of a Mediterranean empire.

We do not have time to examine in very much detail imperial Rome over its course of four or five hundred years beginning after Julius Caesar. We will have to be satisfied with a few telltale signs. Strabo, as perceptive as ever, noted that the Greeks planned their cities with attention to the quality of harbors and the fertility of the soil and occupied themselves with beauty and fortification, while the Romans concentrated on providing their cities with adequate water, streets, and sewers. Indeed, the oldest monument of Roman engineering is the Great Sewer (the Cloaca Maxima). It was constructed in the sixth century B.C. "on a scale so gigantic that either its builders must have clairvoyantly seen, at the earliest moment, that this heap of villages would become a metropolis of a million inhabitants, or else they must have taken for granted that the chief business and ultimate end of life is the physiological process of evacuation."[8] The Great Sewer was built so well that it has been used for over twenty-five hundred years, and is still in use today. Monumental scale and engineering efficiency, however, had little to do with the needs of the urban masses. The sewer line ended at the first floor of the better Roman buildings and was not connected to the crowded tenements of the poor at all. As a result, despite the technological mastery of sewerage, the average Roman was forced to dodge exrement emptied from (in some cases) nine floors above and live with the stench of collected excrement, garbage, and corpses in open cesspools and trenches. The large number of city shrines to the Goddess of Fever attest to the sanitary calamity that ensued. When plagues (as in 23 B.C. and A.D. 65 and 79) added thousands of dead in a single day and the gladiatorial contests made it necessary to dispose of five thousand animals and men in a day, breathing must have been an occupational hazard of living.

Water aqueducts and pavement were equally monumental and equally socially unconscious, if not equally disastrous. There was more than enough water for mammoth public baths, but only the rich enjoyed private baths, and (again) there is no sign of water above the first floor. All roads led to Rome, but once they got there they became parking lots. The congestion was so intense that Julius Caesar banned wheeled vehicles from the center of the city during the day. Then the racket at night kept everyone awake.

## Rome: Streets, Sleep, and Social Insomnia

"It takes a lot of money to get a night's sleep in Rome," the poet Juvenal wrote. Many of the wealthy lived in estates surrounded by gardens on one of the hills above the city. When they ventured to walk through the unlit streets at night, they could afford a retinue of

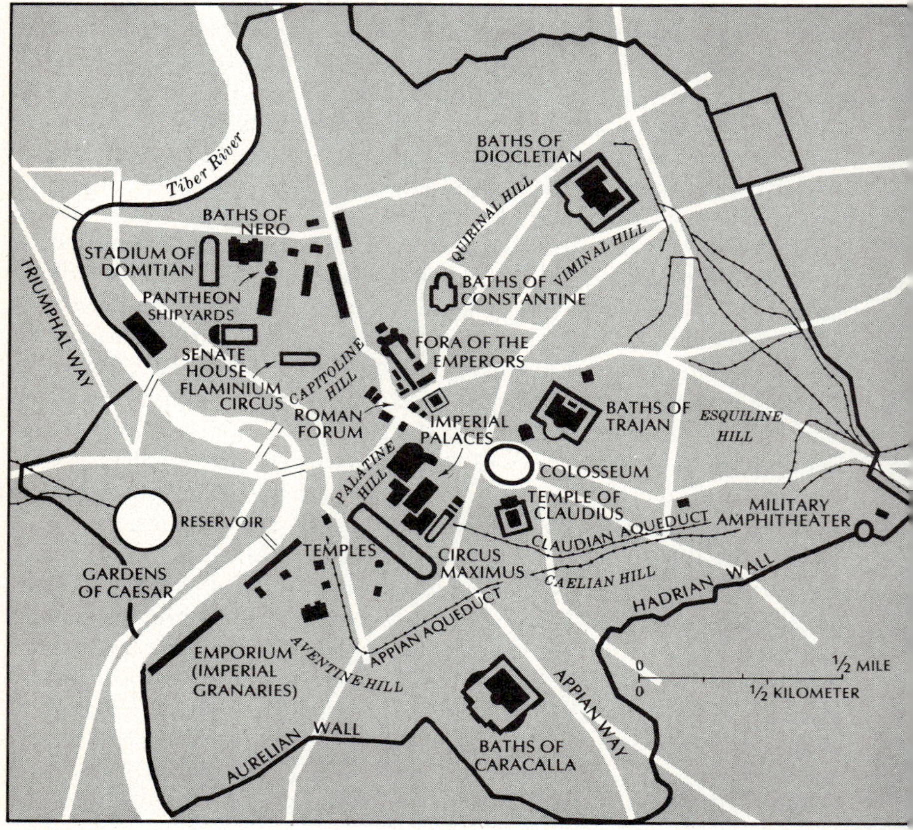


**Imperial Rome**

*Imperial Rome was a city of large public spaces devoted to the relief of boredom from the squalid tenements. Note the size and number of public baths and gladiatorial circuses.*

slaves to light their way with torches and bodyguards for protection. For the poor, nightfall meant locking themselves behind bolts and bars until dawn. Outside, "the poor man's freedom, after being punched and pounded to pieces," Juvenal tells us, was "to beg and implore that he be allowed to go home with a few teeth left."

During the day (and with the introduction of street lighting in the fourth century A.D. even at night) the streets were safer, but impossibly crowded. The population had grown from a hundred thousand in the second century B.C. to over half a million by the second century A.D. The vast majority of inhabitants (who could not afford the hills or suburbs) were crowded into six square miles, most of which was occupied by public buildings and thoroughfares. Only one building in 26 was a private home. Most of the people lived in crowded tenements, five to seven stories high. Generally an entire family lived in a single dingy room off a common balcony and steep staircase. The wooden construction and crowding made fire a regular disaster, despite the fire department of seven thousand freedmen (former slaves) established by Augustus. Fire fighting, police work, and ordinary business was further complicated by the absence of street names (other than those named for their activities, like the "Street of the Money Changers") and the total lack of street signs or building numbers.

Traffic congestion went from bad to worse because nothing was done about the root problem—the overcrowding of the center. The speculators, the contractors, and the landlords were allowed a free hand in buying, building, and renting where profits were highest—in the center of the city:

> [It] was a speculative enterprise in which the greatest profits were made by both the dishonest contractors, putting together flimsy structures that would barely hold up, and profiteering landlords, who learned how to subdivide old quarters into even narrower cells to accommodate even poorer artisans at a higher return of rent per unit. (One notes, not without a cynical smile, that the one kind of wheeled traffic permitted by day in Rome was that of the building contractors.)
>
> Crassus, who made a fabulous fortune in tenement house properties, boasted that he never spent money in building: it was more profitable to buy partly damaged old properties at fire sales and rent them with meager repairs. . . .
>
> The houses of the patricians, spacious, airy, sanitary, equipped with bathrooms and water closets, heated in winter by hypocausts, which carried hot air through chambers in the floors, were perhaps the most commodious and comfortable houses built for a temperate climate anywhere until the twentieth century: a triumph of domestic architecture. But the tenements of Rome easily take the prize for being the most crowded and unsanitary buildings produced in Western Europe until the sixteenth century, when site over-filling and room over-crowding became common, from Naples to Edinburgh.[9]

If the houses of Athens had been no better constructed, at least they were not piled one on top of another to the point of spontaneous combustion or epidemic infestation. More significantly, the houses of Athens were all rude, those of rich and poor alike. Class divisions between rich and poor, powerful and weak, were radically accelerated in the capital city, especially Rome. Housing construction was just another vehicle for widening that gap: builders could afford palaces *because* they packed the poor into cheap tenements and reduced the quality of their lives. Brutalization paid.

Imperial Rome could not offer its urban masses an opportunity to participate meaningfully in community affairs as Athens could for its citizens. Nor could Rome give its inhabitants the Athenian citizen's sense of autonomy nourished by assembly, agora, acropolis, and amphitheater. In Rome the monumental public structures—like the public baths and the arena—provided diversion rather than participation.

## Rome: Monumental Engineering and Mass Diversion

Mumford has written that the whole history of Rome can be seen in the development of the "bath." In the days of the early Republic the bath "was a pool of water in a sheltered place where the sweaty farmer made himself clean." By 33 B.C. the first free public bath set the style of the later empire: huge halls, eating areas, lounging areas, gymnasia, playing fields, separate temples for hot, warm, and cool baths—everything in short that would serve the new religion of the body and take people's minds away from the world outside. The scale of these buildings boggles the imagination. Today (during the summer months) the Roman Opera performs with hundreds of participants and thousands of spectators in a small niche at the ruins of the Baths of Caracalla.

To the Roman engineer, size was everything. Masses of people kept their mass identity in the mammoth baths, markets, amphitheaters, racecourses, and arenas. The special Roman contribution to handling masses, according to Mumford, was the "vomitorium." The word was originally used for a room next to the dining room (in the mansions of the rich). Here the stuffed diner could vomit in order to return to the table or couch for more of the host's rich and exotic food. Then the Romans used the word for the massive exits that they created from public arenas. Like the sewer, the Roman vomitorium was a superb symbol for a civilization that was "poorly digested but splendidly evacuated."

When a city's inhabitants no longer have any control over the life of the city, they must be entertained. The baths and arenas did the job for the Romans in much the same way as spectator sports and television do the job today. The arena, particularly its gladiatorial extravaganzas, combined the contest of sports with the thrill of vicarious violence even more effectively than modern TV. But both the arena and TV perverted the original urban contribution of empathy and mutual understanding into a deadening inability to live except through the lives of others. And where life had been most brutalized, the most exciting vicarious thrill was imagining oneself as the mutilator or murderer of others. The brutalized could only hope to brutalize others. The gladiatorial arena satisfied that dream.

In the first gladiatorial "games" in 264 B.C., prisoners were publically executed.

> Too soon, unfortunately, the ordeal of the prisoner became the welcome amusement of the spectator, and even the emptying of the jails did not provide a sufficient number of victims to meet the popular demand. As with the religious sacrifices of the Aztecs, military expeditions were directed toward supplying a sufficient number of victims, human and animal. Here in the arena both degraded professionals, thoroughly trained for their occupation, and wholly innocent men and women were tortured with every imaginable body-maiming and fear-producing device for public delight. And here wild animals were butchered, without being eaten, as if they were only men.[10]

During the reign of the emperor Claudius (A.D. 41–54) there were 93 days of games a year at public expense. By A.D. 354 there were 175 such days. By then there were enough arenas and theaters to hold almost half the population of Rome simultaneously. Almost a quarter of a million people, unable to find ample work, were supported by the daily dole of bread, and free to dream their revenge, or try to forget at the Circus Maximus. By then the city had become, in Mumford's telling phrase, a Necropolis, a city of the dead:

> From the standpoint of both politics and urbanism, Rome remains a significant lesson of what to avoid: its history presents a series of classic danger signals to warn one when life is moving in the wrong direction. Wherever crowds gather in suffocating numbers, wherever rents rise steeply and housing conditions deteriorate, wherever a one-sided exploitation of distant territories removes the pressure to achieve balance and harmony nearer at hand, there the precedents of Roman building almost automatically revive, as they have come back today: the arena, the tall tenement, the mass contests and exhibitions, the football matches, the international beauty contests, the strip-tease made ubiquitous by advertisement, the constant titillation of the senses by sex, liquor, and vio-

▪ *A reconstruction of the imperial city of Rome as it must have appeared in the reign of the Emperor Aurelian (270–275). (Granger)*

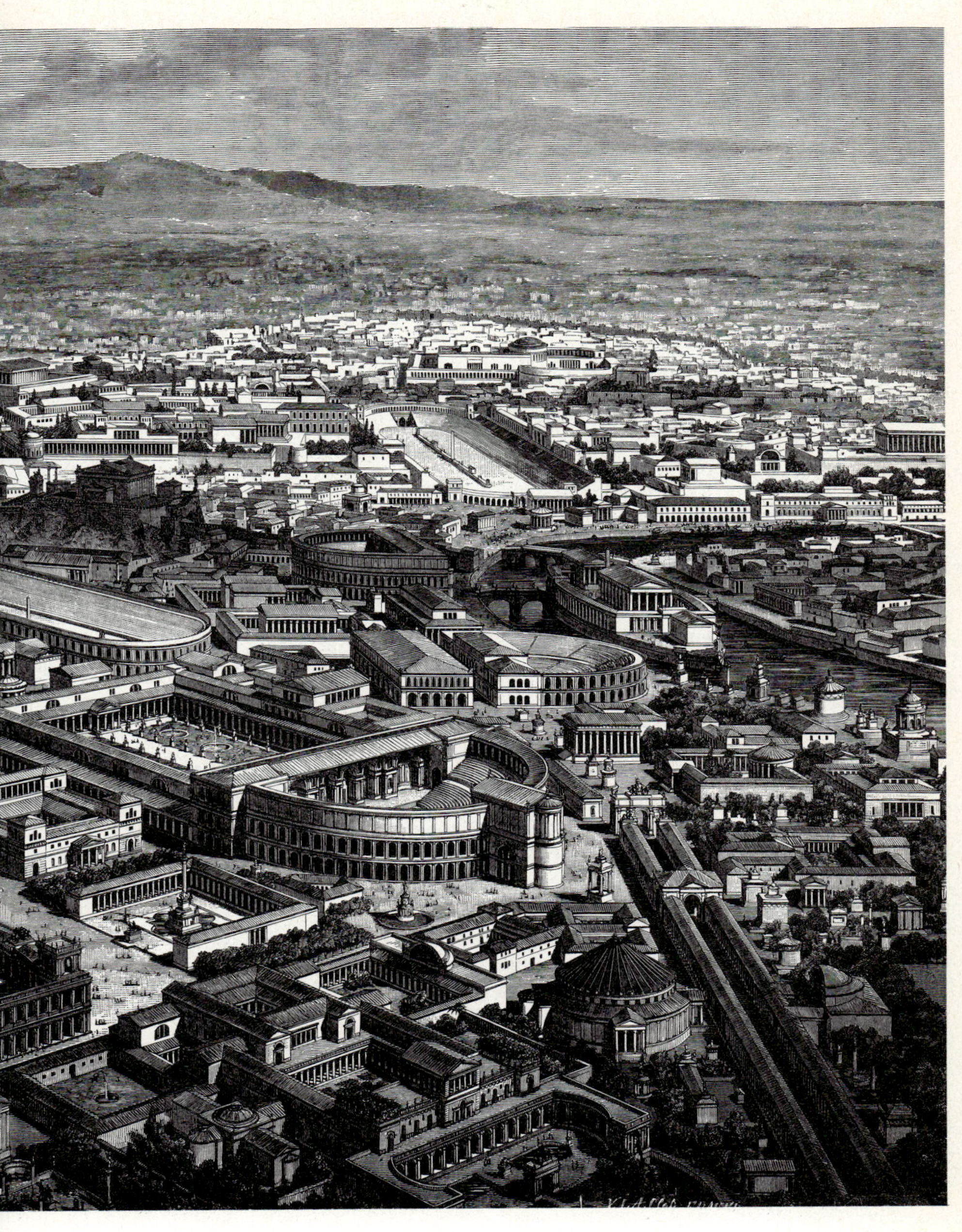

lence—all in true Roman style. So, too, the multiplication of bathrooms and the over-expenditure on broadly paved motor roads, and above all, the massive collective concentration on glib ephemeralities of all kinds, performed with supreme technical audacity. These are symptoms of the end: magnifications of demoralized power, minifications of life. When these signs multiply, Necropolis is near, though not a stone has yet crumbled. For the barbarian has already captured the city from within. Come, hangman! Come, vulture![11]

## *For Further Reading*

Lewis Mumford's **The City in History*** is a masterpiece of interpretive integration, telling detail, and stunning style. It is also eccentric, almost perversely pessimistic, and controversial. To make Mumford more accessible we have followed his argument closely in the text. But this is meant as suggestive stimulation rather than definitive answer.

For a more traditional textbook on Western urban history, the student would do well to read **Western Civilization: An Urban Perspective** by F. Roy Willis.* For a magnificently illustrated book of thoughtful essays on assorted cultural and political capital cities, the student could do little better than **Cities of Destiny,** edited by Arnold Toynbee.

A short, but encyclopedic study of Greek cities can be found in R. E. Wycherley's **How the Greeks Built Cities.*** It is an archeological classic which examines the agora, shrines, gymnasiums, theaters, fortifications, and Greek urban planning in some detail. For a broader view of the society of the Greek polis there are many good books available. Among the best are Frank J. Frost's **Greek Society,*** H. D. F. Kitto's **The Greeks,*** Moses I. Finleys **The Ancient Greeks,*** and the evocatively photographed **Horizon Book of Ancient Greece.**

Among the best of the numerous separate studies of Athens are Angelou Procopiou's beautifully illustrated **Athens City of the Gods,** Charles A. Robinson, Jr.'s **Athens in the Age of Pericles,*** and Robert Flaceliere's **Daily Life in the Athens of Pericles.**

Alexandria is studied in E. M. Forster's **Alexandria: A History and a Guide** and in Kenneth Heuer's readable introduction to Alexandrian astronomy **City of the Stargazers** as well as the chapter in Toynbee's **Cities of Destiny** which is cited in the text. The ambitious student might want to go further with A. H. M. Jones's **The Greek City from Alexander to Justinian.**

Further study of the Roman city might well begin with the influence of Greece. Kathleen Freeman's **Greek City-States*** examines Greek cities in Italy, and Lidia Storoni Massolani in **The Idea of the City in Roman Thought** studies the appeal of the Greek idea of the city for the Romans. The physical appearance of the Roman city is described in some detail in Henry T. Rowell's **Rome in the Augustan Age,*** and the streets come alive in Jérôme Carcopino's **Daily Life in Ancient Rome,*** Harold Mattingly's **The Man in**

* Available in paperback.

**the Roman Street,*** and J. P. V. D. Balsdon's **The Romans.** Besides the many recent Roman histories (most of which place the city in the background), the student might also wish to consult the nineteenth-century classic on the role of religion in almost "primitive" Greece and Rome, **The Ancient City*** by Fustel de Coulanges.

Primary sources that touch on the character of the ancient Greek and Roman cities are almost too numerous to mention. It will have to suffice to suggest the histories of Herodotus and Thucydides, the **Republic*** and **Laws*** of Plato, the **Politics*** of Aristotle, a play of Aristophanes like **The Archarnians** (especially the Douglass Parker translation),* and the Roman histories of Livy, Tacitus, and Suetonius.

## Notes

1. Dicaearchus, quoted by Mumford, *The City in History* (New York: Harcourt Brace Jovanovich, 1961), p. 163.
2. Achilles, Tatius, *Clitophon and Leucippe,* trans. S. Gaselee (London: L.C.I., 1917), bk. V-1-2. Quoted in Edward Alexander Parsons, *The Alexandrian Library* (New York: American Elsevier, 1952), p. 61.
3. Strabo, cited in Claire Preaux, "Alexandria Under the Ptolemies" in *Cities of Destiny,* ed. Arnold Toynbee (New York: McGraw-Hill, 1967), pp. 112–113.
4. Toynbee, *Cities of Destiny,* p. 114.
5. Lewis Mumford, *op. cit.,* p. 201.
6. *Ibid.,* p. 197.
7. *Ibid.,* p. 196.
8. *Ibid.,* p. 214.
9. *Ibid.,* pp. 219–221.
10. *Ibid.,* p. 232.
11. *Ibid.,* p. 242.

# Chapter 5

# Love and Sex

## Passion and Conquest in Greece and Rome

People who have reached adulthood in America since World War II have a problem that would have been an undreamed luxury for the mass of people throughout most of human history. Only some small ruling classes in past history have been able to afford such a problem. The problem is difficult to define. In general, it is that love, sex, and marriage have become problematical for us. A simple way of putting it is that we do not have to get married. The increasing divorce rate is just a symptom of the much greater freedom we have to choose love, sex, or marriage. It is a "problem" of vastly expanded experience, consciousness, and ability to choose. The problem is that since we can enjoy sex without love, and either or both without marriage, we have to figure out what we want. Perhaps no problem is more difficult than self-understanding and self-realization.

Most ordinary people in traditional society never had to ask themselves if they wanted to get married. There were some respectable, especially religious, alternatives, but aside from these, people simply married because they were expected to. People in traditional society had a lot more opportunity for sexual satisfaction outside of marriage than we usually think, but such activities were rarely translated into feelings of love, and even more rarely threatened the basic social institution of marriage. Marriages were arranged by parents and normally were permanent because they formed the only social cement (for those without status and money) that protected people from periodic disaster. Marriage was simply too important to be left to individual feelings.

Modern governments, middle-class mobility, the money economy, and the independent nuclear family have all created a contraceptive technology and a pleasure ethic that make marriage an entirely different arrangement. Instead of a liaison between families, it has become a possible life style to choose for love, sex, children, friendship, or whatever else one desires. We have made it one of many options because we have had the option to do so. We have the luxury to experiment, but that inevitably leads us to ask ourselves what we want.

We will examine one of the first societies in which people in fairly large numbers began to have these experiences and ask these questions. Although still confined to a relative elite, some ancient Greeks and Romans developed much of the self-conscious understanding of sex and love that both burdens us and frees us today. When we think of sex and love, we use ideas and feelings that they developed and passed on.

## Greek Loves

The ancient Greeks spoke of love as if they had invented the word. Actually, they invented two words for love: *eros,* meaning physical or sexual love, and *agape,* meaning spiritual love. They also spoke of *philia* when they meant affection or friendship. They spoke of love often, symbolized it as the heart pierced by Cupid's arrow, diagnosed it as a newly discovered disease, and talked endlessly about its meaning and effects.

It is interesting that in so much of their talk about love, they rarely mentioned marriage. The purpose of marriage had much more to do with housekeeping and insurance against old age. The Athenian aristocrat, soldier, and statesman Xenophon put it this way:

> Did you ever stop to consider, dear wife, what led me to choose you, and your parents to intrust you to me? It was surely not because either

> of us would have any trouble in finding another consort. No! it was with deliberate intent, I for myself, and your parents for you, to discover the best partners of house and children we could find. . . . If at some future time God grant us children, we will take counsel together how best to bring them up, for that, too, will be a common interest, and a common blessing if happily they live to fight our battles and we find in them hereafter support and succor for ourselves.[1]

For the Greeks married life was not expected to yield either *eros* or *agape*. In this respect Greece was no different from other societies. One of them summed up the situation this way: "Mistresses we keep for pleasure, concubines for daily attendance upon our persons, and wives to bear us legitimate children and be our housekeepers."[2]

Greek men entered marriage out of a sense of duty rather than of love. They felt a duty to their ancestors, the city, and their religion to have children. And if they were to lead lives in the city, they needed someone to take care of the children and the household. Wives served this function amply. But a wife was hardly a person to spend time with. Women were not educated, and their lives were occupied with dull trivia.

Marriage was so unpopular that the government of Athens, the leading Greek city, considered making bachelorhood illegal in order to ensure sufficient population growth. Such a law was almost passed as early as the sixth century B.C. During the golden age of Athens (the fifth century B.C.) a law was passed that allowed only married men to become generals or orators (our equivalent of lawyers). So Athenian men learned to carry out duty to the state, but rarely pretended that marriage was anything but such a necessity. The Greek poet Palladas must have expressed the feelings of many when he wrote:

> Marriage brings a man only two happy days:
> The day he takes his bride to bed, and the day he lays
>     her in her grave.[3]

It would be interesting to know if Greek wives wasted any love on their husbands. Since they were not taught to write, we can only guess. Oppressed people sometimes have a peculiar capacity to love their masters, or at least accept their authority as beneficial. But there is some evidence that Greek wives were not always taken in. The great Greek dramatist Sophocles in his play *Antigone* has the heroine, Antigone, who buries her brother in defiance of her uncle's order, say that a brother is irreplaceable while a husband is not. It seems, furthermore, that many Greek wives remained much closer to their own families than they were to their husband. The Greek historian Herodotus approvingly tells a story of a Persian woman who, when given the choice by a conqueror of saving the life of one person, chose her brother rather than her husband.

Who did the Greeks love, then, if not their husbands and wives? The women that Greek men loved were prostitutes. Prostitution was widely developed, if not invented, in almost all of the first patriarchal cities. The city fathers considered it a noble solution to the problem of providing men with seductive and interesting women while ensuring that their own wives (and thus, their own family lines) would remain pure. In short, they created a society of two types of women: the sexless wives and virginal daughters of the men of substance and the women (drawn mostly from the lower class) who were trained to satisfy men's pleasures.

## Greek Prostitution: Love, Death, and Social Disease

Greek prostitution actually became quite specialized by the golden age of the fifth century B.C. There were three types of prostitutes. The common prostitutes, called *pornae,* lived in brothels marked by a large phallus on the door. They were uneducated, cheap and served to siphon off the sexual energy of lower-class men. Above the *pornae* in prestige were the *auletrides* who were trained as entertainers. They were usually hired out by their teachers (who usually owned them as slaves) to play the flute, dance, and amuse men at private dinners and to spend the night with some of the guests. Both of these groups, resembling the streetwalkers and call girls of other patriarchal societies, were frowned on by men of wealth or refinement. They recognized the necessity of such women in maintaining social order, and they might use them themselves, but they did not "love" them even when they enjoyed their company.

The love poems of the poets and the love interests of successful citizens were usually confined to the third type of prostitute—the *hetaerae.* When the word was first used in the sixth century B.C. it meant only an intimate female friend. By the fifth and fourth centuries B.C. it meant high-class courtesans. As the only well-educated and interesting women of Greece, and as women of good families who were often citizens, they ranked higher in social esteem than wives or virgins. They were trained to be not only sexually alluring but also intellectually stimulating. The *hetaerae* lived independently in their own homes, chose as few or as many lovers as they wanted, and frequently became quite prosperous and influential.

■ *One of the Greek* auletrides *plays the double flute as the men drink and spill wine from vases like this one. (Master and Fellows of Corpus Christi College, Cambridge)*

One of these courtesans, Aspasia, was probably the most influential woman of the fifth century B.C. She is said to have trained the philosopher Socrates in the skills of speaking and argument, and even to have written speeches for the greatest Athenian statesman, Pericles, who was one of her oratory students. Aspasia captivated Athenian men with her physical charms as well as her wit and sophistication. After Pericles divorced his wife he took Aspasia to his home as his exclusive mistress. He might have even married her if she had been a citizen.

The settled, almost marital, love of Pericles and Aspasia was the exception, however. Most Greek men were interested in the excitement and bittersweet anguish of love rather than its domestication in married life. No less serious and philosophical a man than Socrates expressed this desire in his reported advice to Diotima, a courtesan renowned for her exquisite beauty:

■ *"You will charm them best if you never surrender except when they are sharp-set." One of the* hetaerae *and one of the sharp set. (Hirmer Fotoarchiv)*

> You will charm them best if you never surrender except when they are sharp-set. You have noticed that the daintiest fare, if served before a man wants it, is apt to seem insipid, while, if he is already sated, it even produces a feeling of nausea. Create a hunger before you bring on your banquet. . . . Seem not to wish to yield. Fly from them—and fly again, until they feel the keen pang of hunger. That is your moment. The gift is the same as when the man did not want it: but wondrous different now its value.[4]

*Hetaerae* were not desired for sex alone. If that were the case they would not have existed. They charged a minimum of 100 drachmas (the equivalent in our economy of hundreds of dollars) for the evening, while the average *porna* charged the equivalent of a couple of dollars. And if they were only desired for their intelligence, they would have been replaced by much cheaper teachers, or free male companionship. They were successful because they offered a tempting combination of both. A cynic might say that the courtesan offered sex without guilt. Certainly these Greeks felt that sex was less vulgar when it was so tastefully introduced. But the Greeks did not feel guilty about sexual drives in the way Christians later did. It would be more accurate to say that the *hetaerae* were sought and loved because they were complex, full-bodied human beings with whom a man could become lost in conversation, as well as in love.

In a society which had no hang-ups about sex, all women could have acquired these attributes, all could have been trained intellectually and sexually, and practiced their skills in or out of marriage. But in patriarchal society where men felt forced to deemphasize the sexuality of some of the women (their wives), and then in compensation to exaggerate the sexual appeal of other women (the courtesans), their relationships with these "ideal" women must have always been full of tension, ambiguity, and frustration. They were interested in conversation, but talk was always a prelude. *Hetaerae* seemed to be genuinely interested in their lovers as people, but they were studiously trained to be so, and it was all for a fee. They were some of the most interesting people in Greece, but they were women—people men had consigned to inferior status. They represented what every man wanted in a companion, but the last thing in the world that he wanted from his wife.

The contradictions in this patriarchal view of women were so great that a man could not simply "love." He could feel *eros* or *agape,* rarely both. And even when he idealized his sexual passion for a courtesan and imagined her to be a noble companion, he was haunted by his unwillingness to allow the women of his own family to become so desirable.

It is no wonder then that the Greeks sensed that their deepest love, their love of these courtesans, yielded as much pain as delight, as much sickness as intoxication, and as much torment as joy. That is the way they wanted it—or rather the love that they idealized and craved could only thrive on the social illness that they created. The courtesans, all Greeks knew as well as Socrates, must tempt and frustrate in order to satisfy. Love in patriarchal society could not be love alone. In the words of the great poet Sophocles,

> Love is not love alone,
> But in her name lie many names concealed;
> For she is Death, imperishable Force,
> Desire unmixed, wild Frenzy, Lamentation.[5]

Love involved death because the ideal love of the courtesan carried to its logical conclusion, allowed to all men and women, meant the death of the Greek patriarchal system. The poet probably did not see things that way. He was thinking of the tragically conflicting emotions of the lover. But these were tragic for Greek men precisely because the social ideals of women and love were so contradictory. The more they attempted to enforce the chastity of their wives and daughters, the more they desexualized them; the more they split the female population in two, the more they compartmentalized their own emotions. The breathless love of the courtesan which the Greeks created was possible only as long as all women were not courtesans. If all women were as exciting and intriguing as the courtesans there would be no need or possibility of courtesan love. That was something the Greeks would not even consider.

## Greek Homosexuality: Ideals and Education

Greek men always felt that there was something imperfect in loving women. The more highly they thought of love, the more foolish it seemed to waste the emotion on their inferiors. It was only natural, then, that the Greeks would develop homosexual love as an even nobler ideal than the love of the courtesan. Since, as all Greeks agreed, men were the most nearly perfect creatures, they were also the most worthy of love. But the most appealing of all, in fact the ideal love, was the love of a mature man for a youth. Some said that it could last until the boy's beard was full; others said that boys could be appealing until their late twenties.

Few Greeks were unaffected by the sight of a beautiful boy. When one entered the room, heads would turn, conversation stopped, grown

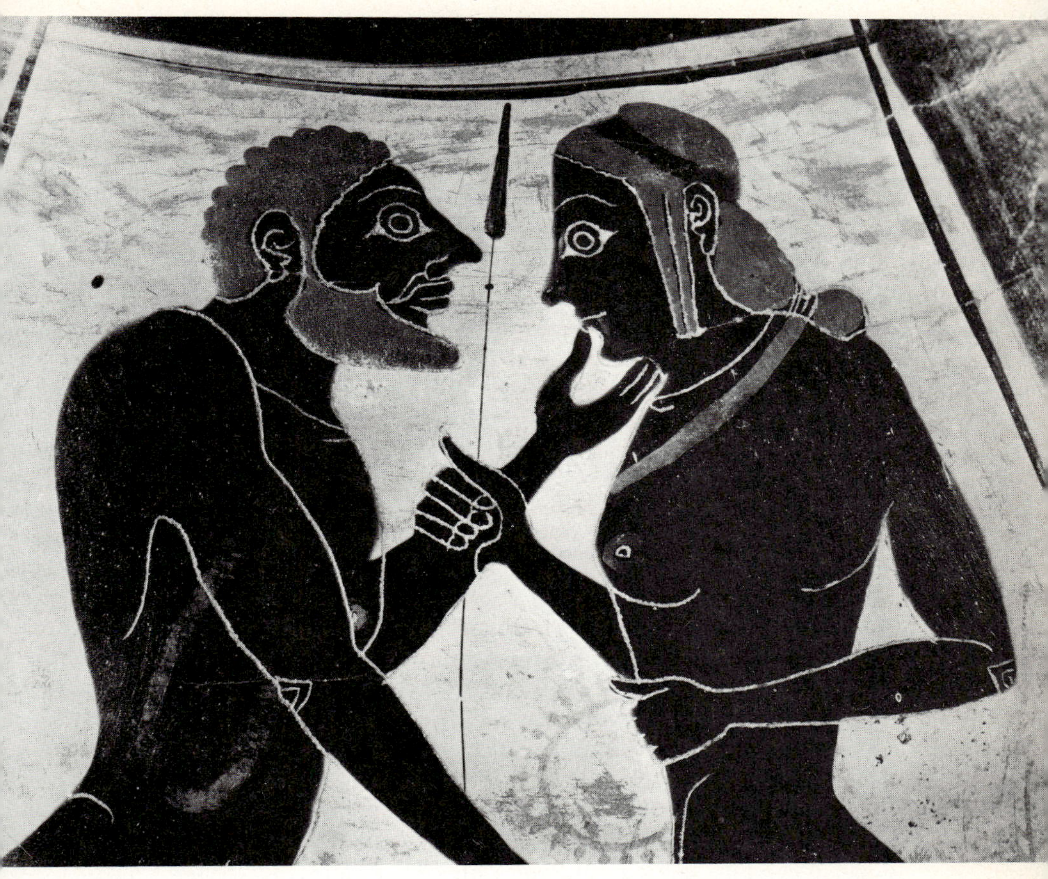

▪ *The Greek gentleman reaches beyond the arrow of love and death to grasp the virility of beardless youth.* (*Hirmer Fotoarchiv*)

men would blush or look foolish. Some men thought that it was improper to have sexual relationships with these youths, but few were untouched by their beauty. Socrates was one of these. According to his student Plato, Socrates always felt a "flame" when he looked at a handsome young man. One, Alcibiades, even tried to seduce the philosopher, but Socrates repressed his desire and treated the youth like a son. Plato (at least in his early life when he was influenced by Socrates) thought that love of a boy was useful in leading men to see the higher, ideal kinds of love—love of the ideas of beauty, virtue, and knowledge. And later Aristotle developed a philosophy of ethics which disapproved of sexual relations with young men, but insisted nevertheless that "love and friendship are found most and in their best form between men."

The avowed homosexuality of Greek philosophers and educators would shock modern educators. Far from being considered a vice or a detriment, love of the pupil was considered a necessary element of the teaching process. When Socrates went looking for students, he said he was "hunting down good-looking young fellows" because he regarded education as "a spiritual bringing to birth of beauty."

Pointing out that all Greek philosophers defined homosexuality in terms of education, H. I. Marrou writes in his *A History of Education in Antiquity:*

> For the Greeks, education—*paideia*—meant, essentially, a profound and intimate relationship, a personal union between a young man and an elder who was at once his model, his guide and his initiator—a relationship on to which the fire of passion threw warm and turbid reflections.
>
> Public opinion—and, in Sparta, the law—held the lover morally responsible for the development of his beloved. Pederasty was considered the most beautiful, the perfect, form of education. Throughout Greek history the relationship between master and pupil was to remain that between a lover and his beloved: education remained in principle not so much a form of teaching, an instruction in techniques, as an expenditure of loving effort by an elder concerned to promote the growth of a younger man who was burning with the desire to respond to this love and show himself worthy of it.[6]

Greek homosexuality may have originated, as Marrou suggests, in the military as part of the recruitment of the young, the training in physical combat, and the "comradeship of warriors." (Plato has Phaedo say in the *Symposium:* "A handful of lovers and loved ones, fighting shoulder to shoulder, could rout a whole army.") It flourished in the gymnasiums where youths exercised and competed in the nude. Despite official disapproval, it became an elaborate preoccupation of the educated, prosperous, and aristocratic men by the fifth century B.C. Although by no means universal, even among the well-to-do, the culture of homosexuality created rituals of flirtation and seduction that later became the repertoire of heterosexual romance as well.

## Greek Romance: The Delicious Disease

Romance is a leisure activity. If the Greek leisure class was the first to afford the cultivation of jealousy and love because of the exclusion of women, foreigners, and slaves from its ideals, their rituals have since been opened to all. Lovers, for instance, would swear their faithfulness, allow themselves to be tested by doing foolish errands or dangerous acts. They would write long letters or poems to their beloved, serenade them, sleep out all night at their doorsteps, become speechless in their presence, or bore their friends with an endless catalog of their lover's virtues. Almost everything that was later integrated into the romance of boy and girl was perfected in the Greek love of man and boy.

These signs of love—blushing, stammering, silly behavior—seemed so new to the Greeks that one of them, Sappho, made a long list which was useful to physicians for hundreds of years. The Greek historian Plutarch, for example, tells the story of a young man who fell in love with his father's young wife. The doctor was called in but was as mystified as everyone else by the young man's behavior. Then the doctor noticed that every time the boy's stepmother appeared, the youth would display all of the symptoms of "love sickness" that Sappho had listed: flushed face, faltering voice, faintness, irregular, violent heart beats, darting eyes, and sweaty skin. With the aid of Sappho's list the doctor was able to diagnose the illness as the youth's love sickness for his father's new wife.

Plutarch's story is interesting because it shows how unknown the symptoms of this new "disease" must have been. Plutarch's story is instructive in another way. He goes on to tell us that when the boy's father learned of the illness he graciously gave his young wife to his son in marriage. The symptoms, we are told, vanished, but with the pain, the joy and ecstasy of love also evaporated. Evidently the romance that the boy found in his father's wife had a lot to do with the impossibility of ever consummating his desire. The Greeks developed romance out of very unlikely material. The love of courtesan, or member of the same sex, or "mother figure" was not the type of love which was ever likely to become permanent. It fed on the obstacles that it created, and thrived on the social instability that it caused.

We should say one other thing about Sappho's contribution to "medical history." Sappho was a woman. Since she happened to live on the Greek island of Lesbos, and since she was sexually attracted to girls, we call her spiritual sisters lesbians today. The point is that her study of love's symptoms, which taught the Greeks so much about the new "delicious malady," was drawn to a great extent from her own experience. And her experience was rich. She was married to a man, raised a daughter, and ran one of the few schools for girls. She fell in love with one after another of her pupils. The poems that she wrote to these girls were considered to be among the finest in Greek. Though some of her art is lost in translation we can get some sense of her passion:

For should I but see thee a little moment,
  Straight is my voice hushed;
Yea, my tongue is broken, and through and through me
'Neath the flesh, impalpable fire runs tingling;
Nothing see mine eyes, and a voice of roaring
  Waves in my ear sounds;
Sweat runs down in rivers, a tremor seizes
All my limbs, and paler than grass in autumn,
Caught by pains of menacing death, I falter,
Lost in the love-trance.[7]

If the Greeks did not invent sex or friendship, they invented romantic love with all of its bittersweet moods that we know today. But the idea of passionate, romantic love that they gave us came out of relationships that were at best temporary and full of difficulty. They burned with a passion that would have been impossible in marriage, and few Greeks seemed to care. They spoke of love as a sickness, but the "cure" was rarely as satisfying as the disease.

Romantic love hardly reached epidemic proportions in ancient Greece. Actually, it was felt deeply by only a minority of sensitive souls. Many Greeks, particularly among the upper class of citizens, had homosexual and heterosexual experiences which they might have called love. Many were infatuated or affected by courtesans and young men, but few could afford to throw all of their time and energy into the wreckless passion that consumed Sappho and some of the poets.

The pursuit of love on such a grand romantic scale began to develop in Greece among an educated, sensitive leisure class. A system of slave labor gave a few people the opportunity to cultivate "the finer things." Since women were degraded, this new sensitivity was directed toward the rare female who magnified the magic that was denied to others and toward other men—the most worthy object of love. The women who were not trained to excite men probably knew very little of love. A few, like Sappho, turned the tables on their masters and found deep relationships or casual sex with other women.

## The Roman Contribution: Love as Sex

When Roman legions marched from nowhere to take over the faded Greek cities that Alexander the Great had united briefly, they paid

▪ *Zeus, the ruler of the Greek gods, abducts Ganymede, the most beautiful boy in the world. Zeus pleased himself with males and females, human and divine, often outwitting the plots of his wife Hera, the goddess of marriage. (Hirmer Fotoarchiv)*

the Greeks the highest compliment possible—they stole their art and imitated their culture.

Returning Roman legions (like American GI's returning from France after World War II) had found sex, and they approved. Within decades after the Roman conquest of the Mediterranean empire in the second century B.C., courtesans had become popular in Rome. Even young boys were bought and sold (sometimes for the price of a nice farm) and the Romans were acclaiming the joys of "Greek love" by which they seem to have meant pederasty. The problem with the Romans was that they (like the Americans) fell in love with sex rather than love. They were not really interested in sex mixed with philosophy, and so the courtesans were never as popular or satisfying as cheaper prostitutes. Nor were the Romans interested in charming handsome young boys for their wit and intelligence. They preferred to seduce them and leave it at that.

Romans looked to Greece in the same way that some Americans have looked to Europe. They recognized the high achievements of Greek culture, but tried to buy it or reproduce it without ever fully understanding it. Some of the better minds would write poetry or plays in the style of the Greeks or spout Greek phrases to impress other Romans with their sophistication. But when most Romans heard about Greek culture, they missed the elaborate, intricate rituals of love, and found the open attitude toward sex which lay beneath these ritualistic restraints.

When Rome consisted of just the city and some other parts of Italy, the people were repressed, or "moral," as many Americans of the 1940s and 1950s. Marriages were valued, not for love certainly, but for the honor that children gave to the family and the prosperity that a virtuous, hardworking wife gave to the husband. But the Rome that had conquered an empire was as different from the early Rome as the American world power was different from the new republic. And just as the small-town culture of America may have lasted long beyond the time that it still made sense (possibly into the 1950s) so did the conservative culture of ancient Rome survive long after the city had become master of an empire. Similarly, the rude awakening of Rome was almost as sudden and complete as the "sexual revolution" in America. If we contrast American films of the 1970s, with their sexual frankness, with those of the 1950s we have some idea of the degree of change. In fact, the French films of the 1950s probably unleashed the pent-up fantasies of Americans in the same way that Greek culture burst through the old Roman morality.

The change, in fact, was so complete that the Americans of the 1950s were unable to imagine the moral life of imperial Rome. In an excellent study of the history of love, *The Natural History of Love* (1959), Morton Hunt writes:

> If the emotional flavor of the earlier moralistic patriarchy is not altogether agreeable, it is at least understandable to us; but that of the later Republic is so alien that few fictional or dramatic treatments of it have dared to be truthful.[8]

Although the readers in 1959 would have been aghast at the sexuality of imperial Rome, America since then has gone through enough of the same changes so that we are today at least prepared to imagine what that society was like. Since 1959 we have, for instance, been treated to Federico Fellini's *Satyricon* on film. The film, so unlike the *Robe* and gladitorial epochs of the 1950s, tells us more about the 1970s *and* imperial Rome than any earlier attempts.

Let us return to Mr. Hunt:

> How many have ever visualized the great Caesar as a fop, a dandy, and a perfumed homosexual? Yet such he was, at least in his youth. His warm reception at the court of the King of Bithynia won him the nickname of The Queen of Bithynia, an epithet thrown at him even on the Senate floor in Rome. He wore his clothing with a studied carelessness, kept his body plucked clean of hair, and fussed so endlessly with his thinning locks that Cicero once said: "When I see his hair so carefully arranged and observe him adjusting it with one finger, I cannot imagine that it should enter into such a man's thoughts to subvert the Roman state."
>
> The same man, however, could not only subvert the state, but also become an indefatigable lecher: the historian Suetonius indicated that his conquests included the wives of almost all his close friends, associates, generals, and the heads of state wherever he went. Partly in admiration, partly in resentment, Romans called him *"Omnium mulierum vir et omnium virorum mulier"*—"The husband of every woman and the wife of every man." His four marriages were all made for political or practical reasons; there is no evidence that love was responsible for any of them. He was past fifty and Cleopatra was twenty-one when they met; she deliberately offered him a queen's body for political reasons, and he found her person and her character alluring enough to keep him overtime in Alexandria, but it is doubtful whether the affair involved more than ambition and cunning on her part, and on his the powerful appeal of having an exotic queen—and so young a one—as his mistress. The woman he was faithful to longest—in his fashion—was Servilia, a matron of a noble family; this affair, in some sense, may have helped undo him, for even in Rome a bastard might hate the man who begot him. Servilia's son, Brutus, was thought to look much like Caesar, and if Suetonius is correct, the dying Caesar said to him not "You too, Brutus?" but "You, too, *my child?*"[9]

## Fashionable Romans: Ovid's Art of War

For the "liberated" upper-class Romans who ruled the empire love meant sex. The fashionable society poet during the reign of the emperor Augustus (the heir and successor of Julius Caesar) was Ovid, whose popular book, *The Art of Love,* was simply a manual for seduction. Ovid's art had nothing to do with the Greek romantic sickness. He cautioned his readers to pretend to be incapacitated in order to manipulate the feelings of the women they desired. The tone of his advice sounds more like *Popular Mechanics* than *Modern Romance.*

Also, the theater's curve is a very good place for your hunting,
 More opportunity here, maybe, than anywhere else.
Here you may find one to love, or possibly only have fun with,
 Someone to take for a night, someone to have and to hold.
(i, 89–92)[10]

Try to find something in common, to open the conversation;
 Don't care too much what you say, just so that everyone hears. . . .
Often it happens that dust may fall on the blouse of the lady.
 If such dust should fall, carefully brush it away.
Even if there's no dust, brush off whatever there isn't.
(i, 142–143, 149–152)

See that you promise: what harm can there be in promising freely?
 There's not a man in the world who can't be rich in that coin.
(i, 443–444)

Also, make it your aim to get her husband to like you;
 If you can make him your friend, he will be useful, you'll find.
(i, 581–582)

Getting really drunk is bad, but pretending to do so
 Does no harm at all, might in fact, be a gain.
Make your cunning tongue stumble and stutter a little,
 So, if you go too far, people will say, "Oh, he's drunk."
(i, 596–599)

After the party breaks up, draw close to her in the confusion,
 Let your foot touch hers, finger the sleeve of her dress.
Now is the time for talk! Don't be an oaf of a farmer.
(i, 603–605)

Play the role of the lover, give the impression of heartache.
(i, 609)

Flattery works on the mind as the waves on the bank of a river:
  Praise her face and her hair; praise her fingers and toes.
(i, 617–618)

Gods are convenient to have, so let us concede their existence. . . .
  What you are eager to be, tell her, is *Only a friend.*
I have seen this work, on the most unwilling of women—
  Only a friend, who was found more than proficient in bed!
(i, 637, 721–723)

Lying, cheating, pretending, are all part of the game for Ovid. The important thing is to win. Women, any women, are the object. And nothing short of sexual conquest is acceptable to the "artist" in love. Even a little muscle is fair in love, as in war.

Once you have taken a kiss, the other things surely will follow,
  Or, if they don't, you should lose all you have taken before.
How far away is a kiss from the right true end, the completion?
  Failure the rest of the way proves you are clumsy, not shy.
Force is all right to apply, and women like you to use it;
  What they enjoy they pretend they were unwilling to give.
One who is overcome, and, suddenly, forcefully taken,
  Welcomes the wanton assault, takes it as proof of her charm.
(i, 669–676)

There are times, however, when Ovid sounds like a highly civilized modern marriage counselor. Not out of sympathy for a woman's needs, but because a happy conquest is more likely to continue to make herself available, Ovid also urges a touch of tenderness.

Take my word for it, love is never a thing to be hurried,
  Coax it along, go slow, tease it with proper delay.
When you have found the place where a woman loves to be fondled,
  Let no feeling of shame keep your caresses away.
Then you will see in her eyes a tremulous brightness, a glitter,
  Like a flash of the sun when the water is clear.
She will complain, but not mean it, murmuring words of endearment,
  Sigh in the sweetest way, utter appropriate cries.
Neither go too fast, nor let her get there before you;
  Pleasure is best when both come at one time to the goal.
(ii, 717–727)

Ovid's ideal of love as mere sexual gratification was probably pretty typical of the Roman ruling class during the days of the empire. It was necessarily promiscuous. Since love was the animal passion aroused in the loins, it had nothing to do with the character or background or intelligence of the beloved. Ovid, for instance, advised his readers to imitate the person desired: the lover, like the politician, should be all things to all women. Be what they want or what they are, he instructs.

> Use a thousand means, since there are thousands of ends.
> Earth brings forth varying yield: one soil is good for the olive,
> One for the vine, and a third richly productive in corn. . . .
> If you seem coarse to a prude, or learned to some little lowbrow,
> She will be filled with distrust, made to feel cheap in your eyes.
> (i, 757–759, 767–768)

Ovid is hardly interested in weighing the comparative merits of the vulgar and the prudish or the intelligent and the lowbrow. "All the stars in the sky, are less than the girls Rome can offer." The rich, poor, mistress and servant, married and unmarried, young and old, coy and aggressive, all are fish for the net. Ovid would probably have nothing but contempt for the romantic Greek ideal of love for "that special someone" with the "special something."

Like any artist, Ovid probably reflected the ideas of the upper class as much as he taught them. Some of the upstanding citizens objected to his frankness, and eventually the poet was banished by the emperor Augustus—but only after Ovid became too friendly with the emperor's granddaughter who was beginning to follow her mother's example of taking on every man in Rome.

Adultery seemed to be the favorite indoor sport of the fashionable set. Love had nothing to do with one's own wife, but everyone else's wife was fair and exciting game. The "smart" women played the game just as eagerly as the men. It was risky in a society without motels or cars, but the risks often made it more delicious.

## Old-fashioned Romans: Pliny Loves Calpurnia?

Of course, there were those who, like Augustus, found this whole "new morality" obscene and corrupt. Some voices from the past spoke of a very different kind of love which they actually found in their relationships with their wives. One of these old-fashioned Romans, Pliny the Younger, looked back at the sexual revolution from the perspective of the second century (when Caesar, and Augustus, and Nero were long dead), and wrote a glowing tribute to the loving marriages of imperial Rome. Pliny was convinced that there were many lovers, even in the most licentious days of the empire, who were married to each other. But almost all of Pliny's examples of loving wives were chosen

■ *In Rome, as in Greece, love was a leisure-class activity. One needed the afternoon free and servants to set the scene and bring on the wine. (EPA; Kunsthistorisches Museum)*

because they killed themselves when their husbands died or were about to die. The emotion that Pliny called love was blind devotion and dependence.

Pliny tips his hand when he talks of his own marriage to Calpurnia, a young girl. He said that he loved her; indeed, he continually swore that he couldn't be away from her. But his letters to friends show that he barely knew the girl, and that her feeling toward him was more like that of disciple to teacher, or servant to master, than lover to lover. In a letter to his aunt he wrote:

> Her mind is keen and her tastes simple. She loves me, which proves her chastity. Besides, she likes literature, to which she was led by her affection for me. She keeps my books, reads them, and even learns passages from them off by heart. She is painfully anxious when I am to conduct a case, and delighted when I have completed it. She appoints people to tell her what applause and shouts I have received, and what the verdict was. If I am reading my work in public she sits near by, behind a curtain, and drinks in the praise of my audience with expectant ears. She also sings my verses, and even sets them to music, taught not by a musician but by love, the best master.[11]

What Pliny seemed to love most in Calpurnia, according to Jérôme Carcopino in *Daily Life in Ancient Rome,* "was her admiration for his writings." And while he missed her admiration while he was away, he was consoled by the chance to "polish the phrases" of his letters to her.

> Even when the couple were living under the same roof they were not together. They had, as we should say, their separate rooms. Even amid the peace of his Tuscan villa, Pliny's chief delight was in a solitude favourable to his meditations, and it was his secretary, not his wife, whom he was wont to summon to his bedside at dawn. His conjugal affection was for him a matter of good taste and *savoir vivre,* and we cannot avoid the conviction that, taken all around, it was gravely lacking in warmth and intimacy.[12]

On the other hand, if Roman divorce statistics are any indication, some Roman husbands and wives must have loved each other as equals. One Roman critic of the high divorce rate claims that men and women were continually getting divorced to be remarried, and getting married to be divorced. Though this is an exaggeration, we know that many of the men and women in the upper class took four and five spouses, one after the other. This means two things: they frequently fell out of love with their spouses, but they also frequently married their new lovers. Again one is led to suspect that the adulterous affairs cooled off when they became legalized.

The Romans may have tried harder than the Greeks to reconcile love and marriage. But it is possible that the Romans wanted little more than a sexually satisfying marriage. The early Greek idea of love could, at times, be passionately physical, but it was more often merely passionate. Since the Greeks were usually interested in the lover as a person (not just an object), there was always a tendency to romanticize the anxiety of a sexless relationship. The romantic lover could idealize the beloved even *because* they "made love" less often. Greek romantic love could thrive even when sexual contact had been eliminated completely. Plato's ideal of *agape* was an extreme case of this sexless love. Love could be noble and enlightening for the Greek philosophers—even without women or sex—partially because these men thought so disparagingly of women. The Christians inherited more of the mysogyny and paternalism of the Greeks than the sexuality of the Romans. It is in this sense that the Christians continued and developed the "romance" of Greek philosophy and practice.

## *For Further Reading*

We have found Morton Hunt's entertaining, anecdotal **The Natural History of Love*** most useful. Among other general studies, there are introductory chapters in Richard Lewinshohn's **A History of Sexual Customs,* Not in God's Image,*** edited by Julia O'Faolain and Lauro Marines, Amaury de Riencourt's **Sex and Power in History,*** and Elizabeth Gould Davis's **The First Sex.***

Sarah B. Pomeroy's **Goddesses, Whores, Wives, & Slaves: Women in Classical Antiquity*** is an excellent history of women in Greece and Rome. Robert Flaceliere's **Love in Ancient Greece** is fascinating. W. K. Lacey's **The Family in Classical Greece** is an absorbing, relevant study. For a more general treatment of Greek social life, Emile Mireaux's **Daily Life in the Time of Homer** is superb for the archaic period, and Robert Flaceliere's **Daily Life in Greece at the Time of Pericles** is an excellent introduction to the classical period. For an intriguing interpretation of the sexuality of a Greek myth, see Erich Neumann's **Amor and Psyche.*** A relevant approach to sexuality in Greece and Rome that is especially valuable on Greek homosexuality and education is H. I. Marrou's **A History of Education in Antiquity.***

There are also good studies of Roman sexuality and social life. J. P. V. D. Balsdon's **Roman Woman** is an interesting historical treatment. Otto Kiefer's **Sexual Life in Ancient Rome** is almost as readable as it was 40 years ago. E. P. Corbett's **The Roman Law of Marriage** is a solid study of legal change and complexities. There is a brilliant essay called "The Silent Women of Rome" (among others) in M. I. Finley's **Aspects of Antiquity.***

* Available in paperback.

Love, marriage, and sexuality are also discussed in broader interpretations of Roman social life. Jérôme Carcopino's **Daily Life in Ancient Rome*** and Frederik Poulsen's **Glimpses of Roman Culture** are especially valuable.

This is one topic which can be most usefully and entertainingly approached through the rich literature of the period. The Greeks and Romans wrote frequently and vividly of love, sex, and marriage. One can approach Homer's **Iliad*** and **Odyssey*** (many editions) from this perspective (as does Mireaux, above). Hesiod's **Works and Days*** is also full of information about archaic social life. Plato's dialogues are treasures of sexual and social attitudes for the classical period, especially the **Symposium,*** **Phaedrus,*** or **Phaedo.*** Xenophon's **Symposium*** and **Oeconomicus (Economics)*** are also rich in detail. The plays of Aristophanes (something of an antihomosexual) are hilarious dramatizations of homosexual and heterosexual relationships, among other themes. All are available as **The Complete Plays of Aristophanes,*** including his **Thesmophoriazusae** (or "Women Celebrating the Thesmophoria") and **Ecclesiazusae** (or "Women in Parliament"). But if you read only one, make it Douglass Parker's modernized translation of **Lysistrata*** about an imagined women's sex strike for peace. Other classical writings on love and sex include Plutarch's **Amatorius, Erotikos,** and **Conjugal Precepts,** Lucian's **Erotes,** and, of course, Ovid's **Art of Love.** The last is published with Ovid's **The Loves, The Art of Beauty,** and **The Remedies for Love** in an excellent translation by Rolfe Humphries called **Ovid, The Art of Love.*** Humphries also has a good translation of **The Satires of Juvenal*** and there is also a good translation by Smith Palmer Bovie of **Satires and Epistles of Horace,*** both of which are more general Roman works. Finally, Robert Graves's translation of **The Golden Ass of Apuleius*** is a joyous classic.

## *Notes*

1. Xenophon, *Oeconomicus,* in *Readings in Ancient History,* trans. H. G. Dakyns (Boston: Allyn & Bacon, 1912), p. 266.
2. Attributed to Demosthenes, "Against Neaera." This and much of the other material in this section is drawn from Morton Hunt, *The Natural History of Love* (New York: Knopf, 1967).
3. Quoted in Hunt, *Natural History,* p. 26.
4. Xenophone, *Memorabilia,* III: xi, quoted in Hunt, *Natural History,* p. 37.
5. Sophocles, Fragment 678, quoted in Hunt, *Natural History,* p. 41.
6. H. I. Marrou, *A History of Education in Antiquity,* trans. George Lamb (New York: New American Library, 1964), p. 57.
7. Sappho, "Ode to Atthis," quoted in Hunt, *Natural History,* p. 45.
8. Hunt, *Natural History,* p. 68.
9. *Ibid.,* pp. 68–69.
10. This and the following selections are taken from Ovid, *The Art of Love,* trans. Rolfe Humphries (Bloomington: Indiana University Press, 1957).
11. Pliny, *Letters,* iv: 19, quoted in Otto Kiefer, *Sexual Life in Ancient Rome* (London: Routledge & Kegan Paul, 1934), and excerpted in Michael Cherniavsky and Arthur J. Slavin, *Social Textures of Western Civilization: The Lower Depths* (Waltham, Mass.; Xerox, 1972), p. 162.
12. Jérôme Carcopino, *Daily Life in Ancient Rome,* ed. Henry T. Rowell, trans. E. O. Lorimer (New Haven: Yale University Press, 1940), p. 100.

# Chapter 6

# War and Peace

## Frontiers and Roman Empire

One of the most frequently expressed opinions about war is that it is natural and inevitable. Ask almost anyone, and you get the same response: "There have always been wars; there always will be; war is part of human nature." That popular attitude may be true, but it is also a pessimistic way of looking at human nature. We could also say there have always been periods of peace, there always will be, and peace is part of human nature. People have been cooperative as well as competitive; friendly as well as hostile; loving as well as violent; and peaceful as well as warlike. Asking if people are naturally peaceful or warlike is like asking if people are naturally stupid or smart. Even if we knew exactly what we meant by those terms, we would find instances of both extremes, and a lot of behavior in between. Even if we could figure out what basic human nature is, we would still have to determine why there is such variety in human behavior.

Psychology may one day explain human nature, but we will still have to study history to account for its enormously different varieties.

The study of history can help us understand changes and causes. In this chapter we will focus on some examples of warrior and military societies in the ancient world in order to deal more knowledgeably with particular social causes of war and the general changes from "primitive" to "civilized" societies. What social conditions make a society particularly warlike or aggressive? Have human societies become more peaceful as they have become more civilized? Are empires less violent than tribes? Is a "frontier experience" or a position of world power (both of which have also been important in American history) particularly conducive to war and violence? These are some of the questions raised by our chapter. We begin by putting Roman history in the broad context of frontier wars. Then we examine the development of the Roman Empire from its earliest beginnings as a city-state. Our thesis is that the Roman Republic (sixth century B.C. to 27 B.C.) had become an empire (in all but name) long before the Principate or early Empire was established by Augustus in 27 B.C. The domestic political effects of Roman expansion during the Republic created the problems of the early Empire (27 B.C. to A.D. 284) and the late Empire (A.D. 284 to A.D. 476). The frontier wars and conquests of the Republic created an imperial society at home that made both the institution of the Empire and its demise all but inevitable.

## Frontiers, Settlers, and Herders: The Longest War

About three thousand years ago when the ancient Hebrews speculated about the origins of war they told a story about two brothers—Cain and Abel. To indicate their belief that war had existed a long time they made these two brothers the sons of the first parents. According to the version of the story in what we know as the Bible (Genesis, chapter 4) Eve gave birth to Cain who became "a tiller of the ground" and then to Abel, "a keeper of sheep." "And in process of time it came to pass that Cain brought of the fruit of the ground an offering unto the Lord. And Abel, he also brought of the firstlings of his flock and of the fat thereof. And the Lord had respect unto Abel and to his offering. But unto Cain and to his offering he had not respect." Jealous that the Lord accepted Abel's animal sacrifice and rejected his agricultural offering, Cain, the farmer, killed his brother Abel, the herder.

As a symbolic account of the origins of war, the biblical tale is very instructive. Cain and Abel are symbols of the two types of lifestyles before the rise of cities. Gradually, after the taming of animals by hunting tribes and the domestication of plants by the food gatherers (about ten thousand years ago), the two styles of life—farming and herding—became more and more distinct. While hunting and gathering were often practiced by the same group, often with only a sexual division of labor, farming and herding became separated ways of life. Herders required vast grasslands for their flocks. Farmers needed river valleys for irrigation or areas with higher rainfall than grasslands. Herders were always on the move in search of new grazing lands. Farmers had to stay with their crops. Herders owned little more than their animals, tents, and what they could carry. Farmers built permanent settlements—villages and eventually cities—which became centers of administration, trade, and numerous occupations.

There must have been almost inevitable tensions between farmers and herders—tensions which had not existed in more primitive hunting-gathering societies. Farming villages were able to accumulate a surplus of food and eventually luxuries that must have been the envy of the wandering herders of the grasslands. At the same time, the settled life of village communities made farmers more vulnerable as they became more "civilized" and prosperous. The herders' rough life in the open country was not far removed from the rigors of the primitive hunt. Herders valued aggression, strength, and stamina. Their tribes were something of a permanent military force, loyal to their leaders, and ready to move at a moment's notice. In short, farming communities were an easy prey and contained attractive booty for the wandering tribes of the grasslands.

Peasant farmers and nomadic herders were, as the biblical story suggests, brothers as well as enemies. Every fall when the grass of the pasture was low, and the crops of the field had been harvested, the herders must have brought their animals to feed on the stubble of the harvested grain. Cattle would be traded for the fruits of the vine and the olive trees, and the produce of the cultivated field. The nomads would also offer precious stones, axes, and decorative shells that they had acquired on their wanderings for the perishable goods and manufactured products of the civilized settlements.

The interaction of farmers and herders, settlers and nomads, villages and tribes, farm and pasture, and eventually city civilizations and barbarians—sometimes peaceful but often violent—was probably the main dynamic of world history until only a few hundred years ago. Organized, sustained warfare began in the conflict between the two groups. Nomadic herders have invaded village settlements for almost ten thousand years; city armies have fought barbarian invaders for almost five thousand years; and since the nomads have learned to ride horseback habitually about three thousand years ago, the confrontations have often been brutal and frequent. If we exclude the very recent past, the last few hundred years in which the last nomadic tribes have been integrated into the laws and customs of cities and countries, the history of war has been the conflict between the settlers and the people of the frontier.

Much of ancient history can be understood in terms of that conflict. The ancient city civilizations of Mesopotamia, Egypt, and India that developed after 3000 B.C. were all overrun after 1700 B.C. by barbarian charioteers (who combined the city invention of wheeled vehicles with their own experience of domesticating horses). The descendants of these invaders had established new empires in Egypt, Mesopotamia, and China when (after 1200 B.C.) a new wave of wandering tribes whose iron weapons and infantry organization proved too much for the ruling aristocracies and their few hundred chariots. These tribes (like the Dorians in Greece and the Hebrews) settled down to agriculture and city life and were, in turn, overrun by a new invasion of nomads (after 900 B.C.) whose perfection of horse riding made their cavalries too powerful for the old infantries.

Successive waves of nomads, spurred by horsemen with bow and arrow, raided and sometimes destroyed or conquered city empires from 900 B.C. until the last significant Mongol invasion in the thirteenth century A.D. Most of them came from the vast grasslands of the Eurasian steppe that stretched from Europe to China. These mounted armies were actually no more than the male members of a tribe or tribal confederacy, moving as they had always moved, but in periods of population growth or pressure from other tribes, forced to carve out new grazing lands without their women and children.

Ancient civilizations were forced to adopt their Iron Age infantries to the new cavalry warfare, hire the nomads as mercenaries to protect their flanks, or succumb to defeat. The Assyrian Empire learned the lesson the hard way: they were overrun by the nomads in 612 B.C. The Persian Empire in Iran hired the nomads as mercenaries. The rulers of the small Asian kingdom of Ch'in were among the few who were able to adopt cavalry warfare on their own. As a result, they were not only able to stave off the nomadic invasion from central Asia, but they were also able to overwhelm rival Asian states and give the Ch'in name to a unified China in 221 B.C. But later nomadic invasions of China proved more successful, and by the fourth century A.D. the 600-year-old Han dynasty had been overthrown and China was again a series of tribal states.

The Western Roman Empire suffered much the same fate as Han China. For almost 600 years the Romans were able to create a Mediterranean empire while keeping the Scythians and other tribal confederacies at bay. Increasingly, however, the Romans were forced to use nomads as mercenaries. Unlike the Chinese, the Roman infantry officers refused to learn the techniques of cavalry or bow and arrow.

By the fifth century A.D. the Western Roman Empire had been overrun by the tribal migrations. The Eastern Romans who combined Latin and Greek culture in Constantinople (which the emperor Constantine had established separate from embattled Rome in the early fourth century A.D.) were able to survive another thousand years. The Eastern Byzantine Empire survived that long primarily because it adopted a new style of cavalry combat which had been developed in Iran to counter the threat from the steppe. Eventually that new style of cavalry—which we know as the armored knight—was to save the very tribes that overran the Western Roman Empire when they, themselves, were threatened by new nomadic invasions in the ninth century A.D.

In many ways, the most dramatic example of the potentialities of nomad warfare—the expansion of the Mongol Empire under Genghis Khan in the thirteenth century—was the last. After 1500 the use of gunpowder and the complicated technology of firearms put the balance of power on the side of the more complex city-based civilizations. After 1500 these civilizations took the offensive against the nomads. While the Europeans moved to "civilize" the pastural corners of their own continent and the "Indian" nomads of the Americas, the new Russian state conquered its own eastern frontier and brought the Bible and the law to the very heart of the Eurasian steppe.

It would not be an exaggeration, then, to say that for most of human history (at least the first forty-five hundred of the last five thousand years) the causes of war have been the disparities between settled and nomadic styles of life. The lure of city luxuries and land has exerted an irresistible pull on the ambitions of nomadic warlords and the populations of pastural society. Perhaps there is some hope that this chief cause of war has come to an end. There are no more barbarians at the gates. Even the conflicts of the American frontier between farmers and cattle herders, or between both and the native tribes, are a hundred years past.

But neither war nor violence has disappeared from our lives. Perhaps a closer look at the Roman Empire will help explain why.

## The Roman Phase of the Longest War: Some Questions

In 391 B.C. a band of nomads, called Gauls, under the chieftain Brennus defeated a small army of Roman patricians (or aristocrats) and proceeded to burn the town of Rome to the ground. Eight hundred years later (in A.D. 410 to be exact) a similar tribe of Goths, led by Alaric, destroyed the city of Rome again. These dates offer convenient markers for the beginning and end of Roman history. The greatness of Rome lies in its achievements during those eight hundred years: the town became an empire which spread its laws, its culture, and its peace from North Africa to England; the capital city of this empire was secure; meanwhile the brutal life of the nomads changed very little. The tragedy is that after eight hundred years of work, Rome was just as vulnerable as it had been before. In fact, it was more vulnerable. The defeat in 391 B.C. had been a cause for revitalization and fantastic development. The defeat in 410 was followed by the "vandalization" of the city again in 455 by another tribe (the Vandals), the murder of the emperor and his son in 476, and the final transformation of the imperial city into pasture land for the herds of any invading tribe. Rome never recovered.

Why was Rome so successful at repelling the barbarians after the defeat of 391 B.C., and so unable to recover after eight hundred years of conquering and civilizing? Why did the imperial armies of the fifth century A.D. fail to provide the security that had been won by the inhabitants of a small town eight hundred years before? Part of the answer may lie with the barbarians themselves. It is possible that the invasions of the fifth century A.D. were much more severe than those of the fourth century B.C. But that is only speculation. We know very little about the earlier nomadic tribes. They left no records, because they could not write. Therefore, most of their activity is still a mystery to us.

It seems more useful to look at what had changed on the Roman side of the equation. The barbarians were always on the frontier. The Roman armies had always responded to their threat. For eight hundred years that response was successful. Then it failed. What had happened in Rome to cause that failure?

## Patrician Response: Republican Constitution and Army

First, what happened after the defeat in 391 B.C.? The invasion of the Gauls convinced the surviving Romans that radical changes were necessary in their military organization. The aristocratic army of patricians was clearly no match against the barbarian tribes in which all men were warriors. A national citizen army which included the common people (called plebeians) seemed to be the only suitable response to the warrior tribes. The plebeians had previously been excluded from the military because they were not full citizens. Without full political rights, they could hardly be expected to give their lives for the city. But these plebeians had been excluded from full citizenship because they owned little or no land. As in other ancient city-states, the Roman patricians were not willing to trust political decisions to those who had no economic stake in the country.

Only a crisis—especially a military crisis—could force the Roman patricians to bring the plebeians into the army. In order to assure the loyalty of the army, these new soldiers had to be given some political and economic power as well. The total defeat of Rome was such a crisis. The egalitarian barbarian armies forced the Romans to democratize their own armies. The creation of a more democratic army meant the democratization of the society as well.

The changes were gradual, and by no means complete. Plebeians were made full citizens. All of the land owning *assidui*, or "settled men" (patrician or plebeians) between the ages of 17 and 65, were bound to answer the summons (called *classis* from which the later meaning of "class" came) for military service. Even the landless men (called *proletarii*) were required to back up the army, and an attempt was made to distribute conquered territory to these landless men and poor plebeians.

According to the new constitution, the popular assembly passed the laws, decided questions of war and peace, and elected the consuls (the executives who were roughly equivalent to later presidents or prime ministers). Plebeians could even become consuls. Further, the officers of the older plebeian assembly, who were called tribunes, were given the right to veto some of the decisions of the whole popular assembly or its consuls.

Despite the maintenance of classes, and despite the existence of landless *proletarii*, the constitution that emerged after 390 B.C. meant a more egalitarian society with a more representative army than had ever existed before in hundreds of years of patrician rule in Rome. "It is certain," according to one historian, "that the new organization of the citizen-body infused fresh strength into the community. The common interest now came home to the heart of each citizen: he felt himself responsible for the state and its prosperity."

Essentially the army had become the people. Since they were all mobilized when war was declared, and since they were the ones who decided when to go to war, they had created the possibility of a peaceful society—able to defend themselves to the last man in the event of an emergency. But as the case of the barbarians (whose solution they had adopted) could show, a nation of warriors might become more accustomed to the discipline of war than the leisure of peace. When the state became the army, the nation could be one of citizens who were also emergency soldiers, or a nation of soldiers who were also part-time citizens. The Romans, like the barbarians, often behaved as a nation of soldiers.

## Preserving Inequality with Foreign Land

The primacy of the army over the state had many causes. It is unlikely that the people simply preferred war to peace. But since the patricians were not about to distribute their own land to the plebeians, military conquest was the least painful way of increasing the citizen base of the army. The poor probably recognized that their own advancement depended on the spoils of war. The more democratic army was necessarily a more imperialistic one. The alternative of genuine economic equality at home may have seemed necessary during the bleak days after the Gauls' invasion, but the patrician class must have quickly recognized the possibility of an imperialistic, military state as an alternative.

Further, despite the constitutional changes, the patrician class always remained in pretty firm control of the government. Though the popular assembly was opened to plebeians, the votes of patricians were weighted more heavily by a complicated process of voting by groups. The wealthy comprised a majority of these groups, called "centuries," and each had one vote. Even this device was usually redundant. Plebeians usually voted for patricians anyway. Whether they were used to authority, or felt more secure with the "big names," or had learned the "chain of command" in their military training, the plebeians consistently elected patricians to be consuls. This was particularly significant because the consuls became increasingly important. (A cynic might say the consuls became more important because patricians were elected.) The consuls served for only a year, but it became customary for them, after that year, to enter an advisory group for future consuls. This group was called the senate. It had a long history as a committee of noble families. It had advised ancient kings as well as the consuls of the recent republic. The reforms that followed 390 B.C. were supposed to force the senate to share some of its power with the popular assembly. Actually, the senate became more and more entrenched as the government of the Roman state. The senate changed from a traditional informal advisory body to the formal legislative body of Rome. The popular assembly voted only on bills which were offered by the consuls, and the consuls offered only bills which had been approved by the senate.

To summarize, the Roman response to the invasion of 391 B.C., reflected in the constitutional developments of the fourth century B.C., was mixed. An attempt at democratization was made in land holding and in politics, but most radically in the army. The changes, however, did not constitute a revolution. The patricians tried to integrate enough of the population into the citizenry so that the army would be popular enough to defend Rome and increase her territory. But the patrician class retained its power. Roman expansion during the next centuries was its show. There was, though, always the implicit understanding that the plebeians would go on strike from military service if they were not satisfied with their role in politics. Such a strike in fact occurred in 287 B.C. Then the plebeians won an important concession: by agreeing to let the patrician-dominated popular assembly continue to decide matters of war and peace, their exclusively plebeian assemblies were given the authority to pass laws which had the same force as the laws of the popular assembly.

## A Roman Peace for All of Italy

From their defeat at the hands of the Gauls at the beginning of the fourth century B.C. to the middle of the third century B.C., the Romans conquered most of Italy. Though their conquests were not as defensive as they insisted (whose are?), they were frequently viewed as the protectors of order and city life. They usually defended the more settled towns against the more nomadic and predatory tribes. Rome was the city to organize other Italian cities and populations in part because of its central location, but also because of its superior military.

Roman soldiers submitted themselves to more rigorous drill and stricter discipline than their neighbors. The power of the commander which was called the *imperium* was absolute during military campaigns. Soldiers who broke ranks or slept on sentry duty were executed. When a whole unit was guilty of serious misconduct the punishment of "decimation" (executing every tenth man) was sometimes employed. Warfare was not a sport as it was for the aristocratic armies of other cities. It was for the Romans a business which tapped the resources of the entire society.

Long before the Romans conquered all of Italy they had adequately secured the defense of their city. The wars after 287 B.C. (when the plebeian strike ended, giving the patricians effective authority over war and peace for sharing legislative authority with the plebeians on other matters) were increasingly directed against other empires rather than nomadic tribes. Rome's conquest of Italy was completed from 281 to 272 B.C. with the victory over the allies of the Greek Hellenistic Empire in southern Italy. But the conquest of Naples and Tarentum in southern Italy brought the Romans face to face with the Carthaginians in North Africa. Rome inherited the rivalries of the cities it conquered along with the conflict of all of southern Italy with the Carthaginians. While the Roman frontier had been a few miles from the city, it was only necessary to defend the city from the Celts, Gauls, and other tribes of central Italy. When the Roman boundaries became the Alps and the Mediterranean Sea, it seemed necessary to defend itself from Greece, Carthage, and the tribes of northern Europe.

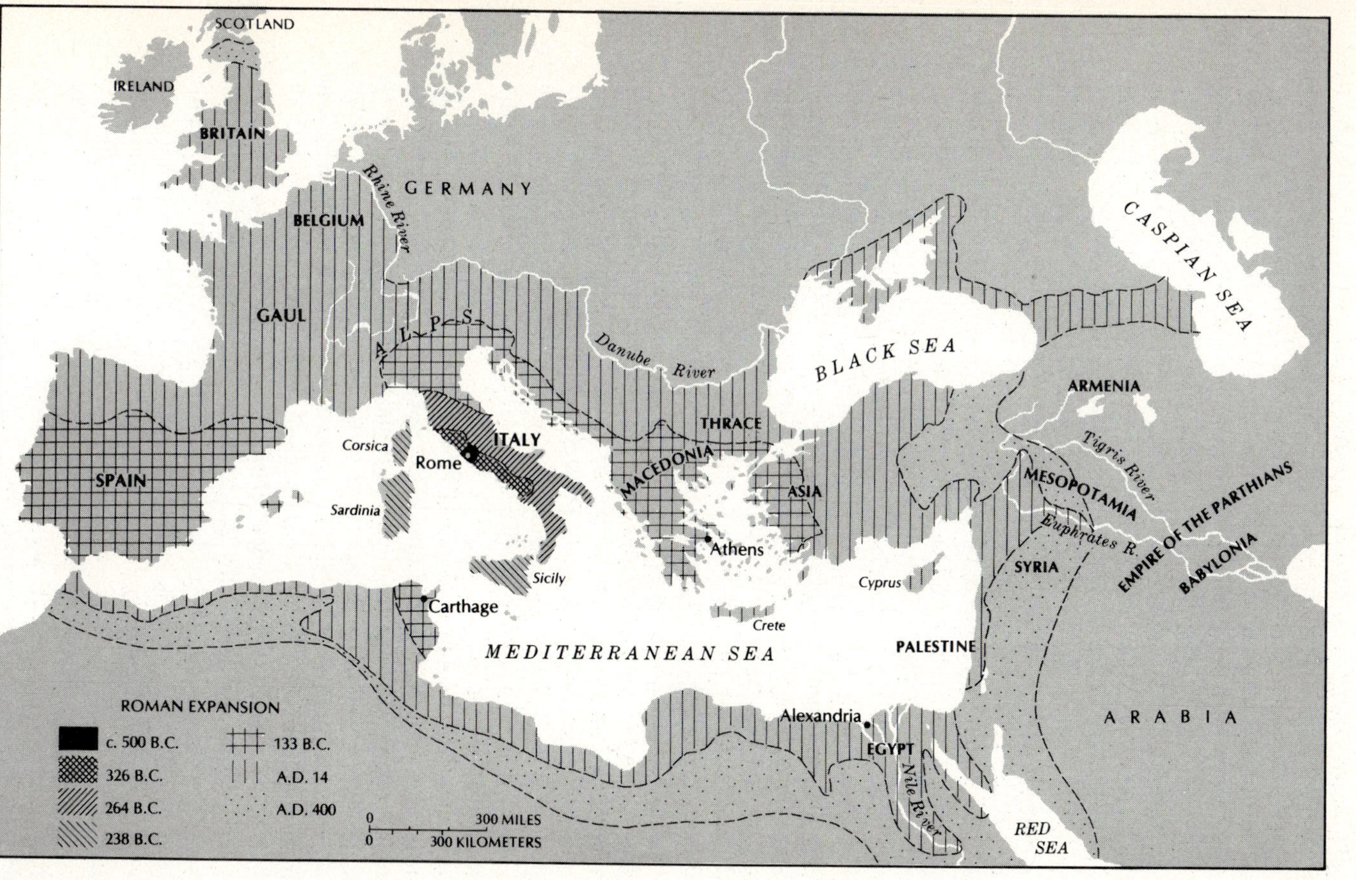


**Roman Expansion**
*With each expansion of Roman boundaries came new neighbors, new defenses, and new potential enemies. Long before the actual Empire, Rome was a militarized society.*

## New Frontiers Make New Enemies: Carthage and Greece

From 262 to 146 B.C. Rome became occupied in continual wars with the Carthaginians and Greek empires. Later Roman historians were fond of viewing the first of these wars outside of Italy as an inevitable burden of Roman responsibility and as an essentially defensive war. The historian Polybius saw all of Roman history as the inevitable expansion of the divinely ordained Roman Empire (much like Americans later invoked "manifest destiny"—another type of divine inevitability). But Polybius (and other Romans) wanted it both ways: they wanted to believe that their expansion had been inevitable so that the Romans were blameless; but they also wanted to believe that their Roman ancestors had been more than passive tools of destiny. Therefore, they argued that each act of expansion was the product of "hard decisions" as well as of fate. They pointed out that each expansion brought Rome into contact with new enemies. They assumed that these new enemies had the will and the ability to conquer Rome (or a Roman province). Consequently, it was necessary—for defensive reasons—to strike first, or when the time was most propitious to Rome. Thus, these "defensive wars" were always blameless since they merely worked the "inevitable" to the best interests of Rome, which (every Roman knew) was to the best interests of civilization.

The first war with Carthage (called the First Punic War) began in 264 B.C. because Rome had recently conquered all of Italy and was in a position to be concerned with Carthage in North Africa, Spain, and part of Sicily. According to the historian Polybius, the Romans feared that the Carthaginians were encircling Rome by threatening Sicily and "all of the coasts of Italy." Few Romans noted that Carthage had been unable to conquer all of Sicily after two hundred years, so that the likelihood of Carthage conquering all of Italy was rather slight. A few more may have urged defensive precautions against a possible Carthaginian attack from Sicily. But the policy that won the day was an armed invasion of the island.

The war for Sicily dragged on for 23 years, from 262 to 241 B.C. The Romans built their first large fleet, conquered a number of Carthaginian cities in Sicily, and, intoxicated by their success, decided to end the war with one final blow. They decided to invade Carthage itself. Success in Sicily increased Roman ambitions and expanded their horizons for "preventive war." But just as success bred more war, so did failure. The Romans were not able to take Carthage, so they kept trying. At the same time, the Carthaginians realized that Rome was their implacable enemy. If the Carthaginians had never before given serious consideration to an invasion of Rome, they now had to mobilize for such a defensive war. Preparations continued after the temporary peace treaty in 241 B.C. that gave Sicily to Rome. The Carthaginian general Hamilcar increased Carthaginian control of Spain, and by 218 B.C. his son Hannibal was able to lead an army into Italy. That invasion, which lasted until 201 B.C., proved as indecisive as the Roman invasion of Carthage. It was possible to do a lot of damage to the countryside, but it was ridiculous to attempt to take the capital city. Hannibal, in fact, failed because the Roman armies harassed him, without confronting him, and the Carthaginian troops and their tribal allies were finally worn down.

The results of the two long wars with Carthage (from 264 to 201 B.C.) were that the Roman citizen army had become a well-trained professional machine, Rome had become a threat to other empires, the Roman senate had become supreme, and the people were tired. The first three results were the ones that mattered.

In 200 B.C. the senate, which had become a virtual dictatorship during the war against Hannibal, saw its chance to defeat the Greek Empire of Macedonia. The time seemed ripe because the king of Macedonia's allies was busy and the Roman war machine was so finely tuned. The fact that the centuries of the popular assembly had almost unanimously rejected the declaration of war made no difference to the senate. The tribune of the plebeians, Q. Baebius, accused the senators of "stirring up war after war to prevent the people ever tasting the fruits of peace." But the senate insisted, had the question restored to the agenda, and finally secured a favorable vote.

If earlier wars had been in any sense "defensive," the wars of the second century were unabashedly imperialistic. Macedonia (in 200 B.C. and in 146 B.C.) was not threatening Rome. There was some talk in the debate that preceded the declaration of war in 200 B.C. about defending the liberties of the smaller Greek city-states from Macedonia. But even that was a projection of a future possibility rather than an immediate threat. Rome had simply become involved in Greek affairs and wanted to prevent the rise of any strong power on its eastern flank. In a sense the wars of the previous century set the stage for further involvement. Between the first and second Punic wars, the Roman armies had pushed eastward in two Illyrian wars which brought Roman power to the edge of Macedonia. One conquest led to another. Sometimes they would be called defensive, but after a while it did not matter.

After conquering Macedonia, Rome involved herself deeper and deeper in Greek politics. For most of the first half of the second century B.C., the Romans were able to support the Macedonian upper class against lower-class movements which were both democratic and anti-Roman. Finally, a revolt of Macedonian "liberation forces" required Rome to govern the colony with her own governors and standing army—after they decisively defeated the rebels in 146 B.C. All of Greece was placed under Roman martial law, the rich commercial city of Corinth was destroyed, and its territory became the property of the Roman people.

The ancient city of Carthage was similarly destroyed in 146 B.C. without provocation. To put it differently, the best that can be said is that the rich wine, olive, and fig plantations of Carthage posed a potential economic threat to Roman landowners who were developing similar plantations in Italy. Roman historians found a sufficient explanation for the destruction of Carthage in a story they told about the leading statesman of the nationalist, landowning party returning from a trip to Carthage. Cato waved a bunch of figs at the Roman senate, recounted the improvements in Carthaginian agriculture since the last Roman-inflicted defeat in 201 B.C., and declared that the new birth of this prosperous state must be aborted.

The landowning class was in charge of the senate, and the senate was supreme. They voted the death sentence for Carthage, and sent Scipio Aemilianus, the general who had just destroyed Numantia, as executioner. Carthage was destroyed. Most of the population was massacred. The territory of Carthage became Rome's African province, and the land was leased to the wealthy landowners back home.

## The Fruits of Empire at Home

In a little more than a half a century, Rome had expanded from a coalition of Italian cities into a Mediterranean empire. Her provinces included North Africa, the previous Carthaginian colonies in Spain, all of the former Greek city-states and kingdoms, and (after 133 B.C.) the Asian empire of Pergamum (Turkey today). The fever of empire had become epidemic. The riches of former empires poured into Rome. This accumulated treasure of centuries, the vast land holdings for Roman agriculture, the investment opportunities for Roman businesses, the graft for Roman governors, and the booty for Roman troops were enough to keep the Roman people occupied for another couple of hundred years. It paid for more Roman wars and more provinces. It financed an elaborate material civilization in Rome. But such wholesale banditry was inevitably shortsighted. Relations with the drained provinces deteriorated. Romans learned to rely more on booty than on innovation. War became the governor of Roman politics and the army its kingpin. And, perhaps most significantly, the Roman people were forced to trade political participation for trinkets: the plebeians lost their farms, their leaders, their political power, their citizen army, and their concern.

It may seem at least slightly absurd to date the decline of the Roman Empire from this half century of expansion (from 201 to 146 B.C.) since the empire did not replace the republic for another century and a half and the empire survived for four hundred years after that. But, in this brief period the events were set in motion which made both an emperor necessary and the empire inherently unstable. The empire was, after all, created in this period. Its only further extensions were into barbarian lands in northern Europe—and that cost more than it was worth. The empire was, itself, the cause of Rome's downfall. Its immediate effect in the next hundred years was internal war. Class wars, civil wars, and wars between Romans and Italians were the fruits of the empire. This violence could be controlled (and some peace restored) by the addition of actual emperors, but the root problems were never solved. Rather than dwell on the long agony, let's look at what the empire did to the Roman Republic.

We have already dropped some clues: the lack of any pretenses about "defensive war" after 200 B.C.; the rise of the landowners and the senate; Cato waving the figs. There are some other clues as to what was happening in Rome. Between 230 and 130 B.C. the population of adult male citizens rose from 270,000 to only 317,000—an insignificant increase considering the expansion of Roman territory. (Compare American population increases in a century of similar expansion. Better yet, imagine the crack troops of something like "the army of the Swiss people" taking over all of Europe, occupying every city from London to Rome, and then looking for troops to send back to Switzerland.) Roman population did not increase at anything like the rate that would have been necessary to maintain even the semblance of a citizen army. There were simply not enough Romans to go around.

To make matters worse, the wealthy senators were not willing to open the Roman army and politics to loyal allies—even those in Italy who were citizens of non-Roman cities or tribes. As in the past, these Italian allies were expected to fight when called by the Roman government, but since they had no voice in declaring war or peace they had little direct interest in a military campaign. The Italian armies were not much more Roman than those of the Greek kingdoms which had assisted the Roman legions in its Asian campaigns.

Not only did Roman citizenship—the basis of the citizen army—increase too slowly to govern an empire, but the character of the citizenry changed as well. The poor and the plebeians were increasingly excluded. The money that poured from the conquered provinces went to those who were already wealthy. Some of it went to the generals and officers of the senatorial class. Some went to the rising business class which had profited from military contracts. The safest investment for this new money was in buying and developing the huge tracts of land that came to the "Roman people," but were administered, leased, and sold by the officers of the senate.

Wealthy Romans were able to buy counties, even countries, of land for the reasonable prices that their friends in the senate set. The Roman treasury could, thus, turn its new possessions into the cash necessary for government, "defense," and more wars. And everyone was happy: everyone, that is, except the Roman poor, the Italian allies, and the subject foreigners.

The foreigners streamed into Rome as conquered slaves or propertyless noncitizens. Eager for work, they were a cheap source of labor for the agricultural plantations that the wealthy Roman landowners bought. Even former Roman citizens were forced to sell their small farms (which had been neglected after years of war) and become tenants on the new large estates. Others gave up their failing farms for the hope of a job in the city. They too gave up their citizenship (which had become almost worthless anyway) and their military service (which had become an intolerable burden) when they gave up their farms.

In many ways the Roman Republic of 150 B.C. looked more like the declining empire hundreds of years later than like the earlier republic of small landholders a hundred years before. The large estates were devoted more and more to commercial crops. Foreign lands were converted to grain production while the Romans converted their own lands to the much more profitable production of wine, olives, and figs. (This was the context of Cato's demand for the destruction of Carthage.) The change in landholding meant a change in the army. The senatorial families still provided generals who were anxious for honors, governorships, and an armed following. Increasingly they recruited their armies from the poor and uprooted with the promise of booty from foreign wars. As long as they were successful, their armies belonged to them. In 88 B.C. the first of a long chain of these armies marched on Rome, itself, and took over the government for its general.

## Radical Reform Rejected

There were a couple of attempts to change the drift toward private armies of paid professional soldiers and the unequal land ownership which made it necessary. One radical reformer, Tiberius Gracchus, a tribune in 133 B.C. with impeccable aristocratic credentials, attempted to win some support in the senate for the idea of military reform. A slave revolt helped underline the problem of a large slave population on the estates, and it was clear to many that the citizen army had been preferable to hired troops. In an attempt to revive the citizen army Tiberius proposed a plan for distributing lands to the displaced peasants who were now tenants on the estates or city *proletarii.* He also proposed shorter military terms so that the people could remain their own soldiers without becoming too attached to war or too absent from their farms. Finally, he urged that the allies in Italy be admitted to citizenship. None of these proposals were popular in the senate. In fact they were so unpopular that Tiberius was murdered, and the senate justified the act as a suppression of a rebellion. Ten years later, Tiberius's younger brother, Gaius Gracchus, revived a similar plan for extending land and citizenship, with added urgency and support. This time the senate found it necessary to justify the massacre of over three thousand of the Gracchi followers as part of a "state of war." Then to divert popular attention from the critical issues raised by the Gracchi, the senate embarked on another series of foreign wars.

The conquest of new territory in North Africa and Gaul (France) in the last quarter of the second century B.C. only intensified the problems. The senate became more venal and dictatorial. The landed ruling class increased their holdings at the expense of the poor. Businessmen, tax collectors, contractors, governors, and generals milked the provinces. The army lost any vestiges of a popular base. Everyone was out for spoils, but the plebeians and allies got the least.

In the midst of these wars, the morale of the allies and peasants who were still called for military service deteriorated to the point of mass desertions. The senate was forced to call on a popular leader, Marius, to put a final end to the myth of a citizen militia and openly to recruit a standing army from the Roman poor. Marius created his professional army with promises of pay and land. To meet these promises he attempted to revive the Gracchi program. The senate refused. Their refusal meant that the standing army they wanted would have to be paid (like everything else) on a "commission basis" through conquest. The same was true for the army of Lucius Cornelius Sulla, a general who supported the interests of the landowners.

## Private Armies and Civil War

When the Gracchi plans were rejected by the senate, the Italian allies declared war on Rome—first for citizenship, and then for equality. The senate sent the armies of Sulla against them. (Marius was loyal but suspect.) By 88 B.C. the three-year war had become a devastating standoff. The allies were given citizenship for laying down their arms, and Sulla's troops lost the hope of the allied lands in southern Italy. They needed land. A war with Mithradates, the Iranian King of Pontus in northern Asia Minor, loomed as their opportunity. But the popular assembly gave the campaign to Marius. Sulla marched on Rome. The ensuing century of civil wars destroyed everything that was left of the citizen republic.

Sulla, like Marius for a short time before him, brought order to Rome with a vengeance. Thousands were tortured and executed. Whole towns were leveled. Cicero later wrote that he "saw the severed heads of senators displayed in the streets of Rome."

After the deaths of Marius and Sulla the struggle continued. The soldiers of their armies were no longer farmers who needed land. They had known war too long to remember how to run a farm. There were two armies of soldiers in Rome who needed work. The only work they knew was fighting. To keep the fighting outside of Italy, they had to be sent on long campaigns into Gaul, Spain, Africa, or the East. Despite their disagreements with him, Pompey was the most loyal general the impotent senate could expect. He trusted them enough (and abhorred civil war enough) to disband his troops on entering Rome. The senate took advantage of Pompey's weakness and, forgetting their own, refused to pay his troops. In effect they asked that future generals make their own senates when they had the army to do so. Julius Caesar learned that lesson well. After a campaign in Gaul, he marched on Rome and concentrated the government in his own hands.

The senate no longer governed. By remaining a club for wealthy Roman patricians, it had lost control of the allies and the mass of Roman citizens and *proletarii*. Without the support of any of these groups it could not hope to control an army. A few senators, like Cassius and Brutus, thought they might regain senatorial initiative by killing Caesar. But Caesar had so completely made the government his own that his assassination resulted in a round of civil wars between his own followers: his lieutenant Antony and his adopted son Octavian. The fact that Caesar could designate Octavian as his heir to the government shows his contempt for the senate and its constitution. Octavian had to win his title by defeating the armies of Antony, but when he became the emperor Augustus, Caesar's contempt was justified.

## Empire and Epitaph

The imperial period of Roman history from 27 B.C. to A.D. 476 was marked by alternating rhythms of chaos and repression. The high point was the reign of the first emperor, Octavian, who was called

■ *Both the public and underlying meanings of a Roman Empire are unintentionally presented on the top and bottom of the beautiful Gemma Augustea, which was carved in onyx about A.D. 10 to commemorate a victory of Tiberius (who descends the chariot on the left top). The majesty of the top panel, where the stars of Capricorn and the Goddess Roma sanction the coronation of Augustus, rests on top of the panel of Roman soldiers taking prisoners and erecting a trophy. The trophy of military conquest over "barbarians" like these was the Empire, the Emperors, its majesty, and renowned works of art like the Gemma Augustea itself.* (Kunsthistorisches Museum)

Augustus. The previous century of civil war had been so debilitating that most Romans and allies willingly gave up freedom for order. Augustus was able to provide peace throughout most of the empire. He was even able to reduce the size of the army by half. But the army became the emperor's personal property, and he gave them land from his personal possessions (among which was Egypt). Augustus decked himself in the trappings of an oriental monarch. The class divisions which had become so great in the preceding centuries were formalized by special symbols to be worn by the senators.

Augustus was followed on his death in A.D. 14 by his stepson (in proper monarchial style) Tiberius. After a wave of violence and assassinations, Tiberius died a madman in A.D. 37, much to the relief of most of his subjects. The next six emperors from 37 to 69 all died by murder or suicide, the last four in the year 68–69 alone.

In 69 Vespasian inaugurated a new line of emperors, reigning until 96, who were not Roman but Italian. Vespasian was able to restore some of the order of Augustus without resorting to an openly military dictatorship. The "five good emperors" that followed from 96 to 180 were actually able to extend the boundaries of the empire slightly, end the worst offenses practiced in the previous century, and restore some confidence with continued peace. But the last of these, Marcus Aurelius, faced renewed frontier warfare which (along with plague and famine) sapped all of his strength.

The year 192, like 69, saw four emperors. One was the tool of the palace guard, beheaded by them when he stepped out of line; another was a wealthy senator who was the highest bidder for the crown. From then on the crown was the prize of the strongest army.

With the reign of Septimius Severus (193–211), the emperor became (without pretensions) the ruling general. "Pamper the army," he told his son, "and despise the rest." Septimius institutionalized the military changes of prior centuries. He outflanked possible Roman rivals by drawing the army from the provinces. By considerably increasing the size and pay of the army he made defense possible but aggravated the heavy tax burden. His son Caracalla (211–217) finally gave citizenship to all free persons in the empire in 212—long after citizenship had ceased to mean anything.

For the rest of the third century the empire was a shambles. From 235 to 285 a total of 26 emperors were put up and pulled down by plundering armies. The frontiers no longer held back the nomads. The riches of past campaigns had been exhausted. Whole provinces declared their independence. Rome itself was threatened. Aurelian (270–275) found it necessary to build a wall around the city.

Two Illyrians (the Roman province of Illyria is now Yugoslavia) postponed the inevitable. They were the emperors Diocletian (284–305) and Constantine (306–337). They divided the empire in two—the Western Empire and the Eastern Empire—and secured the more defensible eastern half for themselves. For defense against the barbarians they relied almost exclusively on barbarian armies. They further increased the bureaucracy to collect taxes and pay the army.

The Eastern Empire was able to survive. The capital city, Byzantium (Constantinople after 330), was almost impregnable. But Rome, capital of the Western Empire, was no more defensible than the barbarian frontiers. Its population was depleted, its money was debased, its treasures had been converted to huge plantations, hordes of slaves, and barbarian troops, and there was no one around who much cared if it remained. Augustine, the church father, was shocked when Alaric sacked Rome in 410, but Augustine was in North Africa, and he was much more concerned with "the city of God."

Perhaps the chief problem was that the government in Rome gave the mass of people no reason to be loyal. Hundreds of years after Romans had forgotten that the Roman Republic and its army belonged to the people, Constantine tried desperately to provide a new basis of loyalty with Christianity. But the new religion was more of an admission of the people's desperation. Its very popularity was a sign that many people felt that the "city of man" was of little importance.

After Alaric's invasion few Romans thought seriously of rebuilding their city as the Roman citizens had eight hundred years before. The imperial city had become one of the two tax collector's offices. It symbolized the oppression as much as the majesty of the empire. Pope Leo I is said to have somehow persuaded Attila and the Huns to leave the city alone, but it is most likely that it offered much less to Attila (especially after Alaric) than the surrounding countryside. A century later the great emperor Justinian of the Eastern Empire (also an Illyrian) attempted to reorganize the remains of the Western Empire, but he found the northern Italian city of Ravenna more suitable than the ancient capital. By the time Rome was not worth ravaging (for Attila) or regaining (for Justinian), it could hardly be worth saving or rebuilding.

## *For Further Reading*

Anthropological studies of war are gathered in **Law and Warfare,*** edited by Paul Bohannan, and **War: The Anthropology of Armed Conflict and Aggression,*** edited by Morton Fried, Marvin Harris, and Robert Murphy, and summarized in a short book on "basic concepts in anthropology" called **Warfare*** by Robert Harrison.

Other anthropological studies include **The Nature of Human Conflict,** edited by E. B. McNeil, Robert Ardrey's **The Territorial Imperative,*** Konrad Lorenz's **On Aggression,*** Desmond Morris's **The Human Zoo,*** and H. H. Turney-High's **Primitive War: Its Practice and Concepts.***

One of the best accounts of the history of the ancient world from the standpoint of warfare can be found in the first half of William H. McNeill's **The Rise of the West,*** a volume which is useful and exciting on so many other subjects and periods as well. His shorter versions of this work, such as **A World History,*** are also superb, if less detailed, on the history of war.

* Available in paperback.

There are simply too many books on Roman political, social, and military history to recommend particular titles. M. Rostovtzeff's **Rome*** still gives a good picture of the socioeconomic effects of military changes (despite the fact that it was written 50 years ago). G. R. Watson's **The Roman Soldier** examines its subject in detail. E. Badian's **Roman Imperialism in the Late Republic*** is good for that period, while T. A. Dorey and D. R. Dudley explore a decisive stage in Roman imperialism in **Rome Against Carthage.** Harold Mattingly's **The Man in the Roman Street,*** especially the chapter on "Peace and War," emphasizes the achievements of peace in the Roman Empire. Tenny Frank's **Roman Imperialism** is still a good discussion of Roman expansion. David Hood's **The Rise of Rome*** and Donald Kagan's **End of the Roman Empire*** are useful collections of the standard interpretations.

The student who wishes to go beyond some of the issues raised in this chapter in Roman history should also be aware of the multivolume **The Cambridge Ancient History** and the earlier multivolume classics T. Mommsen's **The History of Rome** and Edward Gibbon's **The History of the Decline and Fall of the Roman Empire.*** There are also some good shorter, specialized studies of Roman history: H. H. Scullard's **From the Gracchi to Nero: A History of Rome from 133 B.C. to A.D. 68,*** Michael Grant's **The World of Rome,** Lily Ross Taylor's **Party Politics in the Age of Caesar,*** Ronald Syme's **The Roman Revolution,*** and the highly interpretative **The Romans*** by R. H. Barrow.

# Chapter 7

# Individuality and Culture

## Classical and Christian Selves

We are not used to thinking of the emergence of individuality as an historical process. We tend to think that there have been individuals as long as there have been people on the earth. In a sense, of course, this is true. Everyone who has ever existed has been an individual. But the striking thing is that most people throughout most of human history had very little sense of their individuality. The idea of individual uniqueness (as a fact of life or an ideal to live by) developed within human history. We have already seen the early development of the idea of individuality in the first civilizations, five thousand years ago. But this idea was at first the monopoly of pharaohs, priests, nobility, and a few literate people. Even the tombs of the pharaohs are full of images of stick-figures which reflect about as much individual uniqueness as Paleolithic cave painting. Further, the statues of the pharaohs themselves are not very distinguishable one from the other. The most individualized and individualistic figures of the ancient world are the gods and the goddesses. Only very gradually did human beings recognize and picture unique attributes in themselves.

In this chapter, we will look more closely at the discovery of individuality as an historical process. First, we will examine the lack of ideas of individuality in an early twentieth-century tribe of American Indians, as a review of the tribal past of all human groups, and as a reminder of how many perceptions of individuality we take for granted. Then we will compare the emergence of the heroic, aristocratic individuality of the Bronze Age in ancient civilizations with the potential for a more widespread sense of individuality in the Iron Age. Our point here is to call attention to the relationship between technological development and individuality.

The main body of the chapter focuses on the explicit development of ideas and practices of individuality in classical Greece and Rome. Classical Greek culture was the first in human history to evolve a set of individualistic values. Roman and Christian societies further elaborated individualistic ideas in different ways. We will emphasize the uniqueness of the classical and Christian contribution. But we will also notice the social limitations of Greek and Roman ideas of individuality, which often meant very different things to them.

When we speak of individuality or individualism in modern society, it is important to know what we mean by the terms, and it is important to recognize that we are dealing with ideas that have a limited and specific history of meanings. Even at our most "individualistic" we can only express ourselves with the words and signs that our cultural history has passed on to us.

## In the Beginning

Individuality is both much older and much more recent than most modern Americans imagine. It is much older than the American frontier, but it is much more recent than the first man or woman. The biblical story of Adam and Eve has probably been the source of a lot of our confusion about primitive men and women. This is because it was a mythic tale (when it was recorded by the ancient Hebrews about 1000 B.C.) that our much more historically conscious modern society (of perhaps the last thousand years) has translated into an historical account. Our greater historical and archeological knowledge of the last few hundred years has enabled us to recognize the difference between a mythic and an historical explanation, but the tale of Adam and Eve has become so enshrined in our historical religion that we still think (at least unconsciously) that we know the names and acts of the first human beings. The biblical story not only gives us a falsely specific sense of human historical origins, it also contributes to the idea that in the beginning there was the individual, and then the couple, and then the family, and then the tribe.

Actually, the historian and the archeologist cannot name the first human beings. They can point to skeletal remains and label some apes, others humans, depending on their definitions of both. They can speculate about the earliest hunting tribes, and they can say much more about the first agricultural settlements. But there are no names, no individual stories, and no signs that any individual lived apart from the family, clan, or tribe.

The anthropologist can give us much more detail about the lives of hunting and farming tribes of today (or of the last hundred years of anthropological investigation), but we can never be sure how much these tribes resemble people of five, ten, or twenty thousand years ago. Nevertheless, one of the striking things discovered about "primitive" hunting, gathering, and farming societies in the last hundred years is their relative lack of individuality, privacy, and self-expression.

The Wintu Indians of northern California, for instance, do not even have a word for "I" or "myself." A Wintu describing a trip with a friend, White Cloud, instead of saying "White Cloud and I" says "White Cloud—we." The Wintu find little need to distinguish between the self and the other members of the tribe. Little distinction exists, as well, between the self and ancestors. When they are describing a fight, for instance, the anthropologist cannot tell if they mean a personal conflict, a tribal battle, or some ancient war in which ancestors participated. The question which immediately occurs to us—just who is involved?—is not an important issue for the Wintu.

The Wintu sense of the self seems less developed than our own. For us, the self is the measure of all things. We orient nature to ourselves even in the way we use words like "left" and "right." Dorothy Lee, an anthropologist who has lived among the Wintu, has noticed this difference in orientation:

> When we go for a walk, the hills are to our right, the river to our left; when we return, the hills change and the river, while we remain the same, since we are the pivot, the focus. Now the hills have pivoted to the left of me. This has been English language practice for many years, since at least the fourteenth century. To the Wintu, the terms left and right refer to inextricable aspects of his body, and are rarely used. . . . When the Wintu goes up the river, the hills are to the west, the river to the east; and a mosquito bites him on the west arm. When he returns, the hills are still to the west, but, when he scratches his mosquito bite, he scratches his east arm. The geography has remained unchanged, and the self has had to be re-oriented in relation to it.[1]

Dorothy Lee has also studied the stories the Wintu tell, and she has observed that they rarely describe personal feelings. Wintu stories are full of descriptions of action, but

> extremely rarely is there a statement that might be called introspective, such as "she was furious," or "he was happy"; and even here, I am not sure that this is not an observer's statement. The songs the Wintu call love songs refer not at all to the sensations or emotions of love, though they do convey love to us.[2]

Nor are the Wintu used to discussing their own personal lives, as Dorothy Lee discovered:

> When I asked Sadie Marsh for her autobiography, she told me a story about her first husband, based on hearsay. When I insisted on her own life history, she told me a story which she called "my story." The first three quarters of this, approximately, are occupied with the lives of her grandfather, her uncle and her mother before her birth; finally, she reaches the point where she was "that which was in my mother's womb," and from then on she speaks of herself, also.[3]

Sadie Marsh was probably not trying to conceal "her story" from the anthropologist. Indians like Sadie were either not in the habit of thinking about their personal lives, or they had very few separate experiences to think about.

The Wintu Indians seem to be fairly typical of preliterate peoples. The Maori of New Zealand, for example, have a word for "my," but when the Maori says "this is my land" with a wave of a hand over ten thousand acres, it means that it is the land which the tribe and ancestors use. They would be mystified if one suspected that they owned the land privately. They would be unable to understand the meaning of ownership, much less private or individual ownership. Each of the members of the Maori tribe use what is available (whether it be land, tools, weapons, or clothing), but no member of the tribe has a right to monopolize or destroy any of this common property.

Probably the main reason primitive peoples have so little sense of privacy and individuality is that their lives are very much alike. There are very few specialists in primitive society, possibly only a medicine man or a leader. Everyone else takes part in the community job of providing food and pleasing the gods. Since they lead a common life, they have roughly the same ideas about things. There might be some disagreement about the best place to lie in wait for the wild boar, but (if they and their ancestors have always hunted boar) none of them would suggest that they go fishing instead.

Tribal life is public, not private. All of the activities in the village are public and ceremonial. The hunt, the feast, the marriage, the war, are all carried out publicly and according to traditions of ancestors. Tribal peoples simply cannot afford the luxury of letting individuals "do their own thing," and thus no one ever dreams of it. Even the housing is usually public. A person who wants to be alone might sit facing the wall. This is the extent of privacy that is possible.

The idea of "the self" or the individual "personality," then, depends on the breakdown of this tribal life. In the last five thousand years, the tribe has been replaced gradually by the family and the individual. This has occurred only with the rise of cities, which are really societies of specialists. In other words, only as people have led increasingly specialized lives have they thought of themselves as special, unique individuals.

## Metals and Medals: Heroic Bronze and Democratic Iron

Just as stone grinding was the hallmark of the agricultural New Stone Age, the smelting of bronze (from tin and copper) was the hallmark of the first cities. Metallurgy required an investment in labor and specialization of life that villages could not afford, but it created weapons of war that won for cities a permanent claim on the fruits of the countryside. Bronze encouraged the tendency of the first cities to create classes and armies, but since the new technology was available only to the few, the Bronze Age army was upper class. The Bronze Age (after 3000 B.C.) has in fact often been called the age of heroic individualism. Aristocratic warfare was largely an individualistic conflict, like a series of duels. Homer, the father of Greek poetry, told in his *Iliad* of the exploits of Bronze Age warriors of ancient Greece. The climax of the story is the slaying of Hector, the Trojan champion, by Achilles, the Greek hero.

> And when they were come nigh in onset on one another, to Achilles first spake great Hector of the glancing helm: "No longer, son of Peleus, will I fly thee, as before I thrice ran round the great town of Priam, and endured not to await thy onset. Now my heart biddeth me stand up against thee; I will either slay or be slain. . . .
>
> Thus saying he drew his sharp sword that by his flank hung great and strong, and gathered himself and swooped like a soaring eagle that darteth to the plain through the dark clouds to seize a tender lamb or crouching hare. So Hector swooped, brandishing his sharp sword. And Achilles made at him, for his heart was filled with wild fierceness, and before his breast he made a covering with his fair graven shield, and

> tossed his bright four-plated helm; and round it waved fair golden plumes. As a star goeth among stars in the darkness of night, Hesperos, fairest of all stars set in heaven, so flashed there forth a light from the keen spear Achilles poised in his right hand, devising mischief against noble Hector, eyeing his fair flesh to find the fittest place. Now for the rest of him his flesh was covered by the fair bronze armour he stripped from strong Patroklos when he slew him, but there was an opening where the collar bones coming from the shoulders clasp the neck, even at the gullet, where destruction of life cometh quickliest; there, as he came on, noble Achilles drave at him with his spear, and right through the tender neck went the point. Yet the bronze-weighted ashen spear clave not the windpipe, so that he might yet speak words of answer to his foe. . . .
>
> Then with faint breath spake unto him Hector of the glancing helm: "I pray thee by thy life and knees and parents, leave me not for dogs of the Achaians to devour by the ships, but take good store of bronze and gold, gifts that my father and lady mother shall give to thee, and give them home my body back again, that the Trojans and Trojans' wives give me my due of fire after my death.[4]

Bronze Age warrior-heroes like Achilles and Hector are history's first individuals. They are proud of their individual strength and prowess. They face battle, and possible death, alone; they succeed or fail on the basis of their own powers or their influence with the gods. But they are still very public heroes, and public heroism is a weak basis for popular beliefs in individualism. In Bronze Age society just a few aristocrats could be genuine individuals.

Iron was more plentiful than bronze. Once its smelting was known after 1200 B.C., the Iron Age spread throughout the world until the development of steel and industry around A.D. 1800. Iron could afford to make common peasants, as well as aristocrats, individuals. Iron tools were efficient enough to free the average farmer to cultivate personality as well as land. Iron plows made farming less work; fewer people were needed to provide society's food. Iron Age societies were more specialized than Bronze Age societies: there were more individual differences in the jobs people performed and the lives they led.

In general, then, the Iron Age extended individuality in two ways: people became more differentiated from one another and more conscious of themselves—their own personalities, thoughts, and feelings. Iron democratized individuality by giving many of the common people a sense of their own identity. But this process took three thousand years.

The short-range effect of iron technology was just the opposite. Initially, iron destroyed the heroic individualism of aristocrats like Hector and Achilles and left nothing in its place. In fact, for almost a

■ *The "Chigi Vase" depicts the Greek phalanx. Each man's shield covers the next, and the unbroken line charges to a single beat.* *(Hirmer Fotoarchiv)*

thousand years after the introduction of iron, almost all traces of individuality were reduced. The reasons for this lie in the fact that most of the first Iron Age armies were infantries. The common farmer became important as a soldier when armies adopted iron weapons. But he was important as part of a mass formation, not as an individual. A modern historian describes the Greek version of Iron Age infantry—the phalanx—and he dramatizes how limited Greek individualism actually was:

> About 650 B.C. a momentous change in military tactics gave a secure basis to the common farmer's participation in political life. This was the invention of the phalanx—a densely massed infantry formation eight ranks deep whose members were trained to run and charge in unison. A skillful charge delivered by several thousand armored men moving as a single man proved capable of sweeping cavalry or any other kind of opposing force off the field. As this became obvious, every city had to organize and train as big a phalanx as possible from among the citizenry. Anything that interfered with strengthening the phalanx endangered the city. . . .
>
> Every young man who could possibly afford to buy the necessary armor and weapons spent long hours with his fellow youths practicing the rhythms and skills needed to fight effectively in the phalanx. Speed, strength, and courage were only part of what was required. In addition every man had to learn to keep time to the beat set up by the war

chant, so that the wall of shields would not break when the phalanx charged across the field of battle. Every man's safety depended upon his neighbor keeping his place in the ranks, for each man's shield helped to cover the right side of the man next to him. Conspicuous personal feats of arms were as much out of place in such a situation as cowardice or inability to keep pace with the rhythm of the charge, for anything that broke the line threatened immediate disaster. . . .

Every Greek citizen soldier who endured the long hours of training needed for skillful service in the phalanx and had then undergone the fatigues and dangers of a campaign and known the fierce joys and sudden exertions of battle emerged from such adventures marked for life by a deep sense of solidarity with all those who had shared these experiences with him. This intense sentiment became the basis for a fiercely collective pride in the greatness and glory of the city to whom all equally belonged, and in whose service all might find personal fulfillment and an unusually vivid sense of personal freedom by submitting to a common rhythm and demanding regimen.

It is not therefore surprising that with the introduction of the phalanx the Greeks altered their ideal of personal behavior. In the earlier aristocratic age, individual self-assertion and conspicuous consumption had been generally admired. Feats of individual prowess, such as those celebrated by Homer, and personal display of luxury went hand in hand. The phalanx, however, made close conformity to a norm absolutely mandatory in military matters. This principle was soon carried over into civil life as well, so that it became ill-mannered, un-Greek, improper to live luxuriously or, indeed, to differ in any conspicuous way from one's fellows.

Competitive self-assertion was instead transferred to the collective concerns of the polis. Not the individual but the city became the hero.[5]

## Socrates and the Self

Whether we are digging through ruins or looking through an art history, when we reach the statues of the ancient Greeks (about twenty-five hundred years ago) for the first time we see a large number of real individuals. The change is startling. Here are people that we feel we know: real individuals with personal feelings, recognizable "personalities." And we see not only kings, gods, and goddesses, but also fishmongers, widows, soldiers, drunkards, and ordinary peasant farmers.

Some people have said that the Greeks "invented" the individual. At least their artists, poets, and philosophers celebrated individuality and human personality to a much greater degree than anyone ever had before. Between 450 and 400 B.C., the Greek philosopher Socrates taught the children of Athens, including Plato, that wisdom begins with an understanding of one's own self. Socrates was sharply critical of what most people considered common knowledge. He continually challenged traditional ideas with searching questions, asking how such ideas were known and what they meant. Socrates called himself the "midwife" of knowledge because he would force people by continual questioning to realize that they did not know as much as they thought they knew; and this doubt was at least the beginning of real knowledge, or wisdom. Similarly, Socrates believed that all genuine knowledge was inborn in people, and that it only had to be brought out through questioning. When Socrates urged his students, "know thyself," he was telling them to dig deep into their own minds where all truths ultimately lay.

The teaching of Socrates was pretty radical medicine for most respectable Athenians. He was telling their children not only to doubt traditional opinions, but also that the truth was "in" them, if only they would try to pull it out. This meant that even the most uneducated slave had as much potential for wisdom as a philosopher or king.

Though classical Athens could produce a philosopher like Socrates who preached that we should follow the "little god" (or conscience) within us, Athenian society was unable to tolerate such individualism. The Athenian respectables brought Socrates to trial on charges of atheism and "corrupting the youth." Socrates' response to his conviction tells us much about the limits to individualism twenty-four hundred years ago. Offered the choice between death and exile, Socrates chose death. For him, living away from his beloved Athens, outside of the reach of Athenian law and custom, was a fate worse than death.

No Greek, including Socrates, could imagine individual freedom outside of society, tradition, or the community. Freedom meant the quality of life that was possible only in political society, especially in the Greek polis. The community was thought to be the source of all virtue; there could be no morality outside of that community. The Greek word which meant "to take part in community life" was also the word which meant "to live." Human life outside of the community was unthinkable. The philosopher Aristotle, Plato's most famous pupil, makes this assumption clear when he defines man as the political animal. The difference between human beings and the animals, according to Aristotle, is that humans live in a society.

The Greeks of Aristotle's time (the fourth century B.C.) were so interested in individuality that they invented a new type of literature which they called "biography." But, because they were much more concerned with the public society, they wrote biographies about public figures: statesmen, lawgivers, generals, and rulers. Individuality, then, was a virtue for some in ancient Athens, but it was a public virtue.

Some of the other Greek city-states never developed any individualistic culture at all. The Spartans, for instance, built an ancient police state which depended on spies and the total militarization of the ruling aristocracy. Spartan law, according to the Greek historian Plutarch, "made the citizens accustomed to have neither the will nor the ability to lead a private life; but, like the bees, always to be organic parts of their community, to cling together around the leader, and, in an ecstasy of enthusiasm and selfless ambition, to belong wholly to their country."

When the Spartans conquered their neighbors, they made them slaves of the Spartan state. The Spartans could only control this subject population, which outnumbered them twenty to one, by turning their own society into an armed camp, and making every citizen a professional soldier. Spartan law required all male citizens between the ages of 20 and 30 to live and eat in army barracks. From the age of 7, Spartan boys were educated for strict military discipline and an absolute devotion to the state. They were removed from family life and taught by the state to steal, spy on the slaves, and accept strenuous exercise, miserable food, and brutal beatings.

## The Roman Self Possessed: Trimalchio

The Romans allowed slightly more individuality and privacy than the Greeks. The Roman (Latin) word for private, *privatus* (from which our English word comes), meant a lack or absence of the advantages of public life. The Romans felt that the private citizen "deprived" himself of the values of society. Privacy was an error; people who were deprived could not lead a full life. But the Greeks had been much more critical of the private life than the Romans. The Greek word for privacy had been *idiotes* which meant unskilled or uneducated or even "idiotic." The Greeks believed that the private person not only deprived himself of society but became an idiot since all knowledge and intelligence came from society. The private Roman lacked something; the private Greek lacked everything.

There were individuals in ancient Rome who were much more self-centered and selfish than any Greek would have allowed himself to become. The Roman writer Petronius described this kind of socially irresponsible individual in his book *The Satyricon*. He satirized a type of Roman self-made man, called Trimalchio, who was born a foreign

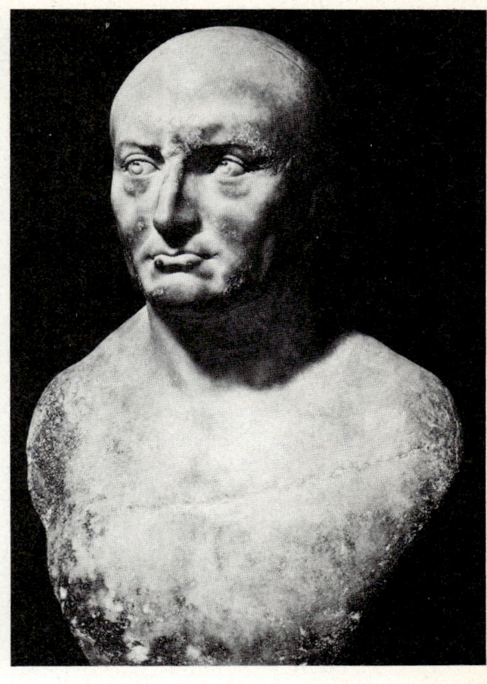

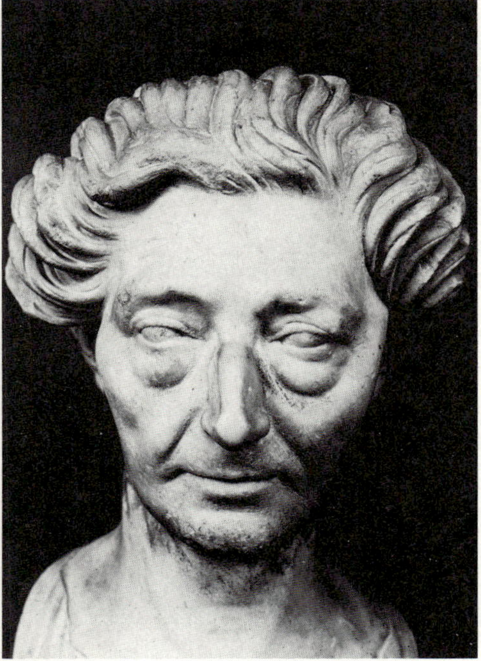

■ *The bust or portrait, which captured individual facial expressions, became, like the biography, an important art in Roman culture. Clearly, individuality was of greater interest to these Romans than it had been before.* (*top left and bottom: Musei Vaticani; top right: Alinari, EPA*)

slave but rose to become a millionaire through his own shrewdness and ambition. Petronius has Trimalchio describe his rise from rags to riches:

> Friends, make yourselves comfortable. Once I used to be like you, but I rose to the top by my ability. Guts are what make the man; the rest is garbage. I buy well, I sell well. . . . It's through my business sense that I shot up. Why, when I came here from Asia I stood no taller than that candlestick there. . . . For fourteen years I was my master's pet. . . . So he made me joint heir with the emperor to everything he had, and I came out of it with a senator's fortune. But we never have enough, and I wanted to try my hand at business. To cut short, I had five ships built. Then I stocked them with wine—worth its weight in gold at the time—and shipped them off to Rome. I might as well have told them to go sink themselves since that's what they did. Yup, all five of them wrecked. No kidding. In one day the sea swallowed down a cool million. Was I licked? Hell, no. That loss just whetted my appetite as though nothing had happened at all. So I built some more ships, bigger and better and a damn sight luckier. No one could say I didn't have guts. But big ships make a man feel big himself. I shipped a cargo of wine, bacon, beans, perfume, and slaves. And then Fortune came through nicely in the nick of time. . . . On that one voyage alone, I cleared about five hundred thousand. Right away I bought up all my old master's property. I built a house, I went into slave-trading and cattle-buying. Everything I touched just grew and grew like a honeycomb. Once I was worth more than all the people in my home town put together, I picked up my winnings and pulled out. I retired from trade and started lending money to ex-slaves. . . .
>
> I built this house. As you know, it used to be a shack; now its a shrine. It has four dining rooms, twenty bedrooms, two marble porticoes, an upstairs dining room, the master bedroom where I sleep, a fine porter's lodge, and guestrooms enough for all my guests. . . . Take my word for it: money makes the man. No money and you're nobody. But big money, big man. That's how it was with yours truly: from mouse to millionaire.[6]

There had never been any Trimalchios in ancient Greece. No Greek would have been so materialistic, and no Greek would have ranted this way about how "I" did this and "I" did that. No character in Greek fiction thinks so much of himself as Trimalchio does. The Romans tolerated brash, egotistical individuals like Trimalchio because they lived in a different world than the Greeks. Roman society was much more fluid and dynamic than Greek society had been. Rome was also much more money conscious and business oriented. An aggressive Roman could easily rise from "mouse to millionaire" because Roman society was always changing so rapidly. Also, Roman society offered the ambitious individual more opportunity to "make it" on his own because it was a much larger society than the Greek city-state. The Romans ruled a vast empire which presented innumerable opportunities for exploitation and personal fame as a businessman, soldier, or government official. There was more room in which the aggressive Roman could maneuver. He not only had the whole Mediterranean world at his disposal, but he also could take advantage of the wide gap that separated him from government. While the Greek had always felt the influence of the city-state, the Roman only had to obey the laws of a distant emperor.

The kind of aggressive, selfish individualism that Trimalchio practiced and preached seems very modern to us. This is because ancient Rome was beginning to develop the expansive, materialistic mentality and the money-oriented, business society which has formed much of our own way of life. But the early development of this business society was cut short in ancient Rome, and it has been revived to reach its fullest possibilities only in the last few hundred years. Of all the ancient peoples, the Romans probably came closest to developing modern business's aggressive individualism. But ancient Rome never fully became a business civilization, and Trimalchio was never more than a writer's exaggeration.

## The Christian Soul Confessed: Augustine

Another kind of individual was created by ancient Rome, one very different from the kind of individual that Trimalchio represents. Rome gave us the spiritualistic individual as well as the materialistic. There are some hints of the individual in spirit, feeling, and thought in ancient Greece. Socrates suggests such an idea of the self when he speaks of his conscience or the "little god" inside him. But it was not really until the Roman Empire that large numbers of people took such an ideal seriously.

There are many types of this spiritual individuality in the Roman Empire. The philosophers of the Roman Empire (Stoics and Epicureans) taught their students to achieve "inner calm," "self-control," and a "mind at peace," and sometimes they argued (as Socrates had) that there was a spark of the divine in everyone. At the same time, many less-educated Romans turned from the formal, official state religious ceremonies to new religions that promised personal experience and an individual life after death. The most successful of these new religions of personal salvation was, of course, Christianity. Its appeal (like that of many religions and philosophies of the empire) was that it offered personal security in a confusing and increasingly impersonal world.

Christianity grew out of the Old Testament religion of the ancient Jews—but with at least one important difference. The ancient Jews had hoped for a social salvation for the whole tribe. They dreamed of the day when they, the "chosen people," would return to "the promised land," their ancestral home. Some Jews, like Jesus, had (at least by the time of Roman occupation) begun to think that their salvation might be personal, not social, and that the future kingdom might be "not of this world." The followers of Jesus traveled throughout the Roman Empire and taught that every individual was born with his own divine "soul," and that he was personally responsible to God for the care of that soul. These Christians insisted that a person might live after dying, but that such a future life depended on what the individual did himself, not on what others did for him.

The idea that God was interested in the behavior and beliefs of every individual must have been very appealing to those who felt lost in the bigness of the empire. But, the immense responsibility to God which this idea implied must have been an awesome burden to those Romans who took it seriously. As a result, the Christians were usually very introspective. They asked questions about themselves, their faith, and their behavior which most ordinary people had never cared to raise. They sought to know themselves in order to know God. They examined all of their past experiences in their search for personal experiences of the divine.

Self-knowledge was the goal of Augustine, the church father, when he wrote his *Confessions* around A.D. 400. This spiritual autobiography was an extreme example of the typical Christian attempt to arrive at a detailed understanding of the inner life, especially sin. Probably no one before Augustine had tried to understand himself so fully.

> I wish to bring back to mind my past foulness and the carnal corruptions of my soul. This is not because I love them, but that I may love you, my God. Out of love for your love I do this. In the bitterness of my remembrance, I tread again my most evil ways, so that you may grow sweet to me. . . .[7]

He confessed his private thoughts (the "sickness of the soul") as well as his acts. In one instance, he asked God's forgiveness for pretending to be as sexually experienced as his companions when he was 16.

> I was ashamed to be remiss in vice in the midst of my comrades. For I heard them boast of their disgraceful acts, and glory in them all the more, the more debased they were.
>
> There was pleasure in doing this, not only for the pleasure of the act, but also for the praise it brought. . . . So they wouldn't make fun of me, I made myself more depraved than I was.[8]

Augustine searched his memory to recall everything, even the most minor acts—such as stealing pears from a neighbor's tree.

> I willed to commit theft, and I did so, not because I was driven to it by any need, unless it was a need of justice and goodness. For I stole a thing of which I had plenty of my own and of much better quality. Nor did I wish to enjoy that thing which I desired to gain by theft, but rather to enjoy the actual theft and the sin of theft.
>
> In a garden nearby to our vineyard there was a pear tree, loaded with fruit that was desirable neither in appearance nor in taste. Late one night . . . we had kept up our street games, and a group of very bad youths set out to shake down and rob this tree. We took great loads of fruit from it, not for our own eating, but rather to throw it to the pigs; even if we did eat a little of it, we did this to do what pleased us because it was forbidden.[9]

A man in his midforties, a bishop in the Roman Catholic church, forced himself to remember a typical 16-year-old's prank. Why? The Christians felt that they were as responsible for childhood sins as they were for sins committed the day before. They believed that the individual would be judged as a total person, for everything he or she had been in the past as well as in the present. Most religions before Christianity saw human sins as particular mistakes or errors which could be "corrected" by the appropriate sacrifice. The Christians, however, believed that sin was a sign of a corrupt personality which had to be converted to Christ before sinning would cease.

Certainly, not everyone in ancient Rome was as intensely self-conscious or individualistic as Augustine or Trimalchio. Probably no more than 10 percent of the inhabitants of the Roman Empire were Christians before Christianity became the state religion (during Augustine's lifetime). As soon as Christianity was established as the official religion of the empire, many people became Christians for political reasons, not necessarily because they were seeking individual salvation.

Nevertheless, there were many Romans who were much more aware of their own individuality than any group of people ever had been before. Roman society was probably more specialized than any previous society. This means that there actually were more individual differences among Romans than previously: there was a greater variety of jobs, living conditions, life-styles, and ways of thinking. Thus, in a real sense, there was a greater degree of individuality in Rome than there had been in Greece or before.

## *For Further Reading*

For anthropological interpretations of "primitive" individuality, Dorothy Lee's **Freedom and Culture*** is a good place to start. Paul Radin's **Primitive Man as Philosopher,*** however, is a good corrective to the frequent assumption that primitive societies have no thinkers.

On the "heroic" individuality of the Bronze Age, the student is invited to read Homer's **Iliad*** and **Odyssey*** (many editions) firsthand. M. I. Finley's **The World of Odysseus*** is an excellent companion. William H. McNeill's **Rise of the West*** and **A World History*** offer suggestive interpretations of the meaning of Bronze Age and Iron Age warfare for individuality in ancient Greece and worldwide.

The story of classical Greece as a "golden age" of individuality is told in almost every text and history of the age. Many of the standard introductions have been noted at the end of the previous chapter. Those students who would like to explore the subject further are alerted to Werner Jaeger's difficult but rewarding **Paideia,*** E. R. Dodds's **The Greeks and the Irrational,*** M. I. Finley's **The Ancient Greeks: An Introduction to Their Life and Thought,*** and Bruno Snell's **The Discovery of the Mind.*** But no understanding of Greek individuality is possible without some sampling of the individuals of the classical age. There are enough editions* of Plato, Aristotle, Herodotus, Thucydides, Euripides, Sophocles, Aeschylus, and Aristophanes (to name only a few) to please any tastes.

We have entered the Roman world of individuality through Petronius' **Satyricon*** and Augustine's **Confessions*** (many editions); both are worth reading in full. For an understanding of the classical Roman individual, the student might also read Cicero, Caesar, Tacitus, Suetonius, Livy, Horace, Juvenal, or Ovid (among so many others). Many secondary sources have already been mentioned, but perhaps Jérôme Carcopino's **Daily Life in Ancient Rome*** stands out. For Roman Christianity, the letters of Paul or Jerome say as much as Augustine. Harold Mattingly's **Christianity in the Roman Empire*** and A. D. Nock's **Conversion*** add (in different ways) to our understanding of the Christian stress on the individual.

## *Notes*

1. Dorothy Lee, "The Conception of Self Among the Wintu Indians" in Dorothy Lee, *Freedom and Culture* (Englewood Cliffs, N.J.: Prentice-Hall, 1959), p. 139.
2. *Ibid.*

* Available in paperback.

3. *Ibid.*, p. 140.
4. Homer, *Iliad*, Bk. XXII, translated by Andrew Lang, Walter Leaf, and Ernest Myers (New York: Grolier, 1969), pp. 337–340.
5. William H. McNeill, *A World History* (New York: Oxford University Press, 1967), pp. 90–91.
6. Petronius, *The Satyricon*, trans. William Arrowsmith (New York: New American Library, 1959), pp. 81–83.
7. Augustine, *The Confessions of St. Augustine*, trans. John K. Ryan (Garden City, New York: Doubleday, 1960), bk. 2, ch. 1, p. 65.
8. *Ibid.*, bk. 2, ch. 3, p. 68.
9. *Ibid.*, bk. 2, ch. 4, pp. 69–70.

# Chapter 8

# Politics and Religion

## Asian Caste and Service

Americans, perhaps more than any other people, pride themselves on their separation of church and state. And yet the symbols of religion are very important to Americans. A recent poll shows that 97 percent consider themselves "religious." Since religion is usually identified with morality, Americans expect their political leaders to be religious. An atheist president would have been more acceptable to Thomas Jefferson or Benjamin Franklin than to most modern Americans.

Consequently most Americans expect politics to be moral. But their ideas of what morality is, and can be, in politics differ widely. In the Watergate hearings that removed President Nixon from office and sent many of his aides to jail, the public responses were interesting in their diversity. Some people said that "politicians are all corrupt, and you cannot expect anything else." Others said that the hearings proved that political corruption was getting increasingly worse in modern society. Still others thought that the hearings themselves proved that American politics were more reformable, and thus less corrupt, than anywhere else. A lot of people, however, were more offended by Nixon's language than his political acts, and seemed to want politicians to be "cleaner" rather than more legal.

In this chapter we will explore some of the possible relationships between politics and religion, politics and morality, or ethics and government. We will examine the expectations of cultures very different from our own, and we will attempt to determine the conditions under which these various expectations arise.

## Politics and Morality in Hindu India

It is sometimes easier to approach a problem through the ideas of a people in a very different time and place. In that way we can put our own culture's ideas into some perspective. Through the eyes of others we can understand the assumptions that we have taken for granted.

In an article called "Ethics and Politics in Hindu Culture" K. Satchidananda Murty has written: "It is very curious that no classical Hindu thinker regarded it as possible to moralize statecraft. Either one would choose to be in it and ignore ethics, or if one wholly wants to be ethical he must remain aloof from statecraft."[1]

The *Mahabharata*, the most ancient and famous of Indian holy books (which took shape as a collection of legends and philosophy from the second millennium B.C. to A.D. 400) is a gold mine of information on ancient Hindu politics and ethics. But like any holy book produced over a long period of time, it is full of contradictions. Much of the book reflects the crude warrior culture of the Indo-European invaders called Aryans who destroyed the ancient Indus civilizations of Harappa and Mohenjo-daro around 1500 B.C. Kings are advised to be ruthless and deceitful; to show humility and sympathy for enemies, especially when they are stronger; but as soon as they have the upper hand, to show no hesitation in destroying enemies. Even a relative or a friend must be killed if it serves the king's purpose. Without cruelty kings cannot govern. On the other hand, most of the *Mahabharata* advises the king to follow the sacred religious scriptures as the guardian of all of the people. Indeed, the central message of the book might be described as extolling the virtues of unselfish, unambitious action and the duty of righteousness (*dharma*).

Why this disparity? What is really meant? A lengthy section of the *Mahabharata* which is called the *Bhagavad Gita* gives a clue. The *Gita* is a long digression in which the warrior Arjuna asks the god Krishna about the ethics of war. Arjuna awaits the start of a battle on his chariot. Among the enemy are old friends, relatives, and teachers, men he has known all his life. Although he is convinced of his cause, he cannot bring himself to destroy those so dear to him. He turns to Krishna who is acting as his charioteer and asks for the god's advice.

The conversation is long, and Krishna's answer complex. First, as we might expect, Krishna tells Arjuna that his loved ones will not really die. The self is "indestructible, eternal, unborn, and immutable." "It is not slain when the body is slain. . . . Just as a person takes off old clothes to put on something new, so does the self cast off worn-out bodies for those that are new." Further, it would be foolish for Arjuna to worry about the unavoidable. "To be born is certain death; for the dead, birth is certain. You should not grieve over what cannot be changed." All of that makes sense in terms of Hindu beliefs in reincarnation and the inevitable recurrence of cycles. But Krishna continues. "Stop thinking of your own desires and selfish needs," he says, referring to Arjuna's concern for his friends. It would be selfish to avoid war simply because his own friends are among the enemy. Such personal and worldly considerations should not obstruct duty.

Arjuna must follow his own *dharma,* Krishna insists. "It is better to perform [one's] own *dharma* poorly, than someone else's well." It is selfish to let personal desires block the free exercise of his own selfless duty to be righteous. And that duty, that *dharma,* for Arjuna is to fight. Fighting is his most basic nature, more basic than particular friendships, because he is a *kshatriya.* "Considering your *dharma,* you should not hesitate. For to a *kshatriya* nothing is better than a proper war. If you refuse, you renounce your *dharma* and your honor. That would be sinful."

In terms of ancient Hindu ethics, it would be sinful for a member of the warrior caste (the *kshatriya*) to shirk the *dharma* or duty which is natural to their caste—fighting and ruling. It would be just as sinful for a *brahmin* (of the priestly caste) or a *vasisya* (of the merchant caste) to fight. That would not be their *dharma.* There is nothing wrong in fighting as such. It is required from soldiers and forbidden to others.

We can understand the complexities of the *Mahabharata* now: A king is urged to practice aggression and religious duty at the same time. The *dharma* of a king (a *kshatriya*) is fighting and ruling; anything that accomplishes that duty is proper.

The caste system offers a simple answer to the age-old question: "How do I get involved in politics, and still stay clean." The answer is that you will if you are a *kshatriya;* you will not if you are of another caste. A *kshatriya* can do anything to continue in politics and still stay "good" because "goodness" for a *kshatriya* is a political-military activity, the obligation of his caste.

Hindu ethics have sometimes been interpreted by Americans who should know better as a kind of Eastern "do your own thing." The reason is that Hindus do not usually speak in terms of absolute standards, but instead urge people to do what is in their own nature. For the Hindu, however, the command to live in terms of one's own *dharma* means to do the duties of one's caste. In other words, Hindu ethics avoid absolute rules in order to satisfy an equally conservative absolute—to keep everyone in his or her place.

The caste ideal of Indian society tended to keep rulers and ethical teachers apart. Thus, the evaluation of politics in terms of ethics (or the moralization of politics that Murty refers to) was impossible. Of course, the four castes were never wholly separated. It was sometimes possible for a person to move from one caste to another. Castes multiplied and changed. By the twentieth century there were over a thousand, mainly based on occupation, which were less hereditary than in the past. For this reason, Murty can talk of *choosing* to be involved in either ethics or statecraft. Despite all these qualifications, even as Hindu society became more fluid, the lives of the priest and the politician were very different. At the most fluid, it was still necessary to make a choice. Hindu moral leaders did not engage in politics, and rulers did not involve themselves in ethical or religious issues. There were few requirements that bound *brahmin, kshatriya, vaisya* and *sudra* (laborer) alike. Loyalty to the special commands of one's caste were still far more important.

## The Arthashastra of Kautilya

Indian Hindus liked to divide things into fours, much as medieval Europeans divided things into threes and we today see things in twos. Perhaps the ideal of four castes explains this division. If there were four kinds of people, there must be four kinds of knowledge. Anyone could see that: there was knowledge of *dharma* (duty, ethics, or righteousness), knowledge of *artha* (material wealth and power), knowledge of *kama* (sex, love, marriage, and family), and knowledge of *moksha* (the final goal of human existence—release, salvation). These four types of knowledge or activity were not identical to the four castes. (As we have seen, every caste had its *dharma*; all strove for *moksha.*) It is just that every Hindu knew that these were the four types of learning or behavior that the world offered (just as we know that there are two: the arts and the sciences).

Thus, when a Hindu wrote a book, he (rarely she) wrote about *dharma, artha, kama,* or *moksha.* The subject of ethics and politics would rarely be discussed. One wrote about either *dharma* or *artha.* The *Atharva Veda* (900–600 B.C.), for instance, deals with such subjects as the success and prosperity of a king, how to deal with enemies, how to ensure the safety of cattle, how to build a house, and how to be successful in trade.

The earliest and most important of Indian studies of politics is certainly the *Arthashastra,* probably written by Kautilya, a half-real, half-legendary advisor to the first king to unite most of India—King Chandragupta Maurya who reigned between 322 and 298 B.C. Kautilya was a *brahmin,* educated at the best orthodox Hindu schools, who did not take too kindly to the newfangled ideas of Buddhists and Jains in northern India. Possibly because the Nanda family who ruled his native kingdom of Magadha had been taken in by the new religions, Kautilya joined forces with the young prince Chandragupta (an orthodox Hindu) and led a successful rebellion. From Magadha they went out to conquer the remaining armies of Alexander the Great and consolidate through India the great Maurya Empire (which lasted from 322 to 185 B.C.).

Kautilya's *Arthashastra* is interesting for our purposes because it ignores what we would consider ethical considerations. Like a similar book of advice to a prince written by Machiavelli in Florence over 1500 years later, the *Arthashastra* treats politics as a separate science with its own justifications. The examination of politics in terms of efficiency and expediency may have been easy in a Hindu culture which thought of politics and ethics as distinct subjects of study. It is also possible that the political situation of numerous competing small states (in India and Renaissance Italy) was the cause of similar cynicism. We will look at Machiavelli later, and return to this question. First, Kautilya's *Arthashastra:*[2]

> The ruler shall acquire balanced wisdom. He shall keep company with the learned. He shall get information through his spies.
>
> Having instituted spies over his chief officers, the ruler should spread his intelligence network over the citizens and the country folk.
>
> The deliberation of the ruler's councils should be made top secret so that not even a bird can whisper. The ruler should be guarded against disclosure. Whoever divulges secret deliberations should be destroyed.

Special precautions are to be taken against contaminated and poisoned food. The following reveal poison: rice sending out deep blue vapour; unnaturally coloured and artificially dried-up and hard vegetables; unusually bright and dull vessels.

The poisoner reveals himself by parched and dry mouth, hesitating talk, perspiration, tremour, yawning, evasive demeanour and nervous behavior.

Wives of actors and persons of that category, trained in various languages and symbols, should be appointed to seduce and liquidate foreign spies.

Any power inferior to another should sue for peace; any power superior in might to another should launch into war; any power which fears no

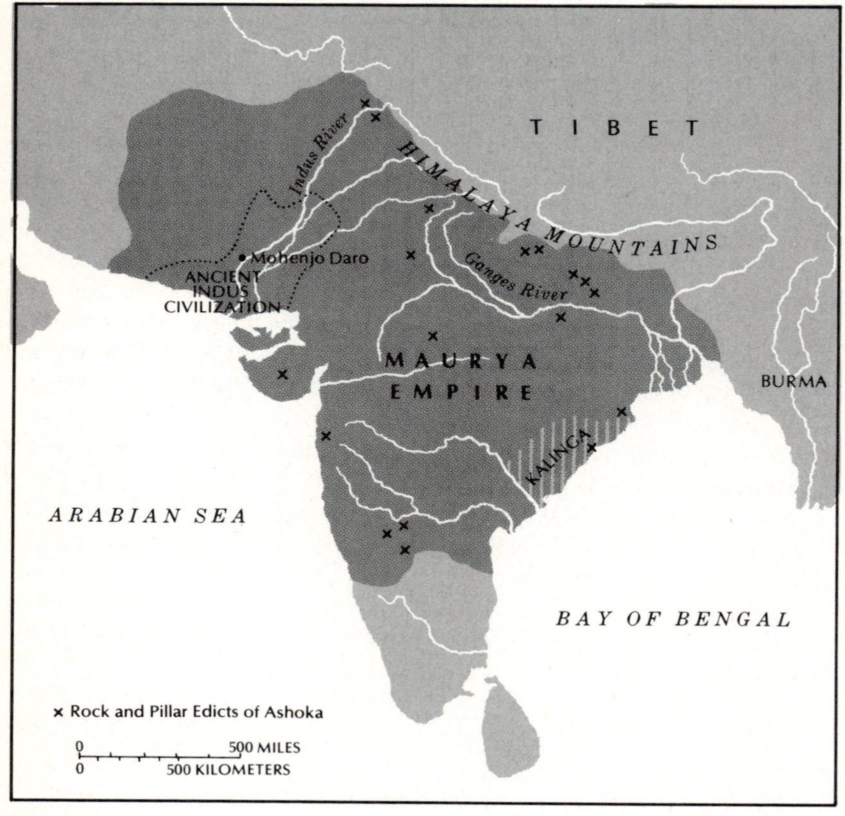


**Maurya Empire, c. 250 B.C.**

> external attack and which has no strength to wage war should remain neutral; any power with high war-potential should indulge in invasion.

Kautilya proceeds to enumerate the kinds of situations in which a state can "augment its resources" with a policy of peace: when peace enables the ruler to prepare secretly for war; when the peace terms allow the ruler to use the other ruler's resources without declaring war; when the peace can be used as a cover for sabotage; when the peace enables the ruler to rebuild, and so forth.

On the other hand:

> A state can increase its own resources by preserving hostility with another state in the following situations:
>
> Where the state is composed of military races and warlike corporations;
>
> Where the state has natural defensive fortifications like mountains, woods, rivers and forts and is capable of liquidating the enemy's offensive; . . .
>
> Where internal disorders sabotage the war potential of the enemy.

In all fairness, Kautilya makes a number of remarks about the importance of moderation in the ruler's behavior, and there are references to the needs of the people that the ruler governs. The remarks about poisoning and foreign spies indicate that these were no easy times for the softhearted. But one looks in vain for any moral principles that the king or state must recognize. When able, declare war. Better yet, make peace and then attack. The world of power politics goes to the strongest. To refrain from taking the offensive when one has the opportunity is to admit irresponsibility and court disaster. Perhaps Kautilya was right.

The amoral power politics taught by Kautilya and practiced by Chandragupta, the first Maurya, may have been necessary in terms of the king's ambitions to unify India and eliminate competitors. The policy may have even been defensible in terms of Hindu ideas. In a sense, Hinduism divided people (castes) instead of dividing human ideas and activities into the good and the bad. Hindus were convinced that all of the world's creatures, ideas, and actions participated in the divine. Everything that existed or occurred was holy, natural, and legitimate. Sex, power, and war were no exceptions because as part of the all-inclusive, divine universe or *Brahma* ("god totality"), they could not be ignored or banned. Everything in nature was natural. But some things were natural for *brahmins,* others for *kshatriyas,* others for *vaisyas,* and others for *sudras.* The exercise of power was natural for kings.

## The Buddhism of King Ashoka: A Different View

The great King Ashoka, who reigned from 273 to 232 B.C., was a grandson of Chandragupta. He was the last ruler until modern times to rule an almost united India. Raised as a Hindu, he was trained in the sacrificial religion of the *brahmins,* read the Vedas, hunted, feasted, fought, and probably learned something from Kautilya as well.

Ashoka's aggressive war against the Kalingas was just the sort of victory that Kautilya would have admired. It added a new kingdom to the Maurya Empire, increased the resources of the state, and demonstrated Ashoka's resolve and mastery. Ashoka was revolted. He was overwhelmed by the suffering and death that his war had caused. Full of remorse, he became a Buddhist and preached the Buddha's Law of Piety to his subjects. We have his own explanation and apology (probably unique in the history of statecraft) engraved on a rock for the people to understand. Here is his story:

> Kalinga was conquered by His Sacred and Gracious Majesty the King when he had been consecrated eight years. One hundred and fifty thousand persons were thence carried away captive, one hundred thousand were there slain, and many times that number died.
>
> Directly after the Kalingas had been annexed began His Sacred Majesty's zealous protection of the Law of Piety, his love of that Law, and his inculcation of that Law. Thence arises the remorse of His Sacred Majesty for having conquered the Kalingas, because the conquest of a country previously unconquered involves the slaughter, death, and carrying away captive of the people. That is a matter of profound sorrow and regret to His Sacred Majesty.[3]

Ashoka's apology continues. He is particularly sorry because so many of those who suffered had lived according to the law. They respected their parents, listened to their teachers, and were courteous to friends, relatives, slaves, and servants "with a steadfast devotion." He makes clear that he regrets the violence done to Hindus and Buddhists equally, "because it never is the case that faith in some one denomination or another does not exist." And by violence he does not only mean death and physical injury. There is another kind of violence, he says, that was suffered by people who were not hurt themselves, but whose loved ones were harmed or killed.

The magnitude of his killing disturbs him. Even "if the hundredth part or the thousandth part were now to suffer the same fate, it would be a matter of regret to His Sacred Majesty. . . . Because His Sacred Majesty desires for all animate beings security, self-control, peace of mind, and joyousness."[4]

"The sound of the drum has become the sound of *dharma*," another rock edict proclaims. To Ashoka *dharma* meant a kind of political morality that signified a greater acceptance of the world than was typical of Buddhism, and less concern for the obligations of caste than was expected of Hindus. The Buddhist monk-king attempted to impose religious toleration and "righteousness" throughout India. Ashoka ignored the priestly caste of brahmins in setting up "*dharma* ministers" who were to "make themselves acquainted with what gives happiness or pain, and exhort the people of the provinces so that they will find happiness in this life and the next." The ministers were to instruct the people in the moral life and report back to Ashoka (even if he were in the women's apartments, "on horseback or in the pleasure orchards") about the "people's business." With the aid of his ministers and other officers of *dharma,* Ashoka was confident that "compassion, liberality, truth, purity, gentleness, and saintliness will thus grow among mankind."

Ashoka's model of a holy king ruling a nonviolent state for the moral elevation and happiness of the people did not last beyond his own life. The state was divided among his heirs, Buddhism passed from India to China and Southeast Asia, and older ideas of Hindu rulership were revived in India. It is impossible to tell how successful a continued Buddhist kingship in India might have been. We know little about the actual workings of Ashoka's rule. Ashoka's ideal was not revived in a unified India until the twentieth century. Gandhi was a Hindu. His notion of nonviolence as an effective political policy and his attempt to moralize politics had more in common with the Buddhist kingship of Ashoka than with traditional Hindu beliefs about the relationship of politics and morality.

## The Crooked and the Straight

There is a line in the *Mahabharata* that reads "both kinds of knowledge, the straight and the crooked, should be available to the king." Kautilya's name comes from the Indian (Sanskrit) root *kutila* which means "crooked." It may be a nickname inspired by his enemies, but it suggests the image of Kautilya in Indian thought. Ashoka, on the other hand, is known as India's greatest king, the very model of moral, "straight," and enlightened politics. But is this justified?

Ashoka preached religious toleration and undercut the power of *brahmins* and the caste structure. But that meant that the people were directly exposed to the whims of the state. Ashoka became the source of a new system of moral legislation, and he had considerably more power to enforce it. His father and grandfather had governed only a political empire. Customs, morals, and ethics were habits of caste, tradition, family, and local associations. Ashoka wanted to determine the spiritual life of the people as well. His empire was to be moral as well as political. He did not succeed, of course. In fact, the scope of his ambition was probably his undoing. The mere administration of so large an area was enough of a job. To "redeem" it as well would have been too much for any man with an ancient communications technology. But even as he failed, he passed on a more ambitious idea of kingship to the warring Hindu kings who followed him, and to the great Gupta dynasty that succeeded his own. Only after Ashoka did Hindu kings sometimes imagine that their rule might be divine.

At least Kautilya limited himself to the actions of a prince, not to the transformation of a whole society. It is true that he argued that the requirements of the state sometimes preceded the rules of religion, but that may have been partly at the urging of the *brahmins* themselves since they felt threatened by new religious authorities. In any case, a recent defender, Charles Drekmeier, argues that Kautilya seems to have always believed that the fundamental purpose of the state was moral: the maintenance of *dharma*.

> When Kautilya remarks that might and self-aggrandizement are more important than religion and morality, he means that moral principles must be subordinated to the interests of the state inasmuch as the moral order depends upon the continued existence of the state. . . . [For] the author of the *Arthashastra* the welfare of the state meant ultimately the welfare of the people, and the well-being of his subjects must be rated higher than that of the king himself.[5]

Kautilya trusts that the moral behavior of the king will result in effective politics. He asks, for instance, who is it better to fight: a wicked king who is powerful or a good king who is weak? His answer is interesting.

> The strong enemy of wicked character should be marched against, for when he is attacked, his subjects will not help him, but rather put him down or go to the side of the conqueror. But when the enemy of virtuous character is attacked, his subjects will help him or die with him.[6]

We may (with Professor Drekmeier) find a healthy attention to morality in Kautilya's answer to that question. The Indian advisor is arguing, after all, that a ruler must be righteous or risk losing the allegiance of his subjects and army. But, we might ask, is it not sometimes easier (and more profitable) to conquer good guys than bad guys? In that light, Kautilya's answer is a cop-out. He assumes that the good will be strong, and the wicked will be weak. We might all wish that were so, but we know better.

Perhaps the differences between Kautilya and Ashoka are not that great after all. Maybe we in modern society have learned to be more cynical and scientific than was possible for an Indian of the third century B.C. It is possible that all ancient Indian society, despite its caste differences, shared in more of a moral universe than we do.

## Politics and Morality in Classical China

We began by saying that we might be able to put our own culture's ideas about political morality in some perspective by studying a culture as different as classical India. We discovered the differences we set out to find. The Hindu caste structure and the teaching of the *Mahabharata* suggest that even our attempt to moralize politics may be unique. And yet, the Buddhist Ashoka attempted just that. In fact, his righteousness and forcefulness remind one of Protestant reformers like John Calvin in Geneva. And we shall see much of Kautilya when we turn later to Machiavelli. So perhaps, the similarities between Indian and Western ideas are most striking. Ancient Indian culture (including the *Mahabharata*) was, after all, largely a product of the invasion of western Aryans. The languages, gods, and myths of India and Europe have been related since that time.[7]

After the invasion of India by Alexander the Great (327 B.C.) Greek ideas of politics and morality were probably influential in the native Maurya Empire. In *The Rise of the West,* William H. McNeill remarks that

> the *Arthashastra* bears a strong imprint of Hellenistic ideas. In particular, its doctrine that the royal law was supreme, overriding sacred precedent and custom, was alien to older, as well as to later Indian tradition. . . . Taken in this light, the *Arthashastra,* as well as the general administrative and military effort of the Mauryas, may be thought of as an attempt to implant upon the refractory body social of India a Greco-Iranian concept of the supremacy of the state as against all other forms of human association.[8]

Consequently, a look at classical China, which remained isolated from Indo-European cultures, may give us a better perspective on our own Western development. The period from about 500 B.C. to the rise

▪ *Confucius (c. 551–479 B.C.). This traditional, conservative image of the Chinese philosopher was made in 1734. (Granger)*

of the Han Empire around 200 B.C., roughly the same period from Buddha to Ashoka in India, included a series of decisive turning points and the fermentation of Chinese classical culture (as in India).

The year 500 B.C. is a convenient starting point, as it marked the maturity of Confucius (whose traditional dates are 550–479 B.C.) and the development of canals and irrigation systems which transformed much of traditional Chinese life.[9] The philosophy of Confucius looked backward to an age balanced between feudalism and the family. Irrigation canals abolished that decentralized world and created the bureaucratic state and the Chinese Empire, first under the Ch'in (whence "China") dynasty (221–207 B.C.), and then under the Han dynasty which ruled from 202 B.C. until A.D. 220, long enough to mark the character of Chinese civilization for two thousand years.

The year 200 B.C. offers a convenient ending point for our investigation since it allows us to catch those changes in their infancy. By then the feudal age of the Chou dynasty (ca. 1027–249 B.C.) had been replaced by empire and bureaucracy under the Ch'in and Han, a new class of scholar-officials (mandarins) had replaced the old feudal landowning class in power, the traditional philosophy of Confucius was out of date, and so (as these things happen) Confucianism became enshrined in the classic education necessary for anyone who wanted to pass the world's first civil service tests.

## Confucius and Mo Tzu: Ritual and Righteousness: Words and Writing

For the last two thousand years, the Chinese have associated the name of Confucius with ritual, righteousness, words, and writing. Confucius is known as the first independent teacher of China. His stock-in-trade was words. He wandered all over China teaching and advising, seeking a prince who would listen. His emphasis on intellectual education, teaching words, led to his followers being called *ju* ("weaklings") because of their neglect of the traditional physical education. Even today *ju* (deprived of its derogatory connotations) means "Confucian" and "intellectual." Confucian scholarship is book learning. Legend attributes the same to Confucius, although there were few books in his day. He is said to have written the Five Confucian Classics: the *Book of Songs*, the *Book of History*, the *Book of Rites*, the *Spring and Autumn Annals*, and the appendices to the *Book of Changes*. Actually most of these were written and edited centuries after his death, but they became the basis of Confucian education and civil service testing nevertheless. Knowledge of what Confucius said became the mark of a gentleman and the path to a political career (in a society which disparaged most other careers).

We do not know what Confucius actually said, and what was added by followers. What we can make out is a Confucian tradition which emphasized the value of certain words: family, respect, moderation, loyalty, decorum, rituals, and righteousness are good Confucian words. The words of traditional religion were largely ignored by Confucius. Devotion to family ancestors was essential, but there is little mention of the traditional Chinese nature spirits or of heaven. Confucianism is a guide to orderly human conduct rather than a religion. Consequently, it is sometimes said that Confucius taught people to live moderately and righteously without "rituals."

> Confucius' insistence upon an internal regulator of conduct—as opposed to the external demands of ritual—was a major innovation in his time. Confucius spoke not of propitiating the spirits, but of cultivating human character. Righteousness, in the broadest possible sense, was his standard for both private and public morals. While respecting the ancient religious ritual, he interpreted it as an aspect of propriety or decorum—a conventional form of social intercourse which directs human behavior into harmonious channels and prevents extremes of emotion.[10]

While this interpretation is valid for much of the thought of Confucius, it overlooks a serious conflict that Confucius faced: the conflict between rituals and words. While Confucius was aware of the inadequacy of traditional *religious* rituals, he was a firm upholder of tradition and ritual. In fact, the appeal of the traditional "old days" for Confucius probably made him favor a world where rituals were more important than words. Ritual was for Confucius what caste was for the Hindu: a mode which combined the political and the moral, the actual and the ethical. As a man of many words, that appreciation of ritual must have created much conflict.

We can get at this conflict with the aid of an excellent article by J. G. A. Pocock called "Ritual, Language, Power." Pocock begins by noticing a paragraph in the writings of the non-Confucian philosopher Mo Tzu (born the year that Confucius died, 479, and died 381 B.C.), who had this to say:

> Of old, when people were first produced, before there were penalties or government, the speech of men had for each a different meaning; for one man it had one meaning, for two men it had two meanings, and for ten men it had ten meanings. As the number of people became great, the meanings which the speech uttered by them had become also great in number. Thus people regarded each his own meaning as right and other people's meanings as wrong, and consequently in their intercourse

> they criticized each other. Consequently at home fathers and sons, elder and younger brothers, became angry with each other, were estranged from each other and could not live in harmony, and the people in the world harmed each other like water and fire, or poison. . . . The disorder in the world was like that of birds or beasts. An examination of this disorder in the world showed that it came from not having government leaders. Therefore the most capable man in the world was chosen and set up as Son of Heaven. . . . Only the Son of Heaven was able to unify all the meanings in the world, so that the world enjoyed order.[11]

Despite the inadequacies of Mo Tzu's view of history, it reminds us of several important things. First, the Chinese written language had so many characters (letters) that it was virtually impossible for those who had to work at anything else to learn to write. Ancient Chinese society (except for a few educated intellectuals) was an oral, speaking society. Second, it is written language which is "able to unify all the meanings." Oral language is continually changing. Writing stabilizes and organizes the meanings of words which speech permits to change. Finally, the way that written words became known to members of the lower classes like Mo Tzu was through laws. Mo Tzu was applauding the creation of written laws because they "unify" meanings, make laws more important than rituals, and unify the people by treating them with the equality of the stable, written word. Mo Tzu preached a kind of primitive communism, equality, universal love, and the abolition of useless ceremony, music, and ritual (*except* religious ritual). The secular ceremonies and rituals so imbued the hierarchies of traditional society that even laws seemed preferable. "The people have three worries," Mo Tzu warned:

> that the hungry will not be fed, that the cold will not be clothed, and that the tired will not get rest. These three are the great worries of the people. Now suppose we strike the great bell, beat the sounding drum [and play other ritual instruments], can the material for food and clothing thus be procured for the people?[12]

Rituals do not feed the people. They celebrate existing inequality. While the people have worries, "to have music is wrong."

With the radical Mo Tzu as foil to the conservative Confucius, we can better understand the latter's ambivalent attitude toward ritual and words. Let us look at ritual from Confucius's conservative perspective. When a society is orderly, there are rituals for every occasion and everyone performs the appropriate rituals. In doing so, the actual, the symbolic, and the proper are all the same. There is no discord and everyone knows what to do. There is no need for force, and there is greater opportunity for spontaneity. It is like dancing.

> How do we know the meaning of dancing? The dancer's eyes do not look at himself; his ears do not listen to himself; yet he controls the lowering and raising of his head, the bending and straightening of his body, his advancing and retreating, his slow and rapid movements; everything is discriminated and regulated. He exerts to the utmost all the strength of his body to keep time to the measures of the sounds of the drum and bell, and has no rebellious heart.[13]

Ritual unites the polar tendencies of men. It unifies discipline and spontaneity, exertion and control, the actual and the ideal, the political and the moral. Ritual unifies society. Words may unify meanings, but they divide men. Once the words are made clear and permanent (as in written laws) they can be interpreted. Order is replaced by argument.

> When the people know what the exact laws are, they do not stand in awe of their superiors. They come to have a contentious spirit and make their appeal to the written words, hoping to be successful in their argument. They can no longer be managed.[14]

For Confucius, the solution was that the nobility could live by ritual, but the mass of people must be awed by the ritual of the nobility, supplemented by law. "The ritual does not extend down to the common people; the punishment of the law does not reach up to the Senior Officer." Those who write make the laws for those who do not, because they have no need of them themselves. A two-class society, composed of scholar-officials and the common people, was the implicit solution of Confucius's conflict between ritual and words in his struggle to retain the past. It was a model that was enormously serviceable in the very different world that was emerging at the end of Confucius's life. That was the world of canals, state bureaucracy, and a Confucian civil service—mandarins who legislated for others.

## Canals, Officials, and the Rule of Words: Legalism and Taoism

Between the fifth and second centuries B.C. the feudalism of Chou times that Confucius had known disappeared. The system of traditional rights and duties in agriculture was undermined by the spread of a money economy, the rise of cities and markets, and the development of a new class of landholders who used tax agents, private armies, and irrigation to increase their prosperity.

Canal irrigation allowed those princes who took advantage of it to extend agriculture to lowlands and plains where natural drainage was poor. This reclaimed land was administered outside of the hereditary feudal system to the advantage of the new class of landlords and their princes. As the treasuries of the larger, frontier principalities were increased, they developed bureaucratic, centralized governments and armies which allowed them to take control over smaller, less efficient states in the interior. After centuries of warfare eliminated one princely state after another, the ruler of the state of Ch'in, Shih Huang-ti, became ruler of all of China by 221 B.C.

The main intellectual force for the consolidation, centralization, and the replacement of feudalism by centralized empire was the philosophy of the Legalists (sometimes also called the "realists," "amoralists," or the "school of power"). The Legalists carried Mo Tzu's demand for unifying laws to its ultimate conclusion. But while Mo Tzu asked that words and laws be used (in opposition to rituals) for the benefit of the people, the Legalists made written laws to serve only the state. Power, conquest, unity, and the state were the only goals of Legalist advisers to the court of Chi'in like Lord Shang.

The *Book of Lord Shang,* written in the early years of the rise of the Ch'in state in the fourth century B.C., argued that fixed laws and penalties were more important than virtuous ministers. Shang believed that laws should be so strict, and penalties so harsh, that no one would dare to commit a crime. He advised that traditional authority of feudal landlords and elder sons be replaced by the division of the state into political units, from districts down to ten-member groups, and that each member of a group be held responsible if one member disobeyed the law. As prime minister, Shang further solidified the power of the central state by replacing titles of nobility with an honorary scale of 18 ranks responsible to the king, depriving towns of their autonomy, and controlling the peasants directly by giving them private ownership of land.

While Lord Shang's policies were motivated by his desire to conquer all of China—an opportunity of a thousand years he called it—his creation of a centralized, military state laid the foundation for such a conquest a hundred years after his death in 338 B.C. The first emperor of China, Shih Huang-ti (founder of the Ch'in dynasty), became known for vast public works projects: canals, roads, a postal system, and the Great Wall of China. But he is also remembered for codifying the laws, unifying the written script, and also for burning the Confucian and other classic books (213 B.C.) and burying many of the living scholars the next year. The power of words was enshrined in the laws of the state. The vision of Mo Tzu had soured.

It is not surprising, then, that the opposition to centralized, bureaucratic despotism took the form, in the philosophy of the Taoists, of a rejection of words. Since the Mohist faith in words had turned from sweet to sour, the Taoists preached a mystical salvation that required neither rituals nor words. When there is argument, Chuang Tzu wrote, "there is something which the argument does not reach; great argument does not require words."[15]

Joseph Needham suggests in *Science and Civilization in China* that the Taoists represented the lower classes (especially in southern China) whose intact village community life offered a basis for criticizing the bureaucracy of written powers. Though Taoism is usually interpreted as a religious withdrawal from all social convention, it may have been directed more specifically at the emerging empire's tyranny of law. The Taoists revived the idea of the *tao* ("the way, the path, the truth") in the same way that Confucius had ritual as a kind of pristine, primitive unifier. By its very nature the *tao* could not be described in words: those who knew it did not have to talk about it; those who talked about it did not know it. Like Confucius's idea of ritual, *tao* was the agreement that needed no discussion.

Thus, the Taoist poetry attributed to Lao Tzu in the *Tao Te Ching* suggests serene calm in the acceptance of the winds and rhythms of the natural world, not political revolution. But accepting the flow of nature meant living in a very different world with very different values than the ethics of activity, power, domination, and the standardization of meanings that the empire encouraged.

> The Way is like an empty vessel
> That yet may be drawn from
> Without ever needing to be filled.[16]
>
> We put thirty spokes together and call it a wheel;
> But it is on the space where there is nothing that
>     the usefulness of the wheel depends.
> We turn clay to make a vessel;
> But it is on the space where there is nothing that
>     the usefulness of the vessel depends.[17]
>
> To remain whole, be twisted.
> To become straight, let yourself be bent.
> To become full, be hollow.
> Be tattered, that you may be renewed.
> Those that have little, may get more,
> Those that have much, are but perplexed.[18]
>
> The more prohibitions that are, the more
>     ritual avoidances,
> The poorer the people will be. . . .
> The more laws are promulgated,
> The more thieves and bandits there will be.[19]
>
> True words are not fine-sounding;
> Fine-sounding words are not true.[20]

Even the radical opposition ethics of the Taoists could be used to good advantage by the proponents of state power, however. Not only was the idea of serene acceptance helpful to those in power, but Legalist political advisors to the Son of Heaven (the emperor's title) also learned the uses of avoidance in governing more effectively. One of the most Machiavellian of Legalist thinkers was Han Fei Tzu (died 233 B.C.). Han Fei (Tzu means "Master" or "Lord") taught rulers who were surrounded by ambitious, self-seeking, potentially treasonous ministers to govern in this den of crocodiles by doing and saying nothing. Han Fei taught rulers the implications of the Taoist maxim, "By non-action nothing is ungoverned."

> Accordingly, the ruler, wise as he is, should not bother but let everything find its proper place; worthy as he is, should not take things on himself but observe closely his minister's motives; and courageous as he is, should not be engaged but let every minister display his prowess. . . .
>
> Thus, the intelligent ruler does nothing, but his ministers tremble all the more. It is the Tao of the intelligent ruler that he makes the wise men exhaust their mental energy and makes his decisions thereby without being himself at his wit's end. . . .
>
> Be empty and reposed and have nothing to do. Then from the dark see defects in the light. See but never be seen. Hear but never be heard. Know but never be known. If you hear any word uttered, do not change it or move it but compare it with the deed and see if word and deed coincide with each other. Place every official with a censor. Do not let them speak to each other. Then everything will be exerted to the utmost. Cover tracks and conceal sources. Then the ministers cannot trace origins. Leave your wisdom and cease your ability. Then your subordinates cannot guess at your limitations.[21]

Han Fei recognized that the ruler, like the Taoist wise man who does by not doing, can wait. Since he has the power that his advisors and appointed ministers desire, they have to come to him. They initiate and plead. The ruler can better determine their sincerity and effectiveness if he rids his mind of all personal ideas. He can best administer the machinery of state if he plays the fool or the philosopher, and says nothing.

The worst excesses of Legalism were associated in China with the Ch'in dynasty, and later Chinese rulers and thinkers vigorously repudiated the policies of Lord Shang, Han Fei, and Shih Huang-ti. The unpopularity of the Ch'in dynasty led to a popular revolt after the death of Shih Huang-ti and the foundation of the more popular Han dynasty, under the less ruthless general-turned-emperor Kaotzu. But although Kaotzu experimented with a more feudal, less centralized administration in the years after his victory in 202 B.C., he too eventually consolidated the state, increased the bureaucracy, and expanded the empire, while trying to rule less autocratically.

During the long Han dynasty China developed the imperial bureaucratic structure—minus the vengeance of the Ch'in—which it was to have for most of its history. Under the reign of Wu-ti (140–87 B.C.) Chinese boundaries were extended into Korea, Vietnam (Annam), and central Asia. Confucianism became the official philosophy of the court, the new class of Confucian scholar-officials took control of everyday decisions of government, and the civil service tests of the bureaucracy were increasingly extended to recruit the new governing class.

The ultimate victory of Confucianism (around 136 B.C.) had nothing to do with the longing of Confucius for the values of the old feudal world. That had ended. Nor did it have much to do with the struggle of Confucius to retain ancient rituals. The bureaucratic state was ruled by the words of the mandarins, the official books, and the endless examinations. Rather, the political ethics of Confucianism (deprived of their bite and nostalgia) appealed to the new ruling class of officials.

> The virtues preached by Confucianism were exactly suited to the new hierarchical state: respect, humility, docility, obedience, submission, and subordination to elders and betters. In comparison with the usefulness of virtues such as these, ancestor worship and the cult of the family were no more than additional, though welcome, features. Moreover, the new elite found it convenient to adopt the Confucian nonreligious, rationalist outlook. Mysticism was usually a cloak for subversive tendencies, and the scholar-officials, anxious above all to maintain the position they had won, felt that it was something to be guarded against.[22]

A dynasty which burned Confucian books and buried alive Confucian scholars was replaced by a dynasty (and thousands of years of dynasties) which made those books and scholars the source and sanction of government. Both acts served the interests of those who ruled.

## Chinese Politics and Ethics: Some Conclusions

Our survey of classical China, in its period of greatest ferment in political and ethical theory, suggests a number of things besides the development of the bureaucratic state. The conflict over rituals and words reminds us that our very questions about politics and ethics are not those of traditional stateless society. The Chinese (like Confucius) emerging from that traditional world, like the Greeks and the Indians of the classical age, only began to experience a conflict between politics and ethics as the certainties of tribe, caste, family, and ritual were breaking down. It was in all cases the rise of the central state that demanded new loyalties, imposed new demands, and thus posed new questions. Words, literacy, writing, and laws were causes and mediums for the expression of that new conflict. One could only ask if a particular political activity was, or could be, ethical, when one was faced with alternatives. Words provided alternatives, while rituals had not.

We are reminded also of a point made by Francis Bacon (1561–1626) much later in Elizabethan England: words are tools. Not only the advocacy of words, but the particular words, theories, and statements that are used "work" to the advantage of a group, class, or particular social need. If merely to advocate words has certain social and political repercussions, certainly the particular words did as well. Ethical and political theories are not merely attempts to define "the good life." They are arguments. They define "the good life" from a particular perspective, in the interests of a particular group. They are spoken or written, consciously or not, in order to do that. They play a social role, and they have social effects.

Finally, we are reminded that the function that words perform changes. Words of Confucius written to celebrate the old order were first villified and then hallowed by the new order. Mo Tzu's words on behalf of words were turned against the common people by the Legalists. When the people spoke through Taoist words against the empire of words, even then a Legalist like Han Fei learned the power of silence. None of these changes means that words are empty of social content, but only (as Confucius knew) that they encouraged interpretation and permitted change. We are lost if we throw up our hands and conclude that political words mean nothing, just as we are lost if we conclude that their meaning is clear, unbiased, and permanent.

## *For Further Reading*

The best general introduction to Indian civilization is A. L. Basham's **The Wonder That Was India.*** For classical India, a good place to start is with a collection of primary sources (including selections from Kautilya's **Arthashastra** and the **Edicts** of Asoka as well as **Bhagavad Gita**) edited by William H. McNeill and Jean W. Sedlar called **Classical India.*** For editions of classical Indian texts that are more complete, one can go to various editions of **The Essentials of Indian Statecraft,** translated by T. N. Ramaswamy, or **Asoka, The Buddhist Emperor of India** by Vincent A. Smith. Charles Drekmeier's **Kingship and Community in Early India** is an astute, modern study. A good series of modern essays on various subjects is offered in **Traditional India,*** edited by O. L. Chavarria-Aquilar.

* Available in paperback.

One can also approach the subject through selections and commentaries on Indian religion. Joseph Campbell's **The Masks of God: Oriental Mythology*** is an excellent study of Indian and Chinese religion. S. Radhakrishnan's **Eastern Religions and Western Thought*** compares Hinduism and Christianity. F. S. C. Northrop's **The Meeting of East and West*** is useful, though mainly Western-centered. The original sources can be found in **The Upanishads,** translated by Swami Prabhavananda and Frederick Manchester* and **The Teachings of the Compassionate Buddha,** edited by E. A. Burtt.* Hermann Hesse's **Siddhartha*** is also a good, modern version of the story of the Buddha.

For classical China, the best place to start is again another volume edited by William H. McNeill and Jean W. Sedlar, **Classical China.*** For further elaboration of the argument of the text, one might want to read J. G. A. Pocock's "Ritual, Language, Power; An Essay on the Apparent Political Meanings of Ancient Chinese Philosophy" in his **Politics, Language, and Time*** which has excellent essays on other subjects in political theory as well. Arthur Waley's **Three Ways of Thought in Ancient China*** is an excellent intellectual history. **The Sayings of Confucius*** are translated by James R. Ware. The **Tao Te Ching** is translated by Arthur Waley as **The Way and Its Power***and by R. B. Blakney as **The Way of Life: Lao Tzu.*** Other sources can be found in Fung Yu-Lan's **A History of Chinese Philosophy,** translated by D. Bodde, or the condensed one-volume **Short History of Chinese Philosophy,* The Book of Lord Shang,** edited and translated by J. J. L. Duyvendak, and **Han Fei Tzu** (two volumes) edited and translated by A. K. Liao. The history of the subject can also be approached through Frederick W. Mote's short **Intellectual Foundations of China*** or Dennis and Ching Ping Bloodworth's **The Chinese Machiavelli,*** an anecdotal survey of Chinese politics.

For general studies of China, Joseph Needham's **Science and Civilization in China** is essential for consultation. Karl A. Wittfogel's **Oriental Despotism: A Comparative Study of Total Power** is stimulating. There are good modern essays on Chinese history in **The Making of China,** edited by Chunshu Chang, and in **Traditional China,** edited by James T. C. Lui and Weiming Tu. **The Legacy of China,*** edited by Raymond Dawson, and **Half the World,** edited by Arnold Toynbee, also have very good recent essays. For the Chinese bureaucracy, besides the classic studies of Wittfogel and Max Weber, there is Etienne Balazs's more recent **Chinese Civilization and Bureaucracy.** Balazs is excerpted in Michael T. Dalby and Michael S. Werthman's **Bureaucracy in Historical Perspective.*** Weber is excerpted in **From Max Weber,*** translated and edited by H. H. Gerth and C. Wright Mills. And China is examined from the perspective of the "sociology of knowledge" not only in Weber and Pocock, but also in Marcel Granet's **Chinese Civilization** and **Chinese Thought** and in an essay by C. Wright Mills called "The Language and Ideas of Ancient China" in **Power, Politics and People.*** A readable study of Chinese technology can be found in Arthur Cotterell and David Morgan's **China's Civilization: A Survey of Its History, Arts, & Technology,*** and a wealth of primary materials are presented in **Sources of Chinese Tradition,*** vol. 1, edited by DeBary, Chan, and Watson.

## Notes

1. *The Ethic of Power,* ed. Harold D. Lasswell and Harlan Cleveland (New York: Harper & Row, 1962), p. 93.
2. *Essentials of Indian Statecraft. Kautilya's Arthasastra for Contemporary Readers,* trans. T. N. Ramaswamy (Bombay: Asia Publishing House, 1962). Reprinted in *Classical India,* ed. William H. McNeill and Jean W. Sedlar (New York: Oxford University Press, 1969), pp. 19–34 *passim.*
3. *Asoka, The Buddhist Emperor of India,* trans. Vincent A. Smith (Oxford: Clarendon Press, 1920). Reprinted in McNeill and Sedlar, *Classical India,* pp. 106–107.
4. *Ibid.,* p. 107.
5. Charles Drekmeier, *Kingship and Community in Early India* (Stanford University Press, 1962), pp. 201, 204.
6. *Ibid.*
7. The language group Indo-European attests to linguistic unity. The unity of myths and deities is explored in Joseph Campbell's *The Masks of God: Oriental Mythology* (New York: Viking Press, 1962).
8. W. H. McNeill, *The Rise of the West* (University of Chicago Press, 1963), pp. 331–332.
9. Karl A. Wittfogel argues that the construction of irrigation canals in China only became important after 500 B.C. His *Oriental Despotism: A Comparative Study of Total Power* (New Haven: Yale University Press, 1957) explains, even if it exaggerates, the importance of that event.
10. William H. McNeill and Jean W. Sedlar, eds., *Classical China* (New York: Oxford University Press, 1970), p. 5.
11. J. J. L. Duyvendak, editor and translator, *The Book of Lord Shang* (London, 1928), p. 105. Quoted in P. G. A. Pocock's "Ritual, Language, Power: An Essay on the Apparent Political Meaning of Ancient Chinese Philosophy" in P. G. A. Pocock, *Politics, Language, and Time* (New York: Atheneum, 1973), p. 52.
12. Fung Yu-lan, *A History of Chinese Philosophy,* translated by D. Bodde, vol. I (Peiping and London, 1937) pp. 89–90. Quoted in Pocock, pp 50–51.
13. Hsun Tzu, third-century Confucian. H. H. Dubs, editor and translator, *The Works of Hsüntze* (London, 1928), pp. 234–235. Quoted in Pocock, p. 46.
14. Tso Chuan, "a pre-Confucian chronicle which may have undergone Confucian editing." Fung Yu-lan, *op. cit.,* pp. 36–37. Quoted in Pocock, p. 45.
15. Arthur Waley, *Three Ways of Thought in Ancient China* (London, 1939), p. 26. Quoted in Pocock, p. 58.
16. Arthur Waley, *The Way and Its Power* (London: George Allen & Unwin Ltd, 1934), p. 146.
17. *Ibid,* p. 155.
18. *Ibid.,* p. 171.
19. *Ibid.,* p. 211.
20. *Ibid.,* p. 243.
21. A. K. Liao, editor and translator, *Han Fei Tzu* (London, 1939, 1959), vol. I, pp. 31–33. Quoted in Pocock, *op. cit.,* pp. 67–68.
22. Etienne Balazs, *Chinese Civilization and Bureaucracy,* trans. H. M. Wright, ed. Arthur F. Wright (New Haven: Yale University Press, 1964), p. 19.

## CHRONOLOGICAL CONTEXT OF
# The Classical World: 1000 B.C.-A.D. 500

| Greece | Rome | Middle East and Africa | India | China |
|---|---|---|---|---|
| Trojan War<br>c. 1200 B.C. | | *Genesis*<br>850–500 B.C. | | |
| Homer<br>c. 700 B.C. | | | *Mahabharata*<br>c. 600–300 B.C. | Lao Tzu<br>c. 600 B.C. |
| | | | Buddha<br>c. 500 B.C. | Confucius<br>551–479 B.C. |
| Socrates<br>469–399 B.C. | | | | Mo Tzu<br>479–381 B.C. |
| Plato<br>427–347 B.C. | | | | |
| | Rome sacked by Gauls<br>391 B.C. | | | |
| Aristotle<br>384–322 B.C. | | | | Lord Shang<br>d. 338 B.C. |
| Alexander<br>356–323 B.C. | | Alexandria<br>f. 331 B.C. | Maurya dynasty<br>322–185 B.C. | |
| | | | Kautilya<br>c. 300 B.C. | |
| | First Punic War<br>264–241 B.C. | | Ashoka<br>273–232 B.C. | Han Fei<br>d. 233 B.C. |
| | Second Punic War<br>218–201 B.C. | | | Ch'in dynasty<br>221–207 B.C. |
| | Third Punic War<br>149–146 B.C. | | | Han dynasty<br>202 B.C.–A.D. 220 |
| | Julius Caesar<br>102–44 B.C. | | | |
| | Augustus<br>r. 27 B.C.–A.D. 14 | Jesus<br>c. 3 B.C.–A.D. 30 | | |
| | Ovid<br>43 B.C.–A.D. 17 | | | |

**c. = circa (about)**
**d. = died**
**f. = founded**
**r. = ruled**

| Greece | Rome | Middle East and Africa | India | China |
|---|---|---|---|---|
| | Petronius d. A.D. 66 | | | |
| | Pliny A.D. 61–113 | | | |
| | Juvenal A.D. 55–138 | | | |
| | Diocletian A.D. 284–305 | | | |
| | Constantine A.D. 306–337 | | | |
| | Alaric defeat of Rome A.D. 410 | | | |
| | Augustine A.D. 354–430 | | | |

# III

The Metropolitan Museum of Art,
The Cloisters Collection, Purchase, 1937.

# PART III

# THE TRADITIONAL WORLD

## 500–1500

# Chapter 9

# Love and Devotion

## Christianity, Chastity, and Chivalry

Have you ever felt guilty about making love? Have you ever felt that sex was dirty? Have you ever wanted to "test" a love by postponing sex?

Then you, like the rest of us, were raised in a Christian culture. Christianity has been so pervasive in Europe and America that most of us, including Jews, Moslems, and atheists, have absorbed some of its values, ideas, and even feelings. Christian attitudes toward love, sex, and marriage have been a basic ingredient of our cultural training. Regardless of our own religion, we can understand ourselves better by understanding Christianity.

This chapter explores our Christian heritage of attitudes toward love and sex. It suggests that we have been trained to think of love as devotion, and sex as sin. Our chapter traces the roots of our modern idea of romantic love to the institutions of medieval chivalry and "courtly love." It argues that our idea of "romance" makes it easy for us to identify love with death, but difficult to relate love or sex with marriage. We have already seen the roots of this problem in ancient Greece. In Christianity it takes on the dimension of what Kazantzakis's character Zorba the Greek called "the whole catastrophe."

## A Christian Dilemma

We have seen the development of two very different ideas of love in the West: the romantic love of the Greeks and the explicitly sexual love of the Romans. Neither of these ideas of love were associated with marriage. The roots of marriage were in social necessity—the needs of the community and the patriarchal family. When the word "love" became fashionable in Roman society, some people like Pliny attempted to read it into marriage. No doubt other Romans attempted to add love to their marriages or began a new marriage based on love. But these were short-lived attempts for the most part, and the most passionate affairs usually lay outside the bonds of matrimony.

The Christians attempted to infuse marriage with love. But their idea of love was not Roman sexuality, not even Greek *eros*. It was the Greek ideal of *agape*, spiritual love. The Christian marriage was to be modeled on the highest type of spiritual love—the love of God. Christian love was to be romantic love, more idealized than the Greeks had ever imagined. Going way beyond the Greek tendency to romanticize the charm of a physical lover, the Christians followed Plato in the belief that all physical love was but an imperfect reflection of the ideal love. The ideal love that the Christians knew was the love for Christ. It was that love which was substituted for Plato's ideal—love of the good, of virtue, of truth, and of knowledge. All Christian love was to absorb as completely as possible the love of Christ. The effect that this belief had on Western sexuality was enormous. Imagine, for instance, what it means to love one's spouse in the same way that one loves God.

Christian love was not practiced by all, of course. No ideal ever is. But Christianity radically changed the Greek idea of love and almost abolished the Roman version. The Roman idea of love as sex revived (at least by the eighteenth century) as the influence of Christianity declined. It is perhaps one of the dominant ideas of love in today's *Playboy* culture. But the romantic idea of love is also very much with us today, sometimes in its original Greek form, but more often in the form that Christianity has made of it during the last two thousand years. Let's examine, then, what Christianity did to the romantic ideal of love which was just beginning to emerge in ancient Greece.

Educated Christians who lived in the Roman Empire were familiar with both the writings of the Greeks and the Jewish Old Testament. From the Old Testament they inherited an un-Roman distaste for adultery, prostitution, homosexuality, and fornication. But the Jews expressed a lusty enthusiasm for sex in marriage. They felt a responsibility to their God as his chosen people to multiply, but the duty was also evidently quite pleasurable. Read the "Song of Solomon" in the Old Testament, for instance.

The attitudes of Jesus toward sex, love, and marriage are not too clear. His closest followers were 12 men but he seems, according to some accounts, to have taken a personal interest in Mary Magdalene, a reformed prostitute, and may even have married her. He seems to have thought highly of constant marriage and opposed divorce, but according to Matthew he also spoke approvingly of those "which have made themselves eunuchs for the kingdom of heaven's sake."

For most Romans, though, Jesus was a minor Jewish troublemaker in a remote corner of the empire until Paul opened the new religion to non-Jews and helped organize groups of these "Christians" throughout the empire. One of the most striking things about these communities of Christians is their obsession with sex as the source of evil. Paul went so far as to develop a whole philosophy based on the casual suggestion in the Old Testament that Eve's sin was sexual seduction and that her sin had been the cause of all human suffering ever since (causing everyone to be born with this "original sin"), and requiring that God purify his people by sacrificing his own son.

## The Ideal of Chastity

We can understand why some of the poorer people in Rome might have taken to the new religion. It offered the meek, humble, and dispossessed eternal salvation from exploitation, sickness, and daily misery. A loving God (even one that urged sexual abstinence) must have been very appealing to people who led loveless lives, especially women who were brutalized in the only intimate relationships they knew.

But Christianity appealed to members of all classes in ancient Rome. One of the early church historians tells us of a wealthy young Egyptian, Ammon, born into a wealthy family which employed servants, who frequented Roman theaters and games, and enjoyed fine foods and stimulating women; but Ammon decided to become a

Christian. Pressured into getting married, Ammon shocked his young bride on their wedding night by reading from Paul:

> It is good for a man not to touch a woman. Nevertheless, to avoid fornication, let every man have his own wife, and let every woman have her own husband. . . . I would that all men were [chaste] even as I myself. . . . I say therefore to the unmarried and widows, it is good for them if they abide even as I. But if they cannot contain, let them marry: for it is better to marry than to burn.

Ammon spoke to his young wife about the spiritual exuberation he felt by keeping his body "pure" of sexual contact, and argued that virginity brought people closer to God. Ammon's bride (probably as afraid of sex as he) pledged that she too would become a Christian and they would live together as brother and sister.

After a while the couple felt they might better serve God if they moved from the sinful city of Alexandria with all its worldly distractions, and they moved into a hut in the desert. There they ate only bread and water, often fasting for two or three days at a time. But even on such a diet they still felt an occasional prompting of the flesh, and so they moved apart to live in two separate huts. Temptation, however, did not even disappear with his wife. Ammon vowed never to remove his own clothing because "it becomes not a monk to see even his own person exposed." Once, in fact, Ammon wanted to cross a river but would have gotten his clothes so wet that he would have had to remove them. So Ammon explained his dilemma to God who, according to the historian, immediately dispatched an angel to lift Ammon across the river dry and pure.[1]

The writings of the early Christians are full of such stories of continent marriages and ascetic behavior that other Romans must have considered bizarre. Another wealthy young man (Injuriosus in the fifth century) and his Christian wife slept in the same bed but refrained from any sexual contact. According to the story, their spiritual love was rewarded after their deaths when their two tombs miraculously came together. Tourists even today are shown the burial place of "The Two Lovers."

Most of these stories were based on some event that actually happened even if they were made more fantastic in the telling. They were self-fulfilling fantasies. They became models of proper Christian behavior. Even when a Christian could not escape from the pleadings of the body (and many certainly did not), he or she would feel guilty. Others no doubt who heard of the innumerable virgins who gave their lives rather than be forced to have sexual intercourse, or of the monks who burned their fingers or castrated themselves in order to free their minds of sex, must have tried to do the same.

■ *A painting commemorating the death of a Syrian Christian shows some of the ascetic practices of Christian monks in the desert, where Christian monasticism originated. One monk, Saint Simeon Stylites of Syria, was said to have lived on top of a column for over thirty years. Some lived as hermits in caves. Other joined together in monasteries. All seem to have avoided women and struggled against the temptations of the flesh.* (Musei Vaticani)

The Christian ideal of love was a sexless passion. Paul urged his fellow Christians to love their spouses in the same way as God loved humankind. This was a difficult, if not impossible, model for mortals to follow.

## The Love of God and Women

The Christians believed that God so loved humankind that he had sacrificed his only son. The God they worshiped seemed to mean that the most complete love ends in the death of the beloved. The greatest act of love is complete self-sacrifice, even death. The more romantic Greeks had sometimes felt this way, but the Christians identified ideal love and death as the central core of their message of salvation.

A human need that is rigidly repressed sometimes bursts free in strange ways. The Christian ideal of love was so sexless that—almost in a Freudian slip—some Christians imagined the love of God to be quite a sensual affair. Listen, for instance, to Jerome's advice to a young virgin:

> Let the seclusion of your own chamber ever guard you; ever let the Bridegroom sport with you within. If you pray, you are speaking to your Spouse: if you read, He is speaking to you. When sleep falls on you, He will come behind the wall and will put His hand through the hole in the door and will touch your belly. And you will awake and rise up and cry: "I am sick with love." And you will hear Him answer: "A garden inclosed is my sister, my spouse, a spring shut up, a fountain sealed."

For devout Christians like Jerome, who genuinely believed that the love of God was the only love for a Christian, and that God was most pleased by those who denied their bodies in order to serve him, all of that sexual energy had a strange way of seducing the divine. A modern observer might say that Jerome, after all of his denials of sex, was agreeing with other Romans that love was little more than the feelings aroused by sexual passion. Even love of God was a passionate affair.

If the early Christians could sometimes think of love of God as if it were a sexual affair, later Christians could imagine love of women to be spiritual devotion. But this did not occur until women could be thought of as worth loving.

There was always a peculiar ambiguity in the attitude of Christian men to women. Of course, this had been the case in Greece and Rome. There were two types of women: the good ones (one's wife) and the really good bad ones (the courtesans and other people's wives). This was a typical attitude of patriarchal culture. But the Christians took it a step further. Christianity offered the world two women—Eve and the Virgin Mary—one of whom was responsible for original sin and all human suffering, and the other responsible for deliverance and salvation. Augustine expressed this conflict in one sentence: "Through a woman we were sent to destruction; through a woman salvation was sent to us."

As long as the early Christians like Paul and Jerome and Augustine were more impressed with the significance of Eve's sin, and as long as Christian society remained preoccupied in licentious Rome with the temptations of sex, they could hardly love women. They could love only God. Gradually, however, after the last Roman emperor yielded power to the church, Christians could view the world with less alarm, even with a certain degree of satisfaction. As a consequence, the destruction wrecked by Eve seemed less important than the gift of the Virgin Mary. By the eleventh century many Christians worshiped Mary as ardently as the earlier Christians had condemned Eve. One churchman in the eleventh century made God himself sound like a love-struck knight. This, according to that churchman, is how the archangel Gabriel asked Mary if she would have a child by the Holy Ghost:

> He, the King and Lord of all things waits for the word of your consent, by means of which He has proposed to save the world, inasmuch as He has approved of your graces. He whom in silence you have pleased, you will please still more by speech, since He cries to you from heaven: O fairest among women, let me hear thy voice. If thou doest this, He will cause thee to see our salvation.[2]

So, by the eleventh century Christians could come around to loving women—at least those women who were virgins like Mary—or they could at least love them as purely as the Lord loved the mother of Jesus.

## In the Service of Woman

This was the immediate background for the revival of the Greek idea of romantic love. There was no *eros,* only *agape.* It was a sexless spiritual love of idealized women, or at least as sexually repressed as the earlier Christian love of God. Young men sang the praises of their beloved as incessantly and romantically as Greek men had praised their boys. But unlike the Greeks, these medieval Christians starved their senses for the spiritual purity that a woman, like Mary, could give. Romance returned to the West with all of its trappings: oaths of fidelity, serenades, and silly or dangerous displays of worthiness.

We are lucky enough to have the autobiography of one of these romantic knights, a minor noble who was born in Austria about 1200. His name was Ulrich von Lichtenstein, and he called his autobiography, appropriately enough, *In the Service of Woman.*

At an early age Ulrich learned that the greatest honor and happiness for a knight lay in the service of a beautiful and noble woman. He seems to have realized, at least subconsciously, that true love had to be full of obstacles and frustrations in order to be spiritually ennobling. So at the age of 12 Ulrich chose as the love of his life a princess. She was a perfect choice: too far above him socially, she was also older than Ulrich and already married. Ulrich managed to become a page in her court so that he could see her and touch the same things that she touched. Sometimes he was even able to steal away to his room with the very water that she had just washed her hands in, and he would secretly drink it.

By the age of 17 Ulrich had become a knight and took to the countryside to joust in tournaments wearing the lady's colors. Finally after a number of victories, Ulrich gained the courage to ask his niece to call on the lady and tell her that he wanted to be a distant, respectful admirer. The princess would have none of it. She told Ulrich's niece that she was repulsed by Ulrich's mere presence, that he was low class and ugly—especially with that harelip of his. On hearing her reply Ulrich was overjoyed that she had noticed him. He went to have his harelip removed, recuperated for six weeks, and wrote a song to the princess. When the lady heard of this she finally consented to let Ulrich attend a riding party she was having, suggesting even that he might exchange a word with her if the opportunity arose. Ulrich had his chance. He was next to her horse as she was about to dismount but he was so tongue-tied that he couldn't say a word. The princess thought him such a boor that she pulled out a lock of his hair as she got off her horse.

Ulrich returned to the field for the next three years. Finally the lady allowed him to joust in her name, but she wouldn't part with as much as a ribbon for him to carry. He sent her passionate letters and songs that he had composed. She answered with insults and derision. In one letter the princess derided Ulrich for implying that he had lost a finger while fighting for her when he had actually only wounded it slightly. Ulrich responded by having a friend hack off the finger and send it to the lady in a green velvet case. The princess was evidently so impressed with the power that she had over Ulrich that she sent back a message that she would look at it every day—a message that Ulrich received like the others "on his knees, with bowed head and folded hands."

More determined than ever to win his lady's love, Ulrich devised

■ *This painting from about the year 1300 to illustrate the poems and songs of love and chivalry contains all the elements: horses, knights, and admiring ladies.* (*Universitatsbibliothek, Heidelberg*)

a plan for a spectacular series of jousts, in which he challenged all comers on a five-week trip. He broke eight lances a day in the service of his princess. After such a showing, the Princess sent word that Ulrich might at last visit her, but that he was to come disguised as a leper and sit with the other lepers who would be there begging. The princess passed him, said nothing, and let him sleep that night out in the rain. The following day she sent a message to Ulrich that he could climb a rope to her bedroom window. There she told him that she would grant no favors until he waded across the lake, then she dropped the rope so that he fell into the stinking moat.

Finally, after all of this, the princess said that she would grant Ulrich her love if he went on a crusade in her name. When she learned that he was making preparations to go, she called it off and offered her love. After almost 15 years Ulrich had proved himself to the princess.

What was the love that she offered? Ulrich doesn't say, but it probably consisted of kisses, an embrace, and possibly even a certain amount of fondling. Possibly more, but probably not. That was not the point. Ulrich had not spent 15 years for sex. In fact, Ulrich had not spent 15 years to win. The quest is what kept him going. His real reward was in the suffering and yearning. Within two years Ulrich was after another perfect lady.

Oh yes. We forgot one thing. Ulrich mentions that in the middle of his spectacular five-week joust, he stopped off for three days to visit the wife and kids. He was married? He was married. He speaks of his wife with a certain amount of affection. She was evidently quite good at managing the estate and bringing up the children. But what were these mundane talents next to the raptures of serving the ideal woman? Love was certainly not a part of the "details of crops, and cattle, fleas and fireplaces, serfs and swamp drainage." In fact, Ulrich might expect that his wife would be proud of him if she knew what he was up to. The love of the princess should make Ulrich so much more noble and esteemed in his wife's eyes.[3]

## Courtly Love

The behavior of Ulrich von Lichtenstein reflected in exaggerated form a new idea of love in the West. Historians have called it "courtly love" because it developed in the courts of Europe where noble ladies and knights of "quality" came together. It was like the Greek idea of love in its appreciation of romance and it's tendency to idealize the beloved. But it was not homosexual. It was closer, perhaps, to the Greek infatuation with the courtesan. On the other hand, the "perfect lady" of the Christians could never be a prostitute. They were too inhibited about sex for that. For the first time since the Greeks a man could idealize a woman, but only if he minimized her sexuality. The evidence is overwhelming that these spiritual affairs would ideally never be consummated.

It is difficult for us to understand how these mature lords and ladies could torture themselves with passionate oaths, feats of endurance, fainting spells when they heard their lover's name or voice, in short the whole repertoire of romance, and then refrain from actually consummating that love. Why did they insist on an ideal of "pure love" which allowed even naked embraces but drew the line at intercourse, which they called "false love"? No doubt the Christian antipathy to sex was part of the problem. Earlier Christian monks had practiced a similar (but less sexual) type of *agape* or sexless marriage. Christianity had always taught that there was a world of difference between love and lust. The tendency of these Christian men to think of their ladies as replicas of the Virgin Mother also made sex inappropriate, if not outright incestuous.

But these lords and ladies were also making a statement about their "class" or good breeding. They were saying (as did Sigmund Freud almost a thousand years later) that civilized people repress their animal lust. They were distinguishing themselves from the crude peasants and soldiers around them who knew only fornication and whoring and raping. They were cultivating their emotions, their sensitivity, and priding themselves on their self-control. They were privileged (as members of the upper class) to know that human beings were capable of loyalty and love and enjoying beauty without behaving like animals. They were telling each other that they were refined, that they had "class."

The statement that they were making was evidently so new that they suffered unendurable frustration to make it. They adapted to the frustration by savoring the tension and the agony. The more they repressed their natural instincts, the more "civilized" they felt. "They put on finer clothing, started to use handkerchiefs, and began to bathe more often; they practiced genteel discourse and sophisticated argumentation."[4] Sexual repression became part of a whole new style of life: a life of manners.

Unlike the Greeks they could afford to let women into their polite, sophisticated, elite company at a level higher than that of paid help. But only a few women could join them, and even these could participate in the game only if they remained perched on pedestals. Men could treat them as living, breathing, thinking human beings, but it was still necessary to idealize them so that both could remain a privileged minority.

Further, despite the new romanticized view of the woman (maybe because of it), wives were just as excluded as they had always been. Noble, uplifting love, genuine romantic love, could not be felt for someone who swept the floor any more than it could be felt *by* someone whose life was preoccupied with such trivia. The lords and one of their special ladies, Marie, the countess of Champagne, issued the following declaration in 1174:

> We declare and we hold as firmly established that love cannot exert its power between two people who are married to each other. For lovers give each other everything freely, under no compulsion of necessity, but married people are in duty bound to give in to each other's desires and deny themselves to each other in nothing.[5]

## The Court of Love

This proclamation was one of many that were made by the "courts of love" that these lords and ladies established in order to settle lovers' quarrels—and to decide for themselves the specifics of the new morality. Some of these trials are summarized by Andreas Capellanus, one of the most famous "judges" of love, in France, in the twelfth century.

One typical case was brought to the court by a knight whose lady found another lover but promised the knight, her first love, that she would return to him if she ever lost her new lover. Accepting this standby role, the knight was asking the court of love to declare that she had lost her lover because she had just married the man.

The queen of France judged this case. She decided in favor of the knight. It was obvious, she said, that the lady had lost her lover when she married him since it was impossible for love to continue in marriage. The lady, according to the queen, should now love the knight as she had promised.

No court, of course, had the power to legislate feelings; certainly not this voluntary, aristocratic "people's court." But by hearing so many cases, the noble ladies and gentlemen were able to devise rules of behavior which made love more polite than the open warfare that Ovid preached, and the crude brutality that most men practiced.

No one did more to formulate these rules than Andreas Capellanus. Andreas not only summarized the numerous cases that came before the court, but he used these decisions to write a manual of polite, courtly love. He called his influential book *A Treatise on Love and Its Remedy*, a title which indicated his debt to Sappho and the Greek romantic idea of love as a sickness. Andreas, however, did not think that he was advocating a "romantic" idea of love. The word was not even used in his day. He considered himself to be a modern twelfth-century Ovid—merely updating the Roman's *Art of Love.* He called himself "Andreas the Lover" and, like Ovid, considered himself to be an expert on all aspects of love.

But Andreas only used the same word as Ovid. The similarity ended there. The "aspects" of love that Andreas taught concerned the loyalty of the lovers, courteous behavior, the spiritual benefits of "pure love," the importance of gentleness, the subservience of the man to his lover, and the duties of courtship. There is none of Ovid's preoccupation with the techniques of seduction. Andreas is not talking about sex. In fact, he clearly advises against consummating the relationship.

Ovid made fun of infatuation and silly emotional behavior, but urged his readers to imitate such sickness in order to get the woman in bed. Andreas valued the passionate emotional attachment that Ovid mocked. Sincerity and honesty were too important to Andreas to dream of trickery, deceit, or pretense. Love, for Andreas, was too noble an emotion, too worthy a pursuit, to be put on like a mask. In short, the Roman had been after sexual gratification, the Christian wanted to refine lives and cleanse souls. They both called it love, but Andreas never seemed to realize that they were not talking the same language.

## Courting and Cavorting

Courtly love was not an absolute disaster for Western men and women. It taught men for the first time to concern themselves with the feelings of at least some women. Among Andreas's 31 basic rules of courtly love we find such new ideas as the following:

> That which a lover takes against the will of his beloved has no relish. . . .
>
> A true lover considers nothing good except what he thinks will please his beloved.

In comparison with Ovid's idea of love as sexual conquest, there is a lot to admire here: concern for human feelings, emotional empathy for others, an honest presentation of the self, a distaste for using other people or treating them like sexual objects.

On the other hand, romantic love was an idealized love. The lovers never permitted themselves to really know each other. They fell in love with ideals, not living, breathing human beings. They created myths to feed their passion; these exaggerated images of each other could only be maintained at a distance. They could not allow themselves to come close enough to see the warts or stay long enough to learn the longings and fears of real people. And so they gloried in everything that kept them apart. They chose impossible love objects, demanded impossible loyalties, and preoccupied themselves in the quest. They cut themselves off from other people by convincing themselves there was only one ideal. But more importantly they cut themselves off from the realities of their relationship and the needs of their own bodies. They could work up a degree of feeling, an emotional intensity, that no other people had known—but that passion was based on repression. They could yearn so deeply only because they could not have what they yearned for. The game of passion could only be played under rules of "civilized" politeness which were repressive enough to ensure that their passions would not be abated. In search of the exaltation of the spirit, they renounced the demands of the flesh.

The Romans, at least, had been in touch with their bodies. Despite their crudity, their boorishness, their manipulation of others as if they were objects, they were able to satisfy real needs, not imagined ones. Both the Christians and the Romans recognized sex as one of the most basic human drives and the greatest source of pleasure. For the Christians that meant that it was evil; for the Romans, pleasure was good. Something has to be said for people who knew how to enjoy what life had to offer.

But people need more than the stimulation of their nerve endings. They need ideals as much as realities. The tragedy of Western love is that it is made up of these uncompromising opposites. We have learned to love in two almost irreconcilable ways. We have learned with the Romans that love can spring from sexual pleasure. And we have learned from the Christians that love can uplift the spirit—especially when it fails to satisfy the body. We have learned the excitement of "romance" and the pleasures of the flesh, and we call them both "love."

In a sense our problem is the one that we began with. We have *eros* and *agape*. But erotic love is more strictly sexual for us than it was for the Greeks. We, like the Romans, understand sexual pleasure in pretty straight physical, even genital, terms. Americans do not go to call girls for intellectual stimulation. Not only is our *eros* more physical, but our *agape* is more spiritual, more idealized, than the Greek. The Christians saw to that by equating spiritual love with the sexless love of God. Later Christians substituted a Virgin Mother model for our *agape*, leaving the ideal as devoid of sex as it ever was. So our problem is more serious than that of the Greeks.

## The Triumph of Romance

But you may object, these are the problems of the Middle Ages. Isn't modern love something very different? Haven't we solved the problem of medieval Christians? The answer is yes and no. Let us briefly look at what has happened since the days of Andreas Capellanus.

The romantic idea of courtly love spread rapidly throughout the royal courts of Europe after the twelfth century. All of the young gentlemen of the fashionable set learned to view women as objects of honor and esteem. Romances (or romantic stories) were invented of ideal love affairs between knights and ladies. According to one, King Arthur's loyal knight Lancelot falls hopelessly in love with the King's bride, Guinevere. His love for Guinevere so overwhelms him that he is unable to refuse any of the lady's foolish or demeaning requests: he shows his obedience by falling off his horse for her, and spends all of his energy distinguishing his illicit love, arranging secret meetings, rescuing her from everything, overcoming one obstacle after another.

In another famous romance, a young knight, Tristan, is instructed to bring the lady, Iseult, to be the bride of his king. Iseult, however, falls madly in love with Tristan when she drinks a love potion by mistake. The rest of the romance describes the feverish attempts of the couple to get together to consummate a love that can only end in death. The romance of Romeo and Juliet, of course, reaches the same conclusion: true love is the complete sacrifice of the self; its passion and ecstasy are too much for this world; its perfection is death.

The romantic story has become one of the most popular types of literature in the modern Western world since the twelfth century. Many of the same old stories have been revived or updated. But even when the names and situations are changed, the same romantic themes have survived intact. Modern romances still describe "ideal" loves which must overcome impossible obstacles. Lovers are still suppposed to be attracted "at first sight" as if they had just swallowed a magical potion. They still are expected to surrender all reason to the "irresistible force" of their love. The fullness of their love is still measured by the extent to which they sacrifice themselves. The most "perfect" loves are still thought to involve passions so intense that they lead the lovers irreversibly to their deaths.

We have all been raised on the same ideas of romance which developed around the twelfth century. We idealize our lovers. We look for the "one and only" expecting some day we will suddenly without warning meet the one person who is best for us. We are sure that we will know when we are in love because we will have "that special feeling" whenever we are near the "special someone." Besides the sweaty palms and quickened heart beat and other symptoms of love sickness that Sappho described, we are trained to hope that bells will ring, and psychedelic lights will flash when we kiss or consummate the love. Love is still for us a world of magic and mystery. And we want to keep it that way. We prefer to romanticize the experience and idealize the beloved, rather than analyze or realistically evaluate either. The fantasies of love still excite us more than the realities of human relationships.

What about sex, someone might ask. If we have kept the "romance" of courtly love, haven't we at least made that romance more sexual than it was in the twelfth century? The answer again is probably yes and no.

We still live in a predominantly Christian culture. That means that men still tend to see women as either seductive, corrupting, but exciting Eves or pure, sexless Virgin Mothers, and they feel guilty about loving the first type and childlike in their love of the second type. It is true that Christian men over the last thousand years have concentrated more on Mary than Eve. They have elevated the status of women—almost to the point where they view them as equals. But because sex was such an evil to Christians, they have usually elevated women by making them less sexual. We have seen that in the early stages of courtly love the knight or poet could most easily idealize the particular woman who was sexually unattainable or "pure." This tendency continued during the European Renaissance (fourteenth to sixteenth centuries). Poets like Dante and Petrarch wrote endless lines to women they loved obsessively, but from afar. Both made their love-ideals, Dante's Beatrice and Petrarch's Laura, the all-encompassing focus of their lives. Dante's love for Beatrice became the model for educated Europeans (including Petrarch) for hundreds of years. The poet never spoke to her, nor did he want to. Rather, he was uplifted by the depth of feeling that her presence gave him. Since he probably had never experienced comparable feelings, he thought of Beatrice as a source of spiritual guidance to the love of God. His feelings for Beatrice (which he called love) were considerably greater than anything he felt for his wife or any of his mistresses. Similarly, Petrarch permitted Laura to enrich his soul with her mere image. He never hoped for anything more from his ideal; Laura had 11 children by her husband and Petrarch had at least two sons by his mistress.

In other societies these lives may have been strange models for people to follow, but in Christian Europe they made some sense. Another Italian of the Renaissance, Castiglione, summarized the new Platonic view of love in a book called *The Courtier*, written around 1500. The lady was loved, according to Castiglione, for her moral virtue as well as her beauty—both of which led the lover to contemplate the divine. Love of the ideal woman was a force that tamed the wild souls of men. "Pure love" could "civilize" men only because it forced them to repress their sexual needs.

In one sense, all that has happened in the last few hundred years is that the ideas of a few upper-class poets in the fourteenth century have become the ideas of almost everyone in the twentieth century. The great American middle class has accepted the earlier aristocratic idea that women are worthy of men's protection and love. Americans no longer feel so close to barbarism that they must repress every physical desire, but women are still expected to be less sexual than men, less experienced and aggressive. Men no longer expect the beauty of a woman to lead their minds to understand the beauty of human nature or knowledge of God, but they still see women as spiritual healers, pacifiers, or peacemakers. The romantic idea of love, then, even in some of its antisexual, spiritual forms, is still a part of us.

While any cultural idea of love, besides the romantic one we have inherited, might harmonize with our sexual needs—as our bodies tell us that we can "love" anyone—our romantic culture insists that there is only one love for each of us. Our bodies are satisfied by sensual gratification, but our romantic culture finds the deepest ecstasy in passion which cannot be satisfied, or in the love of the most idealized, abstract sort. The conflict between the Romans and Christians rages even now, but in each one of us.

## Polygamy, Sexuality, and Style: A Japanese Alternative

At the same time that feudal Europe was developing a code of chivalry that romanticized love and almost desexualized marriage, the aristocracy of feudal Japan was evolving a code of polygamous sexuality without chivalry and almost without passion. We know about the sexual lives of Japanese aristocrats between 950 and 1050—the apex of the Heian period—through a series of remarkable novels and diaries, almost all of which were written by women. These first classics of Japanese literature, like *The Tale of Genji* and *The Pillow Book*, were written by women because Japanese men were still writing the "more important" but less informative laws and theological studies in Chinese (just as Europeans still wrote in a Latin that was very different from the everyday spoken language).

When well-born Japanese in the Heian court spoke of "the world" they were referring to a love affair, and the novels that aristocratic women like Murasaki Shikibu or Sei Shonagon had time to compose in the spoken language were full of stories of "the world."

In *The World of the Shining Prince* Ivan Morris distinguishes three types of sexual relationships between men and women of the Heian aristocracy. (Homosexuality among the court ladies was "probably quite common," he writes, "as in any society where women were obliged to live in continuous and close proximity," but male homosexuality among "warriors, priests and actors" probably became prevalent in later centuries.) The first type of heterosexual relationship was between the male aristocrat and his "principal wife." She was often several years older than her boy-husband and frequently served more as a guardian than as a bride. She was always chosen for her social standing, usually to cement a political alliance between ruling families. Although the match must have frequently been loveless, her status was inviolate; it was strictly forbidden, for instance, for a prince to exalt a secondary wife to principal wife. Upon marriage the principal wife would normally continue to live with her family, visited by her husband at night, until he became the head of his own household on the death or retirement of his father. Then the principal wife would be installed with all of her servants and aides as the head of the north wing of her husband's residence. An aristocratic woman (but never a peasant woman) might also become a secondary wife or official concubine. If she were officially recognized as such (much to the pleasure of her family), she might be moved into another wing of the official residence (leading to inevitable conflicts with the principal wife and other past and future secondary wives), or she might be set up in her own house. The arrangements were virtually limitless. The third and most frequent type of sexual relationship between men and women was the simple (or complex) affair—with a lady at court, another man's wife or concubine, but usually with a woman of a far lower class than the man. Ivan Morris writes of this kind of relationship:

> Few cultured societies in history can have been as tolerant about sexual relations as was the world of *The Tale of Genji*. Whether or not a gentleman was married, it redounded to his prestige to have as many affairs as possible; and the palaces and great mansions were full of ladies who were only too ready to accommodate him if approached in the proper style. From reading the *Pillow Book* we can tell how extremely commonplace these casual affairs had become in court circles, the man usually visiting the girl at night behind her screen of state and leaving her at the crack of dawn.[6]

That emphasis on "the proper style" is what distinguishes the sexuality of medieval Japan from that of ancient Rome, and reminds us of the medieval European's display of form—the aristocracy's mark of "class." Perhaps because the sexuality of the Heian aristocracy was even more potentially explosive than the repressed rituals of European chivalry, style was that much more important. Polygamous sexuality could be practiced without tearing the society apart (and destroying aristocratic dominance in the process) only if every attention were given to style. Listen, for instance, to what the lady of *The Pillow Book* expected from a good lover:

> A good lover will behave as elegantly at dawn as at any other time. He drags himself out of bed with a look of dismay on his face. The lady urges him on: "Come, my friend, it's getting light. You don't want anyone to find you here." He gives a deep sigh, as if to say that the night has not been nearly long enough and that it is agony to leave. Once up, he does not instantly pull on his trousers. Instead he comes close to the lady and whispers whatever was left unsaid during the night. Even when he is dressed, he still lingers, vaguely pretending to be fastening his sash.
>
> Presently he raises the lattice, and the two lovers stand together by the side door while he tells her how he dreads the coming day, which will keep them apart; then he slips away. The lady watches him go, and this moment of parting will remain among her most charming memories.
>
> Indeed, one's attachment to a man depends largely on the elegance of his leave-taking. When he jumps out of bed, scurries about the room, tightly fastens his trouser-sash, rolls up the sleeves of his Court cloak, over-robe, or hunting costume, stuffs his belongings into the breast of his robe and then briskly secures the outer sash—one really begins to hate him.[7]

The stylistic elegance of the lover's departure was one of the principal themes of Heian literature. Perhaps no situation better expressed the mood of the Japanese word *aware* (a word which was used over a thousand times in *The Tale of Genji*) which meant the poignant or the stylishly, even artistically, sorrowful—a style of elegant resignation. The word also suggests the mood of "the lady in waiting" and even the underlying anguish and jealousy of a precariously polygamous existence for the women consorts and writers of the Japanese feudal age. The ladies of the court were trained in caligraphy, poetry, and music; they were dressed in elaborate, colorful silks, painted with white faces and black teeth, and rewarded by sexual attention that always had to be justified by its cultured style.

The rigid rituals of courtship and marriage were highly stylized. The gentleman interested in a lady writes her a 31-syllable poem. The lady responds with a similar effort which is examined meticulously by the gentleman for signs of good breeding: the calligraphy and poetic skill are sure signs of her character. If he is pleased, he arranges for a "secret" night meeting (which the lady's parents or attendants pretend to ignore). The gentleman conventionally keeps the lady awake all night, comments on the rooster's crow with appropriate expressions of dismay, and drags himself away at dawn. On his arrival home he immediately composes his "next-morning" letter which laments his long hours away from the lady and concludes with a love poem that usually includes an image of flowers covered with dew. Everything about the letter expresses the appropriate sentiment: the color of the paper, the type of incense, the style of calligraphy, even the choice of the messenger—who is regaled by the lady's family with abundant presents. If the lady is interested she gives an equally appropriate letter (following the "rule of taste") with the same imagery to the same messenger. The same series of events are followed on the following night.

A third-night repetition, with the addition of rice cakes left by the parents for the gentleman, could seal the relationship in marriage. This time the gentleman remains with his new wife in the morning behind her curtain of state. That evening a feast is held in which the groom meets the bride's family officially, the Shinto priest recites a simple ceremony, and the couple perform the three-times-three exchange of wine cups. The couple are officially married. The groom may visit his bride's house at any time, or even install her in his own home according to her status as principal or secondary wife.[8]

Aristocracies behave in similar ways throughout the world, and throughout history. They demonstrate their "class" or "good breeding" with elaborate rituals that differentiate their world from the ordinary. But the example of aristocratic Heian Japan a thousand years ago points to some of the differences between Eastern and Christian culture. The Japanese developed rituals of courtship and seduction for the leisured few that were sexually satisfying and posed no threat to marriage. They were rituals which showed artistic refinement rather than sexual "purity" or chastity. They could be sexual because Japanese culture did not disparage sexuality. Rather it disparaged lack of "taste." The affair did not threaten marriage because the culture did not insist on monogamy. The new sexual interest could be carried on outside or inside the polygamous estate of the Japanese aristocrat. Perhaps the main difference, then, is that the Japanese aristocrat invented stylized sex rather than romantic love.

## *For Further Reading*

Morton Hunt's **The Natural History of Love*** has offered a treasure of anecdotes and engaging examples. Denis de Rougemont's **Love in the Western World*** has been a profoundly stimulating, if sometimes exasperating, theoretical interpretation. Both are well worth reading. Among other general introductions, the Middle Ages chapters of Julia O'Faolain and Lauro Martines's anthology of sources, **Not in God's Image,*** is invaluable. Also useful are the Middles Ages sections of Richard Lewinshohn's **A History of Sexual Customs,*** Amaury de Riencourt's **Sex and Power in History,*** and Elizabeth Gould Davis's **The First Sex.*** Among more interpretive general introductions, Alan W. Watts's **Nature, Man and Woman*** is an engaging antidote to de Rougemont's defense of Christianity, and E. O. James's **Marriage Customs Through the Ages*** is a sympathetic Christian interpretation that lies somewhere between the two.

On medieval sexual and social life there are a number of good specialized studies. One of the best introductions may be the very unconventional classic by Henry Adams, **Mont-Saint-Michel and Chartres,*** a very personal guidebook to courtly love by perhaps the brightest member of America's most illustrious family. J. Huizinga's **The Waning of the Middle Ages*** is a classic study of manners, morals, and sensibility. Sidney Painter's **French Chivalry*** is the standard since 1940. Ruth Kelso's **The Doctrine for the Lady of the Renaissance** is a recent, scholarly study. Georges Duby's short **Medieval Marriage** is also excellent. Marina Warner's recent **Alone of All Her Sex: The Myth and the Cult of The Virgin Mary*** is thorough and enthralling.

For medieval social life in general, the best introduction is Eileen Power's **Medieval People,*** a classic series of short biographies. Louise Collis's **Memoirs of a Medieval Woman: The Life and Times of Margery Kempe*** is based on a fifteenth-century memoir which is the first autobiography written in English. For a well-written biography of a more famous medieval woman, Jules Michelet's **Joan of Arc*** is a gem. Other useful studies of women are Dorothy Margaret Stuart's **Men and Women of Plantagenet England** and Margaret Labarge's more recent **A Baronial Household of the Thirteenth Century.**

Recent studies of the family in history are extremely valuable beginning with the medieval period. Philippe Ariès's **Centuries of Childhood*** has become the classic introduction in the last few years. It is a remarkable eye-opener on childhood and family. Excellent, recent scholarly articles are gathered in Robert Forster and Orest Ranum's **Family and Society,*** selected from the incomparable French historical journal **Annales,** and **The Family in History,*** edited by Theodore K. Rabb and Robert I. Rotberg.

No study of medieval love should omit the most famous love story of the period. E. Gilson tells it admirably in **Heloise and Abelard,*** and Peter Abelard tells his version in **The Story of My Misfortunes.*** If one had to

* Available in paperback.

select only one other book written during the period, it would be either Baldassare Castiglione's **The Book of the Courtier*** or Andreas Capellanus's **Art of Courtly Love.***

To put the Western Christian tradition in some perspective, we have focused on eleventh-century Japan. The student who wishes to pursue this further would benefit from the introduction by Ivan Morris called **The World of the Shining Prince.*** **The Tale of the Genji*** of Murasaki Shikibu, **The Pillow Book*** of Sei Shonagon, **The Tale of the Lady Ochikubo,*** and other novels are the source of almost all we know of Heian Japan. A brief introduction to the whole feudal history of Japan is **Feudalism in Japan** by Peter Duus.*

There are, of course, many other cultures that would give perspective to the Western Christian experience. The "love literature" of Persia, for instance, in this very period (the eleventh century) includes the **Rubaiyat of Omar Khayyam*** as well as many works on physical and spiritual love.

## *Notes*

1. The story of Ammon is told by Socrates Scholasticus, *Ecclesiastical History* iv: 23; this version is adapted from Morton Hunt, *The Natural History of Love* (New York: Knopf, 1959), pp. 93–95.
2. Saint Bernard de Clairvaus, quoted in Hunt, *Natural History*, p. 148.
3. The story of Ulrich von Lichtenstein is paraphrased from Hunt, *Natural History*, pp. 132–139. Quotations indicate Mr. Hunt's words.
4. Quoted in Hunt, *Natural History*, p. 141.
5. Quoted by Andreas in *Tractatus de Amore*, Bk. 1, ch. 6, Seventh Dialogue; quoted in Hunt, *Natural History*, pp. 143–144.
6. Ivan Morris, *The World of the Shining Prince: Court Life in Ancient Japan* (Baltimore: Penguin Books, 1964, 1969), p. 237.
7. *The Pillow Book of Sei Shonagon*, trans. and ed. Ivan Morris (Baltimore: Penguin Books, 1967, 1971), pp. 49–50.
8. Morris, *Shining Prince*, pp. 226–228.

# Chapter 10

# Violence and Vengeance

## Barbarians, Knights, and Crusaders

Whether or not the United States is a particularly violent or warlike country, we have attitudes toward war and violence that have evolved in a unique way out of Western history. America has sometimes been called the extreme development of Western European culture. In a sense, we have been the most free to develop the potentials of the Europe that took shape in the Middle Ages. Less moored to classical culture than European countries, our country most fully evolved the possibilities inherent in the Christian, dynamic, expansive European beginnings. If Western Europe has been in the last thousand years one of the most aggressive, competitive, colonizing, and crusading societies in human history, then perhaps its most independent and successful offshoot has been least restrained from holding back those impulses.

In this chapter we will seek the roots of American attitudes toward violence and war by looking for the roots of Europe. Certain distinct warrior traditions emerge quite early in European history. The barbarian invaders of Rome and the Christian Crusaders in the Holy Land mark the outlines. In between we can speculate about "styles of violence," the development of justice from vengeance, and the relationship between trading and raiding, praying and preying.

## Children of Attila: The Barbarians

All white Americans are descended (at least in good part) from the barbarian tribes that swept over Rome and Europe from the steppes of Asia. These ancestors were a pretty unruly bunch. The Roman

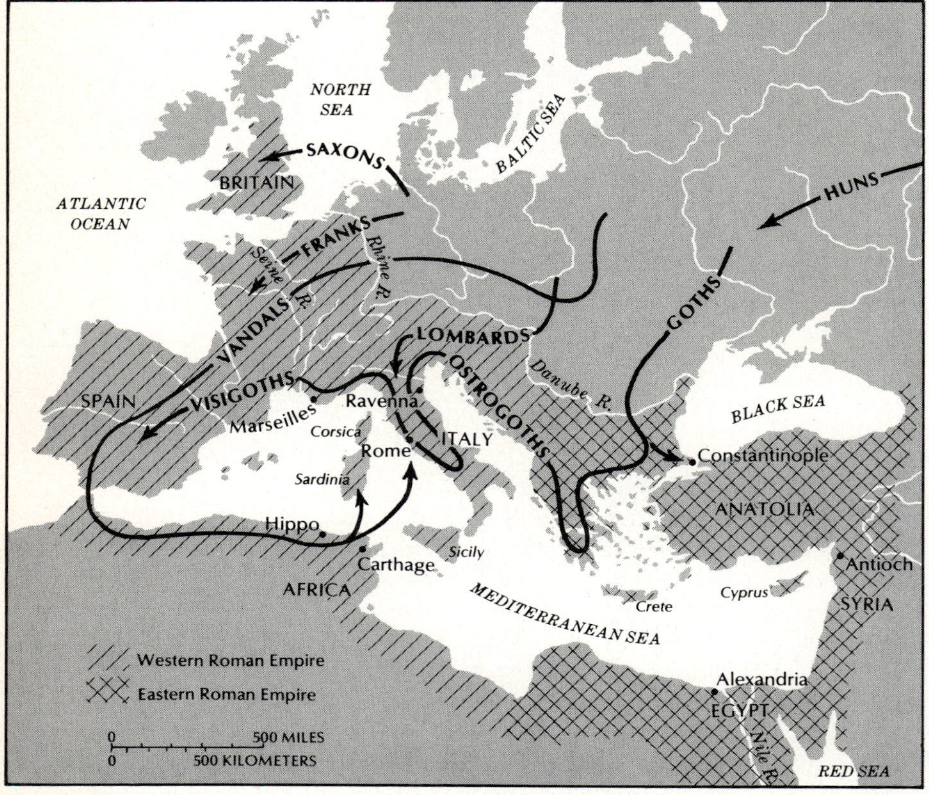


**The Barbarian Invasions, Fourth to Sixth Centuries A.D.**
*Successive waves of barbarian nomads were pushed out of the Eurasian grasslands and northern Europe by the Huns. Some, like the Goths and Vandals, migrated throughout Europe. The Ostrogoths settled in Italy, the Visigoths in Spain, and the Vandals throughout the Mediterranean.*

gentleman Sidonius Apollinaris boasted that he would rather "have braved destitution, fire, sword and pestilence" than submitted to the Visigoths or Gauls. But when these tribes moved into Italy, he resigned himself to rub shoulders with their unkempt chieftains whose hair smelled of rancid butter and whose mouths emitted odors of onion and garlic and strange Germanic sounds.

One of the best of these chiefs, according to their own storytellers, was "good king Guntramn," a leader of the Franks (who settled in what is now France). Guntramn could be as jovial and lustful as the next guy but "when he was with his bishops he conducted himself like one of them." In fact he was made a saint by the early church. The only thing you might say against Guntramn is that he had a taste for murder. Among his many victims were two physicians who were unable to heal his wife.

The Lombard king Alboin, who brought the tribe from the Danube into Italy, killed the king of the Gepids and married his daughter. He might have created a unified Lombard state in northern Italy (in the sixth century) if he had been more sensitive. Paul the Deacon tells a story of Alboin offering his wife some wine in a goblet that was made from her father's skull. It seems she didn't get the joke. Paul tells us that the "silly woman" had the old jokester assassinated.

It is possible that Guntramn and Alboin were not unusual. One seventh-century historian of the tribal invasions has a mother of a barbarian king advise her son: "If you want to accomplish something and make a name for yourself, destroy everything that others have built and massacre everyone that you have conquered; for you are not able to build better monuments than those constructed by your predecessors and there is no more noble accomplishment for you to make your name." Whether or not any mother's son ever heard those words, they certainly express a part of the barbarian consciousness. The leaders of nomadic tribes were particularly sensitive to the issue of proving their abilities in war: courage, strength, and even cruelty must have ranked high among tribal values. The fortunes of these tribes, especially in hard times, was often a direct product of their capacities for destroying and taking. And throughout their lives they were trained to hunt, to wield a sword, to carry out lightning invasions on horseback, and to bring booty and slaves back to camp.

The tribes which penetrated deepest into the Roman Empire were probably less fierce than those which were pushing them from the steppes. (The earliest invaders closest to Rome were actually often semicivilized tribes "retreating" across the Alps.) Even the barbarians told stories about the greater cruelty of other tribes further away from civilization. The Huns, according to Ammien Marcellin were the least civilized and the most feared:

> Their ferocity knew no bounds. They branded their own children's cheeks so that they grew old beardless. These stocky, thick-necked creatures cooked no food, but gorged themselves on wild roots and the raw flesh of the first animal they saw. They had no shelters, no burials, and only rat skin clothing that they wore until it disintegrated. It was said that they were nailed to their horses. They did not dismount to eat or drink. Often they stayed mounted to sleep and dream.[1]

Our tribal ancestors were certainly "barbarians." The word is appropriate. They were barbarians in the sense that the Greeks and Romans used the word: they spoke strange "bar bar" like sounds. But, more significantly, they were barbarians in the two modern senses of the word: they were both violent and primitive (or, more precisely, at a preurban state of development). The brutality of their lives and their lack of the tools, knowledge, arts, or comforts of more advanced city societies are enough to warrant the description "barbarian."

We do not use the word "barbarian" in order to make moral judgments about these people. Some of the early Christians and Romans did. It was enough for some of the educated witnesses to the invasions to point out that the tribes were pagans or Germanic: that was just like saying that the invaders were morally inhuman. This attitude was particularly common in the Roman aristocracy and among the bishops of the church. But at least one monk in Marseilles around the year 440, who called himself Salvien, gives us a different view.

It is true, Salvien wrote in a book that has somehow survived, that the Saxon people are cruel, the Franks untrustworthy, and the Huns immodest. "But," he asks rhetorically, "are their vices any more sinful than our own? Is the lewdness of the Huns more criminal than ours? Is the treachery of the Franks to be blamed more than our own? Is the drunken German more reprehensible than a drunken Christian? Is a greedy barbarian worse than a greedy Christian? Is the deceit of a Hun or of a Gepid so extraordinary?"

The barbarians, Salvien reminds us, had no monopoly on brutality or sin. In fact, they were not much different from the Roman authorities that they displaced. Their invasion was successful because Roman society had become as violent and insecure as nomadic society. From the perspective of the poor in Roman society the barbarians were sometimes preferable masters:

> The castaway Roman poor, the grieving widows, the orphans under foot, even many of the well-born and educated Romans took refuge among their enemies. They sought Roman humanity among the barbarians so that they would not perish from barbarian inhumanity among the Romans. They were different from the barbarians in their manners, their language, and the smell of their clothes, but these differences were preferable to injustice and cruelty. They went to live among the bar-

> barians on all sides, and never regretted it. They preferred to live free under the appearance of slavery, than to be slaves under the guise of liberty. Roman citizenship, once highly esteemed and bought at a high price, is today not only worthless, but despised. Those who did not flee were forced to become barbarians by the persecution of Roman law or the anarchy of Roman lawlessness. We call them rebels and lost men, but it is we who have forced them to become criminals.[2]

Salvien says a lot. Rome had become as violent as the barbarian world. The invasions were accompanied by the revolt of the Roman oppressed and dispossessed. The Roman Empire wasn't assassinated. It committed suicide. At least (since civilizations are not mortal), the owners of Rome allowed their possession to be mangled beyond repair.

Europe was born in this marriage of settled barbarian and barbarized Roman poor. The barbarian had learned that you get from life only what you take from others. The Roman poor had learned that there is no peace or security when a few wealthy families take everything from everyone else. Neither the barbarian nor the Roman knew anything of freedom or the peaceful life. The only world they were allowed to have was chaotic and violent—and even that had to be taken by force.

Life meant very little in early European society. Few writers were concerned with the hardships of the common people, but a few examples taken at random give us an idea of what it must have been like in the first few centuries after the barbarian migration.

One writer, Gregory of Tours, tells a story about the people of Orléans and Blois looting and burning the houses of Chateaudun and Chartres, massacring many of the people, and then receiving the same treatment from the survivors. Another, Gregory I, writes of the tyranny of the tax collectors forcing the inhabitants of Corsica to sell their children and seek refuge among the "unspeakable Lombards." Another, the Venerable Bede, describes how after three years of drought and famine one group of forty or fifty people "exhausted by hunger, went to a cliff top above the sea and flung themselves over, holding hands."

The neutral language of the law codes expresses the cheapness of life: "the fine for cutting off someone's hand, foot, eye, or nose is 100 sous; but only 63 if the hand is still hanging; for cutting off a thumb 50 sous, but only 30 if it is still hanging; for cutting off an index finger the fine is 35 sous; two fingers together is 35 sous; three fingers together is 50 sous."

Written law (like the excerpt from the Salic code above) had little meaning if you fell into the hands of the enemies. When Saint Leger, the bishop of Autun, was captured by an enemy palace mayor in 677, they cut out his tongue; then they forced him to walk barefoot in a pool of sharpened rocks that cut like spikes; then they pierced his eyes. The stories are endless. Another tells of some unfortunate soul being tortured for three days and then tied to the rear of a vicious horse who was whipped until it bolted. Others were killed by being "drawn and quartered": attached to two horses who ran in opposite directions. Cruelty was limitless.

## The Barbarians Civilize Themselves

One thing that is indisputable is that the chaos of the barbarian invasions gradually abated. By the sixth and seventh centuries, the number of invasions declined and most of the nomadic tribes had settled down to an agricultural life. The Goths who had terrorized Roman legions had produced a fairly elaborate culture by the sixth century. One of them, Jordanes, an historian, could boast that the Goths had a king who was a philosopher and scientist and that they had enough professors of philosophy to rival ancient Greece. He exaggerates, of course, but these are not exaggerations that would please a real barbarian.

By the eighth century the sudden terror of barbarian life had given way to the stable regularity of farming, collecting taxes, and making laws. The Franks had established a kingdom with relatively fixed boundaries and laws that was healthy enough to ward off an invading Moslem army from Spain. By 800 Charlemagne had himself crowned by the pope as "Emperor of the Romans," and this was not a completely foolish analogy: his empire included all of France and a good part of current Germany, Austria, and Italy (including Rome). Though he himself could not write, he gathered many of the leading European intellectuals (monks) to his court. One of them, Alcuin, could tell Charlemagne: "If your intentions are carried out, it may be that a new Athens will rise in Frankland."

A new series of invasions from the north (which we'll turn to soon) were to cut short the Carolingian summer of high culture and established law. But stability and prosperity had conditioned even the common peasant to demand "justice" where an ancestor may have needed "blood." The customs of the people were no longer those of barbarians.

Barbarian morality had been based on the need for vengeance. Tribal families were often ripped apart by feuds that continued indefinitely. When an affront was committed against one's family or tribe, honor required that it be avenged. It was impossible to sleep until the wrong had been righted with blood. Gradually, settled barbarian chiefs (and later, kings) were able to insist on a legal settlement of tribal disputes. Money or something of value became a symbolic substitute for blood vengeance. The excerpt from the Salic code (which we quoted disparagingly before) was actually a step toward a less violent society. "An eye for an eye" satisfied the basest human passions for vengeance, but (as the Christian monks taught) the motives of an assailant were also important. What was the point of blinding another merely to even the score? One life could not be brought back by the loss of another, and (as the tribal elder, king, or administrator well knew) the score was never even: the feud or vendetta meant continual warfare and prevented the rise of an orderly state.

Thus, the vendetta was gradually replaced by a system of "blood prices" for various kinds of mutilation and murder. These fines depended on the extent of the damage and the "blood worth" of the victim. The result, as the Lombard king Rothbari explained at the end of his own list of fines, was that "for all of the above-mentioned wounds we have provided a higher compensation than our forebears, so that when such compensation is paid, all hostility will cease."

The blood price should be judged a step beyond barbarism as it made family feuds less frequent as they became more expensive. But even the notion of a blood price was barbaric from the perspective of the Christian church. It limited violence but withheld blame. As long as the price was paid, the matter was settled. The church welcomed the substitution of the blood price for the vendetta but still insisted that a moral issue was involved. Churchmen compiled books of God's punishments for acts of violence. These acts were seen as sins, not just temporary imbalances in the social order. Eventually, the Lombards and other tribes viewed the spilling of blood and taking of life as moral wrongs which should not be committed—even if compensation were possible. This more "moral" attitude toward violence was still not based on any modern humane faith in the sacredness of life. It was based only on the fear of God's punishment. Gradually, the barbarian indifference to death was replaced by a feeling of "shame" for committing antisocial acts. In turn, shame, which was only produced by social pressure, was eventually transformed into Christian feelings of personal guilt. The history of the human conscience has not yet been (and may never be) written, but it seems quite likely that as barbarians became settled, civilized, and Christian, they developed greater capacities for shame and then guilt. Even guilt became increasingly internalized. In medieval Europe guilt was little more than the verdict rendered by the Christian king or his judge. In modern society guilt is still the verdict of the jury, but it is much more: it is the massive internal regulator which responds to so much of what we do.

From indifference to shame to guilt, from vendetta to blood price to responsibility, as barbarian society became more settled, as the individual became more responsible for his or her behavior, as laws and procedure replaced the gut need for vengeance, European society became less violent. Certainly we have evolved in these directions since the Middle Ages.

We have not given up the old ways completely, however. The change has sometimes been agonizingly slow, and in many ways we have only begun to give up our barbarian past. The family feud was a way of life in Appalachian America only decades ago. The vendetta is still common in Italy, Eastern Europe, and other poor regions of the developed world. Banditry, secret societies (like the Mafia), and vigilantes are still more important than the law and the justices of the peace in some relatively "modern" areas. And besides these remnants of the old world in the new, the newest, most developed countries (like the United States) often display a considerable appetite for violence.

The remnants of old world barbarism are easier to understand. The Sicilian home of the Mafia has not changed all that much in the last thousand years, neither has the climate of Latin American revolutions and Indian massacres, nor has the culture of social oppression and natural catastrophe in much of the developing world. These examples remind us that this sort of violence—even in the barbarian period—was the natural life of "hardship society."

Charlemagne's empire was never able to overcome hardship. Its thriving culture and law were only a hint of what was possible. That possibility was shattered by a new series of invasions: Hungarian nomads from the steppes, Viking pirates from the north, and Moslem cavalry from the south.

## Civilized Militarism: Knighthood and Feudalism

The violence of the ninth-century invasions was met by the militarization of European society. We call it "feudalism" and recall images of knights in shining armor riding on large horses and jousting in tournaments with long lances. We don't normally think of medieval knighthood as a process of militarization. Nor do we usually think of it as a response to a particular threat in a particular period. We probably have Hollywood to thank for the image of King Arthur, Lancelot, Camelot, and European knighthood that emphasizes its romance and fun and overlooks the immediate military necessity for its rise. It should have become clear by now that medieval Europeans could not afford to create expensive social institutions for fun. Knighthood, or the existence of aristocratic heavy-armored cavalry, was a most expensive social institution. The armor and horses were expensive investments for the aristocracy, and the development of such an army was a considerable burden on the peasantry (who had to increase their own production to pay for these defenders). Knighthood developed as a response to the new invasions of Hungarians, Moslems, and Vikings.

The earliest sign of this new military institution was in the first defense of the eighth-century Frankish kingdom from the first wave of invading Moslems. The Franks had to meet cavalry with cavalry in order to survive. They turned to a cavalry model which the Byzantine Empire had borrowed from the Persians (Parthians)—the heavily armored cavalry. For hundreds of years the Parthians (second century B.C. to third century A.D.) and the Eastern Romans (third to eighth centuries A.D.) had been able to hold off the barbarians of the steppe with armored warriors on big horses. The barbarians attacked on what we would call ponies. They were swift, and since the nomads had neither the resources nor ability to forge armor, these light animals were sufficient. Further, they required no more grass than the sparse steppes provided.

The Parthians (and from them the Byzantines) were able to provide the resources in land and grazing to raise a breed of large horses that could carry men weighed down in heavy armor. They could also forge the metal and equip a fairly large force with suits of armor. This heavy cavalry was almost invulnerable to the arrows of the barbarian invaders. Shot from any distance, they just bounced off a good suit of mail. The imperial cavalries of Parthia and Byzantium could not follow the barbarians into their own territory at any speed, but neither could the barbarians penetrate or hold imperial territories. It was a standoff.

The problem was that the resources necessary to raise such horses and equip and maintain such a cavalry were enormous. Parthian peasants were taxed so heavily that eventually (by A.D. 226) the empire collapsed. The Byzantine Empire was more successful because of its great wealth, but also because it created a full-time military state: church, state, and army were one and the same.

The Western barbarians, however, inherited a bankrupt empire whose only resource was the land. Most of the workable land was owned by wealthy Roman families, barbarian chiefs, and eventually the church. That land was the only wealth that could be converted into big horses, armor, and a professional cavalry of knights (like those in Byzantium). The first and easiest solution was the response of Charles Martel, the grandfather of Charlemagne. As the Moslems invaded the Frankish Kingdom from Spain, Martel seized the church lands and gave them to his best warriors on the understanding that they would provide their king with the necessary armored knights. They did this by giving parcels of the land to their own subordinates in return for military service. With these knights Charles Martel was able to defeat the Moslems at Tours in 733.

Feudalism was the way to raise an armored cavalry. It involved the exchange of land for the military service of knights. Eventually, most of the chiefs, kings, and large landowners of Europe were forced to exchange portions of their land for such military service. Church lands were not enough. After particularly devastating invasions (like some of the Viking raids) new feudal relationships were the only means for both defense and food. Much of today's European aristocracy can trace its origins back to the land gifts of this period. The peasants, as always, marched on foot, but even they received the benefits of protection that the heavily armored aristocracy provided.

The success of the knights in battle meant the success of the new aristocracy as a class. They were successful in battle because of their adoption of the Byzantine system, but also because of the addition of a new element to cavalry warfare: the simple stirrup. It also appeared in Europe at about the time of Charles Martel, and it became a basic ingredient of the new armored cavalry's repertoire of tricks. It became the basis, in fact, of the Western use of long lances and heavy swords. For some reason the bow and arrow never caught on in the West, but it was just as well. The blow that a mounted, armored warrior could deliver at full gallop, with the full force of his mount, with either sword or lance was virtually invincible when perfected. Without the stirrup, which rooted the warrior to his horse so that he could charge and swing at ease, the European knights would be no better than other cavalries.

The training necessary for such combat was considerable. That is where the jousts and tournaments came in. That was also the reason for the elaborate culture of "valiant knighthood." The knights became a special warrior class because they needed to train continually. Isolated from the rest of society (who worked the land to pay their way), they developed a romantic warrior culture of "chivalry" (from the old French word for horse) which is the basis for the Hollywood image of the Middle Ages. Despite the romance, the knights were the ruling, warrior class of Europe five hundred to a thousand years after the first invasions of their barbarian ancestors. The ideals of the military aristocracy—bravery, courage, daring, and manhood through combat—as well as the "damsel" image of women, the cult of gentlemanly chivalry, and the love affair with the horse are all still an important part of Western culture today.

Beginning with the barbarians, and continuing with feudalism, European culture condoned warfare by giving special honor and prestige to the warrior. Ruling aristocracies of warriors put a stamp on European culture that encouraged later generations to measure their worth on the testing ground of battle, to parade their military prowess in nationalist displays, and to vault their military heroes (Napoleon, De Gaulle, Grant, and Eisenhower) into positions of political power.

Europe and the offshoots of the European West were by no means the only cultures to turn generals into rulers. We have seen how this happened in Rome and Byzantium, and it occurred in other civilizations as well. But it did not happen everywhere. China, for instance, almost always regarded the soldier as one of the lowest social types in terms of prestige. Perhaps the closest analogy to the European creation of an aristocracy whose prestige depended on military prowess was the Japanese development of *samurai*. From the twelfth to sixteenth centuries Japan (just like Europe) was decentralized into competing landowners, each of whom had private armies of professional swordsmen called *samurai*. By the eighteenth century, as the feudal order broke up, the Japanese *samurai* became pirates and merchants in the growing towns. Military activity was channeled into marginally acceptable kinds of trade and profit seeking.

Much the same sort of development occurred in the West. Though waging war remained an important occupation, the aggressiveness of European society was also transformed by more peaceful acquisitions of wealth and power. After knighthood had served its purpose and the growth of towns and kingdoms hastened the decline of decentralized, land-based feudalism, the descendants of the knightly aristocracy turned to other types of aggression—chiefly exploration and trade.

Even before the European aristocracy engaged in worldwide exploration and commercial ventures on a grand scale in the fifteenth and sixteenth centuries, they had carried out a number of "dry runs." In the tenth century the Vikings showed how barbarian raids could lead to exploration and commerce. By the twelfth century Europeans were transforming religious war into profit making and colonization in the course of the Crusades. These were the "respectable" channels that European aggressive culture found. Warrior culture was made "holy" and profitable and adventurous. The warrior cultures of the Vikings and the Crusades paved our particular way of "civilizing" war and the aggressiveness of our culture. They are only two examples among many, but they may offer us insight into what we have become.

## Trading and Raiding: The Vikings

The Vikings are one of the most colorful "warrior societies" of European history. Between the eighth and eleventh centuries Viking ships and soldiers terrorized village settlements from Ireland to Russia, fought and traded in the cities of the Byzantine and Moslem empires, and established European outposts across the Atlantic Ocean. Not too much was known about the origins of these Norse when they first

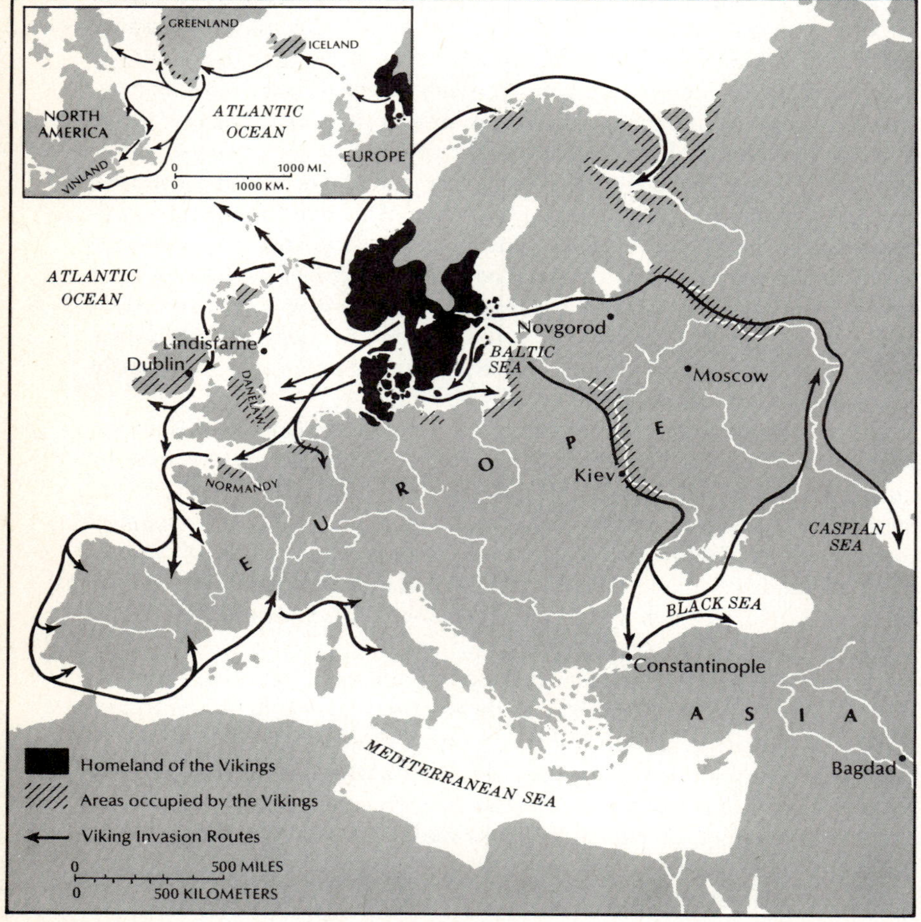


**The Expansion of the Vikings**
*The Vikings (or Norse) spread eastward from Sweden to Russia and Constantinople, and westward from Norway to North America and the Mediterranean.*

struck out from Scandinavia to conquer the English island of Lindisfarne in 793. Their ancestors may have been the "German" tribe which the Roman historian Tacitus called the Suiones in the first century. Tacitus remarks that the Suiones "are strong not only in arms and men but also in their fleets," that their curious ships have "a prow at both ends" but no sail, and that they can be found with their slaves along the ocean and rivers in search of wealth. Apparently, the Suiones were more settled than the nomadic tribes that Tacitus described. We hear no mention of them after Tacitus until the sixth century when the Gothic historian Jordanes reports that the inhabitants of Scandinavia are unusually ferocious and tall. It was not until the end of the eighth century that the European tribes and descendants of the Romans had firsthand experience with the Norse. By that time the Scandinavians had improved their ships, added sails, and realized the potential plunder to be gained from a more settled Europe.

"Out of the north an evil shall break forth." The warning of the prophet Jeremiah must have rung in the ears of the Christian monks at Lindisfarne when the Norse sailed into history in 793. The English scholar Alcuin, who was staying in France at the court of Charlemagne, expressed the shock of European Christians at the sudden "pagan" attack. "Never before had such a terror appeared in Britain," he wrote, than the invasion of Lindisfarne by the Vikings. The Church of St. Cuthbert was robbed of its treasures and "spattered with the blood of the priests of God."

In a matter of decades the Vikings had conquered much of England, Scotland, and Ireland. They came usually as pirates. They murdered unarmed monks, looted sanctuaries, plundered the libraries that had preserved the literary heritage of the ancient world, and burned what they could not carry away. The booty they sought was more precious than the literary achievements of Charlemagne's civilization. They took gold and jewels, valuable objects that they might trade, and they raped and enslaved the wives and daughters of their victims. Sailing first from Norway, and then from Denmark and Sweden, these pirates terrorized the inhabitants of the British Isles especially throughout the ninth century.

In time, the terror of the Norse became modified or institutionalized. In 865 the English began paying a yearly ransom to their Scandinavian overlords which was kind of a "protection" payment called the *Danegeld* (money for the Danes). Much of central England was placed under the Danish king and administered as the *Danelaw*. Scandinavians established their own villages (like Dublin) in occupied territory or set up colonies in existing towns. These settlements were sometimes fortified encampments used for further pirate expeditions, but gradually became more like administrative and trading centers.

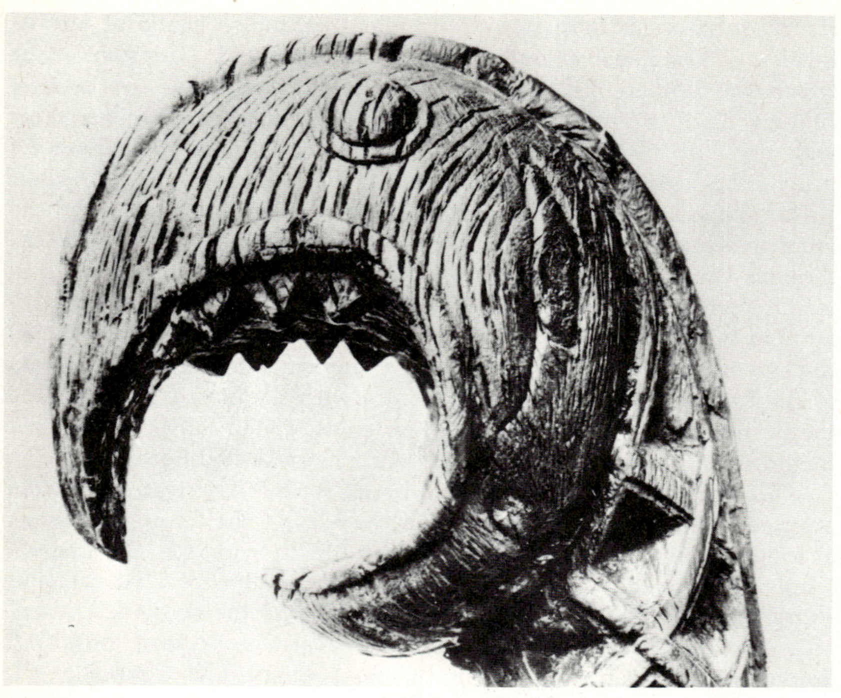

▪ *Head of a Viking ship, probably eighth century.* (*Granger*)

Perhaps there has always been a hazy line between raiding and trading, or maybe the sons of raiders are the ones who can afford to trade. Whatever the case, there is evidence for both continual piracy mixed with trading in Viking history and a gradually increasing emphasis on trade instead of raids. Piracy certainly continued throughout the Viking age, but the raids of the tenth and eleventh century up the rivers of France, along the coast of Spain, and into the Mediterranean Sea often became trading missions. This was especially true when the Vikings established fairly permanent colonies, as in Normandy in northern France and on the island of Sicily in the Mediterranean. It's safer to pillage distant ports than to plunder a neighbor.

Viking expansion was not all piracy and business, even in Western Europe, as the examples of colonization indicate. But colonization was usually a secondary activity in populated Western Europe. It was the major type of Scandinavian expansion in the east along the long rivers of Russia and in the west beyond the edge of the world.

Russia is, of course, the land of the Rus. The Rus were the

Swedish colonists who began settling on the river trade routes between Scandinavia and the Byzantine capital at Constantinople in the ninth century. There the Swedes met some of the older inhabitants, Slavs (whose name reminds us that the Vikings took them as slaves) and Asians. The meetings must have often been violent, but eventually the Swedish towns at Novgorod and Kiev lost their Viking flavor and became the trading centers of the emerging Russian state. From these towns the Rus learned of the magnificence of the Byzantine Empire. The Rus were too weak to pose a serious threat to Constantinople, but Viking courage and military ability were famous enough for the Byzantine emperors to recruit these Rus for a special palace guard and as mercenaries in the Byzantine army. Meanwhile the Rus traded northern furs, honey, amber, wax, and captured slaves in exchange for the fine textiles, spices, wines, and luxuries of the Byzantine Empire at Constantinople and the Moslem Empire at Baghdad. According to a Moslem visitor, the Rus merchants would pray: "O Lord, I have come from distant parts with so many girls, so many sable furs. . . . Please send me a merchant who has many *dinars* and *dirhems*, and who will trade favorably with me without too much bartering."

While the Swedish Vikings turned piracy into colonization, and colonization into commercial activity in the vast eastern lands which were to be known as Russia, the Vikings of Norway explored the Atlantic Ocean. Since Viking society condoned piracy, its criminals and outcasts were not admitted to such a "respectable" calling. They were forced instead, like Erik the Red, to explore and settle in relatively unpopulated areas. Erik the Red had to leave Norway in a hurry "because of some killings" in the late 970s. He went to Iceland which Vikings had taken from Irish priests about a hundred years before. He got into trouble there also, and was outlawed around 980. With another Icelander he set sail westward, arriving finally at a bleak mountainous land which he called Greenland. He ran into more trouble on his return to Iceland so he was forced to make Greenland his permanent home. Soon a colonial settlement had been established on Eric's farm, a haven, probably, for the outcasts of "polite" Viking society.

Bjarni Herjolfsson discovered America about 985. Of course, Asians had arrived there by way of the Bering Sea over a thousand years before. It is also quite possible that the Irish priests who settled Iceland also "discovered" America before Bjarni. In any case, it was an accident (though less accidental than Columbus's later voyage). After a visit to Norway, Bjarni returned to his home in Iceland to find that his parents had left for Eric the Red's colony in Greenland. Bjarni set out to follow them. After a longer trip than expected, Bjarni and his crew finally saw land, but it lacked the mountains of Greenland.

Realizing they had gone too far, Bjarni and his crew did not land but sailed back until they found Greenland and Eric's colony. When they told the colonists of their discovery, Eric's sons Leif and Thorvald gathered a crew to explore the new land. They named part of it *Helluland,* and part of it they called *Vinland,* presumably because of its vine foliage. It's also reported that Thorvald lived there for two years until he was killed by the local inhabitants. The only certain Viking site that has been unearthed so far is at the northern tip of Newfoundland, but it is quite likely that further archeological exploration will yield other sites.

The important thing, of course, is that the colony did not last. That fact tells more about Viking society than the fact of discovery. Viking society was capable of vast oceanic explorations, but it possessed neither the will nor the capability of maintaining all of these far flung colonies for long. The Vikings did not even remain in Greenland. They stayed in Iceland because its climate and vegetation and animal life were much more inviting, and also because it was within relatively easy supply distance of Norway. They remained in Russia because their settlements were prosperous trading centers close to the junction of three thriving cultures: the Byzantine, the Moslem, and the European Christian. Perhaps Viking culture was always more attuned to raiding and trading than to isolated, peaceful settlement.

The causes of Viking failure, as well as success, lie in the character of its militaristic culture. It was a culture in which aggressiveness was channeled into long-distance trade and profit seeking or war. Its long-term success was in the revival of trade and the development of both feudal and capitalistic institutions in Europe. The warrior element in Viking society which was not "civilized" into economic aggression was defeated in battle. The usual closing date is 1066 since that was the year that Harald the Hard Ruler, king of Norway, was killed by the English. The death of King Harald is a fitting symbolic end to Viking ascendency. He represented Viking expansiveness at its zenith. As a boy he had fled from Norway to Kiev. To win back his father's Norwegian crown he prepared himself as a member, and then as the commander, of the Byzantine emperor's palace guard. He fought for the Greeks in Asia Minor, the Caucasus Mountains, and Jerusalem. He returned to Kiev as a seasoned victor, married a Russian princess, and lived to rule Norway, explore the Atlantic, and reconquer England. This "Thunderbolt of the North," an ultimate Viking ruler, was defeated, almost by chance, by Earl Harold Godwinson on September 25, 1066. The Vikings lost England, and gradually thereafter much more of their overseas empire.

The death of a universal Viking king like Harald was the proper symbol for the end of the Viking age. Except for the fortuitousness of his actual defeat, the event had all of the drama of final tragedy—almost the final Twilight of the Gods imagined in Viking legend. But despite the hopes of heroic culture, the death of a single individual never means the end of an age. Actually, Godwinson was killed a few days later by William of Normandy, a descendant of the Vikings who had conquered northern France. In a sense, 1066 marks the final victory, rather than defeat, of Viking culture. At the same time, Scandinavia became disorganized, European armies became better able to cope with pirate raids, and within a couple of hundred years new military techniques and gunpowder made Viking military tactics obsolete.

As a military culture, the Vikings were doomed to fail when their victims learned how to defend themselves. The weakness of Viking culture was that it remained largely militaristic. Only those elements of the raid which could be channeled into trade survived. Much of Viking beliefs and behavior could not. The trading outposts in Normandy, France, made it possible for Vikings sons to conquer England and parts of Italy. By the twelfth century they were engaged in a phase of European expansion called the Crusades.

## Praying and Preying: The Crusades

Western aggressiveness has been culturally acceptable too long to disappear. The development of Western civilization has tempered some of the more extreme forms of barbarian and feudal aggressiveness, but our civilization has been more concerned with the redirection of our aggression into socially useful kinds of activity. In place of war (when possible) we have become occupied in trading, exploring, and competing. Economic competition, the exploitation or conquest of nature, and even sports have fulfilled the old cultural needs for "manliness," power, combat, and being "number one." As raiders have become traders our culture has become less militaristic, but our economic and social life has become unusually aggressive and competitive.

We have also made war "respectable" by giving it high moral purpose. We have become sufficiently "civilized" against war that we need to justify our military actions in terms of high ideals. It is not good enough for us to admit a need for empire or slaves as it was for the Romans. No American senator could argue (as Cato did) that our economic supremacy required the destruction of a foreign city. We could not justify an invasion (as the early barbarians and later Vikings did) in terms of the booty it would bring. We must resort to more idealistic justifications for our wars. We must (even more than the

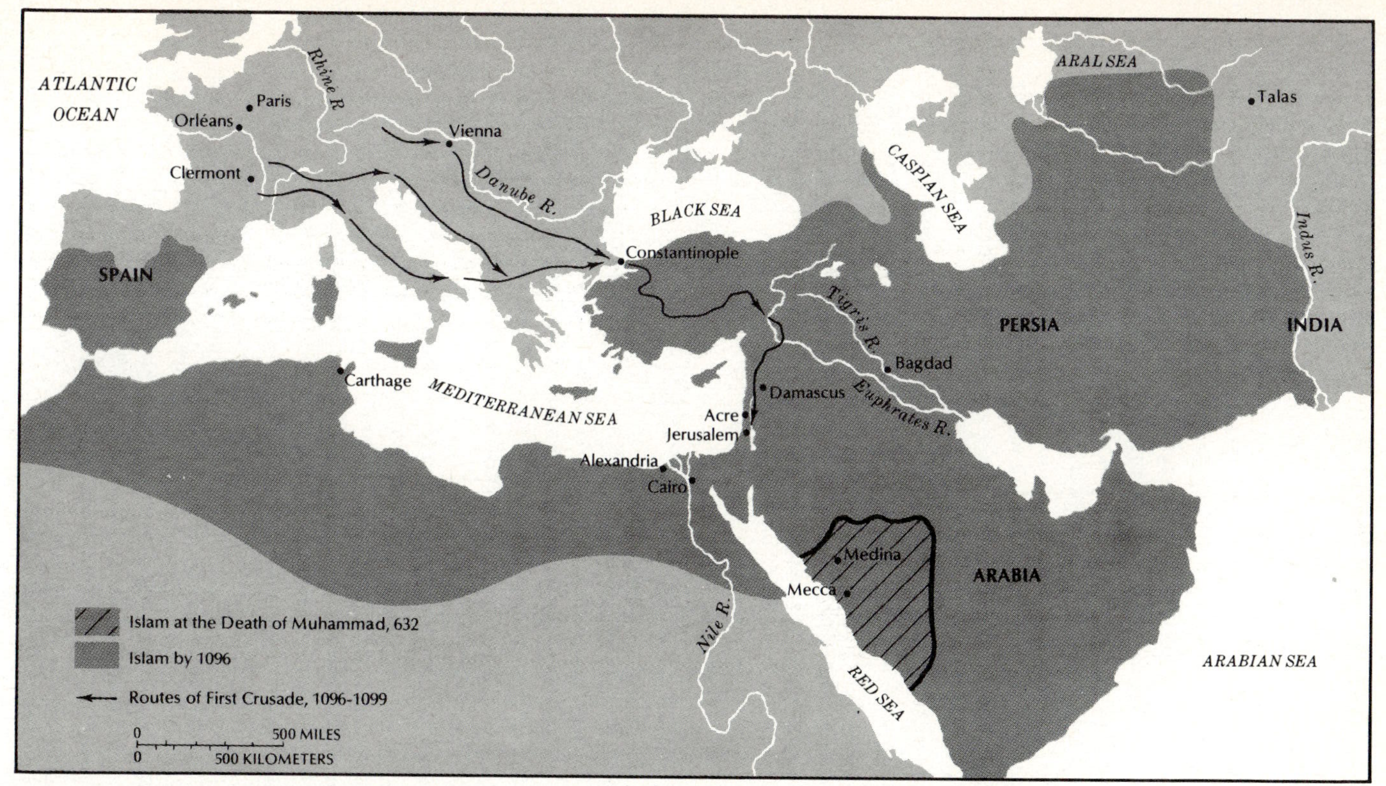


**The Expansion of Islam and the First Crusade**

*Islam spread rapidly throughout the Mediterranean in the century after Muhammad's death. Between 750 and 1096 its boundaries changed slightly. The First Crusade was a brief Christian victory. The later Crusades probably did more to undermine the Byzantine Empire than to arrest the expansion of Islam.*

Romans) find a way to call it defensive. We must convince ourselves that we are making sacrifices to save others. This requires the conviction that others are threatened by a grave, ungodly, almost satanic power, and that we are the specially anointed champions of decency, virtue, and goodness. As the religious words in the preceding sentence suggest, we have learned to make our wars holy by becoming Christian soldiers. Barbarian-feudal ideas of war have come down to us through the intervention of the Christian church. At times, we have seen that the effect of Christian intervention was to pacify, not to inflame, the population. Many of the more violent barbarian customs were softened by the intercession of the church. But the church's insistence that we be moral can cut like a double edged sword. Moral is what you call it. Moreover, the conviction that we are the most moral or most righteous can brew a heady, intoxicating intolerance.

This ability to justify our most barbarous actions in the name of God, or of Christian civilization, or of the secular version we call the "Free World," was learned long before the Crusades. The Hebrew Bible is full of atrocities which the "chosen people" insisted were committed in the name of God: the Egyptians as well as blasphemous tribes were rarely spared the vengeance of the "jealous God." The Christians continued to believe in such a vengeful God. At the end of the fourth century in Rome, many Christians echoed the call of Ambrose to defend their "country" against the inhuman barbarians who were (in the phrase of another bishop) nothing better than "cursed dogs." But European war and European culture did not become fully Christian until after the barbarian invasions. Even Charlemagne's alliance with the papacy was only a start. The church did not become strong enough to direct the actions of princes or mold the morals of the people until the eleventh or twelfth centuries—when feudalism was fully developed. The Crusades, in this perspective, were the successful attempt of the church to take over and use the feudal structure and armies for its own purposes. Documents from the eleventh century in the West reveal a sharp increase in the number of prayers for victory. In the same century we see the first records of sword blessing. Progressively, the knight was expected to live according to the religious standards of the church. Paul's phrase "fighting for Christ" (by which he had meant, and the Byzantine church still meant, a spiritual fight with "the weapons of Christ"—or no weapons at all) had become identified in the West with the service of the knights.

The first Crusade began, ironically enough, after a series of attempts by the pope and his councils to institute a "Truce of God" over rival feudal barons and their armies. Pope Urban II included in his list of reasons for a Crusade the hope that Christian knights would "fight righteous wars instead of iniquitous combats" among fellow Christians. Urban detailed other reasons for a holy war in his speech to the Council of Clermont on November 27, 1095: the Byzantine emperor had asked for help against the Moslem Turks; the Turks not only threatened Constantinople but also occupied Jerusalem and the Holy Land; a Christian conquest of the Moslems might restore Christian rule of Jerusalem and possibly even reunite the Eastern and Roman churches, separate since 1054.

It may have been true that the Byzantine emperor Alexius asked the pope for assistance against the Moslem Turks. But if he made such a request, he was clearly thinking of the usefulness of an aristocratic army of knights. The knights (especially the Norman and Frankish second sons who would not inherit the family lands) formed fairly disciplined armies. They hoped to do holy work at the same time that they might win their fortunes from Moslem infidels (or even Byzantine heretics).

Pope Urban's call struck a responsive chord at the other extreme of the scale of European society as well. As the pope's message was popularized by wandering, barefoot preachers like Peter the Hermit, hordes of poor people hurried out of overcrowded areas to make their lives meaningful in holy war. Untrained and undisciplined "people's crusades" joined the armies of knights in the march across Europe to Constantinople. Before they left to exterminate "the sons of whores, the race of Cain," as they called the Moslems, the vagabond armies seized their own European towns for Christ. The Crusades began with the first large-scale massacre of Jews. "We have set out to march a long way to fight the enemies of the East," one of the Crusaders de-
They must be dealt with first." In France, along the Rhine River
clared, "and behold, before our very eyes are his worst foes, the Jews.
(where Jewish communities had gathered for centuries under the protection of Christian bishops), the mobs demanded the conversion or extermination of the Jews. In May and June of 1096 alone, between four and eight thousand Jews were massacred.

The massacre of Jews was only practice for the real business at hand. The vagabond armies that survived the long walk to Constantinople horrified the Byzantine emperor and the inhabitants of the ancient city. They had no plan or organization, and they could just as readily sack Constantinople as Jerusalem. With a little luck and a good deal of diplomatic skill, the Byzantine ruling class managed to redirect the armies of the dispossessed toward Jerusalem. Since the Moslems were disorganized and did not expect an attack as ferocious and determined as had been executed, the Crusaders were able to take the ancient city where Jesus had lived and died. The city was captured in 1099.

The fall of Jerusalem was followed by a holocaust; except for the governor and his bodyguard, who managed to buy their lives and were escorted from the city, every Moslem—man, woman and child—was killed. In and around the Temple of Solomon "the horses waded in blood up to their knees, nay up to the bridle. It was a just and wonderful judgement of God that the same place should receive the blood of those whose blasphemies it had so long carried up to God." As for the Jews of Jerusalem, when they took refuge in their chief synagogue the building was set fire and they were all burnt alive. Weeping with joy and singing songs of praise the crusaders marched in procession to the Church of the Holy Sepulchre. "O new day, new day and exultation, new and everlasting gladness. . . . That day, famed through all centuries to come, turned all our suffering and hardships into joy and exultation; that day, the confirmation of Christianity, the annihilation of paganism, the renewal of our faith!"[3]

European sources estimate that about ten thousand Moslems were massacred in the wake of that first capture of Jerusalem. Moslem sources put the figure at a hundred thousand killed. Whatever the numbers, the blood bath taught the Moslems (and the Byzantines) to hate the West as they never had before. "The west stands for war and exploitation," a Byzantine diplomat concluded. "West Rome . . . is the mother of all wickedness." The Moslems mourned their losses at the hands of these "Christian dogs," and vowed to fight fire with fire. The Arab poet, Mosaffer Allah Werdis, poignantly expressed the pain and bitterness of the Moslems:

We have mingled our blood and our tears.
None of us remains who has strength enough to beat
off these oppressors.
The sight of our weapons only brings sorrow to us
who must weep while the swords of war spark off
the all-consuming flames.
Ah, sons of Muhammad, what battles still await you,
how many heroic heads must lie under the horses'
feet!
Yet all your longing is only for an old age lapped in
safety and well-being, for a sweet smiling life, like
the flowers of the field.
Oh that so much blood had to flow, that so many women were
left with nothing save their bare hands to protect
their modesty!
Amid the fearful clashing swords and lances, the faces of
the children grow white with horror.[4]

Moslems had not always thought of war with remorse. Their ideal had not always been the poet's vision of the "sweet smiling life, like the flowers of the field." Soon after the death of the founding prophet Muhammad in 632, Moslem armies of Arabian horsemen had conquered the "infidel" in Arabia (632), Syria (635), Jerusalem (637), Egypt (640), and both the ancient kingdom of Persia to their east and the North African tribes to their west by 650. By 750 the "sons of Muhammad" had expanded their religion to the borders of India and what later became southern Russia, and conquered all of Africa north of the Sahara, and the Iberian peninsula of current Spain and Portugal.

The sudden, often violent expansion of Moslem religion (which is called Islam, meaning "submission" to Allah) has sometimes been compared to the invasions of northern European and Asian horsemen in the same period. To the cultured Greeks of the Byzantine Empire there was little difference. Even the Franks and other European kingdoms which were only themselves emerging from barbarism viewed the expansion of Moslem nomads as a threat to civilized life itself.

By the end of the eleventh century, however, Islamic society was more stable and civilized than Europe. It produced philosophers, mathematicians, astronomers, doctors, and artists with the same urgency that Western Europe produced soldiers. The desert horsemen had brought an agricultural technology to Spain that made the land blossom more luxuriously than ever before, more (perhaps) than today. The descendants of horsemen became doctors that staffed the first faculties of European medical schools. Their philosophers taught the West Plato and Aristotle. Their merchants and mariners taught Europeans mathematics, bookkeeping, and maritime travel. In short, the Moslem civilization that was destroyed by the Crusaders at Jerusalem was considerably more sophisticated and peaceful than that of its conquerors.

There was still a tradition of holy war in Moslem culture. They called such wars against the pagans "jihads," which meant roughly the same thing as "crusade." Like the Christians, many Moslems believed that warriors who died fighting the heathen would go straight to paradise. Moslems, after all, believed in the same vengeful, jealous God as the Jews and Christians. But because Muhammad considered himself the last in a long line of Jewish and Christian prophets—such as Abraham, Moses, and Jesus—Moslem rulers were extremely tolerant of these other "people of the Book [the Bible]." The Moslems believed that the Jews (who did not recognize the prophecy of Jesus) and the Christians (who blamed the crucifixion on Jews) worshiped the same God (or Allah) as themselves. The important test for the Moslems was that a subject people worshiped the God of the prophets, not whether they believed in the humanity or divinity of a particular prophet like Jesus or Muhammad.

The Christian Franks who ruled Jerusalem from 1099 to 1185 must have realized that the Moslems were much more tolerant than themselves. They were aware that Christians had for centuries held high positions in the Moslem courts of the Middle East. They found Syrian Christians who were physicians, astronomers, and officials of Moslem princes. They told stories of Moslem generosity, even in battle. One Christian, Oliverus Scholasticus, told of Sultan al-Malik-al-Kamil who defeated one of the later invading armies of Crusaders and then gave the survivors food: "Who could doubt that such goodness, friendship and charity came from God? Men whose parents, sons and daughters, brothers and sisters had died in agony at our hands, whose lands we took, whom we drove naked from their homes, revived us with their own food when we were dying of hunger, and showered us with kindness even while we were in their power." Some Christians, like Arnold of Lubeck, even understood that the Moslem idea of brotherhood was more tolerant than the Christian view of Jews and Moslems as anti-Christs. Arnold put the following words in the mouth of a Moslem: "It is certain, even if our beliefs are different, that we have the same Creator and Father, and that we must then be brothers, not according to our faith but as men. Let us then remember our common Father and feed our brothers."

As tolerant as the Moslems had been, however, they could not be expected to lie back after the Christian massacre of Jerusalem. They had been disorganized at the time of the Christian conquest, but they were able to recapture Jerusalem by 1187, under the leadership of the Syrian sultan Saladin who had unified Syria and Egypt. Although the Christians had launched a second Crusade from 1147 to 1149 (which began with another massacre of European Jews), Saladin treated the descendants of the first Crusaders in Jerusalem with remarkable charity. Those who could afford to buy their freedom were allowed to do so. The poor were freed without payment. Later, Saladin actually bequeathed his wealth to Moslem, Jewish, and Christian poor alike.

Europe's answer was a third Crusade. This time the pope induced three of Christendom's greatest kings to lead armies against the Moslems: Frederick Barbarossa, Holy Roman emperor; Philip Augustus of France; and Richard I (the Lion Hearted) of England. They brought their personal quarrels and national conflicts with them. Only Richard (who relished war) actually made it to the Holy Land to confront Saladin. He captured Acre (just north of Jerusalem) and established a Christian outpost that was to last another hundred years (1189–1291), but he was unable to take Jerusalem. Negotiations with Saladin dragged on too long for Richard's spirited temper. To show his determination he ordered the massacre of two to three thousand of his Moslem prisoners. Then he had their bodies cut open and searched

for gold, which some had swallowed. Last, but not least, he had their bodies burned so that the ashes could be sifted for any gold that might have been missed. Such atrocities soured Moslem toleration for some time.

If Moslems needed the third Crusade to learn the character of Western civilization, the Byzantine Greeks may have needed the fourth. Pope Innocent III asked the kings of Europe in 1202 to capture Jerusalem for the last time. However, Philip Augustus and John of

■ *This thirteenth-century battle scene shows mounted knights, possibly Crusaders, in combat. (University Library, Cambridge)*

England (Richard had been kidnapped for ransom in Germany) were too busy fighting each other. Lesser lords pleaded poverty, but Innocent prevailed upon them, and the city of Venice offered transportation for a percentage of the take. Once the Crusaders had set sail, the Venetian merchants and businessmen were in control. The Doge (or leader) of the city convinced the Crusaders to make a stop at Zara (which he declared had been taken from Venice by the Hungarian king). The Crusaders proceeded to loot, sack, and destroy this perfectly good Christian city. Innocent was horrified. He excommunicated the whole army, then reconsidered. Finally, he lifted the ban so that they could continue on to Jerusalem.

Tempted by a claimant to the Byzantine throne who offered the Crusaders enough to pay the Venetians if their armies would help him take Constantinople, they stopped again. Resistance was minimal, and the Crusaders were successful. But the pretender was slow in paying, or the Venetians cornered most of it. The enraged armies then conquered Constantinople for themselves. The city which had withstood the invasions of barbarians, Hungarians, and Turks fell in 1204 (almost a thousand years after the collapse of Rome) to a motley army of Westerners. The wars for Christ ended in the destruction of the greatest Christian city in the world. Shrines and churches were looted. Priceless art objects were melted down for metal. Altars were broken up and carried away. Mosaics were destroyed for their jewels. Manuscripts of the church and the ancient world were lost forever.

The destruction of Constantinople put an end to the Crusade for the Holy Land. The armies never left for Jerusalem. The crusading spirit, though, became a way of life. Pope Innocent, himself, sought to organize another crusade in 1215. But, for the most part the crusades turned inward. They were launched against the elaborate Moslem civilization in Spain, against Roman Christian heretics in southern France, against foreign nationalities, and (as always) against the Jews. By the end of the thirteenth century, the crusade had a lot to do with national glory, profit, and extermination, and very little to do with prayer. The goals of Christianity had no doubt been perverted, but the shift from praying to preying had been natural and lasting.

## War and Violence: Then and Now

A number of things are implied or suggested in the preceding history which should probably be said directly. The process by which the Christian holy wars became brutal adventures in conquest, looting, and extermination must not be taken out of context. These events occurred nearly a thousand years ago. But such wars were one of the inherent possibilities of the Judeo-Christian culture which arrogantly asserted its belief in a God and prophet that all the world should recognize. Crusades would have been unthinkable in one of the many cultures of the world that believed its god or prophet to be only one of many. Intolerance was an especially strong trait of Western culture. Not all Judeo-Christian societies necessarily waged holy war. Most

Jews and Moslems, and many Christians, have remained relatively free of such arrogance. But the seed germinated more fruitfully in the Judeo-Christian-Islamic tradition than elsewhere. In the thirteenth century, for instance, Western visitors to the Mongol Empire of the Khans were astounded to find European Christians who made no secret of the fact that they had fled Christendom to avoid persecution. Though Genghis Khan was a Taoist, his empire tolerated Buddhists, Confucianists, Moslems, Manichees, Jews, Nestorians, and Christians. Any and all of these enjoyed greater religious freedom in the Mongol Empire than they would in the West.

Consequently, the Crusades were not merely events of the eleventh to fourteenth centuries. The seeds were planted much earlier, and they have germinated since. The past always offers us models for the present, and one of the strong traditions of our own Western Christian past is the holy war. We like to see our wars as sacred ventures. Furthermore, the history of the Crusades should show us that we are capable of justifying almost any degree of brutality or venality if we can sanctify it as part of God's will. In war, as in love, our words may have nothing to do with our actions.

There is no reason to believe that any group of people is biologically more aggressive, warlike, or violent than any other. The distribution of genes is roughly the same in any human population. But the culture (the beliefs, religions, and practices) of a particular society may enhance or repress human aggressiveness, and the culture always channels aggression in particular ways. In our Western society we are used to directing our aggressiveness in religious and commercial channels. We can move easily from praying to preying, or from raiding to trading. In that sense our discussion of the Crusades and the Vikings offers us a view of one of the tendencies of our culture.

The point of the earlier parts of the chapter is a bit different. We can see some of our roots in medieval feudalism. At least our high regard for military prowess, bravery, and "knightly" virtues can be traced back to it. Fortunately, we have even less in common with our barbarian ancestors than with the "flower of European knighthood."

We began with an inquiry into modern American war and violence. We have examined some "warrior societies" to shed light on the origins of our own attitudes toward war and violence and to seek comparisons between our own situation and that of others. In general, whether we looked for origins or comparisons we were looking for similarities. That can be very helpful. Similarities can be very instructive. But so can differences.

In a chapter on war and violence it might be especially soothing as well as useful to conclude with a look at the vast differences between past barbarism and modern civility. Let us return to the Europe of the fourteenth and fifteenth centuries—the end of the period we have just examined. Our examples come from *The Waning of the Middle Ages* by Johan Huizinga.

> The citizens of Mons bought a [bandit], at too high a price, for the pleasure of seeing him quartered. [The people gathered around the spot for the execution with all of the gaiety of a fair. The death was superb.] "The people rejoiced more than if a new holy body had risen from the dead."
>
> . . .
>
> The people of Bruges, in 1488, . . . cannot get their fill of seeing the tortures inflicted, on a high platform in the middle of the market-place, on the magistrates suspected of treason. The unfortunates are refused the deathblow which they implore, that the people may feast again upon their torments.
>
> . . .
>
> In 1427 a noble [bandit] is hanged in Paris. "At the moment when he is going to be executed, the great treasurer of the regent appears on the scene and vents his hatred against him; he prevents his confession, in spite of his prayers; he climbs the ladder behind him, shouting insults, beats him with a stick, and gives the hangman a thrashing for exhorting the victim to think of his salvation. The hangman grows nervous and bungles his work; the cord snaps, the wretched criminal falls on the ground, breaks a leg and some ribs, and in this condition has to climb the ladder again."[5]
>
> . . .
>
> At Brussels a young incendiary and murderer is placed in the center of a circle of burning fagots and straw, and made fast to a stake by means of a chain running round an iron ring. He addresses touching words to the spectators, "and he so softened their hearts that every one burst into tears and his death was commended as the finest that was ever seen."[6]

Not very long ago people went to an execution the way we go to the movies. And they were more involved in the torture than we are in the movie. Until very recently people lived intimately with death. The horrible, macabre, and violent were very familiar. The favorite meeting place of Parisians in the fifteenth century, Huizinga points out, was the churchyard cemetery of the Church of the Innocents.

> Nowhere else were all the images tending to evoke the horror of death assembled so strikingly as in the churchyard of the Innocents at Paris. There the medieval soul, fond of a religious shudder, could take its fill of the horrible. . . . The cemetery was preferred to every other place of burial. . . . The poor and the rich were interred without distinction. They did not rest there long, for the cemetery was used so much,

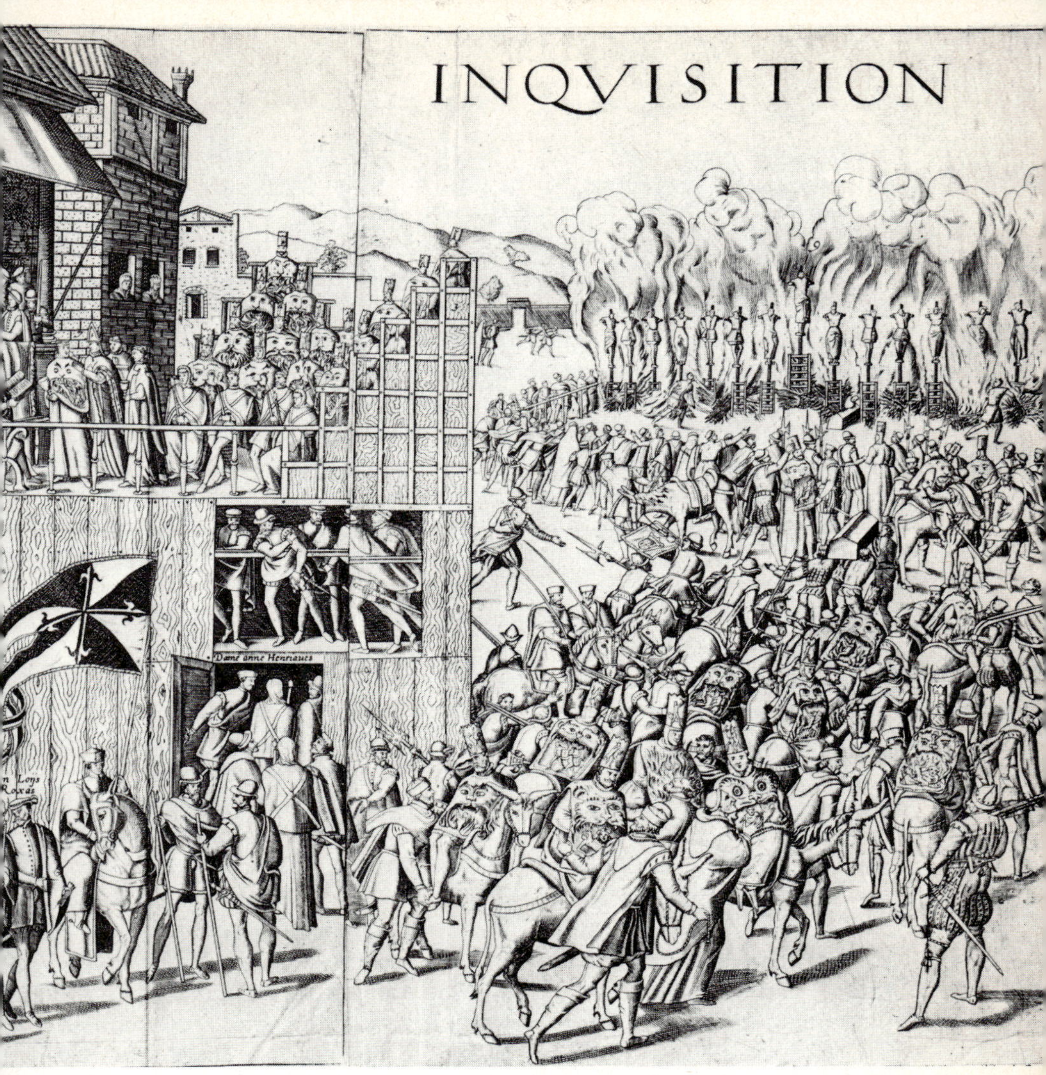


■ *The specter of violence in the fifteenth century. This depiction of the Spanish Inquisition, 1478–1480, shows Jews and heretics being burned to death.* (*Giraudon*)

twenty parishes having the right of burial there, that it was necessary, in order to make room, to dig up the bones and sell the tombstones after a very short time. . . . Skulls and bones were heaped up in charnel-houses along the cloisters enclosing the ground on three sides, and lay there open to the eye by thousands, preaching to all the lesson of equality. . . .

Day after day, crowds of people walked under the cloisters, looking at the figures and reading the simple verses, which reminded them of the approaching end. In spite of the incessant burials and exhuma-

> tions going on there, it was a public lounge and a rendezvous. Shops were established before the charnel-houses and prostitutes strolled under the cloisters. . . . Even feasts were given there.[7]

We are no longer so accustomed to death that we would choose a busy cemetery, piled with decomposing bodies and bones, as a place to stroll, shop, eat, or hang out. Even modern hospitals hide the dying from our view, as if to protect us from the thought of death.

Our uneasiness with death may be a good sign. As we have lost familiarity with death, we have probably become less able to stomach violence, war, and brutality. In traditional society (like medieval Europe) death was too much a fact of everyday life to be ignored. When, as in 1348, a plague could wipe out a third to two-thirds of the population of European cities, life was too obviously cheap. In England almost half of the sons of dukes who were born between 1330 and 1480 died violent deaths. The average life expectancy of the other "more fortunate" half was 31 years.

Some parts of modern civilized society have been able to go quite far in abolishing the specter of violent death. When a London constable shot and killed a bank robber in the last week of 1972 all of England was aghast. Scotland Yard insisted that the event was highly unusual. The only reason that the constable happened to have a gun when he came upon the robbery was because he was on his way to guard the Jordanian embassy. "I think we have to go back to 1909," the Yard spokesman declared, "to find a chap killed by a policeman and that wasn't a bank raid." The London police federation issued a statement saying that "a majority of our police would probably resign rather than carry guns regularly." One London newspaper, *The Evening Standard*, printed an interview with a criminal who asserted that the only reason a robber would carry a gun was "to bang into the ceiling so people will scatter." But, he added, "you see a copper with a gun, you're going to shoot him." "We don't want any of the American business, do we?" he asked. "We don't want any of this 'Stop, it's the law, we'll shoot!' stuff. That's the real danger. Some bloke running down an alley, they shout twice, he's dead. Maybe he's got a hot radio on him. Maybe he's nicked 20 quid. But is a life worth 20 quid?"

When the police have to apologize for killing an armed robber, when a criminal who carries a gun can explain in a public forum why the police should be unarmed, when the public is outraged by the death of one person—even a bank robber—then human life has become sacred. In modern England the respect for life, the absence of domestic violence, and the refusal to engage in war are all related. The "American business" and (for that matter) the violence of the Irish hardship society appear to the average Londoner to be throwbacks to a barbarian past.

Modern America is, however, another example of the future. Like England, the United States has created the technology that makes life worth living. But unlike England, the United States has not minimized war or violence. We have eliminated the enthusiasm for barbarity that sometimes characterized traditional society. We have overcome much of the personal violence of the feud or vendetta that racked traditional society. But we have substituted impersonal for personal violence, and our technology—the handgun or bomb—permit us to do at a distance what most of us would be incapable of doing with our hands. We have not always used our technology to better human life. We have denied the peaceful fruits of our technology to many in our own society. We have bemoaned the rise in domestic violence at the same time that we have tolerated or urged the poverty, inequality, injustice, war, armaments, and capital punishment that belie our preachings about the sanctity of human life. Our cultural heritage enables us to disclaim responsibility for violence at the same time that we reward the military heroes of holy wars and the entrepreneurs who "make a killing." We have created a technology that can end the society of hardship and violent death almost at whim. But we are still part frontier people, and part Roman, part Viking, and part Crusader.

## *For Further Reading*

On barbarian Europe, one of the better, brief introductions is J. M. Wallace-Hadrill's **The Barbarian West.*** His more recent **The Long-Haired Kings** is also valuable. The classical studies (written about 50 years ago) are J. B. Bury's **The Invasion of Europe by the Barbarians,*** Samuel Dill's **Roman Society in the Last Century of the Western Empire,*** and Ferdinand Lot's **The End of the Ancient World and the Beginning of the Middle Ages.*** All are still worth reading. One of the more interesting recent studies is P. R. L. Brown's **The End of Antiquity. The Dark Ages,** edited by D. Talbot Rice, brings together excellent articles. For first-hand accounts of the barbarians, the student can also take advantage of two excellent primary sources: Tacitus's **On Britain and Germany*** and Gregory of Tours's **History of the Franks.***

On the Vikings, there is a well-illustrated introduction in David Wilson's **The Vikings and Their Origins: Scandinavia in the First Millennium*** and a very good history of their culture from 800 to 1100 in Johannes Brondsted's **The Vikings.*** Other useful recent titles are P. G. Foote and D. M. Wilson's **The Viking Achievement,** G. Jones's **A History of the Vikings,** and P. Sawyer's **The Age of the Vikings.**

* Available in paperback.

On the Crusades, various interpretations are brought together in J. A. Brundage's **The Crusades: Motives and Achievements.*** Eyewitness accounts are available in F. T. Marzialis's **Memoirs of the Crusades.*** Arab versions are presented in **Arab Historians of the Crusades,** edited by Francesco Gabrieli. The standard multivolume histories are K. M. Setton's **History of the Crusades** and the older work by Steven Runciman, **A History of the Crusades.** R. A. Newhall's **The Crusades** is a brief, introductory account. The warfare of the period is described in R. C. Smail's **Crusading Warfare, 1097–1193.** Finally, Norman Cohn's superb **The Pursuit of the Millennium*** puts the Crusades into a broader perspective of medieval religious hysteria and relates their popular psychological dimension to modern totalitarianism.

Excellent studies of Muhammad can be found in W. Montgomery Watt's **Muhammad, Prophet and Statesman,** and Maxime Rodinson's **Mohammed.*** For more general studies of Islam, there is Montgomery Watt's **The Majesty That Was Islam** and B. Lewis's **The Arabs in History.***

For general histories of medieval Europe, perhaps the best place to start is with Henri Pirenne's **A History of Europe,** vol. 1,* a book written without the aid of libraries by the French scholar while in a German prison camp during World War I. Another classic French study is Marc Bloch's **Feudal Society.*** One of the more interesting of the modern approaches is Robert Lopez's **The Birth of Europe.*** Norman Cantor's **Medieval History** is also strongly interpretive, and particularly useful on the medieval Church. Among other histories, C. Warren Hollister's **Medieval Europe: A Short History,*** Denys Hay's short **The Medieval Centuries,*** and Joseph R. Strayer's **Western Europe in the Middle Ages*** are fairly easy. Christopher Dawson's **The Making of Europe*** and **Early Medieval Society,*** edited by Sylvia L. Thrupp, are more sophisticated. Hugh Trevor-Roper's **The Rise of Christian Europe*** and Jacques Boussard's **The Civilization of Charlemagne*** are particularly well illustrated.

A few other books are especially valuable for judging the tenor of violence in medieval Europe. T. S. R. Boase's well-illustrated **Death in the Middle Ages*** is rich and disturbing. J. Huizinga's classic **The Waning of the Middle Ages*** is indispensable. Lynn White, Jr.'s **Medieval Technology and Social Change*** is a classic account of the relationship of medieval technology and the warrior society of chivalry. For the richness of contemporary detail there is none better than John Froissart's **The Chronicles of England, France and Spain*** which was completed in 1400.

For comparisons with the world outside of Europe, there are a few good introductions. H. Paul Varley's **Samurai*** introduces the medieval "knights" of Japan. Stuart Legg's **The Heartland,*** Michael Prawdin's **The Mongol Empire,*** and R. Grousset's **The Empire of the Steppes: A History of Central Asia** introduce the Eurasian home of most of the barbarian tribal movements that periodically threatened Europe and Asia.

Finally, a few special studies of societies outside of our time period deserve mention. Erich Hobsbawm's **Bandits*** and **Primitive Rebels*** are superb investigations into the culture of violence in traditional societies, and the report of the National Commission on the Causes and Prevention of Violence, **Violence in America,*** by Hugh Davis Graham and Ted Robert Gurr, is full of good articles on the history of violence in the United States.

## Notes

1. Adapted and translated from Jacques Le Goff's *La Civilisation de L'Occident Medieval* (Paris: Arthaud, 1964), pp. 31–32.
2. Salvien, adapted and translated from Jacques Le Goff, *Civilisation,* p. 36.
3. Norman Cohn, *The Pursuit of the Millenium* (New York: Harper & Row, 1961), pp. 48–49.
4. Friedrich Heer, *The Medieval World* (New York: New American Library, 1961), pp. 135–136.
5. J. Huizinga, *The Waning of the Middle Ages* (New York: St. Martin's Press, 1967), pp. 15–16.
6. *Ibid.*, p. 3.
7. *Ibid.*, pp. 133–134.

# Chapter 11

# Citizen and Subject

## Asian and Western Cities

What is happening to the modern American city? Optimists speak of an urban revival through "gentrification" by which they mean that the wealthy are moving back into the inner city. Pessimists call attention to the abandoned slums, the spiraling costs of welfare and city services, and the near bankruptcies of such large cities as New York and Cleveland in the last decade.

Both are right. The American city is becoming a haven for the very wealthy and a prison for the very poor. The middle class cannot afford to remain. The rich buy apartments that cost more than the poor will earn in a lifetime. Inflation, unemployment, and the withdrawal of the middle class are creating cities divided between the very wealthy and the very poor. The city is no longer a community of equals.

Was it ever? Max Weber, the great German sociologist, pointed out that the European city originated as a community of equals almost a thousand years ago. In fact, Weber argued, ancient and non-Western urban areas should not even be considered "cities" because they did not develop their own community institutions. The whole complex of democratic institutions and ideas that stem from the root word "city"—citizenship, civil, civic, civilian, civility, and civilization—was, according to Weber, the unique invention of the Western communal city of equals. Because the Western city developed as a community, its inhabitants thought of themselves as "citizens." Elsewhere urban inhabitants remained "subjects."

New York City averted bankruptcy when the elected mayor and City Council turned over control of finances to unelected representatives of the banks and securities holders. The mayor of Cleveland chose default instead of corporate ownership of municipal property. When cities are divided between rich and poor, and the poor are (as always) the majority, can democratic institutions weather crises? Are we becoming subjects instead of citizens? Is that what the loss of community means? In this chapter we will examine the history of cities in the light of some of these questions prompted by Max Weber's analysis.

## The Chinese City: Subjects Not Citizens

In the East, especially in China, there was an enormous gap between the city and the village. The great French specialist on China, Marcel Granet, put it this way over 50 years ago:

> The sharpest distinction exists between city people and villagers: the one are *rustics,* the other nobles. The nobles of the city pride themselves on living according to the rites which do not descend to the common people. The country people, on the other hand, refuse to have anything to do with public affairs: It is the *meat-eaters'* business to discuss them they say. The two have neither the same interests, nor the same food. They differ to the point of following opposite systems of orientation: the nobles prefer the left and the peasants the right. The village has at most an Elder. The nobles are vassals of an overlord who is the Master of the Town. At his side they lead a life entirely taken up by court ceremonies. Grouped around the Master, they chant their contempt for the people of the field, the clownish people.[1]

In China the city was the administrative center of the new barbarian chieftain who had taken over the whole country. The city was the most visible realm of his mastery and his exploitation. Each new line of conquerors began his family dynasty by building a capital city and gathering there his nobles, scholars, and servants. No wonder the city always seemed foreign and parasitic to the villagers. The capital and the regional centers of administration all seemed the same to the peasant villagers. They were full of officials and those who served them, and all seemed to live gloriously by taxing the countryside.

We do not know very much about city life in the earliest Chinese dynasties. The earliest city yet uncovered, An-yang, was probably the capital of the Shang dynasty (1525–1028 B.C.). It has left some beautiful art in bronze and jade and some inscriptions in early Chinese writing, but little that tells us about city life. The next dynasty, the Chou, was the longest ruling family in Chinese history (until 256 B.C.). The Chou, though, ruled in name only. China was really divided among a number of feuding noble families. There was no monumental capital city, and most of the achievements of the Chou period have a rural character: iron smelting, the philosophies of Confucius and Mencius, and the nature worship of Taoism. The brief Ch'in dynasty (221–207 B.C.) united China into an empire, and the Han dynasty (202 B.C.–A.D. 220) created a government administration based on civil service exams that was the Rome of the Far East.

The Han were overrun by the same barbarian invasions that swept out of central Asia to destroy Rome, and Han city life, like that of Rome, almost disappeared. In China, however, the recovery came sooner. Under the Sui (589–618) and T'ang (618–907) a sophisticated urban culture developed that was equalled only (if at all) by the Eastern Empire capital, Constantinople. The capital of the Sui, and later of the T'ang, was Changan.

## The Chinese City: Changan

The emperor Wen Ti, founder of the Sui dynasty, chose the site for Changan very carefully. It was close enough to the imperial cities of the Han dynasty to remind people of past glories, but it was distant enough to be distinct. The city was built from scratch. Laid out in a rectangular grid plan with the streets running exactly north-south and east-west (see the map), it was the fitting center of the world for this Son of Heaven. At its fullest development under the T'ang in the eighth century the city contained about one million inhabitants inside the walls and another one million outside. Its life and its inhabitants were as varied as any city in the world. But everything—even the business of the poorest street sweeper or most foreign merchant—was directed toward the pleasure of the emperor and his court.

> No buildings in Changan were built from what we call "civic pride." Building and rebuilding were first of all at the initiative of the imperial

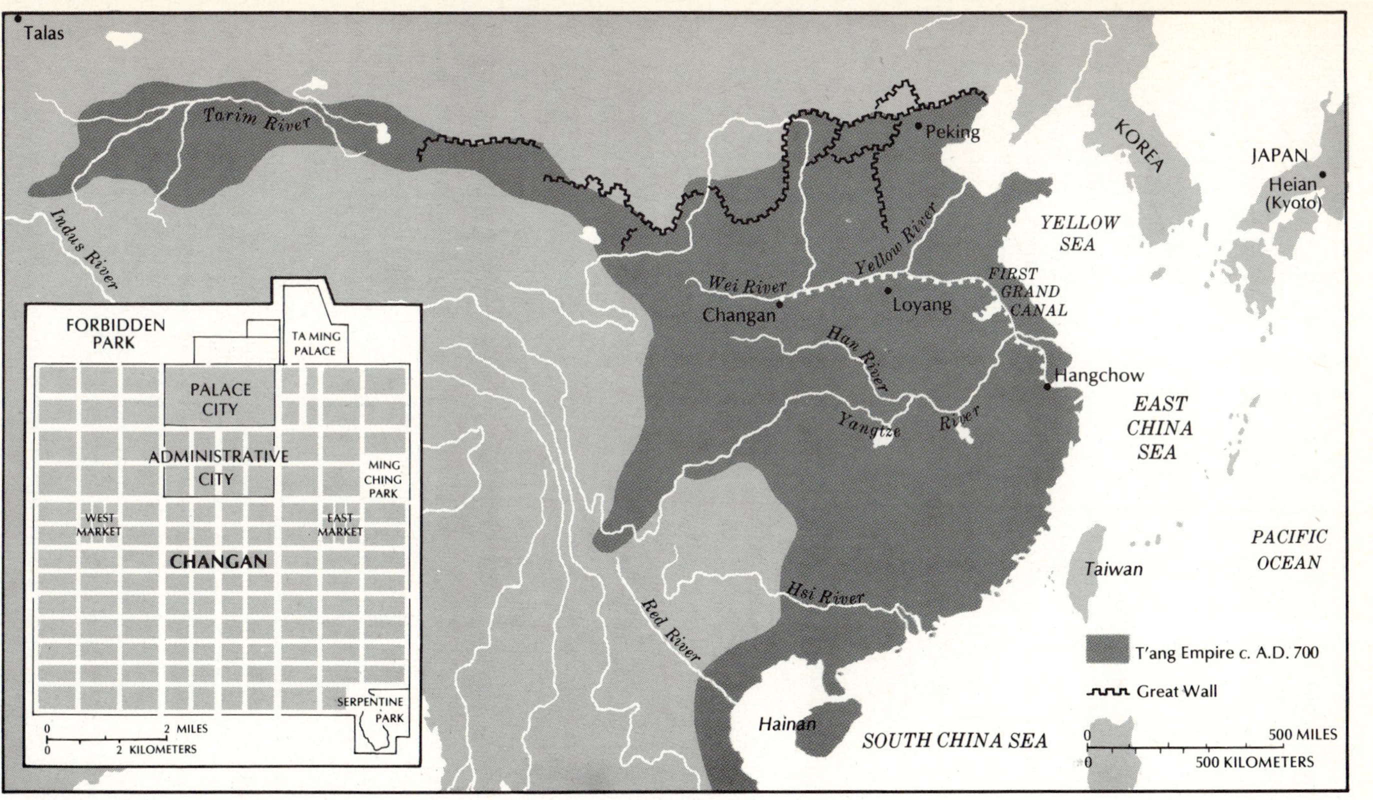


**T'ang China and Changan, A.D. 700**

*Changan was the imperial ideal of a city laid out to pay homage to the Son of Heaven. It was the capital of the vast T'ang dynasty. The map also shows the location of Heian, Japan, at present Kyoto.*

> family, which commanded the resources and could confiscate and relocate property at will. . . . Officials in their public role would frequently petition for funds to build or remodel a particular bureau or to dig a canal. But they argued for these projects in terms of improving the efficiency of imperial administration, not in terms of civic pride or "civic improvement." Although we read much of the parks and pleasances of the great, of their ball-fields and archery halls, there is no mention of any such facilities for the populace. Philanthropy expressed itself through the Buddhist temples with their charitable functions, but the "bread and circuses" of Rome and Constantinople are not to be found. Nor is there anything comparable to the forums, public baths and arcades built by the Roman emperors for the pleasure and convenience of the citizenry. The residents of the city were not "citizens" but the emperor's subjects. This is reflected in the layout of the city, in its administration and in its functioning. . . . There was neither mayor nor city council, and there was no charter. The city and its populace were controlled by the throne through officials of the imperial bureaucracy.[2]

Instead of neighborhoods, there were districts administered by an imperial appointee. Laws forbade the construction of housing facing the main avenues. The gates of each district were closed at sundown and no one was allowed out on the avenues until the drums were beaten in the morning. Any commoner who crossed the wall of a district or entered an official compound without authorization was to be punished with 70 lashes. The large east and west market areas were also strictly regulated: opened at noon, closed at sundown; activity, transactions, and prices checked and regulated.

The Chinese imperial city was to be treated, according to at least one edict at Changan, as the "Mansion of the Emperor." Not only the palaces and imperial offices and gardens, but the whole city was the emperor's preserve. Changan might have made even Rome look like a freewheeling city-state by comparison.

## The Chinese City: Hangchow

The Chinese of the next dynasty, the Sung (906–1279), looked back on T'ang times at Changan the way modern Americans look back at Puritan Boston. Life at the T'ang capital seemed rigid and sterile to the cosmopolitan sophisticates of the Sung dynasty. In many ways they were probably right. The Sung capital at Hangchow by 1275 was the largest and richest city in the world. It was lively, exciting, intellectual, luxurious, beautiful—and even corrupt.

Marco Polo visited Hangchow in 1275, the year before Kublai

■ *This Chinese painting of Hangchow as seen from the West Lake shows only a small part of the city, but it captures the accent on pleasure and the beauty of the tamed natural environment.* (Freer Gallery of Art)

Khan moved to incorporate the Sung capital into his expanding northern empire. The visitor from Venice wrote that Hangchow "is the greatest city which may be found in the world, where so many pleasures may be found that one fancies himself to be in Paradise."

Hangchow offered lowly officials, foreign merchants, and native working people a variety of recreational facilities and amusements which had been unavailable in more circumspect Changan. There were many specialized restaurants: some served everything ice cold, including fish and soups, some specialized in silkworm or shrimp pies and plum wine; even teahouses offered sumptuous decor, dancing girls, and musical lessons of all kinds. On the lake there were hundreds of boats, many of which could be rented, according to Marco Polo, "for parties of pleasure."

> These will hold ten, fifteen, twenty or more persons, and are from fifteen to twenty paces in length. . . . Anyone who desires to go a-pleasuring with the women or with a party of his own sex, hires one of these barges, which are always to be found completely furnished with tables and chairs and all other apparatus for a feast. The roof forms a level deck, on which the crew stand, and pole the boat along whithersoever may be desired, for the Lake is not more than two paces in depth. The inside of this roof and the rest of the interior is covered with ornamental painting in gay colours, with windows all round that can be shut or opened, so that the party at table can enjoy all the beauty and variety of the prospects on both sides as they pass along. And truly a trip on this Lake is a much more charming recreation than can be enjoyed on land. For on the one side lies the city in its entire length, so that the spectators in the barges, from the distance at which they stand, take in the whole prospect in its full beauty and grandeur, with its numberless palaces, temples, monasteries, and gardens, full of lofty trees, sloping to the shore. And the Lake is never without a number of such boats, laden with pleasure parties; for it is a great delight . . . to pass the afternoon in enjoyment with the ladies or their families, or perhaps with others less reputable, either in these barges or in driving about the city in carriages.[3]

Even the soldiers and poor had their "pleasure grounds"—almost two dozen in all. Each was a large fairground with markets, plays, musical groups, instrumental and dance lessons, ballet performances, jugglers, acrobats, storytellers, performing fish, archery displays and lessons, snake charmers, boxing matches, conjurers, chess players, magicians, imitators of street cries, imitators of village talk, and specialists in painting chrysanthemums, telling obscene stories, posing riddles, and flying kites. Gambling, drinking, and prostitution were also part of the scene here as elsewhere in the city.

Market areas were equally a source of entertainment and business. Marco Polo saw so much fish in a single market that he could not imagine it would ever be eaten, but it was all sold in a couple of hours. There were markets devoted to specialized goods and crafts that could hardly be found in the rest of China. Fortunately, one "guidebook" has survived which tells us where we can get the best rhinoceros skins, ivory combs, turbans, wicker cages, painted fans, philosophy books, or lotus-pink rice.

The invention of movable type in the tenth century (five hundred years ahead of Europe) may not have actually increased the number of books available because there were over seven thousand Chinese characters (compared to the European 26 letters) and hand printing had become a work of art that was appreciated in itself. Nevertheless, the resident of Hangchow could find books (hand or mechanically printed) on a fantastic variety of subjects: curious rocks, jades, coins,

■ *The* Diamond Sutra *(868) is the earliest known printed book. It is a Chinese translation of an Indian story of the Buddha. Each of the six "pages" of the scroll was printed with a separate wooden block. The tenth-century invention of moveable type permitted each Chinese character to be printed separately, but there were too many characters for moveable type to replace block printing. (Granger)*

bamboo, plum trees, special aspects of printing and painting, foreign lands, poetry, philosophy, Confucius, mushrooms, and encyclopedias on everything.

Marco Polo, of course, did not know Changan, but he tells a couple of stories that suggest that the imperial capital at Hangchow, for all of its luxury and variety, was not very different from the ancient capital of the T'ang.

> And again this king did another thing; that when he rides by any road in the city . . . and it happened that he found two beautiful great houses and between them might be a small one . . . then the king asks why that house is so small. . . . And one told him that that small house belongs to a poor man who has not the power to make it larger like the others. Then the king commands that the little house may be made as beautiful and as high as were those two others which were beside it, and he paid the cost. And if it happened that the little house belonged to a rich man, then he commanded him immediately to cause it to be taken away. And by his command there was not in his capital in the realms of . . . Hangchow any house which was not both beautiful and great, besides the great palaces and the great mansions of which there were great plenty about the city.

Hangchow like Changan was the emperor's city. And the emperor or his officials were aware of everything:

> There is another thing I must tell you. It is the custom for every burgess in this city, and in fact for every description of person in it, to write over his door his own name, the name of his wife, and those of his children, his slaves, and all the inmates of his house, and also of the number of animals that he keeps. And if anyone dies in the house then the name of that person is erased, and if any child is born its name is added. So in this way the sovereign is able to know exactly the population of the city.

Marco Polo's detailed observations are priceless, but he sometimes seems to have missed the meaning of what he saw. To those of us who are more attuned to the workings of a modern totalitarian state, the listings on each door are a clue to more than the emperor's desire for a population census. Further, the moderately well-off inhabitants were not burgesses, burghers, or bourgeoisie (citizens) in the European sense. That is precisely the point that Max Weber was trying to make. The inhabitants of the Chinese city were not citizens who participated in a common life. The city was not a community concern. The inhabitants of the checkerboard blocks which made up the territory called a city were legally subjects of the emperor. Legally, they were also members of their family and their family's native village in which the temple of their ancestors stood. That was how they perceived their identities. When they came into the city, they came as members of a family, clan, or village. In the city they became subjects as well. Rarely did they think of themselves as members of the city. The city was not their home or their "place," and they had no role in its administration.

## Cities of Castes, Tribes, and Religious Followers

Because the primary identity of the Chinese urban dweller was as subject, the city was always foreign. While imperial power and family membership were as strong as they were in China, it was virtually impossible for groups of urban inhabitants to see themselves as independent citizens with pride or responsibility toward their city. Regardless of the size of the Chinese city, there was no basis for a city-state kind of identity and participation. The merchant class which was most free of family and village ties was in the best position to declare itself citizens. But they did not. They merely became more wealthy and more honored subjects.

In most other non-Western cities the ties of caste, tribe, or religion prevented the development of common citizenship in the same way. In the cities of India caste differences stifled any sense of common city identity. In Africa and the Americas tribal or religious identity usually took precedence over locality or place. Further, in almost all of these other cities, the inhabitants were also subjects of an overlord, emperor, or chief. In general terms tribal identity was strongest in non-Moslem Africa and among the Incas and Aztecs of America. Religious identity was primary in Moslem Africa and among the Mayans in America. Some cities were also primarily cities of subjects. The imperial capital of the Byzantine Empire, Constantinople, was very much like the Chinese city of subjects. In Constantinople, however, the Church was often as strong as the emperor, and religious affiliation was as important as political.

Weber argued that tribal membership blocked the realization of independent citizenship even in Athens and Rome. In a general sense, perhaps, the tribe (or family-clan) identity was always the most persistent obstacle to the evolution of a sense of individual citizen autonomy. We are used to associating tribal organization with Africans and American Indians, but this is not accurate. All preurban societies were tribal. That is why a modified tribal identity was still important in many ancient cities, like Rome. In some cases the city institutionalized tribal organization (in the way that the Roman masses were organized for voting into "tribes" with elected "tribune" leaders). Often that delayed or prevented the development of separate citizenship. But in some cases tribes established cities that were a lot closer to democratic city-states than to the cities of caste or subject societies. The African city of Timbuctoo and the early Aztec city of Mexico, for instance, were cities of tribes who developed a fairly extensive participation in the affairs of their cities. But even in these cities the rule of tribal chieftain or king was more normal.

Most religions have been "in-group" affairs that tended to divide the members of a multireligious city rather than encourage their common identity. Hinduism in ancient Indian cities, for example, enshrined the caste differences that separated city inhabitants. Hindus in Delhi were *brahmans, kshatriyas, vaisyas,* or *sudras,* not Delhians. Other inhabitants might call themselves Moslems or Persians, again not Delhians. Similarly, Jews in Babylonia, Alexandria, or Delhi always considered themselves Jews. To a certain extent, however, Christianity and Buddhism cultivated a sense of communality that allowed city inhabitants to concentrate on collective goals and needs. The cities of Buddhist India were less divided by caste and temporarily came closer than native Hindu cities or the Moslem conqueror's cities to a city-state type of organization. But Buddhism became more important in China than in its native India, and China posed other obstacles to the growth of city community. The cities which were primarily religious centers, like the Moslem Mecca and the Mayan cities of America, might encourage a kind of community of the faithful, but these cities were often "capitals" of the faith that could not be left to local inhabitants. The rulers of Islam and the priests of the Mayans took active direction of these cities. Indeed, in some Mayan cities the priests seem to have been the only inhabitants. Their community was like that of the monastery.

Weber seems right, after all. At least there were serious limitations to the development of urban community in most of the imperial, caste, and tribal societies of the medieval world. Such cities were often splendid, vibrant, and enormously productive, but they offered little opportunity for the democratic participation of the village on a grander scale. The inhabitants of these cities did not normally identify themselves as citizens or take part in governing the life of their cities. These cities did not continue or extend the democratic procedures that originated in the first city-states. That happened in Western Europe. Let us return there.

## The Revival of Cities in the West: The Commune

It may have been the very destructiveness of the barbarian invasions in the West that made regeneration of Rome or any imperial city impossible. City life virtually disappeared, if not completely with the fall of Rome, at least with the rise of Islam in the seventh century. By then there was no one with the power of a Wen Ti to reorganize the empire, or there was little to reorganize. Justinian, a Byzantine emperor (sixth century), codified Roman law and attempted to reorganize the Western empire of the Caesars, but it was hopelessly fragmented. For almost the next thousand years, the West lagged far behind the prodigious accomplishments that continuity gave Chinese civilization, but the West enjoyed the rare luxury of a fresh start. The village again became the center of Western life. The lessons of village community could be relearned. Town and city life could mature gradually and autonomously (we might almost say organically) from the soil of village institutions. There was no emperor around to lay out the grid plan of a new metropolis and then proceed to fill it with subjects. There were, of course, Holy Roman emperors who were sometimes able to actually govern the peasants of a small German state. But none of these feudal lords had the resources of a Wen Ti. And there were other kings to reckon with, too many to name. There were minor princes and barons, each in charge of miles of field and a few villages. And, of course, there was the pope. The medieval Western towns profited from the feuding of the feudal lords, and took the initiative in carving out their own jurisdictions.

Increasingly after the tenth century old towns won from feudal lords grants of independence and self-government that were often put in written, charter form. Towns won the right to hold a regular market, to coin money, to regulate weights and measures, to try their citizens in their own courts, to write their own law, and to protect their cities with their own militia. In return the burghers (inhabitants of the burg or town) offered the feudal lord the services of the militia in case of invasion. The town also provided a variety of crafts, manufactured goods, even foreign luxury commerce that could enhance the lord's style of life on the manor. In many cases the lords founded new towns for these advantages as well as the rent revenue of the land they owned. In short, the lords often gave the towns political freedom in return for military help, economic prosperity, a larger population, and cultural resources that the greatest castle could not afford.

The history of the rise of the medieval town is full of stories of conflict between lord and citizen; towns often demanded rights that threatened even far-seeing feudal lords; and the military and economic power of towns eventually proved more deadly than gunpowder to the feudal regime. But the conflict was often over particulars; many lords built and nourished new towns, and it was the very weakness, poverty, and decentralization of the feudal regime that made free towns possible: the lords, after all, had little to grant but land and rights.

Freedom was in the city air. The serf who remained in the city for a year and a day was legally free. The citizen was free of feudal dues and services. Citizenship itself meant freedom of association, freedom of movement, freedom to own, make, spend, and marry without the lord's permission or dues. Citizenship replaced the ancient ties of blood and soil, family and feudal allegiances. The citizens became autonomous individuals who freely gathered together to establish their own governments and laws, united in a corporate effort, allied in common associations, for the good of the commune.

"The medieval city was a 'commune' from the beginning," Weber said. He meant that it was a corporate or collective association of equals that did not have to be based on ties of family, clan, or tribe. "Commune" was a good word to express common citizenship. Many of the early cities called themselves "The Commune of Florence" (or Pisa or Milan or whatever). It is interesting that we in modern America think of the commune as the antithesis of the urban settlement. Our cities seem so impersonal and competitive that we cannot imagine commune or community away from the countryside. It is also interesting that when American sociologists asked Weber at a meeting in St. Louis early in this century to speak about "rural community" he replied that the phrase was a contradiction in terms. Weber had studied the history of the city well enough to know that it was the only place that had made genuine community possible.

## Late Medieval and Renaissance Cities: Pageantry and Participation

Late medieval and Renaissance towns and cities created a new corporate life which rivaled the best of the ancient city-states. The acropolis returned in the form of the parish church, built by the townspeople, not by imperial decree. Many villages or city parishes of less than a hundred families had their own church. The churches were often named for local saints (whose tombs they frequently were). Their construction and maintenance were a source of civic pride and common work. The village church or the bishop's cathedral offered opportunities for charitable care, refuge, meditation, sociability, and festivity. Hospitals, poor houses, homes for the aged, sanitariums, previously available only to the wealthy or in the monastery, became typical features of the new urban landscape—often forming common neighborhoods with chapel, gardens, and fountains. "All that the territorial state now seeks to do on a wholesale scale was first done," Mumford points out, "in a more intimate way, often probably with more feeling for the human occasion, in the medieval town."

In one important respect the medieval towns and Renaissance city-states were more genuine communities than had existed ever before—even in ancient Athens. The majority of the inhabitants were free citizens, working side by side, without an underlying slave population. Christianity had made work more respectable than it had ever been before. "To labor is to pray," was the way the Benedictine monastic order expressed the Christian attitude. Working associations were as important as religious associations. The first guilds were actually religious fraternities. They never lost their religious coloring. Merchant and producer guilds served the interests of their members and consumers in ensuring the quality of work, just prices, and the economic prosperity of the town. But they were equally engaged in planning and performing religious plays for fellow townspeople, building schools, and chapels, and meeting halls for citizens, and providing their members with insurance, feasts, and festivals.

Festivity and pageantry were the drama and elixir of communal city life. Religious holy days, celebrations of peace, guild-sponsored dances, the completion of the harvest, the safe return of a ship were all occasions for collective rejoicing. The drama, the pageant, the sports contest, even the parade were participatory, not spectator activities. The painter Albrecht Dürer tells us about a parade in sixteenth-century Antwerp:

> On Sunday after Our Dear Lady's Assumption, I saw the Great Procession from the Church of Our Lady at Antwerp, when the whole town

> of every craft and rank were assembled, each dressed in his best according to his rank. And all ranks and guilds had their signs, by which they might be known. In the intervals, great costly pole-candles were borne, and three long old Frankish trumpets of silver. There were also in the German fashion many pipers and drummers. All the instruments were loudly and noisily blown and beaten.
>
> I saw the Procession pass along the street, the people being arranged in rows, each man some distance from his neighbor, but the rows close behind the other. There were the Goldsmiths, the Painters, the Masons, the Broderers, the Sculptors, the Joiners, the Carpenters, the Sailors, the Fishermen, the Butchers, the Leatherers, the Clothmakers, the Bakers, the Tailors, the Cordwainers—indeed, workmen of all kinds, and many craftsmen and dealers who work for their livelihood. Likewise the shopkeepers and merchants and their assistants of all kinds were there. After these came the shooters with guns, bows, and crossbows, and the horsemen and foot-soldiers also. Then followed the watch of the Lord Magistrates. Then came a fine troop all in red, nobly and splendidly clad. Before them, however, went all the religious orders and the members of some foundations, very devoutly, all in their different robes.
>
> A very large company of widows also took part in the procession. . . . Wagons were drawn along with masques upon ships and other structures. Behind them came the Company of the Prophets in their order, and scenes from the New Testament. . . . From the beginning to end, the Procession lasted more than two hours before it was gone past our house.[4]

Like the parade, "singing, acting, dancing were still 'do-it-yourself' activities." Music was composed primarily for the voice, that is, for the singers rather than the listeners. Guilds had their own choral groups. Even the wealthy insisted that an ability to join a family sing—and hold a part—was a prime requirement for a young serving maid.

It would seem as if the city commune were designed for social interaction. Actually, however, the sociability of the commune was due as much to the absence of large-scale planning as it was to the creation of piazzas, plazas, courts, parks, and open space. These meeting and walking areas were not laid out to magnify the power of a prince or to expedite the flow of traffic (as was the case in the later baroque cities). They were instead piecemeal adaptations by the citizens which enhanced rather than abolished neighborhoods. Even the winding medieval streets served to unite neighbors and freshen the view at every turn.

According to the author of a fourteenth-century work in praise of the city of Pavia (a new popular literary style which shows the extent of civic pride), the fifty thousand inhabitants of this Italian city "know each other so well that if anybody inquires for an address he will be told it at once, even if the person he asks lives in a quite dis-

■ *The piazza of Italian Renaissance cities was a public meeting place, a focus of civic pride, or (in darker days) the sight of an execution. In this case the people of Florence put their former monastic leader Savonarola to the stake in 1498.* *(Alinari)*

tant part of the city; this is because they all gather twice a day, either in the 'court' of the commune or in the (adjoining) cathedral piazza."[5]

In some cities (usually smaller than Pavia) the citizens came together in a general assembly to make the laws, very much the way the Athenian citizens had at the Ecclesia. More often, though, in cities of over twenty thousand inhabitants, the citizens would elect representatives to serve (usually for no more than six months or a year) as a legislative council. Sometimes the members of a guild or neighborhood would each choose one of their number (by election or lot) to serve or elect others to serve. The processes of selection varied enormously, as did the size of the councils. Italian city-states, for instance, often had a "great council" of four hundred or a thousand (Modena had sixteen hundred), and an inner council normally closer to 40. The

**The States of Italy, 1494**
*On the eve of the French invasion of Italy in 1494, a few Italian states had already conquered much of Italy. Milan, Venice, Florence, the Papal States, and the Kingdom of the Two Sicilies continued their expansion in the early 1500s.*

meetings of the great councils were not limited to formalities, nor were they necessarily passive rubber-stamping affairs. A council of about six hundred members met in Genoa in 1292 to discuss deteriorating relations with France; over a hundred councillors gave speeches in seven days of sessions.

The degree of political participation must have surpassed that of ancient Athens, considering the commune's larger citizen body and the relative absence of slaves. It has been estimated that Florence drew a thousand of its ninety thousand inhabitants each year for official positions. Smaller cities no doubt required a larger percentage to serve in public office. A budget for the city of Siena in 1257 mentions 860 public offices including 171 night watchmen and others we might call "police," but excluding military—and this in a city whose adult male population could not have been more than five thousand.

But the unpaid citizens, giving speeches in the council and voting on every imaginable question of public interest, are a better clue to the vitality of communal life than the paid officers. It is difficult for us to imagine how these citizens could take time out from their busy lives to deal with all of the vexing questions of public policy. The answer is that the life of the commune was a very important part of their business; the give and take of debate and the burdens of decision making were all of the civic training that they needed.

Since the city-state was itself both a city and an independent state (with surrounding countryside and possibly allied or subordinate villages and towns), questions of war and peace were most crucial. But the records of council debates (carefully recorded by one of the dozens, sometimes hundreds, of the cities' "notaries") show a phenomenal range of interest and legislation. Hygiene and sanitation was perhaps the second most important concern. No one could build without permission in Siena in 1309. At Cremona "no man is to demolish his house except for the purpose of building a better one."[6] Most communes had ordinances requiring the regular cleaning of streets, forbidding the careless disposal of wastes and fouling of the rivers, and preventing the dyers or tanners from contaminating public water sources and hanging their cloths and hides over the street.

On the assumption that the rich man's wasteful expenditure was the people's loss, there were also often ordinances against gluttonous eating in taverns or the wearing of ostentatious crowns of pearls. When class divisions became extreme *and* when the people's parties outvoted the nobles, there were even attempts to use legislation to counterbalance the economic power of the wealthy. Thus, on the assumption that the rich could always find a way to buy their freedom, the popular party made the fines of the wealthy double or triple the fines for poorer citizens convicted of the same offense.

## The Renaissance City: A School of Art

The commune was an education in more than politics, government, and social relations. It was also a school of art. The beauty of the city was part of the "job" of the citizen. The citizens of Florence voted to decide the type of column that was to be used on their Cathedral. A responsibility like that certainly did not turn all Florentines into art critics, but it must have lifted the minds and aesthetic feelings of many. The city of Leonardo da Vinci and Michelangelo could have easily called on "experts," but the city that turns all questions of taste into questions of expertise and hires professionals as decision makers ends with a pretty apathetic public.

Artists were hired by cities like Florence—the way our cities hire engineers. The great Renaissance painter Giotto, called by many today the founder of the modern style of painting, was hired by Florence as architect for many churches, walls, and bridges. He implemented the desires of the public and also broadened their education. Florence could rely on native craftsmen and artists to serve as chapel architects or overseers of public buildings. The artist was another of many craftsmen who was expected, like other citizens, to devote some of his efforts to communal needs. In a city like Orvieto that had to hire outside artists for such work, the citizens would sometimes welcome the newcomer with five or fifteen years of tax exemption—the way our cities attract businesses.

Even the most business-oriented city-states, like Florence and Venice, were works of art. The leading merchants or bankers (like the Medici family of Florence) might direct the finances of distant kings and nations, but the beauty of the public spaces and buildings of their own cities was often more important than their commercial possibilities. With the dedication of a modern city administration that has been sold a bill of goods on a downtown parking lot, office tower, or shopping center, the council of Siena would decide to have a public meadow in the city because

> among those matters to which the men who undertake the city's government should turn their attention, its beauty is the most important. One of the chief beauties of a pleasant city is the possession of a meadow or open place for the delight and joy of both citizens and strangers.[7]

And beauty was as necessary for the homes of the officials as it was for public space, according to the council of Siena:

> It is a matter of great honor to the various communes that the officials occupy beautiful, and honorable dwellings, both for the sake of the

commune and because foreigners often go to their houses upon affairs. This is of great importance for the commune [of Siena] according to its quality.[8]

Siena and Florence show us that small, independent city-states could retain the community and democracy of the village without necessarily succumbing to the tedium and creative stagnation that is all too often typical of village life. Culturally, artistically, and intellectually, Siena and Florence were more dynamic and creative than most cities of any size before or since. Community does not necessarily mean conformity.

The remarkable thing is not only that a Siena or Florence produced giants—Giotto, Dante, Petrarch, Boccaccio, Botticelli, Machiavelli, Leonardo da Vinci, Michelangelo, to name a few—but that it created an environment in which genius was almost institutionalized and expected. The public service required of the artist, and the personal encouragement of artists and philosophers by the Medici family in the fifteenth century, made art and intellect an inspiration to all. Schools (probably half of the male population in Florence had attended), libraries (among them the first public library), Verrocchio's art institute–workshop (where the young Leonardo learned mechanics, mathematics, and music, as well as architecture, bronze casting, goldsmithing, painting, and sculpture), Lorenzo Medici's finishing school for sculptors (where Michelangelo studied), and the city itself were living lessons of a new ideal: beauty and creative expression as the goal of human life and the commune.

Creativity is still possible in a communal city when culture is as important as business. What about larger cities? Are neighborhood communities and a human scale of life impossible in large cities?

## The Renaissance City: The Lessons of Venice

At least one Renaissance city-state, and perhaps the most beautiful one, still says no. Out of necessity as much as foresight, the Republic of Venice found a way to preserve the human dimensions of the neighborhood in a large and most prosperous city. Each of the islands that make up the city of Venice is separated by the canals and lagoon waters that surround it. Each of the island neighborhoods has its own parish, its square, its school, and its guildhall—for each was originally the site of one of the city's six guilds. As Venetian population and prosperity grew, it was impossible to abolish the original neighborhoods by filling in the waters that divided them. Consequently, the Venetians had the good sense to allow each island to perform the function that it did best. One became a shipbuilding center that built the Venetian merchant and warships with a new canal "conveyor belt" system that startled visitors. The Arsenal, as it was called, housed the workers in the shipyard, their magistrates (or elected officials), and their own class of wealthy citizens. On another island, Murano, the Venetian glass industry was established, by an act of the Grand Council by 1255. It was settled by the workers, merchants, and artists active in the industry. Again, they had their own neighborhood organizations, markets, and facilities. In this way the central business and administrative district did not become overly congested and eventually suffocated. This district, the area of the largest island, around St. Mark's church, became the center for international merchants, specialized shops and restaurants, hotels, tourism, and city-wide politics. The larger square in front of Saint Mark's and the administrative Ducal Palace also became the scene of city-wide festivals. It could be enjoyed by the whole population, but they did not have to "commute" there daily to work or shop. Finally, other island neighborhoods were clustered around the separate concerns of religion (the convent of San Georgio), burial (the cemetery of Torcello), and later in the nineteenth century a beach (the Lido).

The great modern architect Corbusier called Venice "an object lesson for town planners." It shows, even today, how neighborhood communities can be retained, how functional zoning can organize the separate concerns of the city, how major thoroughfares can be separated from local streets, and how a large urban area can avoid high-density sprawl. Venice's population has rarely risen beyond the Renaissance peak of one hundred and ninety thousand. There are still no cars permitted beyond the entrance to the city. The Venetian or tourist can take a fast public *vaporetto* up the Grand Canal or out to one of the smaller islands or hire a gondola to wander. On the island he or she can walk. Nothing is very far from the water's equivalent of a subway, bus, or taxi stop. Places to walk and places to ride: the sea has forced Venetians to distinguish between getting there and being there. As a result each "place to be" has retained its particular identity, its neighborhood, and its community.

The model, but not the necessity, is there for any large city to follow. With modern high-speed public transit, even with our socially expensive expressways, the Venetian model might suit a city of 10 or 20 times the size. Today we have the capacity to design our cities to achieve what came to Venice naturally. Large parks, woodlands, lakes, or rivers (instead of the canals and the lagoon) could provide relief from mass sprawl and the refuge of the neighborhood. Separate functions could be separated by location without, at the same time, forcing people to commute long distances to work. Spaces could be designed for social interaction, public activity, and walking and wandering. Instead, we turn every alley into a street, every street into a thoroughfare, and every neighborhood into a block. We forget how to walk, we don't know who our neighbors are, and we find our way by counting the numbered streets. Every part of the city looks the same, and the monotony continues for miles. The city has lost its human scale, and it is not ours.

## The City Since Community: The Baroque and the Broken

Two things have happened to the city-state community in the last few hundred years. It has lost its independence, and the new rulers from outside have broken it up with streets, avenues, and boulevards for easy entry, control, and exit. The two developments are obviously related. Independence went down the avenue.

There are still a few city-states left. At least places like Monaco, Lichtenstein, and Andorra have preserved much of the independence of city-states. Many of the Swiss cities are also relatively free and self-governing. In general, however, the city-state has been consumed, and replaced, by the nation-state. Cities are governed from outside—first by the princes and kings who welded them together as capitals or subjects of the new nation-states, then by national governments, and more recently by national and international corporations. The "corporate community" now refers to something very different from the assembly of citizens in the town council. The new corporate community may run many cities, but has no particular allegiance to any.

The communal city was defeated, however, long before the rise of corporate capitalism or the Industrial Revolution. It was first sacrificed to the baroque quest for power and opulence by the monarchs and ministers of the nation-state. In some ways the city-states defeated themselves. Like the Greek city-states, they experimented with alliances and confederations. Some such larger organization of cities seemed necessary. In half of Italy in 1300 there were more self-governing states than could be counted in the whole world in 1933. Their rivalries often led to war, but even in good times they were frequently unable to keep the peace in the countryside or agree on uniform laws, coinage, or standard weights and measures. The independence of cities was particularly frustrating to the rising class of national and international merchants: the number of tolls that merchants had to pay feudal lords and municipalities along the Rhine

River, for instance, increased from 19 at the end of the twelfth century to 64 at the end of the fourteenth.

Confederation was not impossible. In fact, it worked pretty well in Switzerland and Holland. It was not a viable alternative where there was already a strong monarchy, as in England. But even in Italy where the alternative to civic independence was alliance with a German emperor or a French king, the Italians often chose the foreign monarch. The reason for such a choice probably had a lot to do with divisions within the Italian city-states themselves. Class and economic differences tended to increase during the Renaissance, forcing a noble, merchant, or popular party of "outs" to bargain for foreign intervention. Venice, one of the most stable but least democratic of the Italian city-republics, remained independent until conquered by Napoleon in 1797.

In some cities the merchants and national manufacturers and bankers formed alliances with kings to make the national economy more efficient. In Germany, Scandinavia, and England (but not in Switzerland or the British colonies in America) the Protestant Reformation served the national interest of kings and princes at the expense of city independence. But the most centralized nation-states to be organized in the sixteenth to eighteenth centuries were probably in Catholic France, Spain, and Austria, and in Russia. In any case, the king's capital replaced the commune as the nation-state became the dominant form of political organization. By commanding the main routes of trade, the bureaucracy, and professional armies, the capital city was able to unify the state. The capitals and their subsidiaries (where the king's court ruled) virtually monopolized the population increases of the sixteenth to eighteenth centuries. The capitals' populations reached the hundreds of thousands (London and Paris almost a million) while older cities languished and very few new ones (outside the colonies) were built.

Old cities were transformed and new cities were created often by a single monarch: Henry IV's Paris, Louis XIV's Versailles, Ivan III's Moscow, Peter the Great's Saint Petersburg, Philip II's Madrid, Manuel's Lisbon. Magnificent palaces were built or redesigned or enlarged in line with baroque style and ambitions: opulence, majesty, extravagance, order, and power—to tame the nobility and intimidate the populace. Gathered around the palace in the center of the city were the new town house mansions of the aristocracy (under the king's watchful eye), the official bureaucratic buildings, and the army citadel. Everything was purposely designed on a scale larger than life. These were monumental buildings which were not to be approached by ordinary mortals. Their uniformity of arches, columns, and endless wall and windows is still a forbidding or awe-inspiring sight. The monotony, impersonality, and anonymity of modern city or bureaucratic life is neither accidental nor inevitable. Peter the Great asked that the 12 large office buildings of Saint Petersburg look exactly alike. Henry IV advised his minister in charge of the construction of a street in Paris: "I would be very pleased if you would see to it that those who are beginning to build on the street make the fronts of their houses alike, for it would be a fine ornament to see this street with a uniform facade from the end of the bridge." The king's view was what mattered, and his tastes ran from the uniform-regular to the uniform–extra-large.

Baroque city building was like theatrical stage design. Indeed, many of the new planners got their start by designing stage scenery and props. The monarch's city was to be, as one said, "like a single building," and that, presumably, the theater. Everything was done for effect. Broad vistas of unbroken columns moved the eye to the distant focal point of the palace. The ideal street plan for baroque tastes was radial (a plan Aristophanes had proposed almost two thousand years before as a joke, thinking that the idea of bringing all traffic crashing together at the same spot was a sufficiently obvious satire on the megalomania of ancient planners). Broad avenues converging on the palace, the citadel, or a monumental arch was a theatrical way of attracting attention to the monarch's power, but it was also a very practical way of maintaining that power. Troops could be marched from the central precinct in any direction, for a parade—or for an attack. The architect Alberti distinguished between secondary streets and avenues; the latter he called *viae militares.* Another architect urged that all streets be wide enough so "that there be no place in them where armies may not easily march."

The broad avenue also served the purpose of breaking up the medieval tangle of streets which might be barricaded by the last holdouts of urban liberty. As Mumford remarked, "soldiers cannot fire around corners, nor can they protect themselves from bricks heaved from chimney tops immediately overhead: they need space to maneuver in."[9]

If the baroque style of cities remind us of the ancient imperial capitals, it is because their rulers sought to emulate the pharaohs, Ptolemies, and Caesars. Louis XIV styled himself *Le Roi Soleil* ("the Sun King"). Like lesser monarchs of the period he got his theoreticians and writers to work out new theories of absolute sovereignty and "divine right," ideas that no European since the Caesars had dared to propose. Although some medieval communes had gotten along without any explicit sovereign (or final power) and many others had assumed that the only sovereign was the people or the law, the new theorists, like Jean Bodin, argued that a true state only exists when there is a sovereign and that *he* (or she) must exercise "supreme power over citizens and subjects, unrestrained by law."

As an artistic style the baroque has been dead about three hundred years. The age of absolute monarchy has been replaced by parliaments, congresses, presidents, and prime ministers in the last couple of hundred years. Few presidents these days think they are above the law. But most of our cities are direct descendants of the baroque capitals. The sovereign state is often as absolute as absolute monarchs. City life still means subjection to outsiders.

> The baroque cult of power has been even more tenacious than the medieval ideology: it remained in being and extended its hold on other departments of life, creating Napoleons not merely in statecraft but in business and finance. . . . Armies, governments, capitalistic enterprises took the characteristic animus and form of this order, in all its inflated dimensions. . . . Right on into the twentieth century urban planning itself, at least in the great metropolises, meant chiefly baroque planning: from Tokyo and New Delhi to San Francisco.[10]

The baroque city has always been one of the ways the ruler displayed his power. For the absolute monarchs it was the main theater for such display. Perhaps the new rulers, the sovereign national state and the international corporation, no longer need the city as show place. Like Louis XIV, corporations can build their own Versailles in the suburbs. They and the government can advertise well enough on television. Perhaps television and suburban cultural facilities can even provide the wealthy with the "civilization" that previously depended on cities.

Some of the modern proposals for the renewal of city life have recognized this problem as the "diminishing tax base" of urban areas. The corporations and wealthy who have made their fortunes in the cities have moved out when they were called on to pay the bills. The resulting population of poor people has not been able to pay for the upkeep of the expensive shell. Thus, there have been proposals that the state or federal government assume some of the costs of city management. Such proposals at least have the advantage of recognizing that city independence is a malicious fiction in an age when the real powers are national and international. But movements to spread the tax burden to the suburbs by "regionalization" or to the countryside by a kind of nationalization only mean that the city has been given up for dead. When that happens the cities may become more livable, but they will be administrative areas of the sovereign state (much like Hangchow) rather than communities.

## High Ideals and Sinking Feelings: China and Venice Today

A more imaginative and radical solution which strikes at the root of the problem (economic inequality) and restores urban community (even urban-rural community on a local scale) has been tried by the descendants of Hangchow. Perhaps because the Chinese have had a longer experience with the exploitation of urban ruling classes, they have been more willing to try revolutionary changes. It may also be that they have remained so close to their roots in family and village community that parasitic cities have always been unacceptable. The United States, on the other hand, has always been a most urban nation. We have a heritage of medieval urban community which the Chinese lack, but that heritage rapidly disappeared.

The Chinese Communists have tried a couple of interesting experiments in the cities to cultivate a greater sense of community. As early as 1951 (two years after the revolution) they began experimenting with "street mayors" and street "residents committees." The latter were something like our "tenants associations" except that the Chinese committees were officially recognized powers, not just pressure groups. Thus, the residents were empowered to force the landlord to add a bathroom, admit needy families, institute garbage removal, and also settle disputes among themselves (as a semiofficial neighborhood court) or create teams for repairs, welfare, or child care.

As socialists, however, the Chinese were more interested in "the unity of working and living"—that is, communities of people who lived and worked together, rather than merely residential communities. These took various forms, more or less modeled on the agricultural communes of the countryside. In some cases a whole city would form itself into a commune. The industries, stores, offices, and other facilities would be collectively owned by the commune, and the individual or family would contribute work and be paid by the communal treasury. In other cases, resident neighborhoods would set up new working facilities to be run collectively for extra money. The Kweiyang commune in a neighborhood of 1,920 people, for instance, set up five factories, five stores, one savings bank, kindergartens, public dining halls, and libraries. Women, who were not used to working out of the home, were particularly active in this project: "Some got so excited in working that they forgot to eat, forgot to sleep, forgot to return home. . . . Housewives who earlier simply took care of their own homes now cared about each other and helped each other."[11]

Increasingly in the 1960s and 1970s, however, China has experimented with urban-agricultural communes. As if the unity of working and living were not idealistic enough, they have sought at the same time to achieve this in an environment which unifies urban and rural life. Such communes have consisted of small cities with heavy and light industry and enough farmland to make the whole area self-sufficient. As in the earlier strictly urban communes, all of the facilities including schools, hospitals, factories, and machinery are collectively owned and run. But in addition these communes are designed to acquaint city people with farming—at least as extra hands at harvest times. Such communes also have the obvious additional advantage of providing an environment more natural than asphalt and steel.

If the Chinese have revived the idea of the city commune (so absent from their own experience that they even borrowed Japanese words for burghers and neighborhood associations and Western Marxist ideology), the cities of the West have become subjects of new empires. Sometimes the subjection is pretty clear: Detroit as the subject of the auto empire, Pittsburgh of steel, New York of finance, Paris of France. In most cases, however, the modern Western city is prey to many outside forces. For one of the most dramatic examples of how this works, let us conclude with a brief return to Venice—before it's too late.

Experts calculate that Venice is losing 3 to 4 percent of its artistic heritage to pollution each year. Statues are crumbling from a "bronze cancer" that is not caused by the normal city pollution of exhaust fumes. Venice has no cars, and the motorboats in the canals give off very little exhaust. But when the wind blows from the oil refineries of Porto Marghera on the mainland the sulphurous fumes combine with the salt air to form a poisonous mixture.

More seriously, Venice is sinking. Actually, the waters in the lagoon are rising—about two inches in the last ten years. Much of the responsibility again seems to lie outside Venice with the many uncapped wells drilled by industry in Porto Marghera. These wells are pumping fresh water from the subsoil into the lagoon.

Some of the proposals to reduce the water levels, especially the high flooding of severe storms, seem simple enough. The wells could be capped. Sewage could be dried and converted to fertilizer instead of being dumped into the water. Further, huge locks could be built at the three breaks between the lagoon and the Adriatic Sea. Such locks would automatically close whenever a computerized early warning system signaled a flood alert. (A study has shown that the locks would be closed about 200 hours a year.)

Nothing has been done. The petrochemical industry at Porto Marghera is responsible for solutions as well as the problems. They find capping the wells to be expensive. They are in the business of producing chemical fertilizers, not organic ones. And they oppose the construction of locks because they fear that the tanker traffic will be diverted to another port. They are powerful in Rome as well as in Venice, and so the federal government has been dragging its feet.

Even some of the Venetians have been forced to accept the death of their city. The industrial powers at Porto Marghera have the jobs. Venetians can no longer live and work in their own city. In the last 20 years the population of Venice has declined from two hundred to ninety thousand, and most of those who are left are forced to commute to the mainland for work. The vast concentration of industrial power, as at Porto Marghera, is too much for a mere city, even one that had been (according to the new French ambassador in 1495) "the most triumphant city I ever set eyes on."

## *For Further Reading*

Among general approaches, Max Weber's **The City*** is the classical, if somewhat difficult, starting point. Richard Sennett has edited Weber and a number of other sociological interpretations of the city in **Classic Essays on the Culture of Cities.*** Gideon Sjoberg surveys **The Preindustrial City*** from the perspective of modern historical sociology. Lewis Mumford's **The City in History*** is still the most stimulating, interpretive history of the Western city. **Cities of Destiny,** edited by Arnold Toynbee, offers beautifully illustrated essays on some of the great cities of world history by noted specialists. Fernand Braudel's magnificent **Capitalism and Material Life 1400–1800*** concludes with a fascinating chapter on the world's "Towns." F. Roy Willis offers an urban-centered Western civilization text in his two volume **Western Civilization: An Urban Perspective.*** There is also a collection of articles from **Scientific American** with an introduction by Kingsley Davis called **Cities: Their Origin, Growth and Human Impact*** which is useful, especially for the study of ancient, American Indian, and modern cities. Finally, beyond our time period but worthy of special note is Raymond Williams's study of the city in modern English literature, **The Country and the City.***

For the European city, Weber, Mumford, and Willis are the best introductions, but there are many other useful titles. One of the shortest and best is Henri Pirenne's **Medieval Cities.*** Joseph and Frances Gies explore the daily life of one such city (Troyes in 1250) in the readable **Life in a Medieval City.*** A collection of historical interpretations by Mumford, Pirenne, and others concerning the relationship between commerce and the origins of towns in medieval England is gathered in John F. Benton's **Town Origins.*** For the medieval period there is also Maurice Beresford's **New Towns of the Middle Ages,*** M. V. Clarke's **The Medieval City-State,*** J. H. Mundy and Peter Riessenberg's **The Medieval Town,** and Fritz Rorig's **The Medieval Town.***

* Available in paperback.

There are a number of interesting books on the Italian city-republics of the late medieval and Renaissance period. Daniel Waley's **The Italian City Republics*** is an excellent introduction. D. S. Chambers's **The Imperial Age of Venice, 1380–1580*** is a well-illustrated introduction to Venice. William H. McNeill's **Venice** is more thorough. There is also D. Herlihy's **Pisa in the Early Renaissance: A Study of Urban Growth** and his **Medieval and Renaissance Pistois: The Social History of an Italian Town,** William K. Bowsky's **The Finance of the Commune of Siena, 1287–1355,** and J. K. Hyde's **Padua in the Age of Dante.**

There are libraries on Florence. One might begin with two who were there: Francesco Guicciardini's **History of Italy*** and **History of Florence** and Niccolo Machiavelli's **History of Florence and of the Affairs of Italy.*** Among the better modern accounts are Gene Brucker's **Renaissance Florence,*** J. Lucas-Dubreton's **Daily Life in Florence in the Time of the Medici,** John Gage's **Life in Italy at the Time of the Medici,** Marvin B. Becker's **Florence in Transition,** and Cecilia M. Ady's **Lorenzo de Medici and Renaissance Italy.**

If Asia begins in Byzantium, the city of Constantinople offers a good test of Weber's thesis. Image, poetry, and documents are suggestively combined in Philip Sherrard's **Constantinople: Iconography of a Sacred City.** Glanville Downey's **Constantinople in the Age of Justinian** recreates the age. Dean A. Miller's **Imperial Constantinople*** examines the economy, bureaucracy, and common life of the city. The political and architectural history of the city are studied in Michael MacLagan's **The City of Constantinople** and John E. N. Hearsey's **City of Constantine 324–1453.** For more general studies of the Byzantine Empire, the classic, though dated, account is Charles Diehl's **Byzantium: Greatness and Decline,*** which has an excellent bibliography by Peter Charanis, and the short, readable **Byzantium*** by Rene Guerdan.

On the Chinese city, English-language sources of our knowledge of Hangchow are **The Book of Ser Marco Polo Concerning the Kingdoms and Marvels of the East,** translated and edited by Sir Henry Yule. Its first volume is also available as **Marco Polo, The Description of the World,** edited by A. C. Moule and Paul Pelliot. A shorter version is **Marco Polo, Travels.*** These and Chinese sources are used in Jacques Gernet's absorbing **Daily Life in China on the Eve of the Mongol Invasion, 1250–1276*** and the older work by A. C. Moule, **Quinsai with Other Notes on Marco Polo.** The city of Peking is also lavishly brought to life in Lin Yutang's **Imperial Peking: Seven Centuries of China. The City in Imperial China,** edited by G. William Skinner, offers a number of interesting essays. The symbolism of Chinese city life is discussed in Paul Wheatley's **The Pivot of the Four Quarters, A Preliminary Enquiry into the Origins and Character of the Ancient Chinese City.** Toynbee's **Cities of Destiny** (already cited) offers essays on specific Chinese and other Asian cities.

The city of India and southern Asia is also treated in Richard Fox's **Urban India: Society, Space and Image,** Clifford Geertz's **The Social History of an Indonesian Town,** Kenneth Gillion's **Ahmedabad: A Study in Indian Urban History,** and within the context of Indian culture in Arthur L.

Basham's **The Wonder That Was India: A Survey of the History and Culture of the Indian Subcontinent Before the Coming of the Muslims** and Milton Singer's **When a Great Tradition Modernizes.**

We have said relatively little about the traditional African city, but the interested student can take advantage of the well-illustrated, short survey by Richard W. Hull called **African Cities and Towns Before the European Conquest,*** which also has a good, recent bibliography. Basil Davidson's **The Lost Cities of Africa*** is also a very readable, introductory survey, with a good bibliography of books and articles before 1960. The student can go deeper into specific African cities or Max Weber's thesis with **The Islamic City,** edited by A. H. Hourani and S. M. Stern, **The World of Islam** by Xavier de Planhol,* **Muslim Cities in the Later Middle Ages** by Ira Lapidus, **Fez in the Age of the Marinides** by Roger Le Tourneau, **The Primitive City of Timbuctoo** by Horace Miner, **The Towns of Ghana** by David Grove, and **The City of Ibadan,** edited by P. C. Lloyd and others. On Nigeria alone, there is Akin L. Mabogunje's **Yoruba Towns** and **Urbanization in Nigeria** and Eva Krapf-Askari's **Yoruba Towns and Cities** among other titles.

Finally, there is a series of essays on medieval cities in Europe, Egypt, Byzantium, and the Crusader states in **The Medieval City,** edited by David Herlihy and A. L. Udovitch.

## *Notes*

**1.** Adapted from Marcel Granet, *Chinese Civilization,* trans. Kathleen E. Innes and Mabel R. Brailsford (New York: New American Library, 1964), pp. 175–176.
**2.** Arnold F. Wright, "Changan" in *Cities of Destiny,* ed. Arnold Toynbee (New York: McGraw-Hill, 1967), p. 146.
**3.** This and other quotes from Marco Polo are from Jacques Gernet, *Daily Life in China: On the Eve of the Mongol Invasion, 1250–1276* (Stanford University Press, 1970), pp. 28–32 *passim.*
**4.** Lewis Mumford, *The City in History* (New York: Harcourt Brace Jovanovich, 1961), pp. 279–280. Much of the material in this chapter is from Mumford.
**5.** Cited in Daniel Waley, *The Italian City-Republics* (New York: McGraw-Hill, 1969), p. 53.
**6.** *Ibid.,* p. 99.
**7.** *Ibid.,* pp. 147–148.
**8.** Cited in Helene Wieruszowski, "Art and the Commune in the Time of Dante," *Speculum* 19, no. 1 (January 1944):31.
**9.** Mumford, *op. cit.,* p. 369.
**10.** *Ibid.,* pp. 399–401.
**11.** Cited in Franz Schurmann, *Ideology and Organization in Communist China,* 2d ed. (Berkeley: University of California Press, 1968), pp. 396–397.

# Chapter 12

# Ecology and Theology

## Medieval Religion and Science

Ecology is a problem that we normally identify with modern industrial society. We are not used to thinking of ecology and theology, or ecology in medieval history. But this chapter makes that identification to suggest that our ecological problems lie very deep. Although our generation may have "discovered" an environmental crisis in 1970, its causes go back at least as far as the Western industrial revolution of the last few centuries. The point of this chapter is that the industrial revolution itself, and the transformation of the human relationship to nature that it entailed, had even earlier causes in Western thought and action. Why, after all, was it Western Europe, of all places, that initiated the industrial revolution? This chapter will explore some of the cultural traditions that might have prepared the way.

Specifically, we will examine two Western cultural traditions which have been linked by some scholars to our ecological and environmental problems. They are the Western religious, or Judeo-Christian, tradition, and the development of science. Christianity and modern science might almost be called the hallmarks of Western culture. Although much of Western history is contained in the struggle between these two cultural forms, they also have much in common. We will examine the continuity between Christianity and science in order to explore the roots of Western predominance over nature and the world.

We are therefore raising a number of issues which should be kept in mind. We are asking about the relationship between religion and science, and specifically between Christianity and the development of modern science. We are asking about the validity of tracing such a modern issue as ecology back to the Middle Ages when ecological issues were minimal or nonexistent. We are asking about the different "ideas of nature" that are found in different religious traditions. And we are asking to what extent such ideas matter in people's daily confrontations with the natural environment.

We will proceed by first examining the argument that the Judeo-Christian religious tradition shaped Western ideas of nature in a way that made the natural world more exploitable. Then we will ask if religious ideas really matter all that much by examining some of the inconsistencies between religion and practice in Eastern religious traditions. Then we will survey the link between Western religion and science and examine some of the assumptions about nature which were implicit in the Western scientific revolution.

## The Responsibility of the Judeo-Christian Tradition

Those scholars who have argued that the roots of our ecological problems lie with the Judeo-Christian attitude toward nature emphasize the uniqueness of Judeo-Christian monotheism compared to more "primitive" polytheistic, animistic, and "nature religions."

Arnold Toynbee put the case this way:

> The thesis of the present essay is that some of the major maladies of the present-day world—for instance the recklessly extravagant consumption of nature's irreplaceable treasures, and the pollution of those of them that man has not already devoured—can be traced back in the last analysis to a religious cause, and that this cause is the rise of monotheism.[1]

Why monotheism? What does the ancient Hebrew insistence that there is only one God have to do with our modern ecological problems? Toynbee's answer is to remind us that the monotheism of the Hebrew Bible was an injunction against older forms of nature worship, and that once monotheism was fully accepted in Judeo-Christian culture, nature could be exploited instead of worshiped. "For pre-monotheistic man," Toynbee points out,

> nature was not just a treasure trove of "natural resources." Nature was, for him, a goddess, "Mother Earth," and the vegetation that sprang from the Earth, the animals that roamed, like man himself, over the Earth's surface, and the minerals hiding in the Earth's bowels, all partook of nature's divinity.[2]

The Bible not only deprived nature of its ancient sacred awe in order to acclaim a higher creator God. It also specifically counseled mankind to subdue the natural world. Here Toynbee and others point to the injunction in Genesis 1: 28:

> And God blessed them: and God said unto them, Be fruitful, and multiply, and replenish the earth, and subdue it; and have dominion over the fish of the sea, and over the birds of the heavens, and over every living thing that moveth upon the earth.

It is difficult to know what to make of a logical connection between monotheism and the desacralization of nature, or of any specific statements in the Bible. One wants to know if Jews and Christians actually behaved more arrogantly toward nature because of these ideas. In this regard, the work of Lynn White, Jr., a historian of medieval Christianity, technology, and science, makes a more formidable case for the responsibility of the Judeo-Christian tradition.

White's essay, "The Historical Roots of Our Ecologic Crisis," has become a classic, reprinted many times since its first publication in *Science* in 1967. It was prompted, he tells us elsewhere, by watching Buddhists in Ceylon build a road.

> Noting cones of earth left undisturbed upon the intended roadbed, he discovered that these were the nests of snakes. The Buddhists would not destroy the cones until the snakes departed of their own accord from the scene of activity. Among other things, White could not help reflecting that had the road builders been Christian, the snakes would have suffered a different fate.[3]

White's essay begins with two points worth repeating:

> One thing is so certain that it seems stupid to verbalize it: both modern technology and modern science are distinctively *Occidental*. Our technology has absorbed elements from all over the world, notably from China; yet everywhere today, whether in Japan or in Nigeria, successful technology is Western. . . .

> A second pair of facts is less well recognized because they result from quite recent historical scholarship. The leadership of the West, both in technology and in science, is far older than the so-called Scientific Revolution of the 17th century or the so-called Industrial Revolution of the 18th century.[4]

Lynn White himself has contributed much to the view that Western technological inventiveness and dominance can be traced back to the Middle Ages. His book, *Medieval Technology and Social Change*, shows (among other things) the revolutionary effects of such an apparently simple invention as the stirrup for medieval society. Others (see Lewis Mumford, for instance) have found the origins of modern ideas and methods of work in the medieval monastery. In this essay, however, White draws our attention to the transformation of agriculture in Christian Europe about the time of Charlemagne (whose coronation was in A.D. 800). In this period, White relates, the peasants of Northern Europe began to use a plow which turned over the land more violently than anything known before. Previous plows only scratched the surface of the soil. These new plows not only cut into the soil with a vertical knife, but they also cut underneath with a horizontal knife and turned the land completely over with a moldboard (a curved attachment which twisted the freshly cut sod). This system of plowing (which is still the method of modern tractors) caused so much friction with the soil that it required eight oxen instead of the usual two.

The new plow brought with it a much more aggressive attitude toward nature because of the kind of society that it required.

> In the days of the scratch plow, fields were distributed generally in units capable of supporting a single family. Subsistence farming was the presupposition. But no peasant owned eight oxen: to use the new and more efficient plow, peasants pooled their oxen to form large plow teams, originally receiving (it would appear) plowed strips in proportion to their contribution. Thus, distribution of land was based no longer on the needs of a family but, rather, on the capacity of a power machine to till the earth. Man's relation to the soil was profoundly changed. Formerly, man had been part of nature; now he was the exploiter of nature. Nowhere else in the world did farmers develop any analogous agricultural implement. Is it coincidence that modern technology, with its ruthlessness toward nature, has so largely been produced by descendants of these peasants of northern Europe?
>
> This same exploitive attitude appears slightly before 830 in Western illustrated calendars. In older calendars the months were shown as passive personifications. The new Frankish calendars, which set the style for the Middle Ages, are very different: they show men coercing the world around them—plowing, harvesting, chopping trees, butchering pigs. Man and nature are two things, and man is master.[5]

■ *In this French calendar scene of March from the early fifteenth century, we see the coercion of nature that Lynn White, Jr., refers to. Peasants are clearing the brush, planting and plowing (with an early moldboard plow that requires only two oxen). Above, the signs of the zodiac suggest much older, naturalistic images of the months.* (*From* Les trés riches heures du duc de Berry, *Giraudon, Musée de Condé*)

## Alternate Visions: Polytheism and Eastern Religion

The separation of man and nature that White notices in medieval calendars was certainly not completed by the ninth century, even in the most Christian sections of Europe. The peasant idea of a living nature persisted, we shall see shortly, as an obstacle to the scientific revolution well after 1500. Indeed, even today Greek peasants sing of their mother fields and daughter olive trees. But the question that White poses is whether Judeo-Christian monotheism has been playing a role in creating that separation. To answer this, let us look at some of the alternate visions of nature in "primitive" polytheism and Eastern religions.

As we have seen, most early religions emphasized the ties between humans and nature. They did not make any sharp distinctions between man and nature or between animate and inanimate things. Everything, even the rocks and stones, might be alive. Certainly, animal and plant life were considered as "alive" or as animate as human beings. Hunting tribes would call themselves the Bear or the Buffalo, and feel that they had more in common with that animal of their totem than they had with strangers. "After all," they might say, "our people sleep like the bear in winter," or "like the buffalo, we do not talk unnecessarily." Moreover, because they believed that their totemic animal was their ancestor or their "blood," they would imitate its habits or movements, especially on religious occasions. Thus, they would actually become like the bear or buffalo or their particular totem animal.

One tribe in New Guinea tells a story which explains how they came to be related to the birds. It seems that both the birds and the snakes wanted to be the ancestors of the tribe, so a bird and a snake had a race. The bird won, and ever since the tribe has been descended from the bird. It is true that they do not fly like birds, but they have inherited a much more important characteristic. Like birds, they die. Snakes, you see, never die. Anyone who lives in the woods knows that. Every once in a while you find a snake skin which the snake has crawled out of, and left behind. You never find skins of birds. So, snakes must go on to take one body after another. The tribe believes that they would do that too if the snake had won. But, like birds, they leave behind their whole bodies. They die.

Behind that poetic logic of the New Guinea tribe is the unquestioned assumption that humans and animals are made of the same stuff. Further, since the animals must have been around longer, they decide the fate of humans, not vice versa.

In some ways the cultures of the Far East never lost that primitive sense of nature's priority. Even after cities had developed in ancient India, the Hindus still insisted that the human and natural world were one. Some would not eat cows, others pigs, because they felt a particularly strong relationship to them. But Hindu holy men frequently urged the people to treat all of life in the same way that they treated their "sacred cows." Hinduism preached that all living plants and animals were part of a cycle of reincarnation. A good snake might become a butterfly in the next life. A good ass might become a man.

When the Hindus thought of first things, they thought of the origin of all human beings, not just of a single tribe. Yet, their stories of creation are not too far removed from the explanation of the primitive hunters of New Guinea. Here is one version from a Hindu holy book of around 700 B.C.:

> In the beginning, this universe was nothing but the Self in the form of man. It looked around and saw that there was nothing but itself, whereupon its first shout was, "It is I." . . .
>
> Then it was afraid because it was alone. But then it thought: "Since there is no one here but myself, what is there to fear?" So fear departed.
>
> However, it still lacked delight (just as we lack delight when we're alone). And so it desired a companion.
>
> Well, this universe, this Self, was exactly as large as a man and woman embracing. So it divided itself into two parts; then there was a male and female part of the self or universe.
>
> Then the male embraced the female, and from that the human race arose.
>
> But the female said: "How can he unite with me, since I was produced from him? Let me hide!"
>
> So she hid by becoming a cow; And he became a bull and united with her; And from that union the cattle arose.
>
> Then she hid by becoming a mare; and he became a stallion.
>
> She became as ass; he a donkey, and united with her; and from that the solid hoofed animals arose.
>
> She became a goat, he a buck; she a sheep, he a ram, and united with her; and from that goats and sheep arose.
>
> Thus he poured forth all pairing things down to the ants.
>
> Then he realized: "I, actually, am creation; for I have poured forth all this.
>
> Anyone understanding this becomes, truly, himself a creator in this creation."[6]

Ideas of creation are very important to people. They continually refer to them in order to understand how things are, always were, should be, or will be. This ancient Hindu idea that the universe was the self, and that it merely split itself up into the various animals of the world is, from our point of view, atheistic. There is no God who creates man and the animals. The only god is all of life, and animals are just as much a part of this as people. The Hindu divinity is all of nature, all living things. People who grow up in Hindu culture cannot easily struggle against nature. Hinduism is almost a natural religion of ecology.

Some Hindu holy men went to live in the forest with the animals, insects, and plants as their only companions. They sought continual communion with the divinity of nature. Some of them, like Gautama Siddhartha (around 500 B.C.), who was called the Buddha ("enlightened one") went further than their Hindu teachers in worshiping nature.

A great modern novelist, Hermann Hesse, imagined how Buddha must have insisted on loving nature, even a stone, not because the stone will become soil, plant, animal, or man, but because the stone already was all of these things:

> This stone is stone; it is also animal, God and Buddha. I do not respect and love it because it was one thing and will become something else, but because it has already long been everything and always is everything. I love it just because it is a stone, because today and now it appears to me a stone. I see value and meaning in each one of its fine markings and cavities, in the yellow, in the gray, in the hardness and the sound of it when I knock it, in the dryness or dampness of its surface. There are stones that feel like oil or soap, that look like leaves or sand, and each one is different and worships Om in its one way; each one is Brahman [God]. At the same time it is very much stone, oily or soapy, and that is just what pleases me and seems wonderful and worthy of worship.[7]

Obviously, most people could never become so ecstatic about a stone. The Buddha's worship was unique. But his loving concern for every aspect of nature became an ideal for his Buddhist followers. In a society, like China, where almost everyone was a Buddhist by the seventh century A.D., imagine the obstacles which must have existed to mining a mountain or treating nature as a servant of man.

One man does not change a whole culture, of course. The Chinese imported Buddhism from India because it conformed to very ancient attitudes. At the same time that Buddha was trying to make Indian Hinduism even more sympathetic to nature than it was, Chinese philosophers were saying much the same thing.

One of the most influential of these ancient Chinese "nature religions" was Taoism, named after *tao* ("the natural way") that the poet Lao Tzu, around 600 B.C., taught people to follow. "Let there be no action (contrary to Nature)," the *Tao Te Ching* advises, "and there is nothing that will not be well regulated." Another influential Taoist text expresses the belief that "even insects and crawling things, herbs and trees, may not be injured."[8]

▪ *This is a typical example of the popular Chinese art of landscape painting. As is usually the case in this art form, human beings are barely noticeable. The artist is much more interested in the towering beauty of the natural world. Even when the Chinese artist painted a city (like Hangchow in the previous chapter) nature is predominant. Compare our view of Florence. (Freer Gallery of Art)*

## Ideals vs. Behavior?

One should not assume that all Chinese (even all Taoists or Buddhists) approached nature with such concern, however. The student of traditional China reads of official inspectors of the mountains and forests, prohibitions against cutting trees except at certain times, and other enforced conservation practices. But one also hears why such rules were necessary. "At the beginning of the reign of Chia-Ching" (1522–1566), a Ming dynasty scholar reports, "people vied with each other to build houses, and wood from the southern mountains was cut without a year's rest."[9] Reports of deforestation, soil erosion, and flooding are common. After the tenth century, Chinese manufacturing had so depleted the timber reserves that it became increasingly necessary to substitute coal for wood.

Chinese ecological ideals must also be reconciled with the building of such gigantic cities as Changan and Hangchow. Villages and rural roads were usually laid out according to the principles of *feng-shui:* a preference for following the lay of the land, the natural hills and curves, and a distaste for straight lines, geometrical grids, or structures that seemed to dominate nature. But *feng-shui* was virtually ignored in the construction of Changan. The astronomers who laid out the 31-square-mile site sought conformance to the heavens rather than the earth. They carefully measured the shadow of the noon sun and the position of the north star in order to align the city of the Son of Heaven, its walls and gates, with the four directions. In the process, villages were leveled and (according to legend) all of the trees, except the old locust that shaded the chief architect, were uprooted.[10]

If Changan, with its broad straight avenues, conformed to an astronomer's idea of nature, Hangchow was constructed according to the ideals of a romantic artist. Nature was not followed. It was reconstructed. The many parks and gardens were all carefully constructed, planted, and groomed. Even the West Lake was an artificial construction. The illusion of a natural setting had to be rigorously maintained in the thirteenth century by peasants recruited to clear and enlarge the lake, and by military patrols empowered to enforce the various prohibitions against throwing rubbish or planting lotuses or water chestnuts.[11]

What is one to make of examples, such as these, of a disregard of nature in traditional China? The author who has suggested them, Yi-Fu Tuan, calls them "discrepancies between environmental attitude and behavior." They are that, certainly. But the inference that attitudes are one thing, and behavior is something else (or, more generally, that people never live up to their ideals) skirts a number of issues. If the behavior of the builders of Changan and Hangchow did not conform to the attitudes of Buddhism or Taoism, might it have conformed to the attitudes of some other tradition? We have already suggested that interpretation by writing of astronomers' and artists' attitudes toward nature. That still leaves the construction of such cities within the Buddhist religious tradition, but it extends the behavioral possibilities of that tradition. Yi-Fu Tuan himself uses the traditional Chinese distinction between the *yin* (passive, natural, female) and the *yang* (active, artificial, male) to see city building as assertions of traditional *yang* attitudes, ideas, and ideals. If Buddhism and Taoism are *yin* religious traditions, then emperor worship, ancestor worship, Confucianism, perhaps even astronomy and military rituals can be seen as *yang* religious traditions. In that vein, there is no "discrepancy" between the *yang* religion of emperor worship and the act of moving mountains or digging lakes to build the emperor's city.

Chinese emperor worship may have played a role similar to European Christianity in sanctioning the exploitation of nature. Astronomical and artistic interpretations of Buddhism and Taoism could also serve the cause of redesigning nature. No intellectual tradition is purely naturalistic or entirely hostile to nature. But, on balance, the

Chinese seem to have been more attuned to the natural world (in thought and action) than were their European contemporaries. It is difficult, for instance, to imagine the Western equivalent of the Chinese T'ang dynasty emperor "who went off in the springtime with his court musicians to gladden the flowers with soft music."[12]

It is impossible to imagine the Western equivalent of an inscription in a Japanese monastery which praises the beautiful blossoms of a particular plum tree and warns: "Whoever cuts a single branch of this tree shall forfeit a finger therefor."[13] The Eastern equation of the human and the natural could redound to the disadvantage of humans as well as the advantage of nature.

Medieval Christianity was not entirely lacking in equivalents of Eastern holy men. But the story of one, who appeared around 1200 shows more, perhaps, about the differences than the similarities of the East and West. Like a Christian Buddha, Saint Francis of Assisi led a group of monks who not only humbled themselves by giving up their possessions to live with the poor, but attempted to humble humanity by rejecting human control over nature. Legend describes Saint Francis preaching to the birds and persuading a wolf not to attack an Italian town. Saint Francis believed that animals also had souls. To him all of nature was sacred. He spoke of Brother Ant and Sister Fire and urged his listeners to glorify all of God's creations. He may even have believed in reincarnation; some Christians and Jews in southern France did at this time.

The challenge that Saint Francis and these others made to the Judeo-Christian tradition of dominating nature was so radical that it could not succeed. The group in southern France was suppressed violently. Pope Innocent III was able to bring Saint Francis and his disciples into the church (despite a dream that they might be able to take over) and defuse their message. In the end Francis died, the Franciscans were given a lot of money, and they became the caretakers, rather than the comrades, of the poor and the animals.

That was about as close as Christianity came to nature worship. Saint Francis could never have been a Buddha because Christianity did not even give him the vocabulary for such an extreme. It was a big step for Saint Francis to argue that animals had souls. That had never been an issue for the Hindus. They assumed all along that animals were just as divine as humans. Buddha had been beyond that point when he struggled with the question of the love of stones. Saint Francis shows us the limits of Christianity in two ways: his views were much more moderate than those of Eastern holy men; and there was never much of a chance that he would change the direction of Christian culture. He was much too extreme for the church.

In stressing the different philosophical orientations of the East and

■ *Saint Francis of Assisi preaches to the birds. The Christian tradition approaches the Chinese. But even here the great Florentine artist Giotto places humans in the foreground, and the birds (like the viewers of the painting) are placed at the eye level of the saint. One suspects that a Chinese artist of the period would have preferred the top half of the painting, but with the birds back in the air and trees.* (*Scala, EPA*)

the West, we do not mean to ignore the question of behavior. Lynn White's argument, in fact, depends on a difference between the ecological behavior of the West and that of the East. We have observed examples of ecological damage or avoidance in traditional China. Do such examples refute White's argument?

We think not. First, the damage does not seem that severe. Second, White is not arguing that monotheism is the only cause of environmentally harmful behavior; emperor worship may have had a similar effect. But most importantly, White is arguing that the Judeo-Christian separation of man and nature gave rise to a particular kind of science that has transformed the world. We must turn, then, to the rise of Western science.

## The Responsibility of the Western Scientific Revolution

Science certainly existed long before Christianity. In fact it took the Christians over a thousand years to recover the highly advanced science of the ancient Greeks. This knowledge had been kept relatively intact by the scholars of the Byzantine Empire in Eastern Europe and the Arab scientists in North Africa and Spain. But when, after 1200, the Christians of Europe finally regained Greek science and translated it into Latin, they approached it very differently from the Greeks of Byzantium and the Moslems of the Arab world. The Byzantine Greeks saw science as symbolic communication from God. They viewed the ant as God's message to the lazy. Fire, to them, was God's way of showing the Christian how to rise to Heaven. The rainbow was a symbol of hope—the sign that God sent to Noah after the 40 days of rain and flood.

> However, in the Latin West by the early thirteenth century natural theology was following a very different bent. It was ceasing to be the decoding of the physical symbols of God's communication with man and was becoming the effort to understand God's mind by discovering how his creation operates. The rainbow was no longer simply a symbol of hope first sent to Noah after the Deluge: Robert Grosseteste, Friar Robert Bacon, and Theodoric of Frieberg produced startling sophisticated work on the optics of the rainbows, but they did it as a venture in religious understanding. From the thirteenth century onward, up to and including Leibnitz and Newton, every major scientist, in effect, explained his motivations in religious terms. Indeed, if Galileo had not been so expert an amateur theologian he would have gotten into far less trouble: the professionals resented his intrusion. And Newton seems to have regarded himself more as a theologian than as a scientist. It was

> not until the late eighteenth century that the hypotheses of God became unnecessary to many scientists.[14]

Thus, modern science began as an attempt by very religious philosophers to understand the natural world that God had created and given them. They believed that God had revealed his intentions in a number of ways. He had revealed his word in the Bible—the teachings of the Old Testament and of Jesus; and he had shown his handiwork in the planets and natural environment that he had created for human use.

The first scientific thought was motivated by the hope of understanding God rather than conquering nature. Saint Thomas Aquinas, for instance, declared:

> The Creatures upon earth were not all made, no not the most of them, for mans eating and drinking; but for his glorifying the Wisdom, Goodness and Power of his Creator in the contemplation of them.[15]

By the seventeenth century, however, the work of the first modern scientists—people like Copernicus, Galileo, Sir Francis Bacon, Descartes, and Sir Isaac Newton—had led in two ways to conclusions that Saint Thomas Aquinas and the other theologians of the Middle Ages would not have been able to accept. First, the study of nature led to an increased awareness of the difference between the natural world and human beings. Second, the Europeans who became conscious of that difference became aware of the possibilities of exploiting or controlling nature.

It may seem strange to us that people did not always realize that nature was separate from man. We are so convinced that the grass or the moon or a wooden table are apart from us that it is difficult to imagine how people could think otherwise. The fact remains, nevertheless, that we in the modern Western world make a sharper distinction between people and things, man and nature, ourselves and the things around us, than did anyone before us. It is almost as if our skins have toughened in the last couple of hundred years. They haven't of course, but we have developed a sense of ourselves as separate individuals, operating in a world full of things, that is very recent.

Perhaps modern science has done more than anything else to separate our bodies from nature. We have already seen how primitive tribes could think of themselves as descendants of animals, and how Eastern religions have emphasized the community of the human and animal world. Certainly, the religion of the Jews and Christians began the process of separating the human individual from the animal world. But the scientists of the fifteenth to eighteenth centuries carried this process of separation a lot further. Even when they were religious they thought of themselves as *observers* of a separate reality. Previously, that is, before the last five, six, or seven hundred years, almost all people imagined themselves as *participants* rather than observers of nature.

The feeling of participating in, rather than looking at, nature was particularly common among the lower classes in the Middle Ages. The farming peasants, serfs, and tradespeople were usually unaware of the Christian doctrines which insisted on the separation of the human and the animal world. They were more likely to think like Saint Francis, or they were so involved in the work of farming that they still accepted much older, neolithic ideas about the similarity of soil and human mothers, and they personalized the rain, wind, and harvest.

Even the best educated Christians of the Middle Ages believed that the basic elements of nature—air, earth, fire, and water—were found in varying proportions in human beings just as in the natural world. Just as a high amount of earth would account for the stability of a mountain or a chair, it would also be diagnosed as the cause of human melancholy or laziness. The same thing that made the clouds float—an overdose of air—was thought responsible for making some people giddy or flighty. Fire might ignite the human spirit just as readily as a bale of hay. The same elements were found in man and beast, and even in stones and plows.

The Christians of the Middle Ages also accepted the assumptions of an astrology which may have originated locally or traveled from ancient India. The lives of human beings were thought to be just as determined by the moon and other "stars" as the seasons and the droughts and the quality of the crops.

In short, the people of medieval Europe were almost as sure of nature's power in human life as people had always been. And like earlier civilizations, they imagined that the things of the world lived very much like people. Stones fell because they wanted to; they were attracted to the earth, or they "desired" to be reunited with other stones. The world was full of magic, and everything (including people) participated.

## The World as Garment or Stage: Galileo

We can almost see how revolutionary modern science must have been to these people if, instead of reading the new scientific books, we look at their paintings of themselves. The paintings of the Middle Ages have no three-dimensional perspective. Crowds of people are

■ *The appeal and meaning of modern science: the eyes have it. To see is to measure and possess. How high? How far? How deep? How much? Why are none of these men looking at the man in the tower, or at each other, or at any living thing? Were the trees cut down because they obstructed the view? Are those lines of vision latent rifle shots? No, it is only the gentlemen of the new scientific age celebrating the power of sextant, quadrant, telescope, and compass.* (Deutches Museum)

painted on top of each other as if they occupy the same space. Angels and devils are just as real as people. Halos are just as real as heads. Suddenly, beginning in the 1300s in Italy, and later elsewhere, the artists show people and buildings in three dimensions. They seem suddenly aware that things are placed in space, that people in the foreground appear larger than people in the background because they are separated by distance. Even the rectangular shape of paintings (which we take for granted) became increasingly standardized about this time: a painting was to become like a window on the world. What had happened is that the artist had begun to view the world as an observer. He had detached himself from his surroundings and attempted to duplicate what he saw. This is exactly what the first modern scientists attempted to do. They stepped back to look at the world—the stars or butterflies—as detached observers rather than as participants. They measured things instead of vibrating with them—and that was a revolution. By the 1600s the world had become, in Shakespeare's words, a stage; it was no longer a piece of clothing which one would wrap around, but a spectacle that one would observe.

All of the "discoveries" of modern science had helped bring this about. Perhaps they were not discoveries as much as they were "creations," or new ways of seeing things. To put it another way, we might say that the discoveries of individual scientists were not nearly as important as the new attitude toward the world which led them to these discoveries. The attitude of this new science—the assumption that men and nature were fundamentally different—had enormous ecological implications.

Galileo (1564–1642) is usually credited with improving the telescope, turning it on the heavens, and supporting the theory of Copernicus (1473–1543) that the earth revolved around the sun, rather than vice versa. All of this is true. But the reason that Galileo wanted to use the telescope in the first place was that he believed the planets were not living sources of light (as most of his contemporaries believed), but were instead dead balls of matter like the earth and moon.

The great achievement of European physical science (from about 1500) was that it developed a method of describing the separate physical world in terms that could not be refuted. This was because scientists such as Galileo turned their attention from all of the "subjective" features of the world to its "objective" or measurable qualities. Instead of asking about such subjective qualities as the "hopefulness" of rain, they measured it. Instead of asking about the taste or sound or smell of an object, they asked about its size, shape, or rate of motion. They focused, in short, on those qualities of an object which could be measured because measurements were not open to interpretation. Anyone could disagree about the "meaning" of a falling object. There might even be different interpretations about the sound that such an object made as it struck the ground. But no one could disagree about its rate of motion, once that had been computed. The value of science was that its results were indisputable.

The problem with science (from an ecological point of view) was that the human or "subjective" element had to be overlooked so that the objective qualities could be understood. The result of the scientific approach was to see the objects of the natural world as if they were dead. Listen to Galileo explain his method:

> As soon as I form a conception of an object, I immediately feel the necessity of seeing that it has boundaries of some shape or other; that relatively to others it is great or small; that it is in this or that place, in this or that time; that it is in motion or at rest; that it touches, or does

> not touch, another body. . . . But I do not find myself absolutely compelled to determine if it is white or red, bitter or sweet, sonorous or silent, smelling sweetly or disagreeably. . . . Therefore I think that these tastes, smells, colors, etc., with regard to the object in which they appear to reside, are nothing more than mere names. They exist only in the observer. . . . I do not believe that there exists anything in external bodies for exciting tastes, smells, and sounds, etc., except size, shape, quantity, and motion.[16]

In our terms, Galileo had concluded that only the "primary qualities" (those which could be measured) existed. The secondary qualities which could not easily be measured did not exist. This has been a tendency in modern science ever since. The scientist is concerned with providing exact information. In attempting to be exact, he or she singles out the impersonal, "objective," or quantitative qualities of the object under investigation. That is the only way that measurement is possible. But it means divorcing these measurable qualities from the total organic context of the object.

Let us take the case of butterflies. We can appreciate butterflies for their beauty, their colors, or their grace—or we can attempt to understand them. The job of science is understanding. The process of understanding something like butterflies requires that we ask questions that can be answered: How large do they come, what different types are there, how fast do they fly, and how do they stay aloft? These are all questions that can be answered objectively because they only require that we make certain measurements and computations. We do not ask which butterflies are beautiful because there is no way of measuring that, no way of getting an objective answer.

The job of the scientist can be very useful—even ecologically. We might, for instance, want to know about the different types of butterflies in order to replenish an endangered species. The problem is that the more we become preoccupied with measuring and counting, the less we see natural objects in their totality. We are speaking only of a tendency in science—but the tendency is very real. One tendency of science is to isolate and abstract the qualities of an object that can be measured—to treat such qualities as if they were divorced from the total object. But these are not only the conditions of orderly scientific research, they are also the conditions under which organisms die. Try to weigh and measure a live butterfly.

Modern science has enabled us to understand our world because it has simplified complex organic processes so that they conform to mechanical laws. Galileo and Newton were able to tell us much about the acceleration of bodies by treating moving things as "bodies," whether they be people or animals or balls or meteorites. When you are studying movement, everything that moves is equal. The scientists of the seventeenth and eighteenth centuries could tell us so much about the motion of the planets and the objects of the Earth by imagining that both behaved as so many Ping-Pong or billiard balls. This was a way of simplifying problems of weight, mass, and matter. The answers that science has gained are of invaluable assistance. Such answers were impossible with the medieval assumption that even planets and rocks behaved of their own will or inclination. No science was possible as long as people treated the rocks and planets as if they acted by whim. Science appropriated the whim and the will of natural forces with its mechanical laws, and those laws were used in Christian culture to give "dominion over the fish of the sea, and over the birds of the heavens, and over every living thing that moveth upon the earth."

## *For Further Reading*

Lynn White's "The Historical Roots of Our Ecologic Crisis" is reprinted in **Ecology and Religion in History,*** edited by David and Eileen Spring, in Robert Detweiler's **Environmental Decay in Its Historical Context,*** and in **Western Man and Environmental Ethics,*** edited by Ian Barbour, all of which have other good articles. The contrast between Christian and Eastern attitudes toward nature is discussed both more theoretically and more popularly in Alan W. Watts's **Nature, Man and Woman.*** But the grand interpretative synthesis on the Christian background of Western technology is Lewis Mumford's marvelous history, **Technics and Civilization.***

To understand the medieval Christian attitudes toward nature, one normally thinks of histories of science and of philosophy. There are many good books on each. Perhaps the best history of science is Stephen Toulmin and June Goodfield's **The Fabric of the Heavens*** on astronomy, their **Architecture of Matter*** on physics, and their **The Discovery of Time*** on history and geology. For more attention to medieval science, there is A. C. Crombie's **Medieval and Early Modern Science,** Charles Singer's **From Magic to Science,** and M. Clagett's **The Science of Mechanics in the Middle Ages.** Similarly for medieval philosophy, there is E. Gilson's **History of Christian Philosophy in the Middle Ages,** Gordon Leff's **Medieval Thought,*** H. O. Taylor's **The Medieval Mind,** Maurice De Wulf's **Philosophy and Civilization in the Middle Ages,*** F. B. Artz's **The Mind of the Middle Ages,** and F. C. Copleston's **Medieval Philosophy.***

Almost all of these books, however, concentrate on the discoveries and innovations of intellectuals, leaving the attitudes of most people and even

* Available in paperback.

the unchanging assumptions of the intellectuals between the lines. Thus, the tenor of the medieval attitude toward nature might be better understood with a book like C. S. Lewis's **Discarded Image*** or (equally superb and unconventional) Owen Barfield's **Saving the Appearances.*** Another is Arthur O. Lovejoy's classic, **The Great Chain of Being,*** or E. M. W. Tillyard's **The Elizabethan World Picture*** for a slightly later period. Equally useful is the first chapter of William J. Brandt's **The Shape of Medieval History: Studies in Modes of Perception.*** Two other previously mentioned classics should also be indicated in this regard. They are J. Huizinga's **The Waning of the Middle Ages*** and Lynn White, Jr.'s **Medieval Technology and Social Change.***

For those interested in the comparison with Asian civilization, the same advice is in order. Joseph Needham's multivolume **Science and Civilization in China** is a compendium of insight and information. It is invaluable for comparisons with Western civilization. But the introductory student might better understand the Asian attitude toward nature with Joseph Campbell's **The Masks of God: Oriental Mythology,*** Frederick W. Mote's **Intellectual Foundations of China,*** or even Hermann Hesse's **Siddhartha.*** **The Book of Mencius** is a classic that includes references to wastefulness in energy use, conservation, food storage, and flood control. Leon E. Stover's **The Control Ecology of Chinese Civilization: Peasants and Elites in the Last of the Agrarian States*** is a demanding modern account.

Among the more readable introductions to the conceptual revolution of modern science are Herbert Butterfield's **The Origins of Modern Science,*** Arthur Koestler's **The Sleepwalkers,*** and the Toulmin and Goodfield volumes mentioned above. More theoretical and challenging approaches are E. A. Burtt's **The Metaphysical Foundations of Modern Science*** and Thomas S. Kuhn's **The Structure of Scientific Revolutions.*** For a more thorough history there is Charles C. Gillispie's **The Edge of Objectivity*** and A. R. Hall's **The Scientific Revolution, 1500–1800.**

There are of course many other ways of approaching the subject of ecology—even in the time period we have chosen. Sometimes, in fact, the most innovative and interesting books are those which ignore traditional chronological, geographical, and even topical boundaries. One thinks first of Fernand Braudel's **The Mediterranean and the Mediterranean World in the Age of Philip II.*** The first half of the first volume of this masterpiece discusses "The Role of the Environment" in ways that might serve as a model for future works on other areas and other times. Another monumental starting point for the history of ecology is Emmanuel Le Roy Ladurie's **Times of Feast, Times of Famine: A History of Climate Since the Year 1000.** The subject of ecology can also be approached from the perspective of the single world ecological system which has been emerging in the last five hundred years. **The Columbian Exchange: Biological and Cultural Consequences of 1492*** by Alfred W. Crosby, Jr., begins this study in a most engaging and readable way. Finally, for a very tentative overview of human ecology throughout human history we should note the introductory **Man and Nature: An Anthropological Essay in Human Ecology*** by Richard A. Watson and Patty Jo Watson, and Edward Hyams's **Soil and Civilization.***

## Notes

1. Arnold Toynbee, "The Religious Background of the Present Environmental Crisis," *International Journal of Environmental Studies* 3 (1972):141–146. Reprinted in David and Eileen Spring, eds., *Ecology and Religion in History* (New York: Harper & Row, 1974), p. 146.
2. *Ibid.*, pp. 142–143.
3. Spring, *Ecology and Religion*, pp. 4–5. Lynn White's account is in "Continuing the Conversation" in *Western Man and Environmental Ethics*, ed. Ian Barbour (Reading, Mass.: Addison Wesley, 1973), p. 55.
4. Lynn White, Jr., "The Historical Roots of Our Ecologic Crisis," in Spring, *Ecology and Religion*, pp. 19–20.
5. *Ibid.*, pp. 22–23.
6. *Brihadaranyaka Upanishad* (c. 700 B.C.) adapted from Joseph Campbell, *The Masks of God: Oriental Mythology* (New York: Viking Press, 1970), pp. 9–10.
7. Herman Hesse, *Siddhartha*, trans. Hilda Rosner (New York: Bantam Books, 1971), p. 145.
8. Quoted in Yi-Fu Tuan, "Discrepancies Between Environmental Attitude and Behaviour: Examples from Europe and China," *The Canadian Geographer*, 12, no. 3 (1968), quoted in Spring, *Ecology and Religion*, p. 100.
9. *Ibid.*, p. 103.
10. *Ibid.*, p. 107.
11. *Ibid.*, p. 93.
12. Kakuzo Okakura, *The Book of Tea* (New York: Dover, 1964), p. 54. Okakura's charming little introduction to the Orient was first published in 1906.
13. *Ibid.*
14. White, in Spring, *Ecology and Religion*, pp. 26–27.
15. Quoted in Ernest L. Tuveson, *Millenium and Utopia* (Berkeley: University of California, 1949), p. 84.
16. Adapted from Lewis Mumford, *Technics and Civilization* (New York: Harcourt Brace Jovanovich), p. 49.

## CHRONOLOGICAL CONTEXT OF
# The Traditional World: 500-1500

| West Europe | East Europe | Middle East and Africa | China | Japan |
|---|---|---|---|---|
| | | Parthians develop armored cavalry 150 B.C.–A.D. 200 | | |
| Barbarian invasions 300–600 | Constantinople counters barbarians with heavy cavalry 300–600 | | | |
| | Justinian 527–565 | | | |
| | | | | Importation of Buddhism and Chinese civilization 550–800 |
| | | | Sui dynasty 589–618 | |
| Development of cavalry 600–900 | | Muhammad 570–632 | T'ang dynasty 618–907 | |
| | | Moslem expansion 632–738 | | |
| | | | Height of Changan Eighth century | |
| Battle of Tours, Moslems contained to Spain 733 | | Moslem conquest of Spain 711–715 | | Nara period 710–784 |
| Coronation of Charlemagne 800 | | | | Heian period at Kyōto 794–1185 |
| Viking invasions 793–1066 | | | | |

| West Europe | East Europe | Middle East and Africa | China | Japan |
|---|---|---|---|---|
| | | | Sung dynasty 907–1279 | Dominance of Fujiwara clan 866–1160 |
| Height of feudalism 1000–1200 | | | Printing press Tenth century | *Tale of Genji and Pillow Book* c. 1000 |
| Cult of Virgin, chivalry, and courtly love 1050–1350 | Final schism with Rome 1054 | | | |
| First Crusade 1096–1099 | | | | |
| Second Crusade 1147–1149 | | Saladin 1138–1193 | | |
| Third Crusade 1189–1192 | | | | |
| Fourth Crusade 1202–1204 | | | | Feudalism After 1185 |
| | Constantinople sacked 1204 | | Genghis Khan 1162–1227 | Age of military lords (shōgun), warriors (samurai), and Zen Buddhism 1200–1500 |
| Ulrich von Lichtenstein 1204 | | | | |
| Saint Francis of Assisi 1182–1226 | | | Marco Polo visits Hangchow 1275 | |
| Saint Thomas Aquinas 1225–1274 | | | | |
| More Crusades 1218–1290 | | | | |
| Roger Bacon 1214–1294 | | | | |
| Dante 1265–1321 | | | | |
| Giotto 1276–1337 | | | | Height of feudalism 1300–1600 |
| Petrarch 1304–1374 | | | | |

| West Europe | East Europe | Middle East and Africa | China | Japan |
|---|---|---|---|---|
| Black Death 1348–1350 | | | Ming dynasty 1368–1644 | |
| Printing press 1450 | | | | |
| Leonardo 1452–1519 | Capture of Constantinople by Turks 1453 | | | |
| Dürer 1471–1528 | | | | |
| Michelangelo 1475–1564 | | | | |
| Copernicus 1473–1543 | | | | |
| Sir Francis Bacon 1561–1627 | | | | Tokugawa period 1600–1868, feudal and postfeudal |
| Galileo 1564–1642 | | | | |
| Descartes 1596–1650 | | | | |
| Newton 1642–1727 | | | | |

# IV

# PART IV

# THE EARLY MODERN WORLD

## 1500–1800

# Chapter 13

# Politics and Ideals

## Secular States and Middle Classes

Americans in the last few years, especially since Nixon, have shown a new concern for morality in politics. While some people have become cynical about the possibility of politics ever being ethical, others have sought ways to accomplish confidence in government through institutional reforms and the election of politicians with ideals.

In this chapter we try to understand some of our modern expectations about political morality by focusing on the ideas of three extremely important political theorists of the sixteenth and seventeenth centuries: Machiavelli, Hobbes, and Locke. Machiavelli is important because of his formulation of two ideas that are fundamental to our perception of the relationship of politics and morality. The first is the idea that there can be a science of politics, or political science. The second is the idea that the morals of the modern secular state can and must be different from the political ideals of individuals. We live in a world that values not only science and the state, however. We also value the constitutional and legal forms of government that derive from the middle-class, capitalist revolutions of the seventeenth and eighteenth centuries. Thus, we turn to the political theory of Hobbes and Locke because they were among the first to explore the political and moral implications of these middle-class revolutions.

## Machiavelli

> It is customary for those who wish to gain the favour of a prince to endeavour to do so by offering him gifts of those things which they hold most precious, or in which they know him to take especial delight. In this way princes are often presented with horses, arms, cloth of gold, gems, and such-like ornaments worthy of their grandeur. In my desire, however, to offer to Your Highness some humble testimony of my devotion, I have been unable to find among my possessions anything which I hold so dear or esteem so highly as that knowledge of the deeds of great men which I have acquired through a long experience of modern events and a constant study of the past.
>
> With the utmost diligence I have long pondered and scrutinised the actions of the great, and now I offer the results to Your Highness within the compass of a small volume.[1]

So begins Machiavelli's *The Prince,* perhaps the most praised, damned, and influential "small volume" on political morality ever written. It has been called the work of the devil, the start of political science, a hymn to liberty, a satire, a joke, a warning, a divine inspiration, and a simple description of political reality. Three hundred years after it was written, Napoleon Bonaparte declared that it was the only political book worth reading. Even today, the variety of interpretations seems to multiply. A mere list of the books and articles that have been published on Machiavelli and *The Prince* would be larger than the 80 or so pages of the original "small volume." Although it was written simply and directly, it has given rise to almost as many interpretations as there have been readers. They might all agree only that the book is enormously important.

The opening lines just quoted suggest that Machiavelli viewed his book as a gift to a prince. It was the gift he felt he might best give to Lorenzo de Medici, the new ruler of Florence: a gift of his own knowledge of politics. We might also call this "gift" a letter of application for a job. After 14 years of public service for his beloved city (from 1498 to 1512) Machiavelli had learned a great deal, and now he was out of a job. He had served the "republican" (free, popular) government that had removed the Medici family from power. Although he

■ *Niccolo Machiavelli (1469–1527), from a portrait by Santi di Tito. One interpretation. (EPA)*

may not have considered himself anti-Medici, he had commanded the republic's militia, completed diplomatic missions for the republic, and made important contacts with the family's enemies. Thus, when papal armies were able to return the Medici to power in 1512, Machiavelli's name was on a list of possible republican conspirators. He was arrested, tortured, and then released because he was clearly innocent, but he was not asked to carry on his work for the city. For the next 14 years (until his death) he read, wrote, and attempted to regain the most useful work he knew: service to the city that he "loved more than [his] soul." The great tragedy for Machiavelli was that the Medici never called him back. *The Prince* was largely ignored by the prince it was meant to please. The final tragedy of Machiavelli's life was that when the Medici were overthrown again in 1527 and democratic government was restored, his old "application" (of 1513) came back to haunt him. He hurried back to Florence, but the widely circulated manuscript of *The Prince* had made him too many enemies among the republicans. Before the news of the council's rejection came, he was dead.

*The Prince* is a book of lessons in government, filled with examples from Machiavelli's diplomatic experience and readings in ancient history. As a "how to govern" book, it was similar to dozens of instructional volumes (often called "A Mirror for Magistrates") which rulers had been reading for hundreds of years. But Machiavelli's guide lacked the Christian moral tone of the earlier "mirrors." That was what shocked the council of the Republic of Florence in 1527 and so many readers since.

The lessons that Machiavelli gave were lessons in power and success, grounded in "reality" rather than "imagination":

> For how we live is so far removed from how we ought to live, that he who abandons what is done for what ought to be done, will rather learn to bring about his own ruin than his preservation. A man who wishes to make a profession of goodness in everything must necessarily come to grief among so many who are not good. Therefore it is necessary for a prince, who wishes to maintain himself, to learn how not to be good, and to use this knowledge and not use it, according to the necessity of the case.[2]

The career of Cesare Borgia (whom others viewed as an unprincipled, murderous tyrant) was for Machiavelli most worthy of imitation by a perceptive prince. In discussing how princes could attain order in captured territories, Machiavelli told of Borgia's administration of the Italian territory of Romagna. The province had previously been governed by weak rulers, Machiavelli relates, so that it was "a prey to robbery, assaults, and every kind of disorder." Cesare Borgia "therefore judged it necessary to give them a good government in order to make them peaceful and obedient to his rule." Borgia purposely picked "a cruel and able man" to bring order to the province. Then, after the man had viciously done his job, Borgia "resolved to show that if any cruelty had taken place it was not by his orders, but through the harsh disposition of his minister." Thus, Borgia had his appointed scapegoat "cut in half and placed one morning in the middle of the public square" to satisfy the people's hatred and win their gratitude for himself.

Machiavelli says that Cesare Borgia (whom he had met) sought to preserve in four ways the territories that were given to him by his father, Pope Alexander VI: "[f]irst, by destroying all who were of the blood of those ruling families which he had despoiled," so that none of them could organize to regain their territories; secondly, by gaining allies among the Roman nobles as a check on any future pope who might be hostile; thirdly, by controlling the College of Cardinals so that he could choose his father's successor; "[f]ourthly, by acquiring such power before the pope died as to be able to resist alone the first onslaught." Machiavelli goes on to say that Borgia was almost completely successful in all of these tasks. "For of the dispossessed rulers," he adds, "he killed as many as he could lay hands on, and very few escaped." He had also at least gained veto power in the College of Cardinals over the choice of his father's successor. His only mistake, Machiavelli concludes, was that Borgia let someone he injured become the next pope (Julius II). Otherwise, Machiavelli says:

> I find nothing to blame, on the contrary, I feel bound, as I have done, to hold him up as an example to be imitated by all who by fortune and with the arms of others have risen to power. For with his great courage and high ambition he could not have acted otherwise, and his designs were only frustrated by the short life of Alexander and his own illness.[3]

We get a sense of the limits Machiavelli can accept in the next case he discusses: that of the ancient tyrant of Sicily, Agathocles. First, he dismisses the moral problem by stating that the example of Agathocles is "sufficient for any one obliged to imitate" him. Then, he details Agathocles' "life of the utmost wickedness." Once, for instance,

> he called together one morning the people and senate of Syracuse, as if he had to deliberate on matters of importance to the republic, and at a given signal had all the senators and the richest men of the people killed by his soldiers.[4]

Agathocles was certainly a brilliant strategist and a brave man in surmounting obstacles, Machiavelli says, but we cannot call him "virtuous."

> It cannot be called virtue to kill one's fellow-citizens, betray one's friends, be without faith, without pity, and without religion; by these methods one may indeed gain power, but not glory.[5]

But Machiavelli understands that the wicked may be powerful, and their treachery might even increase their power:

> Some may wonder how it came about that Agathocles, and others like him, could, after infinite treachery and cruelty, live secure for many years in their country and defend themselves from external enemies without being conspired against by their subjects; although many others have, owing to their cruelty, been unable to maintain their position in times of peace, not to speak of the uncertain times of war. I believe this arises from the cruelties being exploited well or badly. Well committed may be called those (if it is permissible to use the word well of evil) which are perpetuated once for the need of securing one's self, and which afterwards are not persisted in, but are exchanged for measures as useful to the subjects as possible. Cruelties ill committed are those which, although at first few, increase rather than diminish with time.[6]

Machiavelli's "moral" is that "the conqueror must arrange to commit all his cruelties at once" so that the people will have an increasing sense of security and improvement.

We can see from the way that Machiavelli uses terms like good and evil that he is speaking the language of tactics, not of morality. This was a new and frightening language to his readers who were trained in the Christian culture of moral absolutes. Traditional Christian values were turned on their heads. "It is much safer to be feared than loved." Although every prince should want to *appear* merciful rather than cruel, he should "take care not to misuse this mercifulness" to the point where disorders arise. *The Prince* is full of such advice: "imitate the fox and the lion"; "be a great pretender and liar"; "be able to do evil."

Statements like these are the cause of Machiavelli's notorious reputation for immorality. But Machiavelli was not immoral. He was simply urging political rulers to recognize the way people really behave, and to act accordingly in the interests of the state. He was rejecting Christian morality for rulers because it would destroy the state. In place of Christian ethics, Machiavelli invented political science (the study of political realities) and created a new version of ancient pagan morality (an ethical system which prized the kingdoms of this world more than those of the next).

Both of these creations—scientific politics and state morality—were Machiavelli's gifts to the modern world. Both were virtually unknown in medieval and Renaissance Europe, and both have shaped our ideas of politics and morality ever since. In traditional Christian society politics and morality were barely separated. The medieval world view recognized a chain or ladder of God's creations, from the lowest to the highest:

> All things whatsoever, spritual and material things, the archangels, the angels, the seraphim and cherubim and all the other celestial legions, man, organic nature, matter, all of them are bound in this golden chain about the feet of God. There are two different hierarchies; the hierarchy of existence and that of value. But they are not opposed to each other; they correspond to each other in perfect harmony. The degree of value depends on the degree of being. What is lower in the scale of existence is also lower in the ethical scale. The more a thing is remote from the first principle, from the source of all things, so much the less is its grade of perfections.[7]

In terms of this medieval perspective, ideal and real were not different. The more "being" or existence a thing possessed the closer it was to God, and the better it was. Humans stood between the animals and angels in both being and value. The king stood above other men in divine sanction as well as power. Such a perspective did not provide the intellectual tools necessary for examining questions about the misuse of power or the gaps between ideal and real. Ethics and politics could barely be conceived of separately.

Machiavelli changed all of that. Or rather, Machiavelli recognized and applauded changes that had begun in Renaissance Italy. Modern secular states were coming into existence. Machiavelli called them "new principalities." They were formed by men like Cesare Borgia. They were based on naked power. They claimed no divine justification. They paid no allegiance to higher feudal lords and set themselves free of medieval hierarchies. They claimed the territory that they could control, and they rested their case with the force of arms. They were neither small city-states, nor divine-right monarchies, nor Holy Roman Empires.

Although secular states proliferated considerably during the Renaissance, many originated a few hundred years earlier. Perhaps the earliest was the state created by Frederick II in southern Italy three hundred years before Machiavelli wrote *The Prince*.

> It was an absolute monarchy in the modern sense; it had emancipated itself from any influence of the Church. The officials of this state were not clerics but laymen. Christians, Jews, Saracens had an equal share in the administration; nobody was excluded for merely religious reasons. At the court of Frederick II a discrimination between sects, between nations or races was unknown. The paramount interest was that of the secular, the "earthly" state.
>
> That was an entirely new fact, a fact that had no equivalent in medieval civilization. But this fact had not yet found a theoretical expression and justification.[8]

## Machiavelli's Morality for the Modern State

Machiavelli provided that theory. He met the issue of political secularism head-on. The church had excommunicated Frederick II twice. Dante, Machiavelli's fellow Florentine, placed Frederick in the flaming ring of heretics in his *Inferno*. Frederick himself justified his state in religious terms, imagining that he had been singled out by divine providence and given the grace of the "highest reason." Machiavelli undercut the needs for religious attack *or* defense. He questioned the desirability of the Christian state itself. "Our religion," he said of Christianity, "instead of heroes canonizes those only that are meek and lowly." That can never be the basis of a strong state. Pagan religions were much more politically serviceable, he thought. "Pagans deified none but men full of worldly glory, such as great commanders and illustrious governors of commonwealths."[9]

In the new secular principalities, Machiavelli felt, the state could again become the source of religion and morality. As in the pre-Christian ancient world, state gods and official priests could harness the energies of the people on behalf of, rather than against, the political institutions. The namby-pamby Christian ethics of love, prayer, surrender, and escape could be transformed by the new secular states into an ethical system that praised strength, power, independence, and ambition. That was the stuff of successful political life for princes and people alike. Religion was an invaluable tool for the maintenance of a state, but it must be a religion of the state—a religion which created soldiers and patriots, not martyrs who turned the other cheek.

Machiavelli's defense of state religion and state morality was too radical for his time. His fundamentally anti-Christian position was too much for anyone then or since (with the exception of Neitzsche in the nineteenth century). The most ruthless rulers have declared their Christian love and humility. But Machiavelli was right about how things were changing. The secular state has become its own authority. Modern religion has become political loyalty, obedience, and patriotism. We still call ourselves Christians, but our loyalties, our attachments, and our feelings go out to Caesar, to Caesar's state, and to the state's symbols of power. Machiavelli saw that this was beginning to occur in the new principalities of the Renaissance, but it has proceeded much more quickly and decisively in the larger nation-states that have arisen since. By including whole ethnic groups (Italians, French, Germans, or English) in the same territorial state, the nation-state could add the appeal of ethnic pride to its arsenal of brute power. The lip service we still give to Christianity disguises the fact that we now worship the state instead.

The transition from a world in which religion was the chief end in life to one in which religion is either ignored or used to prop up the state took many forms. In France absolute monarchy took shape as the kings gained control of the church. Even French cardinals generally associated their interests more with the French state than with Rome. Cardinal Richelieu, who controlled the government for Louis XIII, combined a policy of Gallicanism (establishing a French, "Gallic" national Catholic church) with the development of a theoretical defense called *raison d'état.* Although Machiavelli did not use the French phrase which means "reason of state," or state morality, it expresses the kind of secular justification of state power that Machiavelli defended. Richelieu attempted to justify Gallicanism and the doctrine of *raison d'état* by having one of his aides write an *Apology for Machiavelli in Favor of Princes and State Officials* (1643). More often, the new monarchs of secular states declared their heated hostility to

Machiavelli (as in Frederick II of Prussia's *Anti-Machiavelli*) and then proceeded to follow the master's instructions to the letter. That was exactly what Machiavelli would have advised if he were still alive: condemn me publicly, but read carefully.

"States and people are governed differently than individuals." Only Machiavelli's meaning of "states" made that a new thought. Others had accepted the need for governments to engage in certain kinds of behavior that were denied individuals: legislation, taxation, declaring war, even executing an individual. But Machiavelli first used the word "state" in the modern sense—a secular, territorial power outlasting separate governments, whose ultimate justification was not divine will or popular will but force. The idea that the state could do anything that was necessary to maintain its existence was new. Medieval monarchs did not justify anything for the state. Even the existence of the state was second to God's will. Many medieval rulers had no doubt acted as if their rule were all that mattered. But they invariably did so beyond the pale of the church and their own consciences. They still took their Christian ethics seriously. The fear of God was real. The novelty of Machiavelli's small volume is that it brought power politics back into the ethical cosmos. Machiavelli's new pagan ethical system made force and fraud not only acceptable but necessary for rulers who served the state—a goal more worthy "than my own immortal soul." State morality, an anything-goes ethics of power, the defense of the state, the reasons of state—that was what was new. "It was new and it was a monstrosity," the great historian Friedrich Meinecke wrote in his *History of the Idea of Reason of State* which begins with Machiavelli.

When we ask about the abuse of power in the modern state, we almost have to begin by examining the power that we allow that state without calling it "abusive." Abuse of state power can be so destructive today because the *accepted* power of the state is so enormous. Especially given the fact that we have lost (or transcended—depending on your point of view) the traditional Christian ethical system which kept us honest, our anything-goes ethics make any concentrated power that much more dangerous. The modern state is infinitely more powerful than were the new principalities of Renaissance Europe. Yet, in the name of "national security," "national interest," "national defense," and now even "executive privilege" we allow that state a degree of power over our lives that might make Cesare Borgia blush.

We allow that power to the state, not the particular individuals in the government, of course. But so did Machiavelli. Indeed, Machiavelli assumed more than we do that the ruler would use his power only in the best interests of the state. The problem is that we (like

Machiavelli) often leave it up to the particular ruler or government to determine what the national interest or state needs are. The potential for abuse is implicit in the power.

We said before that two modern developments have followed from Machiavelli's separation of politics and morality. On the one hand, morality was determined by the needs of the state: state morality and state religion replaced traditional Christian ethics of government. On the other hand, politics divorced from Christian morality became a "science." Now that we have examined Machiavelli's first invention, state morality, let us turn briefly to his other contribution, his scientific politics. They are equally important to an understanding of modern attitudes about the relation of politics and morality. We not only have a tendency to accept whatever the state does as moral, we also tend to think of politics as a scientific rather than an ethical activity.

## Machiavelli's Modern Science of Politics

Machiavelli has often been called the father of modern political science. Some of his defenders, in fact, have argued that he was only a scientist: he merely observed how people behaved without imposing his own values. We have said enough to call that interpretation into question. Machiavelli did make value judgments. He applauded Cesare Borgia. He justified state power. The state was in fact his highest value. Machiavelli was unique not only in what he liked but also in his "objectivity" and passion to understand things as they really were. As observer of the human realities behind the veil of sanctimonious rhetoric, Machiavelli was perhaps the first European social scientist. He watched what worked and what did not. He gathered the evidence of the ages and formulated general rules for the power brokers of the future.

Just as Galileo trained his telescope on the heavens and realized that they were made of the same stuff as the earth, Machiavelli turned his perceptive eye to princes and concluded that they behaved just like the beasts of the field. Both "scientists" were more concerned with what "is" than what "should be." In the process of their investigations, both discarded the medieval understanding of an ascending chain of being-and-goodness for scientific laws that applied equally to planets and plows, princes and paupers. Both secularized the world, in order to speak of the capabilities of man. Both tried not to judge in order to understand.

But there were implicit moral judgments in viewing the world without mystery or morals. The scientists insisted that they were only interested in the knowledge that the spectacle of nature offered. Observation was an end in itself. Knowledge was more important than participation and involvement. Though that may have been possible for Galileo the physical scientist (and recent atomic research has raised some doubts), it was not so simple for Machiavelli the scientist of men. He imagined himself to be a mere technician or physician: only showing us how to cure "hectic fevers" in the political body. But even his image of the state as a body or organism had distinct moral implications. If the state is itself a body, it has an instinct for survival which must be satisfied. Part of it is a heart, part a brain, part a stomach, all of which are more important than arms and legs. Disease in the organs might require strong medicine, perhaps even the amputation of a limb. The physician who is willing to prescribe a special diet, blood letting, or surgery is making definite moral judgements when the patient is the "body politic" of the state.

Sometimes Machiavelli's objective, scientific stance is that of a master strategist who is merely watching the game. This ostensibly amoral spectator's role also has decisive moral consequences. In his illuminating study, *The Myth of the State,* the philosopher Ernst Cassirer shows how the "mere observer" of the human game is necessarily engaged in moral judgments:

> Machiavelli looked at political combats as if they were a game of chess. He had studied the rules of the game very thoroughly. But he had not the slightest intention of changing or criticizing these rules. His political experience taught him that the political game never had been played without fraud, deception, treachery, and felony. He neither blamed nor recommended these things. His only concern was to find the best move—the move that wins the game. . . . Sometimes he shook his head at a bad move; sometimes he burst out with admiration and applause. It never occurred to him to ask by whom the game was played. The players may be aristocrats or republicans, barbarians or Italians, legitimate princes or usurpers. Obviously that makes no difference for the man who is interested in the game itself—and in nothing but the game. In his theory Machiavelli is apt to forget that the political game is not played with chessmen, but with real men, with human beings of flesh and blood; and that the weal and woe of these beings is at stake.[10]

The politics of the modern state has become a science and a game. Moral considerations (except the "morals of state") are set aside for discussions of strategy, "scenarios," and "game plans." While political scientists develop "game theory" and social psychologists explore convincing myths, politicians acquaint themselves with the magic of these new priests and make statesmanship an aspect of public relations and advertising.

It is certainly important to understand human behavior, and the model of scientific understanding is still our best guide. Political science can be a tool for greater knowledge of human needs, a testing ground for possible solutions to political problems. It can also be used, however, as yet another device for manipulation, fraud, and personal advantage.

## Protestantism, Absolutism, and Middle-Class Revolution

While Machiavelli argued that politics had nothing to do with ethics, a number of deeply religious "reformers" like Savonarola, Luther, and Calvin insisted that politics must have everything to do with ethics. The Protestant Reformation of the sixteenth century was essentially an attempt to transform the world with the ethics of Christ. Savonarola attempted such a government by God in Florence while Machiavelli was still young. Later Calvin created such a theocracy in Geneva, Switzerland. Luther gained the support of Frederick of Saxony and other German princes in a similar venture to create the holy state.

Although the secular, scientific temperament of Machiavelli was far removed from the religious zeal of the Protestant reformers, and although Machiavelli separated politics from ethics while the reformers sought to reunify them, the results of their labors were almost identical. The Protestants made their states as powerful as any that Machiavelli envisioned. Their states were supposed to legislate the "will of God," but unable to rely on centuries of its interpretation by Catholics, the reformers were forced to interpret it themselves. The results could be only slightly less self-serving than the commands of a secular prince who was mainly concerned with the prosperity of his state. In short, the modern state was created in two forms during the sixteenth century: one secular, the other religious. Both of these enjoyed religious sanction, however, and both were enormously powerful. Protestantism, in fact, served the interests of the national state, the anti-Roman monarch, and the rising national consciousness in some ways better than the state religions that Machiavelli conjured from the pagan past. The patriotism of the English, for instance, was immeasurably deepened by Henry VIII's Protestantism.

In many ways the states that were created between the sixteenth and eighteenth century in Europe (whether encouraged by Machiavellian secular theory or by Protestantism) were ruled by stronger monarchs than any before or since. The eighteenth century was the great age of the absolute monarch and the theory that kings ruled by divine right. After this, the state grew in power, but the rule of the state became legitimized, legalized, and limited. Monarchs were replaced by legislatures, presidents, and parliaments. The rule of the individual was shed for the rule of law.

The unbridled power of the monarch's state became (by the seventeenth century in England and by the eighteenth century in France) too oppressive for the increasingly prosperous middle class to stomach. They revolted to limit the power of the state or open it to themselves. These middle-class revolutionaries spoke the language of new ethical absolutes. It was no longer the absolutes of Christianity or the secular absolutes of *raison d'état*. It was a revival of ancient notions of natural law, a doctrine which again tried to combine the natural and the moral, the actual and the ideal, the political and the ethical. For a brief time—in the midst of revolution—the middle classes of England and France asked that politics be fundamentally moral again.

Maybe those in power are always more interested in "political realities," or "the way things are." Those who are deprived of power may be more conscious of what "should be" and less interested in what "is." Rulers call their subjects to face realities. Much of the status quo operates in their favor. They mouth the required moral phrases, but their attention is more practical than ethical. It is the class of people who are excluded from politics, the "outs," the potential revolutionaries who ask sweeping ethical questions and demand moral politics.

Such revolutionaries call for ethics, but they actually want power. Their idea of justice often does not go beyond the admission of themselves and their followers to political power, but at least their dissent and struggle usually involves the raising of basic questions about the relationship of politics and ethics. Sometimes, when the struggle is successful, the result is a new agreement about the moral possibilities and limitations of politics in general.

In brief, this is what happened during the course of the middle-class revolutions of the seventeenth and eighteenth centuries. Beginning in England in the middle seventeenth century (1640s), the European class of merchants, lawyers, professionals, and artisans, which stood midway between the aristocracy and the poor, challenged the dominance of kings and nobles. This middle class developed a wide ranging body of political theory that was highly moral in tone and purpose. They criticized the idea of the divine right of kings as a guise of tyranny. They condemned the Machiavellian notion of the state as an organic body which set its own ends, and offered instead an image of the state as an artificial creation of people and a means to human ends. They objected to the Machiavellian acceptance of the ruler, prince, or king as interpreter of the public needs and called instead for representative government. They questioned Machiavelli's contention that the exercise of power was always proper and outlined rules and laws which bound ruler as well as ruled. And they went further than Machiavelli in distinguishing between the state (which some still thought to be the eternal sovereign) and the particular governments of that state (which might be replaced at the will of the people).

Similar principles were enunciated continually in the course of the middle-class revolutions: in England in the 1640s and again in 1689, in America in the 1770s and 1780s, in France in the 1780s and 1790s, and in most of the rest of Europe at the end of the eighteenth and beginning of the nineteenth century. Even the revolutions in Russia and Latin America in the early 1800s expressed the new political ethics of the rising middle class: representative government, the rule of law, the limited state, and government as "means" rather than "end."

The most visible feature of these middle-class revolutions was the challenge to monarchy. In England and France the kings were actually executed. Regicide was, however, only one of the possible consequences of the new political and ethical theory. The principles of middle-class theory (which came to be known as liberalism) can be summarized as the limitation of power that had previously been considered absolute and a notion of "ethics as process."

## The Ethic of Process

The new ethic of process requires some explanation. Today it is almost part of our "common sense," but three hundred years ago it was a dangerously subversive idea. Remember that in ancient tribal or caste society (as in India) ethics were dependent on clan or caste membership. The Hindu example is probably only an exaggeration of tendencies in other ancient societies. Members of a ruling caste were expected to behave according to different moral codes than the members of a priestly or peasant caste. To a certain extent this social differentiation of ethical systems continued even into medieval society. In general, however, medieval Christian culture (and Eastern Buddhism) conceived of a unified ethical-political world and argued that ethics were universal. The same set of standards were to apply to rulers, priests, and peasants alike. All were equally divine in the Buddhist view or equal in the eyes of God according to Christian teaching.

The creation of secular states (witnessed by Machiavelli) and of theocratic Protestant states (in the Reformation) made the state and its rulers (whether prince or prophet) the judge of a new state morality. The state flourished. Its morality, official religion, and political control became virtually absolute. Since the authority of the state was in the person of the ruler, it varied from tyranny to "enlightened despotism." It was sometimes benevolent, but that depended on the particular king. Even the advisory assemblies of nobles which had existed since the Middle Ages lost their ancient power of consent or approval. The Estates General (or parliament) of France, for instance, was simply not called to assemble from 1614 until 1789, the year of the revolution, and it virtually ignored the middle class anyway. The English Revolution of 1640 similarly had been precipitated by the attempt of King Charles I to govern without Parliament since 1629. Both revolutions made a middle-class parliament supreme. Unlike the kings, these parliamentarians could not govern in their own names as if they were each appointed by God, nor could they argue that God had directed their class to rule.

Representative government was defended on other terms. It was, the middle class argued, the rule of the people and the rule of law. In effect, they made the *process* of representative government the highest ethical value of politics. We might disagree about the ends of government, they said by their actions, but at least we can give sanction to that disagreement and to an agreed upon means for the resolution of our differences. Machiavelli or Calvin would never have accepted a government concerned with means rather than ends. The notion that means were more important than ends, indeed the idea that the process rather than the goals were the treasure of true citizenship, would have been abhorrent to Machiavelli, Calvin, or the absolute monarchs.

The middle-class revolutionaries really had no other choice. Since government was to be in the hands of the many, there would inevitably be disagreements. Such disagreements could only be resolved in the process of debate, persuasion, bargaining, compromise, and trade-offs. They could never be sure that such a process would always lead to the "right" decision, but they were convinced of fewer absolute "rights" than Machiavelli or Calvin. In effect, they agreed to define the "right decision" as the one which the process of debate and voting produced.

In a strange way the work of Machiavelli and the Protestant reformers led almost inevitably to this modern political ethic of process. Machiavelli led the way by defining politics as a secular activity, but even though he placed the ends of the state above everything else, he was preoccupied with rules, strategy, and process. Much of Machiavelli's work, in fact, was devoted to the examination of political process in the republics of the ancient world. On the other hand, the Protestant reformers were so committed to doing what they perceived as God's will that their only alternative to governing a theocracy was to live as outsiders in a secular state. If their own beliefs were not legislated, then none could be. It was, for example, one of the most religiously committed of American Protestants—Roger Williams—who argued *on theological grounds* in the 1630s for the separation of church and state and for secular, democratic government. God's law was too precious to be interpreted by states; mere governments should not pretend to deal in absolutes.

In a secular state where power was to be shared by many, whether each member of the government was an atheist or a different kind of Protestant, the process of decision making had to be valued more highly than particular ends. The political process itself had to be sacred. Nothing was more serious than tampering with the process because nothing threatened the fragile unity of agreement to disagree more. No single rule was as important as the inviolability of the system of rule making.

The processes of middle-class government may have originated in medieval cities and parliaments, but they developed rapidly in the course and aftermath of revolution. Majorities, parties, parliamentary rules, elections, voting, caucus, clubs, debates, processes to limit and balance powers, constitutions, separated powers, procedures for everything: these were the safeguards of the new system. Government became a serious game with complex rules. A brutal struggle of conflicting interests, in deadly earnest and without appeal, it was carried on, at the least, without bloodshed. Like the similar middle-class economic marketplace (or the new stock exchanges), parliamentary government channeled the most heated confrontations of power into peaceful compromise and resolution. What seemed like a fanatical adherence to procedure kept tempers cool and disputes from getting too personal.

One of the greater achievements of the middle-class revolutions may have been the translation of civil war into party politics. The Italian city-states of the Renaissance often oscillated between civil war and institutionalized struggle, but the institutions rarely held. The "popular party" was never too far removed from a citizen militia. This was essentially the case in the English Revolution of 1640. The first wide ranging debates, creating of programs, and gathering of factions or "parties" occurred in the revolutionary New Model Army among the soldiers. In the French Revolution of 1789, political parties grew out of middle-class clubs (like the Jacobin club) and crystallized around particular programs in the debates of the legislative assembly and the struggles on the street.

At first, political parties were thought to be divisive forces, conspiracies against the rest of the nation. This was particularly the view of monarchists (who favored the restoration of a king) and those who had absolute solutions to which no one seemed to listen. After Oliver Cromwell's revolutionary Commonwealth government began to come apart and the Stuart kings (Charles II and James II) were restored (between 1660 and 1689), party activity fell off in England. Only with the revival of parliamentary power in the Glorious Revolution of 1689 (the second stage of the English middle-class revolution) when Parliament declared the monarchy vacant and selected James's daughter Mary and William of the Netherlands to rule England, did political parties in the modern sense come into being. When real power was in the hands of the many (in Parliament) rather than of the king or the few, political parties became an essential part of the process of disputing and deciding. This took some time. The parties of 1689—the conservative, country Tory party and the moneyed, urban middle-class Whigs—probably had no more than a few thousand members. Even most of the middle class was still excluded. In the 1760s King George III could still hope to play the role of a popular "patriot king" who could set aside party differences and rule arbitrarily. Not until 1770 did an English political theorist of any influence (Edmund Burke) actually advocate political parties.

Parties were probably the most difficult element of the ethics of process to accept. They would originate in periods of revolution and crisis—when the divisions were very real and very important. These were precisely the times when the goals of the parties were much more important than the acceptance of the process or the rights of the opposition. In times of social harmony (at least among the powerful) process could take precedence over special interest, but then the existence of parties itself seemed destructive. Strong leaders, like George III, George Washington, or Napoleon, were suspicious of parties, but the solution of a Napoleon was often to abolish legitimate opposition and drive it into exile or civil war. The ideas of process involved in the separation of state and government, the acceptance of "the loyal opposition" (loyal to the state but not the ruling party), and the willingness to play by the rules (even, or especially, when it meant losing power) were ideas of the antimonarchial, middle-class revolution that took a long time to mature.

The differences between Machiavelli's political ethics and the modern ethics of process are sharpest in this light. We accept the latter today, but we still practice the former when we think we can get away with it. The moral failure of the Nixon administration (and, to be fair, of a number of Democratic city machines) was precisely of this kind. The political process itself was undermined. What better examples could there be of the corruption of the political process than the use of state money and personnel to spy on the opposition, harass their contributors and spokespersons with state agencies, and to use the police power and bureaucracy for partisan ends?

## Some Unfinished Business: The Political Ethics of Liberal Market Society

Just as Machiavelli's secularism and realism had its underside of absolutism and "my country right or wrong" statism, so did the middle-class revolutionary idea of "ethics as process" have its seamier side. To put it as simply as possible, the political process was necessarily closed to all but the propertied class, and (even ideally) the political theory of process offered a sordid, jungle image of humanity and a competitive market idea of society.

Perhaps we can understand these limitations best by examining the political-ethical theory of two of the most famous spokesmen for the English middle-class revolution of the seventeenth century. They are Thomas Hobbes (1588–1679) and John Locke (1632–1704). Their political theories span the century. Although they are usually remembered for only two books, Hobbes's *Leviathan* and Locke's *Second Treatise on Government,* they wrote prolifically. The *Leviathan* was certainly one of the most unpopular books ever written in England. It was rigorously logical and unflatteringly realistic. No party or group accepted the theoretical foundations that Hobbes provided. Most political writers ignored or (like Locke) attempted to refute Hobbes's depressing conclusions. We will look at Hobbes because he was right. Locke, on the other hand, is interesting for our purposes because of his enormous popularity and prestige. His work became the "common sense" of the eighteenth century. His emphasis on constitutionalism, majority rule, individualism, and limited government inspired generations of middle-class revolutionaries in Europe and America. His very vocabulary was enshrined in our own Declaration of Independence and on American minds ever since. We still speak of "natural" or "inalienable rights" of life, liberty, etc. We still profess the same principles of government. Our justifications of our own "liberal democracy" are still essentially the arguments that Locke worked out to justify the approaching Glorious Revolution of 1689. The rule of law, the consent of the people, the preservation of our liberties, the right of election and even of rebellion—these too are principles of John Locke. In short, Locke defended all of the "good things" that we have come to know as democratic theory. The only problem was his logic and that he was speaking solely for the political liberty of his class—the owners of property.

■ *The title page of the first edition of Thomas Hobbes'* Leviathan, *1651. (Granger)*

## Hobbes: A Government for the Competitive Jungle

Hobbes did for the middle class what Machiavelli had done for princes. He surveyed the changing scene of English society, noted the new pervasiveness of buying and selling and market mentality, and swept away the old puffy theories of natural law and moral responsibility because they no longer made sense. Since traditional Christian ethical theory (with all its talk of community and commonwealth, of loyalty and obligation, of divine hierarchy and Christian charity) no longer reflected the way people actually behaved, it was useless as a theory of ethics or government. Hobbes based his theory on actuality. He was looking for a justification of newly emerging secular government which would show people what and why they must obey—without appealing to arguments that had no validity in people's hearts, minds, and guts.

Seventeenth-century England was changing from a feudal, hierarchical society in which the chain of mutual rights and obligations was taken for granted to a capitalist or market society in which rights and responsibilities were bought and sold like everything else. Hobbes recognized the importance of the market. He understood that the elements of market society—private ownership of property, the increasing use of money, and the translation of all relationships into money values—were transforming traditional England. Society was more competitive, less cooperative. Relationships were more fluid, less fixed. Fortunes rose and fell rapidly. Insecurity and war seemed more natural than security and peace.

Hobbes may not have fully realized how new this society was. Seventeenth-century thinkers were still used to thinking, in the style of traditional society, that basic things were always the same, that whatever existed was "natural." Hobbes was the first to accept this new society as the necessary starting point for a viable ethical and political theory. He began with an examination of what he called "the state of nature" which detailed the characteristics of the emerging market society. Only after such a realistic assessment of the way things actually were, he argued, would it be possible to determine what could be. Instead of imposing the "oughts" of traditional theology and natural law (which had worked more or less successfully in traditional society), Hobbes saw the need for a more realistic understanding of the "natural" to suggest the limits of the possible and desirable.

From the vantage point of seventeenth-century market society, the natural state of human life appeared to Hobbes to be "nasty, brutish, and short." Taking market society to its logical conclusion, Hobbes saw a jungle of competitive struggle. Instead of society there were only deals. Instead of creative, emotional, social human beings, Hobbes saw animals with basic appetites—or, more appropriately, rational, calculating machines.

Nothing in Hobbes offended seventeenth-century religious sensibilities more than his materialistic, mechanistic view of humanity. The idea that humans were essentially machines which subtracted potential pain from material advantage before they acted was, no doubt, disconcerting to those who preached love, charity, and spiritual fulfillment. But Hobbes was a realist. The machine model of human behavior made more sense as he looked around him. It also made more sense in terms of the overriding importance of buying and selling decisions in market society.

Hobbes did not use the terms "market society" or "capitalism." These are later words. Further, as we said, he thought he was describing the way things naturally were. His generalizations, however, about the natural state of man suggest that he was considering the requirements and possibilities of a society in which the laws and relationships of the market were primary. Human action, for instance, "is either for gain, or for glory; that is, not so much for love of our fellows, as for the love of ourselves." Individuals are like self-directed, self-willed atoms, each alone trying to maximize its wealth, power, or influence. Values, morals, and ethics have no meaning except in terms of the satisfaction of these desires.

> *Honourable* is whatsoever possession, action, or quality, is an argument and signe of Power. . . . Dominion, and Victory is Honourable; because acquired by Power. . . . Riches are Honourable; for they are Power.[11]

In terms of market morality, the right, proper, or good action is that which increases one's power, wealth, or advantage. All people seek to maximize their desires and to increase their possessions. The market works because people are able to ignore emotional issues and to bargain rationally. The best people are those rational machines which can get the most out of the bargaining process. Value is getting the best price. Since everything is for sale, the best people are those who can command the highest price for their own power.

> The *Value,* or Worth of a man, is as of all other things, his Price; that is to say, so much as would be given for the use of his Power. . . . And as in other things, so in men, not the seller, but the buyer determines the Price. For let a man (as most men do,) rate themselves at the highest Value he can; yet their true Value is no more than it is esteemed by others.[12]

If society is, then, a competitive market, if each man is only out for himself, if power and wealth is its own justification, if everybody has his or her price, and there are no other values than market values, how is it possible for people to agree to any kind of law, ethical system, or government? Hobbes answered that everyone is equally insecure within the market. The market determines not only each person's value and possessions, but also each person's fear that someone will opt for force when he or she loses. As competitive as human relations are in market society, they are still better than open warfare. Some sovereign power is necessary to ensure that people obey the workings of the market without taking things into their own hands. All people, since they are rational, will recognize that an absolute or sovereign power is necessary to enforce the rules of the game: "to appoint in what manner all kinds of contract between Subjects, (as buying, selling, exchanging, borrowing, lending, letting, and taking to hire,) are to bee made; and by what words, and signes they shall be understood for valid."[13]

This is the kind of agreement on politics as process, the agreement to disagree but play by the rules, that we discussed in the previous section. Yet, Hobbes deals squarely with an issue that we only hinted at before. How can we expect a real loser at the social market to continue to play fairly while losing? What is to stop someone from raising an axe or an army when everything is lost? What happens when for some individual or group the controls of market morality and government are more disastrous than the jungle?

Hobbes's answer is twofold. First, remember that he is talking to the property holders. They can recognize that a sovereign power is necessary to ensure the continuance of a market society which allows them private property. Even when they lose some of their holdings, they will still be able to regain and increase their possessions if they have accepted a sovereign power that will permit the game to continue. All property holders, even those who are losing, have a stake in the maintenance of the market system. Secondly, since even a property holder might be made destitute by the market, the sovereign power must be beyond recall, election, or the influence of a particular propertied group. Since the job of the sovereign is to prevent internal war and ensure the opportunity for ownership and gain, it must be subject to none. Its power must be absolute, and it must be self-perpetuating. To preserve the system without yielding to any individual or group (even a majority) it must have no other responsibility. Anything short of this would permit one group to use the sovereign to gain influence or leverage over another group. An electable sovereign would hopelessly divide one property group against another. In a society as fragmented and centrifugal as market society such division among property owners might result in a social revolution and the loss of private property itself. Thus, rational, propertied people would realize that their own interests, individually and as a group, required that they make a compact among themselves to establish an absolute sovereign power that none of them could control. That was the moral basis of government in market society. It was an "ought" that was directly implied in the realities of that society, a moral absolute based on the selfishness of each individual property owner.

It is easy to understand why none of the middle-class groups adopted Hobbes's philosophy. Its assumptions were too unflattering, and its conclusions seemed too severe. But it was logically tight as a drum. If property owners had remained relatively equal in economic power, it would have been necessary for them to put the sovereign beyond the reach of each of them. What Hobbes failed to see was that the same market that created an equality of fear also created inequalities of class. It became possible for classes of property holders to stay cohesive and united enough to minimize the centrifugal pull of the market. Imagine, though, a society in which dozens or hundreds of shipbuilders or cabinetmakers were forced to compete ruthlessly for power. If such owners were the only ones who appointed the sovereign government, imagine how easy it would be for one or a group of them to use that government to their own advantage. An absolute sovereign would be their only protection from other property holders.

Hobbes fully accepted the market morality and ethics of self-interest that was evolving in his time. He used it to show the moral need of the propertied to create and obey a government that maintained the system with absolute power, but, once created, chose its own successors, brooked no objections, and answered to no one. In relation to the sovereign, the kind of political ethics that Hobbes called for was simple obedience. However, since he expected that the sovereign would only enforce the laws of the market, it was the market itself which governed morality. Thus, ethics was the securing of personal advantage, and justice was the striking of a good bargain. Today we call that political corruption. Hobbes might still show us that we can realistically expect little else of market society.

It is interesting that so many modern Americans assume that politics is corrupt but that business is relatively honest. The interesting thing is that by "dirty" or "corrupt politics" we mean just that type of politics that is practiced like business. Political life is "corrupt" for us precisely when it involves buying and selling, when influence is "peddled," when legislators are "bought," when special favors are "sold," in short, when politicians behave like business people or are "too close" to them. We may be justified in our concern that the pub-

■ *John Locke (1632–1704). (Granger)*

lic trust not be put on the market for the highest bidder. Hobbes would have argued, though, that it is unreasonable for us to reward and expect ambition, aggressiveness, selfishness, drive, competitiveness, wealth, and power in all aspects of life except one—and to demand the opposite there. Hobbes might have realistically believed in the seventeenth century that politics could escape the pull of market forces and private interests—but only if the sovereign were absolute and self-perpetuating. Market society has transformed so much of life since then, that his hope sounds as archaic and idealistic as it is oppressive and totalitarian.

## Locke: A Government For Christian Gentlemen

John Locke told the propertied middle class more of what they wanted to hear. He provided a justification for capitalist or market society which did not dwell on the jungle ethic or the selfish, competitive, market-oriented individual. He spoke a glowing language of absolute rights and resurrected much of the traditional teaching of natural moral laws. He refused to see ethics in totally market or utilitarian terms. He argued for the possibility of limited, representative government in market society. And, more significantly, he offered a positive moral basis for capitalist society with the argument that only the propertied class was capable of full rationality, full understanding, and, thus, full participation in the "natural rights of man."

Locke began with a knotty problem. It had been traditionally assumed that God gave the Earth and its fruits to humanity in common. Locke felt that Scripture and "natural reason" compelled him to accept that traditional assumption, despite the obstacle it posed to a defense of private property.

> But this [that the earth was given to mankind in common] being supposed, it seems to some a very great difficulty, how any one should ever come to have a *Property* in any thing. . . . I shall endeavour to show, how Men might come to have a *property* in several parts of that which God gave to Mankind in common, and that without any express Compact of all the Commoners.[14]

Undaunted by the traditional idea of common ownership, Locke set out to show how private property could be justly created, even without the consent of the common people. First, the fruits of the earth are of no use unless they are appropriated (owned): "There must of necessity be a means *to appropriate* them some way or other before they can be of any use, or at all beneficial to any particular Man." Then there must be a right of individual appropriation. This can be derived from the obvious individual right to own oneself, one's labor, and the work of one's labor: "every Man has a *Property* in his own *Person.* This no Body has any Right to but himself. The *Labour* of his body, and the *Work* of his Hands, we may say, are properly his."[15] Well then, if individuals have the right to own their own labor and work, they must have the right to sell it: you cannot own what you cannot sell; and the labor class, after all, sells its labor for wages. The problem is that once the laborer has sold his or her labor, it belongs to a new owner; it is no longer the laborer's. Especially after money has been introduced, a society is created where some people own a lot of the fruits of the earth, their own labor, the labor of others, and the goods produced from all of the labor that they own. In other words, the earth has been justly divided among the propertied, society is divided between owners and workers, and neither owe anything to society, because every individual has the right to his or her labor—even to sell it.

From this "labor theory of value," defense of private property, and acceptance of class divisions, Locke goes on to assume (as did most of his readers) that the laboring class could not possibly be fully rational or participate fully in political life. Their labor is owned by others, and they do not have the time and opportunity to understand politics.

> The labourer's share [of the national income], being seldom more than a bare subsistance, never allows that body of men, time, or opportunity to raise their thoughts above that, or struggle with the richer for theirs.[16]

Except, Locke adds, in a common disaster when the laborers "forget respect" and "break in upon the rich."

Locke's inalienable rights of life, liberty, and property (Jefferson changed "property" to "the pursuit of happiness") could only be upheld in his terms as long as the propertied class monopolized political power. When he urges (against Hobbes) that "the majority" can rule without a self-perpetuating sovereign, he means the majority of the propertied class. He does not even consider the possibility that the majority would abolish private property. He does not have too. The poor only react in revolution. The purpose of government is to ensure the inalienable rights. The liberty to own and sell property is only inalienable if the propertied rule.

It is usually said that Hobbes saw human morality in the jungle and insisted on a dictator, while Locke felt that men could compose their moral and political laws themselves. As we have seen, they were both talking about government by the propertied class. But the difference is even greater than that. Hobbes accepted the morality he found in market society. Locke clung to the traditional belief that there were certain moral "natural laws" that any reasonable or rational man could recognize. He believed that he could hold certain truths to be "self-evident." We might argue, along with Hobbes, that people no longer took any truths to be self-evident; indeed, that was the problem that called for a new justification of government. But Locke would not listen to that. Certainly, he would say, there are moral absolutes that every rational person would accept. And if we objected to one of these—the absolute right to own property, say—Locke could retort: "You're clearly not being rational."

In short, Locke flavored his defense of the new system with the moral absolutism of traditional Christian theology. He sounded good. But he gave that traditional wisdom a class basis. Only the propertied could fully reason. Only they could understand the natural laws of politics and morals. Only their majorities were fit to legislate the self-evident.

## The Unfinished Business of Business Society: Private Ownership or Political Democracy

Locke's language of "inalienable truth" and "natural law" appealed to the eighteenth century. We have become more skeptical since. We are closer today to Hobbes. We are not sure that any moral principle is absolute anymore. We speak today as if morality is "what you feel good after." We fear "value judgments." We shudder at the thought of "imposing our own values." We may not agree with so-and-so but we certainly "defend his (her) right to say it."

All of that is fine, even if it sometimes makes us incapable of outrage. It is all part of the heritage of middle-class liberalism—the Machiavelli-Hobbes variety. One may wish at times that modern Americans expended more effort on moral questions, that they still had the capacity for shock and indignation, that they did not accept so many things with a moral shrug of the shoulders. But no matter. There is value in our tolerance. To that extent we have learned the lesson of the middle-class revolution: we have civilized civil war; we have recognized diversity; and we have moved toward an ethics of process.

At the same time, however, we still live with the legacy of John Locke. It is amazing how many people, like Locke, still deny imposing their own values while they do it all of the time. We no longer speak of "natural laws" but we argue for "objectivity" when we mean "my view of things." We call for "balance" or "the other side" when we mean that we disagree. We find "bias" in everyone but ourselves.

We also still share Locke's specific problem: the moral justification of government. In fact, we have compounded it. Locke may not have fully realized the class basis of his moral absolutes, but he frankly limited government to the propertied. Since Locke suffrage has become virtually universal. Perhaps the laboring classes refused to read between the lines of the noble Lockeian list of universal rights and freedoms. Some would say that they forced the propertied middle class to turn their rhetoric about such rights into a reality for all. Others would say that the liberal, middle-class promise has still not been redeemed. The freedoms and liberties which middle-class revolutionaries proclaimed for all men (while limiting them to themselves) are still not enjoyed by all.

The problem may go deeper than that, however. It may be (as Hobbes and Locke thought) that the freedoms of the middle-class revolution (especially property ownership) cannot be made available to all. The freedom of uninhibited acquisition cannot be given to everyone. Every person on the block cannot have the freedom to own the block. Once one person exercises that freedom, everyone else has lost it. The freedom to be a millionaire means that a million people are a dollar short.

The problem is how to justify complete economic freedom or independence (with all of the potential exploitation of others that is implied) with the goals of a democratic society. Like Locke we still honor absolutes—freedom of opportunity, free enterprise, freedom of ownership. In practical terms the unhindered enjoyment of these freedoms still may mean the suffering and impoverishment of others. Some are born with more of these freedoms than others, and their increasing use of such freedoms is at the expense of the same freedoms for many others.

We are still grappling with the problem that Hobbes and Locke posed three hundred years ago. How do we defend or justify market society? How can we argue for the continuance of a society of class divisions? How can we give an ethical basis to the conversion of the commons into the preserve of the few? Hobbes made no pretense of democracy. Locke began that pretense. Now that we also accept the language of Locke's revolution, we have compounded the problem. Can we have freedom of economic opportunity and democracy too? How do we justify class or economic differences in a democracy? Which is more important: the rights of private ownership or majority will? What happens if the unpropertied majority wants to abolish the "rights" of private ownership? Like Locke we still assert that everyone enjoys the freedom of economic opportunity—even when we do not exactly mean "everybody." Unlike Locke, we think that we *can* mean everybody. Locke would not have to read Hobbes to say that we were being naive.

As ethics have become relative (or at least more relative), so has the nature of politics become less moralistic. We have gone from a politics of goals to a politics of process. In fact, the maintenance of process is the most important, and perhaps the only, goal we can have. That, probably, is the main achievement of democratic theory.

But, as we have observed, the revolution in political and ethical theory that was ushered in by the middle-class revolutions beginning in the seventeenth century also had a darker side. As Machiavelli realized, the state could replace the old religion. As Hobbes recognized, the power of that secular state—especially in market society—might have to be enormous. Locke reminded us of some of the old values of absolutist, but communal, society. Both Hobbes and Locke provided moral justifications for political activity in the new society. But neither Hobbes nor Locke were willing to come to grips with the class divisions and fragmentation that the new economy created.

That problem still remains. We live in a society that makes equal access to the political process its highest ideal. Our political ethic today is democratic process. In part, we said, our problem is that that goal has not yet been fully realized. Our examination of Hobbes and Locke, however, suggests that such a goal was something of a sham from the beginning. Locke glossed over the problem by repeating the high-sounding moral absolutes of the older natural law tradition. The problem however remains. If our only possible political ethic is process, our only absolute imperative is that the process be open to all. The other goals of the middle-class revolution, however—market society, individual acquisition, private ownership of the "capital" (productive facilities), and the acceptance of class (owners and workers, rich and poor)—all mean that the political process cannot possibly be open to all. They all may vote now, but since a single corporation can contribute $400,000 to a presidential campaign, we might well ask how much that vote matters. Economic inequality can make political equality meaningless.

Politics is still the clash of differing interests. That is the model of market society. But some interests have much more power than others. Even with only public financing of political campaigns, we cannot expect the weak to be as well represented as the powerful. The large corporations can pay enough people to outwit the best intentions of democratic government. Their staffs are not only frequently larger than those of government, they are often the same. As long as economic power is private, political power cannot be democratic—except for the few. Hobbes and Locke, of course, knew that. They had no objections. Only the "lunatic fringe" on the left wing of the middle-class revolutions (like the radical Diggers in England) thought of democratizing political power fully by democratizing economic power. Perhaps they were both behind and ahead of their time.

## Opening the Process: From Liberal to Socialist Democracy

"I tooke my spade and went and broke the ground upon George-Hill in Surrey, therby declaring freedome to the Creation, and that the earth must be set free from intanglements of Lords and Landlords, and that it shall become a common Treasury to all, as it was first made and given to the sonnes of men." Gerrard Winstanley explained why he led a group of 20 poor men to cultivate the wastelands of Saint George's Hill as communists in 1649. They invited all of England to join them. The middle-class revolutionaries of Cromwell's new government were horrified by these "Diggers" and their threat to the emerging institutions of the market and private property.

Winstanley wrote 2 years before Hobbes's *Leviathan* and over 30 years before Locke's *Treatise,* but his declaration could have been a direct answer to both as well as to Cromwell. "You are all like men in a mist, seeking for freedom, and know not where, nor what it is," he said with perhaps too much trust in middle-class intentions. "No true freedom can be established for Englands peace, or prove you faithfull in Covenant, but such a one as hath respect to the poor, as well as the rich; for if thou consent to freedom to the rich in the City, and givest freedome to the Free-holders in the Countrey, and to Priests and Lawyers, and Lords of Mannours, and Impropriators [owners], and yet allowest the poor no freedome, thou art then a declared hypocrite," Winstanley wrote a bit more pointedly. "Because this buying and selling is the nursery of cheaters. . . . Therefore, there shall be no buying and selling in a Free Commonwealth, neither shall any one hire his brother to work for him."

In the middle of the English seventeenth century an attack on private ownership, buying and selling, market society, classes, and wage labor was both futile nostalgia and bold dreaming. Not until the nineteenth century, when the middle-class revolution had run its course, did new revolutionary movements arise which found the liberal democracy of the propertied insufficient. Like Winstanley, Marx and the socialists called instead for a radical democracy that would be social and economic as well as political, for the poor as well as the wealthy.

The socialists sometimes seemed to talk as if they rejected the ethics of process. They spoke again of fundamental goals, the priority of ends over means, and they frequently criticized parliamentary process and evolutionary change. In a sense, however, the socialists were asking only that the political process be allowed to operate more fairly, and their attack was implicit in the justifications of middle-class revolution.

The middle class took power from kings and nobles because they were barred from the process of decision making. Implicit in their defense of liberal democracy was the argument that revolution was the only alternative for those who were not allowed to participate. There was nothing unethical or immoral in revolution. It was the only recourse for those whom the process ignored. They created, or re-created, the ethics of process as the most important moral ideal of a politics of full participation. For those who shared access to power, there could be no higher goal than the agreement to follow the rules. That was the only way a shared system of power could work. In that sense, the central core of modern political ethics is the maintenance of a democracy. And in that sense, the democratic socialist parties were in complete agreement. They sought to broaden the process and to make fully representative political decisions more important than those of the market.

## *For Further Reading*

Our concentration on three individuals, indeed three books written in Italy and England between 1500 and 1700, should not lead the student to believe that that small subject has been "covered." Machiavelli, Hobbes, and Locke are even more worth reading after being introduced. (**The Prince, Leviathan,** and **The Second Treatise** are available in many editions*). There are also hundreds of years of interpretations of each. We have found Ernst Cassirer's **The Myth of the State*** and C. B. Macpherson's **The Political Theory of Possessive Individualism*** most convincing. They are strongly recommended. But the student should be aware of other interpretations. A good, standard history of political thought is George Sabine's **A History of Political Theory.** Interpretations of Machiavelli are gathered in De Lamar Jensen's **Machiavelli.*** Herbert Butterfield's **The Statecraft of Machiavelli*** and F. Chabod's **Machiavelli and the Renaissance** caution us against taking Machiavelli out of his time, and any cursory reading of Machiavelli's **The Discourses** shows us his "democratic" side. Other interpretations of Hobbes and Locke can be found in Sabine (above) and in Leo Strauss's **The Political Philosophy of Hobbes: Its Basis and Genesis,*** Howard Warrender's **The Political Philosophy of Hobbes,** Willmoore Kendall's **John Locke and the Doctrine of Majority Rule,*** and J. W. Gough's **John Locke's Political Philosophy: Eight Studies.**

Although we have concentrated on Machiavelli, Hobbes, and Locke, we have done so not to understand every dimension of their thought, but to discuss the emergence of a theoretical justification for the modern state. Students who wish to follow this theme can take advantage of Heinz Lubasz's **The Development of the Modern State,*** Franz Neumann's **The Democratic and Authoritarian State,*** and Judith N. Shklar's **Political Theory and Ideology,*** all of which gather essays on the subject. Our reasons for choosing this topic can be found in two recent studies of the failings of the modern liberal state: Theodore J. Lowi's **The End of Liberalism*** and Peter T. Manicas's **The Death of the State.***

For those students who wish to explore the emergence of the Renaissance, Reformation, and English parliamentary state in greater detail, there are a number of good studies. Arthur J. Slavin presents a number of interpretations in **The "New Monarchies" and Representative Assemblies.*** Garrett Mattingly's **Armada*** and **Renaissance Diplomacy*** are classics. Alfred von Martin's short **Sociology of the Renaissance*** is extremely suggestive.

* Available in paperback.

G. Mosse's **Europe in the Sixteenth Century** is a good survey, as is David Ogg's **Europe in the Seventeenth Century.*** J. H. Hexter's **Reappraisals in History*** offers some recent changes of interpretation. And there is an excellent collection of essays on the whole period in Orest Ranum's **Searching for Modern Times.*** On England, Christopher Hill's **The Century of Revolution, 1603–1714*** is an excellent introduction. Various interpretations of the English Civil War are presented in Philip A. M. Taylor's **The Origins of the English Civil War*** and in the more sophisticated collection by Lawrence Stone, **Social Change and Revolution in England, 1540–1640,*** and in Trevor Aston's stimulating **Crisis in Europe, 1560–1660.***

For comparisons with the political theory of other cultures at approximately the same time, there are a few excellent studies. For Russia, there is Michael Cherniavsky's **Tsar & People: Studies in Russian Myths*** and James H. Billington's **The Icon and the Axe: An Interpretive History of Russian Culture,*** an incredibly thorough and suggestive volume. For China, we have a great Manchu emperor in his own words, **Emperor of China: Self-portrait of K'ang-hsi,** by Jonathan D. Spence,* a beautiful book.

## Notes

1. Niccolo Machiavelli, *The Prince,* trans. Luigi Ricci (New York: Random House, 1940, 1950), p. 3.
2. *Ibid.,* p. 56.
3. *Ibid.,* pp. 29–30.
4. *Ibid.,* pp. 31–32.
5. *Ibid.,* p. 32.
6. *Ibid.,* p. 54.
7. Ernst Cassirer, *The Myth of the State* (New Haven: Yale University Press, 1946), p. 131.
8. *Ibid.,* p. 137.
9. *Ibid.,* p. 138.
10. *Ibid.,* p. 143.
11. Thomas Hobbes, *Leviathan,* edited by A. R. Waller (Cambridge: Cambridge University Press, 1904), p. 58. Cited in C. B. Macpherson, *The Political Theory of Possessive Individualism* (London: Oxford University Press, 1962), p. 37. Much of the argument is based on Macpherson's stimulating book.
12. Hobbes, p. 55. Cited in Macpherson, p. 37.
13. Hobbes, p. 179. Cited in Macpherson, p. 96.
14. John Locke, *Second Treatise,* in *Two Treatises of Government,* edited by Peter Laslett (Cambridge: Cambridge University Press, 1960), p. 304. Cited in Macpherson, p. 200.
15. Locke, pp. 304–306.
16. Cited in Macpherson, p. 223.

# Chapter 14

# Work and Exchange

## Capitalism Versus Tradition

There are growing signs that Western capitalism is in crisis. Socialist parties have been elected to govern much of Europe. The United States' economy struggles with (normally opposite) high rates of inflation and unemployment. A federal study, *Work in America* (HEW, 1972), finds that only 24 percent of blue-collar workers and 43 percent of white-collar workers would choose similar work if they could start again. A survey by the Advertising Council of America reveals that a great majority of Americans have negative attitudes toward free enterprise.

What is capitalism? Where, when, and how did it originate? What problems of working and exchanging has it solved? What relation does it have to freedom, democracy, and our high standard of living? What relation does it have to problems of inequality, jobs, health, environment, and productivity? Has it made us more free? Does it create jobs? Does it give us more pay and leisure? If it once worked well, why the crisis? Or is this talk of crisis only near-sighted pessimism? We will try to answer some of these questions in this chapter.

## Before Capitalism: Traditional Ways of Working and Exchanging

Capitalism has been defined in a lot of different ways. Any useful definition, however, must describe a series of very recent economic developments in Western history over the last five hundred years or so. It will not do to think of capitalism as an eternal or universal economic system. Nor does it make sense to think of capitalism as the system which satisfied basic or natural human needs. The fact is that a capitalist economic system is the exception rather than the rule. It was a new twist in European history after the Middle Ages. It has matured as a recognizable system only in the last couple of hundred years, and it is still predominantly Western.

One of the best ways of seeing the uniqueness of our modern capitalist, market, or business civilization is to examine the ways in which economic activities—like working and exchanging—have been carried out in most of the other places and periods of human history. Anthropologists have found an enormous variety of economic activities in tribal and traditional peasant societies. One anthropologist, Manning Nash, has written:

> The economic life of man shows a great variety over time and space. In the New Hebrides islands (in the South Pacific), the main economic concern is the accumulation of pigs. Men raise pigs, exchange pigs, lend out pigs at interest, and finally in a large ceremonial feast destroy the pig holdings of a lifetime. Among the Bushmen of the Kalahari desert (in Southern Africa) there is no private property in productive goods, and whatever the hunting band manages to kill is shared out among the members of the group. In the Melanesian islands every gardener brings some of the yams from his plot to the chief's house. There the pile of yams grows and grows, and eventually rots, to the greater glory of the tribe. The Indians of Guatemala and Mexico live in communities each with its own economic specialty. One group produces pottery, another blankets, another lumber and wood, and the next exports its surplus maize (corn). These communities are tied together in a complex system of markets and exchange.[1]

There is so much variety in the economic lives of precapitalist societies, that we are sure to find an exception to almost every generalization. Despite this difficulty, however, there are enough similarities among *most* of these societies to enable us to distinguish between precapitalist and capitalist societies.

In the last chapter we referred to capitalist society as market society. We should be careful of using this distinction too loosely. In the passage just quoted Manning Nash pointed to the existence of "a complex system of markets and exchange" in the peasant societies of

Mexico and Guatemala. Indeed, there have been markets of some kind in almost all peasant societies, and some of the first cities were essentially markets—especially for exchanging produce of the countryside, crafts of the city, and imports from far away. Despite this, our notion of modern, capitalist society as a market society is still very useful. The reason for this is the pervasiveness of market relationships in capitalist society. To a great extent, all of the relationships of capitalist society tend to be market relationships. Ideally the market becomes in capitalist society a kind of "invisible hand" that supervises and determines all social relations. "Everything is for sale" a visitor to America said recently: "Everyone is treated like a customer—a buyer or seller." That is the sense in which market society was evolving in England in the seventeenth century. That is what Thomas Hobbes noticed in embryo.

## Premarket Exchange: Householding, Reciprocity, and Redistribution

A market is a system of distribution or exchange. There are other systems too. In fact, for most of human history the market has been only a minor method of distributing and exchanging. Most past societies have relied on systems of exchange which some anthropologists have called "householding," "reciprocity," and "redistribution." In modern, capitalist society the market has replaced most of these earlier forms.

Householding is one of the oldest forms of exchange. The term reminds us of how goods are distributed in the average family household—even to a certain extent today, but much more generally in traditional, farming society. Everyone works, and everyone shares in the produce of the work. This system makes most sense to us in the family. It does not occur to the parents to refuse to feed the children because they do less work; the children have no need to buy or barter their upkeep: it is expected. Prices are not attached to goods and services. The job is done, and everyone benefits.

It may surprise us to realize that householding has been a fairly typical method of exchange in societies much larger than the family. Actually, however, it has worked among extended families, clans, tribes, and other large groups of people throughout history. Householding is essentially the production of goods for use—rather than for sale or gain. In a sense, most precapitalist societies have practiced a kind of householding. The ancient Greeks called it *oeconomia*—the root of our word for economy. Aristotle insisted that the essence of *oeconomia* was the production for the use of the group—householding.

He argued that this had nothing to do with producing for gain, money, or profit through the market: such activity was very different from "economics." Today in capitalist society we define economics in exactly the opposite way.

Householding, production for use and distribution within the group, was the norm in the feudal societies of the Middle Ages as well. The medieval manor was a self-sufficient unit of production and distribution. Markets were largely irrelevant outside of the cities. The manor household, like the Roman *familia* or the Greek clan, could operate quite independently of markets. The degree of authority exercised in production and distribution varied considerably. The Roman head of the household was often something of a tyrant. So were many Western medieval lords. But that was not inevitable in householding. The southern Slav *zadruga* households, for instance, were very democratic. The politics of decision making—about who gets what—are very different from the economics of common work for common use. Manors, families, and communes can be anything from tyrannies to democracies.

A society can allocate resources and exchange goods like a large household. Perhaps most societies have. Within that household of society, and with other households or even strangers, societies have traditionally practiced some form of reciprocity or redistribution.

Reciprocity is an anthropologist's word for giving. The members of a group who think of themselves as a household give their work and the fruits of their work to the other members. They expect that the other members will return (or reciprocate) the gift; and the other members do what is expected. Reciprocity has often worked in tribal societies of many households as well. One of the favorite examples of anthropologists is the custom until recently of the Kwakiutl Indians of the Canadian Pacific. The Kwakiutl astonished American anthropologists, like Ruth Benedict in *Patterns of Culture* (1934), because their custom of gift giving seemed to be such a parody of American capitalist culture's getting and taking. Kwakiutl Indians achieved prestige in their society by giving away (or even destroying) more property than their rivals. Periodic festivals, called "potlaches," were the occasions for a Kwakiutl to show off great wealth by giving it all away. Anthropologists have interpreted this "riches to rags" custom as a way of distributing the property (boats, beads, fish oil, and more important names, songs, and titles) more equally among the tribe. The potlach among the Kwakiutl, and similar practices of giving or destroying property among many societies, was a system of exchange and a system of periodic leveling or equalizing. The custom ensured that everyone would be taken care of, and that no one would be too rich or powerful too long.

Reciprocal exchange was perhaps also the earliest kind of foreign trade. The classic example is the Kula ring exchange of the Trobriand Islanders who inhabit a ring of islands in the Pacific near New Guinea. Each exchange of hard goods (like pigs, yams, canoes, and pottery) is preceded by the ceremonial exchange of armbands and necklaces that the traders value much more highly. The necklaces travel clockwise, and the armbands counterclockwise, around the ring of islands. Some of the shell ornaments are highly prized. They are all thought to be much more valuable than the pigs or canoes. The Trobriander would describe the acquisition of one of these ornaments as the real purpose of the trade. But there is no bargaining for them. There can be no hoarding. Everyone has a season to own each object and then pass it on.

Reciprocal giving and taking is most common in the poorest and simplest of societies. But reciprocity is such an ingrained value in primitive and peasant societies that it fades slowly. Even today in parts of South America, Africa, and Asia that have not yet been commercialized by market attitudes and institutions, people work and live without money as if they were part of a large reciprocal family. An Egyptian who grew up in a small village says that he was surprised to learn when his family moved to Cairo that he needed money to pay for haircuts, shoes, or food. In the village the son of the barber was given bread by the baker, the son of the baker had his shoes mended by the shoemaker, and the son of the shoemaker had his hair cut by the barber, all without money, promises, or notations in an accounting book. In Cairo he needed money, but even there credit, charity, and gifts were a normal part of life. That same Egyptian in the United States struggles today with whether or not to send "thank you cards" when he stays at the homes of other Egyptians in the United States. "To say 'thank you,' " he says, "is an insult because it ends a 'transaction.' We Egyptians are used to taking hospitality for granted. Things that are expected are not 'thanked.' " Perhaps even a "thank you" is our commercial society's polite, but weak alternative to reciprocity. In the less commercialized countries of the world the words "please" and "thank you" are rarely used. That may be a sign of more mutual concern rather than of less politeness, or maybe politeness itself is a sign that genuine feeling has disappeared—"virtue gone to seed" Ralph Waldo Emerson called it.

Redistribution is a kind of institutionalized reciprocity. Redistribution also involves giving and taking without prices, bargaining, money, or calculation. But redistribution is less voluntary or spontaneous. Normally, it is carried out by the chief, king, ruling officials, or otheir specialized agencies. Surplus goods are collected (like taxes) and held in a central store, bank, or granary. In the complex bureaucracies of ancient Mesopotamia, Egypt, India, China, and the American kingdoms of the Aztecs and Incas, large storehouses were maintained for grain, wine, pottery, cloth, ornamental objects, art work, and other goods. Frequently in the case of these empires, the goods were used to support the state bureaucracy, soldiers, and the ruling elite, as well as the emergency needs of the people. In less complex feudal societies, with a less oppressive or top-heavy bureaucracy, both collection and distribution were often more democratic. In some tribal societies, without even a feudal upper class, collection was quite voluntary and distribution benefited everyone but the chief. There was a standing joke among early anthropologists who studied American Indian tribes that you could always find the chief by looking around for the poorest man. Apparently the demands of redistribution could be so great that the chief would give away everything he could collect, leaving himself only the prestige of the tribe.

An account of redistribution among the Creek Indians in the eighteenth century shows how democratic the system could be. Before they carry off

> . . . their crops from the field, there is a large crib or granary, erected in the plantation, which is called the king's crib; and to this each family carries and deposits a certain quantity, according to his ability or inclination, or none at all if he so chooses, this in appearance seems a tribute or revenue to the micro [chief], but in fact is designed for another purpose, i.e., that of a public treasury, supplied by a few voluntary contributions, and to which every citizen has the right of free and equal access, when his own private stores are consumed, to serve as a surplus to fly to for succour, to assist neighboring towns, whose crops may have failed, accommodate strangers, or travellers, afford provisions or supplies, when they go forth on hostile expeditions, and for all other exigencies of the state.[2]

Premarket economic systems of exchange—householding, reciprocity, or redistribution—could be voluntary or forced, democratic or imposed. That depended on the degree of social equality or class stratification and on the extent to which power was shared or monopolized. The important difference between all premarket and market systems is that the premarket systems minimized strictly economic behavior. There was really no such thing as economics or economic activity in premarket society. Everything that we would call economics was understood simply as an aspect of social life. Tradition, religion, custom, and human relationships were the cause and context of working, exchanging, providing, and allocating. One did what was expected. Work, produce, and material goods were not ends in themselves, but means to the life that was sanctioned by one's family clan, tribe, or village.

## The Origins of Capitalism: Markets, Logic, and Desire

The theorists of emerging capitalist society, from Thomas Hobbes to Adam Smith, imagined that selfishness, competition, bargaining, and private ownership were eternal traits of human nature, characteristic of all of human history. The discoveries of human diversity and evolving economic institutions (which we discussed in the previous section) were largely discoveries of the nineteenth century. There were forerunners, of course. One thinks of the recognition of diversity and change in the writings of Montesquieu or Vico in the early eighteenth century. But it was probably the experience of the industrial revolution in the nineteenth century that made European thinkers generally aware of the importance of human change—especially economic change. The nineteenth century was the golden age of historical study, the age of the study of evolution and origins, and the first age to suggest that human nature itself might have changed from one age to the next. The world of Darwin and Marx and anthropology could no longer imagine that the inclinations or institutions of capitalist society had existed for all time.

Defenders of the new economy in the nineteenth century—groups like the English Manchester liberals and utilitarians who spoke for the middle class of merchants and manufacturers—developed a new assumption of the naturalness of capitalist ideas and behavior which was more consistent with the historical consciousness of their age. They reasoned in effect that although capitalism had not always existed, the instinctual need and logic of capitalism had always existed, and that history was the development of that desire and logic. Their ideas were so influential that they have become almost the "common sense" of twentieth-century Americans. They imagined that primitive trading had merely become more complex over the years, that people gradually found it easier to attach price tags (or money values) to the things they bartered, and that local trade led to national and finally international trade as the new knowledge of marketing techniques grew. In effect, these defenders of the new system were arguing that if capitalism had not always existed at least a natural human inclination to barter had become more sophisticated. In many ways this was yet another version of human nature.

Many of us still today assume that capitalism developed logically from the inside out, from the simple to the complex, from the local to the foreign, and from the small scale to the world scale. We assume for instance that barter exchanges among friends led gradually to more efficient money exchanges, that local trade became more monetized as it became more complex, that such capitalist institutions as money, markets, prices, profits, and private property expanded from village to city to state to world as they proved their superiority over simpler ways. There is something very comforting in that assumption. It allows us to think that ideal capitalism began among friends, that it originated in small groups, and that it expanded naturally and gradually because people wanted it to. There is a good deal of comfort in knowing that things have happened in accordance with both logic and human desire.

Actually, however, nothing is further from the truth. One of the most amazing things about the history of capitalism is that most people fought every step of its expansion. The clergyman, the artisan, the farmer, the villager, the worker, the landlord, the tenant, and even many of the slowly emerging middle class fought the expansion of capitalism because it seemed to come from outside to threaten the local and the traditional ways.

The nineteenth-century defenders of capitalism were not completely mistaken, however. There was a kind of logical inevitability in the expansion of capitalism. The logic was the expansion of markets. Market prices were less debatable than barter, and clearer than haggling. Once certain things were bought and sold, a special effort was necessary to prevent people from buying and selling other things. The quest for profit in one commodity or in one area led to negotiations in others. Markets did not have to expand. In fact most ancient civilizations prevented their expansion. But once they were allowed to expand, all of society was increasingly opened to its logic. For that reason we can trace the evolution of capitalism in the development of market society from the first markets.

Markets existed in the most ancient cities. Caravans of merchants often worked out the first roads that connected one urban civilization with another. But the ways of merchants and markets were never important in the internal economies of ancient civilizations. Outside of the urban market square it is not even correct to talk of economies. The word suggests a separate realm of activity that did not even exist in the rest of the city or the countryside. Working and exchanging in accordance with traditions of householding, reciprocity, and redistribution were simply aspects of the rest of life, subject to the same habits and personal relationships as marrying, worshiping, playing, and feuding.

Market society did not come into existence until the ways of the market permeated the whole fabric of working and exchanging. In traditional agricultural society this was all but impossible. Peasants did not even need the city's market. Those who brought a couple of eggs or a blanket into the city on market day were as happy to return with it as to sell it. If anyone had suggested turning their agricultural lives into a gigantic market where they sold their labor as time, bought and sold land as if it were eggs, or used their tools and their skills to make money, they would have been appalled. Yet it was precisely this commercialization and monetization of labor, land, and capital that did occur in one peasant society—late medieval Europe—and that one instance changed the world.

Medieval Europe of 1000 was as unlikely a seedbed for commercialization as were the ancient empires of a thousand or a couple of thousand years earlier. Just as Aristotle had reflected his age's view of the "life of craftsmen or of traders" as "devoid of nobility and hostile to perfection of character," and just as Cicero had expressed a typical Roman view that "those who buy wholesale in order to sell retail" lead "sordid" lives "because they would gain no profits without a great deal of lying," so did the Christian thinkers of medieval Europe condemn the values and activities of the marketplace. "The merchant can scarcely ever be pleasing to God," was the medieval dictum. "It is wholly sinful," Saint Thomas Aquinas wrote, "to practice fraud for the express purpose of selling a thing for more than its just price, inasmuch as a man deceives his neighbor to his loss." The doctrine of the "just price" (a "fair" price that did not take advantage of scarcity or an intermediary's shrewdness), the prohibition against usury (which first meant lending money at any interest), and the general medieval suspicion of money and merchants combined with the agricultural self-sufficiency of medieval society limited commercial activity to towns and periodic fairs.

How then did Europe become a market society? Historians point to a number of changes in European society after 1000 to account for the expansion of market ways and values. Cities multiplied, expanded, and increased their hold over the countryside almost continually after 1000 (though urban population *declines* in the fourteenth century Black Death may have also spurred technological innovation and commercial experimentation). The Crusades introduced Europeans to Eastern markets, luxury goods, commercial techniques, and enough booty to set up thousands of soldiers as entrepreneurs in pepper, spices, and other commodities. European navigational, shipbuilding, and gunpowder technology outdistanced the Islamic and Chinese by 1500. European kings suppressed local trade barriers, fought rebellious nobles with national armies, and created national economic policies and industries. A whole new middle class of merchants, bankers, and manufacturers, richer than many nobles, bought respectability for their activities, their projects, and their ideals. Poor and perceptive nobles commercialized their lands by converting ancient manorial dues into fixed money rents and by enclosing lands that the peasants had used in common (e.g., half of the arable land of England) for their own use as more profitable sheep pasturage. Protective fellowships of medieval craftsmen (called "guilds") became competitive industries hiring landless labor as employees instead of training apprentices and journeymen to eventually take over.

Before 1500 the institutions of market society—money, prices, profits, private property, wage labor, and competition—were developing within the bounds of a feudal society. Feudalism had been a system of laws, customs, and political loyalties that made sense in the decentralized, agrarian, manorial economy of the Middle Ages. Market society required and encouraged a whole new set of legal, social, and political institutions and ideas which we can call capitalism.

Capitalism was the system which gave legal, political, and social sanction to land, labor, and capital as separate market entities, convertible into money terms or prices. In feudal society, a person did not buy land, sell labor, or invest capital for the most part because they each were aspects of life rather than economic categories. Land was home, fields, or place, not real estate. Labor was activity, chores, or giving birth, not time and effort for sale. Capital was not even used to indicate the cattle or plows that were the peasant's or community's investment in future productivity.

When people say that capitalism is a system of private-property ownership, they mean the private ownership of capital—the productive resources of the society. They do not mean the private ownership of personal property like clothes and furniture. That sometimes causes confusion. Almost all societies have recognized the private ownership of personal property. Capitalism recognized the private ownership of what the medieval person would almost call public property—the large scale tools and resources or capital upon which future productivity depended. (Thus, when socialists talk about the abolition of private property they usually mean factories, corporations, banks, and television stations, not televisions, cars, and personal property.) To say that capital is privately owned is to say that it is not owned by everyone, but by the few who are capitalists.

Capitalism did not suddenly replace feudalism after 1500. Even by 1700 the market society had not attained the sanction of laws that legitimated land, labor, and capital as separate economic entities. Serfdom was not formally abolished in France until the revolution of 1789. Guild regulations in England, like the restriction of only two apprentices to each master hatmaker, were in effect until the repeal of the Statute of Artificers in 1813. The English industrial and commercial middle class were not fully represented in Parliament until the passage of the Reform Bill of 1832. Even today in the United States, the most advanced capitalist country in the world, there are still laws which restrict the full commercialization of life: Sunday blue laws in some states curtail shopping time; prostitution is illegal in most places; one cannot use private property or draw up a contract for absolutely any purpose that buyer and seller desire. The market is not even yet entirely supreme legally, politically, and socially. The tendency of capitalism to extend and legitimate the market in all ways of life is still not completed.

We can, however, get some idea of the opposition that capitalism faced in its youth if we look more closely at some of these examples of incomplete development today. Blue laws and antiprostitution laws are clearly on the way out. There is almost a logical inevitability to the expansion of Sunday shopping and the legalization of prostitution. Opposition almost always seems to counter reason and evolution. If people can buy coffee on Sunday, then why not whiskey? If they can shop on Saturday, then why not on Sunday? Are we legislating what people should drink? Are we penalizing Saturday workers or American Moslems who have a Friday sabbath? The same is true of prostitution. Is not legalization preferable to hypocrisy, turning poor women into criminals, and possibly increasing the spread of venereal disease?

The market is imperial. And its expansion is almost always more equitable, rational, and fair. The market eliminates black markets, prejudice, hypocrisy, and inefficiency. But its rush to equalize in commerce also takes its toll of human values: the sanctity of marriage and the family, the need for spiritual renewal, personal loyalty, friendship, and love. We may object to human beings becoming consumers and gamblers instead of sons and lovers, but each step of that protest is as futile, backward, and even illogical as the protests of peasants and artisans centuries ago.

## Capitalism: Work and Pay, Prices and Profits

We are used to thinking that we work less and receive more in a capitalist economy. But the evidence is not that clear. Anthropologists are often amazed at how little time the people of primitive and traditional societies spend working. More than a hundred days of labor seems to be quite rare. Christopher Hill, the English historian, has computed that the average English worker of 1530 worked only 14 or 15 weeks for the year's needs. Two and a half centuries later, a full 52 weeks of over 12-hour days were fairly typical for the working classes.

Similarly, a tabulation of the average real wages of English carpenters from 1250 to 1850 shows interesting fluctuations but no gen-

■ *Sunday "blue laws" and age limits still restrict the market's sway over drinking patterns in the United States today. The spread of gin drinking in England in the eighteenth century was both a result of, and a metaphor for, the spread of market society. Gin oiled the way to social irresponsibility much the way money did. And it destroyed the poor before it atomized the entire society. This is William Hogarth's famous "Gin Lane" etching of 1750. (The Metropolitan Museum of Art, Harris Brisbane Dick Fund, 1932)*

eral improvement. The average wages (translated into kilograms of wheat) look like this:

| | |
|---|---|
| 1251–1300 | 81.0 |
| 1301–1350 | 94.6 |
| 1351–1400 | 121.8 |
| 1401–1450 | 155.1 |
| 1451–1500 | 143.5 |
| 1501–1550 | 122.4 |
| 1551–1600 | 83.0 |
| 1601–1650 | 48.3 |
| 1651–1700 | 74.1 |
| 1701–1750 | 94.6 |
| 1751–1800 | 79.6 |
| 1801–1850 | 94.6[3] |

This table shows us that the English carpenter received the same real wages in 1850 as in 1300. His income increased until about 1450, then declined precipitously from 1450 to 1650, and only gradually returned to the thirteenth-century level by 1850.

Further, there are indications that this pattern was a European, not just an English, phenomenon. The great French historian Fernand Braudel writes:

> From 1350 to 1550 Europe probably experienced a favourable period as far as individual life was concerned. Following the catastrophes of the Black Death (1348–1350) living conditions for workers were inevitably good as manpower had become scarce. Real wages have never been as high as they were then. In 1388, canons in Normandy complained that they could not find anyone to cultivate their land "who did not demand more than what six servants made at the beginning of the century." The paradox must be emphasized since it is often thought that hardship increases the farther back towards the middle ages one goes. In fact the opposite is true, as far as the standard of living of the common people—the majority—is concerned. . . . The deterioration becomes more pronounced as we move away from the "autumn" of the middle ages; it lasted right up to the middle of the nineteenth century. In some regions of Eastern Europe, certainly in the Balkans, the downward movement continued for another century, to the middle of the twentieth.[4]

Braudel's magnificent *Capitalism and Material Life 1400–1800* is full of statistical and literary evidence to support this conclusion. To take only two examples on the single issue of the consumption of meat—so dear to the stomachs of Europeans: there were 18 butchers in the small town of Montpezat in 1550, 10 in 1556, 6 in 1641, 2 in 1660, and only 1 in 1763; and after 1550 there were far more than the usual accounts of the "good old days" when "tables at village fairs and feasts sank under their heavy load," and "we ate meat every day."

Whether we mark the decline from 1450, 1500, or 1550 (and it certainly varied from place to place), one thing is clear. *The standard of living of the majority of Europeans declined drastically with the rise of a capitalist or market economy.* For this was precisely the period in which the ways of the capitalist market replaced those of traditional feudal society.

It would be foolish, of course, to date the origins of capitalism at 1492 because of Columbus's voyage or at 1494 because of the Italian invention of double-entry bookkeeping. A single year, even a single century, is too precise dating for anything so complex. Karl Marx, who began the historical study of capitalism, saw "the first beginnings of capitalist production as early as the fourteenth or fifteenth century, sporadically, in certain towns of the Mediterranean" but marked the "capitalist era from the sixteenth century." The year 1500 may be useful, but symbolically.

Recently economic historians have turned their attention to charting price movements since they are usually a fair indicator of economic activity, and this course seems more fruitful than searching for specific beginnings. Furthermore, old ledgers and account books are full of the prices of things, and modern computer techniques make their compilation and comparison relatively easy. This is what they have discovered. From about 1150 to 1300 there was a rapid rise in prices. As we have seen, this was a period of general prosperity. Population increased, new lands were opened for cultivation, and economic production rose—but all pretty much within a feudal economic and social system.

Then from 1300 to 1450 prices fell. Marxists, who are keen on revolutionary "turning points" where one historical stage dies before another is born, refer to this period as the crisis of feudalism. The figures seem to support something very much like that. The feudal economy may have reached a point (not unlike the Roman slave economy a thousand years earlier) where the system had passed its capacity for exploiting. Feudalism, according to the Marxists, had lasted as long as the feudal barons and clergy could extract an increasing economic surplus (work, food, dues, etc.) from the peasantry in order to keep themselves in the style to which they had become accustomed—often a style of lavish waste. After the depopulation that accompanied the Black Death (1350), the remaining commoners were more powerful. In fact, there were numerous peasant revolts in this period, and we have seen from Braudel and von Bath that the commoners' living standard peaked. Unable to get more work from the peasants, and without a machine technology to replace them, the feudal ruling classes may indeed have reached the limits of the system. As feudal incomes declined, the nobility sent their sons on interminable wars in search of land and booty and borrowed heavily from the new class of merchants and bankers that we spoke of before. Thus—and the Marxist argument is still convincing here—power may have begun to shift from the old feudal class to the new entrepreneurial money class.

It is clear, in any case, that the period from 1450 or 1500 to 1650 was one of phenomenal price rises (inflation). This had a lot to do with the influx of gold and silver from the Americas. The kingdoms of the Aztecs, Mayans, and Incas were ransacked by feudal sons from Spain. Then more gold and silver were mined in Mexico and South America by imported African slaves. Much of the gold, silver, and treasures filled Spanish and Portuguese royal treasuries. But there was so much left for commercial circulation that it fueled one of the greatest inflations that the world had ever known. The bullion probably saved feudalism in Spain and Portugal, but by raising the price level throughout Europe it forced the destitute lords of England and France to deal in the money men and commercialize their own estates. Landlords who were smart enough to adopt the values of the market saved themselves by cutting corners. They studied new methods of cultivation and new ideas of property management. They cut their costs, improved their yields, and brought their surplus to markets for profit. But the easiest corners to cut were the plots of their tenant farmers. In England, the Netherlands, and France (where population increased as quickly as prices) the feudal obligations of numerous peasants were converted into rents. Common lands that had for centuries been used by the villagers and tenants were taken over (or enclosed) by the landlords. Peasants who had barely survived with small plots and an animal or two on the commons found themselves unable to continue. A new class of landless workers was created—people without ancestral rights who could work only for others and for money. In Eastern Europe, the squeeze came as a renewed second serfdom. There peasants were not freed to be poor; their feudal obligations increased with their poverty.

We have seen how the living standard of European farmers and workers was wrecked by the drastic inflation of the long sixteenth-century price revolution. The bullion of the Americas was crucial in inflaming the inflation. But neither gold nor inflation must necessarily destroy the well-being of the people. If the European class structure had been egalitarian enough so that the new bullion could be distributed evenly, all Europeans would have been richer at the expense of the American losers. European peasants would have been able to use the gold to buy Arabian coffees, Indian teas, or Chinese spices and silks. Alternatively, their mercantilist governments would have been able to use the bullion to develop national industries that could have made the lives of all Europeans easier. But the bullion did not enter an economically democratic society. It entered a society where the old feudal ruling class was in debt, and neither they nor the royal governments were as wealthy as the evolving merchant, financial, and industrial classes. As usual in a class-divided society, the new wealth went to the old wealth. And the entrepreneurial class that knew money and its uses used the new money well. Merchant adventuring companies and joint stock companies were created to establish new mines and plantations, build ships, carry on trade, and eventually create the factories and goods of the industrial revolution.

Fernand Braudel noticed the crucial fact about the European expansion that began after 1492: "the gold and silver of the New World enabled Europe to live above its means, to invest beyond its savings."[5] No society develops economically or technologically without saving some of the productive capacity of the present in order to build capital for the future. Merchant ships, machines, or factories can only be built if people consume less (or spend less of their energy and resources on immediate consumption). Investment in future productivity requires savings. Thanks largely to the resources and inhabitants of the Americas and the inhabitants of Africa, Europe was able to invest beyond its savings. The gold and silver savings of centuries of American Indian labor, and the forced labor of native Americans and Africans in mines and plantations, allowed some Europeans to begin the massive investment in future productivity that culminated in the industrial revolution.

Since the more a society saves and invests, the more productive it becomes, and consequently the more it is able to save and invest, some historians have spoken of "takeoff" stages of economic growth. Western Europe experienced its first takeoff into sustained economic growth in this period, 1500–1650. Although much of the bullion was wasted in an economic sense (that is, not invested in future productivity), much of it also fueled economic and technological development. This was especially true of England, so much so that historians have frequently noticed a first industrial revolution in England between 1540 and 1640 that preceded the great industrial revolution by over a century.

"During the last sixty years of the sixteenth century," the historian John U. Nef has written, "the first paper and gunpowder mills, the first cannon foundries, the first alum and copper factories, the first sugar refineries, and the first considerable salpetre works were all introduced"[6] into England. "Between 1540 and 1640," he adds, "the process of iron-making assumed a new and highly capitalistic form," iron output increased several times, coal output increased at least eightfold, and the issue of mineral rights became as much of a political issue as the enclosures of farm land. Private mills and manufactures which employed a thousand workers were not uncommon.

Thus, the period from 1500 to 1650 was one in which a general rise in the price level of three or four times (15 times on the Paris wheat market) both reflected and fueled a capitalistic economic takeoff. In this period capitalists commercialized agriculture, incorporated huge trading companies, banked the mercantilist policies of monarchs, and began applying their fortunes to large-scale industrial production. In this period Europe became the richest and most powerful amalgam of states in the world. Royal, national, and private fortunes were made that had been rare for emperors of the past. And yet—remember von Bath and Braudel—this was precisely the period in which the income and standard of living of the average European declined drastically. The English carpenter had less than a third of the real income in 1650 that he had enjoyed in 1450. Like the African, the American Indian, and the serfs of the European periphery, the common people in the core of capitalist economic growth paid for that growth while others reaped the profits.

We can see the same contradiction between capitalist economic growth and popular living standards if we follow the historians of price movements from 1650 to 1850. Very roughly, the period from 1650 to 1750 was one of falling prices accompanied by declines in population, food production, economic activity, and profits. It was, however, a period in which the English carpenter doubled his real income. Conversely, the period from 1750 to 1850 witnessed rapidly rising prices, population, production, and profits. This was the period of gigantic increases in energy, income, and technological productivity—the full industrial revolution. And average incomes remained constant despite the fantastic new wealth. The conclusion seems inescapable. Capitalist economic productivity has thrived on the sacrifices of the mass of people in order to benefit the few.

After 1850, of course, the industrial technology itself was more than adequate to provide a rising standard of living for descendants of those who made the important initial sacrifices. It did that for some Europeans and North Americans. That it did not do so for the rest of the inhabitants of the world market economy may have been due more to the failures of the economic system than to the limits of the technology.

## Capitalism and the Industrial Revolution

The capitalist economic growth of 1500–1650 was mainly agricultural and commercial rather than industrial. The countryside was transformed into large estates geared to production for market while peasant farmers were dispossessed, often becoming landless day laborers for wages. The largest fortunes, besides those of the landlords, accrued to merchants, traders, and their financial backers, rather than to industrialists as yet. Commercial capitalism was supplanted by industrial capitalism in the process of the great industrial revolution that began after 1750.

We have only to look at the countries of the contemporary underdeveloped world to see how difficult it is to conduct an industrial revolution on a capitalist basis. Over and over again, in Russia, China, and the Third World, industrialization has taken a collectivist or state-sponsored form. How, then, was it possible for the emerging nations of the eighteenth century to industrialize when no one imagined what an industrial revolution might be (the term was not invented until the 1820s), and when the competing interests of capitalist society fought against collective, planned action?

The answer lies in the peculiarities of Britain at the end of the eighteenth century, because it is unlikely that the first capitalist industrialization would have occurred anywhere else. The English had a government that was sympathetic to the interests of private capitalists and industrial development. English agriculture was efficient enough to support a large class of potential workers. Population pressure had been steep enough (and enclosure movements ruthless enough) to ensure a vast quantity of cheap labor after 1750. But, perhaps most significantly, Britain emerged victorious from two centuries of military and naval conflict (first with the Spanish and Dutch, and then with the French) by 1763, which gave it access to the markets and resources of most of the world from India to the Americas.

England in the 1780s (even after the political loss of the United States) was in a position similar to Spain in the 1500s. But while the Spanish nobility choked itself on the booty of colonialism, the English industrial class made money. The British cotton industry was the key. It grew with the English conquest of India, the slave trade, the cotton plantations of the Caribbean and the Americas, and the huge market of its colonies. Indian cottons (calicos) were recognized as the finest in the world. The English East India Company (agents of the older style commercial or trading capitalism) sold the Indian cloth throughout Europe. Some of the profits went from Liverpool into the slave trade and the Caribbean plantations. Eventually the merchants of

Liverpool were outfoxed by the textile mill owners of Lancashire. When Indian revolts interrupted the calicos, Lancashire bought Caribbean cotton and gradually took over the trade. The old vested interests of the East India Company and Liverpool merchants were finally undermined as the producers secured from Parliament import bans on calicos. Industrial capitalism took over. Between 1750 and 1769 British cotton exports increased over ten times. By 1820 the British were exporting over 200 million yards of cotton. By 1840 they exported that much to Europe alone, and over another 500 million yards to the colonies. Even the ancient Indian industry was systematically deindustrialized to become a market for Lancashire cotton. India took 11 million yards in 1820 and 145 million by 1840.[7]

Cotton was more appropriate to lead an industrial revolution than anyone could have known at the time. With slave labor on the plantations the cost of raw materials was miniscule. Slaves did not have to be paid anything close to the value of their work. English spinners and weavers were numerous, disorganized, and consequently also cheap. Under the earlier domestic or "putting out" system, many had learned spinning and weaving at home in order to augment their incomes. Then there was no overhead for the merchants who simply brought them raw materials and bought the finished products. But domestic production was never extensive enough to trigger an industrial revolution. It would never have developed into the mass production which creates its own demand. The world-wide English markets offered the possibility of seemingly insatiable demand. Every slave, every Indian, every South American could be sold a shirt. Thus, cotton, combined with world dominion, was one industry where goods could be produced cheaply on a massive scale. Conversion from domestic to factory production was also relatively simple and cheap. The construction of factories, spinning wheels, and weaving looms could be financed out of profits, because the profits were enormous. Robert Owen started with a borrowed £100 (about $200) in 1789, and twenty years later he was able to buy out his partners with £84,000 in cash. Even the technology of cotton was ideally suited to an industrial takeoff. It benefited enormously from slight improvements. The spinning jenny, the water frame, and later the power loom were adaptations of existing machinery that required little scientific insight and paid for themselves in vastly increased production.

Far more than any other new industry, cotton propelled the British industrial revolution. In 1830 the words "industry" and "factory" were practically synonymous with cotton production. In 1833 1.5 million people were employed in cotton production. Between 1816 and 1848 cotton amounted to 40 or 50 percent of British exports.

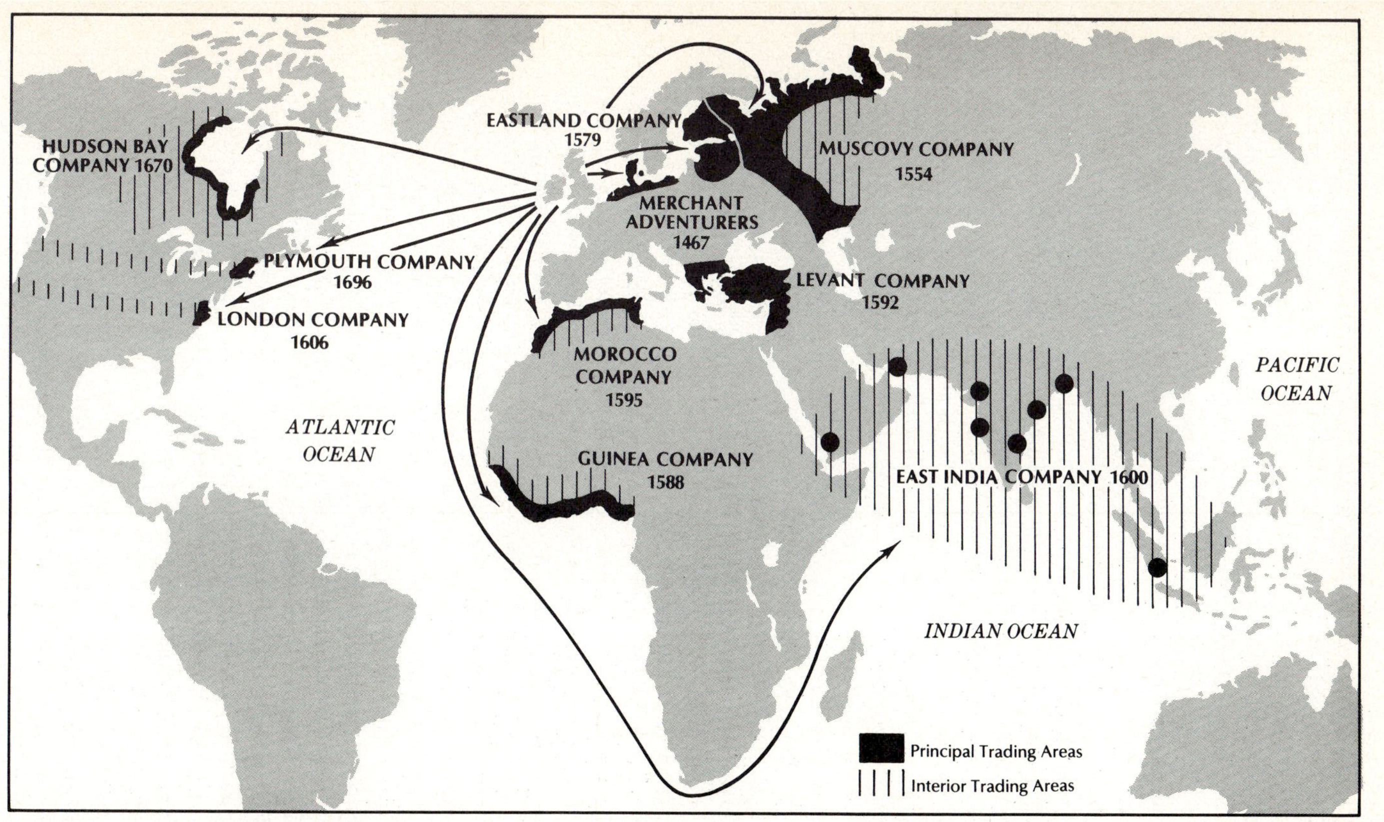


**English Trading Companies, 1450–1700**

*Between 1450 and 1700 English Trading Companies developed markets throughout the world that would enable England in the next century to begin an industrial revolution.*

Cotton was both wind and weather vane of the British economy. It caused and signaled the successes and contradictions of capitalist industrialization.

Its successes were extraordinary. The world was supplied with cotton clothing in vastly greater quantities and at cheaper prices than would ever have been thought possible before. Between 1785 and 1850 British production of cotton cloth increased from 40 million to over 2 billion yards per year. While production increased over 50 times, the price of cloth dropped to about one-tenth of the 1785 level. Competition not only exploded output and trimmed prices, it also forced an endless series of inventions. In cotton spinning alone there were 39 new patents between 1800 and 1820, 51 in the 1820s, 86 in the 1830s, and 156 in the 1840s. Creative energies were unleashed that transformed human productivity more completely in 50 years than in the previous five hundred—perhaps even five thousand.

## Capitalist Contradictions and Contractions

But in the midst of success, there began to appear contradictions in the capitalist economy which were also of imposing scale. The age-old cycle of economic expansion and contraction, which had previously been caused by long-term fluctuations in population growth or by natural catastrophes and agricultural failures, was intensified, shortened, and given artificial human causes. For the first time productivity, rather than want, caused economic contraction. Success in the competitive market depended on continually expanding growth. Without coordination or planning, with only market prices as a guide, entrepreneurs were inevitably drawn to what was momentarily the most profitable enterprise. In the early nineteenth century that was cotton. Because the cotton industry was competitive, many could enter with modest capital; and many did because the profits were so high. But competition cut prices. Costs were more constant. So profit margins shrank. In 1784 the selling price of a pound of spun cotton yarn was 11 shillings, the raw cotton was 2 shillings, leaving a profit margin of 9 shillings. That margin tempted so many that by 1812 the selling price had been trimmed to 2½ shillings, but the cost had been reduced to only 1½ shillings, leaving only a single shilling profit. And since businesses are easier to enter than leave, each entrepreneur had to sell nine times the quantity of 1784 to do only as well. For many that was actually possible in 1812. Expansion was enormous, but a saturation point always loomed on the horizon. By 1832 the selling price had been cut to 1 shilling and the cost of raw cotton to a little more than half a shilling, leaving a profit margin of less than half a shilling. Volume had to increase 18 times, and that was asking too much. By the 1830s and early 1840s, the market that seemed so insatiable was becoming absorbed. The falling rate of profit could no longer be compensated by multiplied sales. The competitors had priced each other out because the market could not continue to expand at a multiplying rate. Indeed, no market can.

There were also social contradictions to this competitive struggle. The gradually tightening profit squeeze forced entrepreneurs to try to cut costs by improving machinery and reducing wages. As a result, the technological capacity of the society (its wealth, power, and energy), and the wealth of the already wealthy, increased as the wages of the poor declined. The average weekly wage of the handloom weaver in Bolton declined from 33 shillings in 1795 to 14 shillings in 1815, and then to 5½ shillings in 1829–1834.

Poverty amidst affluence: that was the hallmark of capitalist industrialization. By the late 1830s and early 1840s the saturated cotton market brought about the first industrial depression, forcing five hundred thousand handloom weavers to starve and a much smaller number of successful entrepreneurs to find a place to invest fortunes which totaled about £60 million a year. Some of the capitalists spent their profits on luxuries and large estates and mansions in an attempt to ape the style of the aristocracy. But far more of this new money class were savers rather than spenders. That is how they had been successful (even when they were forcing others to save), and that is what they hoped to continue to do. If they had all behaved like aristocrats, the windfall profits might have left England in the 1850s not much more productive than Spain in the seventeenth century.

## Railroaded to the Rescue

The industrial takeoff continued because cotton profits were invested —almost by chance—in an industry which would create a stock of capital goods that would transform the world and keep the process going. That industry was railroads. The railroad solved a problem of capitalist industrialization that few could have forseen at the time. More accurately it answered a whole series of questions that sprung from the contradictions of capitalist expansion. Looking back now we can ask those questions. How is it possible for a private enterprise economy to develop a capital goods capacity (that complex of iron- and steelworks, heavy machinery, transportation and communication networks that full industrialization requires) when individual investors (unlike governments) compete in already existing markets for the greatest immediate return? How can individual investors be induced by the market to sink their money into expensive productive facilities that are socially useful but not very profitable? How to keep the economy going, so that it can rebound from each depression? And, what can be done with all of that money that was made by a few—even in the midst of economic collapse?

From the standpoint of the investors of the 1830s and 1840s the question was what to do with their money—that £60 million per year. Giving it to the poor was out of the question, of course, and that would not be a good investment even in a social sense: it wouldn't increase productivity. South American loans were big in the 1820s, but by the 1830s many of them were worthless pieces of paper. Railroads seemed an unlikely alternative. They returned not the hundreds or even thousands percent profits of early cotton expansion, but only 3.7 percent in 1855. The answer is that rails were really the only alternative. There was simply too much money to invest in any other way. And, as John Francis said in 1851, the railroad's "absorption of capital was at least an absorption, if unsuccessful, in the country that produced it. Unlike foreign mines and foreign loans, they could not be exhausted or utterly valueless."[8]

No doubt the otherwise irrational, "railway manias" of investment in 1835–1837 and 1844–1847 were also enflamed by promoters and speculators who catered to the fantasies of the new class for speed and power. The railroad became the symbol of the age and its movers. Even the shrewdest, most calculating investor sometimes puts his money where his heart is. Actually, the market may have played only a secondary role in luring investment where it was needed. And in the United States it was government subsidy (including land grants of over 130 million acres or 7 percent of the nation) combined with Congressional bribes that made rail investment profitable.

Private enterprise, public enterprise, or passion—whatever the reason—the railroad was just what was needed to channel huge profits into productive investments, create a capital goods industry and a transportation network, revive the economy, and send it soaring. Between 1830 and 1850 world railroad mileage rose from a few dozen to 23,500. In the same period British output of both coal and iron tripled. The techniques for the mass production of steel followed naturally in the next decades.

The history of the English industrial revolution between 1780 and 1850, its formative stage, reminds us of the difficulties of capitalist industrialization. We have grown so used to crediting the wealth of industrial society to capitalism, that we have to be reminded from time to time that capitalism and industry are not synonymous. It is possible that the first industrial revolution could not have been achieved in a noncapitalist economy. The power of even the strongest mercantilist rulers in the eighteenth century was probably not sufficient to bring about collectivist industrialization—and besides, the middle class was too willing to play a role. But capitalist industrialization was not entirely a private affair. National mercantilist policy, tariffs, and encouragement were essential. And the private free enterprise aspects of the capitalist industrialization were often mindlessly unplanned and socially disastrous. The highly organized state-planned industrializations of Russia and China in the twentieth century may have sacrificed a generation of workers and peasants. But the unplanned, chaotic, profiteering industrializations of England and the West may have been just as humanly expensive over a longer time.

## *For Further Reading*

Contrary to popular belief, not all books on economics and economic history are impossible to read. Among the most readable (even entertaining) of general introductory economic histories are Robert L. Heilbroner's **The Making of Economic Society*** and Leo Huberman's **Man's Worldly Goods.*** The first is sympathetic to capitalism; the second to socialism.

Our discussion of primitive and traditional economies relies on the findings of a particular school of economic anthropologists. Their work can be pursued through Karl Polanyi's **The Great Transformation,*** and two collections of essays edited by George Dalton: **Primitive, Archaic and Modern Economies: Essays of Karl Polanyi** and **Tribal and Peasant Economies.*** A more diverse set of views can be found in **Themes in Economic Anthropology,*** edited by Raymond Firth. Perhaps the best statement by the opposing school is Harold K. Schneider's **Economic Man.**

For medieval and early modern Europe Robert S. Lopez's **The Commercial Revolution of the Middle Ages, 950–1350*** and Carlo Cipolla's **Before the Industrial Revolution: European Society and Economy, 1000–1700*** are excellent introductions. Lopez's **The Birth of Europe*** and the sourcebook by Lopez and I. W. Raymond, **Medieval Trade in the Mediterranean World: Illustrative Documents*** as well as Cipolla's **Money, Prices and Civilization in the Mediterranean World,** are also very valuable. Robert-Henri Bautier's **The Economic Development of Medieval Europe*** is especially well illustrated. On agrarian society, Marc Bloch's **Feudal Society*** is a beautiful, humanistic classic and Slicher van Bath's **The Agrarian History of Western Europe A.D. 500–1850** is a more strictly economic approach. G. Duby's recent **Rural Economy and Country Life in the Medieval West*** is excellent. Charles K. Warner has gathered a number of good articles in **Agrarian Conditions in Modern European History.***

On the rise of capitalism, Fernand Braudel's **Capitalism and Material Life 1400–1800*** is a superb and suggestive study from a global perspective.

* Available in paperback.

The essays in **Economy & Society,*** edited by Peter Burke, are excellent. **The Rise of Capitalism,*** edited by David Landes, has some very good essays. Maurice Dobb's **Studies in the Development of Capitalism*** is a solid, suggestive volume, written from a Marxist perspective. Karl Polanyi's **The Great Transformation*** is a difficult, but highly rewarding work on what capitalism meant for traditional society.

On the industrial revolution, Philip A. M. Taylor's **The Industrial Revolution in Britain*** and C. Stewart Doty's **The Industrial Revolution*** collect some of the standard interpretations. Lewis Mumford's **Technics and Civilization*** offers an extremely stimulating interpretation of Western technological development. John U. Nef's **The Conquest of the Material World*** surveys early industrialization. Phyllis Deane's **The First Industrial Revolution*** is a good modern account, as is T. S. Ashton's brief **The Industrial Revolution, 1760–1830*** and the classic that coined the term, Arnold Toynbee's **The Industrial Revolution.**

For the social and political background of industrialization, E. J. Hobsbawm's **The Age of Revolution 1789–1848*** is superb. Changes in social class are discussed in Peter N. Stearns's **European Society in Upheaval*** with almost startling clarity. Vincent J. Knapp's **Europe in the Era of Social Transformation: 1700–Present*** covers the same ground well. E. P. Thompson's **The Making of the English Working Class*** is a masterpiece. Val Lorwin's **Labor and Working Conditions in Modern Europe*** excerpts Thompson and some other fine studies.

On the history of economic thought, Robert L. Heilbroner's **The Worldly Philosophers*** makes engaging reading. A delightful Marxist alternative to Heilbroner's liberal view is Joan Robinson's brief **Economic Philosophy.*** Ben B. Seligman's **Main Currents in Modern Economics*** is a solid three-volume study of economic thought. George Friedmann's **The Anatomy of Work*** is a stimulating modern French sociological investigation. An American equivalent might be Reinhard Bendix's **Work and Authority in Industry.***

Finally, the student should be aware of the multivolume **Cambridge Economic History of Europe** and such journals as **Economic History Review, Past and Present, Journal of Economic History,** and **Journal of Social History.**

## Notes

1. Manning Nash, "The Organization of Economic Life," in *Horizons of Anthropology*, ed. Sol Tax (Chicago, Aldine, 1964), p. 171.
2. Adapted from William Bartram, *The Travels of William Bartram*, ed. Francis Harper (New Haven: Yale University Press, 1958), p. 326.
3. Slicher van Bath, *Agrarian History of Western Europe* A.D. *500–1850*, trans. Olive Ordish (London: Edward Arnold, 1963), tab. 1, p. 327.
4. Fernand Braudel, *Capitalism and Material Life 1400–1800*, trans. Miriam Kochan (New York: Harper & Row, 1967, 1973), pp. 129–130.
5. Braudel, "European Expansion and Capitalism: 1450–1650" in *Chapters in Western Civilization*, 3rd ed. (New York: Columbia University Press, 1961), vol. 1, p. 285.

6. John U. Nef, "The Progress of Technology and the Growth of Large Scale Industry in Great Britain, 1540–1640," *The Economic History Review* 1 (1934), reprinted in *The Industrial Revolution in Britain* (New York: Heath, 1958), p. 8.
7. These figures and much of the following discussion are drawn from E. J. Hobsbawm, *The Age of Revolution 1789–1848* (New York: New American Library, 1962), pp. 56–66.
8. *Ibid.*, p. 67.

# Chapter 15

# Racism and Color

## Colonialism and Slavery

Is the racism of modern Western society unique, or has racism always existed? Can it be eliminated by law, or does it thrive on deeply embedded cultural impulses? How deep is the racism of modern, white Western society? When did it begin? How did it develop? Only when we can answer some of these questions will we be able to attempt to eliminate racism from our society and ourselves. This chapter begins with an attempt to answer some of these questions. It will argue that although racism is a very ancient phenomenon, the white racism of modern Western society is particularly severe. This chapter will trace the origins of modern white racism to the European society which created slavery in the Americas.

It will pay special attention to the underlying ideas of whiteness and blackness in Western literature to get a sense of the depth of our cultural color consciousness. Then the chapter will examine the institution of slavery. It will pay special attention to the argument of some historians that the slavery of northern European, Protestant, capitalist countries was more racist than the slavery of Latin America.

## The History of Racism: Eternal or Modern?

There is some debate as to whether racism is an ancient or modern development. One anthropologist, Claude Lévi-Strauss, argues that racism is ancient. He points out that there is something of a paradox in modern civilized people calling other races "savages." According to him, "this attitude of mind, which excludes 'savages' (or any people one may choose to regard as savages) from humankind, is precisely the attitude most strikingly characteristic of those same savages." He is right, of course. Primitive people have always imagined themselves to be the only human beings in the world. When they discovered others they often viewed the intruders as subhuman. Many primitive tribes called themselves "the men." In contrast, foreigners were referred to as the "ground-monkeys," the "lousy eggs," the "wicked," or the "ghosts." These foreigners were rarely, if ever, members of a different race, but primitives have often viewed all strangers as if they were so different as to be nonhuman.

When different races have come together they have each usually wondered whether the other was human. For example, a few years after Columbus discovered America the Spanish sent out commissions to investigate whether the Indians had souls, as a way of finding out if they were human. At the same time that these commissions began their investigation a group of Indians was drowning white prisoners captured from an earlier voyage in order to find out if their bodies decomposed, as did their own human bodies.

While viewing racism as an ancient invention, Lévi-Strauss reminds us that the very idea of brotherhood and common humanity is relatively new. No primitive tribe ever imagined that all the people in the world were children of the same parents or the same god. They believed that every tribe had its own ancestors and its own gods. Only within the last two thousand years have religions emerged which taught the universal brotherhood of all the world's human beings. Christianity, Roman Stoic philosophy, and Eastern Buddhism all developed the concept of "humanity" at about the same time. Earlier religions thought only of *their* tribe, family, or state. Gradually (within the last two thousand years), we have become more and more conscious of our own common humanity.

A different view is offered by another anthropologist, Michel Leiris:

> The first point which emerges from any examination of the data of ethnography and history is that race prejudice is not universal and is of recent origin. Many of the societies investigated by anthropologists do indeed display group pride, but while the group regards itself as privileged compared with other groups, it makes no "racist" claims and, for instance, is not above entering into temporary alliances with other groups or providing itself with women from them.[1]

He maintains that racism was largely absent from primitive and ancient societies. He argues that although the ancient Greeks called their neighbors "barbarians," they meant that these non-Greeks were uncivilized or uncultured, not nonhuman. This is probably true. Greeks accepted foreigners who seemed to be cultured (which is to say, foreigners who learned Greek customs). The Greeks came into contact with a number of different races: Asian Mongoloids, African Negroids, and European Caucasians. In fact, the Greeks were a mixture of various subgroups of these races from the Middle East, Asia, and the Mediterranean. The fantastic flowering of Greek culture is sometimes attributed to this dynamic mixture of peoples. The Greeks looked down on foreigners, but on all foreigners equally, regardless of race. They felt that foreigners lacked the independence and vitality which Greek culture provided. They were not racists, however, because they did not consider the cultural failings of their neighbors an irremediable or incurable problem.

Most Greeks thought that Asians, for instance, were cowardly. But instead of attributing this supposed character deficiency to Mongoloid "yellowness" or racial inheritance, they looked for explanations in Asian culture. Hippocrates, for instance, attributed Chinese military inefficiency to a system that did not adequately reward the bravery of the soldiers; the fruits of victory went to the lords rather than the soldiers.

When the Greek troops under Alexander the Great conquered Persia and India, ten thousand Greek soldiers married Hindu Indian women and Alexander himself married two Persian princesses. Since they imagined that they brought the benefits of Greek culture and civilization, they knew that their sons and daughters would be raised like other Greeks. They had no fear of producing offspring less than human or corrupting a Greek "race" or "blood."

The example of the Greeks is not given to prove that Lévi-Strauss is wrong, and that Leiris is correct. No single example could do that. Certainly Lévi-Strauss is right when he points out that Paleolithic and Neolithic peoples had no idea of the unity of humankind. He is also correct in reminding us that most people in human history have been suspicious of strangers, perhaps especially when those strangers looked different. There were no scientific studies of race before the last couple of hundred years, but that does not mean that people have only become racists since then.

What do we make of the ancient Egyptian tombs which show four colors of people? Is this a sign of racial harmony or racism? Perhaps the distance of each of these figures from the god Horus (in some of the paintings) is an indication of Egyptian ideas of relative superiority and inferiority. Closest to the god is a deep-red-skinned northern Egyptian, next a black-skinned southern Egyptian, next a yellow-skinned Asiatic, and last a white-skinned European. Egypt was a racially diversified civilization, but the balance of power often shifted. When the lighter-skinned peoples of the north were dominant they referred to the southerners as "the evil race of Ish." When these southerners were in power they called the lighter-skinned peoples "the pale, degraded race of Arvad." On the other hand, they lived in relative harmony—at least racial—for most of Egyptian history.

Were there racist elements in ancient Chinese civilization? Around 500 B.C. the philosopher Confucius stated the antiracist position succinctly: "The nature of men is identical; what divides them is their customs." On the other hand, we hear from an historian of the Han dynasty (roughly parallel in scope and time to the Roman Empire) that the yellow-haired, green-eyed people of Europe "resemble the apes from whom they are descended."

How racist are stories of creation which deny a common humanity? Eskimos, for instance, tell a story about the Great Being who created a colorless people called "white men" in his first creation, and then went on to improve on the failures of this trial run with a second creation of perfect *in-nu*, the ancestors of the Eskimos. There is a similar, common North American Indian legend which recounts how the Great Spirit had to create man three times. The first time the creation was not baked long enough and came out white. The second time the Great Spirit kept his creation in the oven too long, and the result was burned black. Only the last time was the Great Spirit able to create a perfectly golden loaf of man.

There is certainly an ingredient in these Indian recipes for humans which gives the flavor of racism. Many American Indians, like many ancient Egyptians, Chinese, and other peoples, seem to have confused race with culture and believed that their own race's culture was superior to others. Before the universalistic ideas of Buddhism, Confucianism, Christianity, and Roman Stoicism were widely accepted, many ancient peoples must have believed that other races were less human than themselves. Lévi-Strauss may be correct when he states that this form of racism is a very common attitude among primitives or precivilized peoples. We should be careful, at least, of considering racism a purely modern development.

On the other hand, the point that Leiris makes is very compelling. The modern racism that accompanied the development of slavery (in the last five hundred years) was so much more extensive than these ancient ideas that it deserves a special place in the history of racism. For the fact remains that despite the American Indian ideas of their own superior creation, they did not enslave other races. And, even when the Egyptians or Chinese enslaved members of other races, racist slavery never became the way of life that it became in the Americas.

Racism in ancient societies was rarely institutionalized in slavery or some other form of domination. There are, of course, cases. In the traditional kingdoms of Rwanda and Burundi in Central Africa, for instance, the Tutsi aristocracy (which comprised about 15 percent of the population) ruled over both the Hutu majority who were physically shorter and the Twa minority who were lighter skinned. Similarly, some Arab Moslems ruled over the darker Hausa of Nigeria and developed associations between light skin and natural domination. But these practices were not common among Moslems or Negroid Africans. Normally, the slavery of Africans (as in Greece and Rome) had nothing to do with race. In fact, the severest forms of slavery in the ancient world (the Greco-Roman rather than the African) were the least racist. The Greeks and Romans used their slaves of all races in the hard work of plantation agriculture while the Africans used their conquests mainly as household helpers and attendants.

Significantly, Western Europeans were the ones who systematically organized large forces of other races (Africans and American Indians) for the fiercely exploitive work of plantations and mines. These Europeans were the ones who moved whole populations to another world, broke up their families, wiped out their identities and traditions, and treated them like animals. Finally, these Europeans were the ones who developed an elaborate set of justifications (ideas, theories, and feelings of racial superiority) which far surpassed the racism of prior societies. No other society developed such an array of poets, philosophers, and diplomats of racism as did the European and American ruling class. No other society committed its religious, ethical, social, and personal values so thoroughly to racism. Maybe, this alone is an indication of the thoroughness of Western racist exploitation. They protested too much, too long, and too hard that what they were doing was only natural.

Western racism was unique in its scope as well as its thoroughness. It not only poisoned European culture, but spread the virus through much of the world. All of the colonial settlements in the New World (both North and South America) prospered with the extermination of the native inhabitants (called Indians) and the slave labor of another race from Africa. Even African soil became a seedbed for European racist institutions: international slave markets, white settler states, white-run, slave-worked plantations and mines. By the end of the nineteenth century Europeans and Americans had carried their racist attitudes to the Pacific islands and the Far East. Eventually they created racist visions of subhuman Chinese, Japanese, and Orientals, which were merely hasty translations of older ideas of blacks and native American Indians. At certain times, some ancient societies had developed racist institutions, even a kind of racist slavery, and sometimes even racist ideas to match. But such an occurrence was rare, almost never became the preoccupation of a people or their culture, and never became the basis of life for a large area or empire. Racism in modern Western society (after about 1500) became a way of life for a continent of Europeans and then for the continents they conquered.

The question to ask is why? It is not enough to say (with Lévi-Strauss) that racism has always existed. The germ of suspicion may have always existed, but it rarely became epidemic—in fact, it rarely developed. Why did modern Western society (of all societies) permit this germ to become a plague which swept almost every institution of their own culture and much of the rest of the world?

Part of the answer, of course, is slavery, particularly the racial kind of slavery that the Western countries developed after their contact with Africa and their discoveries of the Americas. England, France, Spain, and Portugal (to name the most significant examples) built slave societies from scratch in the New World. Unlike the Romans, they built these slave societies with one visibly distinct race of slaves (Africans), and they built them away from home (away from the public eye and in "frontier" conditions). There was a limited market for slaves in Europe: the population was fairly stable, there were too many potential critics, especially the church. If the Europeans had never "discovered" and colonized the Americas, neither slavery nor racism would have become pervasive or extensive.

Thus, another part of the answer is that it was the Western Europeans who opened up vast areas of land which could be exploited by slave labor. After about 1450, the Europeans developed the most advanced naval and military technology in the world. Within a century their merchant ships could travel farther and their cannons could damage more than even the leading Chinese ships and weapons. The Europeans were able to conquer and enslave Africans because of their superior naval and military technology. Yet, it would be inaccurate to say that power alone made the difference. Also, it would be an error to say that the Europeans simply beat the Africans to the punch, as if the Africans would have done the same to the Europeans if they had the chance. There is very little indication in African culture that the Africans would have *wanted* to enslave Europeans and conquer the Americans. African cultures were generally less preoccupied with power and productivity than European culture. Africans were less likely to view Europeans as subhuman or objects of exploitation. Europeans, on the other hand, were more interested in military conquest and empire and more inclined to think in racist terms.

Finally, then, part of the answer lies in European culture. European racism reached extreme proportions because they enslaved Africans. Europeans enslaved Africans because they were more advanced in military technology. But they were more advanced in military technology because they *wanted* to be, and they used that technology to conquer and enslave Africans because their culture encouraged racist ideas about Africans. European racism reached staggering proportions under slavery, but its roots go back in time to before the first African slave was taken. To understand why it was the Europeans who made racism such a world-wide plague, we must first examine these cultural roots. Only then can we determine the damage of slavery and its heritage.

## The Cultural Roots of European Racism: The Problem of Whiteness

Long before Europeans enslaved Africans, they had developed an elaborate Christian culture. One element in Christian religion was particularly prone to encourage a racist attitude toward black people. This was the Christian symbolism of whiteness and blackness. Christians thought of sin as the blackening of a white soul. They thought of God, virtue, purity, and redemption in terms of radiating light or whiteness. Angels and the holy were bathed in white light. Even the Middle Eastern Jesus was gradually whitened until he became a fair-skinned, blond, blue-eyed European in the paintings of the Middle Ages. In striking contrast, the devil was dressed in black; he was the "Prince of Darkness."

According to the *Oxford English Dictionary*, by the end of the fifteenth century (before Africans were enslaved) the meaning of "black" had clearly negative implications:

> Deeply stained with dirt; soiled, dirty. . . . Having dark or deadly purposes, malignant; pertaining to or involving death, deadly; baneful, disastrous, sinister. . . . Foul, iniquitous, atrocious, horrible, wicked. . . . Indicating disgrace, censure, liability to punishment.[2]

The imagery of white and black was not uniquely Christian. Many Paleolithic peoples feared night and welcomed daylight even though they worshipped goddesses as black as the most fertile earth. Perhaps whiteness became associated with divinity in the ancient cities where Sun and Sky Fathers rather than Earth Mothers were worshipped.

One of the ancient religions of the Middle East (Persian Zoroastrianism) developed a vision of the world which spoke of a continual conflict between the "forces of light" and the "forces of darkness." Christians sometimes borrowed the imagery of this Zoroastrian struggle—especially when they felt that things were going so badly that the forces of evil might be just as strong as the forces of good.

The sixteenth and seventeenth centuries were such a time, especially for northern Europeans. Martin Luther spoke for many Germans when he argued that the dark, satanic forces of the Antichrist had taken over the Roman Catholic church. Whether these northern Europeans thought of Roman influence over their own affairs, or the corruption in the Roman papacy, or the materialism of the new class of bankers and merchants, or even the fantastic inflation of the period, they agreed that all was not well with the world. It was easier for these northern Protestants to see human history as a struggle between God and Satan—just as it was easier for the Roman popes to insist that God was in control of the world.

The leaders of the Protestant Reformation naturally found the imagery of Zoroastrian struggle more congenial to their feelings of decay and impending doom. The power brokers of the establishment in Rome could weigh the good with the bad, speak of hopes and failings, and (in general) find the world they ran moderately successful, despite its problems. The Protestants at war with this establishment perceived things more readily in terms of black and white. At the same time, the papacy could insist on seeing things in perspective and considering the shades of gray.

Whiteness may have become more of a problem for northern European Protestant cultures than it was for southern European Catholic cultures for another reason. Not only were the northerners more fearful of the powers of darkness which they believed to be taking over the world, they were also physically whiter and blonder than the inhabitants of the Mediterranean. Whiteness became a mark of beauty for those whose skins were particularly pale. Queen Elizabeth, the Protestant daughter of Henry VIII, was celebrated (as were other women) by the English for the lily-whiteness of her skin:

Her cheek, her chin, her neck, her nose,
This was a lily, that was a rose;
Her hande so white as whales bone,

Her finger tipt with Cassidone;
Her bosom, sleek as Paris plaster
Held up two bowles of Alabaster.[3]

The problem of whiteness was examined indirectly by the great poet of Elizabeth's England, William Shakespeare. Shakespeare may have been a bit more conscious of whiteness as a problem. He had a dark mistress, of whom he wrote half apologetically, and half adoringly:

My mistress' eyes are nothing like the sun; . . .
If snow be white, why then her breasts are dun.

Maybe Shakespeare was particularly conscious of the way he and his fellow English identified blackness with sex. When they thought of their "Virgin Queen" Elizabeth and their respectable Christian wives and daughters, they saw whiteness—the blinding whiteness of purity, loyalty, and chastity which were so important to Christians. Sex was the root of all sin according to these Christians. Paradise had been lost and humankind doomed; all because Eve had tempted Adam. (These Christians were sufficiently aware of the power of sex to know that Eve had offered Adam more than an apple.) Since sin was black, sex was black, because sexual license was the most deadly of all sins.

Some other cultures had thought of sex as black. Neolithic fertility goddesses were sometimes black to represent the most fertile soil. The black Earth Mothers were the most productive. But these Neolithic cults worshipped blackness as the source of life. In general, the Judeo-Christian cultures worshipped whiteness and feared the sexual power of blackness. Christian priests and bishops were not always successful in converting country peasants to the new religion. Many of these uneducated farmers accepted the elements of Christianity which fit in with their ancient Neolithic images. In some cases, for instance, they worshipped a black Virgin Mary more than the official white Jesus.

## Dirty Words and White Lies

Shakespeare and most educated, middle-class Elizabethans, however, were raised on the respectable, official Christianity of cardinals, cities, and universities. For them, sexuality was unambiguously evil as well as black. *Othello,* one of Shakespeare's greatest plays, gives us a clear indication of the Elizabethan Christian responses to whiteness and blackness. The play, which was probably written in 1604 (the year after Elizabeth's death), is based on an earlier Italian story of a black African general's marriage to a fair-skinned Venetian. Shakespeare contributes so much to the original story, though, that we can consider it his own.

Othello is the black Moor (or Moslem). Shakespeare pictures him as especially noble, generous, and loving. Desdemona, his wife, is completely devoted to him. They love each other selflessly and without suspicion. But their love is corrupted by the racism of those around them. For example, the Venetian gentlemen, including Desdemona's father, continually refer to Othello as the "lusty Moor" or the "lascivious Moor." Desdemona's father was dead set against her marriage to the "damn'd" Moor whose "sooty bosom" must, he feels, have won his "fair" daughter's heart by "foul charms." Othello is "damn'd" because he's black; even his name suggests he has come out of hell. His black skin must be only the exterior of a "sooty bosom" inside. It seems unnatural to the father that a daughter as fair or white as Desdemona could be attracted to someone as black as Othello. Therefore, Othello must have used "foul charms" (we would say "black magic") to trick her. All of the elements of white racism are there.

The real force of a racism that identifies black skin with dirt, sex, and sin is displayed in the play by one of Othello's white assistants, Iago. Iago was passed up for a promotion. Perhaps that is why he suspects that Othello has seduced his wife:

> I hate the Moor;
> And it is thought abroad, that 'twixt my sheets
> He has done my office.

It is this fear of black sexuality that eats away at Iago like a virulent disease. He says again:

> For that I do suspect the lusty Moor
> Hath leap'd into my seat; the thought whereof
> Doth, like a poisonous mineral, gnaw my inwards.

Iago is able to save himself from being destroyed by the absurd suspicion poisoning him only by infecting others. He proceeds to attack Desdemona (whom he says he loves) in order to get at Othello (whom he has come to hate). He resolves to "turn her virtue into pitch," in short to "blacken" her image in the eyes of Othello.

Othello is himself so indoctrinated by the racist color scheme of his adopted culture that he easily believes that his loving wife would accept a white lover. Manipulated by Iago to suspect his wife, even Othello can only see her sin in racist terms:

Her name, that was as fresh,
As Dian's visage, is now begrim'd and black
As mine own face.

Finally, the noble Moor (a phrase which meant good nigger or white-washed black to the audience) is driven to kill the loving wife that he calls "the fair devil" (or white black whom he really perceives as a sinful or black white).

It is white racism that really kills Desdemona. Iago uses "dirty" words, spoken from "dark shadows." But the noble Moor is the instrument, the victim, and the accused. After he "puts out the light" of his life, he is condemned by Desdemona's servant:

O! the more angel she,
And you the blacker devil. . . .
She was too fond of her filthy bargain. . . .
O gull! O dolt! As ignorant as dirt!

Shakespeare's play is not racist, but it exposes the racism of Elizabethan society by playing upon the symbols for white and black. *Othello* offers us a mirror image of racism in England *before* the English became involved in the massive projects of enslaving Africans. The first African slaves came to North America only 15 years after *Othello* was written. Even before the English were forced to rationalize their enslavement of African blacks, they had developed a fairly complex color symbolism which had profoundly racist implications.

Before slavery, English Christians had associated blackness with evil and sex. Even before most English had seen any Africans, they were convinced that these Moors or "Ethiopians" were more sexually capable (and thus more sinful) than themselves. It is difficult to tell how much of the slave codes of the Americas was based on a fear of African sexuality. White women were certainly desexualized when they were placed on pedestals by their white masters. One of the deepest fears of the masters of slave society was that the black Africans would rape or seduce their fair, but weak white women. Yet, the most erotic fantasies imagined by the masters depicted their black female slaves because they had convinced themselves that their white women were too pure to be seductive.

In a sense, the slave society created by European Christians from the sixteenth to the nineteenth century was only the logical conclusion of the racist ideas which had already developed in Christianity, especially Protestant Christianity. In another sense slavery was the practical application of the color schemes of a Christianity which had been grafted on to a much older Neolithic or agricultural religion. The conclusion of the Neolithic feeling that blackness was sexuality and the

Christian injunction that sexuality was evil had been reached even before the development of slavery: Shakespeare's audience agreed that blackness was evil; that is why they could enjoy the double meanings and paradoxes of the "noble Moor," the "fair devil," and Othello's innocent crime.

The problem, however, of a culture which made a wholesale commitment against sexuality was that it might become extinct. Christian monastic communities and Protestant sects had on occasion actually disappeared because of their avoidance of sex. As every Neolithic farmer knew, sex was the source of life itself. Christian slave society made such a commitment against blackness that, in symbolic terms, it sometimes meant an opposition to life. Perhaps they feared that the sexuality of blackness was always more vibrantly alive than Christian repression. And perhaps the exclusion of blackness which slavery required was ultimately a call to self-extinction.

## The Whiteness of the Whale

If Shakespeare is the great poet of Christian culture immediately before slavery, Herman Melville may be the poet of mature slave society. As Shakespeare shows us what it means to really believe that sexuality is black and evil, Melville shows us what it means to identify blackness with life, and whiteness with death. Melville's novel *Moby Dick* explores the suicidal implications of the "problem of whiteness" in the same way that Shakespeare had explored its sexual meaning.

On the simple story level *Moby Dick* is about Captain Ahab's fanatical pursuit of Moby Dick, the white whale. The novel tells of the crew, their exploitation by Ahab, life on a whaling ship, and the final destruction of Ahab and most of the crew when they confront the great white whale. This, however, is like saying that *Othello* is about love destroyed by revenge and jealousy. Like all great works of art, both works are about much more than the story tells. Further, the underlying meaning of both has much to do with racism and the problem of whiteness.

Ahab represents the whole white master class of America in its quest for whiteness, or the control over blackness that yields power. It is Moby Dick's whiteness that leads Ahab on his monomaniacal hunt. Melville writes that his most important chapter is the one on the whiteness of the whale. Whiteness, Melville says, is the quality which gives "the white man ideal mastery over every dusky tribe." Whiteness is the control over darkness and the dark demonic powers of the slaves. It is the sign of the intelligence or "enlightenment" of white culture, an indication of the purity of white Christian culture, but also a symbol of the white Christian's fear of the invisible, the ghostly, and the dead. In Melville's terms, whiteness is "at once the most meaning symbol of spiritual things, nay, the very veil of the Christian's Deity; and yet should be as it is—the intensifying agent in things the most appalling to mankind."

Ahab, like white culture, is appalled by whiteness (even while seeking it) because the power of whiteness over blackness means the annihilation of all color, which is to say all of life itself. Ahab, like Western man, is, according to Melville, stabbed "from behind with the thought of annihilation when beholding the white depths of the milky way." Ahab the "wretched infidel gazes himself blind at the monumental white shroud that wraps all the prospect around him. And of all these things the Albino whale was the symbol." White master society gains purity, power, and whiteness through inhumane control of the colorful variety of life. The white masters imagine themselves more purified as their power over dark nature increases. But perhaps, Melville suggests, white masters like Ahab are also aware that the power of whiteness comes at the cost of death; the symbol of purity is akin to the white shroud of death and the colorless, invisible ghost.

The sexist racism that gnawed at the innards of Iago had become by the middle of the nineteenth century a consuming struggle against life itself. It had deep roots in Christian, even Neolithic, culture. Europeans, especially northern European Protestant cultures, had made much more of the differences between whiteness and blackness than other peoples. But despite the ancient pedigree of European racism, despite the increasing quest for whiteness in the Protestantism of the sixteenth century, it was the European colonial society of the nineteenth century which became fixated on the achievement of whiteness at all costs. The reasons for this increasing racist consciousness in Western culture from the sixteenth to the nineteenth century can be found in the institutional changes that transformed the society. Slavery was certainly the most important of these.

## The Institutional Roots of European Racism: The Burden of Slavery

Sometimes the exception proves the rule. Listen to the master of a slave ship, Captain Thomas Phillips, in 1694. The good captain complained of the developing racism of his fellow English, and found it

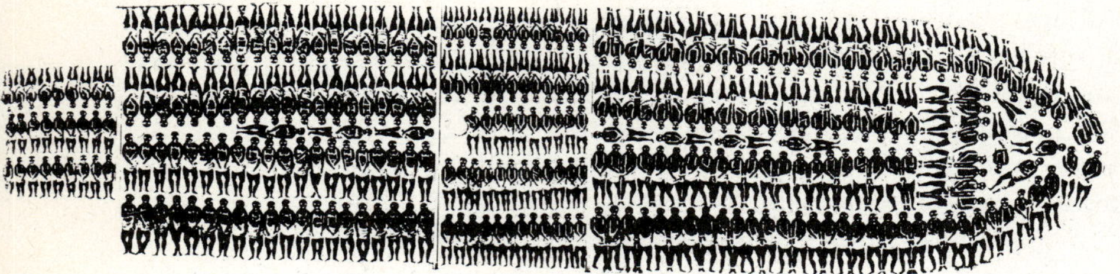

■ *The slaves were packed in the hold of the slave ship for the two- to three-month voyage from Africa "in two rows, one above the other like books on a shelf."* (Abstract of Evidence on . . . Slave Trade, *1792*)

odd that Africans were despised simply because they were black. The good slaver said that he could not imagine why they should be despised for

> their color, being what they cannot help, and the effect of the climate it has pleased God to appoint them. I can't think there is any intrinsic value in one color more than another, nor that white is better than black, only we think it so because we are so, and are prone to judge favorable in our own case, as well as the blacks, who, in odium of the color, say the devil is white, and so paint him.[4]

Statements like that could not have been made by many slave ship captains, nor by many other people who profited directly from the capture, sale, or use of African slaves. The fact that this captain could be so open suggests that there could be good men operating cruelly in a brutal system. But the fact that his statement was unusual also shows that most people were molded by the system, however noble their feelings initially were. It was not possible for many slavers to maintain such views very long and still go about their business. It was almost inevitable that a society which made slavery a way of life would normally think in racist terms, at least when all those slaves were black. Certainly Europeans were better able to tolerate their brutal exploitation of Africans by imagining that these Africans were an inferior race or, better still, not even human. In this sense, slavery encouraged European racism.

It is pretty clear to almost everyone who has thought about modern racism that our history of slavery is one of the major causes of our problem. It is difficult to imagine what the United States would be like today if Africans had been admitted on the same terms as other immigrants. But we would almost certainly have less of a racial prob-

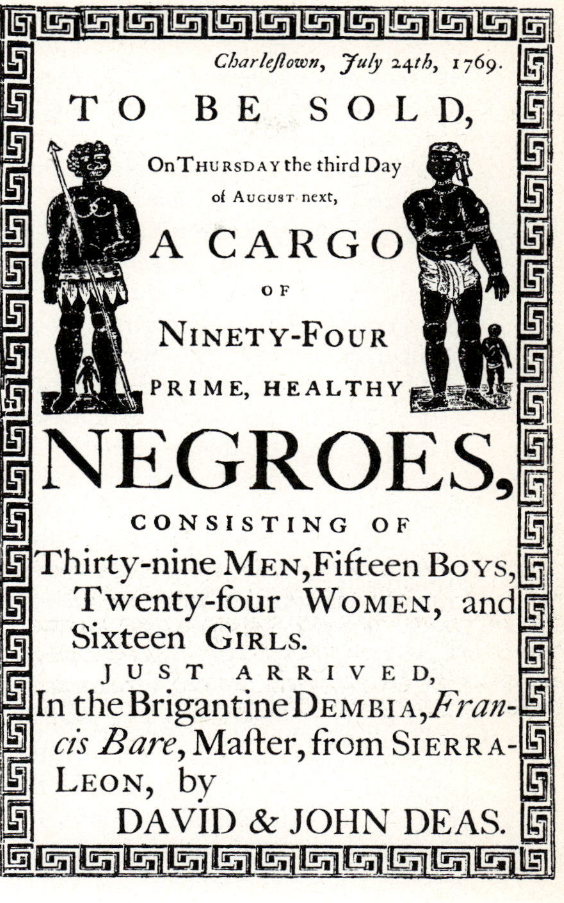
Charlestown, July 24th, 1769.
TO BE SOLD,
On THURSDAY the third Day
of AUGUST next,
A CARGO
OF
NINETY-FOUR
PRIME, HEALTHY
NEGROES,
CONSISTING OF
Thirty-nine MEN, Fifteen BOYS,
Twenty-four WOMEN, and
Sixteen GIRLS.
JUST ARRIVED,
In the Brigantine DEMBIA, *Francis Bare*, Master, from SIERRA-LEON, by
DAVID & JOHN DEAS.

■ *According to conservative estimates, most of the ten- to twenty-million slaves sold came, like these, from West Africa. (American Antiquarian Society)*

lem. Our history of enslaving Africans, breaking up their families, depriving them of much of their own old culture, and forcing them to be totally dependent on white power, created inequalities, prejudice, and discrimination which has lasted centuries. The heritage of slavery encouraged racial fears which inhibited eventual emancipation. When slaves were freed throughout North and South America in the nineteenth century, they were never made first-class citizens. The children and grandchildren of slaves (although legally free everywhere in the Americas by 1900) were politically and economically disadvantaged *because* of their skin color. Their color remained an obstacle to equality *because* of the previous history of slavery. The damage of slavery is pretty obvious.

Having said all of that, however, we can make some distinctions which will be useful in understanding how we arrived at the present point. We have already noticed, for instance, that there was a considerable amount of cultural prejudice (at least in England) before Africans were taken as slaves. Presumably, then, even if the Europeans who immigrated to the Americas had never enslaved Africans, there may have been a certain amount of prejudice against free blacks.

We have also noticed that the prejudice of northern and southern Europeans differed, at least slightly. This difference is especially striking if we compare the prejudice of the Spanish and Portuguese (on the Iberian Peninsula) with that of northern Europeans, especially the British. The Spanish and Portuguese were less prejudiced partially because they had lived with Africans on the Iberian Peninsula since the Moslem invasion in 711. By the time of Columbus the Iberians had spent centuries fighting and loving the dark-skinned Moors of North Africa. The Spanish and Portuguese had learned to admire the rich Islamic culture of Iberia and the "mother cities" of Africa. It was impossible for educated Iberians to identify blackness with backwardness. The English were able to make such an identification because they knew almost nothing of African or Moslem civilization.

The cultural differences between northern and southern Europe around 1500 were probably increased by the different types of slavery which the two areas developed in the Americas. Slavery, like the coexistence of different races, had a much longer history in Iberia than in England. Slavery was a continuous institution in Iberia, almost since Roman times. Over the centuries, the Iberian Catholic church had tempered some of the most brutal aspects of slavery. Custom had enshrined a long list of duties and responsibilities of the slave owner to the slave. Much the same was true of Moslem culture. Wealthy Christians and Moslems often treated their slaves as dependent members of a large household. Slave owners often judged themselves in terms of their generosity, not in terms of the amount of money they could make by exploiting other human beings. Nor was there a clear color line between slaves and free Iberians. Wealthy Christians and Moslems owned white, dark, or black slaves, depending on circumstances. Slavery itself was more of a system of dependence on the rich and powerful than a system of ownership. It was often difficult to tell the difference between slavery and the feudal system of loyalty or obligation which also permeated the social relationships on the Iberian Peninsula.

In England slavery had virtually disappeared by 1500. Even the traditional feudal relationships were largely replaced by a system of relatively free peasants obeying the laws of relatively independent governments. Customary loyalty to the patron or lord had given way to political obedience. Consequently, when the English (and the Danish and Dutch) began to enslave Africans after 1500, they began almost from scratch. The only slaves were Africans. The new slave owners did not have to comply with traditional obligations, responsibilities, or the power of the church. They were in a much better position to write their own slave laws. Since these northern European countries were also more fully on the way to developing a dynamic, capitalist economy, they were also more prone to think of slavery as a system for making money. The English did not take slaves to the new world as part of their extended families. Like the Dutch and Danish, they first traded in slaves for profit, and then set up plantations of slave workers for more profits.

Since the northern Europeans established colonies in the Caribbean and in North America, and the Iberians set up colonies in South America, Mexico, and some of the Caribbean islands, it might be useful to compare some of the differences in these two. They may tell us much about the differences between North and South America today. North American racism has a lot to do with slavery, but it is also a product of a particular type of slavery. There is evidence that the northern, Protestant, capitalist type encouraged the development of a considerably more racist society than the southern, Catholic, precapitalist type of slavery.

## British vs. Latin American Slavery: Racism and Manumission

Let us take a look at some of the evidence. For one thing, it seems pretty clear that bondage was a more permanent condition for the slave in the United States and British Caribbean islands than it was in Latin America. A much higher proportion of slaves in the Spanish and Portuguese colonies were given their freedom than in the British colonies. This attitude toward giving the slave freedom (manumission) is very important because it shows that the white colonizers need not view the Africans as permanently and incurably inferior. In Brazil (settled by the Portuguese) and in Spanish America the law did not declare that a slave was necessarily a slave for his whole life or that his children were necessarily slaves—as was legally the case in the United States after the 1660s.

In Latin America there were a number of ways that slaves might attain freedom. They might purchase it by hiring themselves out on Sundays or one of the 85 holidays on the Catholic calendar. In Cuba or Mexico they had the right to have their purchase price declared, and could pay it in gradual installments. This became a widespread custom, especially in Cuba. A slave who was worth $600 could pur-

■ *The caption of this eighteenth-century engraving reads: "An Englishman from Barbados sells his mistress." In the English colonies taking a black mistress was one thing, freeing her something else entirely.* (Snark International, EPA)

chase freedom in 24 installments of $25 each. Each installment purchased one twenty-fourth of freedom, and the first payment allowed the slave to move from the master's house. Though the cost may have been considerably higher than the price of passage from Africa, slaves who were able to work for their freedom were not different in principle from the white debtors of Europe who were forced to work as servants for a stated period. The relationship between master and slave was almost contractual, based on a legal agreement (though usually unwritten) between two parties (though not entered freely). There were at least some cases of slaves paying everything but the last installment in order to *avoid* complete freedom and the taxes and military service that went along with it.

There were other ways for a Latin America slave to be freed. Thousands of slaves in Venezuela and Colombia were freed by Simon Bolivar when they enlisted in the army for the wars of independence. Similarly, many of the slaves who joined the armies of Brazil and Argentina were freed. Cuba periodically issued a degree that automatically freed slaves who escaped to its shores and embraced Christianity. In most Latin American societies a slave who was unjustly punished could be freed by the judge. A Brazilian slave who had ten children could demand freedom legally.

The legal roads to manumission, however, were probably not as important as the social approval that custom and the church gave to the act of freeing a slave. Even the culture of the slave owners held that manumission was a noble and generous act, a good thing to do. Happy occasions—the birth of a son, the marriage of a daughter, religious and national holidays, and family celebrations—were considered opportunities to ceremonially free one or a number of slaves in Latin America. It was considered appropriate and commendable for a slave child to be freed at baptism with the payment of a small fee ($25 in Cuba,) and many slaves chose a godfather for their children with this hope in mind. In general, in Latin America the moral obligation went even further than the letter of the law, and the law was far more favorably disposed to manumission than it was in the United States.

In the British colonies manumission was frequently viewed with alarm. Most of the British islands placed heavy taxes (often more than the value of the slave) on those slave owners who attempted it. In all cases a slave could not be freed without the owner's consent, and sometimes the consent of others was also required. In most of the British colonies (including the United States) a black or dark-skinned person of African descent was automatically assumed to be a slave. In some cases the slave was allowed to prove that he had been freed (whereas he was presumed free in Latin American courts, and had to be proved a slave). Laws in Georgia, Mississippi, and South Carolina did not even allow the slave to establish a claim to freedom. According to the South Carolina law of 1740 "all negroes . . . mulattoes, or mestizos, who are or shall hereafter be in the province, and all their issue and offspring, born or to be born, shall be and they are hereby declared to be and remain forever hereafter absolute slaves."

Thus, even those few freed slaves in the United States were often forced back into slavery. Virginia required a freed slave to leave the state in a year or be sold "for the benefit of the Literary Fund." In many states of the southern United States, a freed slave could be sold back into slavery for the failure to pay a debt or a fine. The laws of the British West Indies and of the United States offered no hope for the slave to purchase his or her freedom, and these laws assumed that slavery was perpetual. The only hope was manumission by the slave's owner, and though this occasionally occurred there were too many obstacles for it ever to become a widespread practice.

In the slave states of the United States by 1860 only about 6 percent of the black population was free. If we include the equal number of free African Americans who lived in the northern states, only 10 percent of the black population was free. In startling comparison, at the time of Brazilian emancipation in 1888, about 75 percent of the black population was already free. This was the result of different attitudes toward manumission.

These different attitudes toward manumission are significant in two ways. They show that South Americans were more willing to allow black people freedom and independence, and also that South American societies became so populated with free blacks that it was impossible to identify the cultural condition of slavery with the biological condition of black skin. Spanish and Portuguese settlers often spoke of slavery as an unfortunate condition to which anyone might fall prey. They never saw slavery as the mark of an indelible curse or a sign of racial inferiority. They were able to distinguish between a person's color and culture. In that sense, Iberian slavery was the result of less racist attitudes, and it created a society where racism was less pronounced.

We should probably add that we are speaking only of racism, not the brutality of slavery. It is quite possible that South American societies treated their slaves more brutally than North American societies did. The Iberian willingness to manumit slaves only tells us about their attitudes toward black people; it says nothing about their treatment of the slaves who were not freed. Some historians have argued, for instance, that the Spanish and Portuguese slaveholders frequently freed the sick and elderly slaves because they had become too expensive to keep. North American slaveholders were rarely that cruel—or that willing to have a free African population in their midst.

The popularity of manumission in Latin American slave society may not always have been a tribute to their kindness. Since the slave trade continued well into the nineteenth century in Latin America,

■ *The white head of a large Brazilian household typically presided over a racially mixed retinue of wives, children, dependents, and slaves in an extended family. (Snark International, EPA)*

slaves were considerably cheaper than in the United States, which suspended the slave trade in 1808. That meant that Latin American slave owners could afford to work their slaves to death, buy more, and still free some of them. Even if that occurred, however, Latin American slavery still created a less racist society.

Let us return to the evidence. Perhaps the most striking feature for northern visitors to Latin American slave society was that black people were found everywhere. One English visitor to Brazil in the middle of the nineteenth century expressed his surprise this way:

> I have passed black ladies in silks and jewelry, with male slaves in livery behind them. Today one rode past in her carriage, accompanied by a liveried footman and a coachman. Several have white husbands. The first doctor of the city is a colored man; so is the President of the Province.[5]

Another visitor said that the African Brazilian

> seemed to be the most intelligent person he met because every occupation, skilled and unskilled, was in the Negroes' hands. Even in Buenos Aires theirs was the hand that built the best churches. They were the field hands, and in many places the miners; they were the cooks, the laundresses, the mammies, the concubines of the whites, the nurses

■ *Simón Bolivar (1783–1830) comes to the aid of a wounded black soldier in the Latin American struggle for independence. (The Mansell Collection)*

about the houses, the coachmen, and the laborers on the wharves. But they were also the skilled artisans who built the houses, carved the saints in the churches, constructed the carriages, forged the beautiful ironwork one sees in Brazil, and played in the orchestras.[6]

Free Brazilians of African descent achieved positions of considerable prestige, and were recognized in their time and by the Brazilian history books since. They include probably the greatest Brazilian writer, sculptor, and engineer, among so many others. Brazilian literature has always been written by descendants of Africa as well as

Portugal, and many of the most heroic and human of Brazilian heroes and heroines (in fiction and history) are African.

The *United States Magazine and Democratic Review* in 1844 recognized the gap between the treatment of Africans in the United States and Latin America. In Mexico "and in Central America, and in the vast regions still further south," the *Review* observed, "the negro is already a freeman—socially as well as politically, the equal of the white. Nine-tenths of the population there is made up of the colored races; the Generals, the Congressmen, the Presidents are men of mixed blood."[7]

Many North Americans recognized that their own prejudices against black people were much greater in the United States than south of the border. Some like George Bancroft echoed the above quoted sentiments of the *Review* by arguing that the acquisition of Texas would allow black people a way "to pass to social and political equality in the central regions of America, where the prejudices of race do not exist."

It was not true in 1844 that all South American blacks were free; some were still slaves. And it would be an exaggeration to say that no racial prejudice existed in the Iberian colonies: almost no whites were enslaved, and it was much more difficult for an African or Indian to become prosperous and accepted. With that qualification, however, the contrast holds. South American society was much more open for the descendants of Africans. Freedom was easier to attain, and it meant more once it was won. Prejudice was minimal, and there was little of the discrimination (in neighborhoods, schools, hotels, and public accommodations) that became such a hallmark of racial experience in the United States. The lynch law and anti-Negro riots that became such a standard feature of the history of the United States in the nineteenth and twentieth centuries were totally absent from South American experience. In Latin American struggles for independence, blacks (free and slave) were recruited without prejudice. White dockworkers in Brazil worked for the abolition of slavery by refusing to work on slave ships at the same time that North American white workers rioted against Lincoln's draft law by attacking black families instead of Southern troops.

## British vs. Latin American Slavery: Racism and Miscegenation

Why the difference? What accounts for the virulence of British, North American racism compared with the relatively mild prejudice in Latin America? The answers are many, and they have been hotly debated. We have already suggested a few. Perhaps the simple fact that British and other northern Europeans were so white skinned (compared to the more olive-skinned Spanish and Portuguese) made it easier for these northerners to develop a special hang-up with whiteness. Maybe the extreme lack of pigmentation in British skin made it easier for them to think of any darker color as a stain.

As we have seen, there was at least an important sexual dimension to the northern European's struggle with whiteness. They often seem to have preferred the repressed sexuality of the fair Virgin Queen to the robust sexuality that they feared was inherent in blackness and Africans. The earliest Elizabethan explorers of Africa were appalled by the blackness *and* the nakedness of some of the Africans they discovered. They invented myths of the Africans insatiable lust which fitted older Neolithic and Christian fears (and have survived, despite all scientific evidence even down to the present). It is not so much that Iberian colonists overcame the myth of black sexuality. Less fearful of losing their whiteness, and less repressed, they embraced the fantasy of black sexuality eagerly. As one Brazilian has explained, "It was with the black woman that the white man from the cradle, when he was caressed, in bed when he was sexually satiated, that he learned his terms of love: my little black, my precious, my most precious Negro. One hears them from every mouth, from that of the college graduate to that of the exploited worker."[8] Even today, white Brazilians affectionately call their white lovers *minha nega* ("my little Negro") and Spanish Americans use the term *negritta* ("little black") as a term of endearment to those they love, regardless of their color. It is impossible to imagine a white North American using any such term toward another white person.

The Latin American disregard for color in the use of such terms indicates not color blindness (as we shall see). Rather it suggests the association of sexual love with blackness that all American slave societies must have felt, or repressed. Unlike their northern, British neighbors, the Latin American slave owners encouraged the development of the erotic feelings they learned at the breast of a black mammy and in the arms of their black slaves.

It is not enough, of course, to explain the vast differences between Latin American and British American racism by referring to the biological fact of skin color or vague psychological attitudes to sex and blackness. There are distinct historical causes for the less repressed Latin American attitude toward interracial sex. The Spanish and Portuguese conquerors came to the New World without their wives. Many, in fact were not married. From the earliest years of the settlement they developed a permissive attitude toward interracial sex (miscegenation) because they had very little choice. The British settlers of North America, on the other hand, generally came with their wives and families. British wives were also often independent enough to insist that their slave-owning husbands keep their racial affairs private. Even when Iberian women came to the Americas to raise families, they came from a European culture where men and male values (machismo) were more clearly dominant. Iberian men in the Americas flaunted their black mistresses, recognized their black children, and often moved all of their families into the same large patriarchal home. While most states in the United States passed stiff laws against interracial sex (forcing men to be discreet), Latin American societies openly encouraged miscegenation as a proof of male potency and a way of life.

Miscegenation, like manumission, may have been popular in Latin America for less than noble reasons. But both practices created a population and a set of values which made race almost meaningless. How could one talk of "pure" races or even of race when the vast majority of the population was neither black nor white, but shades of olive and brown? How could one speak of the natural abilities (or inabilities) of the Negro when they were neither slave nor free, but both, and when they were planters, writers, masons, and bureaucrats?

By at least the nineteenth century, the majority of Afro-Americans in most countries south of the United States were neither black nor slaves. It became impossible to make generalizations even about the Negro. That was the very least that a racist had to be able to do. In the United States before the War for Southern Independence (usually called the Civil War by the victors) "Negro" meant slave. Neither the northern nor southern states wanted a population of free Africans. Southerners saw free blacks as deadly threats to the slave system: they believed that freed slaves incited slave rebellions, and the mere existence of prosperous or free blacks challenged the official racist doctrine that Africans were inherently inferior. Again, the Brazilian situation offers an interesting contrast. Brazilians not only used free blacks to capture runaway slaves, but Brazilian slaveholders never developed the official North American doctrine of inherent African inferiority. Free blacks were banned from northern territories in the United States as well as from the southern slave states. Even the northern abolitionists (who worked for the end of slavery) often sought the disappearance of Negroes as well. They toyed with schemes to resettle the freed slaves in Africa, or (like George Bancroft) they sought black emigration to Mexico or South America. The United States, North and South, was largely a society of two groups: black slaves and free whites. The North American hostility to miscegenation and manumission kept the descendants of Africans as black (or visible) as possible, and blacks were assumed to be slaves. This in-

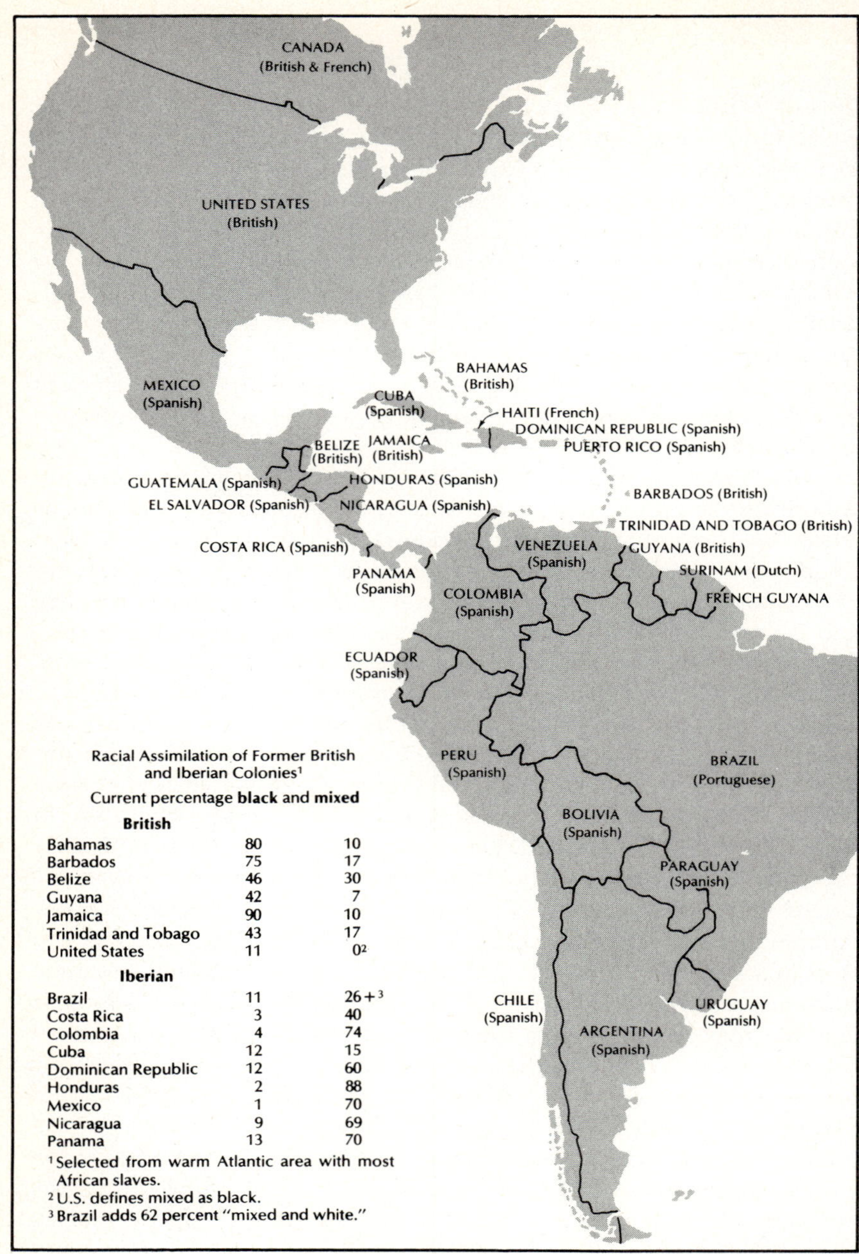


Racial Assimilation of Former British and Iberian Colonies[1]

| Current percentage | **black** | and **mixed** |
|---|---|---|
| **British** | | |
| Bahamas | 80 | 10 |
| Barbados | 75 | 17 |
| Belize | 46 | 30 |
| Guyana | 42 | 7 |
| Jamaica | 90 | 10 |
| Trinidad and Tobago | 43 | 17 |
| United States | 11 | 0[2] |
| **Iberian** | | |
| Brazil | 11 | 26+[3] |
| Costa Rica | 3 | 40 |
| Colombia | 4 | 74 |
| Cuba | 12 | 15 |
| Dominican Republic | 12 | 60 |
| Honduras | 2 | 88 |
| Mexico | 1 | 70 |
| Nicaragua | 9 | 69 |
| Panama | 13 | 70 |

[1] Selected from warm Atlantic area with most African slaves.
[2] U.S. defines mixed as black.
[3] Brazil adds 62 percent "mixed and white."

**Colonization and Racial Assimiliation in the Americas**
*This map shows the principal colonizers of the Americas. The chart shows the current racial distribution of blacks and people of mixed race in selected former British and Iberian (Spanish and Portuguese) colonies. Note that all of the former British colonies currently have more people classified as black than mixed, while the reverse is true for the former Iberian colonies. The figures suggest the difference between British and Iberian cultural attitudes toward miscegenation and racial assimilation.*

sistence on a two-caste society was so strong that even today North Americans classify any light-skinned person with a touch of African ancestry as a Negro. Even today in the United States people must be white or Negro (excluding other races), and they are white only if their ancestry is all white. Negroes include (in common language and official census reports) not only "pure" Africans but anyone who is not "pure" white.

South American whites never insisted that there were only two races (excluding Indians); they did not relegate all people of mixed ancestry to the status of "the other" as if they were mongrel dogs. North Americans persisted in the belief (despite the evidence of their eyes) that there were only two racial types: pure whites and the others. South Americans recognized that there were many, and they encouraged the miscegenation which created many different racial categories between lily white and jet black.

Brazil, again, offers an interesting contrast to our way of thinking of race. In Brazil people are *pretos* (blacks) or *preto retino* (dark black) or *cabra* (dark) or *cabo verde* (dark with straight hair) or *escuro* (less dark) or *mulato escuro* (rich brown) or *mulato claro* (light brown) or *pardo* (lighter still) or *sarara* (light skinned with kinky hair) or *moreno* (light skin and straight hair) or *branco da Bahia* (native whites with slight African ancestry) or brunet whites or blond whites. Spanish Americans think in equally rich racial terms. To the extent that Spanish Americans think of *negro* at all (or Portuguese of *nego*) it means black. No Latin American would think of calling an *escuro* or *pardo* a *negro; escuros* and *pardos* are obviously lighter.

This complex racial vocabulary south of the Rio Grande shows that Latin Americans are not color blind. Instead, they see much greater racial variety than we do. Actually, their extreme sensitivity to racial differences enables them to be less racist than our black versus white vision permits. White racism still exists in Mexico and Latin America, but many frankly recognize that most people are "mixed," and they find value in continuing the mixing. The Mexicans express this goal by calling themselves proudly "a bronze nation." They enthusiastically proclaim the destiny of Mexico to be the miscegenation of Africans, Europeans, and Indians—the "bronzing" of all peoples. Try to imagine the "bronze nation" as a cultural idea in the United States, despite all of our talk of melting pots.

Latin Americans have broken down racial barriers through miscegenation. Partly because they came as soldiers or conquerors without families, but also partly because they took so many Africans as slaves, they almost inevitably established societies which paid scant attention to race. It was never possible for people, the majority of whom considered themselves shades of brown, to work up fears of being overwhelmed by Africans. All but one of the slave states of the United States ended the slave trade before the federal prohibition in 1808. Brazilians continued the slave trade until 1851. By that time over half the Brazilians were black or brown. In the United States never more than 19 percent of the population was classified as Negro, and the percentage declined steadily from that high point of 1790. Brazilians may have been more committed to slavery, but the whites of the United States were more afraid of racial mixture.

## *For Further Reading*

For general discussions of race and racism, the UNESCO (United Nations Economic and Social Council) volume of essays, **Race and Science,*** is an excellent introduction. It includes the articles by Michel Leiris and Claude Lévi-Strauss referred to in the text. **Science and the Concept of Race,*** edited by Margaret Mead and others, is also a good collection of scholarly papers on the general issue.

The best general history of slavery is probably David Brion Davis's **The Problem of Slavery in Western Culture.*** There are a number of good books on slavery in the ancient and classical world. **Slavery in Classical Antiquity,** edited by M. I. Finley, is a good place to start. Finley's **World of Odysseus*** is also valuable. William L. Westermann's **The Slave Systems of Greek and Roman Antiquity** is standard and thorough. On other areas of the ancient world there are Isaac Mendelsohn's **Slavery in the Ancient Near East: A Comparative Study of Slavery in Babylonia, Assyria, Syria, and Palestine, from the Middle of the Third Millennium to the End of the First Millennium,** 'Abd el-Mohsen Bakir's **Slavery in Pharaonic Egypt,** Melville J. Herskovitz's **Dahomey: An Ancient West African Kingdom,** and C. Martin Wibur's **Slavery in China During the Former Han Dynasty, 206 B.C.–A.D. 25.**

On the cultural background of European racism and slavery, Davis's **The Problem of Slavery in Western Culture** is again excellent. Winthrop D. Jordan's **White Over Black: American Attitudes Toward the Negro 1550–1812*** is a deservedly prize-winning study. His shorter version of this book, **The White Man's Burden,*** might be more accessible.

The question of the differences between Latin American and Anglo-American slavery and racism has been a subject of extended debate by historians. The differences are emphasized in Frank Tannenbaum's **Slave and Citizen: The Negro in the Americas*** and Stanley M. Elkins's **Slavery: A Problem in American Institutional & Intellectual Life,*** and deemphasized in Davis's **The Problem of Slavery in Western Culture.*** Also valuable are Kenneth M. Stampp's **The Peculiar Institution: Slavery in the Ante-Bellum South,** Gilberto Freyre's **The Masters and Slaves: A Study in the Develop-**

* Available in paperback.

**ment of Brazilian Civilization,*** and Carl N. Degler's **Neither Black Nor White.***

The work of Eugene D. Genovese is perhaps the best introduction to the world of slave and slaveholders (as well as a model of sophisticated Marxist scholarship). His **Roll, Jordan, Roll: The World the Slaves Made*** is a monument of description and interpretation conveyed with verve and clarity. His earlier **The World the Slaveholders Made: Two Essays in Interpretation*** is the best introduction to the other side of the divided society. The essays in **The Political Economy of Slavery*** and of **In Red and Black*** are first rate.

The work of Clement Eaton also offers an excellent introduction to the Old South. One thinks of **The Civilization of the Old South,** or **The Growth of Southern Civilization, 1790–1860,** and **The Freedom-of-Thought Struggle in the Old South.***

## Notes

1. Michel Leiris, "Race and Culture" in UNESCO, *Race and Science* (New York: Columbia University Press, 1951), p. 214.
2. Winthrop Jordan, *White Over Black* (Baltimore: Penguin Books, 1968), p. 7.
3. [George Puttenham?], *Partheniades* (1959), quoted in Winthrop Jordan, *White Over Black*, p. 8.
4. *Ibid.*, p. 11. Spelling and punctuation are modernized.
5. Thomas Ewbank: *Life in Brazil, or the Land of the Cocoa and the Palm* (London, 1856), p. 266.
6. Frank Tannenbaum, *Slave and Citizen* (New York: Random House, 1946), p. 39.
7. Quoted in Carl N. Degler, *Neither Black Nor White* (New York: Macmillan, 1971), p. 16.
8. Adapted from Luiz Luna, *O Negro na Luta Contra A Escravidão*, quoted in Degler, *Neither Black Nor White*, p. 155.

# Chapter 16

# Energy and Environment

## Industry and Capitalism

In this chapter we continue to try to answer the question we raised in Chapter 12: What is responsible for the disregard of nature that has led to our environmental and energy crises? Here we focus on the most obvious, immediate causes of the modern problem: industry and capitalism. The industrial revolution, almost everyone agrees, has been the basic underlying cause. By suggesting that capitalism may be an alternative explanation, we do not mean to suggest that industrialization is not significant. The question is only whether or not capitalism aggravated the dramatic rupture with nature that industrialization brought about.

The problem is a practical one. Hardly anyone seriously proposes a return to preindustrial, handicrafts industries. Even if a few Americans can put up with that, the masses of people in the developing world will not. They want industrialization. So the question is whether or not they can industrialize (and we can continue industrialization) in a less exploitative way. That is why we ask about capitalism. Is it possible that a noncapitalist industrialization could be more careful of limited energy supplies and less hostile toward the environment?

## The Industrial Revolution Is Responsible?

Almost everyone agrees that the rise of modern science (after about 1500) made possible the series of inventions which we call the industrial revolution. Lewis Mumford, who shows how the early scientists attempted to subject all of organic nature to mechanical laws (in the way we have described) puts it this way:

> What was left was the bare, depopulated world of matter and motion: a wasteland. In order to thrive at all, it was necessary for the inheritors of the seventeenth century idolum to fill the world up again with new organisms, devised to represent the new realities of physical science. Machines—and machines alone—completely met the requirements of the scientific method and point of view: they fulfilled the definition of "reality" far more perfectly than living organisms. And once the mechanical world-picture was established, machines could thrive and multiply and dominate existence: their competitors had been exterminated or had been consigned to a penumbral universe in which only artists and lovers and breeders of animals dared to believe. Were machines not conceived in terms of primary qualities alone, without regard to appearance, sound, or any other sort of sensory stimulation? If science presented an ultimate reality, then the machine was . . . the true embodiment of everything that was excellent. Indeed in this empty, denuded world, the invention of machines became a duty. By renouncing a large part of his humanity, a man could achieve godhood: he dawned on this second chaos and created the machine in his own image; the image of power, but power ripped loose from his flesh and isolated from his humanity.[1]

The scientists stole the life from nature in order to understand it. Then they were forced to fill the world with creatures, and the only creatures they understood were those which followed scientific laws—that is, machines. That's a bit simple, perhaps. But Mumford's analysis at least emphasizes the historical link between modern science and its offspring, the machine technology of the industrial revolution. It is true that the scientists were interested primarily in knowledge while industrialization was a process of harnessing knowledge for practical results. But even the most religiously motivated scientists imagined their work led to an increase of human power. One of the first modern European scientists, Sir Francis Bacon (1561–1626), insisted that knowledge was, after all, power. We might understand the world so that we could control it. The proof of science, ultimately, was in the technology it produced.

The industrial revolution would also have been impossible without the two guiding ideas of modern science: the idea that man was separate from nature, and that man could control this separate natural world. The industrial revolution was the application of modern science to technology. Machines could only take over the work of men after the machine became the model of the natural world. This required not only viewing the objects of the organic world as machines, but also the elimination of the human element from the organic world of time and space.

## Industrialization: Mechanical Time vs. Organic Time

Lewis Mumford suggests that the first requirement for the creation of a machine age was the invention of mechanical time to take the place of organic or natural time. Time had to be understood in terms of its component parts; it had to be divided up. This was accomplished by the invention of the clock.

> The clock, not the steam-engine, is the key-machine of the modern industrial age. For every phase of its development the clock is both the outstanding fact and the typical symbol of the machine: even today no other machine is so ubiquitous. . . .
>
> The clock . . . is a piece of power-machinery whose "product" is seconds and minutes: by its essential nature it dissociated time from human events and helped create the belief in an independent world of mathematically measurable sequences: the special world of science. There is relatively little foundation for this belief in common human experience: throughout the year the days are of uneven duration, and not merely does the relation between day and night steadily change, but a slight journey from East to West alters astronomical time by a certain number of minutes. In terms of the human organism itself, mechanical time is even more foreign: while human life has regularities of its own, the beat of the pulse, the breathing of the lungs, these change from hour to hour with mood and action, and in the longer span of days, time is measured not by the calendar but by the events that occupy it. The shepherd measures from the time the ewes lambed; the farmer measures back to the day of sowing or forward to the harvest: if growth has its

> own duration and regularities, behind it are not simply matter and motion but the facts of development: in short, history. And while mechanical time is strung out in a succession of mathematically isolated instants, organic time . . . is cumulative in its effects. Though mechanical time can, in a sense, be speeded up or run backward, like the hands of a clock or the images of a moving picture, organic time moves in only one direction—through the cycle of birth, growth, development, decay, and death—and the past that is already dead remains present in the future that has still to be born.
>
> Around 1345, according to Thorndike, the division of hours into sixty minutes and of minutes into sixty seconds became common: it was this abstract framework of divided time that became more and more the point of reference for both action and thought, and in the effort to arrive at accuracy in this department, the astronomical exploration of the sky focused attention further upon the regular, implacable movements of the heavenly bodies through space.[2]

As a piece of machinery, the clock was certainly not as powerful as the steam engine. It could not move thousands of tons of railway cars. But the clock produced an attitude toward time which made the steam engine and the railroad and the factory possible. This new attitude was more than punctuality and consciousness about time. It was the feeling that time existed on its own—separate from the world of human need and natural processes. Like the mechanical laws of the new science, time was thought to be an abstract standard which humans were expected to conform to. Mechanical time was more demanding than natural time had been because mechanical time could be used efficiently or wasted. As long as medieval workers thought in terms of "the time it takes to make a table" or "the time for a walk into town" they could never be inefficient or late. There was no way of saying that they made a table in more or less time than "the time it takes to make a table"; it would have been absurd to ask someone to make two tables in that time. That became possible only with the invention of seconds, minutes, and hours—of abstract time. When abstract, measurable time existed independently of human activity, human activity could be timed. Timing permitted jobs to be standardized and coordinated. The modern factory would otherwise have been impossible.

The world could be filled with machines only after time was precisely measurable in nonhuman terms. Machine parts had to do things exactly on time—like "clockwork." But the machine parts also had to be designed and constructed precisely. This meant that each part had to be measured exactly. Standard, abstract measurements of space and weight (meters and centimeters, pounds and ounces) were as necessary as standard amounts of time.

## Industrialization: Standard Space and Interchangeable Parts

In the Middle Ages (as in almost every other society before the industrial revolution) the few machines that existed (like water mills and windmills or potters wheels) were all custom-made as we would say. No two machines were ever exactly alike. Each was made according to the needs or whim of the artisan or the people who would use the machine. One gear would have to mesh with another of course, but there was no standard-size gear or screw or lever or anything else. Each machine was made for the particular job to be done, and the challenge of each new job frequently stimulated the creativity of the artisan.

The unique achievement of the industrial revolution was the mass production of products by the standardization of machines. Goods could be produced on a mass scale because they were made by machines—each one just like the other, the only way machines can make things. Even the machines were identical so that two machines could produce exactly the same products. This meant that machine parts had to be standardized so that they were interchangeable. Exactly similar interchangeable parts were first invented for muskets to meet the needs of war or expected war. This happened almost at the same time in France in 1785 (during the French Revolution) and in the United States in 1800, by Eli Whitney.

We can get some sense of the significance of the invention of interchangeable parts if we recall Thomas Jefferson's amazement when the French inventor Leblanc gave Jefferson (then U.S. minister in France) the locks of 50 guns, all taken apart. "I put several together myself," Jefferson wrote home, "taking pieces . . . as they came to hand, and they fitted in the most perfect manner. The advantages of this when arms need repair are evident."

The first mass-produced goods were the muskets, and later the uniforms, of Western armies. There were no other organizations in Western society around 1800 that could demand the enormous quantities of goods that required machine production. But although the new industrial technology was the child of war, it became (by the early twentieth century) an Aladdin's magic lamp of undreamed of quantities of consumer goods. Today machines produce everything from shirts and ball-point pens to airplanes and houses. It is difficult to buy anything made by hand any more. The advantage of machine production is not only that spare parts are always available because the parts are identical, as Jefferson realized. It is also cheaper for a machine than for an army of medieval artisans on starvation wages to produce a great quantity of identical goods.

There is no way of disputing the human value of machine production over hand manufacture. This is so obvious that it would not be said if it were not for some of the excessive claims of "handicraft" enthusiasts and "back to nature" people. We may complain about the inferior quality of some machine-made products, and we may enjoy making some things ourselves (there can be a real sense of accomplishment in that). But a machine can do anything that an artisan (or even an artist) can do because it is only a mechanical duplication of human labor. And industrial society does not prevent us from doing things ourselves if we like. The machine is only a shortcut for human labor. As such, it is of unquestionable value in doing things more quickly than we can by hand, and in doing more things than human and animal labor are capable of alone.

## Energy Sources: Wind and Water vs. Coal and Iron

The almost "magical" characteristic of machines (doing things automatically, by themselves) is due to the fact that they harness sources of energy other than human and animal muscle. The oldest machines like the waterwheel (which originated over two thousand years ago) and the windmill (in use for the last thousand years) use sources of energy which can never be depleted. Rushing streams and wind are inexhaustible, if sometimes unpredictable. They can never be used up. Their power is not even diminished after their energy has been used. The Dutch countryside of the seventeenth century never faced an energy shortage as more and more windmills were erected. Some of the more rapidly moving streams of England and New England in the eighteenth century could power as many water mills as there was room for.

The central ecological fact about the full-scale industrialization that began in the West in the 1800s is that irreplaceable energy resources were used. Instead of increasing the efficiency of wind and water as power sources, industrialists turned to the fossil fuels of the earth—especially coal, oil, and gas—which could never be replaced because of the time nature took to duplicate them.

Coal, oil, and gas were formed over millions and millions of years by the action of the sun on living organisms, carbon dioxide, and water. It is as if this treasure of energy were suddenly discovered in the last couple of hundred years and immediately used up. We have been living on borrowed time. Some experts agree that these precious reserves will be consumed by the year 2000.

It is always possible, of course, that we will find new sources of energy to replace these fossil fuels. But we have taken the easy way out. We have squandered our treasure as if there were no tomorrow, and it is by no means certain that the new discoveries will come in time or that they will be sufficient to maintain our rate of growth.

Coal, asphalt, oil, and natural gas were occasionally used in ancient times for heating and lighting—but in miniscule amounts. Perhaps we began to live on borrowed time when (during the eighteenth century) the English faced a shortage of wood and found it easier to mine coal in large quantities. By 1800 the world mined about 15 million tons of coal per year. By 1850 the amount had increased to over 100 million, and by 1950 to almost 1,500 million tons per year.

From the early 1800s the rise in coal production was tied to the fortunes of the steam engine. The steam engine was first used to remove water from the mines, and the coal from the mines kept the engines going. Coal-driven steam engines were then used to power the first railroad cars which were used to transport the coal from the mines.

Coal and steam built the iron civilization of the nineteenth century. Coal was the most available and most effective fuel for smelting iron ore as well as for producing steam. The vast new quantities of iron were used to build larger steam engines, railroads, and blast furnaces (requiring more coal to produce more iron).

▪ *The worst abuses of mining civilization were suffered by the children who worked in the low tunnels before illustrations like this in a British parliamentary report brought some reform with the Coal Mines Act of 1842. (Radio Times Hulton Picture Library)*

The civilization based on mining—the industrial West of the nineteenth century—was fundamentally at war with the natural environment. As Mumford has remarked, "mining is a robber industry." The mine robbed the earth of its accumulated energy. It robbed future generations of the savings of eons. It robbed the miners of light and healthy lives, and it robbed their families of clean air and water. The psychology of mining civilization was most evident in the "rushes" of the nineteenth century. Gold, iron, copper, and oil rushes were races to reckless exploitation. The lawless, antisocial life of the mining camp was only the logical conclusion of mining civilization. The get-rich-quick mentality and wasteful destruction of nature in the mineral rushes was only an extension of the feverish, impatient mindlessness of the larger society.

Iron and coal colored every aspect of nineteenth-century industrialization. The color varied from black to shades of gray. Even (Mumford notes) the formal dress of the industrialists—black tie, black suit, black boots, black stovepipe hat—reflected the blackness of coal country, called in England "the Black Country." The gray iron buildings and bridges, the great achievements of mining civilization, were blackened with the soot and cinders of blast furnaces that wastefully belched out as much useful black fuel as they consumed. By 1850 the whole civilization from Pittsburgh to the Ruhr Valley in Germany seemed to be in mourning.

Pollution and waste were two sides of the same coin. Benjamin Franklin had suggested that the soot and smoke that polluted the air might be trapped and reused in the furnaces to provide more energy and keep the air clean. Industrialists realized that their excess smoke and gas was only unburned energy, but they rarely bothered to conserve it. It was always cheaper to dig another well, open another mine, or level another mountain than it was to improve the efficiency of what they had. The symbols of power meant more than the quality of the environment. The smoking factory chimney which shut out natural light with a permanent fog over company towns was a symbol of prosperity. The noise of Watt's original steam engine was preferred as a sign of power—despite Watt's own attempts to quiet the machine—just as automobile engine noise was later increased by manufacturers for its symbolic value.

The nineteenth-century industrial revolution assaulted the environment of Western countries in a number of ways. The mines scarred the countryside, the waste products and smoke of furnaces, refineries, and factories polluted the air and rivers, and railroads cut through forests and farms to make whole countries part of the same industrial system. Perhaps it was the gigantic scale of the new indus-

■ *"The houses of the poor are not the palaces of the rich," an engraving by Gustave Doré of a section of London about 1880, shows how the outdoors could become like a subterranean mining tunnel. Here the steam engine that was created to extract coal in the mines clouds the skys above. The pervasive railroad is imitated by the smoking "cars" of tenements that almost seem about to roll over walls of railroad ties and human cinders.* (EPA)

try which had the most serious ecological effect. When water, wind, and animal power had been the main sources of energy (up until the eighteenth century), mills and factories could be operated on a relatively local scale and each locality could engage in a number of varied occupations. Maybe they did not have to be overconcentrated. There were iron works in the eighteenth century which simply used the iron in local bogs. They were often inefficient, but when they emptied their slag in local streams, they did little environmental damage because they were so few. The miners of the nineteenth century, however, exploited large deposits; they mined whole mountains for their ore or fuel. As a result, industries became concentrated in areas near these rich deposits. Places like Pittsburgh and Detroit became industrial centers because they were close to the source of raw materials or energy. Farming and the smaller industries of these areas became secondary. The concentration of industry near these areas meant a wholesale deterioration of the environment. The discharge from these mines and mills was too much for the surrounding area to absorb. Huge cities were erected near these sites. The human sewage just increased the impossible strain on the atmosphere and rivers.

In some ways the industrial revolution of the twentieth century overcame the handicaps of the earlier industrialization. The discovery of electricity as a power source made it possible for every town or even farm to generate its own power. All that was needed was a small wind or water source of power which could be turned into a local electric generator. Even the cleanliness of the older age of wind power and waterpower could be regained. The possibility was there, but it was rarely employed.

Electricity was also easier to transmit than coal energy. High tension wires lose little power over long distances, and the power can be transmitted much more cheaply than the cost of shipping coal on railway cars. Further, electricity is easily converted into motor energy to do mechanical work, light, and heat. An increase in size does not increase efficiency nearly as much as with the steam engine. When a water turbine is used, the costs of producing energy are reduced to almost nothing. Even when electricity is generated by central power stations, the system can work very efficiently. The current is not wasted when it is not used, and it is relatively simple to provide current to those areas which need it most in times of emergency. Electric power could also allow local areas to satisfy their own needs for food and a complex assortment of industrial goods without making a particular area dependent on a single industry.

In short, the twentieth century provided new sources of energy (some of which, like the water turbine and solar energy and the energy inherent in the different temperatures of the earth's layers, were never adequately exploited) which would not have required the elaborate system of roads and railroads which came into being. The discoveries of the twentieth century allowed industry to become decentralized, but those who were in control of the older energy sources merely added the new sources to their stables, and things changed very little.

## Capitalism Is Responsible?

The industrial revolution which has transformed the Western world in the last few hundred years was based on an organization of the economy and society which was capitalistic. This means that most of the decisions were made in the interests of private profits. This may not have been inevitable. The Russians, the Chinese, and other societies which call themselves socialist have more recently attempted to industrialize on the basis of public, rather than private, ownership and decision making. They have been more or less successful. They have certainly not been free of environmental pollution, depletion of resources, or other affronts to the environment. Their failures and their successes may be a result of their socialistic economy—or possibly of something else. This is very difficult to determine. Perhaps all that we can do is attempt to determine to what extent our own environmental crisis has been caused or aggravated by our particular type of economic organization.

We might put the question in a number of ways. Is our problem the machine or the way a capitalist economy organizes and uses its machinery? Or, if we agree that the machine has done its share of damage (as well as of good), is it possible that a more public or socialized use of the machinery could have averted some of our more serious problems, or that it still might? Lewis Mumford states the case for the prosecution pretty clearly:

> It was because of certain traits in private capitalism that the machine—which was a neutral agent—has often seemed, and in fact has sometimes been a malicious element in society, careless of human life, indifferent to human interests. The machine has suffered for the sins of capitalism; contrariwise, capitalism has often taken credit for the virtues of the machine.[3]

The real question when we compare the ravages of the machine with the disadvantages of capitalism is which of the two (if either) is dispensable. This is the issue that Mumford comes to grips with. He concludes that the machine is neutral, that it can be used for good or bad, that it can revitalize or destroy our ecology. If we accept his conclusion, we are forced to ask why the machine has been used primarily to exploit nature and why it has been used so callously and wastefully. The answer may lie in the realm of our ideas and attitudes toward nature, as we suggested in our analysis of Judeo-Christian culture. It may also lie in the social and economic organization of our society.

Mumford and other social critics have blamed capitalism for our ecological problems for a number of reasons. Their strongest argument is that capitalism is ideally a system of *private* enterprise, control, and profit, whereas ecology is ideally a *public* concern, perhaps our most important public concern. In other words, when capitalism works at its best, and with least interference, all decisions about the use of resources and the production of goods are made privately by those who own them, and they make their decisions solely in terms of what will bring them the most profit. There are times, of course, when private profit can serve public, even ecological, needs. Some private companies today, for instance, make all of their profits by producing and selling antipollution devices. But the critics of capitalism argue that such cases are exceptions to the rule. Normally, they insist, a system of private ownership and profit runs counter to social or public needs. At the very least, they argue, a private enterprise system becomes engaged in social or public causes only when the potential profit is greater than in other activities. These critics would like to see enterprise and industry devoted to social needs all of the time, not just when there is the possibility of a higher profit.

The defenders of capitalism have sometimes argued that the public interest is best served when each individual acts independently in pursuit of his or her self-interest. The Scottish economic philosopher Adam Smith wrote in *The Wealth of Nations* in 1776 that the capitalist market, operating according to the law of supply and demand, would always ensure—like some "invisible hand"—that public and private profit were the same.

> Every individual . . . neither intends to promote the public interest, nor knows how much he is promoting it. . . . [H]e intends only his own security . . . only his own gain. And he is in this . . . led by an invisible hand to promote an end which was no part of his intention. . . . By pursuing his own interest he frequently promotes that of society more effectually than when he really intends to promote it.[4]

According to Smith, manufacturers would always be forced to give society exactly what it wanted at the price it was willing to pay as long as all buyers and sellers acted independently and selfishly. When society wanted more gloves, the prices of gloves would rise so that new people would enter the industry, make more gloves, and eventually lower the price. When the profit on gloves was lower than the anticipated profit on shoes, glove manufacturers would selfishly go into shoemaking. Shoe manufacturers who raised their prices too far beyond the demand price would be forced out of business by new people who undersold them. Manufacturers who tried to underpay their workers would lose them to another company. Each manufacturer could only stay in business as long as he or she produced exactly what society wanted at a price only slightly above costs. Collusion among manufacturers was always impossible; if they artificially inflated prices, there would always be someone else along to undersell them.

Adam Smith's model of capitalist enterprise must have made some sense in 1776 or he would not have been taken seriously. It was a finely balanced scheme. The idea of unbeatable market laws made a lot of sense to Europeans who had recently become accustomed to thinking that the earth and heavens were subject to the clockwork laws of nature. Manufacturers were enthralled with a philosophy which made their selfish behavior into a social virtue. In a sense, Smith's philosophy was even true. The early industrial economy of England was made up of a large number of fairly competitive manufacturers. The technology was simple enough to allow workers and manufacturers to change jobs when the demand shifted. The large number of manufacturers in any one field made competition intense. It must have seemed to many of these enterprising manufacturers that they were acting on the orders of invisible laws, dictated by society's needs. Prices fluctuated rapidly. Fortunes seemed to follow. Individuals went from rags to riches, and back.

There were, however, at least two problems with Adam Smith's model of capitalist society. First, its assumption that everyone had equal buying and selling power never applied to the workers or the poor, even if it were true of a large number of manufacturers. Second, the manufacturers did not stay relatively competitive very long. Some of the more wealthy were able to use their resources, political power, and prestige to prevent challenges by younger, more aggressive companies. They were able to fix prices, pad expenses, monopolize an industry, and use the government for their own ends. Ironically, it was the most successful early capitalists who undermined ideal capitalism. Very shortly after Adam Smith proposed a society regulated entirely by the free market without government intervention, successful manufacturers built national governments stronger than those Adam Smith had complained about. Manufacturers used these governments to charter banks, provide land and resources, subsidize expenses, offer tariff protection, and protect the big companies from possible competitors.

Adam Smith's model may have worked if everyone started with about the same amount of money, and if it were absolutely impossible for the temporarily rich to become permanently rich by converting their money into political power. But everyone did not start on an equal footing, and the market was not the only regulator or the only source of power. Capitalist society has never been a society of equal, independent producers. There were monopolies in Smith's day. (Indeed, his book was written to oppose the monopolies of such companies as the East and West Indies trading companies.) And there have been monopolies since. It is possible that a free market where everyone had the same access to research, patents, manufacture, the courts, the banks, and (today) the media and advertising might have prevented fantastic accumulations of power by the few. But that is something that the successful have never allowed to happen.

Consequently, when we talk about capitalism in the real world we must consider the effects of class differences, inequality, and economic concentration. We can no longer rest assured that the invisible hand of the market will see to the harmony of selfish and public interests. Private profit is no longer (if it ever was) the profit of each of us independently. Private profit is the profit of the few who own most of the stock or manage the boards of the major corporations. We must ask if those who own and direct these corporations act for all of us when they act for themselves. That is a very different question.

## Ecology and Ideal Capitalism

Before we try to answer that question, we should consider one other alternative. What if we were able to make Adam Smith's model really work? The fact that it does not and has not is beside the point. It is at least theoretically possible that we could reform present society by making it *more* capitalistic than it is presently. Some conservative philosophers and politicians have suggested this. In fact, much of the trust-busting legislation and court decisions since the end of the nineteenth century have been directed toward such a goal. What if we could find a foolproof way of avoiding economic concentration, giving everyone a relatively equal opportunity to become rich, and ensure (with something like a 100 percent inheritance tax) that each generation would start at roughly the same line. At the very least, we could force each plant or division of large corporations to become independent, we could eliminate government assistance or force the government to aid small businesses with the same fervor that it aids the aerospace giants. To be more specific, what if General Motors could only make cars, or what if each Chevrolet factory were independent, and forced to compete with the others for workers, steel, and advertising space? What if it were still possible for the small company with ideas and energy to enter a major industry without having to face the corporate power of the giants?

In that kind of society certain social needs might be served much more readily. It would be impossible for the automobile manufacturers to conspire against the public demand for cleaner engines. They would not be able to buy up socially desirable inventions for the sole purpose of squashing them. They might not have the resources to throw away millions in an effort to drive more efficient, but less wealthy, competitors from the market with expensive court cases (that only giants can afford to lose) or temporarily lower prices in the line of products that was challenged. Greater competition would certainly make corporations more responsive to changing public needs.

But there is a problem with this ideal capitalist society which strikes at the root. The more equal, and the more competitive, and the more independent each unit, company, or individual was, the more it would wastefully duplicate efforts and consume common resources. Let us take a simple example. Imagine a piece of pastureland owned by the inhabitants of a village in the Middle Ages. In this precapitalist society, the villagers often made all major decisions about the use of the pasture as a group because they considered the land to be the responsibility of the whole group. The pastureland was recognized as a common resource. It was usually, in fact, called "the commons." If the cows were owned separately by each villager, they would still make group decisions. They might, for instance, take turns bringing all of the cows in from grazing, avoiding any unnecessary duplication of effort. They would also agree on certain procedures to prevent soil erosion, and they might agree on a maximum number of cows for each villager. In short, they would organize to preserve their precious, but limited, resource, the pasture.

Now imagine what would happen if these villagers thought like modern capitalists, each looking out for his or her private profit and competitive advantage. Without any common organization each villager would realize that it was to his or her personal advantage to increase his or her own number of cows. Each additional cow would be an added burden on the limited pasture, but the owner would share that burden with each of the other villagers, and he or she alone would reap the profit from the additional cow. In other words, private interest would force each villager to graze as many cows as possible. Public interest, however, would dictate some limitation in the number of cows to prevent exhaustion of the resource. If everyone acted only in terms of private profit the commons would eventually have more cows that it could support. Ultimately they would starve. Each villager might see the long term disaster, but it would still seem to be in his or her own best personal interests to get as much as possible. If he or she did not, someone else would.

With limited resources, private gain must always be a public loss. Even in an ideal capitalist society where each person has the same economic power, each will gain more than he or she loses individually by depleting the commons.

Think of nature as the commons. The fish in the seas, the trees in the forest, the oil and gas underground, the mineral resources, are all finite, as we have only recently realized. But they have been exploited privately, and competitively. For years, whaling companies have realized that the whale is becoming extinct. But because each company acts independently, they have been unable to avoid the eventual extinction of their own source of profit. In fact, they continue to bring about their own doom as an industry because they attempt to maximize their own profit before it is too late. They hurry their own end because it is profitable (for each separately) to do so.

In ecological terms, private exploitation and private ownership seem to mean the destruction of the commons. The social costs of depletion or pollution or extinction are always shared. Private profit never is. That is why it always pays the private enterprise to be wasteful.

We have recently realized that nature is not inexhaustible, that it is a fixed legacy for all. But it is difficult for us to think of the land, game, energy sources, and mineral resources as common property. In modern capitalist society, especially the United States, everything is privately owned. Even the airwaves are bought and sold privately—with the exception of one or two public stations. But it was not so long ago that even Americans thought primarily in terms of the commons. Though Colonial America was rapidly exploited by private individuals and companies, the young Republic maintained an earlier tradition which the historian Henry Steele Commager calls "devotion to the commonwealth":

> It was devotion to the commonwealth that inspired the generation of the Founding Fathers; it was the sense of obligation to the new nation, to mankind, to posterity that animated Franklin and Washington, Jefferson and Hamilton, John Adams and Tom Paine, John Jay and James Madison, and others who are now part of the American Valhalla. From their earliest youth they gave themselves to serve the commonwealth; they exhausted their energies, their talents, and their fortunes in service to the commonwealth. Modern day politicians and civil servants seem to do pretty well for themselves; it is pertinent to remember that Washington had to borrow $500 to go to his own inauguration; that Jefferson died a bankrupt after fifty years in the public service; . . . that Tom Paine, who served his country well, and France, too, died a pauper. . . . A society obsessed with the vindication of private enterprise does not nourish a generation dedicated to public enterprise. Without that dedication, the commonwealth is betrayed and lost.[5]

## Ecology and Modern Capitalism

So much for ideal capitalism and "ideal selfishness." Let us return to our earlier question about the possibility of social and ecological welfare under modern capitalism. From what we have just said about the ideal of equally independent producers, we might conclude that we are better off today with a high degree of economic concentration. We have beaten the problem of the isolated villagers on the commons. The economic units of modern society (for the most part) have achieved a scale of organization and cooperation that Adam Smith would have found as impossible as it was undesirable. Instead of thousands of competing auto manufacturers, each depleting the public resources by needless duplication, we have only three, to speak of. Instead of hundreds of telephone companies crossing wires at each corner, there is only one. We have, in short, avoided some of the fantastic waste of resources that would have occurred, and to a certain extent did occur, in Adam Smith's ideal of many independent competitors.

Perhaps an ecologist could have told Adam Smith that economic concentration was bound to occur. Modern ecologists, at least, realize that small-scale competitive units are normally replaced by monopolies:

> A cornerstone of ecological theory is the competitive exclusion principle. Simply, this principle states that competing species cannot coexist indefinitely. If two species are utilizing a resource that is in short supply, one of them will be eliminated as a competitor, either by being forced out of the ecosystem or by being forced to use some other resource. . . . Again and again, the evidence seems to indicate that competition reduces the number of competitors. . . . Competition in economic systems has the same effect as competition in ecosystems. It reduces the number of competitors. The more efficient or larger producers force the less efficient or smaller out of business or buy them out, resulting in monopoly. . . . The number of competitors continues to become smaller, prices and profits increase, and the huge corporations and conglomerates are more difficult if not impossible to manage efficiently.[6]

This process was almost completed in the United States by the end of the last century. In the first decades of the twentieth century, all that was needed was for the major corporations to induce the federal government to stabilize their dominant position by creating regulatory commissions that would police the upstart competitors. The historian Gabriel Kolko has shown in a fascinating book called *The Triumph of Conservatism* that this is exactly what happened. Under the guise of regulating business, the administrations of Theodore Roosevelt and Woodrow Wilson created commissions which gave large corporations the monopolies that they had become too fat to gain on their own.

By World War II American corporations had become "public" in their power and responsibility. With the assistance of commissioners in Washington, they were able to avoid most of the excesses (and drawbacks) of competitive capitalism. They planned production and sales like governments in Scandinavia, often with more resources at their disposal. It was possible again to talk of the commons that these corporations controlled and administered. The only difference—and it was crucial—was that these new public overseers of government funds and common resources were privately owned, and operated accordingly. They ran the commons with unanimity, at least, but entirely to increase their own profits.

## *For Further Reading*

There are a couple of very good introductions to the history of human energy use. Carlo M. Cipolla's **The Economic History of World Population*** offers an incredibly brief world history of energy and population growth, full of theoretical insight and statistical generalization. Fred Cottrell's **Energy and Society*** develops in a more leisurely fashion the effect of the industrial revolution. Cipolla's **Before the Industrial Revolution: European Society and Economy, 1000–1700,*** Fernand Braudel's **Capitalism and Material Life 1400–1800,*** and Lewis Mumford's **Technics and Civilization*** are all enormously useful.

Other valuable introductions to the history of technology and industrialization (besides those indicated at the end of Chapter 14) are Friedrich Klemm's **A History of Western Technology,*** Samuel Lilley's **Men, Machines and History,*** and S. Giedion's **Mechanization Takes Command.*** A good introductory study of machines and work is Melvin Kranzberg and Joseph Gies's **By the Sweat of Thy Brow.*** Thomas Parke Hughes's **The Development of Western Technology Since 1500*** is a good collection of scholarly articles. The culture of mechanization is discussed imaginatively in Elting E. Morison's **Men, Machines, and Modern Times,*** and various views of the machine are collected in Arthur O. Lewis, Jr.'s **Of Men and Machines.***

Other useful books on the history of capitalism (again aside from those mentioned at the end of Chapter 14) are Immanuel Wallerstein's **The Modern World System: Capitalist Agriculture and the Origins of the European World-Economy in the Sixteenth Century,*** Christopher Hill's **Reformation to Industrial Revolution,** and Eric Hobsbawn's **Industry and Empire.*** More introductory is W. O. Henderson's **The Industrial Revolution on the Continent: Germany, France, Russia, 1800–1914.**

* Available in paperback.

For recent discussions of energy and economic growth, see the celebrated Club of Rome study by Donella H. Meadows and others called **The Limits to Growth,*** John Kenneth Galbraith's **The New Industrial State,*** and the collection of essays in **Economic Growth versus the Environment,** edited by W. A. Johnson and John Hardesty, and **The Economic Growth Controversy,** edited by Andrew Weintraub, Eli Schwartz, and J. Richard Aronson.

For discussions of capitalism, energy, and environment, see Matthew Edel's **Economies and the Environment,*** K. William Kapp's **The Social Costs of Private Enterprise,*** Robert Heilbroner's **Business Civilization in Decline,*** and Barry Weisberg's **Beyond Repair: The Ecology of Capitalism.**

## *Notes*

1. Lewis Mumford, *Technics and Civilization* (New York: Harcourt Brace Jovanovich, 1934, 1963), p. 51.
2. *Ibid.*, p. 14–16.
3. *Ibid.*, p. 27.
4. Adam Smith, *An Inquiry into the Nature and Causes of the Wealth of Nations*, ed. Edwin Cannan (New York: Modern Library, 1937), Book IV, Chapter II, p. 423.
5. Henry Steele Commager, "America's Heritage of Bigness," *Saturday Review*, 4 July 1970, p. 12.
6. Bertram G. Murray, Jr., "What the Ecologists Can Teach the Economists," *New York Times Magazine*, 10 December 1972, pp. 64–65.

## CHRONOLOGICAL CONTEXT OF
# The Early Modern World: 1500-1800

| European Cultural | European Economic-Political | The Americas |
|---|---|---|
| | Domestic system 1400–1750 | Decline of American Indian empires b. 1500 |
| | Worker wage high 1450 | Destruction of American Indian empires by arms and disease a. 1500 |
| Machiavelli 1469–1527 (w. *The Prince* 1513) | Western naval superiority a. 1500 | |
| | Rise of capitalism a. 1500 | |
| | Drastic inflation 1500–1650 | |
| Martin Luther 1483–1546 | Joint stock companies 1550 | Gold, silver taken, mined 1500–1650 |
| John Calvin 1509–1564 | Wage, living standard Decline 1500–1650 | |
| Sir Francis Bacon 1561–1626 | English "first industrial revolution" 1540–1640 | North European colonization; Iberians lose monopoly 1600–1648 |
| Shakespeare 1564–1616 (w. *Othello* 1604) | Mercantilism 1600–1789 | |
| Hobbes 1588–1679 (w. *Leviathan* 1651) | English Civil War 1640–1649 | |
| | Declining prices, profits; Rising wages 1650–1750 | English ascendance 1655–1763 |
| Locke 1632–1704 (w. *Two Treatises* 1690) | English Glorious Revolution 1689 | |

**a. = after**
**b. = before**
**w. = wrote**

| European Cultural | European Economic-Political | The Americas |
|---|---|---|
| Agricultural Revolution<br>1700–1800 | English Indian empire and cotton<br>a. 1763 | |
| Adam Smith<br>1723–1790<br>(w. *Wealth of Nations* 1776) | Industrialization, rising prices, profits, productivity; Stable wages<br>1750–1850 | Declaration of Independence<br>1776 |
| | French Revolution<br>1789–1800 | |
| | Whitney's cotton gin<br>1792 | Rise in cotton slave plantation<br>a. 1792 |
| | | Simón Bolívar<br>1783–1830 |

# V

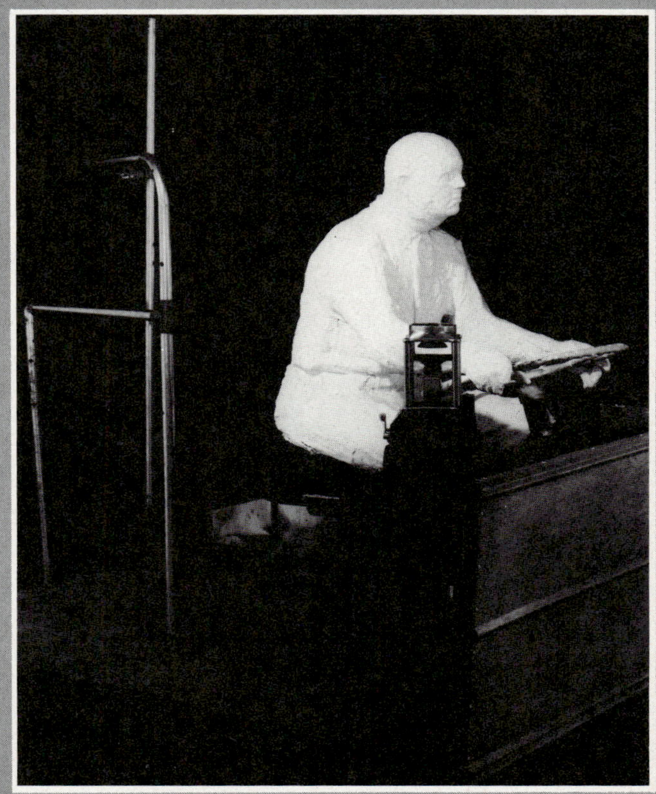

Segal, George. *The Bus Driver* (1962). Figure of plaster over cheesecloth; bus parts including coin box, steering wheel, driver's seat, railing, dashboard, etc. Figure 53½ x 26⅞ x 45″; wood platform, 5⅛ x 51⅝ x 6′ 3⅝″; overall height, 6′ 3″. Collection, The Museum of Modern Art, New York, Philip Johnson Fund.

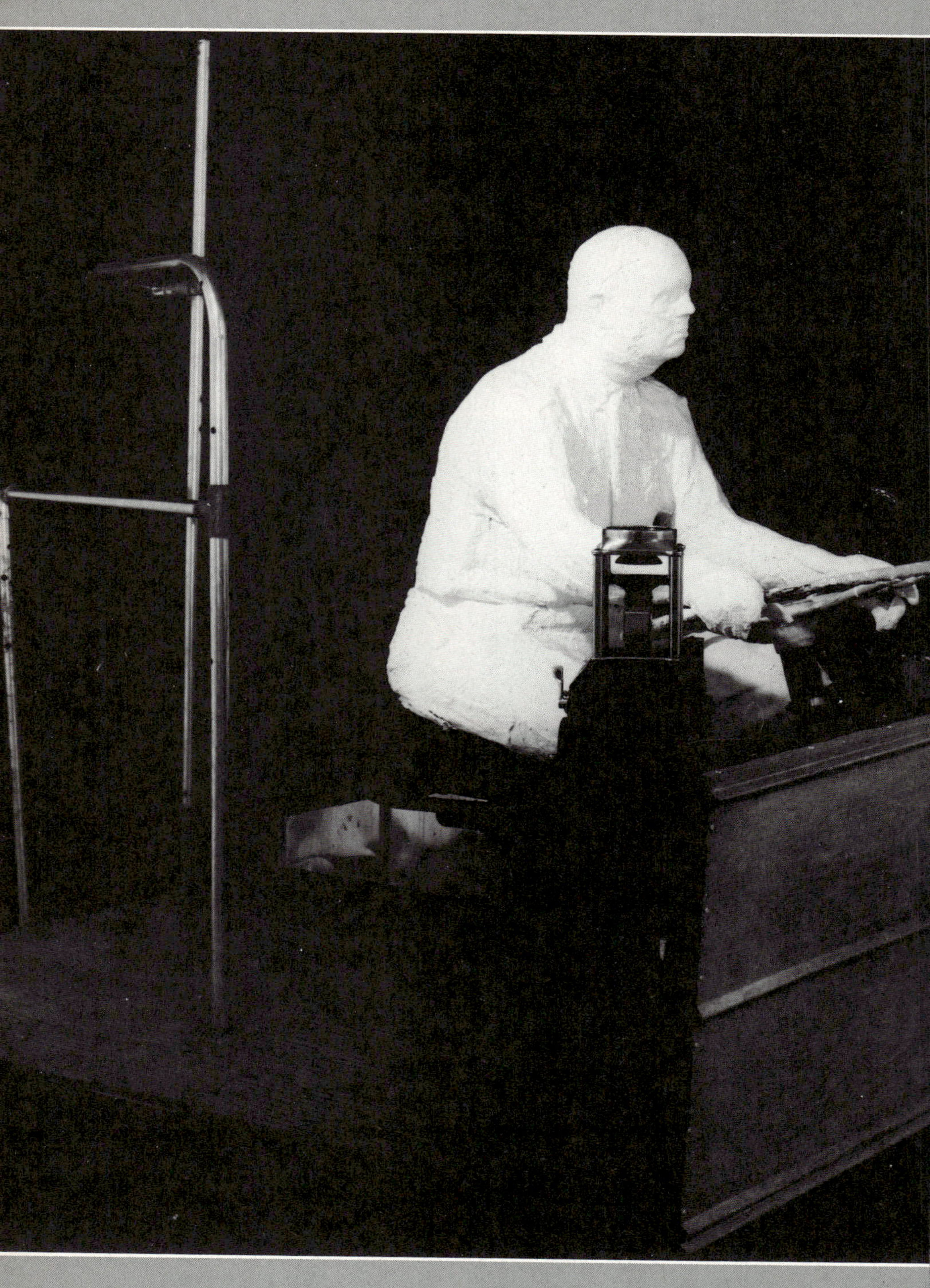

# PART V

# THE MODERN WORLD

## 1800–The Present

# Chapter 17

# Economics and Utopia

## Origins of Socialism

For most Americans the words "socialism" and "communism" evoke images of Russian secret police, single-party governments, state-run newspapers and media, prison camps for intellectuals, and indoctrination posing as education. American mythology identifies capitalism with freedom, and socialism with tyranny. What most Americans miss in that association is the enormous variety of socialism and communism. In this chapter we will explore some of that variety by examining the origins of socialist and communist thought from the French Revolution of 1789 to the *Communist Manifesto* in 1848.

Our chapter will focus on thinkers and theoreticians not because we believe (as so many people say) that socialism is good in theory but bad in practice. We think good theories work, or they are not good theories. Rather, we believe that socialism began as a critique of the capitalist industrialization of this period, that it developed a viable theoretical alternative to that system, but that such an alternative has not yet been tried (except, perhaps, in an introductory way in places like Germany and Sweden) because it depended on the full maturation of capitalism.

## Socialism as Dream

"Most of the people in the world today call the name of their dream 'socialism.' "[1] The songs and stories of the socialist movement are full of the imagery of dreams: dreams of peace and justice, dreams of resurrected martyrs, dreams of promise and hope, dreams of milk and honey. They are always dreams of a future that is better than the present. Perhaps they go back to the ancient Hebrew dream of a promised land—a future time when "the wolf will lodge with the lamb, and the leopard will lie down with the kid; the calf and the young lion will graze together."

Ever since the ancient Hebrews broke with the age-old feeling of cyclical time to imagine a linear time in which God's revelation evolved and became fulfilled, the dream has become a powerful force in Judeo-Christian culture. But if the Hebrews invented the future, the ancient Greeks invented utopia. (Actually the English Sir Thomas More coined the word for his vision of the future in 1516. His title was a pun on the Greek *eutopia,* which means the good place, and the Greek *outopia,* which means no place.) Most Greek utopias were, like Plato's, frankly conservative. But at least one—Iambulos's *Island of the Sun*—suggested an idea that was to become much later a central part of the socialist dream. That was the idea that abundance could junk oppression and create a new humanity.

Utopian dreams surfaced again with the decay of feudalism and the rise of capitalism. In the twelfth century in southern France the Poor Men of Lyons followed a merchant, Pierre Wald, who had given his wealth to the poor and preached a primitive Christian communism. These Waldensians and a similar group from Albi called Albigensians preached against private property and the wealth of the church. As Brothers and Sisters of the Free Spirit they dreamed of ushering in a new age of love, the Kingdom of the Holy Ghost. In the fourteenth century in England the ideas of John Wycliffe inspired peasant Lollards under Wat Tyler to demand the end of feudal dues. In Bohemia the radical theology of Jan Hus had the same effect.

By the sixteenth century radical theology could gain a mass following, especially after Martin Luther's break with Rome enabled others to go one step further. Thomas Muntzer led the German peasants against Luther, the reformed church, the princes, and the lords, preaching revolution and the abolition of property. If Muntzer's secularized utopia, organizational skill, and communistic goals place him at the very beginning of the socialist movement (as the Marxist, Karl Kautsky, said much later), he also ran into the problems that socialist dreamers were to face for at least the next four hundred years. The peasants responded to Muntzer when he said: "Look, the seed-grounds of usury and theft and robbery are our lords and princes, they take all creatures as their property. . . . These robbers use the Law to forbid others to rob." But when Muntzer called for the abolition of private property, he lost the peasants. They wanted their own lands, not common ownership. Oppressed by feudal dues (which, as we have seen, were beginning to become more onerous), the peasants sought to end feudalism and to gain their own fields. They did not want to abolish private property. They wanted some of their own.

Marx would say (over three hundred years later) that the times were not yet ripe for socialism in the sixteenth century (or for that matter in nineteenth-century Russia) because the bourgeois revolution had not yet occurred. The dream of communal ownership could appeal to intellectuals like Muntzer, but bourgeois mass technology had not yet made the socialization of industry an obvious necessity to all—certainly not to peasants. Muntzer was caught in a trap that was to entangle impatient dreamers including Lenin and so-called socialists of underdeveloped countries today. Friedrich Engels described the problem this way:

> The worst thing that the leader of an extreme party can experience is being forced to take power when the moment is not yet ripe for the rule of the class he represents and for the carrying out of those measures that the rule of the class requires. . . . What he *can* do contradicts all of his previous principles and positions and the immediate interest of his party; and what he *should* do is impossible. He is, in a word, forced to represent not his own party and class, but that class for whose rule the movement is really ripe.[2]

Muntzer in the sixteenth century, the English Diggers in the seventeenth century, the French communists in the eighteenth century could all only aid the spread of the bourgeois capitalist revolution's assault on feudalism, as much as they fought to go beyond it. The precondition of the socialist dream was capitalist maturity.

## The Bourgeois Revolution and the Communists: Babeuf's Conspiracy

We have already looked at the English Diggers' response to bourgeois revolution in the seventeenth century. They applauded the middle-class political liberties, representation, parliamentarianism, and suffrage, but they questioned the meaning of political equality that was not based on social and economic equality. Their radicalism made it easier for the English business class to liquidate feudal and monarchial obstacles, and so, despite themselves, they fought for the realization of a bourgeois, capitalist society.

In a similar way, French radicals at the end of the eighteenth century were enlisted in the struggle of their future bosses. The great French Revolution swung increasingly to the left and to the people in the period from 1789 to 1793–1794. It was never a socialist revolution. Middle-class lawyers, business people, and professionals, along with a few liberal nobles, were in charge even in the most radical days of 1793–1794. But the Parisian poor were able to keep the various revolutionary assemblies aware of their own needs through organized political activity and riots. Much of the peasantry was reasonably satisfied as early as August of 1789 when feudal dues were abolished. But the Constituent Assembly (1789–1791) and the Legislative Assembly (1791–1792) were sufficiently businesslike to sell church lands and demand that peasants pay their old feudal lords for the land they tilled. The National Convention (1792–1795) eased the payment requirement, but taxed the peasants even more heavily with a European war and executed their beloved King Louis XVI. (Many peasants supported the execution, despite their traditional conservatism, but found the wartime confiscations of food for Paris unbearable.) The Parisian poor, on the other hand, benefited from the confiscation that kept them from starving, maximum prices on some commodities, and the Constitution of 1793 which gave them suffrage for the first time.

It may have been essential to fight the war to prevent the failure of the revolution. The kings of Europe would have reimposed a monarchy with a vengeance (even after the execution of Louis in January 1793). But the necessary war destroyed the revolution. The drain on soldiers, food, and energies created a militarized society that by 1794 made the old regime seem like the good old days. French revolutionary society during the war years was transformed (like modern wartime societies since) into a barracks warfare state that took good care of its soldiers and forced even the richest and laziest to contribute their share, even when that could only be accomplished by means of official surveillance and terror. Some of the middle-class radicals approved of the rough equality that the terror produced, and the national mission that powered it. But as the ruling Committee of Public Safety under Robespierre failed to put the Constitution of 1793 into effect, and proceeded to devour children of the revolution as well as royalists, it met the combined opposition of popular leaders on the left and the more moderate elements on the right. Robespierre was himself executed in the summer of 1794 and the revolution was over.

A counter revolutionary White Terror followed Robespierre's revolutionary Red Terror, the conservative Constitution of 1795 replaced the radical, but unused, document of 1793, and a corrupt, cynical Directory government (1795–1799) replaced the radical firebrands of the National Convention.

One of the radicals who rejoiced at Robespierre's downfall because he thought it marked a chance for the revolution to continue, rather than its end, was Gracchus Babeuf. Disillusionment led him and others to form in prison and underground a secret Conspiracy of the Equals. It can be called the first communist organization. Under the conditions of the Directory it was necessarily secret, conspiratorial, and revolutionary. It planned to continue the revolution with a popular uprising, directed by its own members. After seizing the government they intended to abolish private property and create (with whatever force was necessary) a society of equal work and equal rewards.

We know Babeuf from the newspapers and posters he wrote to bring about the insurrection between 1795 and 1797, and from the description of organizational structure and strategy which his comrade, Buonarroti, passed on to revolutionary organizations in Europe in 1828. But we know him best from the three days of testimony he gave in April 1797, on trial for his life. His defense was a summary of a life of revolutionary activity, a review of some of the most radical philosophy of the prior century, and a look ahead to a new age.

Babeuf was arrested with 46 associates, mostly workers or *sansculottes* (which meant literally people "without breeches"—a whole class described by the uniqueness of their working clothes: pants). They included people who gave their professions as printer, goldsmith, shoemaker, clockmaker, weaver, laceworker, and embroiderer, among others. They were tried by a special 16-man jury under a law of April 1796 that was passed specifically to stem the rising tide of revolt under the Directory and the Constitution of 1795. The law decreed the death penalty for anyone advocating (even verbally) the overthrow of the government, the reestablishment of the Constitution of 1793, or the division of lands. The state was able to produce agents who had infiltrated the Conspiracy, but even without testimony on the organization's activities Babeuf's words were sufficient for conviction. Consequently his defense centered on denying the legitimacy of the law itself on the grounds that it would mean the execution of many of France's greatest philosophers, respectable bourgeois revolutionaries, and even of some of the leaders of the Directory, who at one time had said the same things that Babeuf was accused of saying.

> The prosecution has drawn up an indictment of our democratic and popular ideas which it has labelled "conspiracy for the confiscation of private property." If, gentlemen of the jury, you find us guilty of such

a conspiracy, it is literally true to say, as I have said, that all the great thinkers whose ashes rest in the Pantheon will stand convicted with us here.[3]

Babeuf referred to one count of the indictment—an article that he had written in his newspaper, *The Tribune of the People*—and told the court that it was true that he had published the allegedly inflammatory language, but that it had been copied word by word from the great philosopher Jean-Jacques Rousseau (1712–1778). In fact, Babeuf continued:

> [A] few words of Rousseau's speak volumes. I remember, still, these terse, sublime sentences of his: "The progress of society depends upon all having enough and none too much—You are lost if you forget that the fruits of the earth belong to all, the earth itself to none—Are you ignorant of the fact that millions of your fellow creatures suffer the pangs of want and perish for lack of those things that you have too much of? And do you not know that you ought to obtain the express and unanimous consent of the human race before taking a larger share of the community's wealth than is rightfully yours? . . . The all-consuming fires of ambition, the lust to make one's fortune, not in order to satisfy a genuine need, but out of an insane frenzy to get ahead of others—this imparts to men an evil inclination for mutual destruction; it endows them with a secret hatred, all the more vile since it assumes a mask of benevolence in order to strike more effectively. We see, in a word, competition and rivalry here and everywhere, an everlasting collision of interests, a bottomless thirst to profit at the expense of others. All these evils are the first result and the inseparable accompaniment of private property. Where there is no private property there can be no wrong."[4]

Babeuf continues. Was it not Diderot, the philosopher of nature who wrote the *Encyclopedia*, who said:

> "From the royal scepter to the shepherd's crook, from the tiara to the monkish cowl, the mainspring of human action is no mystery: it is personal interest. And what gave birth to this monster of selfishness? Private property! You, learned people, who amuse yourselves with discussions about the best form of government, you may wag your jaws till doomsday; all your civic wisdom will not improve the condition of man by one hair's breadth if you do not lay the ax to the tree of private ownership."[5]

Without notes, books, or the use of a library, Babeuf quoted a whole age of philosophic speculation. His case is so convincing that we are led almost to ask what was unique about the ideas of Gracchus Babeuf. Perhaps the answer lies in the word "speculation." The philosophers of the Enlightenment were engaged in speculation. They were committed men to be sure, but they sought truth rather than the transformation of society. Before the French Revolution, certainly before the American Revolution, few dreamed that their ideas could be brought to realization. Babeuf had seen what revolution could accomplish, and what it could fail to accomplish. He grew up in a world where speculation overthrew governments. And that is why Rousseau could receive alternately a prize or exile for his writings, and Babeuf could only receive death. In the age of the Directory, the stakes were too high for "mere speculation," and the revolutionary could not content himself with dreams. Babeuf was a conspirator for revolution (despite his courtroom denials to protect his friends). Ideas had become weapons. It is in that light that we date the origins of communism with the Conspiracy of the Equals, and not with Rousseau or Diderot, or even with the more radical Abbe Morelly and Gabriel Mably, all of whom died before 1789.

In the 1790s it was first possible in France for an ancient dream of equality, elaborated in philosophical speculation about private property and natural rights, to nourish a revolutionary movement with specific objectives. But it was still too early in the 1790s to define a revolutionary communist program in great detail, or to take account of the emerging industrial system, or to gain a mass or working-class following. In practice Babeuf's program would have meant little more than leveling incomes, and thus equalizing poverty. Nobility and clergy would have to work like everyone else. All goods produced would be collected and distributed by a "common store . . . with scrupulous fairness." Babeuf pointed out that this was the procedure for provisioning "twelve armies with their 1,200,000 men. And what is possible on a small scale can also be done on a large one." There was no talk of socializing large-scale industry, because in the 1790s none existed. The private property that would be commonly owned were the possessions of the rich, the food and things produced, and of course the land. At times Babeuf seemed to be suggesting that land be periodically redivided. At his trial, however, he clearly went beyond this traditional peasant dream to a notion of common ownership and farming. In any case his urban movement was more concerned with the private wealth of the middle and upper classes—which is what "property" meant to the Parisian poor.

Even the revolutionary 1790s was still an age of generalities, broad outlines, and guiding principles. Babeuf can speak for himself:

> Society must be made to operate in such a way that it eradicates once and for all the desire of a man to become richer, or wiser, or more powerful than others.

> Putting this more exactly, we must try to bring our fate under control, try to make the lot of every member of society independent of accidental circumstances, happy or unhappy. . . .
>
> Such a regime . . . will sweep away iron bars, dungeon walls, and bolted doors, trials and disputations, murders, thefts and crimes of every kind; it will sweep away the judges and the judged, the jails and the gibbets—all the torments of body and agony of soul that the injustice of life engenders; it will sweep away enviousness and gnawing greed, pride and deceit, the very catalogue of sins that Man is heir to; it will remove—and how important is this!—the brooding, omnipresent fear that gnaws always and in each of us concerning our fate tomorrow, next month, next year, and in our old age; concerning the fate of our children and of our children's children.[6]

On 24 May 1797, Gracchus Babeuf was found guilty by the High Court of Vendome of advocating the reestablishment of the Constitution of 1793. On 26 May he was sentenced to die. "I feel," he wrote his wife and children, "no regrets that I have given my life for the best of causes. Even if all my efforts have been in vain, I have done my duty." He was executed the following day.

The ideals and strategies of the Conspiracy of the Equals were carried throughout Europe by the deported Buonarroti to surface again in 1830 and 1848. By then socialism had developed new roots among the industrial working class, but communism had come to mean the most radical, communal form of socialism.

## A New Old Idea of Work: The Socialism of Fourier

Charles Fourier (1772–1837) is too often dismissed as one of the madmen of early utopian socialism. Mad, he probably was. But his madness was akin to the poet's vision and the romantic's lust for human values which the sober bourgeois, industrial world mocked. It is easy to make fun of his suspicion that the stars had intercourse or that the oceans could be turned into lemonade, but such fantasies should not distract our attention from Fourier's radical critique of the separation of work and life in capitalist industry or from "his prophetic warning that real progress was something other than the mechanical confection of instruments for destroying human happiness."[7]

Fourier grew up in a comfortable middle-class home during the French Revolution. He was given enough of the family wealth (today's equivalent of almost $100,000) on his twenty-first birthday in 1793 to set up his own business as a cloth merchant and importer in the southern French city of Lyon. After a few months he joined Lyon's insurrection against the revolutionary government in Paris, a move that cost him much of his fortune, and almost his life, when Lyon was recaptured. So Fourier was no revolutionary. His socialism did not emerge from the working-class experience of Paris or from the radical politics of journalists and intellectuals like Babeuf.

> If the Lyon insurrection disgusted Fourier with revolutionary politics, it was the financial chaos of the Directory that shaped his economic views. The brief Jacobin experiment in a directed economy was followed by a complete relaxation of economic controls; and the Directory was a period of skyrocketing inflation, industrial stagnation, and widespread food shortages. Fortunes were made overnight through speculation in paper money, profiteering in military supplies, and the creation of artificial shortages. As a commercial employee Fourier saw these abuses at first hand and occasionally participated in them. They strengthened his conviction that there was something wrong with the whole economic system based on free—or as he called it "anarchic"—competition. He began to formulate a general critique of commercial capitalism which emphasized the parasitism of the merchant and the middleman as the chief cause of economic ills.[8]

By 1799 Fourier had arrived at the main outlines of his system for solving social and economic ills. He felt he had discovered the laws of human "natural association," a "geometrical calculus of passionate attraction," and a scheme for organizing a new community in which people would work harmoniously at socially useful jobs because they wanted to. After less than a year of study, however, Fourier had exhausted the rest of his fortune and was forced in June 1800 (shortly after Napoleon took power from the Directory) to return to "the jailhouse of commerce." For the remaining 15 years of Napoleon's rule Fourier filled his notebooks for a few hours every evening "after having spent my days participating in the deceitful activities of the merchants and brutalizing myself in the performance of degrading tasks." His book-length announcement of his discoveries in 1808 was met with derision, as was his offer to Napoleon that the emperor become his "founder of Harmony." Ignored, he declared he would withhold his discoveries until a million troops had been lost in Napoleonic wars.

In 1815, after Napoleon's final exile, Fourier used an inheritance from his mother to quit his clerical and traveling sales jobs to write full time. He devoted himself to his investigations of passion, love, and sexuality. He refined his blueprint for social organization in a community of passionate work. And he began to publish the thousands of pages of his *Grand Treatise* in different versions in 1822.

The question of work was central to Fourier's personal life and to the emerging industrial society in which he lived. The bourgeoisie justified its claim to power by making its own preoccupation with work a virtue. They criticized the poor and some of the unproductive nobility and clergy for not working. They sought ways of indoctrinating the whole society with a work ethic. But the kind of work that they offered in their factories and offices was a new kind of slavery. In chemical plants and glass works it was a form of murder. In textile mills even the easiest manual labor constituted 12 to 15 hours of disciplined, soul-wrecking boredom. The "little people" of the lower middle class were often further removed from physical starvation, but they were prey to the same anxieties, insecurities, and regimentation. In fact the emotional starvation of the clerical worker whose body rotted in shuffled paper was often more severe since the work showed no tangible product.

It is no wonder, Fourier noticed, that work itself was despised. Work had become divorced from life. It was necessary then "*To find a new Social Order* that insures the poorest members of the working class sufficient well-being to make them constantly and passionately prefer their work to idleness and brigandage to which they now aspire." Fourier, of course, was convinced that he had found the new social order, and solved the problem of work.

The solution lay in Fourier's recognition that almost everyone in society had a passion to do something that someone else called work. So instead of concentrating (like the factory owners) on forcing people to work against their instincts at the particular jobs which profited the owners, Fourier suggested the construction of societies which gratified those instinctual needs. Instead of shaping the person to the job, the jobs would be the agencies of passionate, sensual gratification. Society would work to satisfy instincts instead of repressing that deepest and most spontaneous emotional energy for useful work. Fourier could almost define useful work as the work that people would instinctively do, not only because he had faith in human nature, but also because he prized human diversity.

Such a society (even, or perhaps especially, in an experimental form) must have certain preconditions to be possible. Everyone would have to own a share in the community to feel part of it. The working places and residences would have to be comfortable and attractive. And a minimum standard of living would have to be guaranteed to all so that work was clearly spontaneous. Then the diversity of human instincts would allow each person to find his or her most expressive working opportunity. The important thing would be to allow the fullest expression of one's passion. Even a bloodthirsty tyrant like the Roman emperor Nero would be happy as a butcher. His passion expressed, rather than repressed, the young Nero raised in a phalanx

(Fourier's name for the community) "would have begun by the age of four to satisfy twenty other penchants" which his Roman teachers would have stifled "for the sake of morality."[9]

But the Nero type is only the most extreme of 810 personality types that Fourier characterized. A phalanx should have at least one man and one woman of each type. Every passion or combination of passions can be put to use in socially valuable work. The passion of some children for dirt is no exception:

> Two-thirds of all boys have a penchant for filth. They love to wallow in the mire and play with dirty things. They are unruly, peevish, scurrilous and overbearing, and they will brave any storm or peril simply for the pleasure of wreaking havoc. These children will enroll in the Little Hordes whose task is to perform, dauntlessly and as a point of honor, all those loathsome tasks that ordinary workers would find debasing.[10]

Among these are "sewer-cleaning, tending the dung heap, working in the slaughter-houses," and keeping "the roads of Harmony lined with shrubs and flowers and in more splendid condition than the lanes of our country estates."[11] (We might remind ourselves that Fourier was writing in an age when young children were commonly caged in factories and mines for over 12 hours a day.)

Few passions are so strong as to commit one to the same work all day, every day. Many people have multiple passions. And many have a "butterfly passion" which requires that they "flutter about from pleasure to pleasure." Consequently, these people will be aided in designing as often as necessary their preferred series of work attractions. A maximum period of two hours at any job would probably be desirable. Thus a typical summer day of one Harmonian might include five meals, mass, two public functions, a concert, an hour and a half at the library, and eight tasks: hunting, fishing, gardening, and tending pheasants in the morning, and the afternoon at the fish tanks, the sheep pasture, and in two different greenhouses. Finally, he would spend an hour before supper at the "exchange" to plan the next day's activities.

Fourier's revolutionary method of asking what people want instead of what has to be done enabled him to surpass, he felt, even the efficiency of capitalist industry. This is because even the most humanitarian factory owner must repress the worker's source of productive and creative energy—the instincts. A smart owner might be able to find a worker who has the proper physical or tempermental inclinations for a particular job, but the work would always be grudgingly performed as long as it were done for someone else. The problem with work in commercial industrial society (which Fourier called civilization) is that it must inevitably suppress rather than liberate the passions. And not only is that humanly crippling, it is also socially inefficient.

> It is easy to compress the passions by violence [he wrote]. Philosophy suppresses them with a stroke of the pen. Locks and the sword come to the aid of sweet morality. But nature appeals from these judgments; she regains her rights in secret. Passion stifled at one point reappears at another like water held back by a dike; it is driven inward like the humor of an ulcer closed too soon.[12]

How inhuman, and how wasteful to deny such elemental forces with the violence of morality. Human passions always have value when they are allowed expression in a nonrepressive, social setting. Civilization outside of the phalanx makes the error of rejecting and repressing human feelings in the interests of morality or efficiency. But it is wrong on both counts. A morality that ignores human needs must depend on locks and swords, and such institutions of oppression yield a very low level of efficiency.

So far we have described Fourier's system without much attention to its social dimension. This was appropriate because Fourier began with an analysis of passions—an essentially psychological issue—and he sometimes spoke of human society in the idiom of bourgeois liberalism as a collection of separate atoms. Liberals from Adam Smith to John Stuart Mill (and twentieth-century conservatives) looked for social harmony in the competing self-interest of each isolated atomistic individual. Similarly, Fourier argued that his community of Harmony would emerge from "rivalry, self-esteem, and other stimuli compatible with self-interest." The difference is that the liberal defenders of capitalist industrial society interpreted self-interest in narrowly economic terms, and Fourier's psychology led to an idea of self-interest that was deeply emotional, sexual, and social. Liberalism posited an abstract social harmony derived from individuals competing in the marketplace and the job market. Fourier (and most socialists) sought the social harmony that derived from individual drives toward intimacy, cooperation, love, and participation.

Work was to be accomplished in Harmony not only because each individual would give vent to his or her personal passions, but also because it would be performed by individuals who were as attracted to each other as to the work itself. Love, even sexual love, was not to be an obstacle or "a recreation which detracts from work; on the contrary it is the soul and vehicle, the mainspring of all works and of the whole of universal attraction."[13]

Whenever possible work would be done in groups. These voluntary associations would change personnel, but they would always be comprised of men and women of similar inclinations Working would thus provide occasions for meeting new people, developing relationships, and creative social interaction. Groups could compete with others and individuals could show off their talents without creating permanent divisions. Fourier chose to discuss "one of the most difficult administrative problems of civilization: the recruitment of armies" to show how even in the most extreme case love could motivate work. Harmony would recruit young men and women to its training maneuvers and athletic contests with "magnificent feasts" of food and love. In the process of a season's military campaigns the young women would choose partners from the suitors who competed in valor for their attention.

Fourier's discussion of armies touched on a subject that he kept hidden in his notebooks, which he called *The New Amorous World*. Here he imagined a future stage of Harmony which offered complete instinctual liberation with a guaranteed sexual minimum that enabled the inhabitants to transcend sexual scarcity in the same way that the economic minimum allowed spontaneous work. Marriage was to be allowed. But Fourier castigated enforced monogamy for separating love from sexuality and limiting sexuality to copulation or procreation. Christian civilization, Fourier argued, had deprived productive work and civic life of its eroticism by restricting the enjoyment of sexual pleasure to the marriage bed. Harmony's Court of Love would guarantee enough opportunities for sexual gratification so that in the new society of abundance sex would not be a single obsession, but an ever available enjoyment of life. All work was to be passionate play.

## Varieties of Socialism: The Legacy of the French Revolution

What makes Fourier a socialist? His criticism of capitalism (which he called commerce or civilization) certainly qualified him, especially since he proposed the creation of a common cooperative alternative to competitive capitalism: he did not criticize capitalism in order to reform it. His insistence that work serve the interests (indeed, the passions) of the workers (instead of the profits of capital) was socialist. His argument that workers would work for themselves, without whips or wages, because they wanted to—that was socialist. So was his antipathy to markets, sales, production for profit, and his placement of Harmony outside of market society. But perhaps the most socialist aspect of Fourier's philosophy was his radical, revolutionary confrontation of bourgeois civilization. He asked different questions: What are human needs? How can society be organized to satisfy human needs? He made different assumptions: Human nature is various and good; all repression of instincts is destructive. Like Babeuf, "his exposure of pain and suffering that others took for granted and his sympathy for the outcasts of civilized society did much to give socialist thought the moral and humanitarian dimension which was its hallmark"[14] by midcentury.

Fourier's socialism had its peculiarities. He actually sought capital investment in his community, for instance. Shares in the community were to be given to capital, labor, and talent. After the minimum subsistence was paid, the remaining dividends were to go four-twelfths to capital, five-twelfths to labor, and three-twelfths to talent. He also naively expected his program to be adopted by Napoleon or some wealthy financier. That was a peculiar misunderstanding of the revolutionary nature of his proposals. He had little appreciation of the way in which industry was transforming society and creating even more ghastly "jailhouses" of work. His agricultural vision of utopia was becoming outdated as he wrote. Yet, in another sense he was far ahead of his time. The instinctual liberation through creative work that he imagined possible in the 1830s required a technological maturity that is only dawning in the most industrial part of the world today. The industrialization that he despised created the economy of abundance that his vision required. For this reason he deserves our attention. (For an update of Fourier's vision, sifted through Marx and Freud, see Herbert Marcuse's *Eros and Civilization*.)

The varieties of socialism in the first half of the nineteenth century were enormous. There were dozens of Fourierist colonies alone, each with its own version of the master's voice and all understaffed and undercapitalized, on four continents. There were also utopian communities modeled on the socialist theory of Etienne Cabet, Robert Owen, and many others. We cannot do justice to all of the theorists or practitioners of the new way of life. But a look at some of the other socialisms of the 1830s and 1840s can at least give us some idea of the variety of the movement.

Etienne Cabet (1787–1856) in his *Voyage to Icaria* conceived of a communist society on a national scale, with industry supporting a population of a million. Icaria was to exclude private property and eliminate any social inequality. All citizens were to labor equally, and receive from the common store equally, "each according to his needs." And because Cabet grew up in a society which used entirely different types of clothing to indicate social position, the inhabitants of Icaria were to dress alike. Cabet's ideal society reflected much in his own personality. It was austere, authoritarian, almost harshly fair, and deeply Christian. Communism did not become associated with atheism until after 1848. In that year Cabet introduced communism to the

United States, but in the form of experimental communities like those of Fourier and Robert Owen (which he had criticized as so inadequate).

Claude-Henri de Rouvroy de Saint-Simon (1760–1825) was one of the most interesting men of his time. Yet it was his disciples who turned a rather ambiguous legacy into a socialist movement throughout Europe and beyond. Saint-Simon was not only an aristocrat who survived the French Revolution and then went on to launch socialism. He also fought in the American Revolution, undertook canal projects through Central America and in Europe, renounced his title (but not his knack for making money) in becoming Citizen Bonhomme ("Goodman") of the French Revolution, was arrested and nearly executed by Robespierre, became rich under the Directory, found himself an inmate at Charenton insane asylum under Napoleon, became unofficial spokesman for the banking and industrial liberal bourgeoisie in the restoration of constitutional monarchy between 1815 and 1830, but found himself ignored by his former banking friends (who eventually took power in 1830) because at some point in the last decade of his life he had crossed the line from liberalism to socialism without knowing it.

Saint-Simon's route from bourgeois spokesman to socialist was marked not by a change in his own outlook but by a continued effort to carry the arguments of the bourgeois revolution to their logical conclusions. As long as the banking-industrial class was politically weak after the defeat of Napoleon and the restoration of the monarchy in 1815, Saint-Simon's insistence that power belonged to the "producers" satisfied them. They would have preferred Saint-Simon to argue for the power of "property" rather than "producers" or "industrials," but it was clear enough that Saint-Simon meant them. He even honored bankers with the title of "industrial generalists"; and although he included artists, writers, and scientists among the crucial class of "industrials," he did not include the laboring poor. (His disciples made that step.) By the 1820s, however, the upper middle class was powerful enough to sense that its greatest threat was no longer the nobility but the working class. At that point Saint-Simon's espousal of government by the "industrial class" was too vague for them, especially when he described that class as a "majority" of the nation.

Saint-Simon's followers were a diverse group. His secretary, Auguste Comte, sanctified private property and developed a conservative "positivist philosophy" that is often recognized as the first sociology. Some of his followers became the leading capitalists and industrialists of nineteenth-century France. Most of his followers, however, developed the socialist implications of Saint-Simon's thought.

It was the Saint-Simonian journal, *Le Globe,* which popularized the word *socialisme* in February 1832. For them the new word meant not the abolition of private property so much as the assumption that property was social and could therefore be called to public account. The agency of public economic representation was seen as a central banking system which regulated industry, organized production according to public need, and avoided the overproduction or underconsumption that the unplanned economy seemed prone to create.

The tone of the Saint-Simonian movement requires some comment because of arguments since the 1830s concerning the "liberties" of socialism and communism. First, the Saint-Simonians did not advocate a temporary minority dictatorship as some of the radical communists did, though in defense of the communists it should be pointed out that the Saint-Simonians rarely spoke for people whose lives were so desperate that they were frustrating their own needs. Second, the Saint-Simonians almost uniformly embraced the national industrial system, making them often greater proponents of technocracy than the capitalists. In France bourgeois money was so slow to try industry that it had to be prodded and preceded by Saint-Simonian socialists. Finally, Saint-Simonian socialism was a religious movement in many ways. Many thought of themselves as disciples preaching "faith" in the "new Christianity." Thus, the combination of religious commitment and the acceptance of an inevitable, centralized industrial state could have profoundly authoritarian tones. On the other hand, the Saint-Simonians saw the exploitation of nature (through industrialization) as a way of ending the exploitation of human beings, and they were leading proponents of the rights of women and the dispossessed. They pioneered prison reform, employment of paupers, and treatment for the insane. Like the followers of Fourier, they spoke little of economics, aside from criticizing private property, market relations, and inequality, but argued for a general human liberation that, however utopian, began with human needs for sexual gratification, emotional expression, and social participation.

French socialism in the 1830s meant the movements inaugurated by Fourier and Saint-Simon. In general, even the Fourierists took cognizance of a wider world than the self-sufficient commune. Flora Tristan (1803–1844) carried Fourier's vision of worker autonomy toward a program that foreshadowed syndicalism and labor party movements much later. She proposed a union of the working class in a self-governing corporation to which they contributed their own funds for the general emancipation of labor. Every city would have its worker-sponsored "palace of labor" with schools, libraries, hospitals, old-age homes, and recreation facilities that would give the working class the autonomy and training to govern themselves. She also undercut the nationalist rhetoric that divided working classes in the 1840s (and again in 1914) and urged the formation of international labor organizations that would commit socialist movements to peace and international cooperation.

In the 1840s French socialism was dominated by Louis-Auguste Blanqui (1805–1881), Constantin Pecqueur (1801–1887), and Louis Blanc (1811–1882). Born in the age of Napoleon, they spent their youth under the Restoration (1815–1830), came of age under the "bourgeois monarchy" (1830–1848), and participated in the first working-class revolution in the sunny days of 1848. As Marx wrote later, they had all mistaken the birth pangs of capitalism for its death throes. By the winter of early 1849 their dreams had frozen. Perhaps a sign of their strength can be found in the bourgeoisie's panicky, repressive alliance with their old antagonists—the aristocracy—to repress the revolution. But certainly the naive proposals of socialists for government of a world they did not own, as well as the popular support outside of Paris for a new Napoleon, were signs that socialists would have to struggle through a long capitalist ascent. That lesson was reinforced by the failure of the Paris Commune uprising in 1871.

Blanqui, like Babeuf, was always just in or out of jail since he joined the Charbonnerie secret society at the age of 17. We can call him a socialist because he believed that capitalism was inherently unstable and that its periodic crises of overproduction would eventually lead to a cooperative economy. He preferred to call himself a communist, by which he meant to distinguish his own activism from the theorizing of the followers of Cabet, Fourier, Saint-Simon, and almost everyone else.

Pecqueur was an economist. He argued that the new industrial technology was vastly more productive (thus superior) to hand manufacturing, and that it was creating a new way of life—cities, factories, mass markets, monopolies—which were essentially "associational, socialized, agglomerational." In short, the kind of industrial society that capitalism was producing was *social*. It increasingly cried out for socialization of ownership. Private competitors were unwittingly hastening their own obsolescence. The social impact of industrial technology would soon be so enormous that the state would have to take it over as a public trust. Pecqueur felt that the syndicalist goal of worker control of each industry would be impractical, but he was suspicious of the elitism of the Saint-Simonians' "central banking system." So he emphasized the need for public administration of industry by a thoroughly democratic government.

Louis Blanc is best known for his organization of French national workshops after the February Revolution of 1848. The experiment was never allowed to progress, but even its minor successes met with brutal suppression in June. That in turn led to civil war and finally conservative reaction. Blanc's proposal was to guarantee all French workers "the right to work" by creating urban workshops, rural collective farms, as well as shared housing and social services that would compete with those that were privately owned. The public facilities would be administered by autonomous boards (whose directors were to be eventually elected by the workers), and funded by the national bank with guaranteed loans that paid interest. All profit was to be used by the workshops for wages and investment in new facilities. Government subsidies would also be available in low- or no-profit industries where private capitalists were already subsidized. Blanc did not favor a state socialism that nationalized everything. But he believed that, in many cases, the public workshops would prove more efficient because of worker participation than private enterprise. A public sector of the economy would thus be created by giving associations of workers the opportunities that bourgeois governments had normally given to private capitalists. Blanc's program was to avoid the potential confusion of uncoordinated worker-owned factories and the potential rigidity of centralized state socialism. He was adamantly democratic, refusing even to sanction the Paris Commune insurrection of 1871.

## The Origins of Marxism

On the eve of the abortive French social Revolution of 1848 there was still no major socialist movement outside of France. German liberals were allied with a few socialists in an effort to create the parliamentary system, national unification, and middle-class freedoms that France had achieved in the revolution of 1789 and England had been developing since 1689 or even the 1640s.

By 1848 Britain had created the world's only industrial society. Consequently, British thinkers were in a much better position to survey the economics of the new order. After Adam Smith, David Ricardo had taught English economic thinkers to recognize the irrevocable opposition of capitalist and landowning classes as well as the exploitation of labor by capitalists. But Ricardo was a pessimist rather than a socialist. He accepted the exploitation of labor as natural. Some of his followers deduced socialist ideas from the "labor theory of value" which Ricardo (like Locke and Adam Smith) had proposed. They argued that since the value of all industrial production could be measured by the amount of labor that went into it, then labor was the creator of value and the class of laborers had a right to the whole product of industry; capitalists were laborers in so far as they worked, but not because they had acquired capital for investment, especially since their interest or profit came from capital that they had squeezed out of wages due to workers. In this regard the Ricardian socialists of the 1830s and 1840s were saying very much the same thing as the French Saint-Simonian socialists. Their study of economics was more advanced (because the English economy was more advanced) but the Ricardian socialists did not develop a socialist movement.

The "movement" in England before 1848 was Chartist and Owenite. Robert Owen was a successful Fourier. He turned his own textile mill into a model community for the benefit of his workers, aided the creation of utopian worker cooperatives in Britain and America, and pioneered a consumer cooperative, and the organization of British trade unions which eventually became the Labour party. But Owen was naive about economics. He recognized injustice and sought to correct it. But he had little sense of the vested interest of his class in continuing the exploitation that caused the injustices. He was able to put his own house in order and argue that other capitalists should do the same. He thought he could simply show the British industrial class the error of their ways (as he showed his worker-children how to be productive) and everyone would be enlightened, injustice abolished.

British Chartism was a larger mass movement than all of French socialism, but only a few of the Chartists considered themselves socialists. The People's Charter of 1838 demanded only working-class representation in Parliament through universal suffrage for men, the abolition of property qualifications to hold office, and the payment of salaries to elected members of Parliament. Petition campaigns gathered between 3 and 6 million signatures (out of a British population of 19 million). But even with the signatures of half of the adult males of Britain the charter was rejected by Parliament, 287 to 49. Parliament feared that political democracy would threaten the rights of private property and the whole economic system. It took another 80 years before the demands of the charter were passed.

We are left then with something of a paradox. The country which pioneered the industrial revolution, the most advanced capitalist economy of the nineteenth century, the patent office and workshop of the world, waited in the 1840s for a German (or rather two Germans) to analyze its economy along Ricardian socialist lines, to fuse the new study of political economy with the socialism of Owen, and to turn the mass working-class movement from liberal to socialist goals.

In fact, Karl Marx and Friedrich Engels not only used Ricardian theory to study the specific workings of the new economy and the concrete conditions of the new working class, they also directed their

■ *By the middle of the nineteenth century Britain had become "the workshop of the world." This clean, and well regulated, textile factory was not unlike that of an Owen or Engels.* (Granger)

findings to further the development of British economic theory. In the process they created a European mass movement and changed the meaning and importance of socialism for ever.

Marxism is more than the fusion of Ricardo and Owen. It is the fusion of French socialism, German philosophy, and British political economy. For Marx the starting point was the philosophical climate at the University of Berlin in the 1830s. Under Napoleonic occupation German philosophers had confronted the exterior political issues of nationhood and freedom, and they had consoled themselves with intense speculations about such "interior" problems as knowledge, morality, being, reason, judgment, ethics, criticism, substance, mind, and ethics. German philosophers, from Kant in the 1780s and 1790s to Fichte during the occupation and Hegel until his death in 1831, struggled with doubt and faith to reach first principles and universal absolutes in much the way that English thinkers like Hobbes and Locke and French enlightenment thinkers since Descartes had done earlier. But English philosophy was more empirical or concrete and French philosophy was more rational, urbane, and cosmopolitan. The Germans turned inward and contemplated freedom and the world from the standpoint of the soul. Isolated and dominated, they drew

▪ *Karl Marx (1818–1883). (UPI)*

on a rich mystical religious heritage to ask about the relationships between knowing and acting, being and thinking, existence and consciousness.

The young Marx accepted the insight of Kant, Fichte, and Hegel that mind or consciousness is always active. He rejected, however, the tendency of these German philosophical idealists to treat mind, "spirit," or "ideas" as the only reality. At the same time he rejected the tendency of French and English philosophical materialists to imagine that ideas could only reflect or mirror a basic material reality. He wanted to change reality while recognizing its restrictions. He wanted to spend his life working to improve the welfare of humankind, he wrote as early as 1835 at the age of 17 on a final examination. "But," he added, "our relationships in society have already to some extent been formed before we are in a position to determine them."

To recognize what is socially determined, and yet to seek to make a better world—this was the problem that Marx set himself and pursued for the rest of his life. There is little point in accusing him of inconsistency as a determinist and an idealist. He was neither. He confronted the problem of meaningful human action in a fixed world, the problem of freedom and necessity, squarely. He did not shy away from this central problem of his age (and ours) with a one-sided idealist faith in the power of ideas or a one-sided materialist surrender to circumstances. His genius was in confronting an almost impossible problem and in leaving it at his death even more difficult than he found it. For his life work showed that human action was vastly more determined than had been imagined, and also that human liberation was much more possible than had been dreamed.

Marx enlarged his culture's understanding of the depth of necessity *and* the possibilities of freedom by showing people how to think historically about human societies. In the process he practically "invented" sociology and social history. Our debt to Marx is that he gave us new historical and sociological ways of thinking about the problems which are most urgent in modern industrial society.

"History" in the Germany of the 1830s and 1840s meant the philosophy of Hegel. It is often said that Marx took Hegel's philosophy of history, conceived as a dialectical clash of one idea (a "thesis") with its opposite (an "antithesis") leading to the formation of a new idea (a "synthesis"), and that he applied this dialectical process to the study of material society—thus producing a new philosophy or science of history called dialectical materialism. This, however, is a gross simplification of both Hegel and Marx. Hegel's genius cannot be found with a shorthand chart of three or four Greek words. Marx did not simply "apply" Hegel's theory about the evolution of ideas to the evolution of society. Rather, Hegel taught Marx that history is a process which is kept going by its "negative" side, and that a meaning or direction of history could be perceived beyond the turmoil of facts by keeping an eye on the transforming power of the losses, losers, and ashes as well as the steady building.

The idea that there was a logic to history had been developed in the French Enlightenment of the eighteenth century. But this had led to Saint-Simon's and Comte's abstract theories of historical stages, each separated from the preceding by a gulf because there was little thought given to the actual process of change. Hegel, and then Marx, found a motor or propeller of social change in human labor. "The great thing in Hegel's *Phenomenology*," Marx wrote in his *Economic-Philosophical Manuscripts* of 1844, "is that Hegel conceives the self-creation of man as a process . . . and that he therefore grasps the nature of *labor* and comprehends objective man . . . as the result of his *own labor*."

## Marx: From History of Labor to Critique of Alienation

In his doctoral dissertation (1841), the *Manuscripts* (1844–1846), the *Holy Family* (1845), the *Theses on Feurbach* (1845), and the *German Ideology* (1845–1846) Marx developed a philosophy of history and a rudimentary sociology that saw human labor as the creator and beneficiary of history. Through practical activity or labor, Marx argued, people produce themselves and their world. The process is dialectical: people create their environment, and the new environment transforms them. It is social: "the individual is a social being" whose "free conscious activity" is social productivity. It is radically historical: there is no unchanging human nature; human productivity continually transforms human needs, feelings, beliefs, and dreams as it transforms the external world.

Marx went beyond Hegel's philosophy of history in a number of significant ways. The activity of the 90 percent of human working populations was more important to Marx than the abstractions of philosophers. Hegel's vision of history as the progressive realization of freedom was given flesh and blood and sweat. But most significantly, Hegel's closed philosophical system of speculation was discarded for a critical philosophy of history which attempted to unify theory and practice. History for Marx was a revolutionary, critical activity.

Thus, Marx turned his history of human labor into a criticism of labor in capitalist society. The laboring classes did not receive the fruits of their labor. Work was not allowed to be spontaneous, social, creative, and useful. The most fundamental human need—that of expressive activity—was thwarted by capitalist markets and profits. Workers became alienated (cut off) from their own work and their own bodies.

> What constitutes the alienation of labor? First, that the work is external to the worker, that it is not part of his nature; and that, consequently, he does not fulfill himself in his work but denies himself, has a feeling of misery rather than well being, does not develop freely his mental and physical energies but is physically exhausted and mentally debased. The worker therefore feels himself at home only during his leisure time, whereas at work he feels homeless. His work is not voluntary but imposed, *forced labor*. It is not the satisfaction of a need, but only a *means* for satisfying other needs. Its alien character is clearly shown by the fact that as soon as there is no physical or other compulsion it is avoided like the plague. External labor, labor in which man alienates himself, is a labor of self-sacrifice, of mortification. Finally, the external

> character of work for the worker is shown by the fact that it is not his own work but work for someone else, that in work he does not belong to himself but to another person.[15]

In this way the philosophy of history ushers in critical social theory. The world history that shows the self-realization of the individual through labor (and even the gigantic achievements of productivity under industrial capitalism) also reveals the contradictions of the capitalist organization of labor in terms of economic exploitation and psychic alienation. Individuals no longer achieve their identity through creative work because the products of their work are no longer their own. The things that labor produces are now turned against laborers. Just as these products once affirmed their existence, abilities, desires, and identity, they are now under capitalism testaments to their enslavement. Since laborers work at the command of the capitalist, fashion what will bring the capitalist profit, and lose control of whatever they make, the products of their own labor actually deny their identity instead of affirming it. And since capital is acquired by paying laborers less than their products are worth, the power of capital increases while that of labor declines. "The more the worker produces, the greater the power of capital becomes and the smaller the worker's own means for appropriating his products. Labor thus becomes the victim of a power it has itself created."[16]

Under capitalism laborers are alienated from an expanding world of objects which "oppose them." They are alienated from their own powers, from their creative selves. And separated from the objects of their labor, without the self-esteem of making, forming, and shaping, they are treated like objects. Alienated from themselves, they are alienated from other human beings. Bought and sold like objects or pieces of a machine, they think of themselves as objects and treat others similarly. Human relations become "objectified."

Thus, under capitalism according to Marx, it is not work but all of life that is alien to human needs. The problem was more than the greed of capitalists. Rather, the new system of private property had created a complex social system where greed became commonplace, manipulation moral, selfishness natural, and self-sacrifice an ideal.

> Its principal thesis is the renunciation of life and of human needs. The less you eat, drink, buy books, go to the theatre or to balls, or to public houses, and the less you think, love, theorize, sing, paint, fence, etc., the more you will be able to save and the greater will become your treasure which neither moth nor rust will corrupt—your *capital.* The less you *are,* the less you express your life, the more you *have,* the greater is your alienated life and the greater is the saving of your alienated being.[17]

Marx's theory of the alienation of labor in capitalist society transformed his early Hegelian philosophy of history into critical theory—theory unified to practical strategy. His study of the historical importance of labor led to a socialist call for the end of alienation, the reintegration of work and life. This humanistic socialism of 1844 was deepened in the four years that preceded the *Communist Manifesto* of 1848 by Marx's immersion in British economic thought and French historical writing. Just as his earlier Hegelian study of the history of labor had led to a critical evaluation of capitalist labor, now his study of the history of economic and social ideas led to a critical theory of the historical role of ideas under capitalism. Just as the notion of "alienation" had previously provided the link between theory and practice, now the idea of "ideology" offered a new theoretical bridge to action, or "praxis."

## Marx: From History of Ideas to Critique of Ideology

Perhaps it was an essay on political economy written by Friedrich Engels in 1844 that caught Marx's attention. Marx had also been contributing articles to the *German-French Yearbook.* In fact, they had met in 1842 when Engels came to Marx's editorial office at the *Rhineland Times,* a liberal newspaper Marx took over when he was denied a university professorship. Engels stormed into the office spouting a kind of pure communism that seemed clownish and impractical to the serious newspaper editor, so Marx ushered him out. Engels continued his trip to England to learn his father's business in Manchester and use the opportunity to study the Chartist movement and write about the conditions of the English working class. By 1844 Engels was a successful businessman and a pretty well-known communist writer. The essay for the *Yearbook* in 1844 was an interesting study of English economic thought. Engels argued that the political economy or political-economic theories of Adam Smith, Ricardo, and the rest were little more than hypocritical rationalizations of the greedy motives of British capitalists. Their talk of free trade, competition, private ownership, and the wealth of nations was actually a fraud against the British working people, not a neutral science of economics. Marx was so impressed he began corresponding with Engels. He had already gained an understanding of the role of social classes and the revolutionary potential of the proletariat (working class) from his reading of French history while in Paris, and now he set himself to read as much of the British economists as were translated into French.

This time the history of ideas became a critical analysis of ideas. Everything—German philosophy, French historical writing, and British political economy—seemed to fit together. All were responding to the upheavals of the last 50 years. "Marx was struck by the fundamental similarity of certain key concepts employed by philosophers, economists, and historians alike. It appeared to him that, consciously or not, they were reasoning in ways which had gradually been evolved since the seventeenth century by the representative thinkers of one particular social stratum whose pre-eminence was no longer questionable: the bourgeoisie. And from this awareness he was led to the notion that all this complex theorizing constituted, as it were, the 'ideological superstructure' of a particular social reality: 'bourgeois society.' "[18]

Marx was not saying, as Engels had, that these thinkers were hypocrites—mere intellectual hired guns. Nor was he saying that they were simply advocates for their class, like lawyers pleading a case. Marx recognized their sincerity—and the scientific accuracy of much of their writings. But he saw beyond that. He recognized that intellectuals tend to share the guiding ideas, assumptions, and mental categories of their age, and that they are related to the social class alignments of that age in which they live. Almost all of the leading political and economic thinkers since the seventeenth century, for instance, shared a view of human nature which they thought to be eternal but which was actually the kind of human nature that had developed with the bourgeois economic and political revolution.

Many of the ideas of mature Marxism came out of this analysis of the history of ideas. Ideas are always related in some way to the particular historical and social contexts from which they spring. Each historical period produces its own ideas, assumptions, perceptions, art, and truths. In so far as these mental processes reflect the social needs of a particular society or class, they function ideologically, that is, they work to support or challenge some aspect of the social reality. The mental categories of the ruling class are especially effective ideologically in supporting the status quo. Modern modes of thinking can be usefully called bourgeois because they often serve the needs of the ruling entrepreneurial, industrial, middle, or bourgeois, class. We may sometimes be able to speak meaningfully of bourgeois economics, proletarian art, landowner religion, slave-owning ideas of god, feudal ideas of man, peasant attitudes toward time—or any other social form of a mental activity. Ideas, feelings, attitudes, and arts change as the society changes. World history can be understood in terms of these changing styles of mental activity as well as by the changing forms of social organization—and the two spheres are not really separate at all. Ideas never originate in vacuums. They always bear some relationship to social reality. Ideas, therefore, always have some ideological or social role.

The practical implications of these ideas about ideas were enormous. Marx's critical approach was to serve generations of later followers with the tools to cut through the ideological content of much of bourgeois thought. The assumptions of the political economists could be inverted while their insights were absorbed. Working-class ideas, cultures, and arts could be encouraged, separated from oppressive ruling-class models, and given their own respectability. Religions, arts, even social sciences, could be examined for their ideological or social impact—as well as for their abstract "truth" value. History could be written from the bottom up. (In fact, much of this book is written from that perspective; and particular sections, like the preceding discussion of Hobbes and Locke, could not have been written without Marx and the Marxist scholarship tradition.) There is little point then in dwelling on the way Marx and Engels sometimes mechanically and materialistically insisted that the superstructure of ideas copied the structure of social reality. Their ideas of cause and effect were more complex than that. In fact, they accused bourgeois thinkers of imagining that people only worked for money, and the bourgeoisie of creating a society in which one could only work for money. And even when Marx and Engels exaggerated the social roots of ideas, they were themselves reflecting the mechanical and materialistic bias of their industrial age. The important thing is not their mistakes or the limits of vision imposed by their own age but the new questions that they were able to raise and the new methods for critical thought which they devised.

## 1848: *The Communist Manifesto*

Marx the philosopher should not obscure Marx the revolutionary. Philosophy and revolution were not separate occupations for Marx. "The philosophers have only *interpreted* the world in different ways," Marx wrote in 1845, "the point is to *change* it." But an uninformed, mindless desire for change was, for Marx, no better than sterile philosophizing. Successful revolution required a firm philosophical and historical foundation that Marx found lacking in the visions of utopian socialists and the rantings of suicidal revolutionaries.

*The Communist Manifesto* was written in the winter of 1847–1848 as the platform of the Communist League to call for informed revolution. It was a schizophrenic document for a schizophrenic age. In part it looked to the completion of the bourgeois revolution that had only begun in France since 1789 and had barely gotten under way in Germany. And in part it looked to the future socialist revolution that appeared only in embryo in the "hungry forties."

If Marx and Engels had mistaken the birth pangs of bourgeois capitalism in 1848 for its death throes, it was a fault of their broad historical vision. They were able to discern the future developments of the new economic and social system so well that they sometimes imagined it had already occurred. That is why the *Manifesto* exaggerates both the achievements and the failures of bourgeois society in 1848. *The Communist Manifesto* exaggerates the *achievements* of capitalism?

> [Capitalism] has been the first to show what man's activity can bring about. It has accomplished wonders far surpassing Egyptian pyramids, Roman aqueducts and Gothic cathedrals; it has conducted expeditions that put in the shade all former Exoduses of nations and crusades.
>
> The bourgeoisie cannot exist without constantly revolutionizing the instruments of production, and thereby the relations of production, and with them the whole relations of society. . . . All fixed, fast frozen relations, with their train of ancient and venerable prejudices and opinions, are swept away. . . .
>
> The need of a constantly expanding market for its products chases the bourgeoisie over the whole surface of the globe. . . . In place of the old local and national seclusion and self-sufficiency, we have intercourse in every direction, universal interdependence of nations. And as in material, so also in intellectual production. The intellectual creations of individual nations become common property. National onesidedness and narrowmindedness become more and more impossible, and from the numerous national and local literatures there arises a world literature.
>
> The bourgeoisie, by the rapid improvement of all instruments of production, by the immensely facilitated means of communication, draws all, even the most barbarian nations into civilization. . . . It has created enormous cities, has greatly increased the urban population as compared with the rural, and has thus rescued a considerable part of the population from the idiocy of rural life. . . .
>
> The bourgeoisie, during its rule of scarce one hundred years, has created more massive and more colossal productive forces than have all preceding generations together. Subjection of Nature's forces to man, machinery, application of chemistry to industry and agriculture, steam-navigation, railways, electric telegraphs, clearing of whole continents for cultivation, canalization of rivers, whole populations conjured out of the ground—what earlier century had even a presentiment that such productive forces slumbered in the lap of social labor?[19]

Now, certainly all of that had not happened by 1848. National seclusion had not yet been opened to "multinational corporations."

Local provincialism and "rural idiocy" had not yet completely disappeared. National "narrowmindedness" had not yet been replaced by a "world literature." Marx and Engels were able to elaborate the distant future implications of bourgeois capitalism because they understood its dynamic.

The same is true of their exaggeration of the new society's failures. They recognized the transforming potential of the new system and expressed their prophecy in the past tense.

> The bourgeoisie, wherever it has got the upper hand, has put an end to all feudal, patriarchal, idyllic relations. It has pitilessly torn asunder the motley feudal ties that bound man to his "natural superiors," and has left no other nexus between man and man than callous "cash payment." It has drowned the most heavenly ecstasies of religious fervor, of chivalrous enthusiasm, of Philistine sentimentalism, in the icy water of egotistical calculation. It has resolved personal worth into exchange value and in place of the numberless indefensible chartered freedoms, has set up that single, unconscionable freedom—Free Trade. In one word, for exploitation, veiled by religious and political illusions, it has substituted naked, shameless, direct, brutal exploitation.
>
> The bourgeoisie has stripped of its halo every occupation hitherto honored and looked up to with reverent awe. It has converted the physician, the lawyer, the priest, the poet, the man of science, into its paid wage laborers.
>
> The bourgeoisie has torn away from the family its sentimental veil, and has reduced the family relation to a mere money relation.[20]

Again, the future tense would have been more appropriate. European society in 1848 still had significant feudal elements. Serfdom had not entirely disappeared. Aristocracies were still powerful. People had not converted all social relationships into business ones. Cash had not everywhere replaced honor, duty, generosity, and morality. Religion had not completely disappeared. Priests were still honored. Everyone, even physicians, did not work only for money. Absolutely everything was not for sale. Family life was still important. The market economy had not commercialized all of life by 1848.

But today? Just call your doctor and ask. The genius of Marx and Engels was in recognizing the revolutionary nature of the new market, business, or commercial society. They were able to chart the way things were changing by focusing on what was new and elaborating its consequences. They recognized that capitalist or bourgeois society was unleashing forces that would radically change the world—indeed, create a single world. Their historical vision suggested that this world would be immeasurably more productive than the past one—the

■ *"The bourgeoisie has torn away from the family its sentimental veil. . . ." A London street scene by Gustave Doré.* (EPA)

feudal age. But their studies of social classes suggested that the enormous productivity of the new society would also contain the seeds of its own destruction, just as the feudal age had.

The *Manifesto* speaks only generally about these "seeds."

> It is enough to mention the commercial crises that by their periodical return put on its trial, each time more threateningly, the existence of

> the entire bourgeois society. In these crises a great part not only of the existing products, but also of the previously created productive forces, are periodically destroyed. In these crises there breaks out an epidemic that, in all earlier epochs, would have seemed an absurdity—the epidemic of overproduction.[21]

The question of capitalism's crises of periodic depressions was to occupy an important part of Marx's later work for *Capital.* In 1848 it was sufficient to point to the history of commercial crises, and to stress the absurdity of a society drowning in its very productivity because the owners didn't pay the workers enough to buy what they produced.

At times Marx and Engels seemed to agree with their contemporaries that the actual income of the working classes would decline. But they always insisted that the amount of money available to the workers was not the issue. Workers who did not collectively own the factories and other productive means would always be exploited. Private ownership would always mean that the profits of the new productivity would be monopolized by the owning class. Capitalist society would continually increase the gap between owners and workers, but far more importantly it would increase the gap between the potential of its new productivity and its performance. The absurdity of poverty in affluence would deepen, but the absurdity of meaningless, obsolescent, and destructive production would offer no remedy.

## Capitalism, Socialism, and Work: 1850-2050

*The Communist Manifesto* had virtually no effect on the revolutions that swept European society in 1848. The socialist revolution could not be put on the agenda until the bourgeoisie had completed its own revolution and developed capitalist society to the limitations of its power and its contradictions. Despite their exaggerations of the maturity of bourgeois civilization, Marx and Engels realized that the time for socialism was still far off. Later they were to talk of the need to wait possibly 50 years before capitalism had worked itself to death. In 1848 the *Manifesto* spoke of the distant future as if it were the past but concluded with specific proposals geared to the needs of the present. The communists should ally themselves with the bourgeois parties, the *Manifesto* insisted. Only after assuring bourgeois supremacy could the fight against bourgeois society begin.

For a moment after the failure of the revolutions of 1848 Marx and Engels flirted with the idea of speeding up the process. But by

■ *The European revolutions of 1848, which seemed so full of hope in the spring and summer, were crushed in the fall. Here German troops storm a barricade in Frankfurt on September 18, 1848. (Granger)*

1850, and for the rest of their lives, they were committed to a gradual process of study, education, and struggle. Marx worked on *Capital* in London until his death in 1883 and poured his energies into the analysis of the capitalist system. The revolution became increasingly a work of organizing the labor movement and labor parties. Gone was the rhetoric about spontaneous insurrection that had marked some of their writings before 1848. Gone also was the talk of secretive parties and a temporary "dictatorship of the proletariat" that sometimes seemed the only hope in the despair of 1849. The Marxist vision of socialism after 1850 was thoroughly democratic (as it had been before 1849). It awaited the achievements and the contradictions that the *Manifesto* described.

Capitalism recovered from the depressions of 1873 and 1893 with whole colonial territories to lift the burdens of exploitation from the European and North American working classes. The class struggle was abated at home as it became internationalized. Working classes were allowed unions, better wages, social insurance, mass education, and even suffrage as long as they gave their lives to preserve the international imbalance.

The European socialist parties of 1914 screamed that they would never go to war against their brothers in the international working class in order to preserve the colonies that kept capitalism alive. And when war came they enlisted and died in the millions. Modern propaganda created nationalist appeals that no International could drown out.

The Russian Revolution of 1917 offered a foolish moment of hope to the suicidal European movement. Things might have been different if the German socialists had succeeded. But they failed. Socialism and communism became identified with Soviet bureaucracy, Stalinism, and the secret police. European socialists had themselves to blame for accepting the credentials of the Russian Marxists in the first place. They forgot the essence of Marx's historical vision when they imagined that a genuine socialist revolution might occur in the most feudal country of Europe. In 1917 only England and the United States had approached the mature capitalism that would be productive enough to junk oppression. And their colonies gave their system an extended lease on life. Further, the Russian confusion of collectivist industrialization with Marxist socialism allowed the benefactors of Western capitalism to call themselves the democracies and identify socialism with slavery, insolvency, and stupidity. Even Russian industrialization, although more rapid than capitalist, could be compared unfavorably to Western. "See? That's what happens when there's no incentive." Never mind that the Russians were only a generation removed from serfdom.

The collapse of capitalism in 1929 seemed to be the final failure that Marx had predicted. Socialist and communist parties regained some of the strength and prestige they had enjoyed before 1914. But capital had one final option: war. The military state solved the problem of underconsumption (which they called overproduction) by forcing workers to produce things they would never want to buy: bombs.

Capitalism has never fully recovered from the Great Depression of the 1930s except through militarization. Socialism has never fully recovered from Stalinism except by holier-than-thou anticommunist declarations. In some countries—like Italy and France—socialists and communists have revived the "popular front" alliances of the 1930s because communists have become more free of Moscow and socialists have become less xenophobic. In northern Europe—Scandinavia, England, and Germany—democratic socialist parties have governed, but refrained from radically socializing their societies.

European socialist parties have only begun in the last decades to go beyond the social policy of the capitalist welfare state. Before World War II they usually had to satisfy themselves with nationalizing the basic industries—coal, rails, and utilities—that had been bankrupted by private ownership. Nationalizing the losses of capitalists was preferable to leaving them bankrupt. At least necessary social services could be maintained even when they were not profitable in market terms. But the capitalists who favored the nationalization of their own debts were usually powerful enough to prevent governments from entering industries where they might be profitable. As a result, nationalization often gave socialists a bad name. Their administration was always more costly because it had to be.

Since World War II, socialist parties have been more successful at extending public ownership into profitable areas as well. In some cases this has taken the form of nationalization. In others it has taken the form of codetermination of workers and owners at the management level. Recent proposals in Germany, England, and Sweden indicate that the cooperative, egalitarian direction of workers and owners may lead in the near future to elections of majorities of worker, government, and consumer representatives (and the phasing out of stockholder representation entirely) on socially important corporate boards of directors. On the national level, socialist parties have chosen to stake their reputations on comprehensive health care, guaranteed employment, and extensive housing and transportation facilities.

Incredibly enough, it seems to be both the capitalist and communist countries (especially the United States and the U.S.S.R., possibly because of their size) that have taken the most centralized and bureaucratic solutions to economic problems: one is reminded of how Saint-Simonian nationalization can serve the interests of either capitalists or workers. Even the U.S. labor movement generally struggles for centralized solutions: national health insurance, federal employment, U.S. corporate law, and federal regulation of industry. This is because U.S. corporations have historically encouraged state and local governments to bid competitively against each other. Most state and local governments in the United States are too dependent on corporations to even dream of community, worker, consumer, or state and local government ownership and direction of factories, corporations, or even of natural resources.

Perhaps the most interesting proposals for America's third century, however, are those of the modern equivalents of Fourier and Marx, rather than Babeuf or Saint-Simon. Increased national planning is no doubt inevitable (whether for corporations or workers) as economic power has become centralized on national and even international scales. But American democratic socialists like Michael Harrington have revived the possibility of using the federal government to decentralize and democratize economic power. Harrington in his *Socialism* suggests a series of federal initiatives that could increase popular local control of the economy. The federal tax policy could be used, for instance, to channel funds for investment (in new plants and technologies) from corporations (which maximize private profit at a large social cost) to state, regional, and local governments, public corporations, cooperatives, not-for-profit institutions, and even neighborhood associations. A federal "Office of the Future" could also enable regional and local governments to plan new towns, finance public facilities, and purchase necessary plants and resources, backed by federal law that would prevent corporations from playing one locality against another. Similarly, federal law could enable local worker and consumer representatives to sit on the boards of corporations or provide regional governments with the authority to approve or reject the moving or closing of a plant or other major decision that had an important impact on the regional environment, resources, or labor market. Harrington offers a number of other specific proposals that would gradually phase out the use of resources and corporations for private ends: a 100 percent inheritance tax on corporate property every three generations (to encourage fathers to work for their sons, but also to encourage their sons to do the same); opportunities for gainful employment by the gamblers on the stock exchanges (and we might add corporate lawyers, advertising executives, and commercial artists as well); and the encouragement (instead of present prohibition) of public corporation investment in social areas that are profitable as well as marginal.

All of these proposals, Harrington insists, would constitute only a transitional stage from capitalism to socialism. The ideal of a genuinely socialist society in the twenty-first century would be the abolition of compulsory work and money. Perhaps such an ideal would never be fully realized, Harrington admits, but ideals (as Fourier and the utopians realized) are necessary to give direction and energy. This ideal is predicated on the enormous waste of human, natural, and productive resources in capitalist society. A noncompetitive social economy, he suggests, could turn all of the labor devoted to planned obsolescence, arms, duplication, sales, advertising, and other forms of approved confusion and manipulation into creative production. We are rapidly approaching the technological capacity, Harrington implies, that would make Fourier's dream a reality: we can call "work" what people enjoy doing and provide everyone with the fruits of our mutual labors.

## *For Further Reading*

There are a number of good general histories of socialism. Edward Hyams's **The Millennium Postponed: Socialism from Sir Thomas More to Mao Tse-Tung*** is one of the most recent introductory surveys. Edmund Wilson's **To the Finland Station*** is a literary as well as interpretive jewel that traces the tradition back to the philosophy of history of Vico and Michelet and engages the reader with an extensive anecdotal and critical biography of Marx. Michael Harrington's recent **Socialism*** is a demanding, persuasive history of Marxist and democratic socialism. George Lichtheim's **The Origins of Socialism*** is a scholarly history of utopian and Marxist socialism that parallels most closely the period (1789–1848) that we have chosen in the chapter. Melvin J. Lasky's recent **Utopia and Revolution*** includes good selections organized in interesting topical ways.

All of the above are good on the utopian backgrounds of early socialism. One of the best short introductions to utopian thought is still (after 50 years) Lewis Mumford's **The Story of Utopias.*** There is a good collection of modern essays on the history of utopianism (including an excellent one by Lewis Mumford) in **Utopias and Utopian Thought,*** edited by Frank E. Manuel. He and Fritzie P. Manuel have also edited an absorbing collection of French utopian writing, from the late Middle Ages to the present, called **French Utopias: An Anthology of Ideal Societies.*** If the student could read only one early utopian work, Sir Thomas More's **Utopia*** would be it.

On the importance of the Protestant Reformation's expectation of the millennium, Norman Cohn's **The Pursuit of the Millennium*** and Ernest Lee Tuveson's **Millennium and Utopia*** are quite suggestive. Michael Walzer's **The Revolution of the Saints*** and Christopher Hill's **Puritanism and Revolution** and **The World Turned Upside Down*** are especially valuable for the period of the English Civil War. For eighteenth-century utopianism see Carl L. Becker's **The Heavenly City of the Eighteenth-Century Philosophers,*** Kingsley Martin's **French Liberal Thought in the 18th Century,*** and George R. Havens's **The Age of Ideas.*** Manuel's **The Prophets of Paris*** spans the eighteenth and nineteenth centuries with superb studies of Turgot, Condorcet, Saint-Simon, Fourier, and Comte. Sidney Pollard's excellent **The Idea of Progress*** covers the same period more generally.

On the French Revolution, Georges Lefebvre's **The Coming of the French Revolution*** and **The Thermidorians*** are excellent introductions. His **The Great Fear*** is a remarkable specialized study. The best studies of the laboring classes during the revolution are Albert Soboul's **The Sans Culottes*** and George Rude's **The Crowd in the French Revolution.*** Interesting interpretations are Alfred Cobban's **The Social Interpretation of the French Revolution*** and A. de Tocqueville's classic **The Old Regime and the French Revolution.*** For an understanding of the roots of communism in the French Revolution, **The Defense of Gracchus Babeuf,*** edited and translated by John Anthony Scott, has been invaluable. M. J. Sydenham's

* Available in paperback.

**The First French Republic, 1792–1804** is good background. R. R. Palmer's **Twelve Who Ruled** is also useful.

On utopian socialism after the French Revolution, the general introductions mentioned in the first paragraph are the best place to start. The general utopian studies cited in the second paragraph are also invaluable. For Fourier, Jonathan Beecher and Richard Bienvenu's **The Utopian Vision of Charles Fourier*** is excellent. For Saint-Simon, one of the most interesting places to start is the classic by Emile Durkheim, **Socialism and Saint-Simon,** later published as **Socialism.*** Frank E. Manuel's **The Prophets of Paris*** is excellent here also.

On Marx and Marxism, all of the books mentioned in the first paragraph offer good introductions. For introductory biographies, Isaiah Berlin's **Karl Marx: His Life and Environment*** is a good, readable standard interpretation and David McLellan's **Karl Marx*** is a recent lucid introduction. George Lichtheim's **Marxism: An Historical and Critical Study*** is a thorough one-volume analysis. Robert Tucker's **Philosophy and Myth in Karl Marx*** is an interesting theoretical study. Roger Garaudy's **Karl Marx: The Evolution of His Thought*** is a modern French communist interpretation. The first half of Michael Harrington's recent **The Twilight of Capitalism*** also offers (with his **Socialism**) a fascinating new interpretation of Marx.

For interpretations of particular aspects of Marxism, Erich Fromm's **Marx's Concept of Man*** published with a translation from Marx's **Economic and Philosophical Manuscripts** by T. B. Bottomore is an excellent introduction to the early Marx. Herbert Marcuse's **Reason and Revolution: Hegel and the Rise of Social Theory*** is a superb, demanding analysis of Hegel, the Hegelians, and Marx. Istvan Meszaros's **Marx's Theory of Alienation*** is a subtle, thorough treatment of the subject, as is Bertell Ollman's **Alienation.** Schlomo Avineri's **The Social and Political Thought of Karl Marx*** is a more general statement. The economics of Marx are presented in Robert Freedman's **Marx on Economics*** and Ernest Mandel's **The Formation of the Economic Thought of Karl Marx.***

For the writings of Marx, there are many good editions of **The Communist Manifesto*** and a number of collections* of the writings of Marx. There are also a number of small collections of Marxist writings. C. Wright Mills's **The Marxists,*** Sidney Hook's **Marx and the Marxists,*** Arthur P. Mendel's **Essential Works of Marxism,*** and Erich Fromm's **Socialist Humanism*** are all good collections of writings from Marx to Mao.

Background and other approaches to the period between 1789 and 1848 can be found in E. J. Hobsbawm's excellent **The Age of Revolution,*** Jurgen Kuczynski's **The Rise of the Working Class,*** W. Abendroth's **A Short History of the European Working Class,*** and David Caute's **The Left in Europe Since 1789.***

The student who wishes to pursue the study of Marxism, socialism, or communism since 1848 can begin with the general histories mentioned in the first paragraph. Other suggestions for further study can be found in Massimo Savadori's **The Rise of Modern Communism,*** **Revolutions: A Comparative Study from Cromwell to Castro,*** edited by Lawrence Kaplan, and in E. H. Carr's **Studies in Revolution*** or his multivolume **History of Soviet Russia.** Shorter introductions to the Russian Revolution can be found in Theodore H. Von Laue's **Why Lenin? Why Stalin?,*** J. P. Nettl's well-illustrated **The Soviet Achievement,*** and Isaac Deutscher's **The Unfinished Revolution: Russia 1917–1967.*** Bertram D. Wolfe's **Three Who Made a Revolution*** is a mammoth biographical study of Lenin, Trotsky, and Stalin. Of the many approaches to the Chinese Communist Revolution, Jean Chesneaux's **Peasant Revolts in China 1848–1949,*** and Wolfgang Franke's **A Century of Chinese Revolution: 1851–1949,*** and Edgar Snow's personal accounts, especially **Red China Today*** and **The Long Revolution,*** are good places to start. Frederic Wakeman, Jr.'s **History and Will: Philosophical Perspectives of Mao Tse-Tung's Thought*** is difficult but excellent. Two general theoretical studies of revolution deserve special attention: Eric R. Wolf's **Peasant Wars in the Twentieth Century*** surveys the revolutions of Mexico, Russia, China, Vietnam, Algeria, and Cuba; and Barrington Moore, Jr.'s **Social Origins of Dictatorship and Democracy: Lord and Peasant in the Making of the Modern World*** is an enormously challenging interpretation of modern revolutions since the English Civil War.

## Notes

1. Michael Harrington, *Socialism* (New York: Bantam Books, 1973), p. 131.
2. *Ibid.*, p. 22.
3. *The Defense of Gracchus Babeuf: Before the High Court of Vendome*, ed. and trans. John Anthony Scott (New York: Schocken Books, 1967), p. 61.
4. *Ibid.*, pp. 63–64.
5. *Ibid.*, p. 73.
6. *Ibid.*, pp. 57–58.
7. George Lichtheim, *The Origins of Socialism* (New York: Praeger, 1969), p. 32.
8. Jonathan Beecher and Richard Bienvenu, *The Utopian Vision of Charles Fourier: Selected Texts on Work, Love and Passionate Attraction* (Boston: Beacon Press, 1971), pp. 6–7.
9. *Ibid.*, p. 304.
10. *Ibid.*, p. 317.
11. *Ibid.*, pp. 317–318.
12. *Ibid.*, p. 40.
13. *Ibid.*, p. 59.
14. *Ibid.*, p. 68.
15. *Economic-Philosophical Manuscripts*, trans. T. B. Bottomore, in Erich Fromm, *Marx's Concept of Man* (New York: Ungar, 1961, 1966), pp. 98–99.
16. Herbert Marcuse, *Reason and Revolution: Hegel and the Rise of Social Theory* (Boston: Beacon Press, 1941, 1954, 1960), p. 276.
17. *Ibid.*, p. 144.
18. Lichtheim, *Origins*, p. 199.
19. Karl Marx and Friedrich Engels, *The Communist Manifesto*, ed. Samuel H. Beer, trans. Samuel Moore (Northbrook, Illinois: AHM Publishing Corporation, 1955), pp. 12–14.
20. *Ibid.*, p. 12.
21. *Ibid.*, p. 15.

# Chapter 18

# Race and Class

## The Americas Since Slavery

Is American racism declining? Have decades of civil rights legislation abolished racial prejudice and discrimination in the United States? Do black Americans now enjoy the same opportunities as whites? Almost all white Americans would probably answer "yes" to all of these questions. Many white Americans are even convinced that all of the public attention to racism in the last decade has led beyond equality to a privileged status for blacks.

In 1968 *The Report of the National Advisory Commission on Civil Disorders* declared: "Our nation is moving toward two societies, one black, one white—separate and unequal." One of the problems, the commission noted, was the great disparity between white and black family incomes—so important in a society which judges people in terms of the incomes they earn. In 1968 the median black family income was just over $8,000 while the median white family income was just under $14,000. Did that change in the seven years of public attention that followed the commission's report? In 1976 the Bureau of the Census listed the figures (adjusted for inflation) for each year from 1969 to 1975. In each of those years the median black family income was still just over $8,000 while the median white family income had climbed to just *over* $14,000. For each of those years the disparity was essentially the same, but in the six years after 1969 things had gotten worse for blacks.

How is it that things have remained the same, especially when most whites are convinced there has been considerable change? What does that say about America's capacity to create a society of equal opportunity? Is it possible that all of that governmental and media attention of the last decade has only created the illusion of racial progress, and contributed to a white backlash? If so, is the solution of our country's racial inequalities even more difficult than it was then? What is it that has to be done, and why are Americans so slow to do it?

This chapter will try to answer some of these questions in the broader context of the last century. What we have seen as the problem of the last decade is a much broader problem of the history of racism since slavery in the Americas. Just as we expect an end of racism with federal legislation, many of our ancestors expected it to end with the abolition of slavery. Our chapter will suggest that racism did not end, but that new kinds of racism emerged. We will use the insights of sociologists and historians who have seen the newer racism as an emerging problem of class differences: perhaps racial discrimination has become a kind of class discrimination.

## Racism Since Slavery: Class and Race

The relationship between slavery and racism, we have suggested, is a bit more complex than is usually imagined. It almost goes without saying that the development of slave societies in the New World was the cause of an epidemic increase in white racism. But some of the cultural germs of white racism existed in Europe before Columbus, and the societies which imported the most African slaves were frequently the least racist. At the height of slavery (in the middle of the nineteenth century) the United States had one of the lowest proportions of Africans of all the countries in the Americas. At the same time the United States had developed the most sweeping racist doctrines, in the "philosophy" of Southern slaveholders, that existed anywhere.

This fact alone should make us suspicious of the fairly common belief that American racism has declined with the disappearance of slavery. If the most developed slave societies could be the least racist, then the most racist societies might have been those which were least involved in slavery. This was precisely the conclusion of the French aristocrat, Alexis de Tocqueville, when he visited the United States in the 1830s. "The prejudice of race," he wrote in *Democracy in America,* "appears to be stronger in the states that have abolished slavery than in those where it still exists; and nowhere is it so intolerant as in those states where servitude has never been known."[1]

In the same way that racism was more pronounced outside of the Southern states, it became more noticeable after the abolition of slavery. Jim Crow laws which legalized the segregation of the races in everything from maternity wards to cemeteries were first passed in the North before the Civil War. Southern states borrowed such practices only after slavery had been abolished. Whites and blacks had mingled everywhere in the Old South (as on the Latin American plantation). Their contacts were frequently very intimate. They ate at the same table, nursed the same infants, drank, cursed, and made love together. In the language of the sociologist, there was no "physical distance" between the races because the "social distance" was enormous. As long as the slaves "knew their place" they could walk and talk and pray and "rest in peace" right along side their masters.

When blacks were no longer slaves (in the Northern states before the Civil War or in the South after the war) social distance was replaced by physical distance. Slowly, after 1875, the Southern states followed the earlier practice of their Northern neighbors in segregating free blacks from water fountains, toilets, parks, restaurants, schools, hospitals, jobs, and prostitutes. Blacks were forbidden to live in certain places, walk in other places after dark, socialize with whites, or vote. Most of these laws remained in effect until the middle of this century. Many of the practices remain even today.

Maybe the racism of the last hundred years is no worse than the racism of slavery. But it is a different type of racism, and we must understand the difference in order to come to terms with it.

## Paternalistic vs. Competitive Racism

One student of race relations, Pierre L. van den Berghe, in a book called *Race and Racism,* has summarized the differences between the racism of slavery and the modern racism since slavery by calling the former "paternalistic racism" and the latter, more recent variety "competitive racism." In the paternalistic racism of slave society, he says, the members of the subordinate group (the slaves) are viewed as "childish, immature, irresponsible, exuberant, improvident, fun loving, good humored, and happy-go-lucky; in short, as inferior but lovable as long as they stay in 'their place.' "[2] This is the racism of the great slave plantations, celebrated by its defenders in Latin America and the Southern states as a world where master and slave confronted each other as real, living, breathing, thinking human beings. Here social distance allowed for extreme intimacy, as well as the extreme brutality that often accompanies such intimacy. Miscegenation was accepted, and often encouraged. The ruling class mixed its prejudice with oaths of love, service, and loyalty. The slaves either internalized the values of their masters, and (like Uncle Tom) loved their masters, or they rebelled viciously and with dignity, only to be annihilated for their fundamental breach of social order.

These paternalistic societies of masters and slaves duplicate the family relationship of father and children. The master-father loves his children, but only as long as they accept his absolute authority. Like father and child, the master and slave live close to one another. The masters, like fathers, rely on the acceptance of their authority, rather than law. They express their needs as requests (rather than demands) and their subordinates are expected to follow without question. They live "face to face." They have no need of outsiders. The rules are understood by all. Physical intimidation and even coercion is always available, but the paternalistic society operates ideally with the force of custom, habit, and acceptance. In most cases, the slaves are treated by their masters even more like pets than children. When they are "good" they are loved and well cared for. When they bite, they are mercilessly beaten or killed.

The "competitive racism" which replaced the slave regimes in the nineteenth century was almost a polar opposite. Most of these societies were more industrial, and less agricultural. Free blacks lived with free whites in a competitive economy where each was equally able to do the same work. Employers could afford to hire blacks as well as whites ("without prejudice"), and often set one race against another. It is no wonder that poor whites became more racist than the old slaveholders had ever been. The poor whites could no longer accept the slaveowner's image of blacks as good children or pets. As the poor whites themselves took power (after the Civil War in the American South) they saw blacks as "aggressive, insolent, 'uppity,' clannish, dishonest, underhanded competitors for scarce resources and challengers of the status quo."[3]

## Dominative vs. Aversive Racism

The contrast that van den Berghe draws between the racism of slave society and the racism of modern society is not unique. In a more recent book, *White Racism: A Psychohistory,* Joel Kovel suggests a similar comparison. Kovel calls the racism of slavery "dominative racism," implying the same kind of domination of master over slave to which van den Berghe alludes. But instead of using the term "competitive" for the type of racism which has developed on the ashes of slavery, Kovel applies the equally useful term "aversive racism." The term "aversive racism" is valuable in describing the attitudes of whites in the last hundred years because it focuses on one of the central characteristics of modern white racism. Modern racism, Kovel argues, is based on a thorough dislike of (or aversion to) blacks, even to the point of avoiding contact and denying their existence entirely. After emancipation, whites did not expect to lord it over blacks. They simply hoped to avoid them. This is the reason why segregation laws are so new, and segregated housing and schools are such an issue.

The older dominative type of racism did not completely disappear with the emancipation of slaves. The members of the Ku Klux Klan and the poor white leaders of the New South hoped to be just like the slaveholders in controlling blacks. One nineteenth-century poor white leader, Tom Watson, declared that the Negro had "no comprehension of virtue, honesty, truth, gratitude and principle." The South, according to Watson, had to "lynch him occasionally, and flog him, now and then, to keep him from blaspheming the Almighty, by his conduct, on account of his smell and his color."[4]

Meanwhile, the descendants of the slave owners had adopted the more aversive attitude. They spoke of equality, but worked for separation. One of them, Woodrow Wilson, stated in 1912 that he wished to see "justice done to the colored people in every matter; and not mere grudging justice, but justice executed with liberality and cordial good feeling."[5] But President Wilson still issued an executive order which segregated the eating and toilet facilities of federal civil service workers. The hallmark of aversive racism was separate facilities as long as there was some chance of arguing that such facilities were equal.

Race relations since slavery have been based largely on white attempts to ignore the existence of black people. "The nuclear experience of the aversive racist," Kovel writes, "is a sense of disgust about the body of the black person based upon a very primitive fantasy: that it contains an essence—dirt—that smells and may rub off onto the body of the racist. Hence the need for distance and the prohibition against touching."[6]

Le Petit Journal

ADMINISTRATION — 5 CENT. — SUPPLÉMENT ILLUSTRÉ — 5 CENT. — ABONNEMENTS

22me Année — Numéro 1.068

DIMANCHE 7 MAI 1911

SEINE et SEINE-ET-OISE — DÉPARTEMENTS — ÉTRANGER

SCÈNE DE LYNCHAGE AUX ÉTATS-UNIS

Un nègre fusillé sur une scène de théâtre

■ *Dominative racism did not disappear with slavery. Between 1882, when records were first kept, and 1927, 4,951 black men were lynched. Most were hung or shot by mobs, but sometimes it became a sadistic spectacle. In May 1911, the opera house of Livermore, Kentucky, offered one shot with balcony seats and six shots to holders of orchestra tickets. (Snark International, EPA)*

When James Meredith integrated the University of Mississippi, some of his white friends found the walls of their rooms smeared with excrement. When the city of Ann Arbor, Michigan, was in the midst

For improving & preserving the complexion.
Pears' Soap.
Sold everywhere.
unscented tablets
6d each.
larger tablets
scented
1/- each.
Recommended for the complexion.
by Madame Adelina Patti & Mrs Langtry.


■ *This Pears soap ad, from* The Illustrated London News *of 1885 penetrates (as ads often do) the deeper emotional meaning of aversive racism.*

of a civil rights, open-housing drive, the local newspaper made anal typographical errors and printed a letter to the editor which linked the open-housing movement to dogs defecating on lawns.

> Immediately following the civil rights drive, the white citizens became intensely interested in cleaning up their town: a crackdown was ordered on homosexuals, and an antilitter ordinance was frantically passed. The threat had been met with an outburst of moralism and reaction formation: purer and cleaner, the community was able to settle down to business as usual.[7]

## Competitive Racism and Capitalism

Van den Berghe approaches what he calls our modern competitive racism with economic (rather than psychoanalytic) categories that carry much the same meaning. He concentrates on the competitive nature of the modern economy, and finds the roots of postslavery racism there.

> The aftermath of the Civil War marked an abrupt change from a paternalistic to a competitive type of race relations. . . . The old agrarian, feudal world of the slave plantation was destroyed, and with it the traditional master-servant model of race relations. Freed Negroes migrated in great numbers to the cities of the South, and to a lesser extent outside the South, and entered for the first time in direct competition on the labor market with the poor white farmers of the South and the urban white working class of both the North and the South. . . .
>
> Rapid urbanization, the mushrooming of working class slums, high unemployment, massive internal migration, and all the disruptive forces and conflicts of early capitalism contributed to the complete change in patterns of race relations and to a steadily rising tide of racial, ethnic, and religious bigotry.[8]

Though the whole United States economy became transformed by capitalist principles of competition after the Civil War, it did not blossom forth overnight. The Northern economy was based on competitive capitalism long before the Civil War.

Nor were all slave societies paternalistic, feudal remnants from the world of the Middle Ages. Since capitalism was most fully developed in England and the Northern states (after 1800), the sugar plantations in the British Caribbean and the cotton plantations in the South were always more tied to the capitalist market than the Latin American plantations.

Spanish America and Portuguese Brazil were from the beginning colonial operations undertaken by king and church, not businesses. Latin American plantations offered careers for the younger sons of the nobility, a chance for conquest and empire, and an opportunity for the conversion of souls. The Spanish and Portuguese aristocrats had very little sense of maximizing profit by exploiting land and labor to the fullest. When they came to the New World they spent what they earned, saved little, thought less of the productivity of their "enterprise," and sought instead the prestige and honor that came from large households and gracious living. Like the unproductive lords of the Iberian homeland, which was still very medieval, Latin American grandees gave generously when they could, and asked for alms when they could not. They were much more accustomed to leisure than to work. One capitalist visitor to Brazilian slave society told a story which crystallizes the difference between bourgeois capitalist and feudal Iberian psychology. In Rio de Janeiro this traveler came upon a Brazilian beggar who was carried through the streets in a hammock by the two slaves that he owned. When the Brazilian asked the visitor for alms, he replied that the Brazilian might be able to sell the two slaves and use the money to set up a productive enterprise of some kind. The Brazilian beggar replied, "Senhor, I am asking you for money, not advice!"[9]

The roots of aversive racism are not in Brazil, but on the slave plantations of the Caribbean islands, particularly the more directly capitalist ventures—those of British, Dutch, and even Danish business. Here, "the business of the islands was business, the production of agricultural staples; the islands were not where one really lived, but where one made one's money."[10]

Segregation and physical distance, separate black and white housing and facilities, were invented on these islands of black slaves which produced for white men living in London and Amsterdam. Even today, some of these islands bear marks of the most astonishing physical separation. In most cases the only difference is that the pockets of former white luxury are now occupied by black legislators and governors. The physical signs of the two worlds of capitalist slave society remain.

The slave states of the Old South were neither as capitalist as the Caribbean islands nor as feudal as Latin America. Just as North Americans recognized the more human, paternalistic character of Latin American slavery, they realized that their own slave system was less capitalist than that of the West Indies. According to one historian:

> On the generality of the [West Indian] plantations the tone of management was like that in most modern factories. The laborers were considered more as work-units than as men, women, and children. Kindliness and comfort, cruelty and hardship, were rated at balance-sheet value; births and deaths were reckoned in profit and loss, and the expense of rearing children was balanced against the cost of new Africans. These things were true in some degree in the North American slaveholding communities, but in the West Indies they excelled.[11]

Aversive or competitive racism developed in the more capitalist slave societies (like the West Indies) because the businesses in control were less interested in their Africans as people. The slaves were viewed as factory workers or profit-making machines. The European-based entrepreneurs could rest their consciences more easily by living away from the black islands, or by staying clear of the black population when they visited their investments. They never grew to love or hate (or even know) individual slaves, and so they never developed the paternalistic racism of the inbred slave societies of Latin America or the American South.

A certain measure of aversive racism developed in the Northern states before the Civil War. As we have seen, even the liberal abolitionists of the North hoped that once blacks were freed they could be removed to Africa or Latin America. Southern defenders of slavery were often more proslavery than antiblack. The reverse was often true of Northerners. The North kept its racism within bounds, however, simply because there were never too many free blacks who could compete with free whites. After the Civil War that situation changed radically in the South. After the migrations of blacks to the North in the early twentieth century, many whites developed new aversive racial fantasies because the competition with free blacks became so intense.

Since, by its very nature, capitalist society encouraged inequalities in the ownership and control of the country's land, machinery, and resources, the majority of the population was forced to compete for what was left.

In Latin American countries where race had never been a very serious issue, the competition for scarce jobs and resources became, as capitalism replaced slavery, an issue of class. Largely interracial (or nonracial) popular parties channeled the frustrations of the poor into programs which threatened the wealthy families and corporations that controlled so much of the society's resources.

The first semisocialist revolution in the world occurred in Mexico in 1910 (seven years before the Russian Revolution). Insofar as the goals of this revolution were successfully carried out, some of the more flagrant inequalities of capitalist society were abolished. Unfortunately for most Mexicans (like most Russians), the technological development of the country was so minute at the time of the revolution that the main result was only slightly less poverty for 95 percent of the population. But because the popular leaders of the Mexican Revolution were able to see the plight of the poor in class terms rather than racial terms, Mexican society became less racist. Perhaps the fact that Mexico never became very capitalist contributed to the absence of an aversive or competitive racism and encouraged the leaders to seek a social revolution rather than racial oppression. Today Mexicans are working at the same time for a bronze nation, economic development, and a society of relative equality.

Contemporary Brazil is experiencing the kind of capitalist society that the United States passed through in the beginning of this century. Its technological development is also roughly similar. The most capitalist and industrialized section of the country (São Paulo and the south) has clearly entered a stage of competitive (or aversive) race relations. Most observers expect that the rest of the country will follow. Most African Brazilians still do not know when they are discriminated against because of their race and when they suffer because of their lower-class position. Poor Brazilians are torn, more than before, between the prospect of either prejudicially "whitening" their own backgrounds and children or allying themselves with darker members of their class for social change.

After remarking about the surprising absence of African nationalist organizations (like the Muslims) or even civil rights groups (like the NAACP) in Brazil, one American historian suggests that the prejudice which inspires such groups is still developing:

> Yet as Brazil continues to industrialize and the competitive society of classes spreads, the likelihood of increasing discrimination grows, too. Racial tension and color prejudice, as we have seen, already exist in Brazil, but if the experience of Negroes in São Paulo tell us anything, it is that a competitive society encourages discrimination and tension. In part at least, therefore, the history of race relations in the United States may well be in the future of Brazil. For as the social system of Brazil approaches the competitive model of the United States, as the example of São Paulo in this century suggests, then antagonisms between black and white can be expected to rise.[12]

Van den Berghe offers specific evidence that these developments are already happening:

> Rising anti-Negro prejudice in São Paulo, Rio de Janeiro, and elsewhere caused the National Congress to pass a law after World War II making racial discrimination a criminal offense. Such a law had never been necessary before. Even in the cradle of paternalism around Bahia agriculture is being mechanized, and the old emotional ties between white land owners and Negro workers are breaking down. Large industrial sugar mills have replaced the small plantation mills, and the field hands no longer have personal ties to the white employers.[13]

There are still socialist parties in Brazil that urge white and black workers to recognize their class ties rather than their racial differences. It is still possible, since racism has been a minimal force in

Brazilian life, that Brazilians will attempt to rectify the basic inequalities of their society by means of socialist rather than racist solutions. In general, however, the military governments of Brazil have been quite successful in stamping out such challenges to the social system, even when this has meant encouraging racism instead.

There is some comparison between the choice facing Brazilians today and the choice faced by North Americans in the first decades of the twentieth century. But the twentieth-century governments of the United States found it much easier to destroy native socialist parties and create institutional support for competitive racism.

Perhaps, the whites in the United States have always realized that their political freedom, economic opportunity, and prosperity have owed a lot to the suffering of blacks. There was no agreement on independence in the first days of July 1776 among the delegates of the British colonies at Philadelphia until Jefferson changed his Declaration of Independence to permit slavery. Without the concurrence of South Carolina's slaveholding delegates, the colonies lacked the unanimity that was absolutely essential to carry on a successful revolutionary war. Like independence, the Constitution could not have been passed in 1789 if it had abolished slavery. By 1860 slavery had become so important to the way of life of the Southern states that they preferred abolishing the Union to abolishing slavery. The North waged war, not because slavery was racist, but because slavery was part of an almost feudal, paternalistic system which opposed the advance of the new competitive business economy. Lincoln spoke for the material needs (in the moral language) of the new economy. The new industrial corporations required an abundance of free labor, a unified country, and a centralized federal government.

For a brief moment between 1865 and 1875 Congress, under the influence of the Radical Republicans, acted as if it believed that the new competitive economy and racial justice were compatible. The force of this legislation can be seen from the fact that even after the civil rights legislation of the 1960s some of the most sweeping recent court decisions have been based on the less equivocal *earlier* laws.

The period since 1875 must be reckoned as the great age of aversive or competitive racism in the United States. At times, especially in the South, American racism reached and surpassed some of the violent forms of repression of the old dominative, paternalistic period. But more normally, blacks suffered from neglect and segregation and were isolated from the justice of the courts or the material wealth of the society. They were free laborers in the worst jobs the economy offered, granting their employers the freedom to fire them in bad times. They were deprived of police protection, quality education, and public facilities while states and municipalities regained their freedom

■ *The signs of aversive racism were easy to read from the 1890s to 1954 (this one actually from 1956), but have since become more subtle.* (UPI)

to govern themselves. They were free to move from rural squalor to urban ghettos, as long as they didn't follow too closely on the heels of European ethnic minorities or change neighborhoods too quickly.

## Conclusion: From Causes to Solutions

Let us return to the question we raised at the end of our introduction. Why do things keep getting worse? Why has it been so difficult for whites to accept and deal with the conclusions of presidential commissions? The answer is, as we suggested, that racism goes deep. After a long history it has become almost second nature to respond to the warnings of presidential commissions and other studies with the sincere conviction "That's not me; I'm not prejudiced." And yet, to quote another student of American racism:

> To speak of white racism in America does not mean that everyone who is white believes that the white man possesses some innate superiority. It does mean that American society *operates* as though this were the case, that the *nature* of American society is the same *as if* this belief were held by all whites. One must look at the gross effects of the society's institutions and activities to understand that, regardless of individual exception, the total effect of this society is comparable to that of a society based on the ideology of white supremacy.[14]

Now that we have had a look at some of the institutions and activities that have led us to our present crisis, we can begin to piece together some of the answers. First, there is some hope in our conclusion that all societies are not racist. The sense of cultural superiority of some cultures is very different from modern racism. We might also find a bit of encouragement in our finding that modern racism is only partly a product of our heritage in slavery. Just as the racism of some slave societies could be relatively benign, it might also be avoidable with the abolition of slavery. We noticed that Mexico and (to a lesser extent) Brazil have been moderately able to escape the racist heritage of slave society.

The Latin American solution of miscegenation is no longer open to us. At least in the next hundred years or so we cannot realistically expect the people of the United States to eliminate race through intermarriage. But perhaps the more recent element of the Latin American solution is open to us. It might still be possible for us to build a less competitive society where people's common needs are emphasized more than their differences. If our personal and social goals were put in the form of providing meaningful work and leisure, decent housing, adequate medical care and education, and popular political participation *for all,* instead of the opportunity to beat out the next guy to the top, we might have a way of emphasizing commonality rather than difference.

The abolition of social differences (and race, as we have seen is only one of these) is by no means utopian. At least many societies have deemphasized such differences. Our problem is that the abolition of social differences or the competitive mentality has usually been associated with socialism, and socialism is as unpopular as it is misunderstood in the United States.

But what are the alternatives? Until the 1960s many American

■ *The signs of dominative racism were always clear when blacks asserted themselves. This photo was taken "after a near riot erupted during a 'sit-in' by a group of women recipients of city welfare" in Boston on June 2, 1967. According to the National Commission's Report, the chief cause of the "riots" of the summer of 1967 was white racism.* (UPI)

leaders used to suggest that the United States could build such an abundant economy that differences in wealth or prestige would be meaningless; everyone would be able to lead a rewarding, fruitful life; there would be enough to go around twice, and still leave some "more equal than others." That this has not happened does not mean that it cannot, but we are less optimistic than we used to be about the machine abolishing social differences. At least, the differences between rich and poor in the United States are about as great as they ever were, despite the benefits of the machine, and we are now aware that we have been spending more than we possessed. Competition, too, seems as virulent as ever. Further, the assumption that blacks or the poor will be satisfied with their slice of the pie as long as the pie gets larger and larger makes no sense in a stable economy.

Racism as a problem only of class or social differences is still an enormous problem. We are asked to give up some of the basic assumptions and practices which we have acquired over hundreds of years of capitalist development. This has been difficult enough in countries like Mexico and Cuba, which never had as much of a commitment to capitalism, competition, and free enterprise as we do.

Unfortunately, our problem is even greater than overcoming class differences or our competitive second nature. More than the Latin Americans, we have made race a separate issue from the issue of class. We have grown accustomed to believe that we can have a classless society while we forge new racist differences. In fact, we have been doing just that for some time. Ideally, race would only be one type of class or social differentiation. Ideally, people would see only rich and poor, educated and illiterate, powerful and weak, regardless of color. Race has no separate meaning aside from these social distinctions—except to the racist. And white Americans have been racists.

On this level, whites have to deal not only with their attitudes toward class and competition, but also with their ingrained attitudes toward blacks. Here our analysis of our Christian, Elizabethan, and modern cultural heritage is very disturbing. If Kovel is right when he suggests that whites treat black people like dirt, then the problem is almost irremediable. If racism makes whites feel cleaner and purer and more "enlightened" (as it makes them more prosperous), it would be too costly psychologically (as well as materially) to face. It is much easier to continue aversive racism by avoiding it.

## *For Further Reading*

The general studies referred to in this chapter, Pierre L. van den Berghe's **Race and Racism: A Comparative Perspective*** and Joel Kovel's **White Racism: A Psychohistory*** are well worth reading in their entirety. Van den Berghe develops his categories of racism from studies of Mexico, Brazil, South Africa, and the United States, and his presentation is pretty straightforward. Kovel's book is highly intuitive and speculative in its attempt to psychoanalyze all of Western culture. Both have good bibliographies.

C. Vann Woodward's **The Strange Career of Jim Crow*** is still an essential introduction to the development of aversive or segregationist racism since slavery. Thomas F. Gossett's **Race: The History of an Idea in America,*** Winthrop Jordan's **White Man's Burden*** and **White Over Black*** are excellent introductions to the culture of racism. William Stanton's **The Leopard's Spots*** is also a very good study of the history of American racial ideas. There are also a number of good historical and psychological excerpts in **White Racism: Its History, Pathology and Practice,** edited by Barry N.

* Available in paperback.

Schwartz and Robert Disch.* Oscar Handlin's **Race and Nationality in American Life*** is still a useful general statement. **The Report of the National Advisory Commission on Civil Disorders*** is still quite relevant. If the student reads only one literary work on the subject, it should be **The Autobiography of Malcolm X.***

The student who wishes to pursue some of the psychoanalytic interpretations raised in the chapter and in Kovel's book might best begin with Sigmund Freud's **A General Introduction to Psychoanalysis.*** For the use of psychoanalytic categories in the interpretation of Western culture, Erik Erikson's **Young Man Luther*** and Norman O. Brown's **Life Against Death*** are especially suggestive. For an understanding of the psychology of racism in the broader context of authoritarianism (the approach of most modern Freudians), Erich Fromm's **Escape from Freedom*** might be the best place to start. **The Authoritarian Personality,*** by T. W. Adorno and others, is the classic preliminary investigation. Erik Erikson's **Identity: Youth and Crisis*** and **Childhood and Society*** explain racism and authoritarianism in terms of unresolved life crises. Wilhelm Reich's **Mass Psychology of Fascism*** is intuitive and controversial. Herbert Marcuse's **One-Dimensional Man*** and **Eros and Civilization*** are difficult but highly suggestive reformulations of Freud and Marx. Albert Memmi's **Dominated Man*** and Hannah Arendt's **The Origins of Totalitarianism*** are more directly concerned with racism. The work of Frantz Fanon is also invaluable. His **Black Skin, White Masks,* The Wretched of the Earth,*** and **Toward the African Revolution*** are extremely perceptive psychoanalytical investigations of the meaning of racism for blacks. Alex Haley's popular **Roots*** might be read as a literary recreation of the culture of racism and its psychological dimension in America.

On the issue of race and class, the work of Eugene Genovese, especially **In Red and Black,*** is quite perceptive. Harold Cruse's **Crisis of the Negro Intellectual*** is an extensive study of the struggle between racial and socialist solutions in the context of twentieth-century history. For the cross-cultural comparison with Brazil, Carl Degler's **Neither Black Nor White*** is again a useful recent introduction. Also valuable are Gilberto Freyre's **The Mansions and the Shanties,*** Irving L. Horowitz's **Revolution in Brazil,** and **Race and Class in Rural Brazil,** edited by Charles Wagley, and Thomas E. Skidmore's **Black Into White: Race and Nationality in Brazilian Thought.**

## Notes

1. Alexis de Tocqueville, *Democracy in America* (New York: Random House, 1945), vol. I, p. 373. The same point is made by a modern historian, Eugene H. Berwanger, in *The Frontier Against Slavery: Western Anti-Negro Prejudice and the Slavery Extension Controversy.*
2. Pierre L. van den Berghe, *Race and Racism: A Comparative Perspective* (New York: Wiley, 1967), p. 27.
3. *Ibid.*, p. 30.
4. Quoted in Joel Kovel, *White Racism: A Psychohistory* (New York: Random House, 1971), p. 30.
5. *Ibid.*, p. 31.
6. *Ibid.*, p. 84.

7. *Ibid.*, p. 89. Kovel's examples of the University of Mississippi and Ann Arbor are attributed to James Hamilton's "Some Dynamics of Anti-Negro Prejudice," *Psychoanalytic Review* 53 (1966–1967):5–15.
8. Van den Berghe, *Race and Racism*, pp. 85–86.
9. Eugene D. Genovese, *The World the Slaveholders Made* (New York: Pantheon, 1969), p. 59.
10. Winthrop D. Jordon, "American Chiaroscuro: The Status and Definition of Mulattoes in the British Colonies," *William & Mary Quarterly*, 3rd ser., 19 (April 1962):196.
11. Ulrich Bonnell Phillips, *American Negro Slavery* (New York: Prentice-Hall, 1918), p. 52.
12. Carl N. Degler, *Neither Black Nor White* (New York: Macmillan, 1971), pp. 281–282.
13. Van den Berghe, *Race and Racism*, pp. 74–75.
14. Barry N. Schwartz and Robert Disch, ed., *White Racism: Its History, Pathology, and Practice* (New York: Dell, 1970), p. 65.

# Chapter 19

# Individuality and Society

## The Self in the Modern World

On the fifteenth day of the month Xanthicus in the fourth year of the emperor Vespasian (A.D. 73) the 960 Jews at the fortress of Masada near the Dead Sea killed themselves at the urging of Eleazar, rather than surrender to the Roman troops. Men killed their children and wives in a last embrace, then selected ten by lot to kill the rest. The last ten selected one who killed the nine and then himself. The historian Josephus imagined what Eleazar must have said: "For let our wives die undishonored; our children, before they know what slavery is; and, when once they are removed, let us confer a noble favor on one another, preserving our freedom as a becoming shroud."[1]

On 18 November 1978 almost a thousand members of an American religious cult called the People's Temple in Guyana, South America, killed themselves at the urging of their leader, Jim Jones, who imagined American military retaliation for the murder of a Congressman. Parents forced the Kool Aid laced with cyanide down the throats of their children, drank it themselves, and joined hands as they died. The "Dear Dad" letters from members to Jones reflect their complete devotion to their leader and their willingness to die for him and his cause: "Dad has been the best thing that has ever happened to me"; "You freed me"; "I just drink the potion"; "I'm like a banana—just one of the bunch"; "I would gladly die."[2]

What makes an individual commit suicide on behalf of a larger cause? When does a cause, a cult, a religion, or a community become more important than one's own life? Why do children have to be killed by their parents? Does society give us reasons for dying as well as reasons for living? Is religion dangerous to one's health or life? Are people with little individuality more likely to kill themselves? Is the undeveloped self easier to extinguish?

And how have things changed? Is our instinct for self-survival as undeveloped as it was two thousand years ago? Do we have as little sense of individuality as then? If we live in a more individualistic age, how do these things still occur? Is there some hope in the fact that the Masada suicides were praised as noble by Jews and Romans while the Guyana suicides horrified everyone? Do we value individual life more than people used to? If so, why and how? And what accounts for Guyana?

These are some of the questions that prompt this chapter on individuality in the modern world. Our thesis is that our capacity for individuality and self-survival *has* increased since Masada. The causes of that increase can be found in the decline of world views (like religion) that value a "life beyond death" more than this life. They can also be found in the passing of what we have elsewhere called "hardship society" and in the development of societies of abundance. The capacity exists for people in modern society to lead more fruitful, expressive, and individualistic lives than was ever possible (except for the very few) in ancient societies. Especially in the industrialized, literate, specialized, mobile, and democratic Western world, the possibilities for developing creative individualized identities are unique in world history. A contrast with the hardship societies of Asia will underline the possibilities of the West.

But it is also our thesis that the possibilities of individuality in the West have not been realized. There has been a contradiction between the *capacity* for individuality and the *actuality.* The reasons for this are worth exploring. They have something to do with our particular religious heritage, even as it has become secularized. And they have something to do with our particular forms of economic organization. We find in the dynamics of Protestantism and capitalism both the development of individualistic capacity and the limitations of its realization.

## Medieval Social Salvation and Modern Specialization

Modern society, of course, is fantastically more complex and specialized than Roman society was. But modern society has become specialized only in the last few hundred years. During the Middle Ages Europeans lost some of the specialization and individuality that the Romans had known. The Middle Ages produced no Augustines or Trimalchios and nothing as individualistic as Hellenistic art or the philosophy of Socrates. The individual almost seems to have disappeared from the art and writings of the Middle Ages.

The Europeans of the Middle Ages were still Christians. In fact, all of Europe became Christian during this period. But medieval Christianity was very different from the personal religion that Augustine had experienced. The Catholic church which Augustine, and others, were just beginning to establish in the Roman Empire grew into a huge, successful organization in the Middle Ages. Big organizations are rarely interested in encouraging the individual to be his or her own authority. Therefore, organized churches usually teach that the individual cannot know God as well as the organization does. The medieval Catholic church was no exception. Its priests, bishops, popes, and other officials insisted that the individual could only be saved inside the organization. They established institutions like the sacraments and the mass, and insisted that no one could be saved without them. They worked out an elaborate set of beliefs which they felt all Christians must accept. The Christians of the Middle Ages were still intent on saving individual souls, but the saving had become an institutional, or social, process.

Even the word "individual" meant something very different in the Middle Ages than it means today. When we say that someone is a real individual, we mean that he or she is different, unusual, or separate from the rest of us. In the Middle Ages, "individual" meant "inseparable"—almost the exact opposite of what it means today. An individual in the Middle Ages was someone who was representative or typical of, or inseparable from, his or her group. The individual was the person who was the best example of the class, family, trade, nation, or general group that was being described.

The society of the Middle Ages was highly organized into stable, unchanging classes, more appropriately called "castes" or "estates" because a person was virtually unable to work his or her way out of one class into another. Consequently, a man might think of himself first as a member of a particular estate or occupation. He was not primarily John Jones. His main identity was as a priest or bishop in the church's estate, or as a duke or baron in the nobility's estate, or as a farmer or baker in the "third estate." Personal names were used to indicate their membership in a large group. The members of a noble family would be known by their titles: the prince, the count, or the baron of "such and such." A family of metalworkers would come to be known as Smith or Goldsmith. Barrel makers were called "coopers." Hence, a particular barrel maker might be known as Gary the Cooper.

Since identities in the Middle Ages derived from the groups in which individuals were born and died, their hopes and ambitions focused on the group, not on themselves. They wanted things for their village, church, friends and relatives, not for themselves. People felt a great number of responsibilities to others which we have forgotten, and they enjoyed a greater sense of belonging and security than we do.

The modern individual emerged as this secure, stable, estate society of the Middle Ages disintegrated. This happened gradually in Europe a few hundred years ago, and is still beginning to occur in most of the rest of the world. There were many causes of the breakdown of ordered, estate society. One of the most important causes was the rise of a middle class population of merchants and traders who found estate society too confining for their individual talents and ambitions. These early capitalists gradually made money and wealth as important as birth and family, and they turned the largely public land of the Middle Ages into modern private property.

Finally, in the 1700s and 1800s, these new middle-class capitalists began an industrial revolution which continues today to make people's jobs and life styles more and more specialized or individualized. While people in the Middle Ages belonged to only three estates and worked in only 10 or 20 occupations, modern industrial society has created hundreds of thousands of different ways of working, living, relaxing, and thinking. The variety of lives in industrial society has given us a variety of experiences. Each person today has unique experiences which separate him or her from neighbors and allow the development of individuality.

Modern individuality is, then, at least partly the result of the fantastic degree of specialization in industrial society. But some aspects of that specialization were more influential than others in developing our privacy and individuality. Two kinds of specialization —so crucial that they are often taken for granted—are the room and the printed book.

## The Room and the Book: Origins of Modern Individuality

There were no specialized rooms (except for kings and Trimalchios) before the last couple of hundred years. Even in Europe around 1700, both the large town houses of the wealthy and the cabins of the poor contained no special bedrooms, dining rooms, offices, or living rooms. The very rich (as well as the poor) used collapsible beds in each room for sleeping and collapsible tables for eating. Lawyers, bankers, and judges entertained their friends, ate, conducted business and slept in the same rooms (and often at the same time). Visitors, children, and servants frequently slept together in the same rooms, often in the same beds. The toilets of those who could afford indoor plumbing were also located in one of these all-purpose rooms. (The unusually modest would sit behind a special hand-held mask.) Each room led directly into another. Hallways and closed doors were extremely rare in 1700.

Privacy was clearly impossible in this kind of society. Without special rooms and private rooms, no one could ever be alone for very long. The houses of the rich and well-born were crowded with servants, priests, employees, clerks, shopkeepers, doctors, debtors, widows, children, and friends. Swarms of visitors were forever coming and going, staying the night or a few months. Hired teachers constantly complained that they could not teach the master's children because the traffic was too heavy, the rooms were too crowded, and there were too many distractions. Because of these conditions, some of the wealthy even took the chance of sending their sons away to college, even though everyone recognized that colleges were places of vice, moral decay, riots, and violence.

Even the king of France in 1700, Louis XIV, had surrounded himself with most of the French aristocracy in his palace at Versailles. Each day some 20 or 30 of these nobles would receive the special honor of assisting the king at his toilet or participating in the daily ritual of the king's waking and retiring. When the queen gave birth to a child, everyone crowded around to watch and partake in the royal event. Even our most private event, the wedding night, was a publice occasion three hundred years ago. The friends and relatives of the bride and groom would barge in on the couple after they had gone to bed, and they all would drink, dance, and joke most of the night.

Since there was no privacy, there could be very little private identity. All of life was public partly because there was very little private space. Before the 1700s almost everyone lacked the room and rooms to develop private lives and private identities. The "inventions" of the bedroom and the bathroom and the office in the 1700s were significant events in the development of the individual.

However, empty rooms do not alone make individuals; nor do rooms which are full of what everyone else's room contains. Instead, individuality depends on private experience, especially private learning experience. This was made possible after 1500 by the printed book, a source of knowledge and experience which could be (in fact, had to be) read and digested in private.

Before the invention of the printing press around 1450, all written knowledge (literature, philosophy, science) was handwritten. Since copying was such an arduous task, there were very few copies of anything available. As a result, people read very little, or if they acquired something interesting, it was read aloud to others. Most people knew essentially the same things. They read the same limited material, and they read it as a group. Few people had any specialized knowledge.

The invention of printing eventually put books into the hands of almost everyone, and it vastly increased the number of titles which could be "copied." Reading aloud became a waste of time when people (at least among the upper and middle classes) could read for themselves. Private reading was faster than public reading, but is also led to personal interpretations which were not continually checked with the interpretations of a group. As a result, people's ideas no longer developed exactly along the same lines or at the same pace. Books also permitted people to become specialists in certain subjects. Since a single person could no longer know everything that was written, different people learned different things. People became more specialized in their knowledge and more individualistic in their experiences.

In the eighteenth century, a very small percentage of the European population could benefit from the private space of separate rooms and the individualized knowledge afforded by printed books. Only in the nineteenth century did these luxuries of a few begin to become available to the mass of European peasantry and working classes, and even then only gradually. The spread of literacy, the cheap serialized novel that depicted the private worlds of individuals now hidden behind social roles, the public school movements, and the building technology of private space came slowly to the lower and middle classes of Europeans and Americans with the industrial revolution.

## Industrialization and Individuality

The process of industrialization created opportunities for individuality that were unimagined in traditional society. The specialization of labor that industrialization depended upon multiplied the number of job options and the number of job experiences available. By the nineteenth century, one did not have to choose merely between working in the church, working for the state, or pursuing a profession in law, science, or business. A vast host of opportunities presented themselves. Even the laborer, who was bound by the necessity of survival rather than the luxury of choice, would develop differently (which is to say individually) by the job he or she was forced to take. A list of occupations or trades which would have numbered in the dozens in the eighteenth century could be numbered in the hundreds in the nineteenth century, and in the thousands by the early twentieth century. Whether one chose by education, or merely by market demand, it was possible for the first time in human history to lead a life that was vastly different from that of one's neighbors and friends.

The proliferation of choices entered every aspect of life. It was necessary to ask not only what one was to do, but where one was to live, how one was to spend leisure time, what one was aiming for, how one was to bring up the children, and who one was to marry.

Nineteenth- and early twentieth-century literature is full of signs of the new joys and agonies of individual choices and separate lives. While the popular "rags to riches" novels suggested alternative life goals for the working class, the middle-class novels (which had been unnecessary in an earlier, more communal age) opened one's eyes to the privacies of the lives of the boss, the butcher, the mayor, or neighbor in hundreds of pages of details. Newspapers, like novels, had to detail events (as well as purchasing possibilities in the advertisements) that were unknown or unnecessary in a simpler age. At the intellectual apex of society, "romantic" novelists and poets sung of individual insights and feelings in an orgy of introspection and self-awareness.

The new age echoed the sentiments of Rousseau's *Confessions* (completed in 1770), at once more arrogant and vulnerable than Augustine's:

> I am undertaking a work which has no example, and whose execution will have no imitator. I mean to lay open to my fellow-mortals a man just as nature wrought him; and this man is myself.
>
> I alone. I know my heart, and am acquainted with mankind. I am not made like anyone I have seen; I dare believe I am not made like anyone existing. If I am not better, at least I am quite different. Whether Nature has done well or ill in breaking the mould she cast me in, can be determined only after having read me.[3]

The individualistic assumptions of the age of romanticism (from Rousseau to the middle of the nineteenth century) are those of Emerson's essay on "Self-Reliance":

> To believe your own thought, to believe that what is true for you in your private heart is true for all men—that is genius. . . . Trust thyself: every heart vibrates to that iron string. . . . Whoso would be a man, must be a nonconformist.[4]

Nineteenth-century romanticism invented a whole stock of images and ideas that have since become the core of Western individualism. The genius, the hero, the nonconformist, the artist, the intellectual, the pioneer, even the inventor, are inventions of nineteenth-century imagination. The importance of imagination, creativity, personality, self-expression, dreams, the unconscious, self-consciousness has evolved since the nineteenth century in European and American culture. Modern literature, modern psychology, modern art, modern political ideals cannot be understood except as elaborations of this unique departure in world history. Modern men and women are the first to begin with a culture that values individual expression and opportunity above conformity and authority.

## Class and Individuality in the Nineteenth Century

The personal visions of romantic philosophers and poets were expressed for all to read. But in the early nineteenth century few could read. What about the working classes and lower classes of industrial society? Did they also experience greater individuality in the course of industrialization and the expansion of market society? Most of our knowledge of the lower classes comes from the records and the laws of their administrators. Perhaps, if we adjust for their critical eye, we see evidence of a greater freedom of individual expression among the governed as well.

In 1851 the interior ministry of Munich, Germany, issued the following assessment of popular morality:

> Increasing impiety, widespread laziness and pleasure-seeking, the lack of domesticity, the ever-growing overestimation of self, the newly rising indifference to the interest of the community when a question of personal advantage is involved—all these are phenomena which, the more they emerge, the more emphatically they reveal that the basic pillars of the social order are deteriorating.[5]

Public administrators complained of popular "immorality" in dancing, drinking, sexuality, and even dress. "Is it still possible to tell the chambermaid from the lady, the valet from the royal councilor, the countinghouse clerk from the banker?" a Bavarian parliamentarian asked rhetorically. Even the farmer, he added, had adopted the middle-class burger's coat "with its metal buttons."[6]

It is always difficult to tell how much of this is new, and how much is the traditional complaint of the upper class, the administrator, or the older generation. But the complaints of nineteenth-century administrator's are full of new words: self-esteem, emancipation, independence, libertine comportment, social ambition, impudence, isolation, wildness, and egoism. Further, the causes of such behavior were often found in the social changes that accompanied the capitalist industrialization of the period. "All sense of what is just and proper is being lost. . . . The dignity of the family bond, the discipline of the household, is disappearing. . . . The trend to a more independent life-style is predominant. . . . Such a variety of distractions are now offered . . . the bonds have loosened not only between master craftsman and journeyman, between employer and servant, but among the members of the smaller family circle as well."[7]

Although "dating" was a later, twentieth century, source of individual growth, the popularity of dances during the nineteenth century, and the declining influence of the family in matchmaking, seem to have increased individual social contact and romantic experimentation. Statistics from Germany show, for instance, a marked increase in the percentage of bridal pregnancies in the nineteenth century, suggesting both greater moral mobility and romantic choice—key signs of greater self-definition.

The passing of the traditional guild relationship of master and apprentice could also increase the leisure time and opportunity for self-expression. Outside of factories, and before the development of twentieth-century techniques of "scientific management," the worker could follow personal urges and inclinations denied by the earlier watchful master or the later time conscious manager. An observer of a midnineteenth-century New York shipyard describes the morning's work:

> In our yard, at half-past eight a.m., Aunt Arlie McVane, a clever, kindhearted, but awfully uncouth, rough sample of the "Ould Sod," would make her welcome appearance in the yard with her two great baskets, stowed and checked off with crullers, doughnuts, ginger-bread, turnovers, pieces, and a variety of sweet cookies and cakes; and from the time Aunt Arlie's baskets came in sight until every man and boy, bosses and all, in the yard, had been supplied, always at one cent a piece for any article on the cargo, the pie, cake and cookie trade was a brisk one. Aunt Arlie would usually make the rounds of the yard and supply all hands in about an hour, bringing the forenoon up to half-past nine, and giving us from ten to fifteen minutes "breathing spell" during lunch; no one ever hurried during "cake-time."

After this was over, we would fall to again, until interrupted by Johnnie Gogean, the English candy-man, who came in always at half-past ten, with his great board, the size of a medium extension dining table, slung before him, covered with all sorts of "stick," and several of sticky candy, in one-cent lots. Bosses, boys, and men—all hands, everybody—invested one to three cents in Johnnie's sweet wares, and another ten to fifteen minutes is spent in consuming it. Johnny usually sailed out with a bare board until 11 o'clock at which time there was a general sailing out of the yard and into convenient grogshops after whiskey.[8]

One is struck, in passages like this, by both the opportunities for personal growth in the leisurely, convivial atmosphere of the early industrial working place and also by the similarity of individual actions. Working men were still not bound to the routines of the machine (at least outside of the factories), they were still able to gratify individual needs for fun and comradeship at work, but they all, "bosses, boys, and men—all hands," lay out their cent for Aunt Arlie, their couple of cents for Johnnie Gogean, and sail out to the grogshop.

The opportunities for individual expression in leisure activity have increased greatly since the midnineteenth century, but so has the discipline of the working place. By the end of the nineteenth century workers were more often governed by the discipline of the machine than the appearance of Aunt Arlie or the need for grog. "It is no longer simply that the individual workman makes use of one or more mechanical contrivances for effecting certain results," the American economist Thorstein Veblen pointed out in 1904. That used to be the case: machines added to the workman's ability to do his work. But the "particularly modern" character of machine work, Veblen adds, is that the discipline of machine production dominates the workman.

He now does this work as a factor involved in a mechanical process whose movement controls his motions. . . . The process standardises his supervision and guidance of the machine. Mechanically speaking, the machine is not his to do with it as his fancy may suggest.[9]

Instead of encouraging the expression of the worker's creativity (the way tools and simple machines did in the traditional working place), the modern factory of machines requires constant attention, mechanical thinking, and conformity.

His place is to take thought of the machine and its work in terms given him by the process that is going forward. His thinking in the premises is reduced to standard units of gauge and grade. If he fails of the precise measure, by more or less, the exigencies of the process check the aberration and drive home the absolute need of conformity.

> There results a standardization of the workman's intellectual life in terms of mechanical process, which is more unmitigated and precise the more comprehensive and consummate the industrial process in which he plays a part. . . . The machine process is a severe and insistent disciplinarian in point of intelligence. It requires close and unremitting thought, but it is thought which runs in standard terms of quantitative precision. Broadly, other intelligence on the part of the workman is useless; or it is even worse than useless, for a habit of thinking in other than quantitative terms blurs the workman's quantitative apprehension of the facts with which he has to do.[10]

Whether the working classes of industrial society were more or less individualistic at the end of the nineteenth century than they were at the beginning, or middle, of the century would be difficult to say. What is clear is that the capitalist industrial revolution initiated processes which both individualized human experiences and required new kinds of mechanical conformity. We will look first at the positive side of this development—the liberal ideal of the late nineteenth century—and then return to some of the negative features of modern "managed society."

## The Triumph of Liberalism

Any exploration of individuality in the modern age must come to grips with the triumph of Western middle-class liberalism at the end of the nineteenth century. Like the earlier Western ideals of romanticism, liberalism was a uniquely Western credo of the age of industrialization. Like romanticism, it was a philosophy of the new, educated middle class that put individual freedom in the forefront.

One speaks of the "triumph" of liberalism perhaps a bit optimistically. Liberalism never became the majority philosophy in European and American society or elsewhere. But liberal ideals were enunciated with more care and power in the nineteenth century (more broadly, from 1776 to 1914) than before or since. The nineteenth century hosted the only "triumph" that liberalism knew.

Its ideals were freedom of thought, freedom of expression, toleration, diversity, general education and suffrage (voting), the capacity of reason, the power of ideas, and the sanctity of the individual. We could trace its growth in the gradual extension of the suffrage, in the abolition of serfdom and slavery, in the development of mass education, in the developing gospel of free trade, or even in the growth of social welfare legislation (though liberalism always stopped short of socialism).

We prefer to look at one of the most famous documents of the movement and the era, John Stuart Mill's essay *On Liberty,* which he wrote, with his wife, Harriet Taylor, between 1855 and 1858, and published in 1859 (the year Darwin published the *Origin of Species*).

"The object of this essay is to assert one very simple principle," Mill wrote.

> That principle is that the sole end for which mankind are warranted, individually or collectively, in interfering with the liberty of action of any of their number is self-protection. That the only purpose for which power can be rightfully exercised over any member of a civilized community, against his will, is to prevent harm to others. His own good, either physical or moral, is not a sufficient warrant. He cannot rightfully be compelled to do or forbear because it will be better for him to do so, because it will make him happier, because, in the opinion of others, to do so would be wise or even right. These are good reasons for remonstrating with him, or reasoning with him, but not for compelling him.[11]

That statement shows both the liberation and limitation of middle-class, capitalist liberalism. It carries the class concept of liberty (in Hobbes and Locke) into the dawning age of universal suffrage and toleration. (Mill includes the working classes, but excludes children and "barbarians.") It brings to logical conclusion the recognition, implicit in Hobbes, that there are no absolute truths, but only power and human reason. And it magnifies the importance of the individual while further limiting the power of the state and the community. But it accepts a view of the individual as sacred in its separateness (the isolated, free-choosing atom of market society) by its assumption that a line can be drawn between individual action and "harm to others." *On Liberty* is a testament to individual integrity and freedom because it no longer has to assume the community interest and mutual responsibility that market society was annihilating. The doctrine (to put it crudely) that one's freedom ends where another's nose begins is a useful guide to political legislation only in a society where people relate as strangers.

Mill's defense of freedom of thought and expression would (unfortunately) make little sense in a premarket community governed by traditional absolutes. It is based on assumptions that would not be accepted in traditional society: that the majority opinion might be wrong; that even when it is right it must be challenged or it will become dogma or prejudice; that making choices, even "wrong" ones, is essential to individual growth.

Market society created the necessary conditions for Mill's individualism, skepticism, rationality, and preference for process. It freed the individual to have his or her own opinions. Without eternal goals,

■ *John Stuart Mill (1806–1873). (Radio Times Hulton Picture Library)*

it sanctified the creation and discussion (the market exchange) of ideas. Without community, it glorified individual freedom. But individuals without community might find themselves whispering in the wind with nothing to say.

That was never a problem for Mill. He was probably the best-educated person of his time. But what was the meaning of his freedom from restraint for the uneducated and the lower classes? Mill gives a revealing set of examples when he discusses the possibility that free expression can lead to damaging actions:

> No one pretends that actions should be as free as opinion. On the contrary, even opinions lose their immunity when the circumstances in which they are expressed are such as to constitute [by] their expression a positive instigation to some mischievous act. An opinion that corn dealers are starvers of the poor, or that private property is robbery, ought to be unmolested when simply circulated through the press, but may justly incur punishment when delivered orally to an excited mob

> assembled before the house of a corn dealer, or when handed about among the same mob in the form of a placard.[12]

Why those two examples among so many possibilities? Clearly, it is on this side of the political-economic debate that Mill sees the way ideas become actions. The danger he feels to free expression comes not from upper-class ideas of war or racism or from middle-class ideas on hanging thieves, imprisoning debtors, or malicious profiteering in false advertising. The danger line for Mill between ideas and action is when the unruly mob acts according to socialist or anarchist ideas.

Ultimately, Mill is speaking for the freedom of his class, much like Hobbes and Locke. The difference is that his class is not the profit-seeking middle class, but the educated, intellectual middle class. He is speaking for freedom of the "intellectual, and through that to the moral nature of man."[13] That Mill defended freedom of the press in almost absolute terms is a milestone in the history of human freedom and individuality. That it did not occur to him that the poor and working classes of his time had no press or access to the media is a sign of the limitations of middle-class liberalism. The suggestion that he might have objected to the contents of a poor people's press may be a sign of the intentions of middle-class liberalism.

The failure of liberalism in the twentieth century had much to do with the new disillusionment with human reason and goodness in the wake of two world wars. It was also crippled by the numerous strategies of the twentieth century to manage and manipulate rather than educate and listen (as we will shortly see). But it also has much to do with the contradictions in liberalism itself. Mill (like Locke) was attempting to reconcile a particular kind of individual opportunity (albeit the very important opportunity for self-expression and freedom of thought) with the maintenance of a world of private property and the inequalities in power, education, and opportunities for expression that such a world implied. If John Stuart Mill was cautious about encouraging full freedom of individual expression for all classes on all issues, one can imagine the temerity, even the terror, of more self-interested souls.

## Managed Mass Society: Twentieth-Century Corporatism

Any judgment about the state of individuality in the twentieth century must balance the historically unprecedented concern for "the self" in modern culture against the enormous number of ways in which the individual is manipulated and managed. An understanding of some of the methods of modern control might provide a context for understanding the various quests for self-identity.

The workshop is a good place to start. The symbol for most people, and the reality for many, of the controlled working environment is the assembly line. Henry Ford writes in his autobiography that "the idea in a general way came from the overhead trolley that the Chicago [meat] packers used in dressing beef." The first modern assembly line was actually a "disassembly line" developed in the slaughterhouses of Chicago and Cincinnati in the late nineteenth century. Ford first tried the idea in 1913 in the manufacture of generators. Instead of having each man assemble the 29 parts of a generator, he put 29 men on a moving assembly line, and each one fit a single part. By powering the line and raising it for each reach, he was able to produce four times the number of generators in the same man-hours. Later in the year, Ford introduced the assembly line for the production of the entire car. By 1914 the process produced cars in an eighth of the time required earlier.

The world would never be the same. Three hundred thousand Model T Fords were made that year. By 1924 the plant was producing almost 2 million. At $290 each, Ford had halved the price in ten years and put more than half of the world's cars on the road. Mass production had shown the way to mass consumption. The age of the private automobile brought opportunities for privacy, leisure, and personal mobility that must be accounted as one of the chief sources of individuality in the twentieth century. At the same time, Ford's success with the assembly line meant that the division of labor (which some called "the division of man") was to be a permanent feature of industrial society.

More than the assembly line was needed to turn the kind of workers that Aunt Arlie knew into the human machine parts that Thorstein Veblen foresaw. Even before Henry Ford began to engineer the modern workshop, another American engineer, Frederick Taylor, initiated a technique of managing labor which came to be known as industrial engineering. Analyzing each worker's job into a series of machinelike actions—bending, turning, pushing, and lifting—and timing each component of work with a stopwatch, Taylor distinguished the "essential" from "nonessential" actions of the job and designated the most efficient motion and time for each step. "What I demand of the worker," Taylor explained, "is not to produce any longer by his own initiative, but to execute punctiliously the orders given, down to their minutest details."[14]

Taylor expected that the benefits of his "scientific management"

■ *Charlie Chaplin feeds the machine in* Modern Times. *(Culver)*

of work would accrue to the workers and owners alike, but his own account of the process at Bethlehem Steel in the 1890s shows how the lion's share of increased productivity went to company profits.

> "Now, Schmidt, you are a first-class pig-iron handler and know your business well" [he told a strong but untrained worker]. "You have been handling at a rate of twelve and a half tons per day. I have given considerable study to handling pig iron, and feel sure that you could do a much larger day's work than you have been doing. Now don't you think that if you really tried you could handle forty-seven tons of pig iron per day instead of twelve and a half tons?"
>
> [Skeptical but willing] Schmidt started to work, and all day long, and at regular intervals, was told by the men who stood over him with a watch, "Now pick up a pig and walk. Now sit down and rest. Now walk—now rest," etc. He worked when he was told to work, and rested when he was told to rest, and at half past five in the afternoon had his forty-seven tons loaded on the car. And he practically never failed to work at this pace and do the task that was set him during the three years he was at Bethlehem; and throughout this time he averaged a little more than $1.85 per day . . . 60 percent higher wages than were

> paid to other men who were not working on the task work. One man after another was picked out and trained to handle pig iron at the rate of forty-seven tons per day until all of the pig iron was handled at this rate.[15]

In the early days of scientific management workers rankled at a 60 percent increase in pay for almost a 400 percent increase in work. They bristled at the arrogance of the stopwatch and clipboard men, fresh out of college, telling them how to shovel and lift. Often they went out on strike. But throughout the course of the twentieth century, so much intelligence and expertise was devoted to the multiplying disciplines of disciplining workers—sciences of management, industrial psychology, business administration—that workers often lost awareness of how they were being manipulated and mistook manipulation for corporate concern.

As early as 1924 Elton Mayo, one of the founders of "industrial psychology," discovered in his experiments with the workers at Western Electric's Hawthorne Works outside of Chicago that whenever he made changes in the working conditions of an experimental "control group" their productivity increased. Whether he increased or lowered the lighting, humidity, or temperature, or merely returned conditions to what they had been before, production increased. The "Hawthorne effect" that he discovered was that the workers responded favorably to being the objects of an experiment. The mere existence of the clipboard men—hovering, changing something, and watching—was enough to give the workers a feeling of management's concern. The lesson for management was not that the workers could take an active role in the running of the workplace, but that they could be manipulated like children who were eager for parental attention.

Much of twentieth-century education, science, and engineering went into the manipulation of the working place. Efforts at efficiency, productivity, and more "rational" organization often had the effect of making grown men and women workers more mechanical in their behavior and more childlike in their thoughts and feelings. In a similar way, many of the new fields of knowledge of the twentieth century were devoted to the manipulation of the public and the consumer. Though it would be difficult to measure, it is quite probable that the amount of time and resources spent by the fledgling discipline of psychology (for instance) in the twentieth century on manipulation and management has been much greater than that spent on increasing individual autonomy. In the corporate world of the twentieth century there was usually more money available for studies, research, and training in fields that were geared to convincing rather than finding out. Academic departments, whole schools and research institutions, publishing companies, media resources (often with corporate support) were run in the interest of discovering ever new ways of molding public or consumer opinion—designing ever more subtle ways of what an earlier generation, less attuned to public relations, might have called "lying."

The capacity of just two fields—public relations and advertising—to manipulate opinion, to influence individual choice while pretending to broaden the realm of individual choice is enormous. A few examples from the career of just one practitioner of the new techniques in the 1930s, Edward L. Bernays, speaks volumes.

Bernays explains in his memoirs how he helped George Washington Hill of the American Tobacco Company induce women to smoke cigarettes in public. On the advice of a psychoanalyst who said that women view cigarettes as "torches of freedom," Bernays planned an Easter Parade of women smokers in New York City in 1929. He had his secretary send telegrams to 30 leading debutantes in the city that read:

> IN THE INTERESTS OF EQUALITY OF THE SEXES AND TO FIGHT ANOTHER SEX TABOO I AND OTHER YOUNG WOMEN WILL LIGHT ANOTHER TORCH OF FREEDOM BY SMOKING CIGARETTES WHILE STROLLING ON FIFTH AVENUE EASTER SUNDAY.[16]

The event created a national stir. Pictures of the women were printed in newspapers throughout the country. Women responded from New York to San Francisco by smoking publicly. "Age-old customs," Bernays learned, "could be broken down by a dramatic appeal, disseminated by the network of media."[17]

But that was only a beginning for George Washington Hill's American Tobacco Company. Women were not smoking the company's Lucky Strikes because the green package with the red bull's-eye clashed with the colors of their clothes. In the spring of 1934, Hill called Bernays into his office to ask what could be done. Bernays suggested changing the package to a more neutral color. Hill thundered disapproval: he hadn't spent millions of dollars advertising a package to change it. Bernays countered: then change the color of fashion to green. That was the kind of idea George Washington Hill liked. He authorized $25,000.

> That was the beginning of a fascinating six-month activity for me—to make green *the* fashionable color. . . .
>
> Some years before I had asked Alfred Reeves, of the American Automobile Manufacturers Association, how he had developed a market for American automobiles in England, where roads were narrow and curved.

"I didn't try to sell automobiles," he answered, "I campaigned for wider and straighter roads. The sale of American cars followed."

This was an application of the general principle which I later termed the engineering of consent. Like an architect, I drew up a comprehensive blueprint, a complete procedural outline, detailing objectives, the necessary research, strategy, themes and timing of the planned activities.[18]

And what activities! Psychological studies were made of associations with green. The director of the leading fashionable society ball was given the whole $25,000 budget from "a nameless sponsor" to make it a "green ball." A silk manufacturer was encouraged to "bet on green" and gave a luncheon for fashion editors with green menus, all-green food, a talk by a psychologist on green, and a lecture by the head of the Hunter College art department on "green in the work of great artists."

I had wondered at the alacrity with which scientists, academicians and professional men participated in events of this kind. I learned they welcomed the opportunity to discuss their favorite subject and enjoyed the resultant publicity. In an age of communication their own effectiveness often depended on public visibility.[19]

As newspaper stories heralded a "green autumn" and a "green winter," a color fashion bureau was organized. "It alerted the fashion field to green's leadership" in clothing, accessories, and even interior decoration. Fifteen hundred letters were sent to interior decorators and home-furnishing buyers on "the dominance of green" to ensure that they would join the trend. The head of the Green Fashion Ball was persuaded to sail to France to secure the cooperation of the French fashion industry and the French government (which cooperated in recognition of the buying power of American women). An invitation committee for the Green Fashion Ball was formed that included some of the most important names in American society: Mrs. James Roosevelt, Mrs. Walter Chrysler, Mrs. Irving Berlin, and Mrs. Averell Harriman. The committee held a series of luncheons with representatives of the accessory trades to encourage them to make green accessories available for the green gowns from Paris.

As the campaign gained momentum, other manufacturers jumped on the bandwagon. One announced a new emerald nail polish. Another introduced green stockings. Green window displays began to appear in stores, first in Philadelphia, and finally by September in Altman's Fifth Avenue store in New York. *Vogue* and *Harper's Bazaar* featured the new green fashions on their covers. Finally in November, "the unsuspecting opposition" joined the campaign.

"Camel cigarettes showed a girl wearing a green dress with red trimmings, the colors of the Lucky Strike package."[20]

Even the competition had recognized that Lucky Strikes were the height of fashion.

The "green revolution" of 1934 raises a number of interesting questions about the use of resources in corporate, commercial society. What were all of these people doing promoting "green" in the depths of America's economic depression? With fundamental economic issues to tackle, how did so many intelligent and influential people consume their time and energy in activity that was at best meaningless, and ultimately harmful to health? Is this the way that "the best and the brightest" of corporate society confront crisis? Are there no guidelines for more useful activity?

The Lucky Strike campaign raises even more gnawing questions, however, about the meaning and possibilities of individuality in a society dominated by commercial and corporate interests. Who, besides George Washington Hill and Edward Bernays, knew what they were doing? What kind of freedom or compulsion motivated the manufacturers (of accessories, for instance) who hopped on the "green revolution" to their own profit? What kind of individuality was displayed by the intellectuals, journalists, and society people who joined the campaign? When artists and psychologists lectured that autumn on the importance of green, were they saying what they wanted to say? Were they expressing their own choices or individuality? If they were manipulated into thinking that the "issue of green" was important, how about all of the women who thought they had chosen to buy green dresses? When the whole context, the very alternatives, of consumer decision making are created by those who have something to sell, what kind of freedom of choice in fact exists?

## The Triumph of Totalitarianism

In the Great Depression of the 1930s, corporate manipulation of individuality reached its height not in the United States, but in Nazi Germany. The Nazi concentration camps were in some ways only a further extension of the corporate quest for efficiency and profit maximization. When the directors of I. G. Farben (the German multinational corporation that manufactured everything from Bayer aspirin to synthetic gasoline) chose Auschwitz as the site of its synthetic rubber plant, they did so on the promise of slave labor from the concentration camp that they could work to death and supervision by the SS soldiers.

Nor was the policy hidden from the top echelons of I. G. Farben's managerial elite. They were very much involved in the operation and made frequent trips to Auschwitz to see how things were going. According to the affidavit of Dr. Raymond van den Straaten, a slave at Auschwitz, on one occasion, five of I. G. Farben's top directors made an inspection tour of I. G. Auschwitz. As one of the directors passed a slave scientist, Dr. Fritz Lohner-Beda, the director remarked, "The Jewish swine could work a little faster." Another I. G. Farben director responded, "If they don't work, let them perish in the gas chamber." Dr. Lohner-Beda was then pulled out of his group and kicked to death.[21]

Karl Marx's view that capitalism treated workers as things often turned out to be a perceptive metaphor of the managed societies of the twentieth century, but in Nazi Germany it was a literal fact. Major German corporations not only worked the slave laborers of the concentration camps to death, they also used their bodies as guinea pigs for quasi-medical experiments, profited from the manufacture of the gas used to kill them, and then turned their bodies into soap, their hairs into rugs, and their gold fillings into jewelry.

Through it all they behaved not like fanatics, but like thorough business executives. When Himmler informed others of the mass exterminations, "He spoke," according to one observer, "with such icy coldness of the extermination of men, women and children, as a businessman speaks of his balance sheet. There was nothing emotional in his speech, nothing that suggested an inner involvement."[22] Similarly, Hitler's chief architect Albert Speer recalled: "My obsessional fixation on production and output statistics blurred all considerations and feelings of humanity."[23]

In some ways, the business attitudes of Himmler, Speer, and the executives of such corporations as I. G. Farben, Krupp, Audi, and Telefunken that used concentration camp labor are just further extensions of the corporate, commercial mentality that evolved elsewhere (especially in America) in the twentieth century. From the assembly line, industrial engineering, psychological and managerial techniques for increasing production or consumption, public relations and advertising, it is but a series of steps to the world of concentration camp factories, economic revival through militarization, and the propaganda techniques of Goebbels or the technocratic efficiency of Himmler and Speer. Once human values are subordinated to the mechanistic values of output strategies, cost minimization, and profit maximization, the concentration camp becomes little more than an efficient factory. It thus became possible for executives like I. G. Farben's Dr. Fritz Ter Meer to lunch with American counterparts at Standard Oil before the war, secure patent agreements that would prevent Standard Oil from

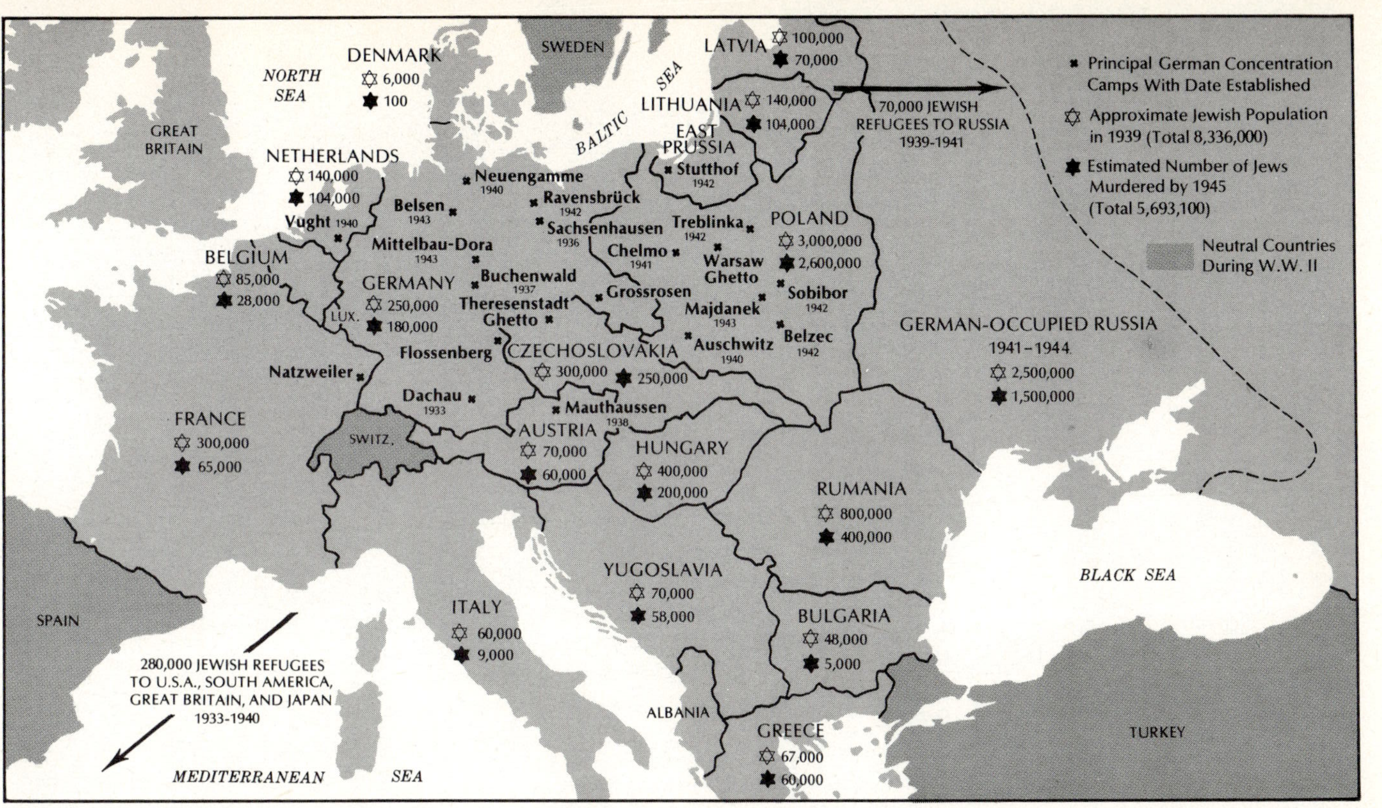


**The Extermination of the Jews, 1939–1945**
*Auschwitz was only one of many Nazi concentration camps. Their number, and the number of their victims, throughout Nazi-occupied Europe is staggering.*

manufacturing synthetic rubber even after the war started, witness the murder of Dr. Lohner-Beda, socialize at Auschwitz while as many as ten thousand inmates were being exterminated daily, and then plead after the war that "no harm had been done" by the Farben pharmaceutical experiments because the inmates "would have been killed anyway."[24]

Market society need not lead inevitably to Auschwitz, of course. In other societies it did not; the Nazi experience of Germany was unique. At the least, however, market society established a "service mentality" of secondary goals that could be used on behalf of any set of primary goals. Hitler's goals of racial extermination, militarization, totalitarian control, and world domination could be implemented as efficiently as any other set of goals. The profit-and-loss mentality could be most effective when it was essentially oblivious or unconcerned with what was being measured. Indeed, in a militarized society where one was expected to follow orders without question, the corporate, technocratic system could work most effectively.

Hitler was able to use the large corporations because he guaranteed them large profits at a time when their very existence was challenged by German socialists and communists. Once German industrialists realized that Hitler's use of the word "socialist" in the National Socialist German Worker's Party was nothing more than a fraud to capture working-class votes, they contributed to the Nazis for their own corporate survival.

Germany's humiliation in World War I, the removal of the emperor, the loss of territory, the war reparation payments, and the admission of "war guilt" demanded by the Treaty of Versailles were sources of frustration that Hitler's nationalist rhetoric promised to counter. The economic breakdown, especially the disastrous inflation of the early 1920s and the continuing high numbers of unemployed—6 million in 1932—turned people to radical solutions. Hitler's anti-Semitism struck deep chords in German culture and offered the Jews as easy scapegoats—for the defeat in war and the economic catastrophe.

The appeal of Hitler, however, had more to do with irrational forces than rational calculation. He offered in his hypnotising speeches and mass spectacles a rigorous certainty in traditional, absolutist values that had been all but destroyed by the successes as well as the disasters of capitalist society. The successes of German capitalism had destroyed the traditional securities of family, village, guild, and church, and created in its place the anonymous, vulnerable, isolated individual of modern society. In Erich Fromm's telling phrases, the individual in modern capitalist society was "free from" the various

■ *In a world that seemed to be falling apart, Hitler mobilized the German masses with a barage of symbols and spectacles—banners, uniforms, parades, salutes, songs, and slogans—that offered certainty for the subordination of personal identity. Without a "self," every German could become part of a new corporate whole.* (UPI)

constraints of the medieval world—free from the obligations of serfdom, guild regulations, religious orthodoxy, and traditional authorities, and thus free from their protection and security. As an isolated competitor, employee, consumer, soldier, or taxpayer, he was only one of the mass audience. He had been divided for conquest, propagandized for sales, and never instructed or encouraged to develop the positive, potential side of his or her new individuality into "freedom to" be something. Thus, since the only freedom people knew was negative, they sought "an escape from freedom." The failure of capitalism was that the system had no advantage in encouraging individual growth. Rather, it profited more by the dependence of the individual as employee or consumer.

Individuals had to be educated to the point of proficiency in their jobs and advertising literacy, but more than that was superfluous, even detrimental. By the 1920s the failure of capitalism in Germany was more general. It not only failed to encourage individual growth;

it failed to provide enough jobs, and the currency was practically worthless.

In *Escape from Freedom,* Erich Fromm attributed the rise of Nazism to Protestantism as well as capitalism. Protestantism, he argued, was a cultural reinforcement of the social disintegration of capitalist society. The classic Protestant posture of the individual alone, answerable only to God, was a religious equivalent of the capitalist isolation before competitors and the market. It too offered only negative "freedom from." The Protestant was free from the institutional structure, rituals, sacraments, and social salvation of the Catholic church. Here too, the result was that the individual did not learn to develop in the necessary give-and-take of an institutional structure.

Thus, according to Fromm, in the collapse of traditional securities and values in Germany in the 1920s and 1930s, the burden of a meaningless individuality was too much to bear. Hitler gave people a new community (the German nation and "master race"), enemies to unite against (Jews, socialists, and communists), and an overriding purpose (world dominion). All of the relativities of advanced market society were abolished by an act of will. All questions were answered. "Hitler is always right."

Hitler frankly recognized the appeal of absolute authority for the Germans who felt their isolation more painfully as their old society disintegrated around them. He wrote in *Mein Kampf:*

> The psyche of the great masses is not receptive to anything that is half-hearted and weak. [They] would rather bow to a strong man than dominate a weakling. . . . The masses love a commander more than a petitioner and feel inwardly more satisfied by a doctrine, tolerating no other beside itself, than by the granting of liberalistic freedom with which, as a rule, they can do little, and are prone to feel that they have been abandoned. They are equally unaware of their shameless spiritual terrorization and the hideous abuse of their human freedom.[25]

Hitler realized the value of the mass meeting, the parade, and the spectacle, in channeling these feelings of loss and loneliness (see his film *The Triumph of the Will*), towards a new hierarchical community.

> The mass meeting is also necessary for the reason that in it the individual, who at first, while becoming a supporter of a young movement, feels lonely and easily succumbs to the fear of being alone, for the first time gets the picture of a larger community, which in most people has a strengthening, encouraging effect. . . . When from his little workshop or big factory, in which he feels very small, he steps for the first time into a mass meeting and has thousands and thousands of people of the same opinions around him, . . . then he himself has succumbed to the magic influence of what we designate as "mass suggestion."[26]

▪ *American films, especially musicals like Busby Berkeley's* Gold Diggers of 1933, *satisfied some of the same longings—to obliterate the self in a larger identity—that the German masses felt. Berkeley's camera angles turned chorus girls into petals for workers who felt turned into machines. He gave unity beauty, and titillation too.* (Culver)

The Nazi state was only the most pernicious of totalitarian regimes that swept Europe in the second quarter of the twentieth century. Much of Hitler's ideology and practice (except for anti-Semitism) was actually borrowed from Mussolini's fascist Italy after 1922. Italian fascism had already developed (by 1930) the system of total (i.e., totalitarian) state control through a hierarchy of corporations administered from the top down, and through the assault on democracy, reason, thought, liberty, and individuality that became pervasive in the fascisms of Germany and Eastern Europe.

Even Stalinist Russia ended the brief experiments with new forms of freedom, individual liberation, and popular participation initiated in the hopeful wake of the revolution in 1917. (In one such experiment, even the position of conductor of the symphony orchestra was dropped for being coercive.) But despite the secret police, the bureaucracy, the purges, and the terror, the worst features of Stalinism were always rationalized as emergency measures to preserve "socialism in one country," and thus create the conditions for an eventual "withering away of the state." Although that was of small consolation to the victims of the regime, the doctrinaire commitment to eventual individual liberation and a democracy more complete than the "bourgeois democracy" of the propertied prevented some of the worst excesses of the fascist regimes. At least the Soviet example of modernization that was championed by various emerging nations meant an ultimate commitment to human rights, greater democracy, and individual freedom, whereas the exportation of fascism (from Spain to the Philippines) did not. Fascism made total individual subordination a matter of faith rather than temporary necessity. Its ideal was the complete suppression of individuality and the brutal extinction of individuals and minorities who were deemed outside of the "national will."

## Modernization and Individuality: The West and the World

From the perspective of the 1980s fascism may appear more historical than prophetic. While it sometimes seemed (at least to Marxists) that fascism was the only alternative to socialism in advanced capitalist society, it now appears that more benign measures of commercial and governmental management are possible in modern mass society. As Western society has become more democratic since World War II, and as fascist or totalitarian regimes have become more common in the developing nations of Asia, Africa, and Latin America, it has become easier to see fascism as an "early" rather than "late" response to the problems of capitalist modernization. Fascism, after all, was most typical in countries with a large peasant population that were just undergoing the wrenching psychological and social dislocations of modernization. It was engineered with relatively primitive mass media (radio, parades, newsreels) for a relatively unsophisticated population, by unnecessarily fearful, short-sighted corporations and dictators not far removed from the feudal, almost tribal, world of peasant vendettas and provincial xenophobia.

If the example of the Western world is any guide, the developing nations have the prospect of greater definition of individual needs as they modernize and more general retreats from the individual isolation, atomization, and alienation that fed the fascisms of Europe. If individualization is as sterile and impoverished as it frequently was in the West, the emerging individuals of the emerging world may

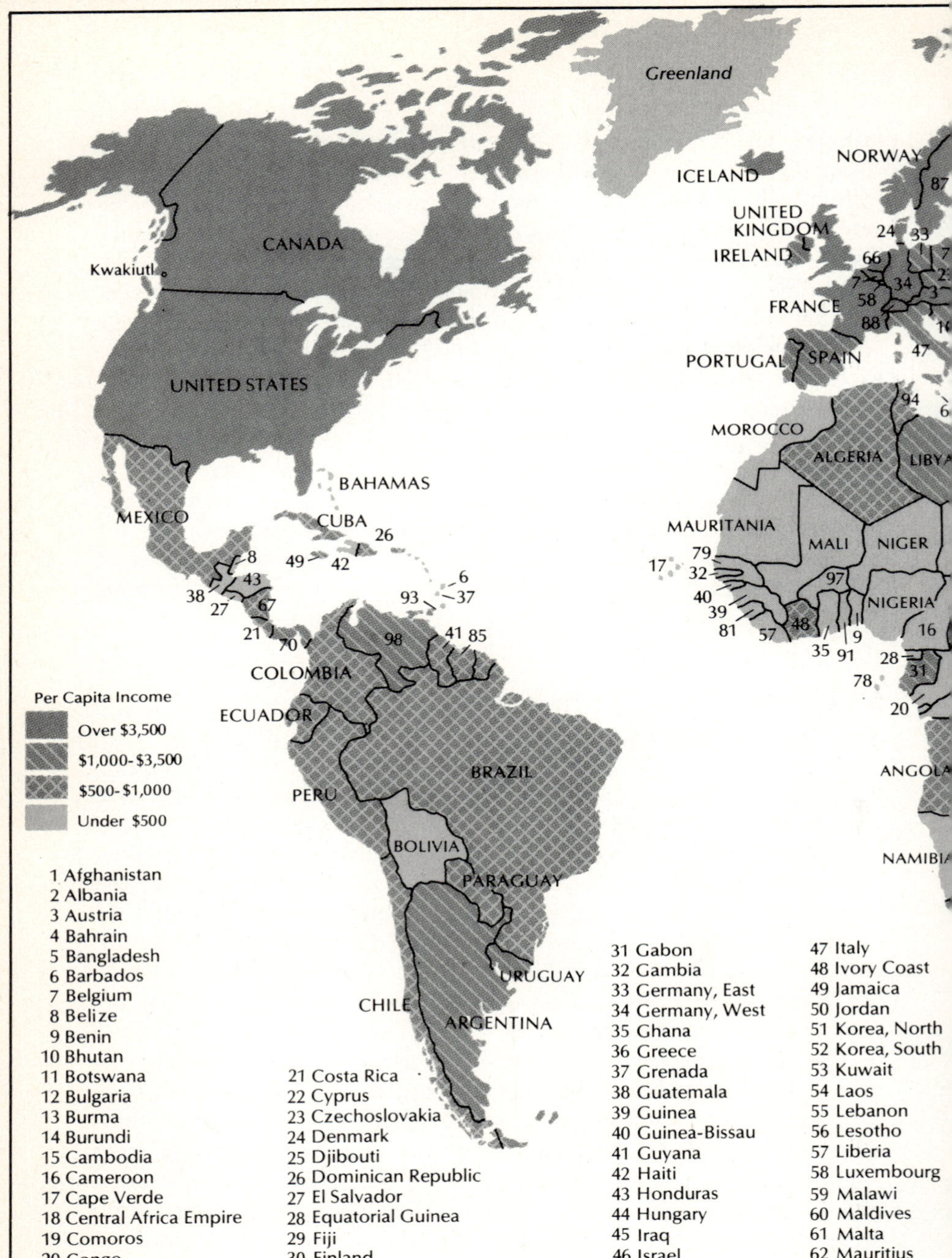


**Wealth and Individuality in the World**

*Most of the countries in the modern world are too poor to afford individualistic ideals and opportunities for the mass of people. As they modernize they face many of the same possibilities of (and threats to) individual expression that were experienced in the West earlier in this century.*

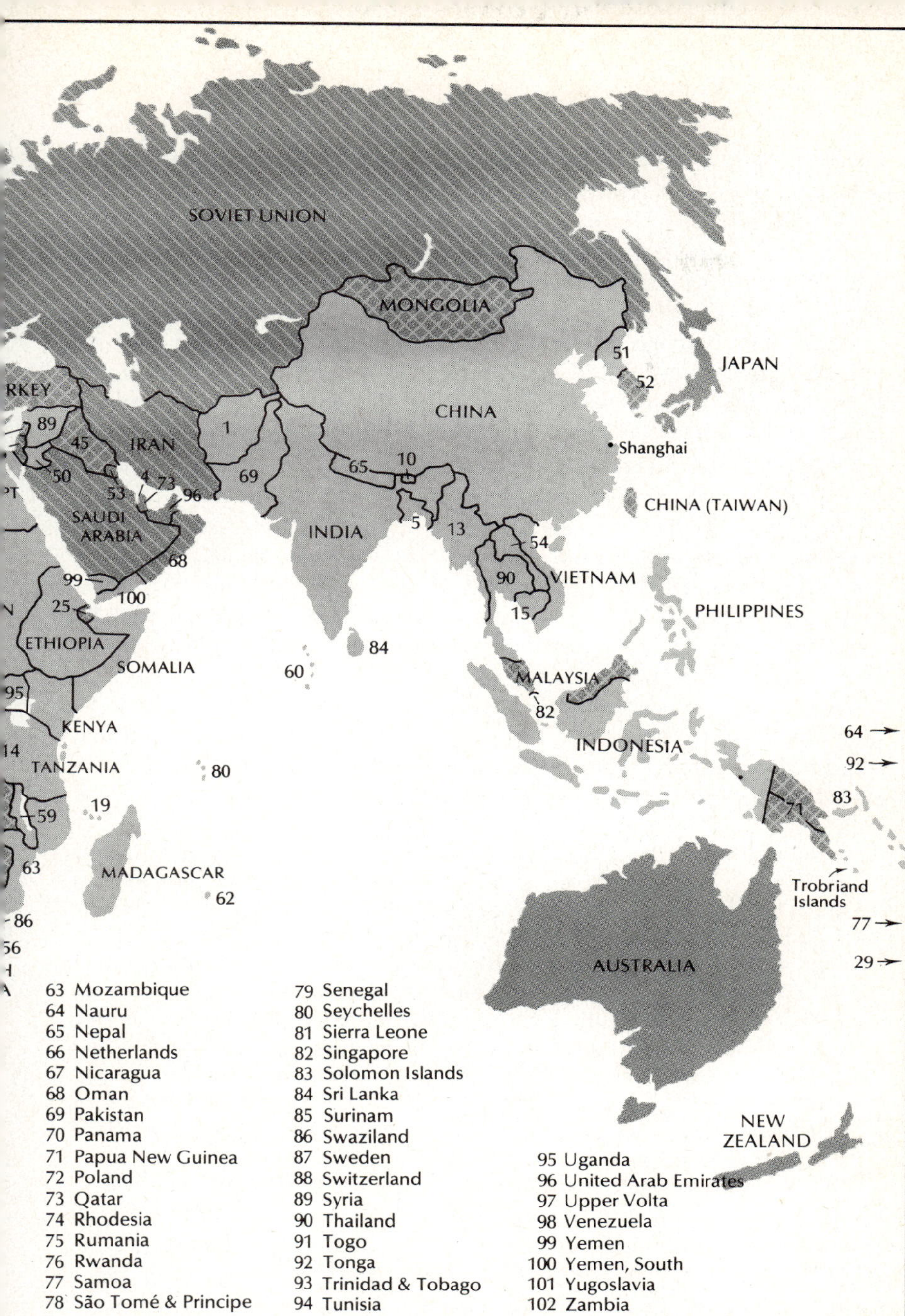
SOVIET UNION
MONGOLIA
CHINA
JAPAN
Shanghai
CHINA (TAIWAN)
IRAN
SAUDI ARABIA
INDIA
VIETNAM
PHILIPPINES
ETHIOPIA
SOMALIA
KENYA
TANZANIA
MALAYSIA
INDONESIA
MADAGASCAR
Trobriand Islands
AUSTRALIA
NEW ZEALAND
63 Mozambique
64 Nauru
65 Nepal
66 Netherlands
67 Nicaragua
68 Oman
69 Pakistan
70 Panama
71 Papua New Guinea
72 Poland
73 Qatar
74 Rhodesia
75 Rumania
76 Rwanda
77 Samoa
78 São Tomé & Principe
79 Senegal
80 Seychelles
81 Sierra Leone
82 Singapore
83 Solomon Islands
84 Sri Lanka
85 Surinam
86 Swaziland
87 Sweden
88 Switzerland
89 Syria
90 Thailand
91 Togo
92 Tonga
93 Trinidad & Tobago
94 Tunisia
95 Uganda
96 United Arab Emirates
97 Upper Volta
98 Venezuela
99 Yemen
100 Yemen, South
101 Yugoslavia
102 Zambia

attempt many of the "escapes from freedom" that offered security in subordination to Westerners in the 1920s and 1930s.

Individuality is still a young plant in the developing world. Nowhere has it taken on the cultural importance that required the new word "individualism" in the West in the nineteenth century. Hardship society cannot allow such extravagances. The caste, the family, the tribe, the village, the church need constant protection and reaffirmation. The individual carves out a separate identity from the group only at great peril. The inevitable crisis—famine, scarcity, catastrophe—might find one cut adrift, without membership.

Such was the threat to Mahatma Gandhi in 1888 when, at the age of 18, he decided to travel from India to England to study law. No one of his caste had been to England before. Foreign travel was forbidden. A section of the caste elders formally declared him an outcaste if he went. He vowed to his mother that he would not touch meat, wine, or women while away, but he was determined to go. Afraid that he would be stopped, but overcome by strong personal longings, he set sail a couple of months sooner than he had planned.

Forty years later, Mahatma Gandhi, one of the most individualistic men his country or caste produced, author of the Indian national independence movement, described his voyage to Southampton in his autobiography, *The Story of My Experiments with Truth:*

> I did not feel at all sea-sick. . . . I was innocent of the use of knives and forks. . . . I therefore never took meals at table but always had them in my cabin, and they consisted principally of sweets and fruits I had brought with me. . . . We entered the Bay of Biscay, but I did not begin to feel the need either of meat or liquor. . . . However, we reached Southampton, as far as I remember, on a Saturday. On the boat I had worn a black suit, the white flannel one, which my friends had got me, having been kept especially for wearing when I landed. I had thought that white clothes would suit me better when I stepped ashore, and therefore I did so in white flannels. Those were the last days of September, and I found I was the only person wearing such clothes.[27]

"That is the voyage," V. S. Naipaul remarks of the above passage. Gandhi's self-identity, although strong by Indian standards, was so fragile by modern Western standards that he was consumed by self-conscious reflection about his food, clothes, and his location. He spent three years in England, Naipaul observes, in which he allowed himself to notice little of English life.

> No London building is described, no street, no room, no crowd, no public conveyance. The London of 1890, to a young man from a small Indian town—has to be inferred from Gandhi's continuing internal dis-

■ *Mahatma Gandhi (1869–1948). (UPI)*

> turbances, his embarrassments, his religious self-searchings, his attempts at dressing correctly and learning English manners, and, above all, his difficulties and occasional satisfactions about food.[28]

Naipaul suggests that Gandhi's "defect of vision" in England, and then again later in South Africa where his 20-year "internal" adventure omits mention of Africans, is the product of the anxieties of an "undeveloped ego." Unable to take in the enormous variety of new people, customs, and places without challenging his own self-identity, Gandhi concentrated on maintaining the fragile self. He turned inward (in the traditional Hindu manner) because the sensory overload was too threatening to the self which had been formed by caste and village India.

Naipaul quotes an Indian psychotherapist who attempted to put Gandhi's response into a broader context. According to Dr. Sudhir Kakar

> [In India] the mother functions as the external ego of the child for a much longer period than is customary in the West, and many of the

> ego functions concerned with reality are later transferred from mother to the family and social institutions.[29]

In traditional India the child's devotion to the father could hamper individual growth as much as protection by the mother. Gandhi also relates in his autobiography how important it was for him to care for his own bed-ridden father when the young Gandhi was 16 and already married.

> Every night I massaged his legs and retired only when he asked me to do so or after he had fallen asleep. I loved to do this service. I do not remember ever having neglected it . . . I would only go out for an evening walk either when he permitted me or when he was feeling well.[30]

Elsewhere in his autobiography Gandhi reveals the tension he felt between caring for his father and the "carnal lust" he felt for his wife. But he seems to have never forgiven himself that his "lust got the better of . . . my devotion to my parents" when he was in his own bedroom the night his father died. The event probably had much to do with his later vows of sexual abstinence and his refusal to allow his own sons to marry.

Even today, parental devotion to the father and family plays a role in Indian society that limits the development of individuality. Arthur Koestler tells a story in *The Lotus and the Robot* (about his stay in India and Japan in 1958–1959) that could probably be told today.

> Mr. X., an Executive, past forty, the father of four children, asked me for lunch. When I offered him a cigarette, he refused, and watched me light mine with a rather wistful look. I asked him why he did not smoke, and he explained, as if it were the most natural thing in the world: "Up to the age of thirty-two I studied in England and smoked quite a lot. I also liked an occasional glass of beer. When I came back, I had to hide these habits from my father who disapproved of them; but I do not enjoy doing things in secret, so I gave them up." I asked, half jokingly, whether he would start smoking again when his father passed away. He answered seriously: "I might."
>
> I told this story to another acquaintance, the elderly Director of a social research institute. He did not think there was anything odd about it. "Why," he said, "my father died when I was forty-five, and until his death I spent all my evenings with him. A few years earlier I used to go occasionally to a lecture, or a debating society to which I belonged, but one evening my father told me that he always felt lonely on the evenings when I went out, so from then onwards I did not go out any more but would talk or read to him instead."

I told both stories to a psychiatrist in Bombay. His only reaction was: "Why yes, the father-to-son relationship among Brahmins is a particularly happy one. My father also lives in my house with my family. I am now over fifty, but it would never occur to me to sit down in his presence until invited by him to do so, although it is my own house. Nor would I consider making any major decision without his advice and consent." "And as a student of the human psyche, you consider this a desirable state of affairs?" "Entirely desirable."

Only one Indian psychiatrist dissented, and he came from southern, Christian stock. He said with an engagingly cynical smile: "Among Hindus it is the oldest son's privilege to set light to his father's funeral pyre; but he has a long time to wait."[31]

Parental authority and family cohesiveness shield the sons and daughters of many developing countries from the insecurities and dramas of personal growth. In the case of India the patriarchal family has exercised such authority longer than elsewhere partly because it was sanctioned by a caste system that survived numerous attempts at reform over the centuries of English rule and independence. Family identity was part of caste identity. Despite its inequities, caste organization served to protect the individual from some of the atomizing tendencies of British imperial market society.

In traditional China the individual was "protected from personal growth" by the family and the imperial court, without an intermediary system like Indian caste. Thus, the defeat of the Chinese imperial system—by the removal of the emperor by the republican forces of Sun Yat-sen in the revolution of 1911 and by the occupation of China by Western and Japanese forces and merchants since the nineteenth century—hastened the disintegration of traditional family life. Poor Chinese families, alone before the landlord or foreign mercenary, were sometimes forced to sell their children or release them to work away from home without traditional protections. But poverty could limit individual growth as rudely as the family shield from poverty. In the China of the 1920s and 1930s poverty was probably the greatest deterrent to the development of individuality.

The human remains of disintegrated Chinese families who lived and died in a city like Shanghai in the 1930s could not begin to experience or understand the meaning of individuality.

Although it is more than thirty years since I first went ashore in Shanghai, some scenes, some impressions of the week I spent there are indelibly etched on my mind.

The beggars. The swarms of beggars of all ages, whole and diseased, vociferous and silent, hopeful and hopeless, blind and seeing. All having in common their poverty, their degradation.

> The prostitutes. The smart ones in the foreign concessions with make-up, high-heeled shoes and skin tight dresses slit to the thigh. The cheap ones in the sailors' districts, unkempt, raucous, brazen. The child prostitutes. The two frightened, bewildered little girls dragged along, one in each hand, by their owner who offered them singly or together for fifty cents an hour.
>
> The poverty. The rows of matsheds where hundreds of thousands lived and died. The hunger-swollen bellies. The rummaging in garbage bins for possible scraps of food.
>
> The children. I can do no better than quote a Canadian hotelier who lived in pre-Liberation Shanghai for more than twenty years and who, on a return visit in 1965, recalled the familiar sights of old Shanghai:
>
> "I searched for scurvy-headed children. Lice-ridden children. Children with inflamed red eyes. Children with bleeding gums. Children with distended stomachs and spindly arms and legs. I searched the sidewalks day and night for children who had been purposely deformed by beggars. Beggars who would leech on to any well-dressed passer-by to blackmail sympathy and offerings, by pretending the hideous-looking child was their own.
>
> I looked for children covered with horrible sores upon which flies feasted. I looked for children having a bowel movement, which, after much strain, would only eject tapeworms.
>
> I looked for child slaves in alleyway factories. Children who worked twelve hours a day, literally chained to small press punches. Children who, if they lost a finger, or worse, often were cast into the streets to beg and forage in garbage bins for future subsistence."
>
> In 1965 he searched without finding, but in the 1930's there was no need to search far for such sights were everywhere to be seen.[32]

The Chinese Communist (or peasant) Revolution has eliminated the extreme inequalities, foreign domination, and market disintegration that impoverished the lives of the mass of Chinese before 1949. Further, the communists created a vastly more productive China through industrialization, land reform, agricultural communes, and institutions of both local and national control of Chinese resources. Begging, prostitution, serfdom, and starvation were abolished in a generation. (There are almost no flies or incidences of venereal diseases in modern China, for instance.) Critics of the regime have acknowledged all of this, but added "At what cost to personal liberty and individuality?" But such critics might be reminded of the people in places like Shanghai before the communist victory. What liberties did they have? What individuality did they know? Clearly they are in a much better position since the abolition of extreme poverty to develop the luxuries of self-identity, freedom, and individuality.

It is also true, however, that the communist victory in China was accomplished by the military discipline of mass armies and by the encouragement and supervision of an enormous party organization. In military success and modernization, it tended to enforce a strict work ethic, an almost puritan sexual restraint, and a consuming dedication to party and people. The uniform blue or gray clothing made economic sense to a society with scarce resources. It was better to provide two suits of blue each year to all of the citizens than fashionable prints to the few while the rest made do with hand-me-down rags. It also made political sense in a society where certain colors and clothes had only recently been the legal and social mark of status or class. But a world where everyone wears blue (or green, for that matter) is also a world where everyone tends to color his or her thoughts uniformly.

Shanghai in the spring of 1978 was a world that could afford colorful prints only for the children, bicycles for those who had saved, and cars, television sets, or private rooms for practically no one. But it was a world where virtually no one earned more than five times the earnings of someone else, and where virtually everyone was well fed, occupied some housing, worked hard, and seemed happy.

I remember more contentment and dedication than either discontent or individuality. I was disconcerted to notice only a single couple holding hands, to watch almost half the entire population doing the *t'ai chi* exercises at dawn to the Western-style marches coming from the loudspeakers overhead, and to hear two Chinese student-guides within minutes of each other use exactly the same words ("Better to serve the people than serve oneself") to the question of how they would feel if they were required to work for the China Travel Service instead of being able to teach English at the university.

But there were already signs of the impending individualistic and Western revolution as well. A few days after watching the traditional Peking opera style of revolutionary propaganda that had been so dear to the heart of Mao Tse-tung's widow (now chastized as one of the "Gang of Four") and thinking both "how sterile" and "how necessary for the young who had forgotten the 1930s," I watched a cultural time bomb explode. A Rumanian movie, dubbed in Chinese, that played to full houses throughout China lavishly portrayed all of the clichés of Western romanticism: the full-face shot of the young hero and heroine, the gypsy violins, the stroll of the lovers through the meadow, the candlelighted supper, the patriot in love. The Chinese were enthralled. The cultivation of personal emotions, the stylish, individualistic camera work, the Rumanian elevation of romance spoke with the power of a thousand wall posters. Duplicated and multiplied by other Western films, the bright yellow dresses of the Western tourists in the spring and the publicity given to the tourists, their presidents, and their ways, Chinese society appeared to have taken a second major step toward Western modernization and Western individualism by 1979.

Back in the United States, one wondered if the individualism championed by Lucky Strikes or Coca Cola was still liable to backfire.

The best-seller lists in the United States were full of psychological self-help titles that were uniformly valuable antidotes to the authoritarianism of working place, family, and commercial media propaganda, but also uniformly lacking in social awareness or concern. The injunctions to "take responsibility for your self," to "be your own best friend," or to "look out for number one" all reflected the uneasy American (Protestant, capitalist?) sense of the isolated, tyrannized individual who could only assert the self by denying the existence or utility of society. The heroic individuals of American culture—the cowboy, the outlaw, the pioneer, or the drifter—were creatures apart, unable or unwilling to develop individuality in a social context.

The heroic individuals of American films often seemed (like Superman) to come from another world. Their motivations, character, personality, or feelings were frequently muted or ignored in Hollywood's quest for action, story, and plot. European filmmakers continued to bore American audiences with their subtle examinations of personality in intricate social settings. In European films one saw the individual at work, the family at dinner, the assorted friends, relatives, lovers, and acquaintances who made the individual (in a net of messy ambiguities) what he or she was. Social context defined individuality. One saw complex, whole people, and understood their conflicting emotions and motivations.

Americans who had been taught that freedom was choosing Chevys or Fords, Aim or Crest, Democrats or Republicans, found greater freedom in rejecting society completely. Those who had been told that they would attain individual worth in purchase or ownership often consumed themselves in their consumption.

Many sought "escape from freedom" in religious absolutism, astrology, cults, and fads that gave temporary meaning and direction to rudderless lives. Individuals often gave religious cults a power over their lives that compensated for their own feelings of impotence. Without the experience or symbols of meaningful social action, the quest for communal identity often faded into submission and self-annihilation. The middle ground of social interaction that could have nourished creative individuality had withered from neglect.

## *For Further Reading*

There are two excellent scholarly studies of the individual in medieval Europe. Colin Morris documents **The Discovery of the Individual, 1050–1200*** in European culture during that period. Walter Ullmann examines the legal and political emergence of **The Individual and Society in the Middle Ages** over a broader period.

On the early modern period, the brilliant modern overview is Fernand Braudel's **Capitalism and Material Civilization 1500–1800,*** although it scarcely mentions a single individual. Philippe Aries's **Centuries of Childhood*** is excellent on the history of individuality as well as of childhood. Marshall McLuhan's **The Gutenberg Galaxy*** is a treasure of exciting insights on the relationship of printing to individuality. Ian Watt's **The Rise of the Novel*** is a superb study of the individual and the social function of print media in the eighteenth century. Lucien Febvre's **The Book** is an excellent recent study.

There is virtually an infinite number of ways of approaching the question of individuality in the nineteenth and twentieth centuries. For the role of the romantic movement, one might turn to Jacques Barzun's **Romanticism and the Modern Ego, Romanticism,*** edited by R. F. Gleckner and G. E. Enssco, Morse Peckham's **Beyond the Tragic Vision: The Quest for Identity in the Nineteenth Century,*** or Arnold Hauser's **The Social History of Art,** vol. 4,* or W. Sypher's **From Rococco to Cubism.***

The significance of individuality in popular culture can be weighed with E. G. West's **Education and the Industrial Revolution,** I. Pinchbeck and M. Hewitt's **Children in English Society,** R. W. Malcolmson's **Popular Recreations in English Society, 1700–1850,** Peter N. Stearn's **European Society in Upheaval,*** or the works mentioned in the text.

For further study of J. S. Mill and liberalism, there are G. Himmelfarb's **On Liberty and Liberalism: The Case of J. S. Mill,** A. Ryan's **J. S. Mill,*** and B. Mazlish's psychoanalytical **James and John Stuart Mill,** as well as J. S. Mill's **Autobiography*** and **On Liberty.***

There are too many studies on modern economic and business history to name a few, but the student might do well to start with M. Kranzberg and J. Gies's, **By the Sweat of Thy Brow.*** Some of the more specialized monuments are E. P. Thompson's **The Making of the English Working Class,*** Thorstein Veblen's **The Instinct of Workmanship and the State of Industrial Art** (or the **Portable Veblen***), Lewis Mumford's **Technics and Civilization,*** or his more recent, two-volume **The Myth of the Machine,*** and Jacques Ellul's **The Technology Society.***

On Nazism a book appears every month. The author recommends Richard Rubenstein's **The Cunning of History,*** Raul Hilberg's **The Destruction of the European Jews,*** John Toland's readable **Adolf Hitler,*** and the bibliography at the end of R. R. Palmer and Joel Colton's **A History of the Modern World.***

* Available in paperback.

Instead of listing the numerous possibilities for studying the Russian Revolution, the Chinese Communist Revolution, the Indian lack of revolution, or current America, the student is best directed to one of the standard bibliographies (like the Palmer and Colton) with the addition of a few exceptional titles that might otherwise go unnoticed: Richard Sennett's **The Fall of Public Man*** (which argues that it is public life, not privacy, which has recently disappeared); Christopher Lasch's brilliant **The Culture of Narcissism** about current America; James Billington's magnificent Russian cultural history, **The Icon and the Axe;*** Barrington Moore, Jr.'s **Social Origins of Dictatorship and Democracy;*** Jean Chesneaux's **Peasant Revolts in China 1840–1949;*** Siegfried Kracauer's too often maligned **From Caligari to Hitler: A Psychological Study of the German Film;*** V. S. Naipaul's **India: A Wounded Civilization;*** Arthur Koestler's **The Lotus and the Robot;** and Warren Susman's **Culture and Commitment 1929–1945.***

A list such as this barely hints at the enormous number of ways one could approach the topics discussed in this chapter. The student should be aware that modern individuality can be studied in many other ways as well. One could, for instance, focus on the appeal of anarchism in the nineteenth century or of existentialism in the twentieth. One could also study the modern personality cults (Stalin, Mao, Hollywood stars), the role of media in mass society, the post-Freudian literature of psychological self-help, advertising, public relations, film, the antihero in the modern novel, the technology or politics of surveillance. The possibilities are endless.

## Notes

1. Flavius Josephus, *The Jewish War*, Bk VII, ch. viii, v. 6, trans. Robert Traill (London: Houlston and Wright, 1868), p. 500.
2. *The New York Times*, November 29, 1978.
3. Jean-Jacques Rousseau, *Confessions*, anonymous trans. of 1783 and 1790 revised by A. S. B. Glover (New York: The Limited Editions Club, 1955), Pt. 1, Bk. 1, p. 3.
4. Ralph Waldo Emerson, "Self-Reliance" in Emerson, *Selected Prose and Poetry*, ed. Reginald L. Cook (New York: Holt, Rinehart and Winston, 1950), pp. 165, 166, and 168.
5. Quoted in Edward Shorter, "Towards a History of *La Vie Intime:* The Evidence of Cultural Criticism in Nineteenth-Century Bavaria" in *The Emergence of Leisure*, ed. Michael R. Marrus (New York: Harper & Row, 1974), p. 43.
6. *Ibid.*, p. 52.
7. *Ibid.*, p. 46–47.
8. Quoted in Melvin Kranzberg and Joseph Gies, *By the Sweat of Thy Brow: Work in the Western World* (New York: Putnam, 1975), pp. 126–127.
9. Thorstein Veblen, *The Portable Veblen*, ed. Max Lerner (New York: Viking Press, 1948), pp. 335–336.
10. *Ibid.*, pp. 336–337.
11. John Stuart Mill, *On Liberty*, ed. Currin V. Shields (Indianapolis: Bobbs-Merrill, 1956), p. 13.
12. *Ibid.*, pp. 67–68.
13. *Ibid.*, p. 67.
14. Kranzberg and Gies, *By the Sweat of Thy Brow*, p. 155.
15. *Ibid.*, pp. 155–156.

16. Edward L. Bernays, *Biography of an Idea: Memoirs of Public Relations, Counsel Edward L. Bernays* (New York: 1965), p. 387, excerpted in Warren Susman, ed., *Culture and Commitment 1929–1945* (New York: George Braziller, 1973), pp. 133–134.
17. *Ibid.*
18. Bernays, p. 390. Susman, pp, 136–137.
19. Bernays, p. 391. Susman, p. 138.
20. Bernays, p. 394. Susman, p. 140.
21. Paul Hilberg, *The Destruction of the European Jews* (New York: Quadrangle, 1967), p. 595.
22. Quoted in John Toland, *Adolf Hitler* (New York: Ballantine Books, 1976), p. 1052.
23. Albert Speer, *Inside the Third Reich* (trans. Richard and Clara Winston (New York: Macmillan, 1970), p. 375.
24. Richard L. Rubenstein, *The Cunning of History: The Holocaust and the American Future* (New York: Harper & Row, 1975), p. 60.
25. Adolf Hitler, *Mein Kampf*, trans. Ralph Manheim (Boston: Houghton Mifflin, 1943, 1971), p. 42.
26. *Ibid.*, pp. 478–479.
27. Mahatma Gandhi, *The Story of My Experiments with Truth* (London: Phoenix Press, 1949), pp. 36–37.
28. V. S. Naipaul, *India: A Wounded Civilization* (New York: Random House, 1976, 1977), p. 103.
29. *Ibid.*, pp. 107–108.
30. Gandhi, *Story*, p. 24.
31. Arthur Koestler, *The Lotus and the Robot* (New York: Macmillan, 1961), pp. 142–143.
32. Dr. Joshua S. Horn, *Away with All Pests* (New York: Monthly Review Press, 1969), pp. 18–19.

# Chapter 20

# Resources and Pollution

## Contemporary America

In the last few years the problems of ecology, energy, and economics have become closely interrelated. Our earlier study of ecology and theology (Chapter 12) suggested that the long-term environmental problem might be seen as a philosophical shift from cooperation with to exploitation of nature. We examined the rise of modern science as a culmination of that Judeo-Christian antagonism to nature. In our later study of energy and the environment (Chapter 16) we examined the role played by the technology of the industrial revolution and the economics of capitalism in furthering that antagonism and exploitation.

To what extent have our energy and environmental problems been caused by each of these factors: science, technology, and capitalism? This chapter will examine the evidence for American society in the recent past, from World War II to 1970. Our conclusion, and that of an increasing number of studies, is that the problems of energy and environment, resources and pollution, are largely economic.

## A Test Case: The American Present Since World War II

We might be able to better understand the interrelationship of some of the causes of ecological disaster (especially science, technology, and capitalism) by concentrating on a short time period. Since for every generation there is no time like the present, let us examine the period in America since World War II. For this period we are fortunately able to draw on an excellent study by the ecologist Barry Commoner called *The Closing Circle.*

Commoner computes that pollution levels in the United States have risen *between 200 and 2,000 percent* since 1946. In accounting for this startling rise, he first discounts the usual explanations: affluence and overpopulation. Affluence (wealth or economic growth) is not the cause, Commoner shows, because we are nothing like 200 to 2,000 percent richer than we were in 1946. Each American eats about the same amount of food as in 1946 (consisting actually of slightly less protein and slightly fewer calories). We each own about the same amount of clothing: the average use of clothing fiber was 45 pounds per person in 1946 and 49 pounds in 1968, an increase of 9 percent. The same is true of shelter: there has been only a very slight rise in the number of housing units available, considering the increase in population.

It is true that we have a lot more "things" than the average American had in 1946. "If affluence is measured in terms of certain household amenities, such as television sets, radios, and electric can-openers and corn-poppers, and in leisure items such as snowmobiles and boats, then there have been certain striking increases. But again, these items are simply too small a part of the nation's over-all production to account for the observed increase in pollution level."[1]

What Commoner means is that even if we consider all of the appliances and gadgets that have become household items since World War II, they still do not approach a 200 to 2,000 percent increase. The most optimistic measure of American economic growth is the Gross National Product (GNP). It is optimistic because it includes all goods and services, regardless of their benefits. This index has risen only about 50 percent per person since World War II, well below the rise in pollution.

Population is an equally limited explanation of our current pollution problem. The population of the United States has grown about 43 percent since World War II. Although that was a considerable increase (which has lately begun to level off) it would account for only a 43 percent increase in pollution, not an increase of 200 to 2,000 percent.

■ *A vision of postwar America by the great photographer Henri Cartier-Bresson. (Cartier-Bresson, Magnum)*

If we take both affluence (or economic growth) and increased population together, the highest estimate of the increase would be the approximately 125 percent GNP rise. Clearly we must look at other factors to determine why pollution levels have increased 200 to 2,000 percent since the war.

## The Technological Flaw

Commoner's conclusion is that the causes lie in the *kinds* of technology that have developed since the 1940s. You may recall that in our discussion of technology we suggested that twentieth-century technology was *potentially* a lot cleaner than the coal and iron technology of nineteenth-century industrialization. This potential was never fully realized. Instead, most of the technological developments of the last 30 years have been more harmful to the environment than earlier technologies. The main difference, especially since the 1940s, is that we have developed a technology of synthetic products and processes to replace an earlier natural, organic technology.

Commoner realized the importance of this change in kinds of technology by computing the postwar growth rate of certain selected products. We will summarize some of these.[2] The production of nonreturnable soda bottles increased 53,000 percent since 1946, to head the list. Synthetic fibers (like nylon and rayon) increased 5,980 percent. Mercury for chlorine production was up 3,930 percent. Air conditioner compressor units increased 2,850 percent. Plastics rose 1,960 percent. Fertilizer nitrogen production was up 1,050 percent. Electrical household appliances increased 1,040 percent. Synthetic organic chemicals rose 950 percent. Aluminum was up 680 percent. Chlorine gas rose 600 percent. Electrical power rose 530 percent. Pesticides were up 390 percent. Truck freight has risen 222 percent. Consumer electronics (like television and stereo sets) has climbed 217 percent. Motor fuel consumption had increased 190 percent. Cement production was up 150 percent.

Some products had grown at the same rate as the population (about 43 percent). Besides food, clothing, and shelter (already mentioned) they included household utilities, steel, copper, and other basic metals.

Those products which had increased slower than the population or actually decreased in production were: railroad freight, up 17 percent; lumber, down 1 percent; cotton fiber, down 36 percent; wool, down 42 percent; soap, down 76 percent; and, at the end of the line, work animal horsepower, down 87 percent.

> What emerges from all these data is striking evidence that while production for most basic needs—food, clothing, housing—has just about kept up with the 40 to 50 percent or so increase in population (that is, production *per capita* has been essentially constant), the *kinds* of goods produced to meet these needs have changed drastically. New production technologies have replaced old ones. Soap powder has been displaced by synthetic detergents; natural fibers (cotton and wool) have been displaced by synthetic ones; steel and lumber have been displaced by aluminum, plastics, and concrete; railroad freight has been displaced by truck freight; returnable bottles have been displaced by nonreturnable ones. On the road, the low-powered automobile engines of the 1920s and 1930s have been displaced by high-powered ones. On the farm, while per capita production has remained constant, the amount of harvest acreage had decreased; fertilizer has displaced land. Older methods of insect control have been displaced by synthetic insecticides, such as DDT, and for controlling weeds the cultivator has been displaced by the herbicide spray. Range-feeding of livestock has been displaced by feedlots.

. . .

> Distilled in this way, the mass of production statistics begins to form a meaningful pattern. In general, the growth of the United States economy since 1946 had a surprisingly small effect on the degree to which individual needs for basic economic goods have been met. That statistical fiction, the "average American," now consumes, each year, about as many calories, protein, and other foods (although somewhat less of vitamins); uses about the same amount of clothes and cleaners; occupies about the same amount of newly constructed housing; requires about as much freight; and drinks about the same amount of beer (twenty-six gallons per capita!) as he did in 1946. However, his food is now grown on less land with much more fertilizer and pesticides than before; his clothes are more likely to be made of synthetic fibers than of cotton or wool; he launders with synthetic detergents rather than soap; he lives and works in buildings that depend more heavily on aluminum, concrete, and plastic than on steel and lumber; the goods he uses are increasingly shipped by truck rather than rail; he drinks beer out of nonreturnable bottles or cans rather than out of returnable bottles or at the tavern bar. He is more likely to live and work in air-conditioned surroundings than before. He also drives about twice as far as he did in 1946, in a heavier car, on synthetic rather than natural rubber tires, using more gasoline per mile, containing more tetraethyl lead, fed into an engine of increased horsepower and compression ratio.[3]

In every one of these cases, Commoner goes on to show, not only have Americans failed to live any better, but the ecological impact of the new technology has been disastrous. Let us follow his examination of the consequences of some of these changes on our environment.

First we should look at what has become of the farm and pasture. Modern American agribusiness has separated the cycle of natural fertilization of the pasture. Cattle are now confined to feedlots instead of being able to wander in the pasture. So that they fatten faster, they are fed grain instead of grass. The ecological result is that manure accumulates in these small feedlots in dense quantities, instead of being spread evenly around the pasture. Feedlots, according to Commoner, "now produce more organic waste than the total sewage from all U.S. municipalities." Some surface water in the Midwest is already hopelessly polluted by the high concentration of manure that bleaches into the ground near feedlots.

Because the animals are confined, and because they are fed grain rather than grass, high amounts of synthetic nitrogen fertilizer are used to replenish the pasture and "supercharge" the grain crops. U.S. farms use 648 percent more nitrogen fertilizer than in 1949, overburdening city water supplies which are already too high in nitrates, to produce approximately the same amount of food on less land.

Pesticides have the same effect. Just as artificial nitrogen fertilizers reduce the growth of natural nitrogen in the soil, pesticides kill off the natural predators as well as the target insects. More and more fertilizers, and more and more pesticides, are necessary each year to achieve the same result. Crop quantities remain the same while they become more poisoned and water supplies become more dangerous.

The modern detergents which are used instead of soap have an environmental impact similar to the nitrates in fertilizer. Like the synthetic fertilizers, detergents require considerably more energy to create than their natural equivalent. And like the nitrates in synthetic fertilizers, the phosphates in detergents tax the oxygen in water with algae growth to the point where our lakes are dying. Soap is made naturally, breaks down easily, without environmental impact, and does the cleaning job as well as detergents. According to a recent textbook in chemical engineering: "There is no reason why old-fashioned soap cannot be used for most household and commercial cleaning jobs."[4]

The synthetic textiles which have virtually replaced organic materials (like cotton and wool) in the last 30 years have had a similar effect. Sheep and cotton plants grow from the natural energy of sunlight, rain, and soil nutrients. There is no pollution. Nylon requires six to ten chemical reactions up to 700° F (the melting point of lead), and high temperature combustion fuel as well as the original raw material, oil or gas. Besides wasting irreplaceable resources, there are waste fumes, pollution, and the final product cannot be broken down, except by fire (and more smoke). The same is true of plastics. Like other synthetic materials, plastics are made to last forever. Our beaches, garbage dumps, and our cities are a testament to that fact.

The greatest single source of urban environmental pollution is, of course, the automobile. Between 1947 and 1968 the number of cars on the road increased 166 percent. The total vehicle miles traveled increased 174 percent. But the amount of lead in the atmosphere (almost totally from automobile exhaust) increased 400 percent. The reason, then, for increased smog and leaded air was the kind of cars and the kind of gasoline that was increasingly produced since the 1940s. Between 1945 and 1968 Detroit built larger and heavier cars with more power, requiring more lead in the fuel to meet the ever higher combustion ratios. Only the force of government legislation has begun to reverse this process since the 1970s.

The rise in truck traffic and the decline of rail freight has had the same consequences. Trucks require six times the amount of fuel as trains, and emit about six times the environmental pollution, for the same haulage. Further, the amount of cement and steel needed for a four-lane highway requires almost four times the amount of energy required for a railroad.

There are numerous other ramifications of the new technology. The production of chemicals has increased about 1,000 percent. Some like mercury and chlorine, needed in the production of plastics and synthetic materials, have increased much more. The electrical power necessary for these chemical processes and for the production of aluminum and cement has increased over 500 percent.

The new technology in general, according to Commoner, accounts for about 95 percent of the added environmental pollution of the last 30 years, except for the case of passenger travel where it amounts to about 40 percent. (And here we should consider how much of our added travel is luxury, and how much is necessitated by the decay of cities, suburban sprawl, and highway lobbies.)

The question in Commoner's analysis of the last 30 years which cries out for an answer is *Why*? We have offered this test case to test the relative importance of science, technology, and capitalism in bringing about our current ecological crisis. In a sense, Commoner's answer is clearly that technology is the main problem. In fact, the chapter of *The Closing Circle* from which we have taken most of this information is entitled "The Technological Flaw." But Commoner was concerned with showing us that the problem was our recent technology, not our population or standard of living. We might well ask, as he does, why our technology has gotten out of hand.

Our problem, as Commoner is at pains to point out, is not technology itself. In a sense, modern technology has done exactly what it was asked to do. It was not flawed but immensely successful in increasing crop yields per acre, in creating synthetic materials that would last forever, and in making more powerful automobiles, among so many other things. We have seen that the new technology has created an enormous amount of problems in its wake, but we cannot blame that on the technologists. They simply performed the tasks that they were asked to perform.

## The Technology of Modern Science

We must now go beyond Commoner's description of the problem and attempt to find out why modern technology has been so shortsighted and so ecologically disastrous. Fortunately, Commoner helps us here also.

One of his answers is that this is the technology of modern science. We have already noticed the tendency of modern science to fragment nature into manageable sections. The scientist separates the object of his or her observation from the total organic context in which that object lives. To measure the butterfly it must be divorced from its environment. To calculate its wingspan, the wing must be—at least theoretically—detached from the body. To understand the parts of any natural process, we must disregard the whole. Scientific knowledge increases as we are able to break down things into their constituent parts. Technology is able to build machines when it understands how "live machines" function. Perhaps it is not so strange that the technique of science which treats organisms as if they were dead should create a technology that kills organisms.

To be less dramatic, it is at least fairly clear that much of modern technology has been flawed by a kind of "tubular vision" that overlooks the total setting. Commoner puts it this way:

> Now the reason for the ecological failure of technology becomes clear: unlike the automobile, the ecosystem cannot be subdivided into manageable parts, for its properties reside in the whole, in the connections between the parts. A process that insists on dealing only with the separated parts is bound to fail. . . . It explains why technology can design a useful fertilizer, a powerful automobile, or an efficient nuclear bomb. But since technology, as presently construed, cannot cope with the *whole* system on which the fertilizer, the automobile, or the nuclear bomb intrudes, disastrous ecological surprises—water pollution, smog, and global radioactive fallout—are inevitable.
>
> . . .
>
> It might be useful, at this point, to show that technology properly guided by appropriate scientific knowledge *can* be successful in the ecosystem, if its aims are directed toward the system as a whole rather than at some apparently accessible part.
>
> . . .
>
> There is, indeed, a specific fault in our system of science, and in the resultant understanding of the natural world, which, I believe, helps to explain the ecological failure of technology. This fault is reductionism, the view that effective understanding of a complex system can be achieved by investigating the properties of its isolated parts. The reductionist methodology, which is so characteristic of much of modern research, is not an effective means of analyzing the vast natural systems that are threatened by degradation. For example, water pollutants stress a total ecological web and its numerous organisms; the effects on the whole natural system are not adequately described by laboratory studies of pure cultures of separate organisms.[5]

The tendency of modern science to fragment nature parallels its tendency to fragment fields of specialization, and to separate science from real-life, human problems. The result is a lack of public awareness about the real choices facing the society, and a lack of knowledge about society's needs among the scientists that make the decisions.

That is one answer—and a compelling one—to explain the direction of modern American technology. But do the scientists really make the decisions, any more than the technologists? Are not most of the decisions about what is to be studied by the scientists, and what is to be made by the technologists, made by their corporate employers? Perhaps, we should look again at the economic system in which American scientists and technologists work.

Commoner, in fact, concludes his argument by examining the relationship between our new pollution and our system of private profit. He asks, "What is the connection between pollution and profit in a private enterprise economic system such as the United States?" He finds the connection pretty clear.

## The Technology of Corporate Capitalism

Soap seems to have been replaced by synthetic detergents because detergents bring a higher profit. "In 1947, when the industry produced essentially no detergents, the profit was 31 percent of sales. In 1967, when the industry produced 30 percent soap and 70 percent detergents, the profit from sales was 47 percent. From the data for intervening years it can be computed that the profit on pure detergent sales is about 54 percent, or nearly twice that of pure soap sales. . . . This helps to explain why, despite its continued usefulness for most cleaning purposes, soap has been driven off the market by detergents. It has benefitted the investor, if not society."[6]

The same is true of the synthetic chemical industry. From 1946 to 1966, "while the average return on net worth for all manufacturing industries was 13.1 percent, the chemical industry averaged 14.7 percent." This Commoner explains is because the particular chemical companies were able to gain temporary monopolies in the industry (and charge monopoly prices) by rapidly developing one new fabric, detergent, or pesticide after another. This "ecologist's nightmare" made it impossible to chart the effect of the new product on the environment before it was replaced by something else. "The very system of enhancing profit in this industry is precisely the cause of its intense, detrimental impact on the environment," according to Commoner. The environmental effect of such products is further complicated by the tendency, which we have already mentioned, for such chemicals like pesticides to become necessary in increasing dosages. Not only is the percentage of profit higher in synthetics, but the amount of their sales also increases.

This phenomenon is particularly obvious in the nitrate fertilizer industry. "To the salesman, nitrogen fertilizer is the 'perfect' product

—it wipes out the competition as it is used. . . . Like an addictive drug, fertilizer nitrogen and synthetic pesticides literally create demand as they are used; the buyer becomes hooked on the product."[7]

The postwar development of bigger and bigger cars also seems to have had a lot to do with profits. Henry Ford II put the matter succinctly when he said that "minicars make miniprofits." This is doubly true. Even if the automakers expected the same 10 percent profit on any size car, they would make more from the larger cars with higher prices. In fact, however, the German and Japanese competition forced Detroit to take less than 10 percent on the compacts, while the manufacturers were able to take more than 10 percent on the most expensive models.

Comparison of the profits of other new technologies is also instructive. In 1969, for example, steel companies made a profit of 12.5 percent of sales and lumber production yielded 15.4 percent. At the same time the new building technologies were getting 25.7 percent (for aluminum) and 37.4 percent (for cement). Similarly, the shareholders of trucking companies took 8.84 percent as profit while railroads were yielding 2.61 percent.

## Private Profits and Social Costs

The axiom that profit is good dominates so much of our thinking that we continually rationalize some of these developments. We think, sometimes unconsciously, as if Adam Smith's world were our own. We argue that high profits mean that these new companies must be doing something right. What we forget is that the thing they are doing right is making a lot of money, and that their achievement may cost the rest of us a good deal.

As long ago as 1950 the economist K. W. Kapp published a book called *The Social Costs of Private Enterprise* in which he pointed out that the conventional thinking of business managers fails to account for the social costs of their productivity. Like the individual in the commons each corporation only considers its private costs for material and labor when it computes its profits. Kapp has shown that if these companies were forced to add the costs of environmental degradation to their balance sheets, many of them would be forced to discontinue production. As long as we consider profit a private matter, and accept private profits as the criterion of success, we may suffer social costs which force the whole society to operate at a loss.

Another rationalization of the present system that we often hear (and sometimes make) is that private enterprise must be making a profit because they are giving the people what they want. This too sounds like Adam Smith. It assumes that large corporations are responsive to public demand. This sometimes seems to be a plausible argument because we can find many people who really want big cars, and who find the new synthetics easier or better in some way. This is partly because industry has not offered us soap chips in a box for laundering or decent materials in wood and steel. But it is also because industry has trained us with all of the power of advertising and the media to believe that we want the things that profit them the most.

It would be difficult to weigh the effect of advertising and the media. How much of our romance with cars was carefully cultivated by ads that enthrall us with the power, prestige, and sex appeal that only a Cadillac or a Ferrari can bring? It is at least interesting to note that we have spent more of our resources in the last 20 years on newsprint for advertising than on newsprint for news, and that we spend about ten times our resources on each minute of TV commercials than on each minute of programming. It is almost impossible to gauge the effect of these ads and commercials, but a study of detergent ads is enlightening. To quote Commoner again:

> A study in England shows that the sales of different brands of detergents are directly proportional to their relative advertising expenditures. Nor is this a matter of merely acquainting the buyer with the virtues of the product with the expectation that these virtues will then sustain further purchases. For, when advertising is cut back, sales fall off. In 1949 Unilever spent 60 percent of the total costs for advertising detergents in England and enjoyed 60 percent of the total sales; by 1951 its advertising budget had been reduced to 20 percent of the total and sales had fallen off to 10 percent. The lesson was learned, however; by 1955 advertising expenditures—and sales—had tripled from the 1951 low.[8]

It seems pretty clear that we often buy what is advertised in almost direct proportion to the advertising. The message of the advertising is almost irrelevant. It is even more disturbing, then, that we insist we are buying the best product. We are manipulated, and then we must assure ourselves of our freedom of choice by denying that manipulation ever occurred.

## Don't Socialists Pollute?

Finally, there is a defense of private enterprise that goes something like this: "It's not only private profit that pollutes our environment. Look at what the 'people's managers' are doing in Russia. Soviet rivers and lakes have been polluted by socialist administrators who are every bit as 'productivity conscious' as capitalist investors are hungry for profits."

Western socialists have, perhaps, been too quick to excuse the pollution of countries which call themselves socialist or communist. Soviet environmental pollution is sometimes defended by Western socialists as an inevitable consequence of rapid industrialization. Sometimes the severity of pollution in the Soviet Union is denied. Sometimes it is accepted as one of the "capitalist" features of the Soviet Union, and is contrasted with a purer, more ecologically sound socialism in China.

None of these arguments will be made here. Even the defense of Chinese environmentalism makes little sense to one who has been reminded of the oil refineries on the New Jersey turnpike when sailing down the Wangpoa River to the city of Shanghai, or been forced to remove contact lenses because of the soot in the air in both Peking and Los Angeles. The low-grade fuel burned by the lawn-mower-like engines of small Chinese vehicles, the filthy exhaust from Chinese buses, and the black smoke pouring out of Chinese smokestacks are reminders of the technological underdevelopment of China, not harbingers of a purer socialism. The city air of Canton, Shanghai, or Peking is somewhat cleaner than that of Tokyo, one suspects, only because most Chinese still must get around on bicycles or buses instead of cars.

The visitor to China does not need the continual, self-conscious reminders of the Chinese guides to recognize that China is a poor country. Although the people are all fed, clothed, and employed for the first time in Chinese history, the distinctive feature of the country is that it is poor, not socialist or communist. The remarkable achievement of what the Chinese wish to call their Communist Revolution is that it has eliminated starvation, begging, servitude, and foreign exploitation in a single generation. China has abolished the grinding, personal poverty and despair that was common before the revolution, and that still exists in India today. One need only venture to walk the streets of the Indian cities of Calcutta or Bombay to measure the enormity of the transformation of China.

But twentieth-century China is in no position to carry out the socialist transformation that Marx envisioned for the advanced capitalist world. Nor was Russia in 1917. The fact that Lenin and Mao Tse-tung imagined that they could leap from a feudal to a modern socialist society does not mean that they could. Even if we accept the attempt by the Russian and Chinese revolutionaries to use the theory of advanced, industrial Marxism for their own revolutionary purposes, even if we agree to call these revolutions socialist or communist (and that concedes more than Marx would have allowed), we would mean something vastly different from the socialism possible today in Western Europe or the United States. The question is not whether Russia or China are better off than the United States. The question is whether a socialist America would be better off than a capitalist America.

## Capitalism and Growth

Some observers insist that there is a single drawback to ecological sanity in capitalist societies. They argue (with Adam Smith, incidentally) that capitalist countries can only prosper as long as they continue to grow and expand. We hear this view from friends and enemies of capitalism. Here is the position of Karl Marx (according to the modern liberal economist, Robert Heilbroner):

> The very essence of capitalism, according to Marx, is expansion—which is to say, the capitalist, as a historical "type," finds his raison d'etre in the insatiable search for additional money-wealth gained through the constant growth of the economic system. The idea of a "stationary" capitalism is, in Marxian eyes, a contradiction in terms.[9]

So that we do not immediately discount this view as the perversity of Marx, it might be worthwhile to quote more "respectable" modern commentators. According to LaMont Cole of Cornell University, "Our fundamental problem is what I would like to call our 'chamber of commerce' syndrome, that growth is good." Paul Ehrlich of Stanford University puts it this way:

> Our entire economy is geared to growing population and monumental waste. Buy land and hold it; the price is sure to go up. Why? Exploding population on a finite planet. Buy natural resources stocks; their price is sure to go up. Why? Exploding population and finite resources. Buy automotive or airline stocks; their price is sure to go up. Why? More people to move around. . . . And so it goes. Up goes the population, and up goes the magical figure, the Gross National Product. . . . We have assumed the role of the robber barons of all time. We have decided that we are the chosen people to steal all we can get of our planet's gradually stored and limited resources.[10]

In all fairness we should point out that this view of expansion as happiness was borrowed by many socialist thinkers. But they did not have too. For the followers of Adam Smith it was essential. Smith was rebelling in 1776 against a kind of economic philosophy—mercantilism—which assumed that the wealth of the Earth was fixed and finite. Wealth, according to mercantilist philosophy, could only be obtained if one were able to "beggar thy neighbor." Since there was only so much to go around, one country's gain could only be viewed as another country's loss. The achievement of Adam Smith was to teach people that industrial wealth could come from the power of the machine and the dynamics of the economy, that real wealth could be much greater than resources. Adam Smith must be honored for shaking his contemporaries (as did Darwin a hundred years later) from the view that the world was stable. Smith showed that a competitive economy could *create* wealth, that industry added new wealth; he showed that the new technology and the new economy could go beyond the age-old mercantilist dream of merely redistributing the wealth that existed.

That is why Adam Smith was able to argue that private profit equalled social profit. Private capitalism was able to create new sources of wealth, and it seemed for a while that this new wealth from machines would answer the needs of the whole society. It did not, as things turned out. But, more significantly, we are now at the point where we have to look again at resources. Machines and capitalism have done a lot to give us a temporary escape from the dilemma of the mercantilists, but that escape has used up much of our resources. Now, again, we have to face the problem of distribution. Ecology is, after all, the problem of the finite. Adam Smith's miracle has transformed society and benefited all of us. For an age of virgin forests and untapped mineral resources, it was valuable to know that wealth could be created. Now that we have accomplished that miracle, we can no longer afford to ignore the natural limitations of our world. Competitive capitalism, and the industrial revolution that it nurtured, has given us the ability to pay back our debt to nature. It has also made that compensation mandatory. As with so many things, the problem and solution come from the same source. We can afford, again, to think of the commons, but we have been taught so long to think of the private that it may be too late. Changing our economy may be as difficult as changing our religion.

## Capitalism, Socialism, and Government: The Case of Nuclear Energy

Many Americans associate capitalism with freedom from government interference and socialism with government control. Thus, they see the United States becoming increasingly socialistic as the government extends its control over new areas of business and public life. The issue is much more complex, however. Big government has actually been the product of advanced capitalist society. Even government regulation has been the creation of corporate business interests, who have seen it as a way of muting popular dissent and eliminating competition. Government regulation can be carried out on behalf of the larger corporations against the interest of smaller competitors, or it can be used to advance the prestige or profits of business in general. There is no automatic correlation between increased government control and an increasing drift toward socialism. The extension of government controls can even enhance the power of business and forestall socialist solutions. Government control can be "socialistic" if it is exercised on behalf of the people in general. It is not if it is exercised on behalf of the people who own capital alone.

The complexity of this issue can be seen in the development of the current debate about nuclear energy. It might be argued that nuclear energy, more than any other source, is a general social concern, rather than a mere matter of business exploitation. The consequences of a nuclear disaster could be enormous in human terms, and no business promise that a disaster is impossible could be satisfactorily redeemed if it did occur. Thus, one would expect this to be an important matter for government regulation and control. In fact, it is, and it is not. The Atomic Energy Commission and its successor, the Nuclear Regulatory Commission, have been given enormous power over the activities of the private companies and public utilities that have developed nuclear power. But the members of these commissions have usually been proponents of the development of nuclear energy, and they have worked closely with, befriended, and later been employed by the directors of the companies concerned. As a result, the interests of the public have often been as poorly represented in government as they are in the industry. When leaks of radiation have occurred at nuclear power plants, the government commissioners have often been as eager as industry representatives to console the public and attest to the essential safety of the enterprise. To many government and industry representatives alike, such "events" (both accept the neutral word) are causes for denial and defense rather than systematic reevaluation.

One could conceivably argue that the question of nuclear energy would be better (more safely) handled by a genuinely capitalist economy than by the current combination of large corporations and their government supporters. If the development of nuclear energy were left to the private sector of the economy without any government intervention, then private energy companies would take their chances, charge their rates, and buy their insurance against disasters. The problem is not only that they would have to do without government support in the importation of plutonium and the building of plants, they would also not get private insurance companies to insure their economic and human losses. The insurance companies find the risk of catastrophe so great that they refuse to insure the power plants. There would probably be no nuclear energy.

Instead, we are faced with a combination of business interests eager to use government to increase their profits and governmental administrators eager to serve the interests of nuclear energy. And the combination has not been limited to regulatory commissioners alone. President Eisenhower told the Atomic Energy Commission in 1953 to keep the public "confused" with its explanations of radioactive fallout.[11] The United States Congress passed the Price-Anderson Act in 1957, and renewed it in 1965 and 1974. The act limited the liability of insurance companies for nuclear disasters to a small fraction of the projected claims, forcing the taxpayer to bear more than 80 percent of the burden for accidents that the insurance companies would not otherwise insure.[12]

Governmental action is not necessarily equivalent to public health or socialism. But as the dominant corporations of the twentieth century have largely extinguished the competitive economy, the government has become the arena for important public decisions. Socialists argue that for all its drawbacks, the government is still a preferable arena to the corporate boardroom. At least, they argue, the public can vote for members of Congress who vote against bills like Price-Anderson, and representatives in local, state, and national government who put the interests of public welfare before those of private profit. The members of the corporate board, or the stockholders of the corporation, would be foolish to do so.

## *For Further Reading*

In this chapter we have concentrated on the argument of Barry Commoner's **The Closing Circle.*** It is well worth reading in full, as is his more recent **The Poverty of Power.*** K. William Kapp's **The Social Costs of Private Enterprise,*** which we have also used, is dated but valuable. Similar, but more recent, approaches can be found in Paul Ehrlich's **The End of Affluence,*** Michael Harrington's **The Twilight of Capitalism,*** especially his chapter on "The Common Good as Private Property," and in John Kenneth Galbraith's **Economics and the Public Purpose,*** especially his chapter on "The Socialist Imperative." All of the books mentioned in the last two paragraphs of the bibliography to Chapter 16 are also useful here.

On the question of population, Carlo M. Cipolla's **The Economic History of World Population*** is an excellent introduction. Paul and Anne Ehrlich's **Population, Resources, Environment** is a good update of the classical view

* Available in paperback.

of Thomas Malthus's **First Essay on Population.*** **Population Crisis: An Interdisciplinary Perspective,*** edited by Sue Titus Reid and David L. Lyon, collects some valuable classic and current articles. E. A. Wrigley's **Population and History*** is a good general historical survey. Elborg and Robert Forster's **European Diet from Pre-Industrial to Modern Times*** collects some good historical essays on food supply and population growth.

Technology, industrial growth, and pollution are explored in **Economic Growth versus the Environment,** edited by Warren A. Johnson and John Hardesty, in **Environmental Quality in a Growing Economy,** edited by Henry A. Jarrett, and in Paul Baran's **The Political Economy of Growth.***

The role of science since World War II is explored in Daniel S. Greenberg's **The Politics of Pure Science.*** Richard Feynman's **Character of Physical Law*** is a readable introduction to the philosophy of science. Hans Thirring's **Energy for Man*** is a valuable account of the physics of energy production. Alfred North Whitehead's **Science and the Modern World*** is a classic statement which is still a valuable introduction. Both the American Chemical Society's **Cleaning Our Environment: The Chemical Basis for Action** and M.I.T.'s **Study of Critical Environmental Problems; Man's Impact on the Global Environment** are good sources on scientific aspects of the problem.

We have already mentioned a number of books here and in Chapter 16's For Further Reading that are useful on the economic aspects of the problem. Other studies which are critical of capitalism are James Ridgeway's **The Politics of Ecology,*** *Ramparts*'s **Eco-Catastrophe,*** and Paul Baran and Paul Sweezy's **Monopoly Capital.*** For criticisms of the Soviet economy's dependence on growth, see Leon Trotsky's **The Revolution Betrayed,*** Milovan Djilas's **The New Class,*** and Raya Dunayevskaya's **Marxism and Freedom.** Samuel P. Hays's **Conservation and the Gospel of Efficiency*** is a good history of the early conservation movement in America.

Finally, a good introduction to Chinese problems and achievements (in agricultural productivity, pest control, and the elimination of grinding poverty) can be found in Keith Buchanan's **The Transformation of the Chinese Earth.**

## Notes

1. Barry Commoner, *The Closing Circle* (New York: Knopf, 1972), p. 139.
2. *Ibid.*, p. 143.
3. *Ibid.*, pp. 143–154.
4. *Ibid.*, p. 156.
5. *Ibid.*, pp. 187–189.
6. *Ibid.*, p. 259.
7. *Ibid.*, p. 153.
8. *Ibid.*, p. 157.
9. *Ibid.*, p. 276.
10. Cole and Ehrlich quoted in Peter Schrag, "Who Owns the Environment?" *Saturday Review*, 4 July 1970, p. 7.
11. *The New York Times*, April 20, 1979, p. 1.
12. Paul Ehrlich, *The End of Affluence* (New York: Random House, Ballantine Books, 1974), p. 71.

# Chapter 21

# Culture and Change

## Beyond Certainty and Relativity

During the last hundred years Western culture—the ideas, values, mentalities, and feelings of men and women in the most industrialized part of the world—has gone through a profound change. It might not be too simplistic to call it a change from certainty to relativity. Over a hundred years ago people were certain about almost everything. God, progress, truth, beauty, human motivation, morality, sexuality, marriage, civilization, war, economics, and nature were all clear concepts about which certain definite, often absolute, statements could be made. Today, as the preceding chapters have shown, such certainty is no longer possible.

We live today in what has been called an age of uncertainty and anxiety, of relativity and cynicism. This chapter will look at how this change to relativity came about. It begins with a survey of the development of modern culture in just one of its many forms—painting from 1863 to 1913. This leads to an investigation into the development of modern ideas of change and culture—one of the sources of modern uncertainty and relativity. Then, our chapter focuses on some of the confrontations with relativity in the twentieth century and some of the attempts to understand it and overcome it. In essence, our concluding chapter asks how we are learning to live with the conclusions of this book.

## Modern Painting: A Visual Barometer of Change

One of the best ways to see the change to modern culture in the last hundred years is to walk through a museum or thumb through a history of painting. Whether you begin with European painting in the Renaissance, the seventeenth century, the eighteenth century, or even the beginning of the nineteenth century, you see (despite changes in style) the same things. You see objects, landscapes, and people. They are identifiable as such. They are shown in three-dimensional perspective: things get smaller and fuzzier the further they recede into the background, just the way we see. They show shadows all going in the same direction. Usually they look beautiful, but even when they show violence or warts it is to look noble, dramatic, or uplifting. They convey messages like "how enchanting," "so real," "how courageous Napoleon was"; they tell stories and show what things look like. There are exceptions, of course, but almost all paintings from the Renaissance to the end of the nineteenth century reflect these interests in visual accuracy, beauty, and "objective" truth. The paintings themselves are framed, rectangular "windows" on the world. As we approach the paintings of the late nineteenth century all of this changes: colors seem wrong; objects are not recognizable; nothing looks like anything anymore. What happened?

We would have been able to see the beginning of this revolution if we had attended the Salon des Refusés ("Room of the Rejected") at the "Exposition des Beaux-Arts" in Paris in 1863. The mere existence of such a room was something of a revolution. The French emperor, Napoleon III, had stepped in on behalf of the artists whose work had been rejected from the official exhibition. He ordered the creation of an annex which would contain the rejected work so that the public could decide for themselves if the official jury had acted wisely. The reaction of the public was derisive laughter and renewed faith in the official jury. Only a few who came to laugh left "serious, anxious, and troubled" or struck by "a certain sincerity . . . novelty and singularity," as two reviewers noted.[1]

The painting which most outraged the public, the jury, and the critics was Edouard Manet's *Le dejeuner sur l'herbe* (*Luncheon on the*

▪ *Edouard Manet's* Le déjeuner sur l'herbe (Luncheon on the Grass). *(Louvre, Jeu de Paume)*

*Grass*). Most professed to be disgusted by the appearance of a nude woman in a public park with two well-dressed gentlemen. The emperor, who had a string of mistresses in private, was said to have been shocked. At least one critic complained of the unconventional technique: the lack of three-dimensional depth, and the flatness of perspective in clothes that seemed to hang without bodies, "boneless fingers and heads without skulls," and "side whiskers made of two strips of black cloth." Most, however, complained of the subject matter. A visiting English critic was impressed by Manet's attempt to translate the Renaissance subject into modern French, and he pardoned its "fine colour," but he too found the subject of "doubtful morality."

The revolution of modern art began as an attack on traditional subject matter. Manet's nude at a picnic could not be dismissed as a classical goddess: she seemed to come out of the Parisian underworld. She was hardly a fitting subject for a great work of art: that is what shocked the critics.

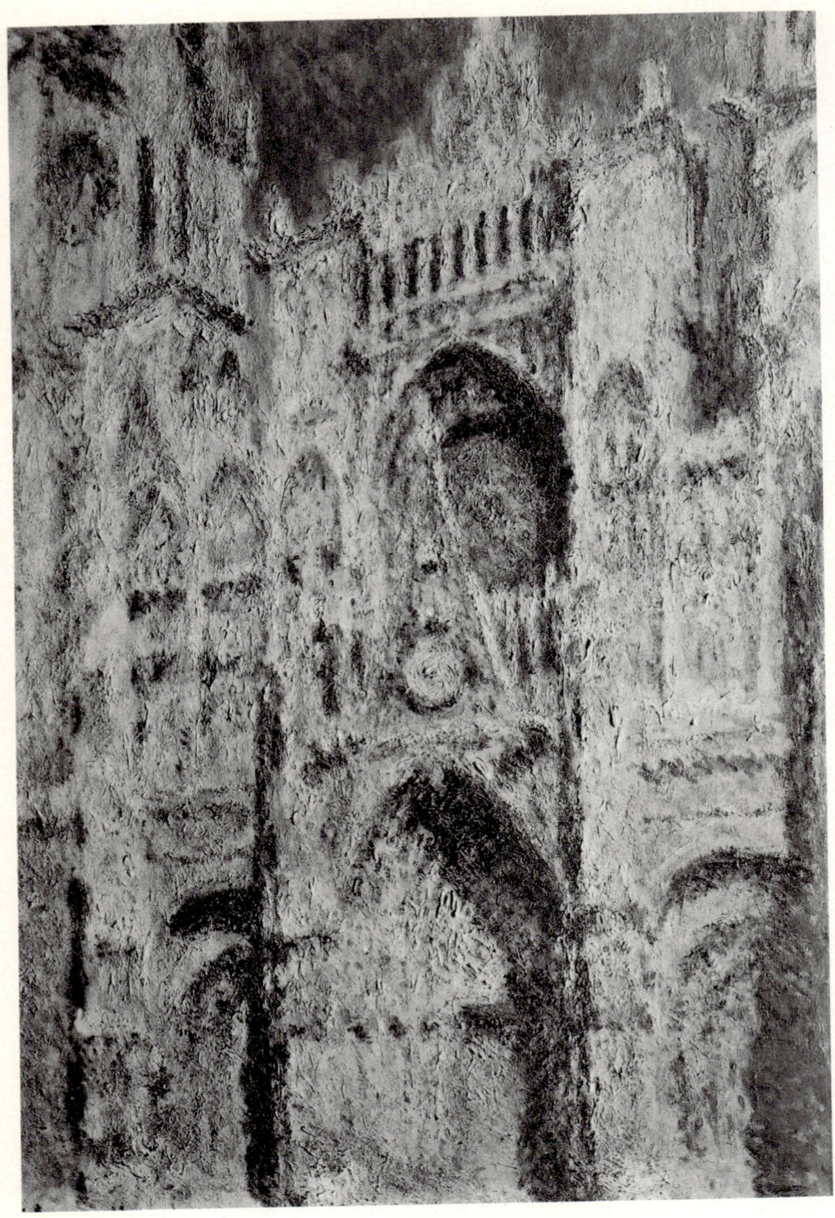

■ *Claude Monet's impressionistic* Rouen Cathedral. *This is one of many paintings Monet did of the Cathedral at different times of day to capture momentary changes of light. (The Metropolitan Museum of Art, The Bequest of Theodore M. Davis, 1915)*

From the perspective of today, however, the most visible shift in the history of modern art occurred not with the new *subjects* of the Salon des Refusés, but with the new *styles* of the next decades: Impressionism and Expressionism. The flatness of Impressionism was already implicit in Manet's work of 1863, and the young group of French Impressionists gathered around Manet in the next decade. The paintings of Claude Monet, Auguste Renoir, Edgar Degas, Camille Pissarro, and Paul Cézanne that were gathered together in the first Impressionist exhibition in 1874 were attacked more for a lack of drawing than a lack of decency. Today we can praise their bold use of color, their meticulous perception of light, their imaginative way of capturing the impermanence of a rapidly changing world, their willingness to paint outdoors, their joyous spontaneity in the ordinary and the transient, or their almost instinctive search for new perceptions that would not be outdone by the developing technology of the camera (the first exhibition was held in a famous photographer's studio). In 1874 the critics treated the show as if it were a hoax. "Do you recall the Salon des Refusés?" the paper *La Patrie* asked. Well, that was the fine museum of the Louvre compared to the paintings of the Impressionist exhibition. "Looking at the first rough drawings—and rough is the right word—you simply shrug your shoulders; seeing the next lot, you burst out laughing; but with the last ones you finally get angry."

The critics saved most of their venom for Cézanne's *A Modern Olympia.* Cézanne had taken a classical theme—the reclining goddess Olympia—which Manet has already modernized in 1865 to the consternation of the Parisian art world. Manet's *Olympia* pictured the goddess as a Parisian prostitute in a setting that looked all too much like a brothel. (Manet's *Olympia* was called the first work of modern art because it was the first to require police protection.) Cézanne modernized the theme and style of Olympia much further. The goddess became a willowy dream, unveiled by her black attendant for the artist on the couch as flowers exploded with expectation overhead.

Cézanne's dreamy confrontation with Olympia, a painting which was already beyond the boundaries of Impressionism, was described over and over again as the work of a madman. Cézanne was to lead the next generation of Western painting into an expressionist style that made the work of the Impressionists look "pretty" and "quaint."

While the Impressionists were still concerned with capturing an objective reality of color and light, if only for an instant, the Expressionists turned inward to express the emotional dimension of the artist's experience. While the Impressionists had relished the flickering, endless changes of their world the Expressionists (perhaps overwhelmed by change) sought universals in their own personal feelings,

■ *Paul Cézanne's* A Modern Olympia.
*(Musée Jeu de Paume, EPA)*

the symbols of dreams, and the abstract structure of materials. In this broad sense, almost all post-impressionist art was Expressionist, and remains so even today.

We can get a more manageable idea of the extent of this change if we look at a few of the works displayed at one landmark exhibition of the twentieth century. The work displayed at the American Armory Show of 1913 reflected a more radical idea of art than that suggested by the canvases of the nineteenth century Salon des Refusés or the Impressionist exhibition. They made Manet's *Dejeuner sur l'herbe* and even Cézanne's *A Modern Olympia* look like continuations of the Renaissance. And we understand the radical departure of modern art even more fully by noticing the responses of the critics and the public to this twentieth-century exhibition. Not only do the paintings seem to come from another planet, but they were also accepted without much of the shock and scandal of the more modest departures of 1863 and 1874.

The organizers of the American Armory Show of 1913 attempted to bring to New York City "the most complete art exhibition that has ever been held in the world during the last quarter century." Allowing for American exaggeration, they were pretty close to the truth. Many of the major Post-impressionists were represented. There were works by Vincent van Gogh, Paul Gauguin, and Pablo Picasso (as well as Cézanne) which were still shocking for their flat perspective, sketchy outline, bright, broad patches of color, and almost cubist, geometrical shapes. But the most radical departures from traditional painting, and the most heatedly debated of the show, were the paintings of Henri Matisse and Marcel Duchamp. Matisse's *The Blue Nude* seemed to assault the viewer's traditional expectations with the pose, look, and setting, but especially the blue color of the model. Duchamp's *Nude Descending a Staircase* showed neither staircase nor nude, but almost a blurred study of machinelike parts in rapid movement.

The reviewers and public had a lot of fun with the more radical exhibits. Almost all tried out their wit at the expense of Duchamp: one concluded that it was actually "a staircase descending a nude." Another called it "an explosion in a shingle factory."

■ *Henri Matisse's* Blue Nude. *(The Baltimore Museum of Art, The Cone Collection, formed by Dr. Claribel Cone and Miss Etta Cone of Baltimore, Maryland)*

NU DESCENDANT UN ESCALIER

> The jibe was perceptive, up to a point. The figure is indeed shattered into shinglelike planes that merge and overlap in a pattern of great energy. But the jibe falls short in that the shattered figure is not chaotic. Contrarily, it is reassembled into a pattern of great order and vivacity, more expressive of bright descending movement than an imitative painting of a nude descending a staircase could be.[2]

The public was infuriated by playful titles, cubist studies of structure and movement, and expressionist uses of color and line. They resented artists that challenged or made fun of their expectations. But given the radical divergence from traditional art, and keeping in mind the charges of scandal, hoax, and madness in 1863 and 1874, the remarkable thing is the good-natured character of the criticism and the degree of public and critical acceptance of these most avant-garde works.

Few viewers responded as sensitively as the American painter John Sloan who described the exhibition as:

> The beginning of a journey into the living past. The blinders fell from my eyes and I could look at religious pictures without seeing their subjects. I was freed to enjoy the sculptures of Africa and prehistoric Mexico because visual verisimilitude was no longer important. I realized that these things were made in response to life, distorted to emphasize ideas about life, emotional qualities about life.[3]

Few were as sympathetic as Stuart Davis the younger American painter who recalled:

> I responded particularly to Gauguin, Van Gogh, and Matisse, because broad generalisations of form and the non-imitative use of colour were already practices within my own experience.[4]

But eighty-seven thousand admissions were recorded in New York, and by the time the show had returned from Boston and Chicago, three hundred thousand Americans had been introduced to modern art. Many of the paintings (including those of Duchamp) were purchased by collectors. There were even many favorable reviews of the exhibition. Surprisingly, it was a great success. But why?

The paintings in the 1913 exhibition were far more radically modern than those of the Paris exhibitions in 1863 and 1874. Not only had modern painting distinguished itself more from the traditional in

■ *Marcel Duchamp's* Nude Descending a Staircase. *(Philadelphia Museum of Art)*

those 40 years, but many Americans were viewing "modern art" for the first time, while Parisians were shocked at slight departures of a few years or a decade. Why, then, did Americans in 1913 respond so much more tolerantly (and even enthusiastically) to much greater changes?

Part of the answer is provided by one of the most notable visitors to the New York Armory, President Theodore Roosevelt. Roosevelt's personal taste in art ran to drawings of wild animals. He admitted that the more extreme paintings in the Armory show were beyond him. He made fun of people who called themselves Cubists. It seemed to him something like calling themselves "Knights of the Isosceles Triangle, or Brothers of the Cosine." He preferred Navajo rugs to Duchamp's *Nude*. But—and here is the point—he insisted that the organizers of the show "are quite right as to the need of showing to our people in this manner the art forces which of late have been at work in Europe, forces which cannot be ignored." He welcomed "newness" and "progress" and agreed that "there can be no life without change, no development without change, and that to be afraid of what is different or unfamiliar is to be afraid of life."[5]

This was the faith of the progressive era of the early twentieth century. It was also a recurring American faith. But, perhaps most significantly, it was one of the only possible attitudes to the sheer enormousness of change that had swept Western society in the preceding half century.

We see, then, a number of things in Western art in the 50 years before World War I. We see the sudden transformation of a traditional, centuries-old style of painting. In 50 years artists abandoned the models of centuries. We see that the artists themselves were responding to, and attempting to show, the changes sweeping their world. We see increasing public acceptance of the artists' radically new perception. But we also see that the public was accepting change more than they were understanding the new art.

If the critics of 1863 and 1874 rejected new departures for the wrong reasons or without understanding them, by 1913 the critics and even much of the general public were *accepting* modern art for similar wrong reasons, without understanding them. In fact, the critics and public of 1863 and 1874 probably understood more of what was happening than did either group in 1913. Art had changed fundamentally. It ceased to communicate with the educated populace. It would have been absurd in 1913 for the president of the United States to urge the public to judge the jurors (as Napoleon III had done in 1863). The organizers of the Armory exhibition had even hoped originally to hang everything submitted. Jury selection, artistic criticism, aesthetic standards no longer seemed to make any sense.

Change had been so rapid that there were no standards available. The new artists had fought against the traditional standards, but their experimentation with new forms was so varied that no new standards were possible. A public that accepted change for its own sake smiled, satirized, or bought, but without understanding what the artists were saying.

## The Discovery of Change and Culture

The idea that change is one of the fundamental ingredients of life (perhaps, in fact, the only one) is very recent. It is an idea which was whispered in the eighteenth century, but has become popular only in the last century. Even today, many people who recognize that everything changes are as unaware of the implications of that idea as was Teddy Roosevelt.

All societies since the Neolithic revolution have recognized that seasons change. Even earlier societies knew that people changed, at least in growing older. But almost all societies before the last hundred years thought that human continuity was much more basic than human change. The ancient Hebrews were probably the first society to understand themselves in terms of change. Their Bible was a history book because they believed that God revealed his promises and commands through the history of his chosen people. Christians continued to believe that God acted through history: the period after Christ was fundamentally different from the period before; Christ would at some revealed time return; the temper of the times had to be understood in order to understand God's design for man. The Christians also placed a premium on the individual's capacity to change: although everyone was born with original sin, conversion gave one a new life, indeed an eternal life. These ideas were quite different from those of Asia, Africa, the Americas, and even Greece and Rome. The Greeks, Romans, Chinese, and some other societies, wrote histories, but in order to understand what had always been, not to understand how things were changing. They believed that time was a succession of repeating cycles and that human nature was always the same. Their history writing was for them a source of moral examples that would show a ruler how to govern and the people why they should behave. In classical Greece and Rome this "exemplar history" became quite sophisticated in explaining the causes of events and the motivations of people—but always in terms of what was imagined to be human nature.

Actually Christian consciousness of change became subordinate in the Middle Ages to the church's control of revelation and interpretation. Medieval Christian history was limited to "lives of the saints" which taught the same examples by telling the same stories. The potential of Christian culture to grapple with change as a fundamental reality lay dormant until the influence of the church was challenged by secular science and the Protestant Reformation.

Western historical writing regained some of the sophistication of the classical world during the Renaissance, partly because historians like Machiavelli and Guicciardini modeled their work on classical histories. We have seen in our reading of Machiavelli, for instance, how he borrowed examples from classical Greece or his contemporary Italy as if both periods were the same in all essentials. He recognized differences, to be sure. In fact, he wrote *The Prince* with an eye to what he saw as the superiority of pagan religion over Christianity. But he imagined that Italians could adopt pagan values because he did not understand that Christianity had brought about fundamental changes. He saw religions, like political strategies, to be interchangeable, because he believed that all people were essentially the same.

But the Europeans of Machiavelli's time were beginning to discover that some people in the world were very, very different. The first letter of Columbus (written on the return voyage of the *Niña* in 1493) was printed throughout Europe and (according to legend) sung on the streets of Italian cities.

> The people of this island, and of all the other islands which I have found and of which I have information, all go naked, men and women, as their mothers bore them, although some women cover a single place with the leaf of a plant or with a net of cotton which they make for the purpose. They have no iron or steel or weapons, nor are they fitted to use them, not because they are not well built men and of handsome stature, but because they are marvellously timorous. . . . They are so guileless and so generous with all they possess that no one would believe it who has not seen it. They never refuse anything which they possess, if it be asked of them; on the contrary, they invite anyone to share it, and display so much love as if they would give their hearts.[6]

The immediate European response to the discovery of vastly different peoples was to place them in the legendary golden age of classical mythology which corresponded somewhat to the Christian idea of the time "before the fall" of Adam and Eve. But this was a literary and mythological solution, not an historical or anthropological one. Eventually, however, the persistent questions which were posed by the existence of such peoples led Europeans to discover "culture" and "change," the inventions of modern anthropology and history.

Three thinkers of the eighteenth-century Enlightenment stand out in the European discovery of culture. They are Montesquieu, Voltaire, and Vico. Both Montesquieu and Voltaire tried to account for the similarities and differences among the world's peoples within an overall framework that would do for human society what Newton's scientific laws had done for the physical world. Both realized that there were certain connections or relationships which taken together made up a people's culture (today we often use the word "life-style"). There were, to use Columbus's information as an example, certain connections between going naked and having no steel or iron weapons, and possibly even a relationship between both of these and the American natives' habit of generosity. The ingredients of a particular culture fit together. They were not completely arbitrary or accidental. It would be highly unlikely, for instance, to find a society whose inhabitants went around naked and also forged steel.

Having read this far, such a conclusion should be obvious to the reader. We have shown continually in these chapters how certain cultural forms were related to each other: farming, containers, villages, fertility symbols, and female deities; cities, kingship, patriarchy, armies, and abstractions; printing, privacy, and individuality; Christianity and exploitation of nature; slavery and dominative racism, to mention only a few. But, perhaps because people like to think that they are themselves free to do whatever they want and, in fact, feel the anxiety of choice every time they do something, they often do not recognize how much their culture determines their very options and choices. As a result, they are slow to recognize the existence of culture as a set of forms which both limits and permits certain kinds of walking, talking, dreaming, and doing. Europeans like Montesquieu, Voltaire, and Vico were beginning to understand this in the eighteenth century. (A good example of the failure of some people to understand these connections even today is the popularity of books like Erich von Daniken's which accept obvious cultural incongruities—electrical batteries, transmitters, and the like—in Neolithic society.)

Both Montesquieu and Voltaire, however, stopped short of allowing their discovery of culture to lead them to a discovery of fundamental change. Montesquieu developed a modern comparative method for outlining the internal relationships of cultures. He organized new information about different peoples into what Max Weber later called "ideal types" or abstract shorthands about cultural forms. But he held to a faith in human nature by suggesting that every cultural variety was a product of a particular "spirit of laws," and that there were only three fundamental types of such spirits. Voltaire argued that a history of customs would reveal more about people than any history of kings and battles, but his own historical writing treated peoples of every age as if they had the same values, motivations, and attitudes as the eighteenth-century French. Both Voltaire and Montesquieu, for instance, refused to believe the observations of the classical historian Herodotus about certain sexual customs of the classical world.

Giambattista Vico's *The New Science* (1725) was the first modern anthropology and the first modern history in that it accepted the uniqueness of primitive and ancient cultures and recognized that all ideas and institutions (even the most sacred) had human histories. It was the first study of culture and change which denied the constancy of human nature. Vico found similarities and even cyclical repetitions in human history, but they were the cycles of the spiral, not of the circle. For Vico, human history changed fundamentally because it was a cumulative process created by human beings. Each age had its own culture—its own morals, myths, and language. Each age created the preconditions for the next, but could only be understood fully on its own terms. For Vico, the recognition of cultural variety led to the recognition of change. It was not enough to explain cultural types in terms of particular environments (as Montesquieu was to do in *The Spirit of Laws* in 1748), because each new environment was a human creation which changed. Human history had a direction which humans determined, consciously or not. Nothing was eternal or natural.

Vico's radical discoveries went unnoticed until the French and industrial revolutions made change a commonplace. After 1789 European intellectuals engaged in a series of studies which developed some of Vico's preliminary insights more fully. The French Revolution stimulated a secular version of the Christian idea of linear, rather than cyclical, time. The growth of human knowledge seemed enough (without religious considerations) to suggest that each age was an improvement on those past. The late-eighteenth-century idea of progress became for some in the nineteenth century an idea of human perfectability (both ideas would have been blasphemous earlier). The French Revolution also encouraged nationalist movements in Europe which sought support from studies of the uniqueness of each national culture and the origins of national identity in medieval folk traditions and myth. In Germany, the study of myth and language led to the systematic study of cultural change which we traced from Hegel to Marx, and to the professional analysis of historical documents in the productive German historical schools of the nineteenth century.

The French historian Jules Michelet actually rediscovered the writings of Vico in 1824, and proceeded to write the history of France as the work of the French people. Both Michelet and the German historians and philosophers insisted that the writing of history was possible only by reliving the experiences of the past. Like Vico, they believed such reliving to be possible because there were still "traces" of older mentalities in the modern mind. But the swiftness of change in the nineteenth century and the logical analysis of philosophers like

David Hume in England and the German historicists made that task increasingly difficult.

The full realization that every culture was unique, and that life is nothing but change—which was historicism's philosophical position in the nineteenth century, and which has become one of our basic assumptions today—was, and is, devastating. It was fought against continually. As we have noticed over and over again, each age wishes to believe that its values and behavior reflect human nature. A belief in human nature was perhaps even more essential for the upholders of market society in the nineteenth century. As we have seen in our discussion of Hobbes and Locke, the defenders of modern market society invented a whole new set of certainties about "human nature" and "natural law" in order to ward off the centrifugal pull and atomistic, fragmenting tendencies of a society modeled on the marketplace.

Many of the new "certainties" that they invented were disputed by the new anthropological discoveries and methods of logical analysis as soon as they were proposed. That had happened since the seventeenth-century beginnings of liberal market theory. In the seventeenth century, Blaise Pascal made a mockery of René Descartes's simple faith that "God has so established the order of things . . . that even if every man were to be concerned only with himself, and to show no charity to others, he would still, in the normal course of events, be working on their behalf."[7]

The varied customs of men showed Pascal that "theft, incest, infanticide, parricide" had all been considered "virtues" by some cultures. To "found the order of the world . . . on the caprice of each individual" seemed a kind of madness. For Pascal the laws of human nature changed with each season and with each crossing of a river. To assume that justice could come from a society without charity, community, or tradition was nonsense. The empty, self-centered morality of the postmedieval world was as frightening as "the eternal silence of infinite space" posited by postmedieval science.

At the end of the eighteenth century, Adam Smith repeated the faith of Descartes. His vision of naturally "economic man" was also refuted by the anthropological knowledge of Columbus. His assumption that the laws of supply and demand and the "natural" human acquisitive instinct would provide a natural harmony of interests was already challenged by David Hume's insistence that the logic of cause-and-effect was much too limited for such generalizations.

Yet nineteenth-century British utilitarians and European positivists had to learn the same lessons again. The need for a society run like a market conspired with the success of machines and science to suggest new laws of human nature—which turned out to be just like the old laws of Descartes, Locke, and Adam Smith. The utilitarians (Jeremy

Bentham, James Mill, and the young John Stuart Mill) attempted to find human nature in the supposed universal ability to rationally calculate pleasures and pains of every atomistic individual. They imagined that "the greatest good for the greatest number" of people could be the goal of social policy, just as the maximization of individual pleasure could be the measured goal of individual action. Positivists like Hippolyte Taine in France went so far as to argue that "virtue and vice are products like sugar and vitriol."

The nineteenth-century versions of human nature and natural law were even less tenable than earlier versions. Opposition was more intense. A lonely Pascal had been replaced by an entire romantic movement of artists, poets, and philosophers whose insistence on the power of passion, irrationality, emotion, and culture could not be ignored. The emerging professional studies of anthropology, sociology, and history brought forward too much evidence of cultural variety to permit universal laws of human nature. The path from the recognition of cultural differences to the recognition of fundamental change had been well cleared and was easier to follow for people raised on Christian time with a faith in progress. But there was still one last refuge from relativity. For at least one generation in the nineteenth century, the crisis of modern consciousness could be averted. Evolution preserved whatever certainty was left.

## Evolution: Certainty's Last Stand

In *Evolution and Society* J. W. Burrow put it this way:

> The evolutionary method in social thinking triumphed, not only or perhaps even primarily because it was in tune with that of the vogue sciences of the period, but because it offered a way of coping with new kinds of experience and new methods of interpreting them—methods which had been germinating throughout the earlier part of the century. . . . The proceedings of the [British Anthropological] Society, during its short life, reveal the impasse reached by mid-nineteenth-century positivism once it had abandoned, for various reasons, the belief that a science of man and society could be deduced from a few cardinal propositions about human nature. The way out of that impasse—in a sense, for the Victorians, the only way—was by some kind of evolutionary theory.[8]

Since it was no longer possible to believe in human nature, one could at least find security in orderly, predictable, almost providential change. Evolutionary theory satisfied sociologists, anthropologists, and historians, as well as geologists and biologists, in the nineteenth century because it kept the lid on suspicions of relativity. In fact, it was a solution which accorded well with the traditional Christian belief that God revealed himself and his design in time. The century that accepted evolution as the fundamental fact of life was the most Christian of centuries in its thought and culture. Sociology was hailed as the new Christianity. Primitive societies could be studied sympathetically without implying criticisms of life in the modern world: primitive and traditional peoples simply represented an earlier stage of human evolution (or of God's revelation).

The furor over Darwin's theory of evolution was largely misdirected. Christian fundamentalists (especially in the United States) found themselves stuck with a particular Biblical literalism (the first parents, the relatively short list of later generations that collapsed the human time scale, and images of world catastrophes like the Flood that seemed to make sudden geological changes and a special human creation tenable). They accepted the same predicament for themselves that the Catholic church had accepted for itself in its conflict with Galileo: since the Bible literally says that Joshua made the sun stand still, that "the foundations of the earth are fixed so firm that they cannot be moved," and that the sun "runneth about from one end of the heavens to the other," it is impossible that the earth revolves around the sun.

By 1859 (the date of publication of Darwin's *Origin of Species*) there were sufficient intellectual tools to understand the Bible as an historical document which reflected a thousand years of Judeo-Christian attempts to understand their God and world (Vico had shown the way). It was even possible to understand the Bible as "the divine revelation" necessary for the particular time and level of understanding that had been achieved in the ancient Near East. God's gradual, historical revelation could still be more fundamental than the Bible. Indeed, if God were a living presence, the revelations of the Bible would have to be dated. But nineteenth-century Christians were often more committed to a literal interpretation of the single revelation of the Bible than they were to the more traditional Judeo-Christian idea of God's continuous revelation throughout history.

## From Certainty to Relativity

If the idea of "evolution" could have been hailed as the culmination of the Christian vision of time, the idea of "natural selection" posed more difficulties. Darwin's work had argued that evolution occurred through a process of natural selection. This meant that nature normally and randomly threw off mutations. Some of these mutations would survive, but only those that were "fittest" or most adaptable to the rest of nature. The problem was that God seemed to have nothing to do with the process. Everything happened spontaneously in nature, according to nature's own laws. One English critic of Darwin noticed this problem when he remarked: "Upon the grounds of what is termed evolution God is relieved of the labour of creation; in the name of unchangeable laws he is discharged from governing the world."[9] To this Herbert Spencer replied that the same objection could be leveled at Newton's law of gravitation, the science of astronomy, or indeed, any scientific laws. The American scientist Asa Gray argued that natural selection was simply an explanation of God's method. God created a nature so that it would produce new species itself. But many wondered if such scientific laws of nature did not remove God too far from his accustomed place of immediate involvement in the world. And Herbert Spencer's reminder that this was the effect of all scientific knowledge was not answered.

Evolutionary theory by natural (or "supernatural") selection did not disprove the existence of God. But like the rest of science, it made (as one French philosopher had said in the eighteenth century) that "hypothesis" less necessary. It replaced the certainty of divine intervention with the certainty of human discovery. But in removing the supernatural further from human life, it made humans more dependent on their understanding of nature. And, in at least one way, the new evolutionary sciences of geology and biology offered less certainty. They were not predictive. The methods of nature could be reconstructed retrospectively, but it was impossible to gauge which one of the millions of new mutations would succeed. A nature evolving according to its own laws was a trip without a destination, or with a continually changing destination. Even the religious had to study science to chart the course.

Much the same could be said about the triumph of the evolutionary method in the "human sciences." Human "selections" were as difficult to predict as natural selections. And increasingly, throughout the end of the nineteenth and the beginning of the twentieth century, Westerners realized that human selections were infinitely more complex, and less predictable, than the positivists and utilitarians had recognized. Philosophers like Arthur Schopenhauer, Friedrich Nietzsche, and Henri Bergson ridiculed the positivist belief that man was a rational, thinking machine. They insisted, instead, that human beings were essentially bundles of animal drives. Will, instinct, energy, and drive were the human motivators. Humankind was swayed more by power, myth, and lies than by reason and evidence. Sigmund Freud found evidence that human behavior was essentially irrational, rather than rational. Sexual urges, the accumulated drives of the subconscious, were what made people do what they do. Reason, in fact, was a tool for self-delusion and confusing others. Rationalizations (or rational, but false, explanations) of our behavior were the defenses of a subconscious able to hide. Since we prevent ourselves from understanding ourselves, how can we possibly understand others? No wonder that one of the frequent themes of drama in the twentieth century was that people do not communicate with one another.

Just as philosophers and Freud revived the insights of romantic poets and artists concerning the irrational in individuals, sociologists became increasingly aware of the irrational fabric of society. People did not create society with a "social contract" as the positivist thinkers had imagined. No one ever agreed to join society like one joined the A.S.P.C.A. Society was like religion, Emile Durkheim pointed out. One accepted its myths and powers because one was a member. One did not choose membership in human society. Society and culture gave one (as Socrates had known and Locke had forgotten) one's humanity and individuality. Similarly, Max Weber noted, people did not obey laws because they agreed to. Often people obeyed leaders because they were magical and charismatic, or they obeyed laws out of traditional thoughtlessness or bureaucratic apathy. Knowledge of the importance of irrational factors in society led some sociologists (from Vilfredo Pareto to modern public relations and advertising) to teach manipulation and mystification. Others (like Georges Sorel) exploited popular myths as a tool of social revolution.

To see that a behavior was socially determined had the same relativistic implications as the anthropologists' discoveries that much of human life was culturally determined. Knowledge itself was subjected to such analysis in the emerging discipline of "the sociology of knowledge" in the twentieth century. Based on Marx's discovery of the ideologies of social classes, Durkheim's investigation of "collective mentalities," and Weber's theoretical and historical studies, sociologists like Karl Mannheim showed that even knowledge was relative (or, as he preferred, related) to the social position of the knower. Different classes developed different kinds of knowledge. Though there might be ways of determining whether a particular piece of knowledge was true or false, the important thing to recognize is that it was knowledge for a particular class in a particular historical situation. Thus, the whole tradition of modern Western scientific investigation reflected the needs of an emerging, individualistic, market-oriented class in its concern for separated observer and observed, its tendency to atomize and particularize, and its emphasis on quantification. The knowledge of Chinese science and the structure of Chinese language, for instance, reflected the different needs of a bureaucratic class of intellectuals. There are an infinite number of types of knowledge. One's social and cultural position determined what one would know.

## Beyond Certainty and Relativity: Understanding and Making Human History

> Karl Mannheim in writing what could be called the "Manifesto of Historicism" declared that this intellectual force epitomizes the world-view of modern man: historicism is of extraordinary importance both in the social sciences and in everyday thinking. Today it is impossible to participate in politics, even to understand a person, without recourse to historicist principles. Modern man, be he social scientist or layman, must treat all realities confronting him as having evolved and as developing dynamically. For also in daily life people use concepts with historicist implications, such as cultural behavior, capitalism, social movement, and so forth. The modern mind copes with these phenomena as potentialities that are always in flux, moving from some point in time to another. Even in our everyday thinking we strive to locate our present situation within a dynamic field and to tell time by the "cosmic clock of history."[10]

We live in a world which is continually changing. Its change is our only certainty. We cannot understand ourselves or our present without understanding these changes, because that is all we are. But the more things change, the more difficult they are for us to understand. We are most able to understand sameness and continuity, but our survival depends on understanding change.

This was the problem that historicism began to confront at the end of the nineteenth and the beginning of the twentieth century. Philosophers (Wilhelm Dilthey, Friedrich Nietzsche, Benedetto Croce, R. G. Collingwood) pushed the problem of historical understanding to the brink of uncertainty. Each age, indeed each event and individual, is unique. To understand it fully we have to transcend our own uniqueness and participate in its particularity. But our reliving of it is necessarily our own. We never fully lose the self. Every explanation and interpretation is, despite our efforts, our own. Understanding the past as an objective reality is absurd. Each person sees it from his or her vantage point or self. The same is true of understanding the present, but the past (beginning a moment ago) is even more lost for us. Thus, there is no such thing as the past, but only as many understandings as there are people in the present. History is thinking about the past.

Though we can determine if a particular fact is true after careful consideration of what that means, there are an infinite number of facts which can be viewed from an infinite number of perspectives. We choose those that interest us because they interest us. Each age rewrites the past in the interests of the present. Every individual does so, and changes it. Myth, memory, nostalgia, and history are only alternative ways of grounding ourselves in time. "Objective" history has no meaning aside from following the rules of verification of the present. That helps us discount errors, but gives no advice in choosing the facts. History is only our imaginative reconstruction of the past in terms of the present.

The recognition that everything changes was possible only in a society that changed everything—the disposable society. But once recognized, it was valid for every society. Many twentieth-century thinkers found the conclusion of historicism so uncomfortable that they sought refuge from change in religion, mythology, or the immediate. Some concluded that since history was not final, it was not worth knowing, or that since everything changed, there was no point in knowing how.

Others found (as Michelet did in reading Vico) an enormous freedom in the discovery that humans make, and continually remake, themselves. For them, the universality of change meant not throwing up one's hands in disgust and confusion, but the opportunity for fresh understanding and planning new directions. This book is written for them.

## *For Further Reading*

For the history of modern painting we have relied heavily on Ian Dunlop's lively, well-illustrated **The Shock of the New.** A much more thorough history can be found in John Canaday's **Mainstreams of Modern Art** or Herbert Read's **A Concise History of Modern Painting;*** Sheldon Cheney's **A Primer of Modern Art*** is a good, readable explanation of the intentions of early modern artists from the perspective of the 1920s. A good introduction to modern music that covers the same period is Leonard Bernstein's **The Unanswered Question.**

For introductions to modern culture more generally, there are excellent readings in Eugen Weber's **Paths to the Present*** and Richard Ellmann and Charles Feidelson's **The Modern Tradition.** John Cruickshank's **Aspects of the Modern European Mind*** is also a useful collection of short selections. For histories of modern culture, H. Stuart Hughes's **Consciousness and**

* Available in paperback.

**Society: The Reorientation of European Social Thought 1890–1930*** is excellent. Roger Shattuck's **The Banquet Years: The Origins of the Avant-Garde in France, 1885 to World War I*** is an engaging study of four artists of the period. Thomas B. Hess and John Ashbery have edited some good articles in **Avante-Garde Art.*** Renato Poggioli's **The Theory of the Avant-Garde*** is a challenging, sophisticated Marxist analysis. Arnold Hauser's **The Social History of Art*** (especially vol. 4 on "Naturalism, Impressionism, the Film Age") is also an exciting Marxist treatment, as are John Berger's **Ways of Seeing*** and the more specialized histories of Raymond Williams's **Culture and Society 1780–1950,* The Long Revolution,*** and **Key Words.**

Good introductions to the history of historical consciousness can be found in Stephen Toulmin and June Goodfield's **The Discovery of Time,*** Frank E. Manuel's **Shapes of Philosophic History,*** Fritz Stern's **The Varieties of History,*** and R. G. Collingwood's demanding, superb **The Idea of History.*** Gunter W. Remmling's conservative **Road to Suspicion*** traces the origins of the sociology of knowledge. A good introductory intellectual history can be found in Harry Prosch's **The Genesis of Twentieth Century Philosophy: The Evolution of Thought from Copernicus to the Present.***

There are also a lot of particular books on modern culture that deserve mention. Leslie A. White's **The Science of Culture,** although not a history, is an excellent statement of cultural determinism. The work of Marshall McLuhan, especially **Understanding Media*** and **The Mechanical Bride,*** is an excellent introduction to the culture of television. So is Raymond Williams's **Television.***

There are too many books on film to mention more than one, Béla Balázs's **Theory of the Film.*** An engaging history of anthropology and anthropologists is H. R. Hays's **From Ape to Angel.***

## Notes

1. These and other quotations in this section are from Ian Dunlop's *The Shock of the New* (New York: McGraw-Hill, 1972).
2. John Canady, *Mainstreams of Modern Art* (New York: Simon & Schuster, 1959), pp. 469–470.
3. Van Wyck Brooks, *John Sloan,* quoted in Ian Dunlop, *op. cit.,* p. 197.
4. Walter Pach, "Queer Thing, Painting," quoted in *ibid.*
5. Quoted in *ibid.,* pp. 184–185.
6. Quoted in Howard Mumford Jones, *O Strange New World* (New York: Viking Press, 1964), pp. 15–16.
7. Letter of 6 October 1646 to Princess Elizabeth of Bohemia, quoted in Lucien Goldmann, *The Hidden God* (London: Routledge & Kegan Paul, 1964), p. 28.
8. J. W. Burrow, *Evolution and Society* (Cambridge University Press, 1966), p. 136.
9. William Ewart Gladstone quoted in A. D. White, *A History of the Welfare of Science with Theology in Christendom* (New York: Dover, 1960), vol. 1, p. 76.
10. Gunter W. Remmling, *Road to Suspicion: A Study of Modern Mentality and the Sociology of Knowledge* (Englewood Cliffs, N.J.: Prentice-Hall, 1967), p. 95.

## CHRONOLOGICAL CONTEXT OF
# The Modern World: 1800-The Present

| Europe | Americas | Asia and Africa |
|---|---|---|
| | | Manchu dynasty in China<br>1644–1912 |
| Industrial revolution<br>a. 1780 | | |
| Cultural romanticism<br>1780–1900 | | |
| Napoleon<br>1800–1815 | | |
| Utopian socialism<br>1800–1848 | British end slave trade<br>1807 | |
| Utilitarianism<br>1800–1870 | | |
| Liberalism<br>1800–1914 | Slave prices increase<br>1808 | |
| First railroad<br>1825 | U.S. ends slave trade<br>1809 | |
| French "July Revolution"<br>1830 | Independence of most of Latin America<br>1810–1828 | |
| Cultural "realism"<br>1830–1914 | | Anglo-Chinese (Opium) War<br>1839–1842 |
| Chartist movement<br>1838–1848 | | Decline of slave trade in Africa<br>1840–1863 |
| Revolutions of 1848 | | |
| *Communist Manifesto*<br>1848 | | |
| Unification of Italy<br>1848–1870 | | |
| Napoleon III<br>r. 1852–1870 | Brazil ends slave trade<br>1851 | Taiping Rebellion in China<br>1851–1864 |

**a. = after**
**r. = ruled**

| Europe | Americas | Asia and Africa |
|---|---|---|
| | | Opening of Japan<br>1854 |
| | | Great Mutiny in India<br>1857–1858 |
| | | Britain rules India<br>1858 |
| Mill's *On Liberty*<br>1859 | | |
| Darwin's *Origin of Species*<br>1859 | | |
| Russian emancipation of serfs<br>1861 | U.S. Civil War<br>1861–1865 | |
| Salon des Refusés<br>1863 | U.S. Emancipation Proclamation<br>1863 | Sun Yat-sen<br>1866–1925 |
| | | Meiji Restoration in Japan<br>1867 |
| | | Mahatma Gandhi<br>1869–1948 |
| | | Opening of Suez Canal<br>1869 |
| Paris Commune insurrection<br>1870 | | End of feudalism in Japan<br>1871 |
| Impressionism<br>1870–1890 | | |
| German Empire<br>1871–1918 | | |
| Internal-combustion engine<br>1876 | Telephone<br>1876 | Height of Western imperialism<br>1880–1914 |
| | Development of legal segregation in U.S.<br>1877–1954 | Organization of Indian National Congress<br>1885 |
| | Brazil emancipation of slaves<br>1888 | |
| Post-impressionism<br>a. 1890 | U.S. finance capitalism<br>a. 1890 | |
| Expressionism in art<br>a. 1893 | | |

| Europe | Americas | Asia and Africa |
|---|---|---|
| Discovery of X-ray 1895 | | |
| Wireless telegraph 1899 | | Open Door Policy in China 1899 |
| Freud's *Interpretation of Dreams* 1900 | U.S. Progressive Movement 1901–1916 | Boxer Rebellion in China 1900 |
| Cubism a. 1903 | | |
| Russian Revolution of 1905 | | |
| Einstein theories 1905–1910 | Mexican Revolution 1911 | Revolution in China 1911 |
| | N.Y. Armory Exhibition 1913 | |
| | Ford's assembly line 1913 | |
| World War I 1914–1918 | | Warlords divide China 1916–1928 |
| Russian Revolution 1917 | | |
| Surrealism a. 1918 | | Height of Indian nationalism 1919–1947 |
| League of Nations 1920–1946 | | Height of Mexican social revolution 1920–1940 |
| Fascist revolution in Italy 1922 | | |
| Death of Lenin 1924 | | |
| Dictatorship of Stalin 1924–1953 | | |
| | E. Mayo's Hawthorne experiments 1924 | |
| | | Nationalist regime in China (Chiang Kai-shek) 1928–1949 |
| Great Depression 1929–1939 | Great Depression 1929–1939 | Triumph of militants in Japan 1936 |

| Europe | Americas | Asia and Africa |
|---|---|---|
| Nazi revolution in Germany 1933 | U.S. New Deal 1933–1939 | Japan invades China 1937 |
| World War II 1939–1945 | Cooling of Mexican Revolution a. 1940 | |
| East, West Europe split 1945 | World War II 1941–1945 | |
| Woman suffrage: France, Italy 1945–1946 | Spread of synthetics in U.S. economy a. 1945 | |
| U.S. Marshall Plan 1947 | Cold War with Russia a. 1946 | British leave India 1947 |
| NATO 1949 | | Communist victory in China 1949 |
| W. German recovery a. 1949 | | African anti-colonial revolts and independence a. 1949 |
| | | Indonesian independence 1949 |
| | Korean War 1950–1953 | |
| Death of Stalin 1953 | Cuban "communism" a. 1959 | |
| End of British, French, Belgian, African colonies 1957–1962 | U.S. war in Vietnam 1964–1975 | Chinese-Russian split a. 1960 |
| Worker, student protests 1968 | Chile's Democratic Marxism 1970–1974 | Chinese cultural revolution 1966–1967 |
| Common Market includes Britain 1973 | | |
| Recession, inflation a. 1973 | Nixon resigns 1974 | |
| Socialist, communist party gains in W. Europe 1974–1976 | | Death of Mao 1976 |
| | | China opens to West 1978 |
| | Energy crisis deepens 1979 | Shah of Iran deposed 1979 |

# Index

# INDEX TO SPELLING OF CHINESE WORDS

The Wade-Giles system of transliterating Chinese was used in this text because most books in the United States are still catalogued according to this system. Since the pinyin system will be used increasingly in the future, a conversion table is provided of words in this text for which the two systems differ:

| WADE—GILES | PINYIN |
|---|---|
| An-yang | Anyang |
| Ch'in | Qin |
| Chou | Zhou |
| Chuang Tzu | Zhuangzi |
| feng-shui | fengshui |
| Han Fei Tzu | Hanfeizi |
| Hangchow | Hangzhou |
| ju *(meaning Confucian, intellectual, or weakling)* | Ru |
| Kao Tzu | Gaozi |
| Kweiyang | Guiyang |
| Lao Tzu | Laozi |
| Mao Tse-tung | Mao Zedong |
| Mo Tzu | Mozi |
| Peiking | Beijing |
| Shih Huang-ti | Shi Huangdi |
| Sung | Song |
| t'ai chi | taiji |
| T'ang | Tang |
| Tao | Dao |
| Tao Te Ching | Daodejing |
| Wangpoa | Huangpu |
| Wen Ti | Wendi |
| Wu-ti | Wudi |

80 81 82 83 9 8 7 6 5 4 3 2